Legal Aspects of SELLING & BUYING

Answers to Questions on Antitrust, Franchising and Current Developments in Distribution Law

Philip F. Zeidman, Editor
Brownstein Zeidman and Schomer

Harvey M. Applebaum
Perry C. Ausbrook
Emmet J. Bondurant
Arthur I. Cantor
Jay Greenfield
Stephen S. Mayne
M. Laurence Popofsky
James F. Rill
Irving Scher
Philip F. Zeidman

SHEPARD'S/McGRAW-HILL, INC.
P.O. Box 1235
Colorado Springs, Colorado 80901

McGRAW-HILL INFORMATION SERVICES COMPANY

New York • St. Louis • San Francisco • Auckland • Bogotá
Caracas • Colorado Springs • Hamburg • Lisbon • London
Madrid • Mexico • Milan • Montreal • New Delhi • Oklahoma City
Panama • Paris • San Juan • São Paulo • Singapore • Sydney
Tokyo • Toronto

45678910 SHCU 892109

Library of Congress Cataloging in Publication Data
Main entry under title:

Legal aspects of selling and buying.

Includes index.
1. Franchises (Retail trade)—Law and legislation—United States. 2. Antitrust law—United States. I. Zeidman, Philip F., 1934- . II. Applebaum, Harvey M.
KF2023.L43 1983 343.73'072 83-4666
347.30372

ISBN 0-07-072750-3

LSBO

To John Fisher Zeidman
1961-1982

Preface

This book had its origins in discussions among the publisher, the editor and several of the contributors, and emerged from some convictions developed during a number of years engaged in the practice of antitrust law. Those convictions can be stated rather simply:

(1) *Much antitrust law is practiced by lawyers who do not consider themselves antitrust lawyers, and most antitrust lawyers do not devote themselves exclusively to that specialty.*

If there were any question about the risks inherent in a lawyer's decision to specialize exclusively in antitrust law, the dual developments of the deregulatory sentiment of recent years and the current administration's antitrust enforcement posture should answer that question persuasively. But there are more fundamental and less narrow vocational explanations: most lawyers want to diversify their practice, for the stimulation of variety as much as for the reduction of risk; few law firms can be so assured of the course which their practices will follow to warrant specializing in antitrust law; and, while most lawyers or firms in most larger cities have an antitrust capability, antitrust problems do not necessarily arise there. In fact, much antitrust counseling, and even antitrust litigation, seem first to appear on the desk of a general practitioner or a house counsel who may have relatively little familiarity with antitrust law or procedure. A study recently completed by the Antitrust Section of the American Bar Association verifies this admittedly unscientific observation: most of its members are lawyers who do not practice exclusively in the field of antitrust law; a great many are simply lawyers who have been or expect during their legal career to be faced with questions that require a sufficient knowledge of antitrust law to deal intelligently with a client's concern—or at least to identify it.

(2) *Antitrust lawyers no longer can, if they ever could, limit themselves to a knowledge of the antitrust laws.*

It has always been the case that, in order to represent and counsel a client effectively, a lawyer must first understand the client's business. But that simple truism is more complex than ever, and no less true. The dramatic changes in communications and in computer technology, for example, may require a lawyer to understand the forces that have led to those developments and that are likely to shape them in the future. By the same token, if the lawyer is accustomed to assuming that the client's problems can be answered on the basis of hornbook antitrust law, counsel is hardly better equipped than the lawyer who can only recall the Rule in Shelley's Case. The lawyer must understand a body of law that did not exist when he or she studied antitrust law: for some, the Uniform Commercial Code; and for most, state and federal franchise laws and regulations, among others. Finally, the steady growth of state antitrust law—and of "little FTC Acts" and of consumer protection statutes—precludes limiting attention to federal antitrust law.

(3) *The antitrust law which lawyers practice is often not the antitrust law about which they hear and read.*

If one were to gauge what is happening in the practice of antitrust law by the subjects of discussion in law journals and in continuing legal education programs, one would conclude that thousands of lawyers are engaged daily in advising on or litigating horizontal price-fixing conspiracies, complex mergers, the fine points of attempts to monopolize, and the like. In fact, of course, only a handful of lawyers is frequently—or ever—concerned with such matters. As to these and even more esoteric areas of law, it sometimes seems that there are more lectures than complaints, more law review articles than decisions. The law of distribution—or, less grandiosely, the law governing the relationship between Seller and Buyer—engages far more of an antitrust lawyer's time than the journals and seminars would suggest; and it is the principal subject of concern for most commercial lawyers and litigators. A recent study conducted in the Southern District of New York revealed that most "antitrust" litigation in fact deals, not with an exotic theory of liability or damages, but rather with the termination of a dealer.

(4) *There is no publication that adequately meets the needs of lawyers—and nonlawyers —concerned with these issues.*

Existing *services* tell the reader what happened last month, or last week, but the reader to whom this book is addressed needs to place those current developments—invaluable, for example, to a full-time litigator in search of a fresh citation—into the context of balanced counseling. Treatises are likely to assume that the reader already knows with some precision how to articulate the question pursued; that the attorney knows within which particular subsection of the antitrust laws it falls and has the leisure to trace the answer in a logical—as well as chronological—fashion. At least one, and sometimes all, of these assumptions is quite likely to be in error.

* * *

From those general observations, some rather specific conclusions were reached about the kind of book needed:

(1) *It should be a desk book—but with the capacity to be used as a more conventional treatise as well.*

By a *desk book,* we mean one that, literally, belongs on a desk, not a library shelf. It should be one which the reader can use easily and often, to provide answers or guidance to questions puzzling the attorney, client or employer. But it should also have the attributes of a more traditional and scholarly work, so that it can be consulted for a comprehensive compilation of the authorities supporting and discussing the principles dealt with in more readable fashion in the first instance.

(2) *It should be organized in the way questions arise, in business and in law, not pigeonholed to accord with a statutory pattern.*

Lawyers rarely convert questions that arise in the course of commercial dealings into the legal framework in which they were first introduced to the governing principles; clients never do. Questions remain practical, business-oriented inquiries: Do I have to do business with this person? Can I sell to this company at whatever price I want? And the most readily usable fashion in which those questions can be grouped is around the basic relationship which is at the heart of commercial undertakings: Buyer and Seller (and, occasionally, the other dramatis personae who make an appearance: the competing seller, the competing buyer, approved supplier, etc.).

(3) *It should be usable by a wide range of readers.*

Writers rarely know in advance the profile of their readers. This book is addressed, then, to a composite audience—

Antitrust lawyers.

General practitioners who wish to consult a reference book but do not need to maintain the full panoply of treatises and services.

House counsel, whose employers want and need rapid answers, but who cannot justify either an extensive library or the expensive practice of referring every question to outside counsel, especially at the threshold stage.

Marketing and other nonlegal personnel of commercial businesses, advertising agencies and other enterprises who must deal with the issues with which this book is concerned. They want help in identifying legal issues—to determine whether they exist, and to be able to discuss them intelligently.

Trade associations, whose members frequently expect some guidance from the association staff as to issues which are the subject of this book.

We recognize that there are pitfalls in reaching out to so broad a range of readers and have tried to avoid them.

(4) *It should be as timely as publishing schedules will permit.*

It was not difficult to write about current topics: the *Sylvania* decision, its progeny, the current enforcement approach of the government, the explosive growth in franchising legislation and litigation. Indeed, in few areas of the law is so large a portion of the subject matter related to such recent developments.

But it is more difficult to keep it current. That is the challenge we will seek to address by pocket part supplements, issued as frequently, based upon our own practices and the reactions of our readers, as they seem to be necessary.

Those objectives are formidable. We hope we have achieved them.

I would like to express my deep appreciation to the publisher for recognizing that each of the contributors is first and foremost a practicing lawyer; to the contributors, for forgiving me on the occasions when I ignored that fact; to my partners who authored certain of the chapters, and to the associates in our firm who ably assisted them; to my partners Daryl A. Nickel and Peter J. Klarfeld, who reviewed most of the text; to Nadine C. Mandel, for careful coordination; and especially to the late Kathleen D. Kennedy, who tempered urgency with patience in her supervision of this complex and challenging project.

Philip F. Zeidman, P.C.

The Authors

Philip F. Zeidman, Editor and Contributor

B.A., Yale College; LL.B., Harvard Law School; trial attorney, Federal Trade Commission, 1960-1961; U.S. Small Business Administration, 1960-1968 (General Counsel, 1965-1968); Special Assistant to the Vice President of the United States, 1968; Stockholder of Philip F. Zeidman, PC, which is a partner in the law firm of Brownstein Zeidman and Schomer, Washington, D.C.; first Chairman, Franchising Committee, Antitrust Section, American Bar Association; Vice Chairman, International Franchising Committee, International Bar Association; Contributing Editor for Antitrust and Trade Regulation, *Legal Times;* member, Advisory Board, Bureau of National Affairs, *Antitrust and Trade Regulation Report;* Washington Counsel, International Franchise Association; member, Washington, D.C., New York, Florida and Alabama Bars; author of numerous professional publications and frequent lecturer on antitrust and franchising.

Contributors

Harvey M. Applebaum

B.A., Yale University; LL.B., Harvard Law School; partner, Covington & Burling, Washington, D.C.; former Chairman of the American Bar Association Section of Antitrust Law; former Antitrust Section delegate to the ABA House of Delegates; former Chairman of the Editorial Board of *ABA Antitrust Law Developments;* former Chairman of the Robinson-Patman Act Committee of the ABA Antitrust Section; former Chairman of the Trade Regulation Committee of the ABA Administrative Law Section; Lecturer of Law, Antitrust, University of Virginia Law School; former adjunct Professor of Law, Georgetown University Law Center; member, District of Columbia Bar; author of professional journal articles and participant in numerous seminars and programs on antitrust and international trade subjects.

Perry C. Ausbrook

B.S., Economics, University of Pennsylvania; LL.B., Harvard Law School; Division of Corporation Finance, Securities and Exchange Commission, 1961-1963; partner, Brownstein Zeidman and Schomer, Washington, D.C.; Advisor to the Franchise Regulation Subcommittee of the North American Securities Administrators Association; member, District of Columbia Bar, the American Bar Association, and the International Bar Association; frequent writer and lecturer on subjects related to franchise law.

Emmet J. Bondurant

A.B., University of Georgia; LL.B., University of Georgia Law School; LL.M., Harvard Law School; Member, State Bar of Georgia, American Bar Association; partner, Bondurant, Miller, Hishon & Stephenson, Atlanta, Ga; author of various articles on constitutional law and local governmental issues; panelist on numerous seminars on legal subjects including antitrust law and criminal antitrust problems.

Arthur I. Cantor

A.B., Columbia College; LL.B., Harvard Law School; trial and appellate attorney, Antitrust Division, U. S. Department of Justice, 1962-1968; Special Assistant to the Assistant Attorney General, Antitrust Division, 1969-1972; partner, Brownstein Zeidman and Schomer, Washington, D.C.; Member, District of Columbia Bar and the American Bar Association; author and lecturer on antitrust and franchise law.

Jay Greenfield

B.A., Cornell University; LL.B., Harvard Law School; trial attorney, Antitrust Division, Department of Justice, 1960-1961; partner, Paul, Weiss, Rifkind, Wharton & Garrison, New York, N.Y.; Fellow, American College of Trial Lawyers; Chairman, Economics Committee, Antitrust Section of the American Bar Association; member, New York Bar; author of numerous professional publications and journal articles.

Stephen S. Mayne

B.A., Brown University; J.D. and LL.M., Georgetown University Law Center; private law practice, Washington, D.C., 1967-1970, San Francisco, California, 1971-present, with Dinkelspiel, Donovan & Reder; member, District of Columbia and California Bars, American Bar Association; frequent author of law journal articles on antitrust law and lecturer on antitrust.

M. Laurence Popofsky

B.A., State University of Iowa; M.A. (Jurisprudence) Oxford University; LL.B., Harvard Law School; Stockholder of M. Laurence Popofsky, PC, which is a partner in the law firm of Heller, Ehrman, White & McAuliffe, San Francisco, California; member, Advisory Board, Bureau of National Affairs, *Antitrust and Trade Regulation Report;* former member, American College of Trial Lawyers; member, California Bar and the American Bar Association; author and lecturer on antitrust issues.

James F. Rill

A.B., Dartmouth College; LL.B., Harvard University; partner, Collier, Shannon, Rill & Scott, Washington, D.C.; member, District of Columbia Bar; Member, American Bar Association Section of Antitrust Law, Antitrust Council; former Chairman, Robinson-Patman Act Committee; member, Advisory Board, Bureau of National Affairs, *Antitrust and Trade Regulation Report.*

Irving Scher

B.A., College of City of New York; J.D., Columbia Law School; Adjunct Associate Professor of Law, New York University Law School; stockholder of Irving Scher, PC, which is a partner in the law firm of Weil, Gotshal & Manges, New York, N.Y.; member, New York Bar; former Chairman, New York State Bar Association Antitrust Section; member, Advisory Board, Bureau of National Affairs, *Antitrust and Trade Regulation Report;* former member, Section on Corporation, Banking, and Business Law, American Bar Association; finance officer, Section of Antitrust, American Bar Association; author of numerous professional publications and journal articles.

Contents

Summary

Detailed

TM

Product F

The Standard of Legality: Per Se or Rule of Reason? 1

M. Laurence Popofsky *

---

*Mr. Popofsky is a member of the California Bar. The author wishes to thank Jessica S. Pers of Heller, Ehrman, White & McAuliffe for her assistance in the preparation of this chapter.

§1.01 What does the law say about the standard of legality?

The statutes under which both private parties and government agencies bring antitrust actions broadly define certain conduct as illegal, without specifying the precise legal standard under which marketplace behavior must be judged. The legislative history of those statutes makes it clear that the courts were expected to give shape to their broad mandate.[1] In interpreting the federal statutes, the courts have defined standards by which the conduct of both Sellers and Buyers is judged.[2]

§1.02 —What is proscribed by Sherman Act §1?

Federal antitrust law had its beginning in the Sherman Act.[3] Section 1 of the

---

[1] National Soc of Professional Eng v United States, 435 US 679, 688 (1978).

[2] §2 of the Sherman Act, 15 USC §2, prohibits monopolization, attempts to monopolize, and combinations or conspiracies with any other person or persons to monopolize any part of the trade or commerce among the several states, or with foreign nations. Since per se concepts have played no role in §2's development, we will not address §2 in this chapter. There may, however, be distribution practices that violate §2.

[3] 15 USC §1.

Sherman Act states: "Every contract, combination . . . or conspiracy, in restraint of trade or commerce among the several States, or with foreign nations, is hereby declared to be illegal." Thus, only restraints of trade arising from a binding agreement[4] (a *contract*), a union of two or more persons or entities for a common end (a *combination*)[5] or a plurality of actors who act unlawfully or seek to achieve an unlawful goal (a *conspiracy*)[6] are reached by §1 of the Sherman Act. Thus, for §1 to apply, two factors must be present—more than two actors[7] and concerted activity.

Questions have arisen as to whether conscious parallel activity by a number of firms constitutes a *conspiracy* or agreement for §1 purposes. Despite an early suggestion by the Supreme Court that such parallel conduct can establish a conspiracy,[8] it is now clear that parallel behavior is merely circumstantial evidence from which a factfinder may infer an agreement.[9]

A situation often arises in which some of a Seller's customers complain about activities of a certain Buyer. If the Seller subsequently terminates its business relationship with that Buyer, is there a *combination* between the Seller and the complaining Buyers for §1 purposes? Generally, complaints, without more, are insufficient to support a §1 claim, since they are considered ordinary marketplace behavior.[10] However, some cases hold that if a Seller acts after receiving customer complaints, there is concerted activity for purposes of the Sherman Act.[11]

---

[4] *See, e.g.,* Sum of Squares, Inc v Market Research Corp, 401 F Supp 53, 56 (SDNY 1975).

[5] *See, e.g.,* Northern Sec Co v United States, 193 US 197 (1904).

[6] *See, e.g.,* American Tobacco Co v United States, 328 US 781 (1946); American Motor Inns, Inc v Holiday Inns, Inc, 521 F2d 1230 (3d Cir 1975).

[7] The issue of *intra-enterprise conspiracy* arises in antitrust cases where a parent and a subsidiary are claimed to have conspired. *See, e.g.,* Ogilvie v Fotomat Corp, 641 F2d 581, 589 (8th Cir 1981).

[8] Interstate Circuit, Inc v United States, 306 US 208 (1939).

[9] *See, e.g.,* Weit v Continental Ill Natl Bank & Trust Co, 641 F2d 457 (7th Cir 1981), *cert denied,* 455 US 988 (1982); Beech Cinema, Inc v Twentieth-Century Fox Film Corp, 622 F2d 1106 (2d Cir 1980); Joseph E Seagram & Sons v Hawaiian Oke & Liquors, Ltd, 416 F2d 71 (9th Cir 1969), *cert denied,* 396 US 1062 (1970); *but see* Bogosian v Gulf Oil Corp, 561 F2d 434 (3d Cir 1977) (allegation of "interdependent consciously parallel action" sufficient to defeat motion to dismiss).

[10] *See, e.g.,* Valley Liquors, Inc v Renfeld Importers, Ltd, 678 F2d 742 (7th Cir 1982); Schwimmer v Sony Corp, 677 F2d 946 (2d Cir 1982); Roesch, Inc v Star Cooler Corp, 671 F2d 1168 (8th Cir 1982); HL Moore Drug Exch Inc v Eli Lilly & Co, 662 F2d 935 (2d Cir 1981); *cert denied,* __ US __, 74 LEd2d 144, 103 S Ct 176 (1982).; AH Cox v Star Mach Co, 653 F2d 1302 (9th Cir 1981) (exclusive distributorship); Oreck Corp v Whirlpool Corp, 639 F2d 75, 80 (2d Cir 1980), *cert denied,* 454 US 1083 (1981); Edward J Sweeney & Sons v Texaco, Inc, 637 F2d 105 (3d Cir 1980), *cert denied,* 451 US 911 (1981); Carr Elecs Corp v Sony Corp, 472 F Supp 9 (ND Cal 1979); AG Rogers Co v Merck & Co, 498 F Supp 5 (ED Tenn 1980).

[11] *See, e.g.,* Cernuto, Inc v United Cabinet Corp, 595 F2d 164 (3d Cir 1979); Donald B Rice Tire Co v Michelin Tire Corp, 483 F Supp 750, 754 (D Md 1980), *affd,* 683 F2d 15 (4th Cir), *cert denied,* 454 US 864 (1981) (combination existed, but restraint found

Section 1 of the Sherman Act seems to imply that all contracts, combinations, and conspiracies are illegal without any inquiry into their purpose or effect. If this were true, any agreement or contract between a Seller and a Buyer would violate the federal antitrust laws. As the law has developed, courts are concerned only with agreements that *unreasonably* restrain competition.[12]

§1.03 —What is proscribed by Clayton Act §3?

Section 3 of the Clayton Act[13] makes certain *exclusive dealing* arrangements and tie-in sales involving commodities or leases of commodities unlawful. The section makes it illegal for a Seller to select a Buyer or determine a price or discount on the basis of the Buyer's agreement not to use or deal in merchandise or goods of a competitor. It also reaches conduct of a Seller who requires a Buyer to purchase one of its products as a condition to purchasing a different product. These arrangements violate the law when they have a substantial adverse effect on competition. Thus, the arrangements proscribed by §3 of the Clayton Act will be deemed illegal only after an analysis of the effect of such arrangements on commerce.

§1.04 —What is proscribed by the Robinson-Patman Act?

The Robinson-Patman Act[14] amends certain provisions of the Clayton Act. It holds unlawful any discrimination in price between different Buyers of commodities of like grade and quality where the effect of such discrimination may be substantially to lessen competition or attempt to create a monopoly in any line of commerce, or to injure, destroy, or prevent competition with any person who either grants or knowingly receives the benefit of such discrimination or with customers of either of them. This act proscribes both price discrimination affecting competition at the Seller's level and price discrimination affecting competition at the Buyer's level.

Related statutory provisions deal with brokerage,[15] promotional, and advertising allowances and services,[16] and Buyer liability for violations of the Robinson-Patman Act.[17] There are also statutory defenses set forth under the

---

reasonable); Battle v Lubrizol Corp, 673 F2d 984 (8th Cir 1982); Spray-Rite Serv Corp v Monsanto Co, 684 F2d 1226 (7th Cir 1982), *cert granted*, __ US __, 75 L Ed 2d 479, 103 S Ct 1249 (1983).

[12] Standard Oil v United States, 221 US 1 (1911); Chicago Bd of Trade v United States, 246 US 231 (1918).

[13] 15 USC §14.

[14] 15 USC §13(a).

[15] *Id.* §13(c).

[16] *Id.* §13(d), (e).

[17] *Id.* §13(f).

law.[18] Finally, the Robinson-Patman Act contains a section that makes some price discriminations a criminal act.[19]

§1.05 —What is proscribed by §5 of the Federal Trade Commission Act?

Section 5 of the Federal Trade Commission Act[20] makes unlawful unfair methods of competition and unfair or deceptive acts or practices in or affecting commerce. The act gives the Federal Trade Commission enforcement authority. There is, of course, some overlap between the Sherman and Clayton Acts and §5 of the Federal Trade Commission Act, but the Federal Trade Commission Act contains no private right of action.[21]

§1.06 —What is the purpose of the antitrust laws that affect distribution?

The antitrust laws that affect the distribution process are designed to protect and encourage competition. Those laws reflect the legislative judgment that ultimately "competition will produce not only lower prices, but also better goods and services."[22] Antitrust laws are primarily concerned with *interbrand* competition. Such competition among manufacturers or suppliers "provides a significant check on the exploitation of intrabrand market power because of the ability of consumers to substitute a different brand of the same product."[23]

In general, the law has been analyzed to ban all concerted arrangements that are adopted for the purpose of reducing competition or which have a significant tendency to reduce competition even if that is not their purpose. Thus, the law does not generally condemn arrangements between Sellers and Buyers that may cause some incidental and inconsequential restraint on competition. Courts have attempted to implement the antitrust laws affecting distribution through the use of two rules: the *per se rule* and the *rule of reason.*

---

[18] *Id.* §13(a), (b).

[19] *Id.* §13a. This section is not an amendment to the Clayton Act.

[20] 15 USC §45.

[21] *See, e.g.,* Fulton v Hecht, 580 F2d 1243, 1249 n 2 (5th Cir 1978), *cert denied,* 440 US 981 (1979); Holloway v Bristol-Meyers Corp, 485 F2d 986 (DC Cir 1973); Carlson v Coca-Cola Co, 483 F2d 279 (9th Cir 1973); Meyer v Bell & Howell Co, 453 F Supp 801, 803 (DC Mo), *appeal dismissed,* 584 F2d 291 (1978).

[22] National Soc of Professional Eng v United States, 435 US 679, 695 (1978).

[23] Continental TV, Inc v GTE Sylvania, Inc, 433 US 36, 52 n 19 (1977).

§1.07 —Why is some conduct illegal per se and other conduct illegal only if unreasonable?

Courts presume that certain conduct is *illegal per se,* without any further analysis into the effect of that conduct on competition. Per se analysis is appropriate only where experience has shown that a particular practice will adversely affect competition.[24] Under those circumstances, it would be time-consuming, expensive, and unnecessary for courts to undertake an economic analysis of the effect of the practice on competition. Based on past experience, courts presume that if such a practice occurs, it has a negative effect on competition and, therefore, is illegal. They will not require an economic investigation into "the entire history of the industry involved, as well as related industries."[25]

On the other hand, where a practice is not one that has been determined through experience to be injurious to competition, the practice is unlawful only if it is *unreasonable*—if it is actually proven to have a negative effect on competition. Using *rule of reason* analysis, courts consider the positive effects of a practice as well as the allegedly negative impact on competition and balance those effects.

When conduct is relatively new and untested, it will generally be analyzed under the rule of reason,[26] at least until courts and those in the marketplace gain familiarity with the practice and its effect on competition.

§1.08 —What results are prohibited?

Under both per se and rule of reason analysis courts are interested in prohibiting injury to competition In per se cases, that injury is presumed because of the nature of the activity in question. In rule of reason cases, on the other hand, a practice is deemed unlawful only after an analysis of how it actually injures competition and a balancing of that competitive injury with any benefits to competition resulting from the conduct.[27]

§1.09 —Does it matter whether the conduct is vertical or horizontal?

For purposes of the antitrust laws, conduct is deemed *vertical* when it affects actors at different levels of the distribution process. In other words, an agree-

---

[24] Broadcast Music, Inc v Columbia Broadcasting Sys, 441 US 1, 9-10 (1979).

[25] Northern Pac Ry Co v United States, 356 US 1, 5 (1958).

[26] Broadcast Music, Inc v Columbia Broadcasting Sys, 441 US 1 (1979).

[27] *See, e.g.,* Broadcast Music, Inc v Columbia Broadcasting Sys, 441 US 1 (1979); Eiberger v Sony Corp, 622 F2d 1068, 1076 (2d Cir 1980) (court weighs enhancement of interbrand competition against effect on intrabrand competition).

ment between a distributor and a customer would be considered a vertical agreement.[28] Where firms at the same level of distribution are involved in a particular activity, it is considered *horizontal*.[29] Thus, if two sellers agree between themselves to allocate markets or fix prices, that would be a *horizontal* agreement.

In some circumstances, an agreement can have both vertical and horizontal elements. For instance, one company may act as both a manufacturer and distributor of merchandise. If that company enters into an agreement with its other distributors, a court may look at that as a *vertical* agreement, between firms on different levels of the distribution process.[30] But, such an arrangement may also be considered horizontal and analyzed as an agreement between distributors on the same level of distribution.[31]

Some conduct is illegal per se whether it is horizontal or vertical—such as price-fixing.[32] This is true because courts have determined price-fixing to be anticompetitive, no matter what the source. For other distribution mechanisms, the vertical or horizontal nature of the arrangement is important for antitrust analysis. Generally, horizontal agreements between competitors to fix prices, to allocate markets, and to control distribution or production will be considered per se illegal. Such agreements tend to injure competition and do not require any detailed analysis into the structure of a particular industry to reach that conclusion. On the other hand, vertical agreements often benefit and encourage interbrand competition, that is, competition between products of different manufacturers. As such, vertical agreements are generally analyzed under the rule of reason, except for the notable exception of vertical price-fixing[33] by a manufacturer enforcing the price at which its goods are sold by

---

[28] *See, e.g.,* Continental TV, Inc v GTE Sylvania, Inc, 433 US 36 (1977).

[29] *See, e.g.,* Catalano, Inc v Target Sales, Inc, 446 US 643 (1980).

[30] Agreements held vertical and not illegal per se: Krehl v Baskin-Robbins Ice Cream Co, 664 F2d 1348 (9th Cir 1982); Donald B Rice Tire Co v Michelin Tire Corp, 483 F Supp 750 (D Md 1980), *affd,* 638 F2d 15 (4th Cir), *cert denied,* 454 US 864 (1981); Abadir & Co v First Miss Corp, 651 F2d 422 (5th Cir 1981); Red Diamond Supply, Inc v Liquid Carbonic Corp, 637 F2d 1001 (5th Cir 1981); Cowley v Braden Indus, 613 F2d 751 (9th Cir), *cert denied,* 446 US 965 (1980); H&B Equip Co v International Harvester Co, 577 F2d 239 (5th Cir 1978); Copy-Data Sys, Inc v Toshiba Am, Inc, 663 F2d 405 (2d Cir 1981); Westpoint Pepperell, Inc v Rea, 1980-2 Trade Cas (CCH) ¶63,341 (ND Cal Apr 8, 1980).

[31] Agreements held horizontal and, therefore, illegal per se: Dougherty v Continental Oil Co, 579 F2d 954 (5th Cir 1978), *vacated on other grounds,* 591 F2d 1206 (5th Cir 1979); Guild Wineries & Distilleries v J Sosnick & Son, 102 Cal App 3d 627, 162 Cal Rptr 87 (1980) (under state Cartwright Act). Pre-*Sylvania* cases holding agreements horizontal: American Motors Inns, Inc v Holiday Inns, Inc, 521 F2d 1230 (3d Cir 1975); Hobart Bros v Malcolm T Gilliland, Inc, 471 F2d 894 (5th Cir 1973); Interphoto Corp v Minolta Corp, 295 F Supp 711 (SDNY), *affd on other grounds,* 417 F2d 621 (2d Cir 1969).

[32] *See, e.g.,* Arizona v Maricopa County Medical Soc, 457 US 332 (1982); United States v Socony-Vacuum Oil Co, 310 US 150, 222-23 (1940) (horizontal price-fixing is per se illegal); Albrecht v Herald Co, 390 US 145 (1968) (vertical price-fixing is per se illegal).

[33] California Retail Liquor Dealers Assn v Midcal Aluminum, Inc, 445 US 97, 102-03 (1980) (dictum); Continental TV, Inc v GTE Sylvania, Inc, 433 US 36, 51 n 18 (1977).

others. Historically, various other vertical arrangements have been analyzed under the per se rule,[34] but current economic and legal thinking applies a rule of reason approach to vertical nonprice restraints, to take into account the benefits of such activity to interbrand competition.[35]

Because the distinction between vertical nonprice restraints and vertical price restraints may become a distinction between permissible and nonpermissible activity, a court's characterization of a distributional restraint is crucial. If a court focuses on the effect a distributional restraint may have on price—even though it is not technical price-fixing—it may still find that restraint illegal.[36] On the other hand, if a court finds valid nonprice considerations supporting a distributional restraint, it may find that restraint lawful under the rule of reason even though it has an effect on price.[37]

§1.10 What kind of conduct is illegal per se?

Conduct that has a "pernicious effect on competition" and lacks "any redeeming virtue" is per se illegal under the antitrust laws.[38] Courts are, therefore, not concerned with benefits that may result from such conduct.

§1.11 —Is the effect of the conduct important?

Although the *effect* of conduct deemed to be illegal per se is important, the effect is presumed using per se analysis. And, of course, that effect is an injury to competition.

§1.12 —Does the market matter?

Using per se analysis, the scope of the market affected by the conduct is of

---

[34] *See* United States v Arnold, Schwinn & Co, 388 US 365 (1967), overruled by, Continental TV, Inc v GTE Sylvania, Inc, 433 US 36 (1977). *Schwinn* itself was an abrupt departure from White Motor Co v United States, 372 US 253 (1963), in which the Supreme Court had refused to endorse a per se rule for vertical restrictions.

[35] See Posner, *The Rule of Reason and the Economic Approach: Reflections on the Sylvania Decision,* 45 U Chi L Rev 1 (1977). In addition, the current Justice Department view would treat both price and nonprice distributional restraints under the rule of reason. See Cutler, Some Antitrust Division Views on Vertical Restraints: Public Policy and Private Actions, Speech before the Twenty-First Annual Advanced Antitrust Seminar on Distribution and Marketing, New York, New York (Dec 8, 1981).

[36] *See, e.g.,* Eiberger v Sony Corp, 622 F2d 1068 (2d Cir 1980) (territorial restriction analyzed as price-related and held unlawful under rule of reason).

[37] *See, e.g.,* Donald B Rice Tire Co v Michelin Tire Corp, 483 F Supp 750 (D Md 1980), *affd,* 638 F2d 15 (4th Cir), *cert denied,* 454 US 864 (1981) (territorial restriction analyzed without price considerations and held lawful under rule of reason).

[38] *See* Northern Pac Ry Co v United States, 356 US 1, 5 (1958). See **§1.14.**

no consequence.[39] This is true because the conduct is presumed to have a negative impact on competition without analysis into the structure of the market. This is not true, however, in tying cases (see **§1.17**), where tying is per se illegal only after the applicable geographic and product markets have been determined for the purpose of showing the economic power of the tying product.

§1.13 —Does the size or power of the actor matter?

In per se analysis, whether or not the firms have economic power is not an issue. In price-fixing cases, for example, if a firm's purpose is to fix prices or if its conduct will fix or stabilize market prices if it is successful, it makes no difference whether or not the firm has economic power in a particular market.[40] Again, this is true because of the presumption in per se cases that certain kinds of conduct always injure competition.

§1.14 What distribution practices are illegal per se?

Certain distribution practices have been determined to be illegal per se. In other words, where these practices are found, courts can impose liability without any further inquiry into the effect of the practice on competition in a particular market. The following distribution mechanisms have been determined to be illegal per se:

1. *Price-fixing,* either by agreement between competitors or between various persons or entities in the chain of distribution[41]
2. *Group boycotts,* that is, agreements by competitors to exclude another firm from competing with them in the market, or a combination between firms at various levels of distribution to exclude a competitor of some of these firms,[42] or an agreement to coerce certain trade practices[43]
3. *Agreements* between competitors to divide markets or allocate customers[44]

---

[39] Northern Pac Ry Co v United States, 356 US 1, 5 (1958).

[40] *See, e.g.,* United States v McKesson & Robbins, Inc, 351 US 305 (1956).

[41] *See, e.g.,* Albrecht v Herald Co, 390 US 145 (1968); Kiefer-Stewart Co v Joseph E Seagram & Sons, 340 US 211 (1951); Simpson v Union Oil Co, 377 US 13 (1964); United States v Socony-Vacuum Oil Co, 310 US 150, 222-23 (1940).

[42] *See, e.g.,* United States v General Motors Corp, 384 US 127 (1966); Fashion Originators Guild v Federal Trade Comm, 312 US 457 (1941).

[43] Certain trade association practices may fall into this category. *See, e.g.,* Radiant Burners, Inc v Peoples Gas Light & Coke Co, 364 US 656 (1961).

[44] *See, e.g.,* United States v Topco Assoc, 405 US 596 (1972); Addyston Pipe & Steel Co v United States, 175 US 211 (1899).

4. *Tie-in sales,* whereby a Seller requires a Buyer desiring a particular product or service to purchase some other product or service as well, if the Seller has economic power in the desired product or service, and a not insubstantial amount of commerce is affected[45]
5. *Reciprocal dealing arrangements,* in which one firm agrees to buy from another on the condition that the selling firm agrees to purchase something else from the buying firm[46]

§1.15 —Is vertical price-fixing per se illegal?

Vertical price-fixing, or resale price maintenance as it is sometimes called, refers to arrangements between firms or persons at different points in the chain of distribution to establish the resale price (or price range) of goods or services. It may entail a manufacturer's setting the price at which wholesalers can market the manufacturer's goods,[47] a manufacturer's setting the price at which its goods may be sold at retail,[48] or a wholesaler's setting the retail price of the goods it distributes.[49] Whether the prices set are minimums or maximums,[50] the party setting the price is liable for vertical price-fixing.

Although vertical price-fixing has been condemned as illegal per se, without regard to economic power or competitive effect, a manufacturer or Seller may still influence the price at which its goods are sold at another level of distribution through unilateral action, outside the scope of the Sherman Act. Thus, a manufacturer is entitled to suggest retail prices for the sale of its products and announce in advance its intention to deal only with retailers who sell at the sugggested price.[51] However, a manufacturer can do no more than suggest

---

[45] *See, e.g.,* Fortner Enters, Inc v United States Steel Corp, 394 US 495 (1969); International Salt Co v United States, 332 US 392 (1947).

[46] *See, e.g.,* United States v General Dynamics Corp, 258 F Supp 36 (SDNY 1966); Southern Concrete Co v United States Steel Corp, 535 F2d 313, 317 (5th Cir 1976).

[47] *See, e.g.,* Albrecht v Herald Co, 390 US 145 (1968); Kiefer-Stewart Co v Joseph E Seagram & Sons, 340 US 211 (1951); Simpson v Union Oil Co, 377 US 13 (1964).

[48] *See, e.g.,* Simpson v Union Oil Co, 377 US 13 (1964); United States v Parke, Davis & Co, 362 US 29 (1961).

[49] *See, e.g.,* United States v Bausch & Lomb Optical Co, 321 US 707 (1944).

[50] Arizona v Maricopa County Medical Soc, 457 US 332 (1982) (horizontal agreements to fix maximum prices are on same legal footing as agreements to fix minimum prices); Albrecht v Herald Co, 390 US 145 (1968).

[51] United States v Colgate & Co, 250 US 300 (1919); *see also* California Retail Liquor Dealers Assn v Midcal Aluminum Inc, 445 US 97 (1980). In Russell Stover Candies, Inc, 1982 Trade Cas (CCH) ¶21,933 (FTC July 1, 1982), the Federal Trade Commission made it clear that the *Colgate* decision affords little protection for vertical price-fixing. The commission determined that Russell Stover violated §5 of the Federal Trade Commission Act by terminating dealers who refused to abide by the candy manufacturer's suggested retail prices. The commission found that an unlawful *agreement* exists

prices and announce its policy; it can in no way enforce adherence to a suggested price by a customer, either itself or through third parties, nor can it threaten a customer with termination or any other penalty for selling at a price other than the one suggested by the manufacturer.[52] However, a manufacturer may use its power of persuasion to encourage a customer to follow its suggested prices as long as it does not *coerce* adherence.[53]

Recently, the Federal Trade Commission in *Russell Stover Inc.*[54] determined that the candy manufacturer's policy of suggesting retail prices and terminating dealers who refused to abide by those prices violated §5 of the FTC Act. The commission found that an unlawful vertical agreement existed between the manufacturer and its dealers when unwilling dealers complied with the manufacturer's prices to avoid termination. The commission stated, however, that Russell Stover could initially choose to distribute its products through nondiscounting dealers without violating the FTC Act.

Some scholars and other commentators have recommended that retail price maintenance be analyzed under the rule of reason,[55] since it can encourage interbrand competition by insuring that retailers obtain enough for a product to allow them to provide services to consumers, such as promotion, sales help, and advertising. Resale price maintenance helps maintain a uniform product image and discourages "free riding" by nonservice-oriented Sellers who might be tempted to charge a lower price and cut back on consumer services. Thus, retail price maintenance may, in reality, be pro-competitive, even if it limits intrabrand competition among Sellers of the same product. However, such benefits to competition are not considered under the current approach to vertical price-fixing.

---

where a dealer unwillingly complies with a manufacturer's pricing policies to avoid termination. The commission held that a manufacturer could still decide initially to distribute its products through non-discounting dealers, without running afoul of the Sherman Act or the FTC Act, but could not condition continued dealing on any particular conduct by the dealers.

[52] *See, e.g.,* United States v Parke, Davis & Co, 362 US 29 (1960); Lehrman v Gulf Oil Corp, 464 F2d 26 (5th Cir), *cert denied,* 409 US 1077 (1972) (cannot threaten sanctions), Interphoto Corp v Minolta Corp, 295 F Supp 711 (SDNY), *affd per curiam,* 417 F2d 621 (2d Cir 1969) (cannot require manufacturer's approval for deviation from list price).

[53] *See, e.g.,* Hanson v Shell Oil Co, 541 F2d 1352 (9th Cir 1976), *cert denied,* 429 US 1074 (1977); Knutson v Daily Review, Inc, 548 F2d 795 (9th Cir 1976), *cert denied,* 433 US 910 (1977).

[54] Russell Stover, Inc, 1982 Trade Cas (CCH) ¶21,933 (FTC July 1, 1982).

[55] See Cutler, Some Antitrust Division Views on Vertical Restraints: Public Policy and Private Actions, Speech before the Twenty-First Annual Advanced Antitrust Seminar on Distribution and Marketing, New York, New York (Dec 8, 1981). Judge Posner recommends a rule of per se legality for vertical arrangements. Posner, *The Next Step in the Antitrust Treatment of Restricted Distribution: Per Se Legality,* 48 U Chi L Rev 6 (1981).

§1.16 —Is horizontal price-fixing per se illegal?

Horizontal price-fixing, that is, agreements between competitors to affect, stabilize, or determine the price at which they sell a particular product[56] or service,[57] are illegal per se under §1 of the Sherman Act and §5 of the FTC Act. Such agreements are per se illegal even if the prices fixed are themselves reasonable.[58]

Horizontal price-fixing agreements clearly discourage competition between Sellers on one of the most important subjects of competition—the price at which a product is sold. If Buyers cannot choose among Sellers on the basis of price, competition among those Sellers is severely hampered.

Some agreements among competitors directly affect price and are easy to characterize as illegal per se. Some other agreements between competitors—which are not direct price-fixing—may also affect price competition. Where such agreements aim to manipulate price in the market, they will be treated as price-fixing.[59] No evidence of reasonableness, lack of power, or minimal effect will change the analysis and the finding of per se illegality.

Where actions taken by competitors have a pro-competitive purpose, with some ancillary effect on price, they are generally not held unlawful per se. Where the action is designed to facilitate the market mechanism, the price effect will be judged under the rule of reason, and may or may not be found unlawful.[60]

§1.17 —Are all tying arrangements illegal per se?

A Seller imposes a *tie* by refusing to sell a desired product (the *tying* product) to a Buyer unless the Buyer also purchases another product (the *tied* product) from the Seller. Using this arrangement a Seller can extend its power in the tying product market over the tied product. Courts have stated that tying arrangements serve hardly any purpose beyond the suppression of competition:

> They deny competitors free access to the market for the tied product, not because the party imposing the tying requirements has a better product or a lower price but because of his power or leverage in another market. At the same time, buyers are forced to forego their free choice between

---

[56] *See, e.g.,* United States v Socony-Vacuum Oil Co, 310 US 150 (1940).

[57] *See, e.g.,* Goldfarb v Virginia State Bar, 421 US 773 (1975).

[58] Catalano, Inc v Target Sales, Inc, 446 US 643 (1980).

[59] *See, e.g.,* FTC v Cement Inst, 333 US 683 (1948) (basing point system for determining price); Las Vegas Merchant Plumbers Assn v United States, 210 F2d 732 (9th Cir), *cert denied,* 348 US 817 (1954) (bid-rigging); National Macaroni Mfrs Assn v FTC, 345 F2d 421 (7th Cir 1965) (agreement to depress prices for raw materials).

[60] *See, e.g.,* Chicago Bd of Trade v United States, 246 US 231 (1918) (practice held reasonable).

competing products.[61]

Tying arrangements can be analyzed under both §1 of the Sherman Act and §3 of the Clayton Act.[62] Although the standards under the two statutes are not identical, by now, they have become virtually interchangeable and all tie-in arrangements are subject to the tests articulated in the Clayton Act cases.[63]

Although courts have repeatedly stated that tying arrangements are illegal per se,[64] in fact, a finding of illegality is proper only after consideration of the Seller's power in the market for the tying product and the effect of the tie on commerce in the tied product.[65] In other words, three elements must be established to make out a per se tying violation: (1) there must be two separate products;[66] (2) the Seller must have sufficient economic power in the tying product market to appreciably restrain competition in the tied product market; (3) a "not insubstantial" amount of commerce in the tied product must be affected.[67] At times, market power may be presumed if the tying product is patented,[68] copyrighted,[69] or otherwise clearly differentiated in the minds of

---

[61] Northern Pac Ry Co v United States, 356 US 1, 6 (1958).

[62] *See, e.g., In re* Data General Corp Antitrust Litigation, 490 F Supp 1089, 1100 (ND Cal 1980).

[63] *See In re* Data Gen Antitrust Litigation, 490 F Supp 1089, 1100-01 (ND Cal 1980); Spartan Grain & Mill Co v Ayers, 581 F2d 419, 428 (5th Cir 1978).

[64] *See, e.g.,* International Salt Co v United States, 332 US 292 (1947); United States Steel Corp v Fortner Enters, Inc, 429 US 610, 612 n 1 (1977); Fortner Enters, Inc v United States Steel Corp, 394 US 495, 498-99 (1969).

[65] *See, e.g.,* United States v Mercedes-Benz, 517 F Supp 1369 (ND Cal 1981); *In re* Data Gen Antitrust Litigation, 529 F Supp 801 (ND Cal 1981) (granting judgment for defendant notwithstanding the verdict). In fact, the current Justice Department view recommends that tie-ins be analyzed under the rule of reason. See Cutler, Some Antitrust Division Views on Vertical Restraints: Public Policy and Private Actions, Speech before the Twenty-First Annual Advanced Antitrust Seminar on Distribution and Marketing, New York, New York (Dec 8, 1981).

[66] For example, a franchisor's trademark has been determined to be a separate product for tying analysis. Siegel v Chicken Delight, Inc, 448 F2d 43 (9th Cir 1971), *cert denied,* 405 US 955 (1972). The Ninth Circuit has recently interpreted *Chicken Delight* to mean that "under certain circumstances, a trademark may be sufficiently unrelated to the alleged tied product to warrant treatment as a separate item." Krehl v Baskin-Robbins Ice Cream Co, 664 F2d 1348 (9th Cir 1982). Baskin-Robbins's trademark served merely as a representation of the end product marketed by trademark licensees and, therefore, was not a separate product for tie-in purposes. *See also* Principe v McDonald's Corp, 631 F2d 303, 309 (4th Cir 1980), *cert denied,* 451 US 970 (1981), in which the court held that McDonald's requirement that its franchisees lease land from it and pay a security deposit were not separate products tied to the McDonald's trademark. On the contrary, the court held that the lease and deposit were integral components of the business method being franchised.

[67] *See, e.g.,* Fortner Enter, Inc v United States Steel Corp, 394 US 495, 499 (1969).

[68] International Salt Co v United States, 332 US 392 (1947).

[69] United States v Paramount Pictures, Inc, 334 US 131 (1948); United States v Loews, Inc, 371 US 38 (1962).

Buyers. And the amount of commerce affected need not be very substantial.[70]

Thus, although courts continue to assert that tying arrangements are illegal per se, they generally do not find illegality without some degree of economic analysis. In addition, under exceptional circumstances, business justifications may render lawful a tie-in that otherwise possesses the necessary elements for per se illegality. However, the scope of the business justification exception is still unclear.[71]

§1.18 —Are boycotts illegal per se?

A boycott is group action designed to keep a particular firm from competing with the boycotting group. For example, a group of retailers may join together to exclude a competitor from the market. The group may do this by coercing a distributor (expressly or by implication) not to deal with a competing retailer[72]—or by influencing consumers not to deal with that retailer.[73] The retailer group may seek to dissuade a distributor from integrating vertically and entering the retail business by threatening to cease dealing with the distributor unless it stays out of retailing. The group may not directly seek to exclude a competitor, but rather may coerce certain trade practices that effectively destroy competition or make it impossible for a certain firm to compete effectively.[74] In all of these circumstances, the purpose of the group action is to drive out competition or discourage a competitor from entering the market.

Boycotts are generally analyzed as horizontal, and, at least if more than two firms at one level agree to exclude a competitor, they are per se illegal.[75]

---

[70] In International Salt Co v United States, 332 US 392 (1947), the Court found an illegal tie where annual sales of the tied product amounted to only $500,000.

[71] *See, e.g.,* Susser v Carvel Corp, 332 F2d 505, 520 (2d Cir 1964), *cert dismissed,* 381 US 125 (1965); United States v Jerrold Elecs Corp, 187 F Supp 545 (ED Pa 1960), *affd per curiam,* 365 US 567 (1961). *Cf* Siegel v Chicken Delight, Inc, 448 F2d 43, 51 n 9 (9th Cir 1971), *cert denied,* 405 US 955 (1972) (A tying arrangement might be justified where some "extraordinary condition forcloses specification, *e.g.,* where it would divulge a trade secret.").

[72] Where a manufacturer chooses not to deal with a particular retailer because of pressure from *one* competing retailer (not a group), that action could technically be considered a *boycott,* but is more likely to be viewed as a vertical agreement or unilateral action on the part of manufacturer. *See* Ron Tonkin Gran Turismo, Inc v Fiat Distrib, Inc, 637 F2d 1376 (9th Cir 1981). *But see* Spray-Rite Serv Corp v Monsanto Co, 684 F2d 1226 (7th Cir 1982), *cert granted,* __ US __,75 L Ed 2d 479, 103 S Ct 1249 (1983); Com-Tel, Inc v DuKane Corp, 669 F2d 404 (6th Cir 1982); Cernuto, Inc v United Cabinet Corp, 595 F2d 164 (3d Cir 1979); Alloy Intl Co v Hoover-NSK Bearing Co, 635 F2d 1222 (7th Cir 1980).

[73] *See, e.g.,* United States v General Motors Corp, 384 US 127 (1966); Klors, Inc v Broadway-Hale Stores, Inc, 359 US 207 (1959); Eastern States Retail Lumber Dealers Assn v United States, 234 US 600 (1914).

[74] *See, e.g.,* Fashion Originators Guild v FTC, 312 US 457 (1941); Radiant Burners, Inc v Peoples Gas Light & Coke Co, 364 US 656 (1961).

[75] *See, e.g.,* Klors, Inc v Broadway-Hale Stores, Inc, 359 US 207 (1959); Com-Tel, Inc v DuKane Corp, 669 F2d 404 (6th Cir 1982). *But see* United States v Realty Multi-List,

However, courts may look at arrangements with some characteristics of a boycott as vertical—as long as they do not amount to a wide-ranging combination of firms at various levels of the distribution process.[76] This outlook may lead a court either to find that *no* agreement exists or to find a purely nonprice vertical agreement to be judged under the rule of reason.

§1.19 —Is horizontal market division per se illegal?

Decisions by competitors to allocate markets or customers are per se illegal, since they clearly limit competition among the firms agreeing to the allocation.[77] Such agreements are illegal, whether or not they also involve price-fixing, without any inquiry into economic power or the effect of the arrangement. Where competitors boldly agree to divide territories, customers, or markets, courts have had no difficulty determining that their agreements are per se unlawful. But where an agreement between competitors *may* segregate markets, courts must decide whether to characterize the agreement as market division and per se illegal, or as an arrangement to be reviewed under the rule of reason.[78] Generally, where the purpose or primary effect of an agreement between competitors is to divide markets horizontally, it will be considered to be horizontal market division and analyzed under the per se rule.

§1.20 —Is reciprocal dealing per se illegal?

In a reciprocal dealing agreement, one firm agrees to buy from another on the condition that the selling firm agrees to purchase something else from the buying firm. The possibility of reciprocal dealing is enhanced where firms are involved in a variety of enterprises, and where they enter the market as both buyers and sellers. However, it is not enough that a firm acts as both a seller and a buyer with respect to another firm. There must be some agreement on reciprocity, some fact to show that a purchase or sale is made to encourage a reciprocal response. When such agreements affect a substantial volume of

---

Inc, 629 F2d 1351 (5th Cir 1980) (court refused to hold real estate multiple listing service admission requirements per se illegal as a boycott, but held them "facially unreasonable" because of the listing service's market power and because the rules lacked sufficient grounding in the defendant's competitive needs and were broader than necessary to accomplish any legitimate objectives).

[76] *See, e.g.,* Ron Tonkin Gran Turismo, Inc v Fiat Distribs, Inc, 637 F2d 1376 (9th Cir 1981); Borger v Yamaha Intl Corp, 625 F2d 390 (2d Cir 1980); *see also* Oreck Corp v Whirlpool Corp, 579 F2d 126 (2d Cir) (en banc), *cert denied,* 439 US 946 (1978).

[77] United States v Topco Assocs, 405 US 596 (1972); Timken Roller Bearing Co v United States, 341 US 593 (1951).

[78] *See, e.g.,* United States v Columbia Pictures Corp, 189 F Supp 153 (SDNY 1960); United States v American Smelting & Ref Co, 182 F Supp 834 (SDNY 1960).

commerce, they will most likely be found illegal per se.[79]

§1.21 What kind of conduct is illegal only if unreasonable?

As stated before, the goal of antitrust laws is to encourage competition—primarily between different products or services. Some conduct that increases interbrand competition may simultaneously decrease intrabrand competition.[80] Where that is the case, courts do not judge the conduct to be illegal until they have looked at its effects in the particular industry involved, weighing both the benefits and the drawbacks of the practice. If the practice is found to be an unreasonable restraint, it will be struck down.

Thus, conduct that may have competitive benefits—especially conduct that is untested or otherwise new to a given industry[81]—is generally characterized to fall outside the categories of behavior deemed illegal per se. Instead, the conduct is viewed under the rule of reason.

§1.22 —How is conduct that is illegal only if unreasonable distinguished from conduct that is illegal per se?

Courts generally determine conduct to be illegal per se only after experience has shown that conduct to be generally anticompetitive, no matter what firm engages in the conduct or what industry is involved. On the other hand, conduct judged under the rule of reason has not been found through experience to be anticompetitive whenever it occurs. The conduct will be illegal only if it is unreasonable given the actors involved, the structure of the market and the actual effect of the conduct on competition.

For example, a manufacturer is generally able to choose how it wants to distribute its products—directly to retailers, through wholesalers, or using a combination of the two. Moreover, a manufacturer's decision to change its methods of distribution ordinarily escapes antitrust scrutiny in the absence of

---

79 *See, e.g.,* Betaseed, Inc v U&I Inc, 681 F2d 1203 (9th Cir 1982); Southern Concrete Co v United States Steel Corp, 535 F2d 313, 317 (5th Cir 1976); United States v General Dynamics Corp, 258 F Supp 36 (SDNY 1966). *But see* WIXT Television, Inc v Meredith Corp, 506 F Supp 1003 (NDNY 1980) (requiring a plaintiff to demonstrate that a reciprocal agreement was coerced with a reciprocal motivation or entered into with an understanding that the patronage would be mutual, "causing a substantial foreclosure of competitors from the marketplace"). The Supreme Court has stated that reciprocity is anticompetitive, but has not had occasion to declare it per se illegal. *See* FTC v Consolidated Foods Corp, 380 US 592, 594 (1965).

80 *See* Continental TV, Inc v GTE Sylvania, 433 US 36, 51–52 (1977).

81 *See* Broadcast Music, Inc v Columbia Broadcasting Sys, 441 US 1, 9-10 (1979).

an anticompetitive purpose or effect.[82] Thus, a decision to curtail distribution through wholesalers,[83] to replace one distributor with another,[84] or not to increase the number of existing distributors[85] will not be unlawful in the absence of an anticompetitive purpose or effect.

§1.23 —How is reasonableness determined?

Courts determine whether conduct is reasonable by looking at the market in which the conduct occurs, in terms of geography and products, the size and power of the actors, and the positive and negative effects of the conduct on the market. Under this rule, the factfinder must consider

> the facts peculiar to the business to which the restraint is applied; its condition before and after the restraint was imposed; the nature of the restraint, and its effect, actual or probable. The history of the restraint, the evil believed to exist, the reason for adopting the particular remedy, the purpose or end sought to be attained are all relevant facts.[86]

Rule of reason analysis thus focuses directly on the challenged restraint's impact on competitive conditions. But the rule is not used to decide whether competition is a worthy goal of the antitrust laws. As recently stated by the Supreme Court:

> [t]he purpose of the analysis is to form a judgment about the competitive significance of the restraint; it is not to decide whether a policy favoring competition is in the public interest, or in the interest of the members of an industry. Subject to exceptions defined by statute, that policy decision has been made by the Congress.[87]

---

[82] *See, e.g.,* Fuchs Sugars & Syrups, Inc v Amstar Corp, 603 F2d 1025 (2d Cir), *cert denied,* 444 US 917 (1979); Bowen v New York News, Inc, 522 F2d 1242 (2d Cir 1975), *cert denied,* 425 US 936 (1976).

[83] *See, e.g.,* Knutson v Daily Review, Inc, 548 F2d 795 (9th Cir 1976), *cert denied,* 433 US 910 (1977).

[84] *See, e.g.,* Carlson Mach Tools, Inc v American Tool, Inc, 678 F2d 1253 (5th Cir 1982); Chandler Supply Co v GAF Corp, 650 F2d 983 (9th Cir 1980); Westpoint Pepperell, Inc v Rea, 1980-2 Trade Cas (CCH) ¶63,341 (ND Cal 1980).

[85] *See, e.g.,* Borger v Yamaha Intl Corp, 625 F2d 390 (2d Cir 1980); Ron Tonkin Gran Turismo, Inc v Fiat Distribs, Inc, 673 F2d 1376 (9th Cir 1981).

[86] Chicago Bd of Trade v United States, 246 US 231, 238 (1918).

[87] National Socy of Professional Engs v United States, 435 US 679, 692 (1978).

§1.24 —Does the market affect the reasonableness of conduct?

Since rule of reason analysis focuses on the impact of particular conduct on competitive conditions, courts must define the relevant market in which the restraint operates. The inquiry must, therefore, begin by defining the relevant geographic and product markets.[88] Those markets set the boundaries within which a distributional restraint is to be judged.

With respect to vertical restraints, Judge Richard Posner has recommended a test that expressly takes into account the market position of the supplier. Under this view, if a firm does not have power in a given market it cannot affect the price of its product and therefore any vertical restraint imposed by that firm cannot be anticompetitive. Thus, proof of a defendant's *substantial* market power would be a first step in rule of reason analysis.[89] If the court finds insignificant market power, no further inquiry will be required.

§1.25 —How is the geographic market determined?

Courts have not been excessively rigorous in defining the *geographic market* in which a distributional restraint must be analyzed,[90] although the concept of geographic market is certainly well-known in monopoly and merger cases.[91] In its simplest formulation, the relevant geographic market is one in which the "goods and services at issue are marketed to a significant degree,"[92] or a commercially significant area which can be said to confine the activity at issue.

In truth, the market must reflect commercial reality, and many factors may influence its proper size and scope. For example, transportation costs must be considered. A small mom and pop grocery store may attract customers from

---

[88] *See, e.g.*, JBL Enters, Inc v Jhirmack Enters, Inc, 698 F2d 1011 (9th Cir 1983) (cosmetic manufacturer's territorial and customer restrictions did not unreasonably restrain trade in view of manufacturer's insignificant market share; Red Diamond Supply, Inc v Liquid Carbonic Corp, 637 F2d 1001, 1005-06 (5th Cir), *cert denied*, 454 US 827 (1981) (plaintiff in vertical restriction case failed to show relevant market).

[89] Posner, *The Next Step in the Antitrust Treatment of Restricted Distribution: Per Se Legality*, 48 U Chi L Rev 6, 16 (1981). *See also* Muenster Butane, Inc v Stewart Co, 651 F2d 292, 298 (5th Cir 1981).

[90] *See, e.g.*, Eiberger v Sony Corp, 622 F2d 1068 (2d Cir 1980); Donald B Rice Tire Co v Michelin Tire Corp, 483 F Supp 750 (D Md 1980), *affd*, 638 F2d 15 (4th Cir). *cert denied*, 454 US 864, (1981).

[91] The relevant market must be identified in both monopoly cases under §2 of the Sherman Act and merger cases under §7 of the Clayton Act. *See, e.g.*, United States v EI DuPont de Nemours & Co, 351 US 377 (1956) (in monopoly case, market defined as flexible packaging material in which du Pont had 20% share rather than cellophane in which it had 75% share); Brown Shoe Co v United States, 370 US 294 (1962) (men's, women's and children's shoes taken as submarkets for purposes of analyzing merger).

[92] *See, e.g.*, United States v Marine Bancorporation, Inc, 418 US 602, 621 (1974) (merger case).

a radius of a few city blocks. A larger grocery may pull customers in from miles away, especially if it advertises throughout a wide area, offers parking facilities, etc. And, a nationally known chain grocery store may draw customers from a much wider metropolitan area. In determining the effect of a distributional practice, how the market is characterized may determine whether *significant* competition is affected.

§1.26 —How is the product market determined?

Similarly, the *product market* may become relevant in a rule of reason case, since the court must gauge the probable effect of a distributional restraint on a particular market. One of the competitive conditions to be considered is what products compete in that market and therefore, how much competition is actually foreclosed by the restraint.

The market generally affected by purely vertical restraints is the market for the particular brand of product that is the subject of the restraint. This is true because vertical restraints generally limit intrabrand competition (between dealers of the same brand of product) and encourage interbrand competition (between different brands and types of products). Therefore, to assess the effect of a vertical restraint on competition, a court must know what products actrually compete with each other and how the restraint may affect that competition.[93]

Although analysis of distributional restraints under the rule of reason is in the process of articulation and embellishment, the question of relevant product market has been addressed in tying cases,[94] monopoly cases under §2 of the Sherman Act,[95] and merger cases under §7 of the Clayton Act.[96] In those cases, the basic rule formulated by the courts is that if one product is competitive with another, it will be included in determining the market. To determine competitiveness, courts look at whether the products are reasonably interchangeable[97] or if there is cross-elasticity of demand between products, so that

---

[93] *See, e.g.,* Ron Tonkin Gran Turismo, Inc v Fiat Distribs, Inc, 637 F2d 1376, 1379-80 (9th Cir 1981) (relevant market was all cars, not just Fiats); JBL Enters, Inc v Jhirmack Enters, Inc, 509 F Supp 357, 366-69, 376 (ND Cal 1981), *affd,* 698 F2d 1011 (9th Cir 1983) (relevant market was beauty products sold to professional outlets, not shampoo and conditioners sold to consumers for home use); Mesirow v Pepperidge Farm, Inc, 1981-2 Trade Cas (CCH) ¶64,292 (ND Cal Aug 31, 1981) (market was biscuit crackers, not "premium cookies").

[94] *See, e.g., In re* Data Gen Antitrust Litigation, 529 F Supp 801 (ND Cal 1981) (granting judgment for defendant notwithstanding the verdict); United States v Mercedes-Benz, 517 F Supp 1369 (ND Cal 1981).

[95] *See, e.g.,* United States v EI DuPont de Nemours & Co, 351 US 377 (1956); United States v Aluminum Co, 148 F2d 416 (2d Cir 1945).

[96] *See, e.g.,* Brown Shoe Co v United States, 370 US 294 (1962); United States v Marine Bancorporation, Inc, 418 US 602 (1974).

[97] *See, e.g.,* United States v EI duPont de Nemours & Co, 351 US 377 (1956); United States v Continental Can Co, 378 US 441 (1964) (glass and metal containers were reasonably interchangeable).

consumer demand shifts freely from one product to a possible substitute.[98]

§1.27 —What market effect is considered unreasonable?

Rule of reason analysis must assess the effect of a particular restraint on the relevant geographic and product markets. Only if the restraint has an anticompetitive effect will it be deemed unreasonable. This analysis includes a determination of how interbrand competition is enhanced and how intrabrand competition is limited by the restraint.[99] For example, a territorial restriction may insulate a distributor from competition by other distributors of that same product within its territory. At the same time, it can increase competition between the exclusive distributor and distributors of other products, since the exclusive distributor may be encouraged to provide promotion or after-sale services along with the product, and thereby attract customers away from competing goods.[100]

Recently, Judge Posner has recommended a *market power* rule—if a firm does not have substantial market power, any restraint it might impose cannot conceivably have an anticompetitive effect.[101] Thus, the question of market and market share would be a threshold inquiry under the rule of reason.

§1.28 What kind of distributional practices are illegal only if unreasonable and how are they analyzed under the rule of reason?

Generally, exclusionary buying arrangements and, since the Supreme Court's decision in *Continental TV, Inc v GTE Sylvania*,[102] vertical nonprice restrictions are illegal only if they are unreasonable—if they have an anticompetitive effect in the relevant market. The following distributional practices are currently analyzed under this standard:

1. Exclusive dealing arrangements
2. Requirements contracts

---

[98] *See, e.g.*, Brown Shoe Co v United States, 370 US 294 (1962).

[99] *See, e.g.*, Eiberger v Sony Corp, 622 F2d 1068 (2d Cir 1980); Muenster Butane, Inc v Stewart Co, 651 F2d 292 (5th Cir 1981). Some courts have raised the question of whether a detriment to intrabrand competition alone is a sufficient basis to hold a restraint unreasonable. *See, e.g.*, Eiberger v Sony Corp, 622 F2d 1068, 1081 (2d Cir. 1980).

[100] *See, e.g.*, Westpoint Pepperell v Rea, 1980-2 Trade Cas (CCH) ¶63,341 (ND Cal Apr 8, 1980).

[101] Posner, *The Next Step in the Antitrust Treatment of Restricted Distribution: Per Se Legality*, 48 U Chi L Rev 6, 16 (1981); *see also* Valley Liquors, Inc v Renfield Importers, Ltd, 678 F2d 742, (7th Cir 1982) (Posner, J.).

[102] 433 US 36 (1977).

3. Vertical customer restrictions
4. Vertical territorial restrictions
5. Vertical location restrictions
6. Trademark licenses

In analyzing these restraints, courts look at their effect on both interbrand and intrabrand competition in a particular market.

§1.29 Are exclusive dealing arrangements illegal only if unreasonable?

Exclusive dealing arrangements are those in which a Seller agrees to sell its products to only one Buyer in a particular area—an *exclusive dealership*[103]—or where a Buyer agrees to carry only the products of a particular Seller.[104] In each instance, the legality of the arrangement is determined under the rule of reason.[105] In an exclusive dealership, a manufacturer insulates a dealer from intrabrand competition within a certain territory on the assumption that interbrand competition will be encouraged; thus, this is the classic arrangement for which rule of reason treatment under *Sylvania* is appropriate. In the other form of exclusive dealing, a Seller agrees to sell to a Buyer on the condition that the Buyer does not deal in competitive products. Thus, a competitor of the Seller is foreclosed from the market represented by that Buyer. The anticompetitive danger of such arrangements is that one Seller may obtain a sufficient number of them to make it difficult, if not impossible, for another Seller to compete in a given market.

Historically, exclusive dealing arrangements were judged under either the quantitative substantiality test or the qualitative substantiality test.[106] The *quantitative* substantiality test was carried over from tie-in cases, and required a showing of the amount of commerce affected by the arrangement, either in relative or in absolute terms. The *qualitative* test, on the other hand, is more akin to rule of reason analysis and requires an investigation of economic

---

[103] Exclusive dealerships or distributorships generally arise in the context of franchising. They are often combined with a *primary responsibility* provision whereby the franchisee agrees to focus its sales efforts in a particular territory. The term *exclusive dealing* usually describes an exclusionary buying arrangement, in which a Buyer agrees not to handle goods that compete with the Seller's goods.

[104] Exclusive dealing contracts are only one form of exclusionary buying agreement. Others include requirements contracts and tie-in sales. All such arrangements can be reached under §1 of the Sherman Act or §3 of the Clayton Act.

[105] Tampa Elec Co v Nashville Coal Co, 365 US 320 (1961).

[106] Quantitative substantiality test: Standard Oil Co & Standard Stations v United States, 337 US 293 (1949); Dictograph Prods, Inc v FTC, 217 F2d 821 (2d Cir 1954), *cert denied,* 349 US 940 (1955). Qualitative substantiality test: Tampa Elec Co v Nashville Coal Co, 365 US 320 (1961); Precision Dynamics Corp v American Hosp Supply Corp, 241 F Supp 436, 447 (SD Cal 1965).

factors, potential justifications for the arrangement, and its actual competitive effects.

Since the Supreme Court's decision in *Tampa Electric Co v Nashville Coal Co*[107] the qualitative test is used. In that decision, the Court required that the product and geographic markets be defined and the extent of foreclosure as a percentage of the market be estimated to determine the competitive effect of an exclusive dealing arrangement.

§1.30 —Are requirements contracts illegal only if unreasonable?

Requirements contracts, in which a Buyer agrees to purchase all or a substantial portion of its needs from one Seller, are really a variant of an exclusive dealing arrangement. As with an exclusive dealing contract, the Buyer, in effect, agrees not to deal with a competing Seller with respect to a particular product. Requirements contracts are analyzed under the rule of reason in much the same way as exclusive dealing arrangements, although requirements contracts are somewhat more acceptable to courts since they have advantages for Buyers as well as Sellers. The Supreme Court noted the following reasons a Buyer might want to enter into a requirements contract: "[T]hey may assume supply, afford protection against rises in prices, enable long-term planning on the basis of known costs and obviate the expense and risk of storage in the quantity necessary for a commodity having a fluctuating demand."[108] With respect to Sellers, other advantages may accrue: "[R]equirements contracts may make possible the substantial reduction of selling expenses, give protection against price fluctuations, and—of particular advantage to a newcomer to the field to whom it is important to know what capital expenditures are justified —offer the possibility of a predictable market."[109]

§1.31 —Are vertical customer restrictions illegal only if unreasonable?

Between 1967 and 1977, vertical distributional restraints—restrictions on the customers to whom and territories in which a distributor could sell, or the locations from which a distributor could sell—were deemed per se illegal.[110] Since the Supreme Court's decision in *Sylvania* recognizing the competitive

---

[107] 365 US 320 (1961).

[108] Standard Oil Co & Standard Stations v United States, 337 US 293, 306 (1949).

[109] *Id* 306-07.

[110] United States v Arnold, Schwinn & Co, 338 US 365 (1967), *overruled by,* Continental TV, Inc v GTE Sylvania, Inc, 433 US 36 (1977). Even under *Schwinn,* however, where consumer safety was an issue, vertical restrictions were upheld. *See, e.g.,* Tripoli Co v Wella Corp, 425 F2d 932 (3d Cir), *cert denied,* 400 US 831 (1970).

benefits of such arrangements, vertical nonprice restrictions are judged under the rule of reason. As the Court in *Sylvania* recognized:

> Economists have identified a number of ways in which manufacturers can use [vertical] restrictions to compete more effectively against other manufacturers. . . . For example, new manufacturers and manufacturers entering new markets can use the restrictions in order to induce competent and aggressive retailers to make the kind of investment of capital and labor that is often required in the distribution of products unknown to the consumer. Established manufacturers can use them to induce retailers to engage in promotional activities or to provide service and repair facilities necessary to the efficient marketing of their products. Service and repair are vital for many products, such as automobiles and major household appliances. The availability and quality of such services affects a manufacturer's goodwill and the competitiveness of his product. Because of market imperfections such as the so-called "free rider" effect, these services might not be provided by retailers in a purely competitive situation, despite the fact that each retailer's benefit would be greater if all provided the services than if none did.[111]

Although *Sylvania* concerned a location restriction, the decision applies to all vertical nonprice restraints—customer and territorial restrictions as well. Thus, a manufacturer's policy of selling only to retailers for subsequent sale to consumers and not to other retailers, an "anti-wholesaling" customer restriction, is to be analyzed under the rule of reason.[112] Similarly, a policy prohibiting a distributor from selling to particular customers[113] will also be judged under the rule of reason.

Although such arrangements restrict intrabrand competition at either the wholesale or the retail level, they may have significant interbrand benefits. For instance, a manufacturer may correctly believe that unauthorized retailers will not provide the promotion and sales efforts the manufacturer requires to enable its product to compete with others in the market. What is more, such unauthorized accounts may *free ride* on the promotional and sales efforts of

---

[111] Continental TV, Inc v GTE Sylvania, Inc, 433 US 36, 54-55 (1977).

[112] *See, e.g.,* JBL Enters, Inc v Jhirmack Enters, Inc, 698 F2d 1011 (9th Cir 1983); Sports Center, Inc v Riddell, Inc, 673 F2d 786 (5th Cir 1982); Davis Watkins Co v Service Merchandise Co, 686 F2d 1190 (6th Cir 1982); Donald B Rice Tire Co v Michelin Tire Corp, 483 F Supp 750 (D Md 1980), *affd,* 638 F2d 15 (4th Cir), *cert denied,* 454 US 864, (1981).

[113] *See, e.g.,* Abadir & Co v First Miss Corp, 651 F2d 422 (5th Cir 1981) (limiting sales to Asian customers is reasonable); Clairol, Inc v Boston Discount Center, 608 F2d 1114 (6th Cir 1979) (manufacturer's prohibition against selling professional beauty products to the general public is reasonable); H&B Equip Co v International Harvester Co, 577 F2d 239 (5th Cir 1978) (manufacturer's prohibition against distributor's bidding on government sales or sales to rental yards not unreasonable).

authorized dealers.[114] As a result, the authorized dealers might be unwilling to engage in promotion and sales efforts, thereby decreasing the position of the manufacturer's product vis-á-vis competitive products. To avoid this result, the manufacturer may prohibit wholesaling by one dealer to other unauthorized dealers.

§1.32 —Are vertical territorial restrictions illegal only if unreasonable?

Similarly, vertical territorial restrictions, whereby a Seller restricts the geographic area in which a Buyer can resell products, are now judged under the rule of reason.[115] These restrictions may not prohibit extraterritorial sales completely, but may make them economically unfeasible or less profitable.[116] Such territorial restrictions are often necessary to encourage interbrand competition, since a dealer who is insulated from intrabrand competition within its territory will expend resources on promotional and service activities to improve its competitive position vis-á-vis retailers of other products. The dealer does not face the possibility that another retailer of the same product in its territory will "free-ride" on the services provided.[117] A manufacturer's desire to grant exclusive territories to retailers is a legitimate goal and, without more, does not suggest any forbidden anticompetitive motive or effect.

Issues often arise when a manufacturer seeks to terminate one of its distributors, or replace it with another distributor. The terminated distributor often tries to implicate its competitors in the decision and characterize the action as a horizontal *boycott* and therefore per se illegal.[118] Ordinarily, however, the

---

[114] *See, e.g.,* Donald B Rice Tire Co v Michelin Tire Corp, 483 F Supp 750 (D Md 1980), *affd,* 638 F2d 15 (4th Cir), *cert denied,* 454 US 864 (1981); Posner, *The Rule of Reason and the Economic Approach: Reflections on the Sylvania Decision,* 45 U Chi L Rev 1 (1977).

[115] *See, e.g.,* Muenster Butane, Inc v Stewart Co, 651 F2d 292 (5th Cir 1981); Abadir & Co v First Miss Corp, 651 F2d 422 (5th Cir 1981); Copy-Data Sys v Toshiba, Inc, 663 F2d 405 (2d Cir 1981). Eiberger v Sony Corp, 622 F2d 1068 (2d Cir 1980); Cowley v Braden Indus, 613 F2d 751 (9th Cir), *cert denied,* 446 US 965 (1980); Mesirow v Pepperidge Farm Inc, 1981-2 Trade Cas (CCH) ¶64,292 (ND Cal Aug 31, 1981).

[116] For example, see the Sony warranty fee system at issue (and held unreasonable) in Eiberger v Sony Corp, 622 F2d 1068 (2d Cir 1980). In Cowley v Braden Indus, 613 F2d 751 (9th Cir), *cert denied,* 446 US 965 (1980) distributors could sell outside their own territory only if: (1) the goods came first to their territory; (2) the items were placed in stock; and (3) the distributors were not "actively soliciting business outside their assigned territory." Thus, sales outside an assigned territory were not prohibited outright, but they became economically unfeasible or significantly less profitable.

[117] *See, e.g.,* Muenster Butane, Inc v Stewart Co, 651 F2d 292, 297 (5th Cir 1981).

[118] *See, e.g.,* Ron Tonkin Gran Turismo, Inc v Fiat Distribs, Inc, 637 F2d 1376 (9th Cir 1981); Borger v Yamaha Intl Corp, 625 F2d 390 (2d Cir 1980); Oreck Corp v Whirlpool Corp, 579 F2d 126 (2d Cir 1978) (en banc), *cert denied,* 439 US 946 (1979).

action is not characterized as a boycott.[119] In fact, courts are generally sympathetic to a manufacturer's attempts to replace an unsuccessful distributor with one who promises better service and an increase in interbrand competition.[120]

§1.33 —Are vertical location restrictions illegal only if unreasonable?

A third form of nonprice vertical restraint—a location restriction—is also analyzed under the rule of reason.[121] In this arrangement, a Buyer is authorized to sell a manufacturer's products only from a specified location. Once again, a manufacturer's purpose in requiring a location restriction is to encourage interbrand competition. Many manufacturers choose their distributors because of the way their outlets look, to insure that their products are offered and displayed in well-equipped and well-designed locations. If a Buyer could sell merchandise from any unapproved location, the benefits accruing to the manufacturer from carefully choosing its dealers would diminish.

§1.34 —What if vertical restrictions affect price?

As stated earlier, vertical nonprice restrictions are judged under the rule of reason while vertical price restrictions—i.e., resale price maintenance—are per se illegal.[122] Thus, whether a restraint is characterized as affecting price may

---

[119] *See, e.g.,* Carlson Mach Tools, Inc v American Tool, Inc, 678 F2d 1253 (5th Cir 1982); Borger v Yamaha Intl Corp, 625 F2d 390 (2d Cir 1980); Westpoint Pepperell, Inc v Rea, 1980-2 Trade Cas (CCH) ¶63,341 (ND Cal Apr 8, 1980). *But see* Com-Tel, Inc v DuKane Corp, 669 F2d 404 (6th Cir 1982) (although pressure on distributor was applied vertically by manufacturer, competition was affected horizontally, warranting application of per se boycott rules); Cernuto, Inc v United Cabinet Corp, 595 F2d 164 (3d Cir 1979); Alloy Intl Co v Hoover-NSK Bearing Co, 635 F2d 1222 (7th Cir 1980); Contractor Utility Sales v Certain-Teed Prod Corp, 638 F2d 1061, 1072 (7th Cir 1981), holding that a per se violation of §1 of the Sherman Act may be established upon proof that a manufacturer terminated its relationship with an existing dealer/distributor/agent if: (1) the termination was at the request of a competing dealer/distributor/agent, and (2) the termination was motivated by a desire to reduce or eliminate price competition for its products. The United States Supreme Court recently granted certiorari in a case raising this issue. Spray-Rite Serv Corp v Monsanto Co, 684 F2d 1226 (7th Cir 1982), *cert granted,* __ US __, 75 L Ed 2d 479, 103 S Ct 1249 (1983). In *Spray-Rite* the Seventh Circuit affirmed a jury verdict of $10.5 million for the plaintiff. One of the issues before the Supreme Court is: can a per se unlawful vertical price-fixing conspiracy be inferred solely from evidence that a manufacturer, concerned about retail prices, received complaints from a distributor's competitors and subsequently severed its relationship with the distributor?

[120] *See, e.g.,* Chandler Supply Co v GAF Corp, 650 F2d 983 (9th Cir 1980); Marquis v Chrysler Corp, 577 F2d 624 (9th Cir 1978).

[121] *See, e.g.,* Continental TV, Inc v GTE Sylvania, Inc, 694 F2d 1132 (9th Cir 1983) (affirming summary judgment on remand).

[122] Continental TV, Inc v GTE Sylvania, Inc, 433 US 36 (1977).

be crucial to its legality.[123] One court noted the reason for the distinction: "Restrictions on price have a tendency to reduce price competition, interbrand as well as intrabrand. Restrictions on customers and territory tend to restrict intrabrand competition only and have the potential of strengthening interbrand competition."[124]

Where nonprice vertical restraints have been held unreasonable and, therefore, illegal, at least one court has found an impact on price, which clearly influenced its decision.[125] On the other hand, in finding customer and territorial restraints reasonable, another court ignored the impact of those restraints on price.[126] And, a third court expressly recognized that a territorial restriction coupled with a price restriction is no more anticompetitive than a pure territorial restriction and, therefore, should be analyzed under the rule of reason and not deemed a per se violation.[127] The United States Supreme Court recently granted a petition for certiorari to decide, among other issues, whether nonprice vertical restraints should be subject to per se treatment because they are alleged to be part of a vertical price-fixing conspiracy.[128]

§1.35 —Are trademark licenses illegal only if unreasonable?

Often, when a manufacturer licenses others to use its trademarks, it imposes certain vertical restraints to insure uniformity of quality and to protect the trademark. This ordinarily arises in the context of franchising. Even before *Sylvania* held that all vertical nonprice restrictions should be judged under the rule of reason, vertical restrictions ancillary to a valid trademark license have been held to be illegal only if unreasonable. Thus, a trademark licensor may set specifications for finished products, prohibit licensees from carrying certain types of goods, and specify sources of supply or methods of inspection without running afoul of the antitrust laws.[129] Problems may arise, however,

---

[123] It may be that all vertical restrictions have some impact on price and therefore, the characterization of a particular restraint as *price-related* becomes very important in determining the standard under which it is judged. See Posner *The Next Step in the Antitrust Treatment of Restricted Distribution: Per Se Legality,* 48 U Chi L Rev 6 (1981). See **§1.28.**

[124] JBL Enters, Inc v Jhirmack Enters, Inc, 519 F Supp 1084, 1088 (ND Cal 1981), *affd,* 698 F2d 1011 (9th Cir 1983).

[125] Eiberger v Sony Corp, 622 F2d 1068 (2d Cir 1980).

[126] *See, e.g.,* Donald B Rice Co v Michelin Tire Corp, 483 F Supp 750 (D Md 1980), *affd,* 638 F2d 15 (4th Cir), *cert denied,* 454 US 864 (1981).

[127] Eastern Scientific Co v Wild Heerbrugg Instruments, Inc, 572 F2d 883 (1st Cir), *cert denied,* 439 US 833 (1978).

[128] Spray-Rite Serv Corp v Monsanto Co, 684 F2d 1226 (7th Cir 1982), *cert granted,* __ US __, 75 L Ed 2d 479, 103 S Ct 1249 (1983).

[129] *See, e.g.,* Susser v Carvel Corp, 206 F Supp 636 (SDNY 1962), *affd,* 332 F2d 505 (2d Cir 1964), *cert dismissed,* 381 US 125 (1965) (franchisor of soft ice cream could prohibit franchisees from selling hamburgers and hot dogs); Phillips v Crown Central

if a licensor unlawfully *ties* the trademark to purchases from it of other products that are not an integral part of a trademarked business method.[130]

§1.36 Is there a middle ground between per se and rule of reason analysis?

Per se rules are based on a determination that certain conduct may be deemed illegal without any further economic analysis. On the contrary, rule of reason analysis requires a full-scale inquiry into the market affected by a particular practice and the competitive impact of that practice. Recently, a middle ground analysis has been advanced, which requires a less detailed economic inquiry to determine illegality.

In *United States v Realty Multi-List, Inc*[131] the government challenged the membership policies of Realty Multi-List (RML), a real estate multiple listing service in Georgia. RML's policies amounted to a boycott of those brokers denied membership. Despite the boycott label, the Fifth Circuit refused to apply a per se rule, since the multiple listing service had procompetitive effects. The court noted: "We need to know more about the justifications for the particular restraints imposed and their competitive significance before we can judge their legality. This type of analysis takes place under the rule of reason."[132]

However, the court did not engage in traditional rule of reason analysis. Instead, it held that RML's membership policies were *facially unreasonable* because of RML's significant market power and the fact that the particular membership policies could not be justified by RML's competitive needs and were broader than necessary to fulfill the association's legitimate objectives. The court noted that a restraint which survived analysis under the facial unreasonableness standard might still be condemned under traditional rule of reason analysis when the court considered its actual effects in the marketplace.

Thus, the decision in *Realty Multi-List* may signal the development of a new intermediate level of antitrust scrutiny for distributional restraints—between the inflexibility of per se rules and the unlimited, time-consuming, and expensive rule of reason approach.

Petroleum Corp, 395 F Supp 735 (D Md 1975), *affd in part on other grounds, revd in part on other grounds & remanded,* 602 F2d 616 (4th Cir 1979), *cert denied,* 444 US 1074 (1980) (gas station lessor could require lessees to carry only top-quality accessories); Evans v SS Kresge Co, 394 F Supp 817 (WD Pa 1975), *affd,* 544 F2d 1184 (3d Cir 1976), *cert denied,* 433 US 908 (1977) (licensor of K-Mart trademark could limit the products licensee could sell, prohibit licensee from issuing trading stamps, and require licensee to maintain competitive prices).

[130] *See, e.g.,* Siegel v Chicken Delight, Inc, 448 F2d 43 (9th Cir 1971), *cert denied,* 405 US 955 (1972). *But see* Krehl v Baskin-Robbins Ice Cream Co, 664 F2d 1348 (9th Cir 1982); Principe v McDonald's Corp, 631 F2d 303 (4th Cir 1980), *cert denied,* 451 US 970 (1981).

[131] 629 F2d 1351 (5th Cir 1980).

[132] United States v Realty Multi-List, Inc, 629 F2d 1351, 1369 (5th Cir 1980).

Refus de Vente

Must Seller Sell to Buyer?

*Arthur I. Cantor**

2

*Mr. Cantor is a member of the District of Columbia Bar. The author wishes to thank Warren Josephson of Brownstein Zeidman and Schomer for his assistance in the preparation of this chapter.

Seller believes that Buyer is not creditworthy; or
Seller believes that Buyer will not purchase a specified minimum quantity of Seller's products?

§2.01 Introduction

This chapter deals with the question: Under what circumstances does Seller's refusal to sell to Buyer—an action taken countless times every business day—violate the federal antitrust laws?[1] This chapter treats the general question in five groups of sections, each group focusing upon a single circumstance which affects antitrust liability. Each group is, in turn, divided into several sections which deal with various aspects of the main principle of the group.

Sections **2.03** through **2.14** address the situation in which Seller, in refusing to sell, acts completely on its own. The refusal is not based on Buyer's breach of a contractual commitment; indeed, there may be no contract between Seller and Buyer. Seller neither consults nor communicates with competing Seller or

---

[1] Seller's refusal to sell to Buyer generally does not transgress other bodies of law absent contractual commitments, a law controlling Buyer/Seller relationships in a particular industry or a particular location, or unlawful discrimination under federal or state laws. Cf **ch 7,** focusing on Seller's termination of Buyer. State antitrust laws often mirror the federal scheme, but a detailed discussion of these state laws is beyond the scope of this chapter.

competing Buyer concerning the decision to refuse to deal. Furthermore, Seller does not attempt to influence Buyer's selling practices by entering into understandings with Buyer or announcing to Buyer the conditions upon which it will refuse to deal.

Sections **2.15** through **2.29** discuss the lawfulness of Seller's refusal to deal with a Buyer who does not comply, or who Seller believes will not comply, with Seller's previously announced sales policy. Seller often announces the terms upon which it will refuse to sell in order to influence Buyers' sales practices. This announcement may create antitrust exposure if it is accompanied by acts taken to secure compliance with the policy.

Sections **2.30** through **2.40** analyze communication between Seller and competing Buyer which results in Seller's decision to refuse to sell to Buyer; **§§2.41** through **2.45** focus upon Seller's communication with competing Seller(s). The term *communicate* is used in these two sections to encompass interaction between the parties in its broadest sense. For example, in certain circumstances, liability may hinge upon Seller's refusal to deal preceded by unsolicited complaints made to Seller by competing Buyer.

The final sections in this chapter, **§§2.46** through **2.59,** focus upon the right of monopolist Seller to refuse to deal. The rules change when Seller so dominates a market that Buyers do not have adequate alternate sources of supply. When monopolist Seller refuses to deal, it may violate the Sherman Act even if it acts entirely on its own.

In the business world, facts rarely fit neatly into particular categories. Sellers' decisions to refuse to deal are influenced and motivated by many different factors, and are carried out by many techniques. This chapter seeks to analyze the situations which arise most frequently in commerce. If no section in this chapter is on point for a given set of facts, at least one, and probably several, sections should be sufficiently analogous to provide meaningful guidance. In preparing the chapter, the authors have sought to reflect the principal antitrust cases in which courts have decided the legality of seller's refusal to deal. The reader is also referred to Chapter 7, which concerns termination of dealers, a species of refusals to deal.

§2.02 What statutes and legal principles govern refusals to sell?

The two statutes most pertinent to refusals to deal are §§1 and 2 of the Sherman Act.[2] Section 1 of the Sherman Act proscribes joint action—"contract, combination, or conspiracy"—which unreasonably restrains trade. To determine whether a particular refusal to deal violates §1 thus requires a two-step analysis: (1) Is there joint action? (2) Does it unreasonably restrain trade?

One focal point of this chapter is to determine whether in particular cases,

---

[2] 15 USC §§1, 2.

Seller's decision to refuse to deal involves joint action. If Seller's decision to refuse to deal does not involve joint action, it is *unilateral* and there is no antitrust liability unless seller is a monopolist.[3] Joint action consists of collaborative conduct involving a plurality of actors, whether it be an express agreement or merely a unity of purpose, common design, tacit understanding, or meeting of the minds.[4] The *joint action* requirement does not mean that Seller's decision to refuse to deal must actually have been a product of agreement with someone else. Rather it is a term of distinction, designed to differentiate between unilateral action, which lies outside the jurisdictional reach of the "contract, combination or conspiracy" language of §1 of the Sherman Act, and conduct within the ambit of the statute. Its meaning is thus more accurately derived from a review of the decided cases than by attempts at logical analysis. Joint action is most often found in two refusal-to-deal settings. First, the refusal may be grounded in a contract between Seller and Buyer; for example, Buyer breaches an undertaking to Seller. Even though Seller may be said to have decided unilaterally to terminate Buyer for the breach, Seller's refusal to deal is traceable to an explicit agreement, and this is sufficient to satisfy the joint action requirement. (The legality of the refusal will turn on the nature of the contractual provision.)[5] Second, the refusal may be a product of Seller's dealings with others, typically with competing Buyers. For example, Seller may refuse to deal with Buyer because Seller has already granted an exclusive distributorship to competing Buyer. Here, too, the refusal is grounded in a contract, albeit with a third party, and thus is treated as joint action subject to the statute. However, a finding of joint action may also result from much less formal dealings between Seller and Buyer, or between Seller and third parties.[6] And such a finding is critical to liability under §1 of the Sherman Act because the statute does not apply to unilateral action by the Seller regardless of its effect on competition.

The second focal point of this chapter is to determine when a Seller's refusal to sell to Buyer constitutes an unreasonable restraint of trade. Antitrust jurisprudence groups all restraints of trade into two categories which are governed by different standards of judicial scrutiny. A limited category of restraints subject to the *per se* standard of review—those practices which courts have found are nearly always harmful to competition and lacking in redeeming virtue—are presumed unlawful without case-by-case consideration of their competitive impact or business justification.[7] All other restraints are subject to

---

[3] *See* Byars v Bluff City News Co, 609 F2d 843, 854 (6th Cir 1979) (a manufacturer has no duty to deal so long as its decision is unilateral).

[4] *See generally* Kiefer-Stewart Co v Joseph Seagram & Sons, 340 US 211 (1951).

[5] In Perma Life Mufflers, Inc v International Parts Corp, 392 US 134, 142 (1968), the Supreme Court stated that an illegal combination could exist between the franchisor and a franchisee who unwillingly complied with a restrictive franchise agreement.

[6] *See* United States v Parke, Davis & Co, 362 US 29, 44 (1960); *see also* Yentsch v Texaco, Inc, 630 F2d 46 (2d Cir 1980).

[7] "[T]here are certain agreements or practices which because of their pernicious effect on competition and lack of any redeeming virtue are conclusively presumed to

the *rule of reason* standard of review; a plaintiff must prove that the restraint reduces competition in a relevant market, a difficult and often unsuccessful task.[8] Therefore, whether a restraint is subject to the per se rule or to the rule of reason is often decisive in an antitrust case. These two concepts are discussed in detail in Chapter 1.

Under current law, joint action which results in a refusal to deal is subject to the per se rule primarily in two situations: (1) if the motivation for the refusal to deal was the Buyer's pricing practice;[9] or (2) if the joint action was engaged in by at least two competitors.[10] The latter situation could arise if two competing Buyers act together to convince Seller to refuse to deal with Buyer, or if Seller acts jointly with one or more competing Sellers to refuse to deal with Buyer. However, the courts have carved out numerous exceptions to these rules, applying the per se standard to certain conduct not within the two categories and at times refusing to apply the per se standard to conduct within them. The body of this chapter discusses which standard of review attaches to each particular restraint.

Section 2 of the Sherman Act prohibits companies from monopolizing or attempting to monopolize a relevant market.[11] Unlike §1, where a plurality of actors (joint action) is necessary, §2 also proscribes specific types of behavior by a single firm; joint action is not required. In certain circumstances, monopolists, or companies dangerously close to becoming monopolists, may violate §2 by refusing to deal. Section **2.46** discusses those circumstances.

---

be unreasonable and therefore illegal without elaborate inquiry as to the precise harm they have caused or the business excuse for their use. . . ." Northern Pac Ry Co v United States, 356 US 1, 5 (1958). *See* United States v Socony-Vacuum Oil Co, 310 US 150, 218 (1940) (price-fixing agreements illegal per se, and plaintiff not permitted to introduce evidence of competitive abuses that agreements were designed to eliminate); United States v Trenton Potteries Co, 273 US 392 (1927).

[8] *See* Continental TV, Inc v GTE Sylvania, Inc, 433 US 36 (1977) (TV manufacturer's dealer location restriction upheld as reasonable); Valley Liquors, Inc v Renfield Importers, Ltd, 678 F2d 742, 745 (7th Cir 1982) (plaintiff failed to prove harm to competition in a relevant market).

[9] Spray-Rite Serv Corp v Monsanto Co, 684 F2d 1226, 1238 (7th Cir 1982), *cert granted,* __ US __, 75 L Ed 2d 479, 103 S Ct 1249 (1983) (applied per se rule where distributor's complaints to manufacturer about competing distributor's discounting practices resulted in termination of the latter distributor). *See also* Battle v Lubrizol Corp, 673 F2d 984 (8th Cir 1982); Com-Tel, Inc v DuKane Corp, 669 F2d 404 (6th Cir 1982); Cernuto v United Cabinet Corp, 595 F2d 164 (3d Cir 1979). See **§§2.30-2.59.**

[10] *See* United States v General Motors Corp, 384 US 127, 145 (1966) (joint, collaborative action among distributors designed to eliminate competing discounting distributor from access to market is per se illegal).

[11] §5 of the Federal Trade Commission Act proscribes "unfair methods of competition." 15 USCA §45. Courts have interpreted §5 to condemn conduct which violates §1 or §2 of the Sherman Act and, in certain circumstances, conduct which would not violate the Sherman Act. *See* FTC v Texaco, Inc, 393 US 223 (1968) (Supreme Court condemned conduct under §5 of FTC Act, indicating §5 of FTC Act condemned a broader range of conduct than §1 of Sherman Act).

§2.03 May seller unilaterally refuse to sell to buyer?

Seller, a manufacturer of widgets, distributes its products directly to hundreds of independent retail outlets located throughout the country. Seller, like many manufacturers, is extremely interested in the quality and creditworthiness of the retailers who sell its widgets and the techniques by which its widgets are resold. Seller receives a written request from Buyer, a local retailer already selling products similar to widgets, to become a dealer in Seller's widgets. Seller reviews the application and, for one or more reasons, turns it down. Has Seller incurred antitrust liability?

§2.04 —What does unilaterally refuse to sell mean?

This section considers whether Seller may unilaterally refuse to sell to Buyer without violating the antitrust laws. The term *unilaterally refuse to sell* means that Seller reaches the decision to refuse to deal entirely on its own, rather than as a result of communication or agreement (*joint action*) with others. Specifically, the discussion in this section presupposes the following facts: (1) Seller is not a monopolist, or dangerously close to becoming a monopolist (see **§§2.46** through **2.59**); (2) Seller has no existing contractual relationship with Buyer and is not currently selling to Buyer (see **§§2.15** through **2.29**); (3) Seller has not had communication with competing Buyer(s) relating to Seller's decision not to sell to Buyer (see **§§2.30** through **2.40**); (4) Seller has had no communication with competing Seller(s) relating to Seller's decision not to sell to Buyer or to a class of customers similar to Buyer (see **§§2.41** through **2.45**).

In addition to the facts contained in the hypothetical (see **§2.03**), the principles of this section also apply to the following situations involving simple refusals to deal: (1) Seller is a distributor selling to retailers; (2) Seller is a manufacturer selling to distributors, wholesalers, jobbers and/or retailers; (3) Seller sells services rather than products; or (4) Seller sells to only a few select buyers.

§2.05 —What principles of law govern the legality of Seller's unilateral refusal to sell?

The courts have uniformly held that, in the absence of monopoly (see **§§2.46** through **2.59**), the antitrust laws do not restrict the right of Seller unilaterally to select its customers. Seller's decision to deal or not to deal with Buyer is a unilateral act not within the scope of §1 of the Sherman Act.[12] (As discussed

---

[12] For example, in Anaya v Las Cruces Sun News, 455 F2d 670 (10th Cir 1972), the defendant newspaper requested all carriers to provide a list of all subscribers. When

in **§2.02,** joint action is a necessary element of a §1 violation.) The sections which follow address the legality of refusals to sell in various situations. It is essential to recognize that the presence of additional facts, such as complaints from competing Buyer(s) or competing Seller(s) (see **§§2.30** through **2.40** and **§§2.41** through **2.45**), or prior agreements or communication between Buyer and Seller (see **§§2.15** through **2.29**), may affect the lawfulness of a particular refusal to sell because they may supply the joint action element and bear upon the purpose and effect of Seller's decision.

§2.06 —What if Seller unilaterally refuses to sell to Buyer because Seller believes that: Buyer's store is of poor quality; Buyer is not creditworthy; or Buyer will not purchase a specified minimum quantity of Seller's products?

Seller's unilateral refusal to sell to Buyer based upon quality, credit, or purchase volume criteria generally does not violate the antitrust laws, because it satisfies neither of the two prerequisites for a violation of §1 of the Sherman Act: joint action and an unreasonable restraint of trade. Courts have uniformly recognized Seller's prerogative to select its buyers based upon whether the quality of their stores or business in general is adequate,[13] whether Buyer is an acceptable credit risk,[14] or whether Buyer is likely to meet a minimum volume purchase requirement.[15]

---

the plaintiff failed to furnish this list, the defendant refused to do further business with plaintiff. The court held that this type of unilateral refusal to deal did not violate the antitrust laws. *See generally* Reeves v Stake, 447 US 429 (1980).

[13] *See* D&M Distribs, Inc v Texaco, Inc, 1970 Trade Cas (CCH) ¶73,099, at 88,292 (CD Cal Feb 13, 1970) (refusal by Texaco to deal with wholesaler of petroleum products who was supplying retail outlets not of preferred quality image is not illegal).

[14] *See* Belk-Avery, Inc v Henry I Siegel Co, 457 F Supp 1330, 1336 (MD Ala 1978) (unilateral termination after distributor fell behind in payments and had continual poor credit record not an unreasonable restraint of trade and not illegal).

[15] *See* Business Equip Center, Ltd v DeJur-Amsco Corp, 465 F Supp 775, 785 (DDC 1978) (declining sales volume of dealer was a legitimate reason to terminate); North Penn Oil & Tire Co v Phillips Petroleum Co, 358 F Supp 908 (ED Pa 1978) (unilateral termination of low-volume dealers and withdrawal from unprofitable market was not a conspiracy under §1).

§2.07 —What if Seller unilaterally refuses to sell to Buyer because Seller believes that: Buyer's sales area is adequately represented; Buyer's business format is not compatible with Seller's products or image; or Buyer will transship Seller's products to other retailers?

Seller's unilateral refusal to sell based upon these factors does not violate §1 of the Sherman Act because Seller's refusal is not the product of joint action.[16] Buyers have filed numerous lawsuits claiming that Sellers' refusal to deal for these reasons was illegal. Absent proof of collaboration between Seller and competing Buyer(s) or competing Seller(s), courts have uniformly dismissed such claims.

§2.08 —What if Seller unilaterally refuses to sell to Buyer because Seller believes that Buyer will discount Seller's products?

While price-related conduct is scrutinized most carefully under the antitrust laws, a unilateral refusal to sell based upon Seller's belief that Buyer will discount its product does not violate the antitrust laws because it is not joint action.[17] Prescreening prospective customers is one of the few techniques by which Seller can seek to some degree to maintain its suggested resale prices with relative safety.[18] For example, if Seller manufactures watches and desires that they be sold only at a suggested retail price, it may carefully select only those retail outlets which it believes will not discount, although Seller may not obtain their assurance that they will not do so. If a Buyer who otherwise meets

---

[16] *See* Interstate Camera Stores, Inc v EI du Pont de Nemours & Co, 1970 Trade Cas (CCH) ¶73,077, at 88,227 (EDNY Jan 30, 1970) (refusal to permit additional dealer to enter market was reasonable where 19 dealers already provided adequate distribution). Weather Wise Co v Aeroquip Corp, 468 F2d 716, 718 (5th Cir 1972), *cert denied,* 410 US 990 (1973) (unilateral refusal to deal with manufacturers that did not manufacture complete air conditioning systems was not illegal); D&M Distribs, Inc v Texaco, Inc, 1970 Trade Cas (CCH) ¶73,099, at 88,292 (CD Cal Feb 13, 1970).

[17] *See* United States v Colgate & Co, 250 US 300, 306 (1919) (manufacturer has right to refuse to sell to distributors who sell at discounted prices). *Cf* Russell Stover Candies, Inc, No 9140, slip op at 57 (FTC July 1, 1982) (FTC expressly approved discounting as basis to refuse to sell to prospective Buyers. Russell Stover appealed the decision to the Eighth Circuit Court of Appeals in October 1982).

[18] *See* United States v OM Scott & Sons, 303 F Supp 141, 154 (DDC 1969) (court dismissed complaint against seller that selected dealers that it believed would be likely to sell products at the suggested prices, without further inducements or coercive practices).

Seller's criteria applies to purchase Seller's watches, Seller may, in most instances, lawfully refuse to sell if it believes Buyer will discount its products.

In order to avoid antitrust liability for refusing to deal with Buyer on this basis, Seller should not have any prior communication with competing Seller(s)[19] or with competing Buyer(s),[20] nor should Seller utilize a third party to investigate Buyer's sales practices.[21] If Seller's refusal to deal is the result of joint conduct with any party, it may be held to be per se unlawful.[22] If Seller prescreens Buyer based upon its resale price policies, Seller should avoid consulting with any persons other than its own personnel with respect to implementing that policy. (Different employees of one business organization cannot engage in joint action vulnerable under §1 of the Sherman Act unless, under certain circumstances, they work for separate affiliates or subsidiaries.[23]

§2.09 —What if Seller unilaterally refuses to sell to Buyer because Seller does not like Buyer?

The antitrust laws, in general, condemn acts which are economically motivated. Unilateral refusals to deal based upon noneconomic criteria ordinarily do not violate the antitrust laws, not only because they do not constitute joint action but also because they are not cognizable restraints of trade.[24] It is important to note that refusals to deal which are motivated by social, ethnic, racial, or religious discrimination may violate other federal or state statutes.[25]

---

[19] *See* Fashion Originator's Guild of Am, Inc v FTC, 312 US 457, 465 (1941) (boycott of retailers and manufacturers that decline to comply with restricted distribution held to be per se illegal).

[20] *See* Uniroyal, Inc v Jetco Auto Serv, Inc, 461 F Supp 350, 354 (SDNY 1978) (Uniroyal's communication with competitor of one of its dealers amounted to combination).

[21] *See* Albrecht v Herald Co, 390 US 145, 149 (1968) (combination existed when Seller hired third party to induce customers to cease purchasing from disfavored dealer).

[22] In United States v Parke, Davis & Co, 362 US 29, 45-46 (1960), the Supreme Court stated:

> In thus involving the wholesalers to stop the flow of Parke Davis products to the retailers, thereby inducing retailers' adherence to its suggested retail prices, Parke Davis created a combination with the retailers and wholesalers to maintain retail prices and violated the Sherman Act . . . [T]he entire policy was tainted when Parke Davis used. . . [the Net Price Selling Schedule] as a vehicle to gain the wholesalers' participation in the program to effectuate the retailers' adherence to the suggested retail prices.

[23] See generally **§2.40.**

[24] See generally **§2.02.**

[25] See **§7.07.**

§2.10 —Must Seller base its refusal to deal on accurate information?

The antitrust laws establish no affirmative duty on Seller to sell to Buyer.[26] The preceding sections of this chapter demonstrate that, where there is no joint action, Seller, if not a monopolist, may unilaterally refuse to deal with Buyer for any reason whatsoever. Seller is under no legal obligation to verify the accuracy of the information upon which it based its unilateral decision to refuse to deal. However, Seller often seeks to verify information which may lead to a refusal to deal, for two reasons. First, Seller's primary interest is to maximize the number of units sold; Seller may therefore want assurance that its reasons for rejecting Buyer are accurate. Second, Seller may wish to maintain good relationships with other businesses and to avoid disputes and litigation; arbitrary refusals to deal do not promote those objectives.

§2.11 —Must Seller notify Buyer of its reasons for refusing to sell?

The antitrust laws do not obligate Seller to notify Buyer of its reasons for refusing to deal. However, Seller often does so in order to maintain good business relations with potential customers. Such communications should, of course, be carefully drawn so as not to create a risk of antitrust exposure; if that cannot be done, silence may be the more prudent course. If Seller's reason pertains to the quality of Buyer's operations, an offer of rectification by Buyer should pose no problems; this is not true if Seller's decision rested on the fact that buyer is a discounter. See **§2.13**.

§2.12 —Must Seller grant Buyer an opportunity to cure its faults?

When Seller refuses to sell to Buyer, it is not obligated under the antitrust laws to inform Buyer of its reasons (**§2.11**) or to give Buyer an opportunity to eliminate the basis for the refusal. For example, if Seller refuses to sell to Buyer because its store is of poor quality, it need not sell to Buyer ever, even if the quality of the store were to be markedly improved. Similarly, if Seller refuses to sell because buyer discounts most products in its store, Seller is not required to sell if Buyer stops discounting.

Seller must carefully draft any rejection notices in order to avoid creation of an expectancy which might result in a contractual or equitable obligation to sell to Buyer. For example, a rejection notice which stated that Seller would

---

[26] In Byars v Bluff City News Co, 609 F2d 843, 854 (6th Cir 1979) the court stated that, as a general rule, "there exists no duty to deal, so long as the determination is made unilaterally." The court then noted: "Franchisees and distributors which have been unilaterally terminated have discovered to their chagrin that ordinarily the law offers them no remedy absent proof that a conspiracy against them took place."

sell but for Buyer's dilapidated store front might create an obligation to sell if Buyer were to expend funds to repair.

§2.13 —Should Seller seek or accept assurances or commitments from Buyer?

A Seller who decides to sell to a Buyer after soliciting the Buyer's assurance that it will, for example, refrain from discounting, has engaged in joint action.[27] Under the two-step analysis discussed in **§2.02,** the legality of the conduct depends upon whether the purpose or effect of the assurance is to unreasonably restrain trade. Seller should not, for example, sell to Buyer based upon Buyer's assurance that it will not discount. Seller should also consider antitrust ramifications when selling to Buyer based upon Buyer's assurance that it will not sell outside a specified territory or to a particular class of customers.[28]

§2.14 —Does it make any difference if Seller has previously sold to Buyer?

Seller may unilaterally refuse to sell to Buyer, despite the fact that it previously sold products to Buyer, without incurring antitrust liability. However, when there have been prior dealings between the parties, Seller should exercise even greater care. Thus, if the refusal to sell is the result of Buyer's breach of a previous agreement or commitment, the refusal will be construed as a product of joint action, not unilateral action;[29] its legality would depend upon whether that underlying agreement or commitment was itself lawful. For example, if Buyer ignores an agreement to promote Seller's line, Buyer may be terminated without Seller's incurring antitrust liability; the same is not true if Buyer reneges on a pledge to adhere to Seller's *suggested* prices. Furthermore, as a practical matter, the termination of an existing customer is more likely to trigger litigation than a refusal to deal with a new one.

Seller's right to refuse to sell to a Buyer to whom it had previously sold or is currently selling is sometimes governed by state statutes, including, where applicable, state franchise laws.[30]

---

[27] In United States v Parke, Davis & Co, 362 US 29, 44 (1960), the Supreme Court found a combination resulting from the dealer's assurance that it would comply with the manufacturer's pricing policy.

[28] See generally **ch 4.**

[29] In FTC v Beech-Nut Packing Co, 257 US 441 (1922), the Supreme Court found a violation of §5 of the FTC Act and §1 of the Sherman Act based, in part, on Beech-Nut's reinstatement of dealers terminated because of discounting.

[30] See generally **ch 7, 9.**

§2.15 May Seller announce a sales policy and refuse to sell to Buyer if it believes Buyer will not, or if in fact Buyer does not, comply with that policy?

Seller manufactures widgets and sells them to hundreds of independent retailers located throughout the country. Seller determines that efficient distribution of its widgets requires that its retailers comply with certain conditions, including: maintaining high quality operations; prompt payment of bills; purchase of a minimum volume per order and per year; not selling outside a specified territory; not selling to unauthorized customers; and not discounting. Next, Seller considers how to assure that the retailers meet these conditions. Seller determines that it cannot achieve its distribution goals solely by prescreening potential retailers. It is Seller's experience that many retailers quickly depart from Seller's preferred selling practices despite rigorous preliminary evaluations. On the other hand, Seller has also decided not to incorporate the conditions in a *dealer contract,* which could be terminated upon Buyer's noncompliance, for two reasons. First, Seller prefers the flexibility of selling to Buyer on an order-by-order basis, without the obligations of a formal, long-term contractual relationship. Second, Seller believes that to include certain of the conditions in a dealer contract would violate the antitrust laws; the agreement would constitute joint action, and the conditions themselves would constitute an unreasonable restraint of trade.

Based upon these considerations, Seller adopts the following procedure: Before accepting Buyer's first order, Seller informs Buyer, either orally or in writing, that it is Seller's policy to sell only to Buyers who comply with Seller's conditions of sale, which it describes. Without seeking Buyer's promise to abide by the conditions, Seller makes clear to Buyer that Seller will cease selling to Buyer if Buyer fails to comply.

This scenario raises numerous antitrust issues. Under what circumstances may a Seller announce a policy of refusing to deal with Buyers who do not adhere to specified conditions? When does Buyer's adherence to the conditions constitute joint action which violates §1 of the Sherman Act? When does termination of a Buyer for failure to abide by the announced policy constitute an illegal act? These matters are treated in **§§2.16** through **2.29.**

§2.16 —What does *announce a sales policy* mean?

We use the phrase *announce a sales policy* to mean any communication from Seller to Buyer setting forth the conditions upon which Seller will refuse to sell, or will cease selling, to Buyer. Seller may announce its policy orally or in writing, to one, several, or all of its Buyers. A basic assumption here is that Buyer does not *agree,* either formally or informally, to abide by the policy. Such an agreement would constitute joint action, and Seller would lose certain legal benefits which might otherwise be available to it, as discussed in the following sections.

§2.17 —What principles of law govern announced sales policies and subsequent refusals to deal?

In 1919, the Supreme Court, in *United States v Colgate & Co* stated that Seller is free "to exercise his own independent discretion as to parties with whom he will deal. And of course, he may announce in advance the circumstances under which he will refuse to sell."[31] Under the *Colgate* doctrine, if Seller merely announces a sales policy and refuses to sell to Buyers who do not comply with that policy, Seller has not engaged in joint action within the meaning of §1 of the Sherman Act; its decision is unilateral.

The *Colgate* doctrine has engendered considerable controversy in the courts. Theoretically, it permits Seller to obtain strict adherence to its sales policies while insulating it from antitrust liability. The impact of the *Colgate* doctrine is particularly significant in the context of Seller's *no discount* policy. Chapter 6 concludes that an agreement between Seller and Buyer obligating Buyer to resell Seller's products at specified prices is unlawful per se. Under the *Colgate* doctrine, however, Seller may achieve the same result without, in theory, incurring liability.

Since 1919, courts have markedly narrowed the circumstances to which the *Colgate* doctrine applies. Almost *any* steps taken by a Seller beyond simply announcing its policy and refusing to sell to Buyer if it does not comply, have led to a finding of joint action. For example, courts have held that Seller's use of third parties to police compliance,[32] Seller's conduct of a surveillance program,[33] or Seller's repeated announcements of the policy may result in a

---

[31] 250 US 300, 307 (1919). The FTC has recently interpreted the *Colgate* doctrine, finding that it no longer constitutes binding precedent. In *In re* Russell Stover Candies, Inc, No 9140 (FTC July 1, 1982), the FTC held that a company's suggestion of prices, announcement to its dealers of a *no discount* policy, termination of discounting dealers, and evidence that certain dealers did not discount in order to avoid termination constituted an illegal combination under §1 of the Sherman Act. The FTC reasoned that where a manufacturer's announcement of a policy constrains a dealer's distribution policies, the manufacturer has coerced the dealer into combining with it to restrain trade. Russell Stover appealed the FTC decision to the Eighth Circuit Court of Appeals in October, 1982.

[32] *See* Albrecht v Herald Co, 390 US 145 (1968) (newspaper publisher's use of third party to solicit customers away from distributor to secure compliance with specified prices constitutes illegal combination); United States v Bausch & Lomb Optical Co, 321 US 707, 720 (1944) (use of surveillance and other tactics to secure compliance coupled with refusal to deal constitutes violation of §1); FTC v Beech-Nut Packing Co, 257 US 441, 454 (1922) (finding joint activity where seller used special agents and other dealers to report deviations from price maintenance scheme). See also **§2.27.**

[33] *See* United States v Bausch & Lomb Optical Co, 321 US 707 (1944).

finding of joint action.[34] For this reason, Seller should recognize that, despite *Colgate,* it may incur liability if its announced policy would constitute an unlawful restraint of trade were it incorporated in a contract with Buyer; the protection granted by the *Colgate* doctrine is not hard to lose.

§2.18 —May Seller announce a policy of refusing to sell to Buyer if Buyer does not: maintain adequate quality; purchase a specified quantity; or pay its bills on time?

Announced policies such as these, which do not impose unreasonable restraints of trade, are lawful under the antitrust laws. Courts have consistently recognized Seller's right to insure the quality of its dealers, to impose minimum purchase standards based upon legitimate economic criteria, and to establish terms of payment.[35]

§2.19 —May Seller include quality, volume, or credit terms in a dealer agreement without risking antitrust liability?

Inclusion of these terms in a contract generally does not violate the antitrust laws because they do not constitute unreasonable restraints of trade.[36]

§2.20 —May Seller announce a policy of refusing to sell to Buyer if Buyer: sells outside of its prescribed territory; sells from an unauthorized location; sells to unauthorized customers; purchases products from Seller's competitors; or does not purchase Seller's full product line?

The lawfulness of Seller's policy announcement which incorporates any of

---

[34] *See* Yentsch v Texaco, Inc, 630 F2d 46, 53 (2d Cir 1980). In *Yentsch,* the seller told the buyer at least 10 times to drop its price or risk termination. The court was persuaded that multiple threats of termination which secure adherence to fixed prices go beyond the boundaries of *Colgate,* and are thus illegal combinations under §1.

[35] See generally **§2.06.**

[36] *Id.*

these terms[37] depends primarily upon whether the terms themselves constitute unreasonable restraints of trade.[38] In addition, Seller could argue that, even if the terms were deemed to be unreasonable restraints, under the *Colgate* doctrine the joint action element necessary for any violation of §1 of the Sherman Act is not present. The success of this argument would depend upon whether Seller took any action beyond merely announcing the policy and refusing to sell to Buyers who did not comply with it. The types of conduct which may result in a finding of joint action are discussed in **§§2.23** through **2.28** of this chapter.

§2.21 —May Seller include territorial, location, customer, or product restrictions in a dealer agreement without risking antitrust liability?

Inclusion of these terms in a dealer agreement does entail a greater risk under the antitrust laws than incorporating them in a policy announcement. The dealer (or franchise or distributor) agreement by definition constitutes joint action. The sole remaining issue is whether the restraint is unreasonable.[39]

§2.22 —May Seller announce a policy of refusing to sell to Buyer if Buyer does not adhere to Seller's suggested prices?

An agreement between Seller and Buyer which restricts Buyer's freedom to determine its resale prices is per se unlawful under the antitrust laws.[40] Under

---

[37] For sales outside prescribed territories, in unauthorized locations, or to unauthorized customers, see **ch 5.** For products purchased from seller's competitors or failure to purchase Seller's full product line, see **ch 4.**

[38] *See* Knutson v Daily Review, Inc, 548 F2d 795, 808 (9th Cir 1976) (designation of area of primary responsibility or mere suggestions of territorial allocation without an express prohibition do not by themselves violate §1), *cert denied,* 433 US 910 (1977). The court added, however, that if a plaintiff can show a course of conduct by which a manufacturer prohibits sales outside a specified territory, a §1 violation may occur; Beverage Distribs, Inc v Olympia Brewing Co, 440 F2d 21, 32 (9th Cir), *cert denied,* 403 US 906 (1971) (no violation of §1 where seller had policy of limiting distributors' sales to certain customers).

[39] *See* Continental TV, Inc v GTE Sylvania, Inc, 433 US 36 (1977) (Supreme Court held vertical nonprice restraints subject to rule of reason standard of review). *But cf* Eiberger v Sony Corp of Am, 622 F2d 1068, 1076 (2d Cir 1980) (warranty service plan designed not to promote warranty service but to enforce territorial division had an unreasonable impact on intrabrand competition); *In re* Coca-Cola Co, 642 F2d 1387 (DC Cir 1981). See generally **ch 5.**

[40] *See* California Liquor Dealers Assn v Midcal Aluminum, Inc, 445 US 97, 103 (1980) (wine producer's requirement that dealers charge specified price violated §1 of Sherman Act).

the *Colgate* doctrine, however, Seller's mere announcement of a resale pricing policy, and its subsequent refusal to deal with Buyer if it does not comply with that policy, is lawful.[41] As discussed in **§§2.23** to **2.28,** courts have found joint action, and a violation, when the announcement is accompanied by any additional conduct on the part of Seller that coerces or compels compliance with its suggested retail prices.[42]

The matter of defining the sort of conduct beyond mere announcement which may result in a finding of joint action has engendered significant controversy within the legal community.[43] For that reason, the legal standards distinguishing lawful from unlawful conduct are imprecise and subject to change.[44] The following sections explore some of the applicable concepts.

§2.23 —May Seller solicit assurances from Buyer that it will abide by Seller's pricing policies?

An assurance given by Buyer in response to Seller's request that Buyer not discount constitutes a per se violation of the Sherman Act.[45] The solicitation coupled with the assurance is an agreement to fix prices. In order for Seller to minimize antitrust exposure, it must merely announce its policy and then terminate Buyers that do not comply with the policy, even though that action in and of itself may be found to violate the antitrust laws.[46] Any understandings or side agreements which Seller and Buyer enter into concerning resale prices are illegal per se.

---

[41] United States v Colgate & Co, 250 US 300, 307 (1919); *cf* Klein v American Luggage Works, Inc, 323 F2d 787 (3d Cir 1963) (manufacturer's termination of discounting dealer held lawful under *Colgate* doctrine).

[42] *See, e.g.,* FTC v Beech-Nut Packing Co, 257 US 441, 454 (1922) (use of third parties to report deviations from price maintenance scheme is joint action); Yentsch v Texaco, Inc, 630 F2d 46, 53 (2d Cir 1980) (multiple communications to dealers to drop price or risk termination constituted joint action).

[43] See **§2.17.**

[44] See **§2.17.**

[45] *See* United States v Parke, Davis & Co, 362 US 29, 44 (1960) (dictum) (Supreme Court stated that although induced by manufacturer's announced pricing policy, retailer that observes specified prices without more is not involved in illegal combination); *cf* United States v Colgate & Co, 250 US 300 (1919) (mere announcement of policy with no request of compliance held not to constitute a combination).

[46] See **§2.22.**

§2.24 —Does Buyer's unsolicited assurance that it will comply with Seller's pricing policy constitute an antitrust violation?

Seller announces to Buyer its policy of refusing to deal with customers that discount its products. Buyer responds by stating to Seller that it understands Seller's policy and will not discount. Does Buyer's response transform Seller's unilateral announcement into an agreement to fix prices?

Although this issue does not appear to have been decided by the courts, the risk of antitrust liability is reduced if Seller's policy announcement did not solicit a response from Buyer specifically, or if Seller merely stated what would happen to Buyer if it chose to discount. Seller can further reduce the risk of obtaining a response from Buyer by stating at the end of its announcement that Seller neither seeks nor would accept an assurance that Buyer will not discount.

§2.25 —What if Buyer is a franchisee?

The Supreme Court has held that an oil company's announcement of a policy that its dealers must purchase equipment from specified suppliers, coupled with dealer compliance, constituted joint action and violated the Federal Trade Commission Act.[47] The Court distinguished this case from the typical Seller-Buyer situation because of the inherent economic power which it found the oil company had over its dealers. Some lower courts have applied this reasoning and have held that oil companies may not announce to their dealers a *no discount* policy without violating the Sherman Act.[48] These cases may not apply in other franchise settings not marked by the enormous leverage which the oil companies were found to enjoy over their dealers.[49]

§2.26 —What if Seller repeatedly announces its policy?

The *Colgate* doctrine protects only a simple announcement of a policy of refusing to deal with discounters, not repeated statements of the Seller's policy which cause Buyer to maintain the suggested retail price. A federal appellate court recently held that Seller's repetition of its retail pricing policy to Buyer

---

[47] FTC v Texaco, Inc, 393 US 223 (1968). This case was decided under §5 of the FTC Act, which the Supreme Court indicated condemned a broader range of conduct than §1 of the Sherman Act.

[48] Broussard v Socony Mobil Oil Co, 350 F2d 346 (5th Cir 1965) (oil company's power to terminate plaintiff's entire service station operation made policy announcement inherently coercive and resulted in combination). *But see* Quinn v Mobil Oil Co, 375 F2d 273 (1st Cir), *cert dismissed,* 389 US 801 (1967) (court found no violation based upon absence of general price maintenance scheme or compliance).

[49] See generally **ch 9.**

on approximately ten separate occasions coerced Buyer into following Seller's policy and thus constituted unlawful joint action.[50]

§2.27 —What if Seller polices Buyer's selling prices?

By engaging a third party to enforce or monitor Buyer's compliance with Seller's announced *no discount* policy, Seller may be found to have conspired with that third party to fix retail prices.[51] If Seller or its own employees determine whether Buyer is complying, liability will be unlikely. However, if Seller or its employees, while ascertaining Buyer's pricing practices, threaten or otherwise coerce Buyer into complying with Seller's policy, liability may arise.[52]

§2.28 —What if Seller solicits pricing information from competing Buyer(s)?

Seller sells to two Buyers in a small town. Seller might ask Buyer A to report on whether Buyer B is discounting. This conduct may result in a per se violation of the Sherman Act.[53] Seller should therefore not enforce Buyer's compliance with Seller's pricing policy by soliciting pricing information from competing Buyers.

§2.29 —Must Seller grant Buyer an opportunity to cure its faults?

The antitrust laws do not impose any such limitation on Seller's right to terminate Buyers. However, state law and/or a contract between Seller and Buyer, if any, might restrict a Seller's authority to cease selling to Buyer.[54]

---

[50] Yentsch v Texaco, Inc, 630 F2d 46, 53 (2d Cir 1980). The court was persuaded that threats of termination which secure adherence to fixed prices go beyond the boundaries of *Colgate,* and are thus illegal combinations under §1.

[51] *See* Albrecht v Herald Co, 390 US 145 (1968) (newspaper publisher's use of third party to solicit customers away from overcharging distributor constitutes an illegal combination); United States v Bausch & Lomb Optical Co, 321 US 707, 720 (1944) (use of wholesalers to enforce resale price maintenance scheme constitutes a violation of §1); FTC v Beech-Nut Packing Co, 257 US 441, 454 (1922) (manufacturer's surveillance of dealers' retail pricing practices coupled with refusals to deal with noncomplying dealers constitutes a violation of §1).

[52] *Id.*

[53] *See* FTC v Beech-Nut Packing Co, 257 US 441, 455 (manufacturer's use of dealers to report on pricing practices held illegal).

[54] See generally **ch 7.**

§2.30 May Seller refuse to sell to Buyer as a result of Seller's communication with competing Buyer(s)?

Seller manufactures widgets and sells them to hundreds of retailers located throughout the United States. Seller receives a request from Buyer to become a widget dealer. Seller contacts competing Buyer, one of its dealers located in a town close to that of Buyer, and asks whether Buyer has the type of store consistent with Seller's image and whether sales to Buyer would substantially harm competing Buyer's widget business. As a result of competing Buyer's response, Seller decides not to sell to Buyer.

This section discusses the legality of the many situations where Seller refuses to deal with, or terminates,[55] Buyer after communication with, complaints from, or an agreement with, competing Buyer(s). This is a more precarious area for Seller than those previously considered, in which (aside from the policing issue, see **§§2.26** through **2.28**) we have been dealing with only two actors: Seller and Buyer. In the two-party setting, it may be somewhat simpler to decide whether Seller and Buyer have agreed, and Seller may enjoy the benefit of the *Colgate* presumption that it is entitled to choose its customers and of the courts' reluctance to intrude into unilateral decision making.[56] Here, however, a third party has entered the picture; and because that third party is a competitor of Buyer, the possibility arises that the refusal of Seller to deal with Buyer had an anticompetitive purpose or effect. The cases in this area are not uniformly unfavorable to Seller, but it is well to recognize the heightened risk which the presence of competing Buyer presents.

§2.31 —What are the relevant statutes and principles governing the legality of communication between Seller and competing Buyer resulting in Seller's refusal to sell to Buyer?

Two or more parties who engage in joint action for the purpose of, or having the effect of, unreasonably restraining trade violate §1 of the Sherman Act.[57] Under this standard, courts have condemned seller's refusal to sell to, or termination of, Buyer when it resulted from competing Buyer's complaints about Buyer's aggressive pricing practices.[58] Courts are less inclined to find a violation when competing Buyer's complaints are not prompted by Buyer's discounting.[59]

---

[55] See **§2.32.**

[56] *See* United States v Colgate & Co, 250 US 300 (1919).

[57] United States v General Motors Corp, 384 US 127 (1966).

[58] See **§2.37.**

[59] See **§§2.35, 2.36.**

The hypothetical facts in **§2.30** involved one Seller and one competing Buyer. The standard is apparently even stricter where Seller's refusal to deal results from communication with its own competitors[60] or from communication between Seller and more than one competing Buyer.[61]

§2.32 —Are dealer terminations resulting from communications between Seller and competing Buyer subject to the same standard of law as initial refusals to sell?

The antitrust analysis is virtually identical whether communication between Seller and competing Buyer results in a refusal to deal with a prospective new Buyer or in the termination of an existing Buyer. To avoid repetition, the two situations have been consolidated here, and the latter is not discussed in Chapter 7. Most cases in this area in fact involve termination of active accounts. Competing Buyer is more likely to know about, and more apt to complain to Seller about, the conduct of an actual competitor who is cutting into its sales, than about the potential for lost sales if Seller decides to sell to a new Buyer.[62]

§2.33 —When does communication between Seller and competing Buyer constitute joint action?

A plaintiff must prove that two or more parties engaged in joint action to establish a violation of §1 of the Sherman Act. Joint action may consist of any form of collaborative conduct, whether it be an express agreement, or merely a unity of purpose, common design, tacit understanding, or meeting of the minds.[63] For purposes of this section, the crucial inquiry is usually whether Seller's refusal resulted from, or was independent of, competing Buyer's complaints.

---

[60] See generally **§§2.41-2.45.**

[61] See **§2.38.**

[62] *Compare* Oreck Corp v Whirlpool Corp, 579 F2d 126 (2d Cir) (en banc), *cert denied,* 439 US 946 (1978) (large distributor, Sears, complained to vacuum cleaner manufacturer that plaintiff, a competing distributor, should be terminated), *with* Borger v Yamaha Intl Corp, 625 F2d 390 (2d Cir 1980) (stereo manufacturer refused to sell to prospective dealer based upon consultations with established dealerships).

[63] In American Tobacco Co v United States, 328 US 781, 809-10 (1946), the Supreme Court stated:

> The essential combination or conspiracy in violation of the Sherman Act may be found in a course of dealing or other circumstances as well as in any exchange of words. . . . Where the circumstances are such as to warrant a jury in finding that the conspirators had a unity of purpose or a common design and understanding, or a meeting of the minds in an unlawful arrangement, the conclusion that a conspiracy is established is justified.

The courts have uniformly held that a written contract,[64] an oral contract, an implied contract,[65] or even a noncontractual understanding, will support a finding of joint action. A noncontractual understanding may arise, for example, if in response to a competing Buyer's complaints, Seller assures competing Buyer that Seller will cease selling to Buyer. Without more, Seller is not legally obligated to competing Buyer to terminate Buyer. However, the facts might support a finding of joint action under the Sherman Act if Seller does, in fact, terminate Buyer.[66]

A more difficult question arises where Seller receives complaints from competing Buyer about Buyer, gives competing Buyer no commitments or assurances, and proceeds to terminate Buyer. Buyers have initiated numerous lawsuits in recent years based on such a scenario, alleging that Seller and competing Buyer have conspired to force Buyer out of business. Courts have dealt with this issue inconsistently—in some cases finding joint action,[67] and in other cases refusing to infer joint action, holding that Seller could base its refusal to sell on information received from competing Buyer without entering into a conspiracy.[68] The courts have not set forth clear guidelines which delineate whether or not joint action is present. The most important fact necessary to establish joint action appears to be a causal link between competing Buyer's complaint and Seller's decision to refuse to deal. Direct evidence of causation will, of course, suffice. Courts, however, may infer that link if Seller solicits competing Buyer's comments, or if Seller's decision immediately follows communication with competing Buyer, or if competing Buyer, rather than Seller, has the economic motivation not to allow Buyer to distribute Seller's

---

64 *See* Dr Miles Medical Co v John D Park & Sons, 220 US 373 (1911) (dealer agreements which required dealer pricing compliance held illegal).

65 In United States v A Schrader's Son, 252 US 85, 99 (1920), the Supreme Court held that the Sherman Act prohibited manufacturers from entering into "agreements—whether express or implied from a course of dealing or other circumstances . . . which undertake to bind them to observe fixed resale prices."

66 *See, e.g.,* Quality Mercury, Inc v Ford Motor Co, 542 F2d 466, 468 n 1, 469 (8th Cir 1976), *cert denied,* 433 US 914 (1977) (car manufacturer's understanding with existing dealer granting it veto power over new dealers within 10-mile radius held to constitute joint action under §1 of Sherman Act).

67 In Spray-Rite Serv Corp v Monsanto Co, 684 F2d 1226, 1238 (7th Cir 1982), *cert granted,* (Feb 28, 1983) the Seventh Circuit stated, "proof of termination following competitor complaints is sufficient to support an inference of conspiracy"): (The petition for certiorari filed by the United States Department of Justice argued that proof of termination following competitor complaints was not sufficient, as a matter of law, for a jury to infer an agreement. If the Supreme Court addresses this issue in its decision, the decision should assist in reconciling the current inconsistent holdings among the United States courts of appeal.) *Accord* Battle v Lubrizol, 673 F2d 984 (8th Cir 1982).

68 Bruce Drug, Inc v Hollister, Inc 688 F2d 853 (1st Cir 1982); Valley Liquors Inc v Renfield Importers, Ltd, 678 F2d 742 (7th Cir 1982); Schwimmer v Sony Corp of Am, 678 F2d 946 (2d Cir 1982); Roesch, Inc v Star Cooler Corp, 671 F2d 1168 (8th Cir 1982); Edward J Sweeney & Sons v Texaco, Inc, 637 F2d 105 (3d Cir 1980), *cert denied,* 451 US 911 (1981).

products.[69] If the plaintiff cannot persuade the trier of fact that Seller's decision was, at least in part, in response to competing Buyer's complaints, then there probably will be no finding of joint action.

§2.34 —When is joint action between Seller and competing Buyer, resulting in Seller's refusal to sell to buyer, unlawful?

Once the element of joint action has been established, courts turn their attention to the impact of that joint action upon the marketplace. As discussed in the sections which follow, the legality of Seller's refusal to sell which was motivated by competing Buyer turns primarily on the reasons for the Seller's action. If the purpose was to eliminate a discounter from the marketplace, the action is legally suspect. If, however, the purpose was to maintain the quality standards associated with Seller's products, the action is probably lawful. As we shall discuss, the law governing the many situations which lie between these extremes is far less precise.

§2.35 —What if the purpose of the refusal to sell is to maintain quality or other standards associated with Seller's product?

Seller, its distributors, and its retailers often have a strong interest in maintaining a high quality image for Seller's products. In many instances, Seller becomes aware through complaints from competing Buyer that Buyer is not maintaining prescribed quality standards. Seller's decision to cease selling to Buyer in this situation does not constitute an antitrust violation. Maintaining quality standards is not a restraint of trade within the meaning of the antitrust laws.[70] If, however, quality control is merely a pretext for other, anticompetitive motivations, liability may result. Thus, litigation in this area often involves a dispute as to the real reasons for the refusal to deal.[71]

---

[69] *See* Spray-Rite Serv Corp v Monsanto Co, 684 F2d 1226, 1238 (7th Cir 1982), *cert granted* __ US __, 75 L Ed 2d 479, 103 S Ct 1249 (1983).

[70] *See* Dalmo Sales Co v Tysons Corner Regional Shopping Center, 308 F Supp 988 (DDC) (shopping center's refusal to grant lease to plaintiff in response to complaints by other tenants upheld where evidence indicated motivation for refusal to lease one plaintiff's incompatible image), *affd*, 429 F2d 206 (DC Cir 1970).

[71] *Cf* Business Equip Center Ltd v DeJur-Amsco Corp, 465 F Supp 775 (DDC 1978) (court dismissed terminated dealer's complaint holding, in part, that real reason for termination was dealer's declining sales record).

§2.36 —What if the purpose of the refusal to sell is: to protect competing Buyer's exclusive territory; or to protect competing Buyer from Buyer's competition?

Sellers are frequently called upon to referee disputes between adjacent buyers of their products. A common source of such disputes is the resale of Seller's products by Buyer which cuts into the sales of competing Buyer. Chapter 5 addresses the question whether the grant by Seller of an exclusive territory violates the antitrust laws. If a grant of exclusivity in a particular situation is lawful, Seller generally may terminate Buyer for transgressing competing Buyer's territory, even if the decision is based upon the complaints of competing Buyer.[72]

The outcome may be different if competing Buyer does not already have the protection of an exclusive territory. Assume, for example, that Buyer and competing Buyer are Seller's only dealers in a city. Competing Buyer purchases approximately twice the annual volume from Seller that Buyer does. Competing Buyer informs Seller that, unless Seller terminates Buyer, it will stop purchasing Seller's products. Seller acquiesces and ceases selling to Buyer.

Courts addressing this fact pattern have reached inconsistent holdings. Some decisions have found liability, holding that competing Buyer's motivation to eliminate its competitor Buyer renders the refusal to deal with Buyer subject to the per se standard of review.[73] Other courts have held that, notwithstanding competing Buyer's motivation,[74] Seller is entitled under the antitrust laws to structure its distribution system by terminating Buyer, and may consult with competing Buyer in reaching its decision.[75] The majority of recent cases

---

[72] *See* Muenster Butane, Inc v Stewart Co, 651 F2d 292, 296 (5th Cir 1981) (manufacturer's termination of dealer, in part, for selling outside of its assigned territory did not unreasonably restrain trade even though prompted by complaints of competing dealer).

[73] Com-Tel, Inc v DuKane Corp, 669 F2d 404 (6th Cir 1982); American Motor Inns, Inc v Holiday Inns, Inc, 521 F2d 1230 (3d Cir 1975). *See* Sport Shoe, Inc v Ralph Libonati Co, 1981-2 Trade Cas (CCH) ¶64,230, at 73,930 (D Del Apr 14, 1981) (conspiracy among defendant franchisee, franchisor, and supplier to refuse to deal with competing franchisee within defendant franchisor's territory, held to be subject to per se rule).

[74] If competing Buyer's motivation is to eliminate Buyer's discounting, the conduct may be held to be per se illegal. See **§2.37**.

[75] *See, e.g.,* Ron Tonkin Gran Turismo, Inc v Fiat Distribs, Inc, 637 F2d 1376 (9th Cir 1981), *cert denied,* 454 US 831 (1982) (car distributor's termination of dealer at behest of competing dealer held not to constitute an unreasonable restraint of trade); Oreck Corp v Whirlpool Corp, 579 F2d 126 (2d Cir) (en banc), *cert denied,* 439 US 946 (1978) (vacuum cleaner manufacturer's termination of mail order distributor at behest of competing distributor retailer, Sears, held lawful); Joseph E Seagram & Sons v Hawaiian Oke & Liquors, Ltd, 416 F2d 71, 76 (9th Cir 1969), *cert denied,* 396 US 1062 (1970) (no per se violation for supplier to agree with one distributor to grant it an exclusive franchise even if it required termination of another distributor); Packard Motor Car Co

addressing this question have not found a violation (except where Buyer was a discounter). The presence of inconsistent precedent renders Seller's termination of Buyer at the behest of competing Buyer not free from risk under the antitrust laws.

§2.37 —What if the purpose of the refusal to sell is to protect competing Buyer from Buyer's price competition?

When competing Buyer's complaints are prompted by Buyer's discounting, Seller's subsequent termination of Buyer is highly suspect under the antitrust laws. If Seller's refusal to deal with Buyer resulted from joint action between Seller and competing Buyer, most courts have found a per se violation in this situation.[76] Whether competing Buyer's complaints and Seller's termination of Buyer amount to joint action has been the subject of considerable recent controversy.[77] If Seller did not engage in joint action with competing Buyer, Seller's termination of Buyer for the purpose of eliminating its discounting may be found not to violate §1 of the Sherman Act.[78]

---

v Webster Motor Car Co, 243 F2d 418 (DC Cir), *cert denied,* 355 US 822 (1957) (termination of car dealership at behest of competing car dealership held lawful).

[76] Spray-Rite Serv Corp v Monsanto Co, 684 F2d 1226, 1238 (7th Cir 1982), *cert granted,* (Feb 28, 1983); Battle v Lubrizol, 673 F2d 984, 990 (8th Cir 1982) in which the court stated:

> If a distributor can establish that a manufacturer or common supplier terminated its existing supply relationship at the request of a competing distributor and the termination was motivated by a desire on the part of the manufacturer to reduce or eliminate price competition for the other distributor, then a per se violation of §1 of the Sherman Act has been established; . . .

Alloy Intl Co v Hoover-NSK Bearing Co, 635 F2d 1222, 1224 (7th Cir 1980); Cernuto, Inc v United Cabinet Corp, 595 F2d 164 (3d Cir 1979). *But cf* Valley Liquors, Inc v Renfield Importers, Ltd, 678 F2d 742, 744 (7th Cir 1982) (court denied plaintiff's motion for a preliminary injunction based upon insufficient evidence of joint action, but indicated per se rule should not apply even if joint action was present).

[77] In Spray-Rite Serv Corp v Monsanto Co, 684 F2d 1226, 1238 (7th Cir 1982), *cert granted,* ___ US ___, 75 L Ed 2d 479, 103 S Ct 1249 (1983) the Seventh Circuit stated, "proof of termination following competitor complaints is sufficient to support an inference of conspiracy"); *accord* Battle v Lubrizol, 673 F2d 984 (8th Cir 1982).

[78] Valley Liquors, Inc v Renfield Importers, Ltd, 678 F2d 742 (7th Cir 1982); Schwimmer v Sony Corp of Am, 677 F2d 946 (2d Cir 1982), Roesch, Inc v Star Cooler Corp, 671 F2d 1168 (8th Cir 1982); Edward J Sweeney & Sons v Texaco, Inc, 637 F2d 105 (3d Cir 1980), *cert denied,* 451 US 911 (1981).

§2.38 —Is joint action between Seller and more than one competing Buyer, resulting in Seller's decision to refuse to deal with Buyer, unlawful?

A stricter standard of law applies when two or more competing Buyers act together to convince Seller not to deal with Buyer. Courts review such conduct under the per se doctrine.[79] Although the essence of such an antitrust violation may be the agreement between the competing buyers to foreclose competition, Seller's participation in the arrangement would subject Seller to antitrust exposure as well.

To illustrate, assume that Seller sells to three Buyers in a metropolitan area. Buyer A adopts aggressive sales techniques that begin taking sales away from competing Buyers B and C, who agree to pressure Seller to refuse to deal with Buyer A. Seller's refusal to deal in this situation may be found to violate the antitrust laws.

§2.39 —What if Seller is also a distributor or retailer and competes with Buyer and competing Buyer?

If Seller competes at the wholesale or retail level with Buyer and competing Buyer, Seller's termination of Buyer at the behest of competing Buyer may risk antitrust liability.[80] A court could view the refusal to deal as an illegal horizontal boycott between Seller and competing Buyer.[81] Seller's motivation for refusing to deal would be important in determining liability. If Seller's interest is in enhancing the efficiency of its distribution system, a court would probably not find a violation. If, however, Seller's intention is to divide the market in the distribution of its products between competing Buyer and itself, a court might find that the Seller conspired to restrain trade unreasonably.

---

[79] *See* United States v General Motors Corp, 384 US 127, 140 (1966) (collaborative action by dealers and General Motors to eliminate discounting dealer from market is per se illegal); Com-Tel, Inc v DuKane Corp, 669 F2d 404 (6th Cir 1982) (complaints by dealers to manufacturer to terminate bootlegging dealer held per se illegal); American Motor Inns, Inc v Holiday Inns, Inc, 521 F2d 1230, 1242 (3d Cir 1975) (objections by existing franchisees, which operated as a veto, to application of another franchisee constitute per se illegal horizontal conspiracy).

[80] *See* **ch 8.**

[81] *See e.g.,* Copy Data Sys, Inc v Toshiba Am, Inc, 663 F2d 405 (2d Cir 1981) (manufacturer's integration forward to distribution level held lawful despite termination of independent distributor); American Motor Inns, Inc v Holiday Inns, Inc, 521 F2d 1230 (3d Cir 1975) (franchisor operating company-owned hotels held to have entered into horizontal market allocation scheme with franchisees that vetoed approval of plaintiff).

§2.40 —What if competing Buyer is a subsidiary of Seller?

Under §1 of the Sherman Act, Seller, in most instances, will not be found to have engaged in joint action with its wholly owned subsidiary. The law generally views the parent and subsidiary as a single entity.[82] For example, a subsidiary Buyer complains to the parent Seller that competing Buyer is cutting, or will cut, into its sales. If the subsidiary is wholly owned, Seller probably may terminate, or refuse to sell to, Buyer without engaging in joint action. However, if the subsidiary holds itself out to the public as an independent entity, or if Seller does not control the subsidiary's day-to-day operations, courts might view the transaction for antitrust purposes as if the subsidiaries were an unaffiliated Buyer and capable of conspiring with Seller.[83]

§2.41 May Seller engage in joint action with competing Seller(s) to refuse to sell to Buyer or to a class of Buyers?

Seller, a widget manufacturer, attends the annual widget manufacturers trade association meeting. Seller and competing Sellers unanimously adopt and agree to abide by certain conditions under which the members will and will not sell to categories of Buyers.

Any agreement between competitors regarding the terms under which they will operate is suspect under antitrust law. Determining the lawfulness of such an arrangement involves the same two-step analysis discussed in the prior sections of this chapter: (1) Does the conduct constitute joint action, or is it the unilateral act of a single party? (2) Does the conduct constitute an unreasonable restraint of trade? Courts will find joint action to be present when any communication between competitors is directed towards a common purpose.[84]

---

[82] *See* Ogilvie v Fotomat Corp, 641 F2d 581, 588-90 (8th Cir 1981) (Fotomat could not conspire with its wholly owned subsidiary). In *Fotomat,* the Eighth Circuit used a two-part test to determine whether two corporations could conspire with each other. First, are they controlled and operated by the same management; and, second, do they hold themselves out as distinct entities? *Cf* Fuchs Sugar & Syrups Inc v Amstar Corp, 602 F2d 1025, 1029 n 1 (2d Cir), *cert denied,* 444 US 917 (1979) (agreement under §1 must be between independent businesspersons).

[83] *See* United States v Yellow Cab Co, 332 US 218, 227 (1947) (restraint of trade may result among those affiliated or integrated under common ownership); Kiefer-Stewart Co v Joseph E Seagram & Sons, 340 US 211, 215 (1951) (common ownership and control of two subsidiaries does not liberate corporations from the impact of the antitrust laws). The First, Third, and Fifth Circuits have interpreted these Supreme Court decisions to reject the defense that affiliated parties may not be found to combine to restrain trade in violation of §1, regardless of the degree of affiliation between the parties. George R Whitten, Jr, Inc v Paddock Pool Builders, Inc, 508 F2d 547 (1st Cir 1974), *cert denied,* 421 US 1004 (1975); Cromar Co v Nuclear Materials & Equip Corp, 543 F2d 501 (3d Cir 1976); Battle v Liberty Natl Life Ins Co, 493 F2d 39 (5th Cir 1974), *cert denied,* 419 US 1110 (1975).

[84] *Compare* Klor's, Inc v Broadway-Hale Stores, Inc, 359 US 207 (1959), *with* United

A restraint will be held unreasonable if it is intended to, or has the effect of, maintaining or promoting the Sellers' market position.[85] The following four Sections apply these standards to different situations in which Sellers act together to refuse to deal with Buyers.

§2.42 —What if Seller and competing Seller(s) agree to sell only to Buyers who meet certain standards?

In limited circumstances, Sellers may jointly refuse to sell to a Buyer or to a group of Buyers if the purpose of the action is to promote legitimate procompetitive goals. A joint refusal to sell designed solely to protect the health of end-users of a product or otherwise to promote health and safety would, absent any anticompetitive purpose or effect, probably not violate the antitrust laws.[86] For example, an agreement among manufacturers to establish sanitary specifications for their dealers and to refuse to sell to dealers that do not comply with those specifications may withstand antitrust attack. However, courts traditionally scrutinize such agreements very closely. If the joint action does restrict competition, even indirectly, and if a less restrictive approach would accomplish the same goal, the agreement may be held to be illegal.[87]

§2.43 —What if the purpose of the joint refusal to sell is to create an orderly market or course of dealing?

A series of federal court decisions has upheld the right of competing businesses to agree among themselves to organize a market, and to refuse to deal outside of that market, where the purpose is to enhance, not diminish, competition.[88] There are some businesses which cannot, as a practical matter, operate

---

Shoppers Exclusive v Broadway-Hale Stores, Inc, 1966 Trade Cas (CCH) ¶71,727 (ND Cal Nov 24, 1965).

85 *See* Fashion Originators' Guild of Am, Inc v FTC, 312 US 457 (1941) (agreement among dress designers to boycott retail stores purchasing "pirated" patterns held per se illegal).

86 *See* Neeld v National Hockey League, 594 F2d 1297 (9th Cir 1979) (league bylaw prohibiting participation by persons with vision in only one eye is reasonable safety measure, and not a per se illegal boycott among NHL teams).

87 See **§2.44.**

88 *See* Broadcast Music, Inc v Columbia Broadcasting Sys, Inc, 441 US 1, 20-21 (1979) (arrangement by which all licensing agencies issue blanket licenses for copyrighted musical compositions in exchange for flat fee is a reasonable restraint because it creates more orderly and less expensive transactions); Chicago Bd of Trade v United States, 246 US 231, 240 (1918) (exchange of information in commodity market promotes orderly and efficient marketplace); Bridge Corp of Am v American Contract Bridge League, Inc 428 F2d 1365, 1370 (9th Cir 1970), *cert denied,* 401 US 940 (1971) (imposi-

without various kinds of restrictions on dealings with third parties. Based upon this reasoning, courts have sanctioned joint refusals to deal in the context of commodity markets, stock exchanges, and sports leagues. In these situations, as in all settings involving joint action among competitors, courts seek to determine whether there is an anticompetitive purpose or effect.[89]

§2.44 —What if the purpose of the joint action is to restrain competition among Buyers?

Agreements among Sellers not to sell to Buyers who bootleg (that is, who sell to unauthorized dealers), sell outside of their assigned territories, discount, or purchase from Sellers not party to the agreement, are suspect under the antitrust laws. In limited circumstances, courts may rely on business justifications to uphold such agreements.[90] Most decisions addressing these agreements, however, have found them to be per se unlawful.[91]

§2.45 —Does it make a difference if Seller agrees with only one, rather than with several, competing Seller(s)?

Agreements between two competing Sellers are analyzed under the same strict legal standards as agreements among several or all competing Sellers in a given market.[92]

§2.46 May monopolist Seller refuse to deal with Buyer?

Monopolist Seller produces 80 per cent of the widgets sold in the United States. There are no close substitutes for widgets. Widgets are a high-technology consumer product and take many years to develop. Monopolist Seller distributes its widgets to hundreds of independent retail stores located throughout the United States. Monopolist Seller seeks to increase its market

---

tion of conditions on supplier of computer scoring system is reasonable to promote the integrity of the master point system and tournament play).

89 *See* Silver v New York Stock Exch, 373 US 341, 347 (1963) (action by stock exchange which removed access of broker to essential services held to be an unreasonable restraint of trade).

90 See generally **§2.42.**

91 *See* United States v Crescent Amusement Co, 323 US 173, 181 (1944) (combination designed to restrict ability of competitors to license films so that buyer could preserve exclusive territories is illegal); Fashion Originators Guild of Am, Inc v FTC, 312 US 457, 465 (1941) (agreement among dress designers to boycott retail stores purchasing "pirated" patterns held per se illegal).

92 See **§2.38.**

share by announcing to its retail Buyers that it will refuse to sell to Buyers that carry any products made by monopolist Seller's competitors. As a result of this policy, several of monopolist Seller's fledgling competitors lose sales and/or go out of business.

§2.47 —What are the statutes and principles which govern monopolist Seller's right to refuse to sell?

Section 2 of the Sherman Act proscribes monopolization of, attempts to monopolize, or conspiracies to monopolize all or any part of a relevant market.[93] Monopolist Seller is, of course, also subject to prosecution under §1 of the Sherman Act for engaging in joint action which unreasonably restrains trade. Buyers challenge the conduct of Sellers under §1 far more often than under §2, because few Sellers are so dominant in their lines of commerce as to qualify as monopolists. However, a charge of monopolization or attempt to monopolize is often the only technique by which Buyer can challenge Seller's unilateral refusal to deal.

In order to establish that Seller's refusal to deal, or threat of refusal to deal, with Buyer violates §2 of the Sherman Act, two elements must be proved in addition to the refusal itself. First, Seller must possess monopoly power, or demonstrate a dangerous probability of obtaining monopoly power, in the relevant product and geographic markets. Second, Seller's refusal to deal must act to obtain, maintain, or extend its monopoly power. The concepts embodied in these two elements are discussed in the three sections which follow.

§2.48 —What is a relevant market?

The term *relevant market* is, in essence, an economic concept used to determine whether a firm or firms possess monopoly power.[94] Two variables, product description and geographic area, define every market. For example, *cellophane sold in the United States* describes a market. The following test illustrates whether that market is economically relevant for antitrust purposes: If the price of cellophane were significantly raised or production significantly curtailed, would competition from substitutes restore the old price and volume within a reasonable period of time? If the answer is yes, the market is defined too narrowly and must be expanded to incorporate the competing source of supply. Thus, if the prices of cellophane were doubled, and enough customers switched to aluminum foil and wax paper to drive the price of cellophane down, perhaps the relevant market should be *food packaging materials sold in the*

---

[93] *See generally* United States v Grinnell Corp, 384 US 563 (1966).

[94] *See generally* Brown Shoe Co v United States, 370 US 294 (1962); United States v EI Dupont de Nemours & Co, 351 US 377 (1956).

United States.[95]

§2.49 —What is monopoly power?

Once the relevant market has been defined in terms of both product and territory, a court is able to ascertain whether a particular firm in that market possesses monopoly power. The generally accepted measure in antitrust cases is that a firm that manufactures or sells two-thirds or more of the products or services in a relevant market has monopoly power.[96] The fraction may vary in any particular case in response to numerous factors, including the number of firms in the market, the price structure in the market, and the ability of the nondominant firms to maintain their presence.

§2.50 —When does monopolist Seller violate §2 of the Sherman Act?

Section 2 of the Sherman Act does not proscribe monopoly power that is obtained or maintained only through the Seller's "skill, foresight or industry."[97] For example, a manufacturer of widgets that obtains 80 per cent of the United States widget market solely because it makes the best widgets at the lowest price has not violated the Sherman Act. Monopolist Seller illegally monopolizes a market when it abuses its market power to obtain or maintain a monopoly, to the detriment of competition.[98] In the situations which follow,

---

[95] United States v EI DuPont De Nemours & Co, 351 US 377 (1956) (Supreme Court held food packaging materials, not cellophane, constituted relevant market within which to measure market power of cellophane manufacturer).

[96] *See* United States v Grinnell, 384 US 563, 571 (1966) (existence of monopoly power may be inferred from predominant share of the market); Byars v Bluff City News Co, 683 F2d 981, 982 (6th Cir 1982) (monopoly power exists where firm controlled 90% of the relevant market); United States v Aluminum Co of Am, 148 F2d 416 (2d Cir 1945) (2/3 market share held sufficient to establish monopoly power).

[97] *See* United States v Grinnell Corp, 384 US 563, 570-71 (1966) (no violation of §2 where monopoly power acquired through superior product, business acumen, or historic accident).

[98] *See* United States v EI Dupont de Nemours & Co, 351 US 377, (1956) (monopoly illegal where power used to control prices or unreasonably restrict competition); Eastman Kodak Co v Southern Photo Materials Co, 273 US 359, 375 (1927) (refusal to sell to Buyer at dealer discount for purpose of perpetuating monopoly is question for jury); Murphy Tugboat Co v Shipowners & Merchants Towboat Co, 467 F Supp 841, 850 (ND Cal 1979), *cert denied,* 455 US 1018 (1982) (refusal to work on ships run by competitors enhanced monopoly power and excluded competition); Lorain Journal Co v United States, 342 US 143, 155 (1951) (refusal to accept advertising from buyer is illegal if purpose to create or maintain monopoly); *cf* Homefinders of Am, Inc v Providence Journal Co, 471 F Supp 416 (DRI 1979), *affd,* 621 F2d 441 (1st Cir 1980) (no purpose to drive out competitors in refusing to sell advertisements to buyer); National Tire Wholesale, Inc v Washington Post Co, 441 F Supp 81 (DDC 1977), *affd,* 595 F2d 888 (DDC 1979) (in absence of intent to monopolize, nonmonopolist may refuse to deal

it is assumed that monopolist Seller first acquired its monopoly power by lawful means.

§2.51 —May monopolist Seller refuse to sell to a Buyer because: Seller disapproves of Buyer's quality; Buyer's business format is not compatible with Seller's products or image; Seller believes that Buyer is not creditworthy; or Seller believes that Buyer will not purchase a specified minimum quantity of Seller's products?

Monopolist Seller, like a nonmonopolist Seller, may refuse to sell to Buyer for legitimate business reasons, such as quality, credit, and minimum purchase criteria.[99] Monopolist Seller has no absolute duty to deal. Nevertheless, monopolist Seller may not use these reasons as a pretext for refusing to sell to Buyer in order to enhance its market power. For example, Seller informs Buyer that it will not sell to it because its store is too small. Seller informs Buyer, however, that it would reconsider its decision if Buyer stopped selling products manufactured by Seller's competitors. Both Buyer and competing Seller may have a valid cause of action under §2 of the Sherman Act against Seller based upon its abuse of its monopoly power.[100]

---

with others or choose to deal on terms it specifies). *See also* Otter Tail Power Co v United States, 410 US 366, 377 (1973) (refusal to transfer power to competing power company is an illegal use of monopoly power). The Supreme Court noted that Otter Tail abused its existing dominance in the transmission of power in foreclosing potential entrants into its markets from obtaining power from other sources.

[99] *See* America's Best Cinema Corp v Fort Wayne Newspapers, Inc, 347 F Supp 328 (ND Ind 1972) (refusal by newspaper to accept advertisements for X-rated movies is not an unreasonable restraint of trade); *cf* International Rys of Cent Am v United Brands Co, 532 F2d 231, 239 (2d Cir) (act of abandoning unprofitable operation does not constitute monopolization), *cert denied,* 429 US 835 (1976).

[100] *See, e.g.,* Eastman Kodak Co v Southern Photo Materials Co, 273 US 359 (1927) (manufacturer's termination of dealer prompted by dealer's purchase of goods from another manufacturer constituted unlawful monopolization).

§2.52 —May monopolist Seller refuse to sell to Buyer because it believes that: Buyer's sales area is adequately represented; Buyer would transship Seller's products to unauthorized customers; or Buyer would sell outside of its designated territory?

Monopolist Seller's imposition of territorial or customer restrictions on Buyer may be found to constitute an unreasonable restraint of trade under §1 of the Sherman Act.[101] Similarly, monopolist Seller may not announce a policy of terminating Buyers that do not comply with its territorial or customer restrictions, or coerce Buyers into complying with these restrictions, without risking antitrust liability.

The courts, however, have offered little guidance as to whether monopolist Seller may simply refuse to sell to Buyer if it believes Buyer would not comply with its distribution program. A court would not be likely to find a violation unless monopolist Seller's conduct augmented its market power or was the product of joint action with competing Seller or competing Buyer.

§2.53 —May monopolist Seller refuse to sell to Buyer because Buyer is located within a preexisting dealer's exclusive territory?

The courts have not directly addressed the question of whether monopolist Seller may establish an exclusive dealer network and refuse to sell to Buyer in order to maintain the integrity of that network. Faced with that situation, a court would be likely to balance Seller's interest in achieving the most efficient distribution of its products against the harm to competition resulting from the absence of competition between Seller's customers.

§2.54 —May monopolist Seller refuse to sell to Buyer because it believes that Buyer will discount its products?

No cases directly address the right of monopolist Seller simply to refuse to deal with Buyer because it believes Buyer will discount its products. A court would probably attempt to determine whether Seller's intent was to augment

---

[101] *See* Eastman Kodak Co v Southern Photo Materials Co, 273 US 359 (1927); United States v Klearflax Linen Looms, Inc, 63 F Supp 32, 39 (D Minn 1945) (monopolist's termination of distributor to secure for itself a preferred customer held illegal under §2 of Sherman Act). See generally **ch 5.**

its monopoly power. However, courts would subject this action to much greater scrutiny than a refusal based upon nonprice factors.

Monopolist Seller may not announce a policy of refusing to deal with discounters without risking antitrust liability. The Supreme Court has stated that such a policy would result in a violation.[102]

§2.55 —May monopolist Seller refuse to sell to Buyer if the purpose of the refusal is to protect or maintain Seller's market position?

Section 2 of the Sherman Act prohibits Sellers that have monopoly power from refusing to deal with Buyers for the purpose of augmenting that monopoly power. For example, monopolist Seller violates the Sherman Act if it seeks to drive its competitors out of the market by refusing to sell to Buyers that purchase products from competing Sellers.[103]

§2.56 —May monopolist Seller refuse to sell to Buyer solely because it does not like Buyer?

The antitrust laws focus upon economic motivations. Monopolist Seller's refusal to deal based upon noneconomic factors does not violate the Sherman Act.[104] It might, however, violate other federal or state antidiscrimination statutes.[105]

§2.57 —May monopolist Seller refuse to sell to Buyer if the effect of such refusal will be substantially to impair Buyer's business?

If monopolist Seller controls a product or resource essential to Buyer's business, and Buyer has no alternate source of supply, §2 of the Sherman Act might prohibit monopolist Seller from refusing to sell to Buyer.[106]

---

[102] *See* United States v Colgate & Co, 250 US 300, 307 (1919).

[103] Eastman Kodak Co v Southern Photo Materials Co, 273 US 359, 375 (1927).

[104] *See* America's Best Cinema Corp v Fort Wayne Newspapers, 347 F Supp 328, 333 (ND Ind 1972) (refusal to accept advertisements based on fear of losing family image and burden of policing objectionable theater advertisements is based on noneconomic considerations and is not a violation of §2).

[105] See generally **chs 7, 9.**

[106] *See* Otter Tail Power Co v United States, 410 US 366, 377 (1973) (requiring Otter Tail to transfer power over its service lines from another source, where it had a strategic dominance in electric power, and used such dominance to foreclose potential entrants); United States v Terminal Ry, 224 US 383 (1912) (exclusive ownership and control of

§2.58 —Does monopolist Seller have a duty to notify Buyer of the reasons for refusing to deal?

The antitrust laws do not require monopolist Seller, or any party, to specify its reasons for refusing to deal. Sellers sometimes do provide such information to promote good will and eliminate the need to respond to Buyer's questions. Chapters 7 and 9 discuss the duty of a franchisor to specify its reasons for terminating a franchisee under certain state laws.

§2.59 —How do the antitrust laws treat the right of large, but not monopolistic, Sellers to refuse to sell?

If Seller is dangerously close to becoming a monopolist, it may violate §2 of the Sherman Act by refusing to deal with Buyer for the purpose of obtaining a monopoly.[107] In order to prevail on a charge of attempt to monopolize, a plaintiff must prove that Seller specifically intended by its refusal to deal to gain monopoly power.[108]

---

railway access constitutes attempt to monopolize); *cf* Official Airline Guides, Inc v FTC, 630 F2d 920 (2d Cir 1980), *cert denied,* 450 US 917 (1981) (discussing legitimacy of monopolist's ability to discriminate among classes of airline carriers so as to place one class at a significant competitive disadvantage); *see* Byars v Bluff City News Co, Inc, 683 F2d 981, 983 (6th Cir 1982) (upholding district court's determination that efficiency and business reasons justified refusal to deal); International Rys of Cent Am v United Brands Co, 532 F2d 231 (2d Cir) (refusal to provide Buyer with shipping trade because of abandonment of unprofitable banana operation is not an attempt to monopolize), *cert denied,* 429 US 835 (1976).

[107] In Swift & Co v United States, 196 US 375, 396 (1905), the Supreme Court stated:

> Where acts are not sufficient in themselves to produce a result which the law seeks to prevent, for instance, the monopoly,—but require further acts in addition to the mere forces of nature to bring that result to pass, an intent to bring it to pass is necessary in order to produce a dangerous probability that it will happen.

Compare United States v Empire Gas Corp, 537 F2d 296, (8th Cir 1976) (proof of dangerous probability must include a showing of the relevant market within which that probability occurred), *cert denied,* 429 US 1122 (1977); *with* Lessig v Tidewater Oil Co, 327 F2d 459, 474-75 (9th Cir) (proof of dangerous probability need not include a showing of relevant market; specific intent to monopolize is the only evidence §2 requires); *cert denied,* 377 US 993 (1964).

[108] *E.g.,* Times-Picayune Publishing Co v United States, 345 US 594 (1953); Lorain Journal Co v United States, 342 US 143 (1951); Hiland Dairy, Inc v Kroger Co, 402 F2d 968 (8th Cir 1968), *cert denied,* 395 US 961 (1969).

Déterm° du Prix.

At What Price May Seller Sell?

*James F. Rill**

3

§3.01 What laws restrict the price at which a Seller may sell?
§3.02 What conditions led to the passage of the Robinson-Patman Act?
§3.03 What are the elements of a Robinson-Patman Act offense?
§3.04 Is price discrimination anything more than a net price difference?
§3.05 Is availability of goods to all customers a defense to a charge of unlawful price discrimination?
§3.06 What transactions are in interstate commerce?
§3.07 What are transactions in commodities?
§3.08 What is a sale?
§3.09 Who is a purchaser?
§3.10 What are sales for resale?
§3.11 What are commodities of like grade and quality?
§3.12 What kind of injury to competition will violate the act?
§3.13 What are the elements of competitive injury to competitors of the seller?
§3.14 What are the elements of competitive injury to customers of the Seller?
§3.15 What is a functional discount?
§3.16 When can a functional discount cause injury to competition?
§3.17 May Seller pay a broker who facilitates a sale?
§3.18 Are discrimination and competitive injury relevant to a brokerage section violation?

---

*Mr. Rill is a member of the District of Columbia Bar. The author wishes to thank Oleta J. Hamilton for her assistance in the preparation of this chapter.

§3.01 What laws restrict the price at which Seller may sell?

Several provisions of the antitrust and trade regulation laws have an impact on the price at which suppliers may sell commodities. For example, discriminatory, predatory pricing may be attacked as evidence of an attempt to monopolize under §2 of the Sherman Act.[1] Similarly, of course, price-fixing conspiracies are per se violations of §1 of the Sherman Act.[2]

Of principal concern in this chapter, however, are the statutory provisions which deal with Seller's conferring preferential treatment on one or more of its customers vis-á-vis other customers in either the same or different geographic areas. Such treatment may be accorded through the mechanism of discriminatory prices, or disproportional promotional allowances or services, or brokerage payments or allowances. The Robinson-Patman Act, enacted in 1936 as an amendment to the Clayton Act, undertakes to cover in extensive detail the circumstances under which price and price-related discriminatory

---

[1] *See, e.g.*, William Inglis & Sons Baking v ITT Continental Baking Co, 668 F2d 1014 (9th Cir 1981), *cert denied*, 103 S Ct 57 (1982) (No 81–2083) (ITT), *cert denied*, 103 S Ct 58 (1982) (No 81–2289) (Inglis).

[2] *See, e.g.*, United States v Socony-Vacuum Oil Co, 310 US 150 (1940).

practices are unlawful.[3] Section 2 of the Clayton Act, as enacted in 1914,[4] dealt primarily with geographic price discriminations and was not effective to challenge buyer inducement of preferential treatment.

Separate provisions of the amended act deal with price discrimination, discriminatory promotional allowances and services, unlawful brokerage payments or allowances, and buyer liability. While the basic thrust of the statute is the prevention of commercial discriminations which may adversely affect competition, certain of the collateral provisions do not refer at all to an impact on competition and, hence, tend more to be viewed as aberrant absolute proscriptions of certain pricing behavior. The Supreme Court has, nevertheless, with some frequency admonished that the provisions of the act must be construed so as to harmonize them with the broader antitrust focus on the general competitive vigor of the economy.[5] This harmonization effort has involved a continuous process of statutory interpretation which occupies the courts and the Federal Trade Commission to the present day.

In addition to the Robinson-Patman Act, §5 of the Federal Trade Commission Act[6] has been employed by the FTC to challenge various discriminatory practices. These practices, including, particularly, Buyer's inducement of discriminatory promotional allowances, are not covered by the Robinson-Patman Act but have been held by the courts to be within the grasp of the flexible provisions of §5.[7]

A provision of the Robinson-Patman Act, which is not one of the antitrust laws and is, therefore, not amenable to private actions, deals specifically with predatory pricing. Added almost as an afterthought during the legislative deliberations in 1936, §3 of the Robinson-Patman Act authorizes actions by the federal government against geographic price discriminations or sales at unreasonably low prices for the purpose of destroying competition or eliminating a competitor.[8]

Finally, there are numerous state laws which deal with Seller's pricing practices. Of foremost importance among these are several state statutes which prohibit below-cost selling for the purpose of injuring competition or destroying a competitor.[9] A discussion of these statutes is beyond the scope of this chapter.

---

[3] 15 USC §13. The amendments to the Clayton Act effected by the Robinson-Patman Act are included within the definition of the antitrust laws and, as such, may provide a basis for private suits as well as governmental actions. *See* 15 USC §§12, 15.

[4] 15 USC §12.

[5] Great Atl & Pac Tea Co v FTC, 440 US 69 (1979); *see e.g.*, Automatic Canteen Co v FTC, 346 US 61 (1953).

[6] 15 USC §45.

[7] *See* Grand Union Co v FTC, 300 F2d 92 (2d Cir 1962).

[8] 15 USC §13a.

[9] *See, e.g*, Cal Bus & Prof Code §17000 *et seq* (Deering 1982).

§3.02 What conditions led to the passage of the Robinson-Patman Act?

By the time the Robinson-Patman Act was considered in 1936, the distribution system in the United States had been in a state of significant transformation since before the beginning of the twentieth century, with the increasing popularity of the chain store method of distribution. By 1936, through the use of multiple outlets and the vertical coordination of the wholesale and retail functions, entrepreneurs were able both to achieve real economic efficiency and to consolidate their purchases so as to make maximum use of quantity and similar discounts from suppliers.

The Great Depression caused independent retailers, particularly in the grocery and drug industries, to suffer severe economic hardship. It also exacerbated the tension that had already existed between the independent and chain store methods of operation. The independents both at the retail and wholesale level, carried their complaints to Congress with the result that a number of anti-chain legislative efforts were undertaken.[10]

Unquestionably, the Robinson-Patman Act[11] was the offspring of this legislative onslaught. The chain stores were held out as the primary source of the independents' economic distress and it was believed by supporters of the act that if equality in pricing treatment were assured, the independents would be profitable. Thus, the Robinson-Patman Act reflects a strong populist trend in American antitrust legislation, one which arguably seeks to codify equality of treatment as an independent goal of the antitrust laws.

The act's principal sponsor left no doubt as to the roots of the statute, commenting significantly as to the law's enactment "[O]ne certain big concern had really caused the passage of this Act, the A&P Tea Co."[12]

Some of the legislative history is even more colorful, for example: "[The bill] will restrict the chain-store and mail-order octopuses which are gradually but surely destroying the small businessman in every section of the country."[13]

The proponents of the legislation, nevertheless, were required to make certain concessions to economic efficiency. Thus, only those price discriminations which threatened an adverse competitive impact would be prohibited and, even then, the defense that they were justified by cost savings might be asserted.[14] Legislative efforts to mandate functional discounts were unsuccess-

---

[10] The best discussion of the political forces at work in the adoption of the Robinson-Patman Act and of the conflicting positions taken in the legislative debates are found in J. Palamountain, The Politics of Distribution (1955).

[11] 15 USC §13.

[12] *Hearings Before the Antitrust Subcomm of the House Comm on the Judiciary on Bills to Amend Sections 2 and 3 of the Clayton Act,* 84th Cong, 2d Sess 57 (1956) (statement of Rep Patman).

[13] 80 Cong Rec 8102 (1936) (remarks of Rep Sabbath).

[14] 15 USC §13(a).

ful.[15] In view of the unique forces which brought about its creation and its somewhat distinctive underlying rationale, it is no surprise that judicial and administrative constructions of the Robinson-Patman Act have been tortured.

§3.03 What are the elements of a Robinson-Patman Act offense?

The bulk of this chapter consists of a discussion of the various elements of offenses arising under the Robinson-Patman Act[16] and collateral construction of the Federal Trade Commission Act.[17] For present purposes, it is sufficient to note that the statute deals with discriminatory practices in connection with the sale of commodities in interstate commerce. While its primary focus is expressly on those discriminatory practices which may have an adverse impact on competition, competitive effect is not mentioned in the subsections dealing with promotional allowances,[18] promotional services,[19] or brokerage.[20] The extent, if any, to which the competitive concerns underlying the principal antitrust laws are even relevant to these provisions remains an issue which is the subject of checkered judicial consideration.

Further, while the defense that a discriminatory price has been made to meet the equally low price of a competitor is available as well in cases involving discriminatory promotional allowances and services, it does not appear to be available in brokerage allowances cases.[21] The cost justification defense, moreover, appears available only in §2(a) price discrimination cases.[22]

As a consequence, it often appears that the various subsections of the statute are freestanding with elements that may bear little relationship to one another. The extent to which these distinctions persist or have been reconciled constitutes a principal topic for the remainder of this chapter.

§3.04 Is price discrimination anything more than a net price difference?

As with many critical elements of the Robinson-Patman Act, the term *discriminate in price* was not clearly defined when the statute was enacted. Judicial crafting has been necessary to give shape even to this threshold concept.

---

[15] Provisions which would have required the granting of functional discounts based on the level at which the buyer resold products were deleted by the conference committee. *See* HR Rep No 2951, 74th Cong, 2d Sess (1936).

[16] 15 USC §13.

[17] *Id.* §45.

[18] *Id* §13(d).

[19] *Id* §13(e).

[20] *Id* §13(c).

[21] *See* FTC v Washington Fish & Oyster Co, 282 F2d 595 (9th Cir 1960).

[22] 15 USC §13(a).

Part of the difficulty arises from the divergent economic and legal concepts of discrimination. To the economist, a discrimination can consist of pricing behavior which results in the Seller's realizing a difference in net profits from two or more sales through, for example, the failure to recognize cost savings differentials in pricing goods. Under this approach, identical prices can be discriminatory.[23] The Federal Trade Commission experimented briefly with this notion in the *Rigid Steel Conduit Association* case in the 1940s.[24] The commission attacked the seller's uniform zone delivered pricing system as unjustifiably discriminating against nearby customers, and the agency's order to cease and desist was affirmed by the court of appeals and the Supreme Court. Inexplicably, the commission did not pursue the economic discrimination approach, and uniform zone delivered pricing which did not effect a potentially injurious discrimination in actual prices charged was tacitly sanctioned by the Supreme Court's 1945 decision in *FTC v AE Staley Manufacturing Co.*[25]

Confirmation that, in essence, a price discrimination is nothing more than a price difference was explicitly provided by the Supreme Court's 1960 *FTC v Anheuser-Busch Inc* decision.[26] Charged with an unlawful geographic price discrimination, respondent had argued that, to be actionable, a discrimination must involve two or more customers who are direct competitors. The Supreme Court disagreed, concluding that,

> an independent and important goal of § 2(a) is to extend protection to competitors of the discriminating seller. [T]he limitation of that protection by the alien factor of competition among purchasers would constitute a debilitating graft upon the statute. . . . *Rather, a price discrimination within the meaning of that provision is merely a price difference.*[27]

This decision does not, however, resolve all questions relative to the meaning of *price discrimination.* Identification of the price charged customers for commodities creates some difficulty. The courts have construed the term *price* to mean *net price,* arrived at by adjusting the price to account for various discounts or rebates offered by the Seller.[28] An actionable discrimination can result, for example, if the seller establishes discriminatory sales terms which cause two or more customers to pay different prices. Discriminatory credit and

---

[23] R. Posner, Antitrust Law: An Economic Perspective 62–65 (1976).

[24] 38 FTC 534 (1944), *affd sub nom* Triangle Conduit & Cable Co v FTC, 168 F2d 175 (7th Cir 1948), *affd sub nom* Clayton Mark & Co v FTC, 336 US 956 (1949).

[25] 324 US 746, 757 (1945).

[26] 363 US 536 (1960).

[27] *Id* 546, 549 (emphasis added); Palmer News, Inc v ARA Servs, Inc, 476 F Supp 1176 (D Kan 1979).

[28] Although a uniform zone pricing system is not discriminatory under the act, some adjustment must be made in considering a delivered price to one customer and an f.o.b. price to the customer's competitor. In such circumstances, a discrimination may be acknowledged and its legality tested by considering availability, the potential for competitive injury, and functional pricing.

prompt payment discount rates can have such an effect.[29]

§3.05 Is availability of goods to all customers a defense to a charge of unlawful price discrimination?

The existence of a price discrimination can be contradicted by facts showing that the lower price was reasonably available to the disfavored customer. The notion that availability of the lower price to competing customers would preclude the finding of a Robinson-Patman Act §2(a) violation is implicit in the Supreme Court's 1966 *FTC v Borden*[30] decision which intimated that there would have been no offense had the seller's private label milk been available for purchase by all customers. The principle was expressly stated by dissenting Justice Stewart: "So long as Borden makes private label brands available to all customers of its premium milk, is is unlikely that price discrimination within the meaning of §2(a) can be made out."[31]

Since the *Borden* decision, the lower courts have, apparently without exception, treated availability as a defense, or, similarly, unavailability as an element of a prima facie case. Thus, the Third Circuit, in *EJ Sweeney & Sons, v Texaco, Inc,*[32] concluded that a seller's customer pickup allowance which resulted in a buyer's paying a higher net price for gasoline than its competitors was not discriminatory, since the allowance was available to all customers pursuant to a nondiscriminatory, mileage-related formula.

Whether *availability* is a defense to a §2(a) charge, however, or *unavailability* an element of the offense as to which the plaintiff must carry the burden of proof, is unsettled. Logically, since the issue of availability relates to the existence of a discrimination vel non, the obligation of proving unavailability of the lower price should fall upon the one attempting to establish the offense. The courts and the commission, however, have tacitly dealt with availability as an affirmative defense to be established by the defendant or respondent. For example, in its *Mueller Co v FTC* decision, the Seventh Circuit held, while conceding that the Seller's willingness to offer a stocking-jobber discount to all qualifying customers might make the discount available and, therefore, nondiscriminatory, that it was incumbent on the Seller seeking to rely on such availability to show that clear and objective qualifying criteria had been set forth and announced to the trade.[33]

In the wake of the *Borden* decision, high-level enforcement officials at the

---

[29] *See* Craig v Sun Oil Co, 515 F2d 221 (10th Cir 1975), *cert denied,* 429 US 829 (1976); Robbins Flooring, Inc v Federal Floors, Inc, 445 F Supp 4 (ED Pa 1977).

[30] 383 US 637 (1966).

[31] *Id* 659 n 17 (Stewart, J, dissenting).

[32] 637 F2d 105 (3d Cir 1980), *cert denied,* 451 US 911 (1981).

[33] Mueller Co v FTC, 323 F2d 44, 46 (7th Cir 1963), *cert denied,* 377 US 923 (1964); Century Hardware Corp v Acme United Corp, 467 F Supp 350 (ED Wis 1979).

Federal Trade Commission argued that *if* there were an availability defense, the lower price must be *functionally* available to all customers; i.e., must be reasonably suitable to and usable by each.[34] This position was the outgrowth of the FTC's pre-*Borden* stand that a discount was not available if *any* change in the buyer's practices—increasing the volume of purchases, for example—were required to earn it.[35] The commission itself, however, in dealing with the closely-related element of proportional availability under §2(d) of the act, approved a modest quantity-discount requirement that was not beyond the reach of smaller customers.[36] Similarly, purchase-quota discount programs, based on a buyer's cumulative volume of purchases over a specified time period, have been viewed as available and, therefore, nondiscriminatory.[37] Accordingly, it may be concluded that qualifying criteria which can be satisfied by the Buyer with reasonable modifications in purchase volume or are based on, e.g., prompt payment, function performed, or other purchase conditions, will meet the test of nondiscriminatory availability. It is highly unlikely, however, that this test will be satisfied by, for example, a volume-purchase requirement that is beyond the practical reach of some customers.[38]

Thus far in this section, the question of availability has been discussed from the standpoint of the availability of a lower price from the Seller charged with a §2(a) violation. There is some authority to the effect that a violation does not occur if the goods (or goods of like grade and quality), while not available at the lower price from the defendant, are also available from a competing Seller.[39] It seems, however, that such availability cannot logically be related to the threshold question of jurisdiction but should be considered in connection with whether the discrimination has the capacity for competitive injury.

An important caveat to consideration of the availability issue is that the defense (or element) is probably not applicable to primary line cases, involving potential competitive injury at the Seller level. Thus, in the context of a geographic price discrimination, the fact that the lower price may be available to all customers in a particular area would not cause the pricing practice to be

---

[34] See Remarks by Joseph E. Sheehy, Director, Bureau of Restraint of Trade, FTC, *Some Special Problems Under the Robinson-Patman Act,* 30 ABA Section on Antitrust Rep 41, 56 (1966) (panel discussion).

[35] Universal-Rundle Corp, 65 FTC 924 (1964), *revd,* 352 F2d 831 (7th Cir 1965), *revd,* 387 US 244 (1967); Dayton Rubber Co, 66 FTC 423 (1964), *revd on other grounds, sub nom* Dayco Corp v FTC, 362 F2d 180 (6th Cir 1966).

[36] Sunbeam Corp, 67 FTC 20 (1965); Yale & Towne Mfg Co, 52 FTC 1580 (1956).

[37] Rod Baxter Imports, Inc v Saab Scania of Am, Inc, 489 F Supp 245 (D Minn 1980).

[38] *See* FTC v Morton Salt Co, 334 US 37, 42 (1948).

[39] Hanson v Pittsburgh Plate Glass Indus, 482 F2d 220 (5th Cir), *cert denied,* 414 US 1136 (1973); Tri-Valley Packing Assn v FTC, 329 F2d 694 (9th Cir 1964); Ark-La-Tex Warehouse Distribs, Inc, 73 FTC 846 (1968); *But see* Fowler Mfg Co v Gorlick, 415 F2d 1248 (9th Cir), *cert denied,* 396 US 1012 (1970).

nondiscriminatory when evaluated from the standpoint of a competing Seller.[40]

§3.06 What transactions are in interstate commerce?

Unlike the Sherman Act,[41] and other provisions of the Clayton Act,[42] the Robinson-Patman Act contains a fourfold nexus requirement with respect to the interstate character of an offense. It is certainly not enough for jurisdictional purposes that a discriminatory practice affect commerce. Under the Robinson-Patman Act:

1. The Seller must be engaged in commerce
2. The discrimination must occur in the course of such commerce
3. Either or any of the purchases involved in the discrimination must occur in the course of commerce
4. The commodities must be sold for use, consumption, or resale within the jurisdiction of the United States[43]

The Supreme Court confirmed the narrow reach of the Robinson-Patman Act in its 1974 *Gulf Oil Corp v Copp Paving Co,*[44] decision, expressly rejecting the plaintiff's contention that the statute covers discriminatory practices which only affect interstate trade. Thus, purely local discriminations, even those effected by large interstate Sellers, are not subject to the act.[45]

Although its jurisdiction depends on either the higher or lower priced commodities actually crossing state lines, the scope of the act has on occasion been expanded by judicial resort to the *flow of commerce* theory. Under this approach, goods which come to rest for a brief period, and even those subjected to minor processing, may in some circumstances be covered.

Thus, the Supreme Court, in *Standard Oil Co v FTC,*[46] ruled that the stream of commerce had not been broken by an interstate shipper's bulk storage of petroleum products. Similarly, the Fifth Circuit in 1965 concluded that milk which was processed and stored intrastate after interstate shipment was never-

---

[40] Continental Baking Co v Old Homestead Bread Co, 476 F2d 97 (10th Cir), *cert denied,* 414 US 975 (1973).

[41] 15 USC §1.

[42] *See, e.g.,* §7 of the Clayton Act, 15 USC §18.

[43] 15 USC §13(a).

[44] 419 US 186 (1974).

[45] *See* Willard Dairy Corp v National Dairy Prods Corp, 309 F2d 943 (6th Cir 1962), *cert denied,* 373 US 934 (1963); *see also* Mayer Paving & Asphalt Co v General Dynamics Corp, 486 F2d 763 (7th Cir), *cert denied,* 414 US 1146 (1973), *rehearing denied* 417 US 978 (1974); Littlejohn v Shell Oil Co, 483 F2d 1140 (5th Cir), *cert denied,* 414 US 1116 (1973).

[46] 340 US 231 (1951).

theless in the flow of commerce.[47]

The judicial application of the flow of commerce theory has been erratic and, in recent years, less than generous. It appears that passage of title after interstate shipment will invariably be held to sever the flow of commerce, and that jurisdiction will not attach where a Seller's interstate sales are de minimis.[48] Further, it has been held that the interstate shipment of a component accounting for 5 per cent of the value of the product will not cause a subsequent discrimination if the sale of the finished product is to be in intrastate commerce.[49] In summary, it now appears that the interstate flow will be broken unless goods are shipped from out of state with the expectation of prompt resale, or are only briefly stored in the Seller's owned or controlled facilities, and unless processing, if any, is insignificant.

The courts have uniformly ruled, moreover, that sales at the retail store are not in commerce. A retailer's sales in different stores at different prices are, therefore, not subject to the act, even if the stores are located in different states.[50]

Finally, the act does not cover sales for export,[51] and import sales cannot be compared with higher-priced foreign sales under the act.[52] These results are mandated by the statutory provision that the commodities be sold for use, consumption, or resale within the jurisdiction of the United States. Thus, *dumping* cannot be reached by the Robinson-Patman Act.

§3.07 What are transactions in commodities?

Section 2(a) of the Robinson-Patman Act relates only to discrimination in *commodities*.[53] The general rule is that the act does not apply to intangibles.[54] Thus, transactions in real estate,[55] mutual fund shares,[56] and travelers' checks[57] have been held not to be covered. In an increasingly service-oriented

---

[47] Foremost Dairies, Inc v FTC, 348 F2d 674 (5th Cir), *cert denied*, 382 US 959 (1965).

[48] Zoslaw v MCA Distrib Corp, 693 F2d 870 (9th Cir 1982).

[49] RSE, Inc v Pennsy Supply, Inc, 489 F Supp 1227 (MD Pa 1980); *but see* Paceco, Inc v Ishikawajima-Harima Heavy Indus, 468 F Supp 256 (ND Cal 1979).

[50] *See* Cliff Food Storoes, Inc v Kroger, Inc, 417 F2d 203 (5th Cir 1969); Food Basket, Inc v Albertson's, Inc, 383 F2d 785 (10th Cir 1967).

[51] General Chems, Inc v Exxon Chem Co, 625 F2d 1231 (5th Cir 1980).

[52] Zenith Radio Corp v Matsushita Elec Indus Co, 402 F Supp 244 (ED Pa 1975).

[53] 15 USC §13(a). §2(c) refers to "goods, wares or merchandise" and §2(d) refers to "products or commodities." The terms appear to be indistinguishable for purposes of the act's enforcement.

[54] *See* ABA Section on Antitrust, Report on Price Discrimination in Non-Sale and Non-Commodity Transactions (1973).

[55] Export Liquor Sales, Inc v Ammex Warehouse Co, 426 F2d 251 (6th Cir 1970), *cert denied*, 400 US 1000 (1971).

[56] Baum v Investors Diversified Servs, Inc, 409 F2d 872 (7th Cir 1969).

[57] American Bankers Club, Inc v American Express Co, 1977-1 Trade Cas (CCH) ¶61,247 (DDC 1977).

society, however, the line is difficult to draw. Typically, the courts have looked to the dominant characteristic of a goods-service package in determining whether the act applies, with cost serving as the primary indicium of dominance. Thus, the combined provision of a product and repair service,[58] and of a bookkeeping service together with supporting forms,[59] have been held not to constitute covered commodity transactions. Cost alone, however, is not the sole measure of whether a transaction is subject to the act, and a qualitative factual analysis may be required.[60] Although the problems of proof may be formidable, it seems that the proper rule may be that where a commodity constitutes a significant element of a mixed transaction such that a discriminatory price for the commodity alone might reasonably be found to cause injury, the matter should not be stopped at the jurisdictional stage.

There is a split of authority over whether advertising price discriminations are cognizable under the act. The Federal Trade Commission[61] and at least one district court[62] have held that newspaper advertising is covered. The commission reasoned that the purposes of the act would best be served by finding jurisdiction to exist and that newspaper advertising, unlike construction work and professional services, is fungible so as to facilitate intercustomer price comparisons. The Second Circuit[63] and another district court[64] disagree.

Having decided that newspaper advertising rates may be subject to the Act, however, the Commission has reconsidered the undesirability of its attempting to challenge discriminations in the newspaper medium. The agency ultimately dismissed its pilot complaint, expressing the concerns that small business might be disproportionally damaged by FTC's invasion of the field and that newspapers might be disadvantaged vis-a-vis other media.[65]

§3.08 What is a sale?

Inherent in the focus on discrimination in price is the jurisdictional requirement that there be a sale to two or more purchasers.[66] A lease[67] or true

---

58 Aviation Specialties, Inc v United Aircraft, 586 F2d 1186 (5th Cir 1978); General Glass Co v Globe Glass & Trim Co, 1978–1 Trade Cas (CCH) ¶61,998 (ND Ill 1978).

59 Advanced Office Sys v Accounting Sys, 442 F Supp 418 (DSC 1978).

60 *See* May Dept Store v Graphic Process Co, 637 F2d 1211 (9th Cir 1980).

61 Times Mirror Co, [1976–1979 Transfer Binder] Trade Reg Rep (CCH) ¶21,448 (July 27, 1978) *complaint dismissed,* 3 Trade Reg Rep (CCH) ¶21,937 (July 7, 1982).

62 Sun Communications, Inc v Waters Publications, Inc, 466 F Supp 387 (WD Mo 1979).

63 Ambook Enters v Time, Inc, 612 F2d 604 (2d Cir 1979), *cert dismissed,* 448 US 914 (1980).

64 National Tire Wholesale, Inc v Washington Post Co, 441 F Supp 81 (DDC 1977), *affd,* 595 F2d 888 (DDC 1979).

65 Times Mirror Co, 3 Trade Reg Rep (CCH) ¶21,937 (complaint dismissed 1982).

66 *See* ABA section on Antitrust *Report on Price Discrimination in Non-Sale and Non-Commodity Transactions* (1973).

consignment[68] of goods is beyond the reach of the act. Similarly, a sale of goods to a favored customer compared only with an offer to sell others the goods at a higher price does not constitute a price discrimination, since there are not at least two sales.[69] By the same token, a Buyer's unsuccessful coercive effort to obtain a preferential price does not give rise to a cause of action under the Robinson-Patman Act.[70] On the other hand, a concluded sales *agreement* may be enough to satisfy the two-sales requirement.[71]

Considerable litigation has involved the question of whether a transfer of goods between different levels of a single enterprise can be considered a sale for purposes of the act. The trend of court decisions is toward a categorical refusal to consider such intra-enterprise transfers as sales.[72] Other decisions, which may still reflect the law in certain circuits, determine whether such a transfer might constitute a sale based on the degree of autonomy in the intra-enterprise relationship, especially with regard to pricing decisions.[73]

§3.09 Who is a purchaser?

Section 2(a) of the Robinson-Patman Act makes it unlawful, inter alia, "to discriminate in price between different purchasers of commodities."[74] The courts and the Federal Trade Commission have generally construed this provision so as to require that both the preferred and the disfavored customer be purchasers from the discriminating Seller, at least in a case asserting secondary or tertiary line injury.[75]

In the germinal leading case of *Klein v Lionel Corp*,[76] the court dismissed the Robinson-Patman Act claim of a plaintiff retailer who complained that the

---

67 Export Liquor Sales, Inc v Ammex Warehouse Co, 426 F2d 251 (6th Cir 1970), *cert denied,* 400 US 1000 (1971).

68 Students Book Co v Washington Law Book Co, 232 F2d 49 (DC Cir 1955), *cert denied,* 350 US 988 (1956).

69 Highspire, Inc v UKF Am, Inc, 469 F Supp 1009 (SDNY 1979).

70 Paint Prods Co v Minwax Co, 448 F Supp 656 (D Conn 1978).

71 Harper Plastics, Inc v Amoco Chems Corp, 617 F2d 468 (7th Cir 1980); Aluminum Co of Am v Tandet, 235 F Supp 111 (D Conn 1964). A plaintiff would, of course, have difficulty in establishing competitive injury and antitrust damage to himself or herself on the basis of a contractual offer to sell at a higher price.

72 *See, e.g.,* Security Tire & Rubber Co v Gates Rubber Co, 598 F2d 962 (5th Cir), *cert denied,* 444 US 942 (1979); Island Tobacco Co v RJ Reynolds Indus, 513 F Supp 726 (D Hawaii 1981).

73 *See* Schaben v Samuel Moore & Co, 606 F2d 831 (8th Cir 1979); Parrish v Cox, 586 F2d 9 (6th Cir 1978); Brown v Hansen Publications, Inc, 556 F2d 969 (9th Cir 1977).

74 15 USC §13(a).

75 The same requirement applies in primary line cases; however, in such cases the purchasers need not be in competition with one another. *See* FTC v Anheuser-Busch, Inc, 363 US 536 (1960); Palmer News, Inc v ARA Servs, 476 F Supp 1176 (D Kan 1979).

76 138 F Supp 560 (D Del), *affd,* 237 F2d 13 (3d Cir 1956).

wholesalers from whom he purchased were paying the same price as direct buying retailers. The district court expressed the rule as follows: "[A] plaintiff has no cause of action for a discrimination under 15 USC §13(a), where it appears that the plaintiff was not a purchaser from the Seller but a retailer purchasing from a jobber. . . ."[77] This general principle, which has been endorsed in a number of subsequent cases,[78] makes sense. There is no logical or economic justification for requiring a Seller that does not itself effect a discrimination to be responsible for the downstream pricing of its customers. A contrary rule would involve the courts and the commission in the public utility-type regulation of prices reminiscent of the mandatory functional discount legislation which Congress did not see fit to enact.[79]

The FTC, with court endorsement, has fashioned a theory, however, whereby a Buyer who does not purchase directly from the discriminating Seller, but is adversely affected by the discrimination nevertheless, may be found to be a purchaser within the meaning of §2(a). This theory, labeled the *indirect purchaser doctrine,* holds that a purchaser from a direct customer of the Seller may be the subject of an unlawful discrimination where the Seller exercises such control over the terms of sale to the indirect Buyer and maintains such contacts with it that the relationship is tantamount to that between a direct Buyer and Seller. The indirect purchaser doctrine was invoked by the Commission in the *Purolator Products* case where:

1. Seller provided the direct Buyer with contract forms for use in selling to the indirect Buyer
2. These forms provided that the indirect Buyer must maintain a certain level of inventory of the Seller's product
3. Seller maintains and implements a suggested price list covering prices to the indirect customers
4. Seller promoted the product through direct contact with the indirect purchaser[80]

Under these circumstances, an actionable discrimination was found to have occurred through the Seller's granting of a lower price to direct buying warehouse distributors, some of whose sales were to retailers, than to indirect buying jobbers who also resold to retailers.

Critical to the successful invocation of the indirect purchaser doctrine is Seller's control over the prices charged by the direct customer in resales to the

---

[77] 138 F Supp at 566.

[78] *See, e.g.,* Wales Home Remodeling Co v Alside Aluminum Corp, 443 F Supp 908 (ED Wis 1978).

[79] *See, e.g.,* HR 12562, 94th Cong, 2d Sess (1976).

[80] Purolator Prods, Inc v FTC, 352 F2d 874, 880 (7th Cir 1965), *cert denied,* 389 US 1045 (1968). The indirect purchaser doctrine has its roots in some of the earliest commission decisions under the act. *See* Kraft-Phenix Cheese Corp, 25 FTC 537 (1937); Luxor, Ltd, 31 FTC 658 (1940).

indirect purchaser. Subsequent cases to *Purolater Products v FTC*[81] have found an indirect Buyer not to be a *purchaser* within §2(a) where resale price maintenance is absent. For example, in *Barnosky Oils, Inc v Union Oil Co*,[82] the Sixth Circuit ruled that direct promotional contacts by Seller with the indirect purchaser were not enough to invoke the doctrine where there was no attempt to control the direct buyers' resale prices.

The strict limits of the indirect purchaser doctrine applicable in §2(a) proceedings have been relaxed by the United States Supreme Court with respect to cases involving promotional allowances and services under §§2(d) and 2(e).[83] In *FTC v. Fred Meyer, Inc*,[84] the court expressly rejected application of the indirect purchaser analysis to these sections and held broadly that a Seller who undertakes promotional activity at the retail level is responsible under the act for insuring proportional equal treatment to all Buyers at that level, no matter how remote they are from the Sellers in the chain of distribution. The courts have not applied this sweeping rule to §2(a) cases, in part because of concern with the resale price maintenance implications of such an approach.[85]

There has been surprisingly little discussion in the recent cases concerning the impact of the Supreme Court's *Illinois Brick Co v Illinois*[86] on the indirect purchaser doctrine. It may be that the courts have either not focused on the issue or assumed that facts sufficient to invoke the indirect purchaser doctrine would also satisfy the *control* exception to the *Illinois Brick* rule.[87] If the latter is the case, the assumption is faulty, since the complexity in proof of injury and damages with which the *Illinois Brick* decision is concerned can arise very readily in an indirect-Buyer discrimination context, even after the purchaser threshold has been crossed.

One district court has carved out an exception to the direct purchaser rule applicable to situations where the indirect purchaser's supplier is charged a *higher* price by the Seller than is a direct-buying competitor of the indirect purchaser.[88] In reaching this result, the court concluded, "[I]f plaintiff, even as an indirect purchaser, can show that it has suffered competitive injury at the secondary level from conduct proscribed under the Act, it has the right to maintain a price discrimination action."[89] This rationale reflects, at present, a view very much in the minority.

---

[81] 352 F2d 874 (7th Cir 1965), *cert denied*, 389 US 1045 (1966).

[82] 665 F2d 74 (6th Cir 1981). *See also* Blatt v Lorenz-Schneider Co, 1980–81 Trade Cas (CCH) ¶63,670 (SDNY 1980) (independent retailers not customers of Seller where distributor was free to set prices to them).

[83] 15 USC §§13(d),(e). See discussion at **§§3.19–3.21.**

[84] 390 US 341 (1968).

[85] FLM Collision Parts, Inc v Ford Motor Co, 543 F2d 1019, 1025 (2d Cir 1976), *cert denied*, 429 US 1097 (1977).

[86] 431 US 720 (1977).

[87] *Id* 736 n 16. *See* Diehl & Sons v International Harvester Co, 445 F Supp 282 (EDNY 1978) (discriminatory price could be traced through parent to subsidiary).

[88] Paceco, Inc v Ishikawajima-Harima Heavy Indus, 468 F Supp 256 (ND Cal 1979).

[89] *Id* 263.

Finally, insofar as secondary line injury cases are concerned, the purchasers must buy the goods at approximately the same time,[90] and the price discriminations must occur in the same general geographic area.[91]

§3.10 What are sales for resale?

With dual distribution prevalent in the marketing system, it is not surprising that the question of preferential treatment of consumers has arisen from time to time. The issue has been presented in several contexts.

Customers of the supplier have complained of the supplier's sales to consumers at lower prices through the supplier's own retail outlets. The courts have held that such a discrimination is not actionable in a secondary line injury case since the reselling customer would not have been able to compete even if the price to the consumer had been the same as the price to it, a clearly nondiscriminatory pricing practice.[92]

Another situation involves Seller's distribution of coupons directly to consumers who subsequently redeem them at the stores of the supplier's retail customer and pay a reduced price for the goods. The retailer is reimbursed by Seller for the discount stated on the coupon and for its handling costs. It has been held that no discrimination in price has occurred since the coupons benefit the consumer rather than the retailer and the consumer is in no sense a purchaser from the Seller.[93]

Nevertheless, at least for purposes of primary line injury cases, sales to consumers may serve as one leg of a discrimination where the consumer is a direct Buyer from Seller and the interstate commerce element is satisfied.[94]

§3.11 What are commodities of like grade and quality?

Another element of a prima facie discrimination case is that the commodities involved in the sales being compared must be of "like grade and quality."[95] The issue is a threshold one, and if different grades or qualities[96] are involved, the situation is beyond the reach of the Robinson-Patman Act regardless of the extent of the price difference.

---

[90] Atalanta Trading Corp v FTC, 258 F2d 365 (2d Cir 1958).

[91] Palmer News, Inc v ARA Servs, Inc. 476 F Supp 1176 (D Kan 1979).

[92] Secatore's Inc v Esso Standard Oil Co, 171 F Supp 665 (D Mass 1959).

[93] Indian Coffee Corp v Procter & Gamble Co, 482 F Supp 1104 (WD Pa 1980).

[94] *Cf* Littlejohn v Shell Oil Co, 483 F2d 1140, 1143 (5th Cir), *cert denied,* 414 US 1116 (1973) (dicta).

[95] 15 USC §13(a).

[96] Neither the legislative history nor the cases suggest that there is any difference between the term *grade* and the term *quality.*

Perhaps because it is a threshold aspect of a discrimination case, the courts have not been expansive in finding distinct grade and quality where there are marketing but not physical differences in the commodities.

The United States Supreme Court's landmark decision in *FTC v Borden Co*[97] establishes that the distinction between a private label item and a manufacturer's brand does not constitute a difference in the grade and quality between physically identical products even though they command different prices throughout the chain of distribution. The Court declined to stop the Federal Trade Commission at the initial stage of a prima facie case, indicating instead that label differences could be taken into account in the evaluation of competitive injury. Adopting this suggestion on remand, the Fifth Circuit found no competitive injury, concluding, "We are of the firm view that where a price differential between a premium and nonpremium brand reflects no more than a consumer preference for the premium brand, the price difference creates no competitive advantage to the recipient of the cheaper private brand product on which injury could be predicated."[98] The court opinion is unclear as to how one might determine whether a price difference reflects "no more than a consumer preference for the premium brand." Circular as it may appear, the existence of a customary price differential could suffice.

Where a brand difference is coupled with commercially significant physical differences, even the commission has been willing to conclude that commodities are not of like grade and quality. In *Universal-Rundle Corp*, the question was stated in the following terms: "The issue here is whether a showing of physical variations between two products of such a nature as to create a consumer preference for one over the other will support a conclusion that the two products are not of like grade and quality."[99] Responding affirmatively, the commission found that physical differences, particularly in size, between private brand bathtubs sold to Sears and Universal-Rundle's own brand were such as to create a consumer preference for the latter. The commission has also applied the preference test to goods for further processing. The fact that a type of flour required reprocessing by the customer caused it to be of distinct grade and quality from flour which did not.[100]

The courts also have been inclined to find distinct grade and quality where there is a physical difference between the commodities in question, at least where the difference is responsive to consumers' preference. Whether physical differences are such as to affect consumer use or preference is a question of

---

[97] 383 US 637 (1966).

[98] Borden Co v FTC, 381 F2d 175, 181 (5th Cir 1967).

[99] Universal-Rundle Corp, 65 FTC 924, 955 (1964), *revd on other grounds,* 352 F2d 831 (7th Cir 1965), *revd,* 387 US 244, *on remand,* 382 F2d 285 (7th Cir 1967). The commission's decision reflects a departure from its earlier view, which was rejected by the court of appeals, that all products in a broad category are of like grade and quality. Atalanta Trading Corp, 53 FTC 565 (1956), *revd,* 258 F2d 365 (2d Cir 1958).

[100] Quaker Oats Co, 66 FTC 1131, 1192 (1964).

fact to be resolved by the factfinder in a damage action.[101] The plaintiff bears the burden of establishing like grade and quality, and the failure to come forth with probative evidence of likeness may result in an adverse summary judgment.[102] The statutory language and the cases suggest a stricter test for determining like grade and quality than for identifying the products to be included in a relevant market for purposes of assessing probable competitive injury under §2(a) or other sections of the Clayton Act.

§3.12 What kind of injury to competition will violate the act?

The Robinson-Patman amendments to §2 of the Clayton Act created a different and arguably broader standard of competitive injury than applies to any other provision of the antitrust laws.[103] In addition to the general focus of the Clayton Act on substantial injury to competition and tendency toward monopoly, the Robinson-Patman Act proscribes discriminations which have the capacity "to injure, destroy, or prevent competition with any person who either grants or knowingly receives the benefit of such discrimination, or with customers of either of them."[104]

The inclusion of this language has precipitated an enduring debate over whether the Robinson-Patman act was designed by Congress in 1936 to preserve the process of competition or, rather, to safeguard individual competitors. Concern that the latter objective might have an influence on the outcome of cases arising under the act stemmed from some broad dicta in the Supreme Court's 1948 *FTC v Morton Salt* decision to the effect that the Clayton Act was amended such that a finding of competitive injury could rest on a finding that a competitor had been injured by a discriminatory price.[105] The prospect that commission and court decisions would focus solely on the plight of individual competitors prompted the Attorney General's National Committee to Study the Antitrust Laws to contend that "we emphasize that it is not 'injury' to competitors but adverse effects on 'competition with' parties privy to discriminations that the statute expressly forbids."[106] This philosophical dispute has not had any practical impact on the construction of the act, however, and the competitive injury standard is applied with reference to a discrimination's probable impact on competition as a whole. This result has been encouraged

---

[101] Checker Motors Corp v Chrysler Corp, 283 F Supp 876 (SDNY 1968), *affd,* 405 F2d 319 (2d Cir), *cert denied,* 394 US 999 (1969).

[102] Wire Mesh Prods, Inc v Wire Belting Assn, 520 F Supp 1004 (ED Pa 1981); Lombino & Sons v Standard Fruit & Steamship Co, 1975–2 Trade Cas (CCH) ¶60,527 (SDNY 1975).

[103] *Compare* 15 USC §13 *with* 15 USC §§14, 18.

[104] 15 USC §13(a).

[105] 334 US 37, 46–47 (1948).

[106] Report of the Attorney General's National Committee to Study the Antitrust Laws 165 (1955).

by the Supreme Court's repeated admonition of the need to interpret the Robinson-Patman Act in harmony with the broader, procompetitive goals of the antitrust laws as a whole.[107]

Nevertheless, it is clear that actual injury to competition is not a requisite to a finding of illegality under §2(a). The Supreme Court has held that a violation can be established by proof that there is a reasonable probability that a discrimination will have a significant adverse competitive consequence.[108] This assessment of probabilities has led the commission and the courts into drawing inferences of injury to competition in both primary line (injury to Seller's competitors) and particularly secondary line (injury to Seller's customers) cases. The liberality of the commission and some courts in drawing inferences of competitive injury at the secondary level has generated considerable criticism that the act has been used to undermine effective competition.[109]

Finally, Congress in 1936 adopted, as subsidiary provisions of the act, subsections dealing with unlawful brokerage payments or allowances and the provision of advertising and merchandising allowances and services.[110] These provisions define illegal practices without regard to their effect on competition and, in the case of the brokerage section, possibly without regard even to discrimination.[111]

§3.13 What are the elements of competitive injury to competitors of the Seller?

The language of the Robinson-Patman Act does not differentiate between the primary line and secondary line with respect to a test of competitive injury. In both instances the Federal Trade Commission and the courts have relied to an extent on inferences of injury. The standard for establishing injury to competition at the Seller level, however, has evolved such that it is substantially

---

[107] Great Atl & Pac Tea Co v FTC, 440 US 69, 80 (1979); Automatic Canteen Co of Am v FTC, 346 US 61, 74 (1953).

[108] FTC v Morton Salt Co, 334 US 37, 50 (1948); *see also* Corn Prods Ref Co v FTC, 324 US 726 (1945). A controversy existed for a brief period as to whether it was the *reasonable possibility* of competitive injury as suggested in *Morton Salt* or the *reasonable probability* as indicated in *Corn Products* which the act condemned. As with the *competition* versus *competitors* dispute, no doctrinal significance has attached and the courts have dealt with probabilities. *See, e.g.,* Whitaker Cable Corp v FTC, 239 F2d 253 (7th Cir 1956), *cert denied,* 353 US 938, *rehearing denied,* 353 US 962 (1957). *But see* Falls City Indus, Inc v Vanco Beverages, Inc, 1983–1 Trade Cas (CCH) ¶65,282 (US Mar 22, 1983) where the Supreme Court resurrected the "reasonable possibility" standard.

[109] C. Edwards, The Price Discrimination Law 627 (1959); the Justice Department's 1976 report on the Robinson-Patman Act criticized the mechanical approach to secondary line injury and proposed to amend the act so as to limit findings of unlawful discriminations to injuries effected through larger, systematic discriminations. United States Dept of Justice Report on the Robinson-Patman Act, app C, 276–93 (1976).

[110] 15 USC §13(c)-(e).

[111] See **§3.17.**

more rigorous than that applicable at the customer level. This fact may be attributable to a recognition that territorial, functional, or brand discriminations may be an effective way whereby a Seller might engage in price experimentation leading to a generally lower or, at least, less rigid market price structure.[112]

Mere proof of diversion of business from a competitor is insufficient to support the conclusion that a Seller's price discrimination is injurious to competition.[113] Rather, a more probative analysis of a discrimination and the market in which it occurred is necessary for a finding of primary line injury.

The principal basis for a determination of primary line injury has come to be Seller's predatory pricing. Below-cost pricing has been deemed sufficient to create the inference of predatory intent from which the inference of probable competitive injury can be drawn.[114] Although predatory pricing is not a prerequisite to a finding of primary line injury,[115] and some older cases have based injury determinations on other factors,[116] the recent focus has been almost entirely on predatory intent based on below-cost pricing.

The Supreme Court's *Utah Pie Co v Continental Baking Co*[117] decision found primary line injury through the breakdown of the market's competitive structure as the result of defendant's price discriminations. Although the Court noted that the pricing was below cost, supplying the inference of predatory intent, it did not identify the nature of the costs involved.[118] Similarly, in *National Dairy Products Corp,*[119] the commission inferred predatory intent by the Seller of fruit spreads from the Seller's extensive market analysis which forecast the dramatic increase in its sales volume which would result from a below-cost promotion program and the corresponding inability of its competitors to withstand such a program. Again, the decision was not specific as to the costs below which prices were offered.

A major effort to establish objective standards for a cost-based test and a significant contribution to the development of the law concerning predatory pricing is set forth in a 1975 law review article by Professors Areeda and Turner.[120] Although directed principally to the development of a rule relative to predatory pricing as evidence of an attempt to monopolize under §2 of the

---

[112] See Backman, *An Economist Looks at the Robinson-Patman Act,* 17 ABA Section on Antitrust Rep 343 (1960).

[113] Anheuser-Busch, Inc v FTC, 289 F2d 835 (7th Cir 1961).

[114] Utah Pie Co v Continental Baking Co, 386 US 685, 697 (1967).

[115] FTC v Anheuser-Busch, Inc, 363 US 536, 552 (1960).

[116] Continental Baking Co v Old Homestead Bread Co, 476 F2d 97 (10th Cir), *cert denied,* 414 US 975 (1973); Forster Mfg Co, 62 FTC 852 (1963), *revd on other grounds,* 335 F2d 47 (1st Cir 1964), *cert denied,* 380 US 906 (1965).

[117] 386 US 685 (1967).

[118] *Id.*

[119] 71 FTC 1333 (1967), *modified,* 412 F2d 605 (7th Cir 1969).

[120] Areeda & Turner, *Predatory Pricing and Related Practices Under Section 2 of the Sherman Act,* 88 Harv L Rev 697 (1975).

Sherman Act, the concepts expressed in the article have been applied to primary line injury determinations under the Robinson-Patman Act. The test proposed is that pricing below marginal cost, or its surrogate, average variable cost, should be considered presumptively predatory.[121]

Although some commentators have strongly disagreed with the Areeda–Turner approach,[122] numerous court decisions have endorsed it. The approval has not been uniformly unqualified, however, and some courts have refused to embrace a solely cost-based test[123] or to signify that pricing below average variable cost will be considered to the exclusion of other evidence of possible predatory intent.[124] Nevertheless, where the test has been accepted even on a qualified basis, other factors have not been influential and the defendant has prevailed on the basis that there was no showing that it had priced commodities below average variable cost.

In recent cases in the Second and Third Circuits, the acceptance of the Areeda-Turner theory has been nearly complete. The Second Circuit, in *Northeastern Telephone Co v American Telephone & Telegraph Co,*[125] explained that a rule based on marginal cost pricing most closely comports with competitive efficiency, is consistent with consumer welfare, and discourages underutilization of capacity. It concluded, "[W]e agree with Areeda and Turner that in the general case at least, the relationship between a firm's prices and its marginal costs provides the best single determinant of predatory pricing."[126] In *O Hommel Co v Ferro Corp,*[127] the Third Circuit examined the small and declining share of the defendant who had made selective price reductions within a geographic market and the secrecy it had employed in effecting the pricing discriminations in concluding that *below average total cost* pricing could not, under these circumstances, give rise to a presumption of predatory intent. Although the court was attracted to the Areeda-Turner thesis, it expressed doubt that any cost-based theory could give rise to liability under the facts of the case.

A decision by a panel of the Ninth Circuit stands out in concluding that, in general, a plaintiff need not establish prices below average variable cost to prevail in a primary line §2(a) case. In *William Inglis & Sons Baking v ITT Continental Baking Co,*[128] the court concluded that, while proof of pricing below

---

[121] *Id* 712.

[122] See Williamson, *Predatory Pricing: A Strategic and Welfare Analysis,* 87 Yale LJ 284 (1977); Scherer, *Predatory Pricing and the Sherman Act: A Comment,* 89 Harv L Rev 869 (1976); Posner, Antitrust Law: An Economic Perspective 189 (1976).

[123] Pacific Eng & Prod Co v Kerr-McGee Corp, 551 F2d 790, 797 (10th Cir), *cert denied,* 434 US 979, *rehearing denied,* 434 US 977 (1977); Chillicothe Sand & Gravel Co v Martin Marietta Corp, 615 F2d 427 (7th Cir 1980).

[124] International Air Indus v American Excelsior Co, 517 F2d 714, 724 (5th Cir), *cert denied,* 424 US 943 (1975).

[125] 651 F2d 76 (2d Cir 1981), *cert denied,* 102 S Ct 1438 (1982).

[126] *Id* 88.

[127] 659 F2d 340 (3d Cir 1981), *cert denied,* 102 S Ct 1711 (1982).

[128] 668 F2d 1014 (9th Cir 1981), *rehearing denied,* 668 F2d 1060 (9th Cir 1981), *cert denied,* 103 S Ct 57 (1982) (No 81–2083) (ITT), *cert denied,* 103 S Ct 58 (1982) (No 81–2289) (Inglis).

variable costs might create a presumption of predatory intent, failure to establish such pricing is not fatal to the plaintiff. Other evidence sufficient to establish competitive injury could include whether the prices were set with the anticipated benefit of destroying competition and whether other alternatives such as higher prices or even termination of operations might "have been better means of minimizing losses."[129] The decision has the obvious capacity for injecting extreme uncertainty into primary line injury determinations.

§3.14 What are the elements of competitive injury to customers of the Seller?

The Robinson-Patman Act was enacted partly in response to the apparent inability of the original §2 of the Clayton Act to reach discriminations whose sole adverse impact was at the customer level.[130] Legislative concern was expressed with the need to preserve equality of competitive opportunity among those engaged in the distribution of commodities.[131] Thus, the statute was amended in 1936 to add language making it unlawful for a Seller to discriminate in price where, inter alia, the effect of such discrimination may be substantially to lessen competition or tend to create a monopoly in any line of commerce, or to injure, destroy, or prevent competition with any person who either grants *or knowingly receives the benefit of such discrimination, or with customers of either of them. . . .*[132]

The Federal Trade Commission's enforcement activity and the preponderance of private litigation under §2(a) have concentrated on Buyer-injury situations. Since the statute permits a finding of competitive injury at the level of the preferred customer's customers, a discrimination may be illegal if its impact is exerted not merely at the secondary level but at the tertiary level. Thus, the Supreme Court has found cognizable injury in a Seller's higher price to an integrated wholesaler-retailer than to a wholesaler who passed the lower price through two subsidiary operations to the retail level.[133]

As explained in **§3.12,** actual competitive injury is not a prerequisite to a finding that the Robinson-Patman Act has been violated; instead, the critical issue is whether there is a reasonable probability that injury will occur. The leading Supreme Court decision, *FTC v. Morton Salt Co,*[134] involved a Seller's graduated aggregate annual volume discount schedule. Only the very largest-

---

[129] 668 F2d at 1037.

[130] *See* HR Rep No 627, 63 Cong, 2d Sess 8–9 (1914).

[131] *See* S Rep No 1502, 74th Cong, 2d Sess 3 (1936).

[132] 15 USC §13(a) (emphasis supplied).

[133] Perkins v Standard Oil Co, 395 US 642 (1969). The secondary and tertiary line injury test does not confer standing on a person who is not a direct or indirect purchaser from the Seller. See **§3.09.** In addition, it is unsettled whether the principles of Illinois Brick v Illinois, 431 US 720 (1977), prohibiting suits by those who do not deal directly with an antitrust defendant, are applicable in Robinson-Patman Act cases.

[134] 334 US 37 (1948).

volume Buyers could qualify for the largest discount; thus the discount schedule was not functionally available to all customers.[135] The Court concluded that the Seller's system created a reasonable probability of competitive injury at the buyer level since it involved substantial price differences in effect over a significant period of time with respect to a competitively significant product in a highly competitive industry where profit margins are typically low. The Court rejected Seller's argument that salt is but one of a multitude of items sold in a grocery store, reasoning that unless substantial discriminations affecting single products in multiproduct customer industries can be brought within the scope of the act, there is no way that the act could prevent competitive injury in such markets until it was too late.

The *Morton Salt* approach has generally been followed in subsequent cases where a chronic discrimination has been established as to a single product or group of products and there is evidence of intense competition and low profit margins at the buyer level. The auto parts cases of the 1950s mark the furthest reach of the injury-predictive capacities of the courts.[136] Even those decisions, however, contain suggestions that the ability to perceive possible injury at the buyer level from every Seller discrimination is not limitless. Nevertheless, the general principles expressed in the Supreme Court's *Morton Salt* decision remain applicable to secondary line cases.[137]

Where, however, a discrimination is small, or sporadic, or there is an absence of proof relative to competitive conditions at the buyer level, a probability of competitive injury will not be found. Thus, the FTC has exonerated a 3 per cent price discrimination on toy products where there was insufficient proof of competitive conditions at the resale level.[138] In the same vein, the Seventh Circuit reversed a commission finding of probable injury where the discrimination arose in the context of a price war which was of only 17 days' duration.[139] In addition, a sales quota system based on customers' performance over the preceding calendar quarter has been deemed not to cause probable competi-

---

[135] See **§3.05.**

[136] *See, e.g.,* E Edelmann & Co v FTC, 239 F2d 152 (7th Cir 1956), *cert denied,* 355 US 941 (1958); Moog Indus v FTC, 238 F2d 43 (8th Cir 1956), *cert denied,* 355 US 411 (1958); Whitaker Cable Corp v FTC, 239 F2d 253 (7th Cir 1956), *cert denied,* 353 US 938, *rehearing denied,* 353 US 962 (1957).

[137] In a decision announced on March 22, 1983, the United States Supreme Court reaffirmed the principles of *Morton Salt* and explained that competitive injury could be inferred from a substantial, persistent price discrimination even when granted to a relatively small buyer. Falls City Indus v Vanco Beverage Inc, 44 Antitrust & Trade Reg Rep (BNA) 658, 660 (US Mar 22, 1983). *See* Great Atl & Pac Tea Co v FTC, 557 F2d 971 (2d Cir 1977), *revd on other grounds,* 440 US 69 (1979); United Biscuit Co of Am v FTC, 350 F2d 615 (7th Cir 1965), *cert denied,* 383 US 926 (1966).

[138] Fred Bronner Corp, 57 FTC 771 (1960); *see also* General Glass Co v Globe Glass & Trim Co, 1978-1 Trade Cas (CCH) ¶61,998 (ND Ill 1978).

[139] American Oil Co v FTC, 325 F2d 101 (7th Cir 1963), *cert denied,* 377 US 954 (1964). *See also* Marty's Floor Covering Co v GAF Corp, 604 F2d 266 (4th Cir 1979), *cert denied,* 444 US 1017 (1980).

tive injury.[140]

The conclusion that competitive injury is likely to result from a discrimination is less readily reached where the products in question are not standardized or fungible. The FTC, in denying complaint counsel's motion for summary decision in the *Times Mirror* case, held that greater proof of capacity for injury is required where it is not clear that the products (or services) are fungible.[141] A more searching analysis is also required where the product in question is resold only as a component or part of the formulation of another product. In such situations, the courts will consider the importance of the component to the final product and the extent to which its costs can be traced to an influence on the final product's price.[142] Similarly, in comparing the price of private label and seller-branded products, the courts will consider, in connection with competitive injury, whether the price difference reflects no more than a recognized consumer preference for the Seller's brand.[143]

The burden of proving probable competitive injury is on the party initiating the suit. This burden involves establishing a causative link between the discrimination and probable injury.[144] The Second Circuit, however, has adopted a rule which gives rise to a rebuttable presumption of competitive injury at the secondary level once a showing of discrimination has been made.[145]

In sum, the courts are showing an increasing inclination to require probative evidence of the capacity for injury rather than relying on the mere fact of discrimination. It may be that probable injury findings will be limited to those situations involving chronic discriminations favoring large Buyers where there is a threat that either Seller or Buyer market power will be enhanced.

§3.15 What is a functional discount?

The term *functional discount* is not found in the Robinson-Patman Act; nevertheless, the existence of functional differences among purchasers has been found by the courts and, albeit somewhat erratically, by the Federal Trade Commission, to sanction price differences. Both the original Robinson bill and the Patman bill contained provisions which would have expressly authorized functional discounts to those operating at the wholesale and higher levels of

---

[140] Rod Baxter Imports, Inc v Saab-Scania of Am, Inc, 489 F Supp 245 (D Minn 1980).

[141] Times Mirror Co, [1976–1979 Transfer Binder] Trade Reg Rep (CCH) ¶21,489 (FTC July 27, 1978), *complaint dismissed,* 3 Trade Reg Rep (CCH) ¶21,937 (July 7, 1982).

[142] *Compare* Corn Prods Ref Co v FTC, 324 US 726 (1945), *with* Minneapolis-Honeywell Regulator Co v FTC, 191 F2d 786 (7th Cir 1951), *cert dismissed,* 344 US 206 (1952) *and* Quaker Oats Co, 66 FTC 1131 (1964).

[143] Borden Co v FTC, 381 F2d 175 (5th Cir 1967).

[144] Chrysler Credit Corp v J Truett Payne Co, 670 F2d 575 (5th Cir 1982).

[145] John B Hull, Inc v Waterbury Petroleum Prods, Inc, 588 F2d 24 (2d Cir 1978), *cert denied,* 440 US 960 (1979); Samuel H Moss, Inc v FTC, 148 F2d 378 (2d Cir), *cert denied,* 326 US 734 (1945), *modified,* 155 F2d 1016 (2d Cir 1946).

the distributive chain, based solely on the level to which the customer *sold*.[146] As the legislation was approved by each house, however, inconsistent provisions were fashioned, and the conference committee deleted all reference to functional pricing from the statute.[147] The consensus view of the legislative history is that Congress, in electing neither to approve nor to disapprove functional discounts expressly, intended that their legality be judged under the various elements of the act, particularly that relating to competitive injury.[148]

It is clear that Congress did not intend to mandate that functional discounts be made available at various levels of distribution. On several occasions in the years following enactment, various bills were introduced which would have amended the act to require functional discounts based solely on a purchaser's resale level.[149] None was accorded serious attention. Thus, consistent with an early ruling by the Federal Trade Commission,[150] the law does not prevent a seller from establishing identical prices for all purchasers regardless of their level of distribution.

Because of the absence of any clear statutory guidelines, the identification of lawful functional discounts has been left to the commission and the courts. A variety of functional differences have been considered, subject to the prerequisite that the differences be real and not artificial.[151]

Functional discounts frequently involve discounts to entities that resell at higher levels of distribution than retailers, e.g., in the form of lower prices to wholesalers who resell to retailers than are available to retailers. Absent circumstances which give rise to analysis under the *indirect purchaser* rule,[152] such discounts have not been questioned. Considerable controversy, however, still surrounds the status of a discount to an entity which operates at various levels, e.g., one which buys at the wholesale level but resells to consumers. The current legal posture of such discounts is considered in **§3.16.** What is clear is that the functional discount rubric cannot be used to justify a discount to a firm operating only at a lower level of distribution, a *pure* retailer, that is not allowed to one operating only at a higher level, a wholesaler.[153]

Although functional discount analysis has typically involved different prices to two or more firms operating at different levels of distribution, it is also relevant to different prices to firms at the same level based on functions performed or on the category of customer to which the product is resold. Thus,

---

[146] S 3154, 74th Cong, 1st Sess (1935); HR 8442, 74th Cong, 1st Sess (1935).

[147] HR Rep No 2951, 74th Cong, 2d Sess (1936).

[148] See ABA section on Antitrust, The Robinson-Patman Act: Policy and Law 58 (Monograph No 4 1980); *see also* Calvani, *Functional Discounts Under the Robinson-Patman Act,* 17 BC Indus & Com L Rev 543, 545–46 (1976) (suggesting tacit legislative approval).

[149] *See* S 315, 86th Cong, 1st Sess (1959); HR 3465, 87th Cong, 1st Sess (1961); HR 2710, 88th Cong, 1st Sess (1963); HR 12562, 94th Cong, 2d Sess (1976); HR 12688, 94th Cong, 2d Sess (1976).

[150] Bird & Son, 25 FTC 548 (1937).

[151] *See* FTC v Ruberoid Co, 343 US 470, 475 (1952).

[152] See **§§3.09, 3.16.**

[153] *See* Krug v International Tel & Tel Corp, 142 F Supp 230 (DNJ 1956).

whether a customer performs a warehousing function,[154] or whether it performs a delivery function for a seller who otherwise employs zone delivered pricing,[155] has been considered within the framework of functional pricing analysis. Similarly, whether auto dealers resell replacement parts to consumers or to repair shops has been considered a legitimate basis for functional pricing differences, even though the purchasers operate at the same level of distribution.[156]

Although the analytical framework for assessing the legality of functional discounts strongly implicates the element of competitive injury,[157] it does not involve the same considerations raised by the cost justification defense.[158] With respect to the defense, the focus is on the actual cost savings to Seller resulting from the different methods or quantities in which it sells or delivers commodities to different purchasers. Functional discount analysis, on the other hand, may not involve different methods of sale or delivery to purchasers at all. Rather, it may involve the functions performed by the purchaser, at some cost to it, which have a value to Seller in accomplishing the efficient distribution of commodities. Nevertheless, an increasingly hospitable judicial and FTC approach to functional pricing may offset a narrow and rigid approach to the cost justification defense.

§3.16 When can a functional discount cause injury to competition?

New uncertainty surrounds the legality of functional discounts granted by Sellers to purchasers who operate at more than one level of distribution. This uncertainty was created by the Federal Trade Commission's stated willingness in *Boise Cascade Corp* to reexamine the legality of a functional discount granted to a vertically integrated purchaser based on the functions it performs *as a buyer* rather than based merely on the level to which it resells commodities.[159] In a separate statement accompanying the *Boise Cascade* complaint, Commissioner Pitofsky endorsed the view that allowing functional discounts based on the value of the distributive services performed by the customer, irrespective of the level to which it resells, would enhance competition by encouraging distribu-

---

[154] Mueller Co v FTC, 323 F2d 44 (7th Cir 1963), *cert denied,* 377 US 923 (1964). The *Mueller* case is considered in more detail in connection with the dual-level purchaser issue, **§3.16.**

[155] *See* Edward J Sweeney & Sons v Texaco, Inc, 478 F Supp 243 (ED Pa 1979), *affd,* 637 F2d 105 (3d Cir 1980), *cert denied,* 451 US 911 (1981).

[156] FLM Collision Parts, Inc v Ford Motor Co, 543 F2d 1019 (2d Cir 1976), *cert denied,* 429 US 1097 (1977); *but see* Knoll Assoc, 70 FTC 311 (1966), *revd on other grounds,* 397 F2d 530 (7th Cir 1968) (functional discount pricing favoring furniture retailers over interior decorators not valid because of competition between two functions).

[157] See **§3.16.**

[158] See **§3.24.**

[159] 3 Trade Reg Rep (CCH) ¶21,684 (Apr 23, 1980) (FTC complaint).

tors to take advantage of the efficiencies that may result from vertical integration.[160]

In its 1955 *Doubleday & Co*[161] decision, the commission adopted the position that a wholesale functional discount granted to integrated wholesaler-retailers would be lawful if there were a relationship between the amount of the discount and the value of the distributive services performed by the integrated customer. Functional pricing was not precluded by the fact that the integrated Buyers sold at the retail level where discounts were not available to firms which did not undertake the wholesale distribution function.

Starting with its 1962 decision in *Mueller Co,*[162] the commission reversed its position and held that a functional discount must be viewed exclusively from the standpoint of the customer's resale level. Competitive injury would be found if the magnitude of the discount and the other factors establishing a prima facie case of injury[163] were present at that level, regardless of the value of services which a vertically integrated entity might perform.

In a commission proceeding shortly after *Mueller,* respondent argued that competitive injury did not arise from its functional discounts of 4 per cent to warehouse distributors who redistributed to branches even though such discounts were not available to distributors who did not perform this service. It was contended that the discount merely offset the expense to the favored customers of performing the branch warehousing function, which provided more efficient distribution. The commission rejected this argument and concluded that a discount granted on such a basis reimbursed the integrated distributor for the costs of a system which it voluntarily elected to adopt and injured its competitors who did not establish such a system.[164] This position has consistently been taken by the commission[165] subject to the re-evaluation presaged with the issuance of the *Boise Cascade* complaint.

A hint of a more flexible approach to functional pricing is found in the Second Circuit's *FLM Collision Parts Inc v Ford Motor Co*[166] decision. The Seller had granted its dealers a discount on auto crash parts resold to independent repair shops, which was not available on such parts resold by the dealers to other customers, including parts wholesalers. In approving this discount structure, the court observed that the Robinson-Patman Act does not mandate uniform pricing to all customers and that the discount was lawful since all *dealers* were subject to the same discount structure. The pricing system was found to be lawful, even though its practical effect was to put wholesale dis-

---

[160] *Id* at 21,852.

[161] 52 FTC 169 (1955).

[162] 60 FTC 120 (1962), *affd,* 323 F2d 44 (7th Cir 1963), *cert denied,* 377 US 923 (1964).

[163] See **§3.14.**

[164] Purolator Prods, Inc, 65 FTC 8 (1964), *affd,* 352 F2d 874 (7th Cir 1965), *cert denied,* 389 US 1045 (1968).

[165] *See* Monroe Auto Equip Co, 66 FTC 276 (1964), *affd,* 347 F2d 401 (7th Cir 1965), *cert denied,* 382 US 1009 (1966).

[166] 543 F2d 1019 (2d Cir), *cert denied,* 429 US 1097 (1976).

tributors of crash parts at a disadvantage in competition with dealers for resales to repair shops. The case cannot be viewed as directly rejecting the commission's more rigid view, however, since the court also ruled that the parts wholesaler was not the direct or indirect customer of the Seller. Thus, the answer to the question of whether a more liberal view of functional discounts will ultimately be adopted must await the outcome of pending and future litigation.

§3.17 May Seller pay a broker who facilitates a sale?

Section 2(c) of the Clayton Act, as added by the Robinson-Patman Act—the *brokerage section*—constitutes one of the most curious anachronisms in antitrust legislation. It provides:

> It shall be unlawful for any person engaged in commerce, in the course of such commerce to pay or grant, or to receive or accept, anything of value as a commission, brokerage, or other compensation, or any allowances or discounts in lieu thereof, except for services rendered in connection with the sale or purchase of goods, wares, or merchandise, either to the other party to such transaction or to an agent, representative, or other intermediary therein. . . .[167]

An offspring of the real or imagined concern that powerful food chain retailers were employing a variety of devices to exact preferential treatment from Sellers, the brokerage section was aimed at preventing Seller payments to dummy brokerage houses which were established, owned, and operated by the Buyers.[168] Cases under this section have, however, dealt with all aspects of pricing in sales transactions insofar as they relate to the functions performed by brokers or sales representatives.

The section is virtually self-contained; read literally, it does not depend on any other provision of the Robinson-Patman Act or, for that matter, the other antitrust laws for its construction or enforcement. Because of the ease with which an offense might be established, its enforcement at the hands of the Federal Trade Commission once threatened to swallow the other provisions of the statute. The brokerage section:

1. Permits suits against the buyer[169] and broker[170] as well as the seller

---

[167] 15 USC §13(c).

[168] *See* HR Rep No 2287, 74th Cong, 2d Sess 14–15 (1936); FTC v Henry Broch & Co, 363 US 166, 169 (1960).

[169] Southgate Brokerage Co v FTC, 150 F2d 607 (4th Cir), *cert denied,* 326 US 774 (1945).

[170] FTC v Henry Broch & Co, 363 US 166 (1960).

2. Does not expressly require a showing of competitive injury[171] or even discrimination[172]
3. Does not incorporate the meeting competition[173] and cost justification defenses[174]
4. Might prevent brokerage payments to an independent intermediary, acting primarily in its own interests, which expedites sales transactions[175]
5. Has been used to challenge the conduct of buying groups which render valuable services to independent retailers, with whose survival the Robinson-Patman Act is most concerned[176]
6. Has been used to challenge price discounts to Buyers who bypass brokers in making purchases[177]

Given the rigid language of the section and the literal approach of most of the earlier cases, Buyers and Sellers might well have been concerned that the brokerage section would present an all-intrusive vehicle for the public utility-type regulation of sales transactions. Every transaction with a buying group and every transaction with direct Buyers who also employ, or primarily employ, brokers would be vulnerable to attack under a per se statute and to treble damage claims by offended competitors or brokers.

The cases following the Supreme Court's 1960 *FTC v Henry Broch & Co*[178] decision, however, have gone far to alleviate these concerns by eroding and even tacitly overruling some of the inconsistent earlier constructions. The Supreme Court in that case refocused analysis under §2(c) by announcing that the central concern of the provision was with preferential payments to dummy brokers, controlled by powerful Buyers, who performed no services deserving such treatment.[179]

Subsequent cases have held that brokerage payments may be made by Sellers to an independently owned intermediary which facilitates sales transactions even though it also renders valuable services to the Buyer.[180] These decisions

---

[171] FTC v Washington Fish & Oyster Co, 282 F2d 595 (9th Cir 1960); Webb-Crawford Co v FTC, 109 F2d 268 (5th Cir), *cert denied,* 310 US 638 (1940); Great Atl & Pac Tea Co v FTC, 106 F2d 667 (3d Cir 1939), *cert denied,* 308 US 625 (1940).

[172] Southgate Brokerage Co v FTC, 150 F2d 607 (4th Cir), *cert denied,* 326 US 774 (1945). See **§3.18.**

[173] FTC v Washington Fish & Oyster Co, 282 F2d 595 (9th Cir 1960).

[174] Union Malleable Mfg Co, 52 FTC 408 (1955).

[175] *See* FTC v Herzog, 150 F2d 450 (2d Cir 1945).

[176] Independent Grocers Alliance Distrib Co v FTC, 203 F2d 941 (7th Cir 1953); Modern Mktg Serv, Inc v FTC, 149 F2d 970 (7th Cir 1945); Biddle Purchasing Co v FTC, 96 F2d 687 (2d Cir), *cert denied,* 305 US 634 (1938).

[177] Venus Foods, 57 FTC 1025 (1960).

[178] 363 US 166 (1960).

[179] *Id* 169, 173.

[180] Tillie Lewis Foods, Inc, 65 FTC 1099, 1111 (1964) *revd on other grounds sub nom* Flothill Prods, Inc v FTC, 358 F2d 224 (9th Cir 1966), *revd,* 389 US 179 (1967); Food

have obviated reliance on intricate proof in brokerage cases of the balancing of benefits from a broker's services to resolve which side might properly pay a fee.

Perhaps more important, the courts and even the commission have begun to recognize that a direct Buyer or a buying group might properly receive price discounts or allowances for performing distributional functions benefiting Seller even where some of those functions might otherwise be performed by a broker. Thus, the FTC in *Hruby Distributing Co*[181] held that a discount from Seller to Buyer was in reality a functional discount for distributive services, even though denominated a brokerage payment by the parties. The Fifth Circuit, in *Thomasville Chair Co v FTC,*[182] ruled that a reduction in price to direct buyers attributable in part to the savings in salesmen's services in transactions with those Buyers was lawful because of the services rendered by the Buyers. Even the FTC indicated that services rendered by Buyer might validate its receipt of a brokerage-related allowance where those services result in genuine value to Seller.[183]

As a result of this trend, a considerable measure of flexibility has invaded the enforcement of §2(c) and neither the commission nor the courts seem prone to disrupt either payments to independent brokers or discounts to Buyers which reflect genuine services rendered.[184] An even more forthright step toward harmonizing the brokerage section with overall antitrust objections, however, would be a recognition by the courts and the commission that the statute is concerned only with discriminatory payments or allowances having a potentially adverse competitive impact. The likelihood that this principle will be adopted is addressed in the next section.

§3.18 Are discrimination and competitive injury relevant to a brokerage section violation?

A derivative of the absolute congressional condemnation of payments by

---

Fair Stores, Inc, 83 FTC 1213, 1226 (initial decision), *affd,* 83 FTC 1273 (1974). In affirming, the commission noted that it did not necessarily agree altogether with the rationale of the initial decision. *See also* Fuchs Sugars & Syrups, Inc v Amstar Corp, 447 F Supp 867 (SDNY 1978); *revd on other grounds,* 602 F2d 1025 (2d Cir), *cert denied,* 444 US 917 (1979).

[181] 61 FTC 1437 (1962).

[182] 306 F2d 541 (5th Cir 1962). *See also* Central Retailer-Owned Grocery, Inc v FTC, 319 F2d 410 (7th Cir 1963).

[183] Gibson, 95 FTC 553 (1980), *affd,* 1982–2 Trade Cas (CCH) ¶64,971 (5th Cir Aug 13, 1982).

[184] A parallel development has been the unwillingness of the courts to infer that the grant of discounts to a direct Buyer made contemporaneously with Seller's elimination of broker's services constitutes a §2(c) violation. *Compare* Robinson v Stanley Home Prods, Inc, 272 F2d 601 (1st Cir 1959) *with* Venus Foods, 57 FTC 1025 (1960).

sellers to dummy brokers based and operated by large retail chains[185] is the widely accepted view that neither discrimination nor competitive injury is an element of a Robinson-Patman §2(c) offense.[186] In fact, there is a paucity of authority directly ruling that discrimination, at least, is not part of a brokerage section violation, and the trend seems to be to the contrary.

While some earlier cases did hold that the per se character of §2(c) permits a finding of illegality without regard to discrimination,[187] the Supreme Court's watershed *FTC v Henry Broch & Co*[188] decision has stimulated a re-analysis of the brokerage section resulting in a respectable body of authority holding that discrimination is at least a relevant consideration. In *Broch,* the Supreme Court strongly suggested that its approval of the Federal Trade Commission's brokerage cease and desist order was based on the absence of proof that the Buyer had performed any services or functions that justified its receipt of a *discriminatory* discount.[189]

Three courts of appeals' decisions have followed the *Broch* suggestion. The Fifth Circuit's *Thomasville Chair v FTC* decision construed *Broch* as permitting a finding that §2(c) is violated by a reduced price to a Buyer coupled with a reduction in commission rates only where the conduct effects a discrimination.[190] Similarly, in *Empire Rayon Yarn Co v American Viscose Corp,* the Second Circuit explained that application of §2(c) in cases other than those involving discrimination at the same functional level would jeopardize procompetitive pricing.[191] The most forthright appellate court statement merging the principles of §§2(c) and 2(a) is found in the First Circuit's *Allen Pen Co v Springfield Photo Mount Co* decision.[192] Ruling that a wholesaler had not made out a brokerage section violation by proof that it was required by its supplier to buy through a brokerage firm whereas its competitor, which paid a lower price, bought direct, the court explained that a plaintiff

> must show that the sales agent . . . was interposed as a device or sham to give the favored customer a competitive advantage through a lower price . . . [E]ven if [the plaintiff] had made such a showing, *it still would have had to establish injury,* for §2(c) is designed to prevent violation of the

---

[185] See **§3.17.**

[186] See Mezines, *Brokerage—When Is It Permitted Under the Robinson-Patman Act,* 7 BC Indus & Com L Rev 821 (1966); Bison, Jr, *Services Rendered' Provision in the Brokerage Section of the Robinson-Patman Act,* 41 NDL Rev 326 (1966).

[187] FTC v Washington Fish & Oyster Co, 282 F2d 595 (9th Cir 1960); Southgate Brokerage Co v FTC, 150 F2d 607 (4th Cir), *cert denied,* 326 US 774 (1945); *see also* FTC v Simplicity Pattern Co, 360 US 55, 65 (dictum) (1959).

[188] 363 US 166 (1960).

[189] *Id* 173.

[190] 306 F2d 541, 545 (5th Cir 1962); *but see* Gibson v FTC, 1982-2 Trade Cas (CCH) ¶64,971 (5th Cir 1982).

[191] 364 F2d 491, 493 (2d Cir 1966) (en banc), *cert denied,* 385 US 1002 (1967).

[192] 653 F2d 17 (1st Cir 1981).

basic §2(a) price discrimination prohibition under different guise.[193]

The FTC has followed a more erratic course with respect to discrimination under §2(c). In some of its early post-Broch brokerage decisions, the commission employed language indicating a receptivity to the notion that there can be no violation without discrimination.[194] In *Gibson,* however, its only detailed consideration of the brokerage section in more than a decade, the commission ruled that, at least as a general matter, discrimination need not be proven to establish a §2(c) violation.[195]

The Fifth Circuit, in apparent conflict with its earlier *Thomasville Chair* decision, affirmed the Commission's *Gibson* ruling, concluding that discrimination need not be proven, at least where Seller makes payments to a dummy broker who is the *alter ego* of Buyer.[196] Possibly the *Gibson* holding that discrimination is not an element of the offense can be limited to such dummy broker situations.

The thrust of most current decisions seems clear. Much the same showing will be necessary to make out a §2(c) violation as is applicable under §2(a).[197] This showing includes, at least in the First Circuit, probable injury to competition. Thus, the brokerage subsection may no longer be of greater concern to Sellers in the granting of functional or other cost-based discounts to Buyers than the principal statutory subsection, even though the decisions in this regard are not uniformly comforting.[198]

§3.19 What are promotional allowances and services?

One of the principal market abuses effected by powerful Buyers, as perceived by the advocates of the Robinson-Patman Act, was the ability of the retail chains to exact hidden price concessions from their suppliers in the form

---

[193] *Id* 25 (emphasis supplied).

[194] *See* Tillie Lewis Foods, Inc, 65 FTC 1099, 1138 (1964); Garrett-Holmes & Co, 67 FTC 237, 254 (1965); Modern Mktg Serv, Inc 71 FTC 1676, 1685–86 (1967), *revd on other grounds,* Flothill Prods, Inc v FTC, 358 F2d 224 (9th Cir 1966), *revd,* 389 US 179 (1967).

[195] Gibson, 3 Trade Reg Rep (CCH) ¶21,692, p 21,866 (FTC Apr 30, 1980), 95 FTC 553 (1980), *affd,* 1982–2 Trade Cas (CCH) ¶64,971 (5th Cir 1982).

[196] Gibson v FTC, 1982–2 Trade Cas (CCH) ¶64,971 (5th Cir 1982).

[197] See **§§3.12** to **3.14.**

[198] An apparently ineradicable aberration in the antitrust scheme created by §2(c) is the continued application of the brokerage section to instances of commercial bribery. *See* Burch v Goodyear Tire & Rubber Co, 554 F2d 633 (4th Cir 1977); Grace v EJ Kozin Co, 538 F2d 170 (7th Cir 1976); Calnetics Corp v Volkswagen of Am, Inc, 532 F2d 674 (9th Cir), *cert denied,* 429 US 940 (1976); Rangen, Inc v Sterling Nelson & Sons, 351 F2d 851 (9th Cir 1965), *cert denied,* 383 US 936 (1966); Fitch v Kentucky-Tennessee Light & Power Co, 136 F2d 12 (6th Cir 1943).

of promotional payments or services. As summarized by the Chairman of the Senate-House Conferees:

> The existing evil at which this part of the bill is aimed is, of course, the grant of discriminations under the guise of payments for advertising and promotional services which, whether or not the services are actually rendered as agreed, results in an advantage to the customers so favored as compared with others who have to bear the cost of such services themselves.[199]

As a consequence, §§2(d) and 2(e) were added to the Clayton Act to deal with a particular form of discrimination which, if the conditions of the provisions were met, would be unlawful irrespective of the absence of any potential adverse impact on competition.[200] The absolute (per se) character of these sections was confirmed by the Supreme Court's 1959 *FTC v Simplicity Pattern Co*[201] decision, which also determined that the defense of cost justification was unavailable in promotional allowance and service cases.

Thus, it is extremely important in counseling and litigation to differentiate carefully between an unvarnished price concession and a promotional payment or service. There may, moreover, be conflicting objectives between Buyer and Seller in this regard. While the Seller may enjoy the advantage of competitive injury as an element of the offense and the cost justification defense available in a §2(a) case, the buyer liability subsection of the act[202] deals only with the inducement and receipt of unlawful *price* discriminations. Although the Federal Trade Commission has successfully challenged Buyers' knowing inducement and receipt of discriminatory promotional allowances under §5 of the FTC Act,[203] that statute is not one of the antitrust laws and, therefore, does not

---

[199] 80 Cong Rec 9418 (1936) (remarks of Rep Utterback).

[200] §§2(d) and 2(e) provide:

> (d) It shall be unlawful for any person engaged in commerce to pay or contract for the payment of anything of value to of for the benefit of a customer of such person in the course of such commerce as compensation or in consideration for any services or facilities furnished by or through such customer in connection with the processing, handling, sale or offering for sale of any products or commodities manufactured, sold, or offered for sale by such person, unless such payment or consideration is available on proportionally equal terms to all other customers competing in the distribution of such products or commodities.
>
> (e) It shall be unlawful for any person to discriminate in favor of one purchaser against another purchaser or purchasers of a commodity bought for resale, with or without processing, by contracting to furnish or furnishing, or by contributing to the furnishing of, any services or facilities connected with the processing, handling, sale, or offering for sale of such commodity so purchased upon terms not accorded to all purchasers on proportionally equal terms.

15 USC §13(d),(e).

[201] 360 US 55 (1959).

[202] 15 USC §13(f).

[203] *Id* §45.

provide a vehicle for treble damages or, for that matter, other private actions.[204]

It has been held that the same payment by a supplier cannot be attacked both under §2(d) and as a price discrimination under §2(a).[205] A threshold determination must, therefore, be made as to the character of a payment or discount.

The key to a determination of whether a Seller's payment or allowance is covered by §2(d) is whether it is conditioned on the performance of services by the customer in connection with the resale of the product involved.

Thus, a discriminatory discount to a customer for which little or no services are performed will be subject to question, if at all, as a price discrimination.[206] The Second Circuit's *RH Macy Co v FTC*[207] decision constitutes the most expansive judicial perception of a payment for promotional services benefiting the Seller, the court ruling that the Buyer's use of the Seller's money for its own institutional advertising brought the payment within the ambit of §2(d).

Allowances made directly to consumers, in the form of consumer coupons, for example, have been held not to constitute payments to retailers for promotional services.[208] The FTC has also adopted a narrow view of §2(d) in ruling that Seller's payments for trade show booth rentals to a franchisor which promoted sales to franchisees were related to the original sale, not the resale, and, therefore, were not subject to §2(d).[209]

In the same vein, the courts have held that various seller-rendered services which are not related to the Buyers' resale of the products are not subject to §2(e). These rulings have applied, for example, to discriminatory credit terms.[210] One decision of the Seventh Circuit suggests that delivery preferences may be covered by §2(e).[211] This decision has not been followed elsewhere, however, and is inconsistent with the rationale of the subsequent *Kirby*

---

[204] *See, e.g.,* Holloway v Bristol-Myers Corp, 485 F2d 986 (DCC 1973).

[205] Kirby v PR Mallory & Co, 489 F2d 904 (7th Cir 1973). A single promotional vehicile can, however, involve separate payments which are respectively price and promotional allowances. Thus, in the *Fred Meyer* case, it was held that Sellers' payments for advertising in the retailers' coupon book were promotional allowances, while the reimbursement to the retailer for the shelf-price discounts offered by the coupons themselves was price discrimination. Fred Meyer, Inc, 63 FTC 1 (1963), *revd on other grounds,* 359 F2d 351 (9th Cir 1966), *revd,* 390 US 341 (1968).

[206] *See* Miami Wholesale Drug Co, 28 US 485 (1939); Yakima Fruit & Cold Storage, 59 FTC 693 (Sept 28, 1961) (interlocutory order).

[207] 326 F2d 445, 450 (2d Cir 1964).

[208] Indian Coffee Corp v Procter & Gamble Co, 482 F Supp 1104 (DC Pa 1980).

[209] Gibson, 95 FTC 553 (1980), *affd on other grounds,* 1982-2 Trade Cas (CCH) ¶64,971 (5th Cir Aug 13, 1982). The FTC's *Gibson* decision overruled the commission's earlier decision in Alterman Foods, Inc, 82 FTC 298 (1973), *affd,* 497 F2d 933 (5th Cir 1974).

[210] Craig v Sun Oil Co, 515 F2d 221 (10th Cir 1975), *cert denied,* 429 US 829 (1976).

[211] Centex-Winston Corp v Edward J Hines Lumber Co, 447 F2d 585 (7th Cir 1971), *cert denied,* 405 US 921 (1972).

v PR Mallory & Co[212] decision in the Seventh Circuit which expressly limits the scope of §2(d) and (e) to payments and services which promote the resale of goods.[213]

§3.20 When is a promotional allowance or service available to competing customers?

The provisions of the Robinson-Patman Act require that promotional allowances or services be "made available" (§2(d)) or "accorded" (§2(e)) to all customers on proportionally equal terms.[214] The act does not prescribe any specific method or system whereby Sellers are required to satisfy its availability requirement. Two concepts merge in connection therewith: (1) notice and (2) functional availability.

The obligations of Seller to notify its customers of promotional allowances or service offers are considered in detail in guides issued by the Federal Trade Commission.[215] These guides constitute a reasonable and practical response to the decision by the Supreme Court in *FTC v Fred Meyer, Inc,*[216] where the Court held that a Seller bears the responsibility for assuring that promotional allowances granted to direct-buying retailers be made available to all retailers, whether they purchase directly or through wholesalers, if they compete with the recipient in the resale of the promoted product in the trade area of the promotion.

The guides adopt a *rule of reason* approach to notification: "The seller should take reasonable action, in good faith, to inform all his competing customers of the availability of his promotional program."[217]

The guides also set forth nonexclusive examples of various means whereby Sellers can convey such information to Buyers. They include both direct and indirect communications and initial contact which sets forth either all the details of a program or merely a summary. The use of wholesalers to perform the notice function is expressly approved by the guides,[218] as are trade publication advertising and inserts or flyers distributed with the merchandise.[219] It is suggested in the guides that the notice be in writing so that Seller will be in a position to demonstrate that it has made reasonable efforts to communicate the essential details of its plan to its customers.[220]

---

[212] 489 F2d 904 (7th Cir 1973), *cert denied,* 417 US 911 (1974).

[213] *See also* L&L Oil Co v Murphy Oil Corp, 674 F2d 1113 (5th Cir 1982).

[214] 15 USC §2(d),(e).

[215] FTC, Guides for Advertising Allowances and Other Merchandising Payments and Services, 16 CFR pt 240.

[216] 390 US 341 (1968).

[217] 16 CFR §240.8.

[218] 16 CFR §240.8(b)(1) example (5); *id* §240.13.

[219] 16 CFR §240.8(b) example (3).

[220] 16 CFR §240.8(a).

The cases dealing with notice have primarily involved circumstances where the Seller made either no effort or only a superficial effort to inform customers of the availability of advertising allowances. For the most part, these cases involve alleged oral instructions to sales representatives to communicate advertising allowance or service programs to Buyers. In some instances, Buyers testified that no such communication was ever received. The courts and the FTC have uniformly held that passive availability, i.e., allowances being available to any customer who asks, is not sufficient.[221]

The concept of *functional availability* presents more complex problems. Under the guides, an allowance must be usable in a practical business sense by all customers: "The Seller should not either expressly, or by the way the plan operates, eliminate some competing customers . . ."[222] This requirement stems from the Seventh Circuit's landmark *Women's Day* case in which it was held that a seller might not limit advertising allowances to those customers who publish a store-distributed magazine.[223]

It is not, however, necessary for a Seller to construct a plan every feature of which must be usable by every customer to whom an offer must be made.[224] Some aspect of the program must, however, be usable by each such customer, and proportionally equal payments must be made to all participating customers. The FTC has held that the form of participation and the amount of payment cannot ordinarily be individually negotiated with each Buyer.[225]

In identifying those customers to whom an offer must be made, Seller may select the particular product,[226] time period,[227] and, within reason, geographic territory[228] for its cooperative promotional venture. In addition, Seller may elect to limit its promotional program by its customers' functional level, *e.g.* it may fashion a program exclusively for wholesalers and not make payments available to retailers and vice versa.[229]

---

[221] Alterman Foods, Inc v FTC, 497 F2d 993, 1001 (5th Cir 1974); Vanity Fair Paper Mills, Inc v FTC, 311 F2d 480, 484–86 (2d Cir 1962); Henry Rosenfeld, Inc, 52 FTC 1535 (1956).

[222] 16 CFR §240.9.

[223] State Wholesale Grocers v Great Atl & Pac Tea Co, 258 F2d 831 (7th Cir 1958), *cert denied,* 358 US 947 (1959).

[224] Sunbeam Corp, 67 FTC 20 (1965).

[225] House of Lord's, Inc, 69 FTC 44, 82–83 (1966).

[226] Atalanta Trading Corp v FTC, 258 F2d 365 (2d Cir 1958).

[227] *Id.*

[228] 16 CFR §240.12 example (2).

[229] Kirby v PR Mallory & Co, 489 F2d 904 (7th Cir 1973), *cert denied,* 417 US 911 (1974).

§3.21 What is meant by proportionally equal terms?

The Robinson-Patman Act provides that promotional allowances and services granted by Seller to Buyer must not only be available to Buyer's competitors but must be structured so that they can receive the payment or services "on proportionally equal terms."[230] It is clear that the statute does not require that each participating customer receive the same payment, or the word *proportionally* would be meaningless; however, neither the law nor the legislative history clarifies the meaning of the term.

Accordingly to the Federal Trade Commission guides "No single way to proportionalize is prescripted by law. Any method that treats competing customers on proportionally equal terms may be used."[231]

The guides suggest that a relationship between the dollars paid by Seller for Buyers' advertising services and the volume of goods purchased by Buyer during the promotional period would serve as the basis for an acceptable means of proportionalization.

Difficulties have arisen where vague plans for proportionalizing payments have been developed or payments have been tailored to the particular programs developed by Buyers.[232] Generally, promotional programs under which Seller agrees to pay a portion of the cost of a cooperative advertisement, an amount up to a stated percentage of Buyer's purchases during a promotional period, has been acceptable.[233]

In 1972 the FTC amended its guides purportedly to add a new element to the requirement of proportionalization: that of a relationship between the amount paid by Seller and the cost to Buyer of performing the promotional services. According to the amended guides "Allowances that have little or no relationship to cost or approximate cost of the service provided by the retailer may be considered to be a violation of §2(d) or subject to the prohibitions of §2(a) of the amended Clayton Act."[234]

This position is inconsistent with that stated in prior decisions of the FTC[235] which were cited with approval in an opinion by the United States Supreme Court.[236] Moreover, the commission has not undertaken to enforce its payment–cost relationship theory in any adjudicatory proceeding. It may be that the commission was primarily concerned with grossly disproportionate payments to different Buyers who performed essentially identical services and

---

[230] 15 USC §2(d), (e).

[231] FTC, Guides for Advertising Allowances and Other Merchandising Payments and Services, 16 CFR pt 240.

[232] Colonial Stores, Inc v FTC, 450 F2d 733 (5th Cir 1971).

[233] 16 CFR §240.7.

[234] *Id.*

[235] Giant Food, Inc, 58 FTC 977 (1961), *affd on other grounds,* 307 F2d 184 (DC Cir 1962) *cert denied,* 372 US 910 (1963); Lever Bros, 50 FTC 494 (1953).

[236] FTC v Simplicity Pattern Co, 360 US 55, 61 n 4 (1959).

with simply admonishing Sellers to establish some reasonable proportion between the amount of payment and the service. In any event, mathematical equivalence does not appear to be required.

§3.22 What defenses exist to charges of price discrimination?

The principal defenses to a Robinson-Patman Act charge are the cost justification proviso of §2(a)[237] and the meeting competition defense of §2(b).[238] These defenses are considered in detail at **§§3.23** and **3.24.**

There is one other specific statutory defense which exonerates price discriminations made as a result of changed conditions such as deterioration or obsolescence affecting the marketability of commodities.[239] Although perishability and seasonality are identified in the statute as nonexclusive examples where the marketability defense would apply, judicial decisions have tended to confine the application of the defense to these circumstances.[240] Where changes in supply or demand conditions have produced a change in price, the discrimination resulting therefrom has been sanctioned on the basis that the sales before and after the change were noncontemporaneous.[241] In sum, the marketability defense has not been an important factor in the enforcement or interpretation of the Robinson-Patman Act.

Although not specifically arising under the rubric of a statutory defense, the question of the statute's application to sales to charitable and governmental entities has recently received considerable attention in the courts. The Nonprofit Institutions Act[242] expressly excludes from the scope of the Robinson-Patman Act sales to such charitable institutions as hospitals and schools, provided such sales involve supplies for the institutions' own use. The Supreme Court has held that the exemption does not apply to sales to nonprofit hospitals for resale at retail in competition with commercial entities.[243]

There is no specific statutory exemption for sales to governmental entities;

---

[237] 15 USC §2(a).

[238] *Id* §2(b).

[239] *Id* §(2)(a) provides in relevant part:

> And provided further, That nothing herein contained shall prevent price changes from time to time where in response to changing conditions affecting the market for or the marketability of the goods concerned, such as but not limited to actual or imminent deterioration of perishable goods, obsolescence of seasonal goods, distress sales under court process, or sale in good faith in discontinuance of business in the goods concerned.

[240] Lombino & Sons v Standard Fruit & Steamship Co, 1975–2 Trade Cas (CCH) ¶60,527 (SDNY 1975); *See* Moore v Mead Serv Co, 190 F2d 540, 541 (10th Cir 1951), *affd on other grounds sub nom* Moore v Mead's Fine Bread Co, 384 US 115 (1954).

[241] *See* Guyott Co v Texaco, Inc, 261 F Supp 942 (D Conn 1966).

[242] 15 USC §13C.

[243] Abbott Laboratories v Portland Retail Druggists Assn, 425 US 1 (1976).

nevertheless, it has been held that sales to the federal government are exempt under the doctrine of sovereign immunity.[244]

The Supreme Court in a 1983 decision ruled, 5–4, that sales of pharmaceuticals to state and county hospitals for resale through their pharmacies in competition with local druggists were not exempt from the Robinson-Patman Act.[245] The Court assumed, without so deciding, that state entity purchases for their own use were not covered by the Act.

§3.23 —What facts support a meeting competition defense?

Section 2(b) of the Robinson-Patman Act provides, in pertinent part, that "nothing herein contained shall prevent a Seller rebutting the prima facie case [of discrimination] thus made by showing that his lower price or the furnishing of services or facilities to any purchaser or purchasers was made in good faith to meet an equally low price of a competitor, or the services or facilities furnished by a competitor."[246]

The early, overly restrictive, interpretation of the defense, which often resulted in its failure, may safely be said to have given way to a more reasonable and flexible approach, which acknowledges the defense as enhancing vigorous competition. The more flexible rein is apparent in both lower court decisions and the relatively few Supreme Court decisions addressing the defense.[247]

Although the general contours of the defense have been fairly well defined, substantial questions about the scope and proof of the defense still remain to be addressed by the Supreme Court.

An early controversy over whether the defense was procedural or substantive was settled by the Supreme Court in 1951. In one of a series of cases involving the Standard Oil Company, the court held that the defense was substantive and absolute.[248] The defense is applicable both to price discrimination made under §2(a) and to discrimination in allowances and services under §§2(d) and (e).[249] It has been held inapplicable to charges of §2(c) (illegal

---

[244] Champaign-Urbana News Agency v JL Cummins News Co, 632 F2d 680 (7th Cir 1980).

[245] Jefferson County Pharmaceutical Assn v Abbott Laboratories, 51 USLW 4195 (US Feb 23, 1983) (No 86–212).

[246] 15 USC §13(b).

[247] See generally, ABA section on Antitrust, The Robinson-Patman Act: Policy and Laws 116–40 (Monograph No 4 1980).

[248] Standard Oil Co v FTC, 340 US 231 (1951).

[249] Although the defense, by its terms, appears to apply to §2(e) but not §2(d) this anomaly has been ignored by the courts and, now, by the commission in holding the defense available to rebut charges of promotional allowance discriminations. *See, e.g.*, Exquisite Form Brassiere, Inc v FTC, 301 F2d 499, 501–06 (DC Cir 1961), *cert denied*, 369 US 888 (1962); Continental Baking Co, 63 FTC 2071 (1963).

brokerage) violations.[250] However, the competitive product need not be of "like grade and quality," but one which is of comparable "saleability.'[251]

The statutory requirement of good faith is the key to successful use of the meeting competition defense.[252] The Seller offering a discriminatory price must have reason to believe in good faith that it is meeting an equally low competitive offer. Typically, a showing of good faith requires some attempt at verification, particularly when there is reason to doubt the customer's veracity, or where Seller's business experience should suggest that the reported competitive offer is not realistic.[253]

One question concerning the extent to which Seller's verification efforts must reach to satisfy the good faith requirement was answered in the Supreme Court decision in *United States v United States Gypsum Co*,[254] a case brought under the Sherman Act. Defendants were convicted of price-fixing, based in part on evidence of competitor-to-competitor price information exchanges. Defendants claimed the exchanges were for the purpose of verifying competitive price offers and were necessary to qualify for the meeting competition defense. The Third Circuit had concluded that a defense to a Sherman Act charge based on price exchanges would prevail where the exchanges were solely for the purpose of establishing the meeting competition defense, at least where there was reason to doubt the customer's veracity.[255] The Supreme Court, although upholding the circuit court's reversal of the convictions, rejected the §2(b) verification exception and held that intercompetitor information exchanges could not be justified on the basis of alleged requirements of the §2(b) defense.[256] Although the Court declined to explicate what verification attempts would establish good faith as a matter of law, it suggested several circumstances to be considered in evaluating Buyer's report. These included reports from other customers tending to substantiate the report, prior experience with Buyer, knowledge of the market, and Buyer's threat to refuse to deal absent

---

[250] FTC v Washington Fish & Oyster Co, 271 F2d 39, 44 (9th Cir 1959). It may, however, be open to a defendant to argue that a payment allegedly in lieu of brokerage is in actuality a discriminatory price, cognizable under and subject to the defenses of §2(a).

[251] Callaway Mills Co v FTC, 362 F2d 435, 440–41 (5th Cir 1966).

[252] United States v United States Gypsum Co, 438 US 422 (1978).

[253] FTC v AE Staley Mfg Co, 324 US 746, 758 (1945). *See also* Forster Mfg Co v FTC, 335 F2d 47 (1st Cir 1964), *cert denied,* 380 US 906 (1965) (rejecting commission's position that verification insufficient where Buyer would not divulge name of competing offeror and precise price); Viviano Macaroni Co v FTC, 411 F2d 255 (3d Cir 1969) (investigation required when experienced salesman doubted customer's report).

[254] 438 US 422 (1978).

[255] United States v United States Gypsum Co, 550 F2d 115, 126 (3d Cir 1977), *affd,* 438 US 422 (1978). The court of appeals also reversed the conviction on the ground that the jury instructions could have been construed to permit conviction regardless of defendants' intent.

[256] 438 US at 459.

a matching offer.[257]

The Court concluded with the troublesome suggestion that Buyer who, despite all reasonable attempts, cannot satisfy its doubts about the purported competitive offer, might not in good faith be able to meet that offer.[258] The Court, however, appeared to abandon that reservation the following year in *Great Atlantic & Pacific Tea Co v FTC*.[259] In that case, the Court made it clear that the historic judicially developed limitation of the defense to prices that meet but do not beat the competition[260] may be relaxed where the Seller acts in good faith. In *A&P*, the Court held the defense was available to the Seller who had made the good faith verification efforts but who nevertheless undercut rivals' offers.[261]

It generally has been accepted that the prices met must be lawful, that Seller cannot successfully assert the defense if the lower prices met are themselves unlawful under the Robinson-Patman Act.[262] However, it would seem unreasonable, especially in the wake of the *Gypsum* and *A&P* decisions, to make Seller responsible for knowing with certainty that its rival's price was lawful before it could avail itself of the meeting competition defense. And, in fact, a subjective standard was developed whereby the question is whether Seller knew or should have known that the competitive price was illegal. The question is essentially one of burden. The Federal Trade Commission has established the requirement that Seller bear the burden of proving facts which would lead a reasonable person to believe that the lower prices it met were lawful.[263] One court, to the contrary, required either the FTC or private plaintiff to come forward with proof that the price met was illegal and that Seller knew or should have known that fact.[264]

One major issue resolved by the Supreme Court on March 22, 1983 in the

---

[257] *Id* 454–55.

[258] *Id* 456 n 31.

[259] 440 US 69 (1979).

[260] *E.g.*, National Dairy Prods Corp, 70 FTC 79 (1966), *affd*, 395 F2d 517 (7th Cir), *cert denied*, 393 US 977 (1968); Balian Ice Cream Co v Arden Farms Co, 231 F2d 356 (9th Cir 1955); *Cf* Beatrice Foods Co, 76 FTC 719 (1969), *affd sub nom* Kroger Co v FTC, 438 F2d 1372 (6th Cir), *cert denied*, 404 US 871 (1971) (undercutting permissible in competitive bidding context).

[261] 440 US at 84. *Cf* Hillside Dairy Co v Fairmont Foods Co, 1980–2 Trade Cas (CCH) ¶63,313 (ND Ohio 1980), *affd*, 1981–2 Trade Cas (CCH) ¶64,375 (6th Cir 1981) (granting judgment for defendant on meeting competition defense where defendant, in good faith, undercuts competitor. Court required defendant to show both substantial effort to verify competitor's actual price and that the lower price bid did not require defendant to operate at a loss).

[262] *E.g.*, Standard Oil Co v FTC, 340 US 231 (1951) (dictum); Cadigan v Texaco Inc, 492 F2d 383 (9th Cir 1974); Corn Prods Ref Co v FTC, 144 F2d 211 (7th Cir 1944), *affd*, 324 US 726 (1945); Tri-Valley Packing Assn, 60 FTC 1134, 1173 (1962), *revd on other grounds*, 329 F2d 694 (9th Cir 1964).

[263] Tri-Valley Packing Assn, 60 FTC 1134, 1173 (1962), *revd on other grounds*, 329 F2d 694 (9th Cir 1964).

[264] Standard Oil Co v Brown, 238 F2d 54 (1956).

case of *Falls City Indus, Inc v Vanco Beverages, Inc*[265] is whether Seller may rely on the defense to justify a pricing system adopted in response to a competitor's pricing system, or whether the defense is limited to meeting individual or specific competitive situations. Previously, language in the Supreme Court's *FTC v AE Staley Mfg Co* decision,[266] dealing with adoption of a competitor's unlawful basing point system, had been interpreted as holding that the defense is not available to meet a competitor's pricing system. The District of Columbia, Second and Seventh Circuits adopted this view.[267] The Fifth Circuit recognized that a systemwide lowering of prices may, however, be a valid defense to a competitor's systemwide offering of discounts to all of the customers of defendants.[268]

Vanco involved an attempt by an Indiana beer distributor to recover damages for price discrimination from its supplier, who charged higher prices to its Indiana beer distributors than to its Kentucky beer distributors. The supplier defended on grounds of meeting competition with respect to its Kentucky prices, alleging that it had simply adopted its own competitors' system of charging higher prices in Indiana than in Kentucky.

Reversing the Seventh Circuit, the Supreme Court ruled that Seller might successfully invoke the defense if an areawide response to overall pricing conditions, rather than customer- and competitor- specific, was necessitated by competitive conditions. According to the Court, Seller may invoke the defense as to area wide meeting of competition, "by showing that a reasonable and prudent businessman would believe that the lower price he charged was generally available from his competitors throughout the territory and throughout the period in which he made the lower price available."[269]

The Court also rejected plaintiff's contention that the defense is unavailable to Seller who has raised its prices in the higher-priced geographic area rather than lowered its prices in the lower-priced market. Nothing in §2(b) of the Robinson-Patman Act, the Court explained, compels Seller to subtract from rather than add to its prices in response to a competitive situation.[270] Seller, thus is not deprived of the defense if it increases its prices in some markets to realize increased profits, while keeping prices low in markets where it faces more intense competition. The Court distinguished *Staley* on the ground that

---

[265] Falls City Indus, Inc v Vanco Beverages, Inc, 44 Antitrust & Trade Reg Rep (BNA) 658 (US Mar 22, 1983).

[266] FTC v AE Staley Mfg Co, 324 US 746, 753–56 (1945).

[267] Exquisite Form Brassiere, Inc v FTC, 380 F2d 492 (DC Cir 1965), *cert denied,* 384 US 959 (1966); Standard Motor Prods, Inc v FTC, 265 F2d 674, 677 (2d Cir), *cert denied,* 361 US 826 (1959); E Edelmann & Co v FTC, 239 F2d 152, 156 (7th Cir 1956), *cert denied,* 355 US 941 (1958).

[268] Callaway Mills Co v FTC, 362 F2d 435 (5th Cir 1966). *See also* Wm Inglis & Son Baking Co v ITT Continental Baking Co, 668 F2d 1014, 1046 (9th Cir 1981), *cert denied,* __ US __ (1982).

[269] Falls City Indus, Inc v Vanco Beverage, Inc, 44 Antitrust & Trade Reg Rep (BNA) 658, 664 (US, Mar 22, 1983).

[270] *Id* 662, 663.

in the earlier case the prices being met were unlawful, the result of collusion among sellers.[271]

The Supreme Court's *Vanco* decision also puts to rest the long-standing controversy regarding whether the defense may be used to obtain new customers as well as to retain old ones. The FTC's historic position has been that the defense may be used "defensively" only,[272] and the Second Circuit has agreed.[273] Other lower courts had declined to acquiesce in this limitation.[274] The Supreme Court in *Vanco* has ruled that to hold that the defense is available only to a Seller who is seeking to retain old customers "would be inconsistent with that section's language and logic."[275]

Finally, the defense is available only to meet the competition of the Seller's competitor, not to meet the price of a competitor of Seller's customer.[276] In its *FTC v Sun Oil*[277] decision, however, the Supreme Court left the door open to use of the defense in two situations involving meeting the competition posed by Seller's customer's competitor. The first is when the customer's competition is integrated, such that the particular competitor is actually a customer of the discriminating Seller. The second would be when the customer's competitor is receiving a price break from its own supplier, who is a competitor of the Seller.[278] The FTC has approved the use of the defense in both situations,[279] and the Tenth and Fifth Circuits have applied that approach.[280]

§3.24 —What facts support a cost justification defense?

One method of rebutting a prima facie case of discrimination,[281] that of

---

[271] *Id* 661.

[272] Sunshine Biscuits, Inc, 59 FTC 674 (1961), *revd,* 306 F2d 48, 51–52 (7th Cir 1962).

[273] Standard Motor Prods, Inc v FTC, 265 F2d 674, 677 (2d Cir), *cert denied,* 361 US 826 (1959).

[274] Cadigan v Texaco, Inc, 492 F2d 383 (9th Cir 1974); Hanson v Pittsburgh Plate Glass Indus, 482 F2d 220 (5th Cir), *cert denied,* 414 US 1136 (1973); Sunshine Biscuits, Inc v FTC, 306 F2d 48 (7th Cir 1962).

[275] Falls City Indus, Inc v Vanco Beverage, Inc, 44 Antitrust & Trade Reg Rep (BNA) 658, 663 (US Mar 22, 1983).

[276] FTC v Sun Oil Co, 371 US 505 (1963).

[277] *Id.*

[278] *Id* 512 n 7.

[279] FTC, Report on Anticompetitive Practices in the Marketing of Gasoline, *reprinted in* 3 Trade Reg Rep (CCH) ¶10,373 (1967).

[280] Covey Oil Co v Continental Oil Co, 340 F2d 993 (10th Cir), *cert denied,* 380 US 964 (1965); Hampton v Graff Vending Co, 478 F2d 527 (5th Cir), *cert denied,* 414 US 859, *rehearing denied,* 414 US 1987 (1973).

[281] The cost justification defense is not, by its terms, available to rebut prima facie cases of promotional discrimination under §§2(d) and 2 (e) or the Robinson-Patman Act. FTC v Simplicity Pattern Co, 360 US 55 (1959); FTC v Henry Broch & Co, 363 US 166, 176 (1960).

proving that the differences were cost justified, is so fraught with difficulties that in 1955 it was called "largely illusory in practice."[282] Today, considerable uncertainty remains as to whether and how a workable pre-complaint cost justification program can be developed that will withstand post-complaint scrutiny.

Section 2(a) of the Robinson-Patman Act provides simply "[t]hat nothing herein contained shall prevent differentials which make only due allowance for differences in the cost of manufacture, sale, or delivery resulting from the differing methods or quantities in which such commodities are sold or delivered. . . ."[283]

The language affords guidance only as to the broad types of cost differences that may be considered. It does not detail what specific costs may be considered; how those costs may be computed; and how they may be allocated among customers or groups of customers. Compounding the proviso's problem for Seller seeking advance assurance that its prices will withstand scrutiny is the fact that the burden of proving cost justification is on the defendant.[284] It is not settled whether introduction of a good faith pre-complaint cost study will shift the burden of going forward back to the government or private litigant.

The courts have provided guidance in some but not all of these areas. It has been accepted for 20 years that costs need not be computed, or differences justified, on a customer-by-customer basis. According to the decision in *United States v Borden Co*,[285] differences may be justified on the basis of the average costs of dealing with various customer groupings. The Supreme Court in the *Borden* case, however, cautioned that such customer groupings must not be arbitrary, nor may differentials be justified on the basis of customer classifications which are merely representative of a numerical majority of the individual members. Rather, the groupings must be such that the individual members of each customer group must closely resemble each other on the essential point or points which determine the costs considered.[286] Thus, in *Borden,* the Court disallowed a cost justification defense where the costs attributable to the disfavored class of customers were not incurred with respect to many members of that class.[287] On the other hand, the Sixth Circuit distinguished *Borden* in

---

[282] Report of the Attorney General's National Committee to Study Antitrust Laws 171 (1955).

[283] 15 USC §13(a).

[284] FTC v Morton Salt Co, 334 US 37, 44–45 (1948); United States v Borden Co, 370 US 460 (1962); Utah Pie Co v Continental Baking Co, 386 US 685 (1967). Although the burden is Seller's in a §2(a) case, a Buyer defendant in a §2(f) case may defend based on a good faith belief that seller had a valid defense. Great Atl & Pac Tea Co v FTC, 440 US 69 (1979); Automatic Canteen Co of Am v FTC, 346 US 61 (1953).

[285] 370 US 460 (1962).

[286] *Id* 469.

[287] *Id. See also* Foremost Dairies, 62 FTC 1344 (1963), *affd on other grounds,* 348 F2d 674 (5th Cir), *cert denied,* 382 US 959 (1965) (defense disallowed because discounts were not granted to all customers within the purported group); National Dairy Prods Corp, 70 FTC 79, 194 (1966), *affd,* 395 F2d 517 (7th Cir), *cert denied,* 393 US 977 (1968)

approving a Seller's grouping of some 6,000 disfavored customers of various sizes in a single class for comparison with four favored customers, citing Seller's avoidance of averages and estimates in developing its cost justification system.[288]

The requirement that manufacturing, sale, or delivery cost differences relate the differing *methods* or *quantities* in which the commodities are sold or delivered eliminates some items of cost from consideration, but provides little guidance as to the specific costs that may be considered. Not all cost savings which a Seller might find reasonable, or even preferred business practice, to attribute to the quantity or method of sales to a favored customer or group of customers, have been allowed. For example, Seller might reasonably suppose that it may consider the cost of producing a large quantity order as including only the marginal cost of producing that additional quantity, or may consider that it has achieved a reduction in unit cost to such Buyer merely as a result of having more total volume over which to spread fixed costs. The Federal Trade Commission and the courts disagree.[289]

Differences in manufacturing costs are not often relied on, although they have been recognized.[290] The 1956 FTC Advisory Committee on Cost Justification opined that manufacturing costs are likely to be segregated to allow cost differences only where goods are made on customer order, and that manufacturing costs applicable for cost justification purposes are those which vary either directly or indirectly with the factors on which the price differential is based.[291] At the time of the Robinson-Patman Act's passage, it was suggested that cognizable cost differences would include those involved in producing in advance and storing for spot deliveries during the rush season to a customer who lacks storage facilities.[292] The 1956 advisory committee listed other costs which *may* vary with the size of specifications (or timing) of customers' orders, including product development and design, tooling up, and employee train-

---

(averaging cost of serving individual stores in a chain disallowed because of lack of relation to actual cost of dealing with each store).

[288] American Motors Corp v FTC, 384 F2d 247 (6th Cir 1967), *cert denied,* 390 US 1012 (1968); *cf* FTC v Standard Motors Prods, Inc, 371 F2d 613 (2d Cir 1967) (disapproving an overly strict grouping method advocated by the FTC possibly requiring Seller to individually cost out its customers).

[289] Champion Spark Plug Co, 50 FTC 30 (1953); *and see* United States v Borden Co, 370 US 460 (1962) (by implication); FTC v Morton Salt Co, 334 US 37 (1948) (by implication); see F. Rowe, Price Discrimination Under the Robinson-Patman Act, 281 (1962).

[290] *See, e.g.,* Thompson Prods, Inc, 55 FTC 1252 (1959); United States Rubber Co, 46 FTC 998 (1950).

[291] Advisory Committee on Cost Justification, Report to the Federal Trade Commission, app A (1956), *reprinted in* II Oppenheim & Weston, The Lawyers Robinson-Patman Act Sourcebook 1018–41 (1971).

[292] 80 Cong Rec 9417 (1936), *reprinted in* F. Rowe, Price Discrimination Under the Robinson-Patman Act, 282 (1962).

ing, as well as methods and standards development.[293]

Sale and delivery costs are most often relied on in justifying cost differentials, and a wide variety of such costs has been recognized. Differing freight and delivery costs tend to be the principal components of such cost justification.[294] Clerical expenses are recognized, as are advertising expenses, but only when they can properly be allowed to a particular customer or product line.[295] A question remains as to whether savings in brokerage allowances, achieved by a Seller's dealing directly with one customer or group of customers, may be used to justify a favorable price to such customer, relative to customers with whom Seller deals through brokers. The Supreme Court has suggested that the commission's opposition to recognizing brokerage savings is limited to situations where the brokerage savings were passed on to a single Buyer who was not shown in any way to have deserved favored treatment.[296] The Fifth Circuit held subsequently that such savings may be offered in defense of a price discrimination where the reduced commissions were incurred in selling to an entire class of customers, but the commission announced its refusal to acquiesce in that decision.[297]

The FTC has applied, with court approval, a de minimis rule, disregarding minor differences between price differentials and the justified cost differences in defense of those price differentials.[298] The limits of the de minimis exception are unclear, but are generally on the restrictive side. Discrepancies of 1 per cent have been accepted,[299] but discrepancies of 3.5 per cent have not.[300]

Cost justification defenses are likely to fail if they rely only on post-complaint studies. The commission and the courts have insisted on concrete, formal studies, employing actual, not estimated costs, and formal studies supporting the allocation of those costs.[301] This is not to say that no estimates or sampling

---

293 Advisory Committee on Cost Justification, *supra* note 291, at App A, 1036, at 20–21 n283.

294 *See, e.g.,* American Motors Corp v FTC, 384 F2d 247 (6th Cir 1967), *cert denied,* 390 US 1012 (1968); Thompson Prods, Inc, 55 FTC 1252 (1959).

295 Southern Cal Jobbers, Inc, 68 FTC 1039 (1965).

296 FTC v Henry Broch & Co, 363 US 166 (1960).

297 Thomasville Chair Co v FTC, 306 F2d 541 (5th Cir 1962); Thomasville Chair Co, 63 FTC 1048 (1963). Buyer's receipt of a discount equal to the usual brokerage fee does not, in any event, necessarily prove a violation of §2(c), inasmuch as the discount may be defensible as a functional discount **(3.17)**, Empire Rayon Co v American Viscose Corp, 364 F2d 491 (2d Cir 1966) (en banc), *cert denied,* 385 US 1002 (1967); Central Retailer-Owned Grocers, Inc v FTC, 319 F2d 410 (7th Cir 1963).

298 United States v Borden Co, 1961 Trade Cas (CCH) ¶69,946 (ND Ill 1961), *revd on other grounds,* 370 US 460 (1962); American Metal Prods Co, 60 FTC 1667, 1684 (1962) (initial decision); Hamburg Bros, 54 FTC 1450 (1958).

299 United States v Borden Co, 1961 Trade Cas (CCH) ¶69,946 (ND Ill 1961), *revd on other grounds,* 370 US 460 (1962).

300 Thompson Prods, Inc, 55 FTC 1252 (1959).

301 *See, e.g.,* Beatrice Foods Co, 76 FTC 719 (1969), *affd sub nom* Kroger Co v FTC, 438 F2d 1372 (6th Cir), *cert denied,* 404 US 871 (1971); Alhambra Motor Parts, 68 FTC 1039, 1080 (1965); Reid v Harper & Bros, 235 F2d 240 (2d Cir 1956).

techniques may be used.[302] Reliable sampling techniques, and studies of particular customers or areas, if truly representative, may serve for an entire class.[303] The unfortunate fact remains that clear standards for determining what will prove to be an acceptable accounting or costing technique are lacking.

§3.25 Can Buyer violate the Robinson-Patman Act?

Unquestionably one of the principal objectives sought by the proponents of the Robinson-Patman Act in Congress was an expansion of the Clayton Act's coverage so that the practices of Buyers might be challenged. The legislative concern was that existing law would not reach the allegedly coercive tactics of Buyers in inducing and receiving discriminatory pricing and promotional benefits.[304] Nevertheless, §2(f) dealing with liability for Buyers' inducement of discriminatory prices was adopted virtually as an afterthought with little legislative deliberation.[305] Moreover, there has been very little litigation, in both absolute and relative terms, initiated under this subsection.

There are three statutory provisions under which Buyer inducements of preferential treatment have been challenged.

Section 2(f) of the amended Clayton Act[306] expressly covers the knowing inducement and receipt by Buyers of price discriminations which are prohibited by the act. Although broader interpretations of this subsection might be possible, its use has been essentially limited to the challenge of Buyer conduct in the context of a Seller's discriminatory *pricing* violative of §2(a).[307]

Section 2(c),[308] dealing with unlawful brokerage transactions, is the only statutory provision which incorporates both Seller and Buyer violations. Under this provision, both granting and receiving of unlawful payments or allowances are prohibited.[309]

Since the early 1960s, the Federal Trade Commission has successfully used

---

[302] Champion Spark Plug Co, 50 FTC 30, 43 (1953) (the fact that estimates were used does not render cost justification effort wholly void of probative value).

[303] *See, e.g.*, Standard Oil Co, 41 FTC 263 (1945) (FTC rejecting cost survey of sales in one geographic area to one class of customer as having no probative value in determining cost differential between two types of sales to different class of customer in a different geographic area).

[304] F. Rowe, Price Discrimination Under the Robinson-Patman Act, 3 (1962); see C. Edwards, The Price Discrimination Law 12–13 (1959); Great Atl & Pac Tea Co v FTC, 44 US 69, 75–76 (1979).

[305] See F. Rowe, *supra* note 302, at 421.

[306] 15 USC §13(f).

[307] See **§3.26.**

[308] 15 USC §13(c).

[309] According to dicta in one Supreme Court decision, Buyer's knowledge that it had received an unlawful brokerage payment might have relevance in a case charging it with violating §2(c). FTC v Henry Broch & Co, 363 US 166, 169 (1960).

§5 of the FTC Act[310] to challenge Buyer inducement and receipt of unlawful promotional allowances and services. In the seminal *Grand Union Co v FTC*[311] decision, the commission was affirmed by the Court of Appeals for the Second Circuit in ruling that §5's broad proscription of unfair methods of competition could be used to fill the interstices left by Congress in its failure to deal directly with Buyer conduct in the field of cooperative promotional activity.

Despite the substantial congressional concern with Buyer misconduct, §2(f) has seldom been used by the FTC, and lately its use has been almost nonexistent. Between 1970 and 1977 only two FTC complaints and two cease and desist orders were based on §2(f).[312] In fact, there has not been a final §2(f) order issued since 1972,[313] and evidently only one complaint charging Buyer inducement of an unlawful price discrimination has been issued in recent years.[314]

§3.26 —When has a Buyer knowingly induced or received an unlawful discrimination in price?

Under the language of §2(f) of the Robinson-Patman Act Buyer liability is dependent on Seller's having violated §2(a): "[I]t shall be unlawful for any person engaged in commerce, in the course of such commerce, knowingly to induce or receive a discrimination in price which is prohibited by this section."[315] This principle was confirmed by the United States Supreme Court in its *Great Atlantic & Pacific Tea Co v FTC*[316] decision.

One possible exception to the foregoing rule involves the case of a "lying" Buyer who knowingly misleads the Seller into believing that Buyer has received a lower price offer when such is not the case. The Sixth Circuit in the *Kroger Co v FTC*[317] decision held that a Buyer who knowingly provides such false information to Seller may be held to have violated §2(f) even though Seller may have a valid meeting competition defense and, therefore, would not have violated §2(a). The Supreme Court implicity pretermitted this issue in its *A&P* decision.[318] There appears, however, to be little justification from the standpoint of the antitrust laws for drawing fine lines between a lying Buyer and one who simply neglects to advise Seller that there is no lower-priced offer out-

---

[310] 15 USC §45.

[311] 300 F2d 92 (2d Cir 1962).

[312] HR Rep No 1738, 94th Cong, 2d Sess 132 (1976).

[313] *Hearings Before the Subcomm on Antitrust and Restraint of Trade Activities Affecting Small Business of the House Comm on Small Business, Testimony of FTC Bureau of Competition Director Thomas J. Campbell, App Question 5,* 97th Cong, 2d Sess (1982).

[314] Boise Cascade Corp, 3 Trade Reg Rep (CCH) ¶21,811 (Mar 12, 1981) (FTC complaint).

[315] 15 USC §13(f).

[316] 440 US 69 (1979).

[317] 438 F2d 1372 (6th Cir), *cert denied,* 404 US 871 (1971).

[318] 440 US at 75 n 6.

standing. The latter conduct was held lawful by the Federal Trade Commission in the *A&P* case.[319]

The principal focus in those §2(f) cases which have been litigated has been on the sufficiency of proof to establish that Buyer has knowledge of the illegality of the discriminatory price which it receives. In the landmark *Automatic Canteen Co v FTC*[320] case, the Supreme Court held that the FTC could not rest its case and switch the burden to Buyer merely by showing the existence of a discrimination and probable competitive injury, together with Buyer's knowledge of these elements. The Court held that the commission must also show Buyer had reason to know that none of the statutory defenses were available to Seller. With specific reference to the cost justification defense, the Court suggested that the commission's burden might be satisfied by a demonstration that Buyer was aware that the methods and quantities under which it purchased merchandise from Seller were substantially identical to those in transactions involving its competitors.[321]

Proof of Buyer's knowledge of the elements of discrimination and competitive injury has often been satisfied through a bare showing that Buyer is experienced in the marketplace and had general knowledge of market conditions. Of course, Buyer is in a poor position to argue lack of knowledge as to a discrimination if it has insisted that an allowance be made exclusively to it during a specified period or has particularized the terms of an allowance to suit its business needs.[322] On the other hand, courts' reliance on such factors as Buyer's general experience in the marketplace[323] seems an inadequate basis for imputing to Buyer knowledge as to both discrimination and competitive injury.

With respect to proof of Buyer knowledge that Seller would not have a valid cost justification defense, the FTC responded to the *Automatic Canteen* decision by challenging cooperative buying groups whose basis of organization was such that there was little question of their awareness that competitors were buying in essentially the same volume and using essentially the same delivery methods.[324] The question becomes more difficult in situations where different brands, volumes, and delivery methods are involved. The Second Circuit's decision in the *Great Atlantic & Pacific Tea Co* case does not appear to perceive

---

319 87 FTC 962 (1976), *affd on other grounds,* 557 F2d 971 (2d Cir 1977), *revd,* 440 US 69 (1979).

320 346 US 61 (1953).

321 *Id* 80.

322 *See* Fred Meyer, Inc v FTC, 359 F2d 351 (9th Cir 1966), *revd on other grounds,* 390 US 341 (1968); Grand Union Co v FTC, 300 F2d 92 (2d Cir 1962); Furr's, Inc, 68 FTC 584, 686 (1965).

323 Great Atl & Pac Tea Co v FTC, 557 F2d 971 (2d Cir 1977), *revd on other grounds,* 440 US 69 (1979). *But see* Texas Gulf Sulphur Co v JR Simplot Co, 418 F2d 793 (9th Cir 1969).

324 *See, e.g.,* Mid-South Distribs v FTC, 287 F2d 512 (5th Cir), *cert denied,* 368 US 838 (1961); American Motor Specialties, Inc v FTC, 278 F2d 225 (2d Cir), *cert denied,* 364 US 884 (1960).

the potential distinctions in law as between sales to that respondent and to its competitors. Rather, it suggests that the failure of Seller to give assurances to A&P that its price was cost justified amply served to warrant the imputation of knowledge to Buyer that there was no available cost justification defense.[325] It is at least arguable that a requirement that Buyer conduct a cost study or insist that Seller do so would seriously inhibit procompetitive price negotiations.

Finally, the Supreme Court in *Automatic Canteen* suggested that Buyer might more readily be presumed to have culpable knowledge with respect to the absence of the meeting competition defense in a particular transaction.[326] While this suggestion may be appropriate where in fact Seller does not have a valid meeting competition defense, it appears that where Seller reasonably believes that such a defense is available, Buyer cannot be held to have violated §2(f), even though it knows that Seller is, in fact, beating and not meeting competition.[327]

§3.27 —When has Buyer unlawfully received a promotional allowance or service?

It is somewhat surprising that there has been very little effort made to challenge Buyer inducement of discriminatory promotional allowances or services under §2(f) of the Robinson-Patman Act It is certainly arguable that such conduct could be tantamount to the inducement of an indirect price discrimination and that §2(f) might appropriately be employed against Buyer who causes Seller to violate §2(d) or §2(e). While such an argument would be consistent with the legislative history of the act, it has not been pursued on any widespread basis.[328]

In the early 1960s, the Federal Trade Commission issued several orders which were affirmed by various appellate courts, and tacitly approved by the Supreme Court, under which §5 of the FTC Act was used to prohibit Buyers from knowingly inducing and receiving disproportional allowances and services.[329] It seems no longer open to question that §5 may be used for that purpose.

---

[325] Great Atl & Pac Tea Co v FTC, 557 F2d 971, 981 (2d Cir 1977), *revd on other grounds,* 440 US 69 (1979).

[326] Automatic Canteen Co v FTC, 346 US 61, 79 n 23 (1953).

[327] Great Atl & Pac Tea Co v FTC, 440 US 69 (1979).

[328] See **§3.25.** *But cf* Krug v International Tel & Tel Corp, 142 F Supp 230, 237 (DNJ 1956) (apparently assuming that §2(f) might be used against a Buyer who had induced and received a promotional allowance unlawful under §2(d)).

[329] Fred Meyer, Inc v FTC, 359 F2d 351 (9th Cir 1966), *revd on other grounds,* 390 US 341 (1968); Grand Union v FTC, 300 F2d 92 (2d Cir 1962); Giant Food, Inc v FTC, 307 F2d 184 (DC Cir 1962), *cert denied,* 372 US 910 (1963); RH Macy & Co v FTC, 326 F2d 445 (2d Cir 1964); Colonial Stores, Inc v FTC, 450 F2d 733 (5th Cir 1971); Alterman Foods, Inc v FTC, 497 F2d 993 (5th Cir 1974).

The elements of a §5 discriminatory promotional allowance or service inducement case are much the same as those applicable to a §2(f) price discrimination inducement proceeding. The enforcement agency must establish Buyer's knowledge that the allowance or service conferred a discriminatory benefit on it. In most litigated cases, Buyer had demanded exclusivity[330] or had specially tailored allowances to its own business circumstances.[331] Under these conditions it was not difficult to establish Buyer's awareness that it was receiving preferential treatment. In addition to showing that Buyer had knowledge of the discriminatory nature of the allowance, it would seem that the commission would also have to show that Buyer was aware that the meeting competiton defense was not available to seller.[332] The cost justification defense, however, is not applicable to §2(d) and §2(e) offenses[333] and, therefore, presumably not to a §5 buyer liability case.

While the commission has prohibited both inducement and receipt of discriminatory promotional allowances, the courts have not upheld orders prohibiting inducement in the absence of receipt.[334] By the same token, it would seem difficult for the commission to sustain a challenge against Buyer's receipt of a disproportional allowance which it did not initiate. Where Seller was the initiator of the allowance, it would seem that only in unusual circumstances might Buyer properly be held to be aware of any discriminatory benefit which might be accorded.

While §5 might properly be used to challenge the Buyer inducement and receipt of disproportional allowances and services, private actions may not be maintained under that provision.[335] As a consequence, to the extent that §5 is the only vehicle whereby such inducement and receipt might be challenged, Buyers would not be amenable to treble damage exposure for such conduct.

§3.28 What liability arises for violation of the Robinson-Patman Act?

With the exception of the rarely used §3,[336] criminal sanctions do not attach

---

[330] Fred Meyer, Inc v FTC, 359 F2d 351 (9th Cir 1966), *revd on other grounds,* 390 US 341 (1968).

[331] *See, e.g.,* Colonial Stores, Inc v FTC, 450 F2d 733 (5th Cir 1971).

[332] *Cf* Exquisite Form Brassiere, Inc v FTC, 301 F2d 499 (DC Cir 1961), *cert denied,* 369 US 888 (1962). Under the Supreme Court's *A&P* decision, it seems unlikely that Buyer could be held to have violated §5 for inducing and receiving a disproportional promotional allowance or service unless Seller has also violated §2(d) or §2(e). Great Atl & Pac Tea Co, 440 US 69 (1979).

[333] FTC v Simplicity Pattern Co, 360 US 55 (1959).

[334] *See* Grand Union Co v FTC, 300 F2d 92, 99–101 (2d Cir 1962).

[335] *See* Holloway v Bristol-Meyers Corp, 485 F2d 986 (DC Cir 1973).

[336] §3 of the Robinson-Patman Act, 15 USC §13a, **§3.01,** makes it a crime: (1) to discriminate in discounts, rebates or allowances among competing purchasers of like quantities; (2) to engage in geographic price discrimination with the purpose of destroying competition or eliminating a competitor; or (3) to sell goods at unreasonably low prices for the purpose of destroying competition or eliminating a competitor.

to violations of the Robinson-Patman Act. The act is enforced primarily by the Federal Trade Commission[337] and by private litigants.

The FTC enforcement mechanism involves the issuance of an administrative complaint, followed by an adjudicative hearing before an agency administrative law judge and appeal to the full commission. Upon the finding of a violation, the commission issues a cease and desist order. No penalties attach at this stage, but subsequent violations of a final commission order can subject the violator to penalties of up to $10,000 per violation, per day.[338] Although the act does not provide for buyer liability for receipt of discriminatory allowances or services, as opposed to discriminatory prices, the commission may proceed against a Buyer who receives a discriminatory promotional allowance, under its general authority under §5 of the FTC Act.[339]

Private persons injured by violations of §2 of the Clayton Act may sue for treble damages and costs, including reasonable attorney's fees[340] as well as for injunctive relief.[341] There is no private right of action against a Buyer who receives or induces discriminatory allowances or services prohibited under §2(d) or §2(e) of the act.

Section 3 of the Robinson-Patman Act[342] is not one of the antitrust laws. It is not enforced by the FTC, and it creates no private right of action.[343] The Department of Justice, the agency charged with the responsibility for the enforcement of §3, has brought very few cases under the statute.

§3.29 —When does a private plaintiff have standing to sue for a Robinson-Patman violation?

Numerous appellate court decisions have limited the seemingly broad language of §4 of the Clayton Act to authorize suits only by persons who are more than incidentally injured in their business or property by an antitrust violation.[344]

---

[337] 15 USC §§13(b), 21.

[338] 15 USC §45(1). This section applies to any order issued pursuant to the commission's §5 authority. Typically a commission discrimination complaint will allege a violation of §5 as well as of the Robinson-Patman Act.

[339] *See, e.g.,* Grand Union v FTC, 300 F2d 92 (2d Cir 1962).

[340] 15 USC §15.

[341] *Id* §26.

[342] 25 USC §13a.

[343] Nashville Milk Co v Carnation Co, 355 US 373 (1958); Safeway Stores, Inc v Vance, 355 US 359 (1958).

[344] The Supreme Court has not addressed the issue directly. Its decision in Illinois Brick Co v Illinois, 431 US 720 (1977), limiting the right to sue direct dealers, with certain exceptions, even if viewed as resting on standing rather than injury, is probably inapplicable to Robinson-Patman Act cases. Unlike the Sherman Act, at issue in *Illinois Brick,* the Robinson-Patman Act evidences a congressional concern with competitive

These standing tests range from the *target area* test used by the First, Second, and Third Circuits,[345] which are closely related to an earlier *proximate injury* test,[346] and an expanded target area test of the Ninth Circuit, which would include all persons who, with reasonable foreseeability, would be affected by the antitrust violation,[347] to the *zone of interest* test of the Sixth Circuit.[348]

Essential for standing in a private Robinson-Patman action brought by a disfavored Buyer, i.e., one alleging secondary or tertiary line injury, is a competitive nexus between the favored customer and the plaintiff. A panel of the Third Circuit has held that the Buyer-plaintiff must be a direct purchaser from the discriminatory Seller to get into court.[349] That test has not been applied elsewhere and has been expressly rejected[350] or distinguished[351] by other courts.

Instead, it is generally accepted that persons who did not deal directly with the discriminating Seller may have standing to sue. Two approaches are employed to permit this result. The first is the indirect purchaser doctrine (see **§3.09**) adopted by the Federal Trade Commission[352] and several courts.[353] The doctrine confers standing on a plaintiff as an indirect purchaser where the discriminating seller controlled the terms or conditions of the direct purchaser's resale to the plaintiff and had direct contracts with the plaintiff.

Second, the Court of Appeals for the Second Circuit, while adopting the rationale of the indirect purchaser doctrine, conditions standing on the further

---

impact on levels other than that of the direct Buyer; moreover, most courts have adopted the *indirect purchaser* doctrine to accommodate that concern.

[345] *See, e.g.*, Engine Specialties, Inc v Bombardier, Ltd, 605 F2d 1, 17 (1st Cir 1979); Billy Baxter v Coca-Cola Co, 431 F2d 183 (2d Cir 1970), *cert denied*, 401 US 923 (1971); Harrison v Paramount Pictures, Inc, 115 F Supp 312 (ED Pa 1953), *affd*, 211 F2d 405 (3d Cir), *cert denied*, 348 US 829 (1954).

[346] Adopted in Loeb v Eastman Kodak Co, 183 F 704 (3d Cir 1910); Ames v American Tel & Tel Co, 166 F 820 (D Mass 1909).

[347] *See, e.g.*, Mulvey v Samuel Goldwyn Prods, 433 F2d 1073 (9th Cir 1970), *cert denied*, 402 US 923 (9th Cir 1971).

[348] Malmaud v Sinclair Oil Corp, 521 F2d 1142 (6th Cir 1975).

[349] Klein v Lionel Corp, 237 F2d 13 (3d Cir 1956).

[350] FLM Collision Parts, Inc v Ford Motor Co, 406 F Supp 224, 237–38 (SDNY 1975), *affd in part on other grounds*, 543 F2d 1019 (2d Cir 1976), *cert denied*, 429 US 1097 (1977).

[351] Paceco, Inc v Ishikawajima-Harima Heavy Indus, 468 F Supp 256, 261 (ND Cal 1979).

[352] First articulated in Kraft-Phenix Cheese Corp, 25 FTC 537, 546 (1937); *see also In re* Luxor, Ltd, 31 FTC 658, 663 (1940).

[353] Hiram Walker, Inc v A&S Tropical, Inc, 407 F2d 4 (5th Cir), *cert denied*, 396 US 901 (1969); American News Co v FTC, 300 F2d 104 (2d Cir), *cert denied*, 371 US 824 (1962) (although not a private action case, the court commented with approval on the commission's *indirect purchaser* rule articulated in *Kraft-Phenix*); Roorda v American Oil Co, 1981–1 Trade Cas (CCH) ¶64,153 (WDNY 1981); Siew Corp v Royal Petroleum, Inc, 1979–2 Trade Cas (CCH) ¶62,775 (SD Fla 1979); Paceco, Inc v Ishikawajima-Harima Heavy Indus, 468 F Supp 256 (ND Cal 1979); Wales Home Remodeling Co v Alside Aluminum Corp, 443 F Supp 908 (ED Wis 1978); KS Corp v Chemstranel Corp, 198 F Supp 310 (SDNY 1961).

requirement that plaintiff be in the target area of the alleged price discrimination.[354] Under this formulation,

> . . . an indirect purchaser is considered a "target" of a seller's price discrimination if there is evidence that the discrimination was "aimed at" the indirect purchaser by virtue of the nature and foreseeable effect of the antitrust conspiracy. Relevant factors to consider in this connection are the anti-competitive purpose or object of the seller's price discrimination.[355]

It remains to be seen whether this formulation would deny standing to any plaintiff who would qualify under the general indirect purchaser doctrine; it is not likely to so restrict standing.

The Ninth Circuit, alone for the present, employs a much broader *foreseeability* standing test in buyer-line cases.[356] It would permit almost unlimited standing; if plaintiff is too remote, however, it will be unable to meet the jurisdictional requirements of the Robinson-Patman Act.

In primary line cases, standing is limited to plaintiffs who can prove competition with the discriminating Seller. Competition may be established by means of the indirect purchaser doctrine.[357]

§3.30 —What injury must a private plaintiff prove in order to recover damages for price discrimination?

Since §2 of the Clayton Act as amended by the Robinson-Patman Act is one of the antitrust laws,[358] private treble damages[359] and private injunctive[360] actions may be maintained for violations. A plaintiff seeking to recover damages under §4 of the Clayton Act for a secondary line Robinson-Patman violation, however, must show that it suffered actual injury to its business or property as a result of an antitrust violation.

Until very recently, there have been sharp differences among the circuits as to whether such injury could be established with respect to a Robinson-Patman Act violation merely through proof of an unlawful discrimination, with damages being measured by the extent thereof. This approach, known as the *automatic damage theory* was employed in the Seventh, Eighth, and Ninth Cir-

---

[354] Schwimmer v Sony Corp of Am, 637 F2d 41 (2d Cir 1980).

[355] *Id* 47, n 15.

[356] Mulvey v Samuel Goldwyn Prods, 433 F2d 1073 (9th Cir 1970), *cert denied,* 402 US 923 (1971).

[357] Gas-A-Car, Inc v American Petrofina, Inc, 484 F2d 1102 (10th Cir 1973).

[358] 15 USC §12.

[359] *Id* §15.

[360] *Id* §26.

cuits.[361] The contrary approach, accepted in the Second, Third, and Sixth Circuits, held that a plaintiff seeking to recover damages would have to demonstrate that the favored customer used its preferential price to draw sales from the disfavored customer or cause it to suffer a profit diminution.[362]

In *J Truett Payne, Inc v Chrysler Motors Corp*,[363] the Supreme Court rejected the automatic damage rule. It did not unqualifiedly adopt the alternative approach which would require the tracing of a preferential price through its use by a favored customer; however, it explained that a plaintiff's case would be weak in the absence of such proof. The Court concluded that a particularized showing of injury must be made by a plaintiff and remanded the case to the court of appeals for a determination of whether a violation had occurred.[364] It explained that a more liberal injury standard might be available to a plaintiff once it is demonstrated that a violation has occurred.[365]

The cases subsequent to *Truett Payne* illustrate various aspects of its application. The First Circuit has held that there must be some proof linking the discriminatory price to its use by the favored customer or customers with a resultant business disadvantage to the plaintiff. It held that a relatively insubstantial discrimination affecting commodities accounting for only 1.5 to 2 per cent of the plaintiff's business would not create any inference of such adverse impact.[366] The Seventh Circuit suggested that a reduction in price by the disfavored customers coupled with a loss of sales and a loss of profits contemporaneously with the sale's discriminatory pricing would be enough to satisfy the *Truett Payne* standard.[367] The case was remanded to the district court, however, since it had been tried on the automatic damage theory.

It might be argued that the automatic damage theory could still be applied

---

[361] Fowler Mfg Co v Gorlick, 415 F2d 1248 (9th Cir), *cert denied*, 396 US 1012 (1970); *see also* Grace v EJ Kozin Co, 538 F2d 170 (7th Cir 1976); Elizabeth Arden Sale Corp v Gus Blass Co, 150 F2d 988 (8th Cir), *cert denied*, 326 US 773 (1945).

[362] Enterprise Indus v Texas Co, 240 F2d 457 (2d Cir), *cert denied*, 353 US 965 (1957); *see also* Edward J Sweeney & Sons v Texaco, Inc, 637 F2d 105 (3d Cir 1980), *cert denied*, 451 US 911 (1981); Kidd v Esso Standard Oil Co, 295 F2d 497 (6th Cir 1961).

[363] 451 US 557 (1981).

[364] On remand, the 5th Circuit held that plaintiff had not introduced sufficient proof to create a jury question of probable competitive injury and directed the entry of judgment for defendant. Chrysler Credit Corp v J Truett Payne Co, 670 F2d 575 (5th Cir 1982). See **§3.14.**

[365] J Truett Payne Co v Chrysler Motors Corp, 451 US 557 (1981).

[366] Allen Pen Co v Springfield Photo Mount Co, 653 F2d 17 (1st Cir 1981). *See also* Crowl Distrib Co v Singer Co, 1982-2 Trade Cas (CCH) ¶64,907 (D Kan 1982) (no injury where no lost sales caused by discrimination).

[367] Vanco Beverage, Inc v Falls City Indus, 654 F2d 1224 (7th Cir 1981), *revd on other grounds*, 44 Antitrust & Trade Reg Rep (BNA) 658 (US Mar 22, 1983). The Supreme Court reversed on the issue of the meeting competition defense. It strongly suggested, however, that the Court of Appeals was correct to infer injury to the plaintiff from lost sales attributable to favored customers' lower prices. 44 Antitrust & Trade Reg Rep (BNA) 658, 660 n 8. *See also* Hasbrouck v Texaco, Inc, 663 F2d 930 (9th Cir 1981), *cert denied*, 51 USLW 3224 (Oct 4, 1982).

to offenses arising out of §§2(d) and (e) of the act, the injury under these per se sections allegedly arising from the failure of the disfavored customer to receive the promotional allowance or service. This approach has been rejected by the First Circuit.[368]

§3.31 What government agencies enforce the Robinson-Patman Act?

There has been a marked decline in governmental enforcement of the Robinson-Patman Act over the past 15 years. The Department of Justice has never taken an active interest in enforcing the statute and cases initiated by it under the act have generally involved a combination with charges under other antitrust laws.[369] In fact, in 1976 the Department of Justice authored an extensive report on the Robinson-Patman Act in which it included proposed draft legislation seriously restricting the statute's scope.[370]

Once a major aspect of the Federal Trade Commission's antitrust activity, the Robinson-Patman Act case volume at the commission has virtually disappeared in recent years. The following table[371] furnished to a congressional committee in 1982 by the director of the FTC's Bureau of Competition sharply demonstrates this fact:

Fiscal Year	Complaints Issued	Consents Issued	Litigated Orders
1966	4	68	0
1967	1	6	0
1968	2	9	2
1969	2	11	0
1970	6	6	2
1971	1	9	0
1972	2	3	0
1973	0	4	1
1974	0	4	0
1975	0	3	0
1976	1	1	1
1977	1	1	0
1978	2	0	0
1979	0	4	0
1980	1	0	0

368 15 USC §13(d), (e). *See* Allen Pen Co v Springfield Photo Mount Co, 653 F2d 17, 24–25 (1st Cir 1981).

369 United States v Borden Co, 370 US 460 (1962); United States v Safeway Stores, Inc, 1957 Trade Cas (CCH) ¶68,770 (ND Tex 1957) (consent decree).

370 US Dept of Justice, Report on the Robinson-Patman Act (1976).

371 *Hearings Before the Subcomm on Antitrust and Restraint of Trade Activities Affecting Small Business of the House Small Business Comm, testimony of FTC Bureau of Competition, prepared statement of Director Thomas J Campbell, App Question 4,* 97th Cong, 2d Sess (1982).

Fiscal Year	Complaints Issued	Consents Issued	Litigated Orders
1981	1	2	0
1982	0	0	0

Nevertheless, the commission continues to pay lip service to the statute and claims to be continuously vigilant for cases where price discrimination facilitates attempted monopolization or predatory conduct, where *power Buyers* have exacted preferential treatment and where Sellers attempt to confer market power on Buyers in return for reciprocal preferential treatment.[372] According to a recent report, 23 Robinson-Patman Act investigations were opened by the FTC during the 12-month period October 5, 1981 to October 5, 1982.[373]

Despite the commission's persistent avowals of continued interest in the act, it is not likely that the stream of Robinson-Patman Act cases initiated by the FTC will ever again amount to more than a trickle. The act has, in fact, been ignored on a bipartisan basis by Democratic as well as Republican chairmen of the FTC since the mid-1960s.

§3.32 Will the Robinson-Patman Act continue to have a substantial impact on the distribution of goods?

The steady reorientation of antitrust goals toward a very nearly exclusive focus on consumer welfare has been in large measure responsible for the decline of Robinson-Patman Act enforcement by the federal agencies. There has simply been less emphasis on the protection of small business as an appropriate antitrust goal in and of itself.

Nevertheless, it is unlikely that the Robinson-Patman Act will become unimportant to business planning and antitrust litigation. While the absence of government enforcement may be one reason for the relative paucity of cases in recent years, the level of compliance has also improved markedly over the same period. This improvement can be traced in part at least, to such effective guidance programs as the Federal Trade Commission's promotional allowances and services guides.[374]

Finally, private treble damages actions remain an important source of activity under the Robinson-Patman Act. There are a sufficient number of unresolved questions, raising both substantive and injury and damage issues, so that the level of private enforcement is not likely to abate significantly in the near future. As a consequence, counseling in the Robinson-Patman Act area remains an important part of an antitrust compliance program.

---

[372] *Id* 4.

[373] FTC, First Year of the New Administration: A Progress Report 11 (1982).

[374] FTC, Guide for Advertising Allowances and Other Merchandising Payments and Services, 16 CFR pt 240.

May the Seller Restrict What the Buyer Buys and Resells?

*Harvey M. Applebaum**

4

---

*Mr. Applebaum is a member of the District of Columbia Bar. The author wishes to thank Timothy A. Harr of Covington & Burling for his assistance in the preparation of this chapter.

§4.01 Do the antitrust laws prohibit Seller from restricting what Buyer buys?

As a general rule, competition is enhanced if Buyer has a free choice among all possible suppliers each time it desires to purchase or lease an item. Therefore, arrangements whereby Seller eliminates or restricts Buyer's free choice of suppliers are, under certain circumstances, prohibited by the antitrust laws. The two types of restrictive arrangements most often the subject of antitrust actions are tying arrangements and exclusive dealing arrangements.

Tying occurs when Seller will sell or lease a product, service, or other item desired by Buyer only if Buyer will agree to also buy certain other less desired items from Seller. Tying is treated in **§§4.02-4.37.** Exclusive dealing occurs when Buyer agrees to purchase a particular item only from Seller in the future. Exclusive dealing is discussed in **§§4.38-4.53.**

Both tying arrangements and exclusive dealing arrangements may be challenged under §1 of the Sherman Act, §3 of the Clayton Act, or by the Federal Trade Commission under §5 of the FTC Act. The courts generally have been much tougher on tying arrangements than exclusive dealing, on the apparent theory that tying is usually highly anticompetitive and without legitimate benefit, whereas exclusive dealing is often not anticompetitive or is justified. For this reason, tying is generally subject to a type of per se standard, while exclusive dealing is more often tested under a rule of reason analysis. Of course, tying or exclusive dealing may also constitute activity that violates other antitrust laws, including §2 of the Sherman Act (monopolization) where the conduct is intended to achieve or maintain market power. Certain variations on tying and exclusive dealing arrangements are also discussed below, including *full-line forcing* (**§4.34**), quality requirements (**§4.36**), *requirements contracts* (**§4.40**), and *reciprocal dealing* (**§4.54**) which are restrictions on Buyer subject to the same antitrust statutes and to similar analysis.

Tying

§4.02 May Seller condition or tie its sale or lease of one item to the purchase or lease by Buyer of a second item offered by Seller or a related third party?

A Seller ordinarily may not condition—or *tie*—its sale or lease to Buyer of one highly desired product or service, the *tying* item (item A), on buyer's agreement to purchase or lease a less-desired second item, the *tied* item (item B), from seller or from a third party in which Seller has a financial interest. The courts have generally treated tying as per se unlawful, finding that its primary effects are to prevent Buyer from making a free choice among competing suppliers of item B and to permit Seller to use its leverage over item A to gain power over the market for item B.[1] The Supreme Court observed in a leading tying case, *Northern Pacific Railway v United States,*[2] that, where there is such tying, Buyer, rather than selecting the competing item having better quality or a lower price, instead chooses Seller's item B only because Buyer wants Seller's item A. This diminishes competition in the market for item B.

Section 3 of the Clayton Act directly prohibits tying between two separate "commodities" whenever the effect "may be to substantially lessen competition or tend to create a monopoly in any line of commerce."[3] Section 1 of the

---

[1] The Supreme Court held in International Salt Co v United States, 332 US 392, 396 (1947) that "it is unreasonable, per se, to foreclose competitors from any substantial market" in holding a tying arrangement unlawful. Two years later, in Standard Oil Co v United States, 337 US 293, 305-06 (1949) the Supreme Court found that tying arrangements have "hardly any purpose beyond the suppression of competition." The per se rule was again supported in Times-Picayune Publishing Co v United States, 345 US 594, 611 (1953), which found that tying is prohibited because Seller is attempting to exploit its dominant position in one market "to expand its empire into the next." Per se treatment of tying arrangements has been upheld by the Supreme Court as recently as 1977 in United States Steel Corp v Fortner Enters, Inc, 429 US 610 (1977) (*Fortner II*).

[2] 356 US 1 (1958).

[3] The full text of Clayton Act §3 is as follows:

> It shall be unlawful for any person engaged in commerce, in the course of such commerce, to lease or make a sale or contract for sale of goods, wares, merchandise, machinery, supplies, or other commodities, whether patented or unpatented, for use, consumption, or resale within the United States or any Territory thereof or the District of Columbia or any insular possession or other place under the jurisdiction of the United States, or fix a price charged therefor, or discount from, or rebate upon such price, on the condition, agreement, or understanding that the lessee or purchaser thereof shall not use or deal in the goods, wares, merchandise, machinery, supplies, or other commodities of a competitor or competitors of the lessor or seller, where the effect of such lease, sale, or contract for sale or such condition, agreement, or understanding may be to substantially lessen competition or tend to create a monopoly in any line of commerce.

Sherman Act prohibits unreasonable restraints of trade and has been interpreted to prohibit as a per se violation tying between any two separate items, including services, licenses, trademarks, or commodities, where (1) Seller has sufficient economic power with respect to item A to appreciably restrain free competition in the market for item B, and (2) the tying affects a "not insubstantial" amount of commerce.[4] Where one of the elements of a per se §1 violation is not found, the tie may nevertheless be found to violate §1 under the rule of reason test if it is found to be an unreasonable restraint of trade.[5]

The Federal Trade Commission, under §5 of the FTC Act, also may challenge tying as an "*unfair method of competition*".[6] Indeed, the FTC may even attack conduct that, although not technically tying, involves Seller's use of its power in the market for item A to influence sales in the market for item B.[7] Finally, tying may violate numerous state antitrust laws.[8]

---

15 U.S.C. § 14.

[4] Northern Pac Ry v US, 356 US 1 (1958).

[5] Fortner Enters, Inc v United States Steel Corp, 394 US 495, 499-500 (1969) (*Fortner I*); Bogus v American Speech & Hearing Assn, 582 F2d 277, 287 (3d Cir 1978); Ware v Trailer Mart, Inc, 623 F2d 1150, 1154 (6th Cir 1980); Greenville Publishing Co v Daily Reflector, Inc, 496 F2d 391, 400 (4th Cir 1974). The relevant text of Sherman Act §1 is as follows: "Every contract, combination in the form of a trust or otherwise, or conspiracy, in restraint of trade or commerce among the several States, or with foreign nations, is declared to be illegal. . . " 15 USC §1. Some courts have made the broad statement that where conduct does not violate §3, it does not violate §1 (*see, e.g.*, Tampa Elec Co v Nashville Coal Co, 365 US 320, 335 (1961); Mercantile Natl Bank v Quest, Inc, 303 F Supp 926, 935 (ND Ind 1969)); but these statements are almost certainly too broad (see **§4.03**).

[6] Times-Picayune Publishing Co v United States, 345 US 594 (1953). The full text of FTC Act §5 is as follows: "Unfair methods of competition in or affecting commerce, and unfair or deceptive acts or practices in or affecting commerce, are declared unlawful." 15 USC §45(a)(1).

[7] Under §5 of the FTC Act, the FTC is authorized to take such measures as are necessary to prevent anticompetitive effects at their incipient stage. *See* FTC v Brown Shoe Co, 384 US 316, 321-22 (1966), where the Supreme Court stated that the commission, under §5, has the power to prevent practices which are contrary to the policy of §1 and §3 "even though such practices may not actually violate these laws." In Atlantic Ref Co v FTC, 381 US 357, 369 (1965), the Supreme Court found that the FTC had properly ruled that a sales commission plan was an unfair method of competition under §5, because the effect of the plan was the same as that of a tying arrangement. Under the prohibited plan, a tire manufacturer selling tires at a service station had to pay the oil company a commission on sales of tires, batteries and accessories. *But see* Texaco, Inc v FTC, 336 F2d 754, 763 (DC Cir 1964).

[8] Some states have their own laws which would prohibit tying. For example, NY Gen Bus Law §340 (Consol 1968) provides that

> every contract, agreement, arrangement or combination whereby . . . competition or the free exercise of any activity in the conduct of any business, trade or commerce or in the furnishing of any service in this state is or may be restrained . . . is hereby declared to be against public policy, illegal and void.

Because tying would or could certainly restrain the other supplier's ability to compete and Buyer's free exercise of choice, tying would appear to fall clearly within the prohibition of the New York statute.

While the courts generally have held that tying is per se unlawful, they often have not applied a true per se standard. In many instances tying has been found to be *justified* because the competitive benefits of tying the two items (for example, tying a trademark and the trademarked product to protect Seller's goodwill) outweigh the anticompetitive effect.[9] In other instances where tying of certain items is deemed reasonable and not significantly harmful, courts have avoided the per se rule by finding a necessary element of per se tying to be missing. Most often, the courts in these cases have held that the items are part of a single package, and thus not separate items tied together[10] or have found lack of the necessary economic power to impose an unreasonable tying condition.[11] These per se avoidance tactics have led one court to conclude that the established per se tying "principles are honored as much in the breach as in the execution and as a result the courts as well as industries are left without consistent guidance."[12]

The increasing tendency of the courts in cases such as *Continental TV Inc v GTE Sylvania,*[13] and of the Justice Department and the FTC, to test vertical restraints under a competitive injury rule of reason analysis rather than treat

---

Other states have statutes which essentially parrot §3 of the Clayton Act. *See* Mo Rev Stat, §416.031(3) (1969 & Supp 1975); Mass Gen Laws Ann (1978) ch 459 §6 (West). Other states, such as Maryland, have attempted to improve on the language, while aiming at the same conduct. Md Com Law, Md Com Law Code Ann (1975) §11-204(6) states that a person may not

> lease or make a sale or contract for the sale of a patented or unpatented commodity or service . . . on the condition, agreement or understanding that the lessee or purchaser will not use or deal in the commodity or service of a competitor of the lessor or seller if the effect of the lease, sale, or contract for sale or the condition, agreement or understanding may: (i) substantially lessen competition; or (ii) tend to create a monopoly in any line of trade or commerce.

In cases brought under state antitrust laws, the courts have relied heavily on federal precedent for standards and analysis. For example, in Hamro v Shell Oil Co, 674 F2d 784 (9th Cir 1982), the court applied California's Cartwright Act, §§6720, 16726 and 16727, which were patterned on the federal antitrust laws. Throughout its analysis, the court treated the case as one brought under the Sherman and Clayton Acts, relying on federal precedent from across the country. *See also* Golden West Insulation v Stardust Inv Corp, 1980-81 Trade Cas (CCH) ¶63,616 (Or Ct of App July 28, 1980).

Other jurisdictions, such as the District of Columbia and Ohio, have no statutes that seem directly aimed at tying. Texas, curiously, has a prohibition on tying arrangements only with respect to newspapers and news agencies. Tex Bus & Com Code Ann, §15.06 (Vernon 1967).

[9] See **§4.28.**

[10] See **§4.13.**

[11] See **§§4.22, 4.27.**

[12] United States v Mercedes-Benz of N Am, 517 F Supp 1369, 1377-78, n 9 1380 (ND Cal 1981).

[13] Continental TV, Inc v GTE Sylvania, 433 US 36 (1977); Metrix Warehouse, Inc v Daimler-Benz Aktiengesellschaft, 1982-2 Trade Cas (CCH) ¶64,861 (DMd June 4, 1982).

them as per se violations[14] may generate increased competitive effect analysis

---

[14] There is some evidence of this developing attitude on the part of the two antitrust enforcement agencies. For example, in a 1983 *amicus* brief supporting certiorari in the Supreme Court in Jefferson Parish Hosp Dist No 2 v Hyde (No 82-1031) (where the Fifth Circuit held that a hospital's exclusive contract with a medical corporation for anesthesia services was per se illegal (Hyde v Jefferson Parish Hospital Dist No 2, 1982-2 Trade Cas (CCH) ¶64,945 (5th Cir Sept 20, 1982)), the Solicitor General, on behalf of both the Antitrust Division of the Justice Department and the Federal Trade Commission, urged that the rule of reason should be applied to certain vertical arrangements alleged to be tie-ins. 44 Antitrust & Trade Reg Rep (BNA) No. 1103, at 385-86 (Feb 24, 1983). The Solicitor General argued that the *Jefferson Parish* arrangement was more akin to exclusive dealing and should be tested under the rule of reason, and urged the Court to follow "the better-reasoned decisions of courts that have recognized that the economic efficiencies may be achieved through purported tie-ins," referring to decisions such as Hirsh v Martindale-Hubbell, Inc, 674 F2d 1343 (9th Cir 1982), and Dos Santos v Columbus-Cuneo-Cabrini Medical Center, 684 F2d 1346 (7th Cir 1982). *Id* 386. He urged review of the *Jefferson Parish* decision because it "eshewed any such analysis and instead found [a *per se* violation simply because the court found] it 'clear that we are dealing with two distinct services which a buyer should be able to obtain separately.' " *Id.* The brief concluded that the "failure even to consider the possible efficiencies and advantages to the [h]ospital and consumers serves to emphasize the inherent problems of a wooden application of the per se rule." *Id.* The Supreme Court, on March 7, 1983, granted certiorari. 44 Antitrust & Trade Reg Rep (BNA) No 1105 at 537 (Mar 10, 1983).

Similarly in Shop & Save Food Mkts Inc v Pneumo Corp, 1982-2 Trade Cas (CCH) ¶64,832 (2d Cir 1982), a private action, the Department of Justice filed a brief as amicus curiae in support of reconsideration by the court of its previous decision applying a per se tying analysis. In its conclusion in that case, the court agreed with the Department of Justice and the defendants, finding that it would not invoke the per se rule. The court noted, "[i]n deciding whether to invoke the *per se* rule, we must be cognizant of the teachings of the Supreme Court that 'easy labels do not always supply ready answers' " (citing Broadcast Music Inc v CBS, Inc, 441 US 1, 8 (1979)). 1982-2 Trade Cas (CCH) ¶64,832, at 72,145. In another example, Assistant Attorney General William F. Baxter, Chief of the Antitrust Division, announced in March 1982 that after a thorough review of the case, the Justice Department was dismissing its suit against Mercedes-Benz of North America, Inc in which the government had alleged that there was tying between the sale of automotive replacement parts and the granting of a franchise to handle Mercedes-Benz automobiles. CCH Trade Reg Rep, No 534 (Mar 22, 1982). The Justice Department concluded that tying arrangements of this sort did not injure competition or create unreasonable market power.

FTC Chairman Miller has suggested that vertical restraints, including even price restraints, be challenged only where they have an unreasonable adverse effect on competition. See, e.g., Miller's dissenting opinion in *Russell Stover Candies,* 3 Trade Reg Rep (CCH) ¶21,933 at 22,372 (July 1, 1982). Miller has urged that many restraints, while they may have anticompetitive effects with respect to a certain brand, may in fact enhance interbrand competition, and that the principal focus should be on this interbrand competition. Because tying does, to a certain extent, limit interbrand competition, it is unclear how the FTC position will evolve in this area. However, it seems likely that the FTC will not adopt a per se test. The latest in depth FTC analysis of the question was not with respect to tying, but rather with respect to the related area of exclusive dealing. In Beltone Elecs Corp, FTC No 8928, 3 Trade Reg Rep (CCH) ¶21,934 (July 6, 1982), the FTC essentially reversed an earlier decision concerning Beltone's exclusive dealing, citing the Supreme Court decision in *GTE Sylvania.* In

of tying arrangements, particularly under §1. Under such an analysis, tying is unlawful only if it *unreasonably* restricts competition.[15] Application of a rule of reason approach may have caused the government to drop tying cases that it previously might have brought as per se cases,[16] and has caused some courts to engage in more in-depth analysis of the Seller's role in the market and the actual competitive effects of the tying conduct rather than relying on a simple per se rule.[17]

Beltone, the FTC stated "[i]n returning to a rule of reason analysis for non-price vertical restraints, the *Sylvania* decision emphasized two points: (1) that all such restraints, regardless of form, can serve legitimate pro-competitive purposes, and (2) that interbrand considerations are of primary importance", 3 Trade Reg Rep (CCH) at 22,391-92. (Footnotes omitted.) The FTC went on to state: "To summarize, it is not sufficient for a party challenging a vertical restraint to show only a resultant loss of intrabrand competition. Rather, current judicial precedent indicates that the party must show that the restraint also has a probable adverse effect on interbrand competition", *id* 22,393. The broad language used by the FTC in *Beltone* suggests that the same analysis may be used in tying cases.

[15] A discussion of the rule of reason in general is contained in **ch 1.**

[16] Perhaps one of the best recent examples of this is the Justice Department's decision to drop the *Mercedes-Benz* case. In United States v Mercedes-Benz of N Am, Inc, 517 F Supp 1369, 1377 (ND Cal 1981), the court stated that it was unwilling to find that the rule of reason had yet replaced the established per se tying principles. The court noted the dilemma of application of the per se rule where it was not appropriate, but felt bound to apply it. It was in the face of this favorable decision that the Justice Department decided nevertheless to dismiss the case, apparently solving the dilemma for the court.

[17] For a possible shift in one court's position recently, *compare* Fifth Moorings Condominium, Inc v Shere, 81 FRD 712, 716 (SD Fla 1979), *with* Sandles v Ruben, 89 FRD 635, 636 (SD Fla 1981); the latter case stated four necessary elements for unlawful tying, the fourth being anticompetitive effect; the former case stated that only the first three elements were needed: tying, economic power, and substantial volume of business affected.

In *In re* Data Gen Corp Antitrust Litigation, 529 F Supp 801 (ND Cal 1981), the court found that the manufacturer had not imposed a per se unlawful tying arrangement by refusing to license its software for use with other manufacturers' computers because the competing manufacturers failed to show that their inability to compete was attributable to the licensing limitations. The court's decision turned on the question of market power and whether there was sufficient market power to require a per se determination. The court stated: "To require market evidence identical to that appropriate in a rule of reason case would effectively eradicate the distinction between rule of reason cases and per se cases." But the court required the plaintiffs to introduce sufficient evidence to show their "competitors were prevented from developing competitive software, and . . . to find an appreciable restraint of trade." 529 F Supp at 809. The court found that in Fortner Enters, Inc v United States Steel Corp, 394 US 495 (1969) (*Fortner I*) and United States Steel Corp v Fortner Enters, Inc, 429 US 610 (1977) (*Fortner II*), the Supreme Court "expressed its dissatisfaction with the evolution of the *per se* analysis and suggested that some degree of market analysis is necessary even in a *per se* case." 529 F Supp at 808.

Other courts have also used a market analysis similar to the traditional rule of reason to determine whether seller's economic power is sufficient to meet the per se test. These courts have thereby introduced a significant effect on competition analysis into cases where the per se standards were nominally used. *See, e.g.,* JBL Enters, Inc v

§4.03 Does it make any difference whether the items tied together are commodities as opposed to services, licenses, or other intangible items?

As stated in **§4.02,** tying may be found unlawful under either §1 of the Sherman Act, §3 of the Clayton Act, or §5 of the Federal Trade Commission Act. However, §3 of the Clayton Act only applies where both item A and item B are "goods, wares, merchandise, machinery, supplies, or other commodities," and therefore §3 is not available where the items involved are not commodities.

This distinction is significant because a per se violation of §3 may technically require less market power and effect on competition than does a per se violation of §1. The Supreme Court has held that in order to establish a per se §1 violation, it must be shown *both* that Seller had sufficient economic power over the market in item A to appreciably restrain free competition for item B *and* that the tie-in had a not insubstantial effect on commerce in item B. But, the Court held, *only one* of these showings need be made to establish a §3 violation.[18] However, because substantial tying seldom occurs without sufficient economic power, this distinction between §1 and §3 is often ignored or even said not to exist.[19] Therefore, there is often little practical importance to whether a tying arrangement is tested under §3 or §1.

Jhirmack Enters, Inc, 509 F Supp 357, 378-79 (ND Cal 1981) and Kingsport Motors, Inc v Chrysler Motors Corp, 644 F2d 566, 572 (6th Cir 1981).

[18] This distinction was clearly set out in Times-Picayune Publishing Co v United States, 345 US 594, 608-09 (1953), where the Court stated:

> When the seller enjoys a monopolistic position in the market for the "tying" product, *or* if a substantial volume of commerce in the "tied" product is restrained, a tying arrangement violates the narrower standards expressed in §3 of the Clayton Act because from either factor the requisite potential lessening of competition is inferred. And because for even a lawful monopolist it is "unreasonable, *per se,* to foreclose competitors from any substantial market," a tying arrangement is banned by §1 of the Sherman Act whenever *both* conditions are met.

Since the *Times-Picayune* decision, the "monopolistic position in the market" requirement has been modified so that now all that is required is "sufficient economic power with respect to the tying product to appreciably restrain free competition in the market for the tied product." Northern Pac Ry v United States, 356 US 1, 6 (1958). See also **§4.23.**

[19] One court has concluded that "the neat distinction between tying arrangements that violate Sherman §1 and those that violate Clayton §3 has faded beyond recognition," and determined that the established test for per se violations of §1 should be used for §3 as well. *In re* Data Gen Corp Antitrust Litigation, 490 F Supp 1089, 1100 (ND Cal 1980). *See* United States v Westinghouse Elec Corp, 471 F Supp 532, 545 (ND Cal 1978), *affd,* 648 F2d 642 (1981); Smith-Kline Corp v Eli Lilly & Co, 427 F Supp 1089, 1114 (ED Pa 1976), *affd,* 575 F2d 1056 (3d Cir), *cert denied,* 439 US 838 (1978); Greenville Publishing Co v Daily Reflector, Inc, 496 F2d 391, 400 (4th Cir 1974); Robert's Waikiki U-Drive, Inc v Budget Rent-a-Car, 491 F Supp 1199 (D Hawaii 1980); *see also,* Northern Pac Ry v United States, 356 US 1, 6 n 4 (1958). As a practical matter, there is seldom a case where either ecomonic power or substantial tying could be shown, but both could not be shown. As the Supreme Court suggested in Northern Pac Ry v United

§4.04 —What is a commodity?

A *commodity* is generally held to be a tangible item other than real property, the value of which is based on its actual physical properties, e.g., an automobile, coal, or food. Because a commodity is often equated with a tangible good, there has been some disagreement as to whether semitangibles, such as natural gas or electricity, are commodities. At least one court has found that items such as natural gas or electricity are not commodities, but other decisions have found the opposite.[20] Real property or items whose value is not in their physical properties, such as a service, money, credit, or a license, are not commodities.

§4.05 —Is the definition of commodities in the tying context different than that used for analysis of exclusive dealing arrangements or under the Robinson-Patman Act?

The definition of commodities under §3 with respect to tying arrangements is identical to that used in analyzing exclusive dealing arrangements under §3,[21] and to that used under the Robinson-Patman Act with respect to price

---

States, 365 US 1, 6 (1958), "where the seller has no control or dominance over the tying product . . . tying arrangements would obviously be insignificant at most." In United States v Loew's Inc, 371 US 38, 45 (1962), the Court found that sufficient economic power could be "inferred from the tying product's desirability to consumers or from the uniqueness of its attributes," and suggested that, where tying has been successful, it should not be necessary to do a full economic analysis to determine the real level of market power. *Id* at n 4.

If the courts continue to move away from application of a per se rule to tying in line with *Continental TV, Inc v GTE Sylvania, Inc,* 433 US 36 (1977), however, the importance of the §1 versus §3 distinction may increase. The courts may be more willing to embrace a traditional rule of reason analysis under §1 of the Sherman Act, where it is often applied in other contexts, than under §3. Section 3 has its own built-in *competitive effect* test—i.e., tying that "*may* substantially lessen competition"—that does not require actual unreasonable injury. As a result, in the future a seller imposing a tying arrangement with incipient effects on competition may avoid §1 but violate §3. See also **§4.21**.

[20] Auto Acetylene Light Co v Prest-O-Light Co, 276 F 537, 543 (6th Cir 1921) (natural gas not a commodity); City of Newark v Delmarva Power & Light Co, 467 F Supp 763, 773 (D Del 1979) (electricity not a commodity). *But see* Pennsylvania Water & Power Co v Consolidated Gas, Elec Light & Power Co, 184 F2d 552, 559 (4th Cir), *cert denied,* 340 US 906 (1950); B & W Gas Co v General Gas Corp, 247 F Supp 339 (ND Ga 1965).

[21] See **§4.42**.

discrimination.[22]

§4.06 —What are examples of items that have been held to be commodities?

Examples of items that have been found or assumed to be commodities under §3 are tractors,[23] automotive products,[24] electricity,[25] liquified natural gas,[26] gasoline,[27] bedding,[28] tabulating cards,[29] clothing,[30] food,[31] machinery,[32] electronic equipment,[33] automobiles[34] and coal.[35] Tying involving such commodities may be attacked under §3, and also under §1 or by the Federal Trade Commission under §5 of the FTC Act.

§4.07 —What are examples of items that have been held not to be commodities?

Examples of items which have been held not to be commodities under §3 are services (e.g., insulation subcontracting,[36] towing services,[37] and electron-

---

[22] See **§3.25.**

[23] United States v J I Case Co, 101 F Supp 856, 865 (D Minn 1951).

[24] Reisner v General Motors Corp, 511 F Supp 1167, 1177 (SDNY 1981); Englander Motors, Inc v Ford Motor Co, 267 F2d 11 (6th Cir 1959).

[25] Pennsylvania Water & Power Co v Consolidated Gas, Elec Light & Power Co, 184 F2d 552, 559 (4th Cir), *cert denied,* 340 US 906 (1950). *But see* City of Newark v Delmarva Power & Light Co, 467 F Supp 763, 773 (D Del 1979).

[26] B&W Gas Co v General Gas Corp, 247 F Supp 339 (ND Ga 1965).

[27] United States v Richfield Oil Corp, 99 F Supp 280 (SD Cal 1951), *affd,* 343 US 922 (1952), Davis v Marathon Oil Co, 528 F2d 395, 398 (6th Cir 1975), *cert denied,* 429 US 823 (1976).

[28] 2361 State Corp v Sealy, Inc, 263 F Supp 845, 854 (ND Ill 1967).

[29] IBM v United States, 298 US 131 (1936).

[30] Fashion Originators' Guild of Am, Inc v FTC, 312 US 457 (1941); Standard Fashion Co v Magrane Houston Co, 258 US 346 (1922).

[31] Detroit City Dairy, Inc v Kowalski Sausage Co, 393 F Supp 453 (ED Mich 1975); Automatic Canteen Co v FTC, 194 F2d 433 (7th Cir 1952).

[32] United States v American Can Co, 87 F Supp 18, 27 (ND Cal 1949).

[33] United States v Jerrold Elec Corp, 187 F Supp 545, 558 (ED Pa 1960), *affd per curiam,* 365 US 567 (1961).

[34] Bob Maxfield, Inc v American Motors Corp, 637 F2d 1033 (5th Cir), *cert denied,* 454 US 860 (1981).

[35] Tampa Elec Co v Nashville Coal Co, 365 US 320 (1961).

[36] Hudson Valley Asbestos Corp v Tougher Heating & Plumbing Co, 510 F2d 1140, 1144-45 (2d Cir), *cert denied,* 421 US 1011 (1975).

[37] Centanni v T Smith & Son, 216 F Supp 330, 339 (ED La), *affd,* 323 F2d 363 (5th Cir 1963).

ics maintenance[38]) money,[39] travelers' checks,[40] credit,[41] real property,[42] cemetery plots,[43] advertising,[44] licenses,[45] privileges,[46] vending machine space,[47] security deposits,[48] copyrights,[49] and broadcast time.[50] Tying involving such items may not be attacked under §3, but may be attacked under §1, or by the Federal Trade Commission under §5 of the FTC Act.

§4.08 —Is a trademark a commodity?

Although it seems clear that a trademark is not a *commodity,*[51] the courts ordinarily do not have to face this question because the tying claims in cases involving trademarks are usually brought under §1 which covers noncommodities as well. Trademarks nevertheless are often the subject of tying litigation

---

[38] United States v Jerrold Elecs Corp, 187 F Supp 545 (ED Pa 1960), *affd per curiam,* 365 US 567 (1961).

[39] Wendkos v ABC Consolidated Corp, 379 F Supp 15, 18 (ED Pa 1974).

[40] American Bankers Club, Inc v American Express Co, 1977-1 Trade Cas (CCH) ¶61,247 at 70,741 (DDC 1977).

[41] Fortner Enters, Inc v United States Steel Corp, 394 US 495 (1969); Anderson v Home Style Stores, Inc, 381 F Supp 402, 407 (ED Pa 1974), *affd,* 511 F2d 1392 (3d Cir 1975).

[42] Northern Pac Ry v United States, 356 US 1 (1958).

[43] Moore v Jas H Matthews & Co, 473 F2d 328 (9th Cir 1972), *after remand,* 550 F2d 1207 (9th Cir 1977), *after second remand,* 682 F2d 830 (9th Cir 1982).

[44] ALW, Inc v United Air Lines, Inc, 510 F2d 52, 57 (9th Cir 1975); Times-Picayune Publishing Co v United States, 345 US 594 (1953).

[45] Principe v McDonald's Corp, 631 F2d 303 (4th Cir 1980), *cert denied,* 101 S Ct 2047 (1981)

[46] Columbia Broadcasting Sys v Amana Refrigerators, Inc, 295 F2d 375 (7th Cir 1961).

[47] GO Coin Serv, Inc v Ace Vending Co, 1978-1 Trade Cas (CCH) ¶61,882 at 73,694 (SD Ohio Mar 15, 1978).

[48] Principe v McDonald's Corp, 631 F2d 303 (4th Cir 1980), *cert denied,* 451 US 970 (1981).

[49] *See* United States v Loew's, Inc, 371 US 38 (1962).

[50] Columbia Broadcasting Sys v Amana Refrigerators, Inc, 295 F2d 375 (7th Cir 1961).

[51] In Schuler v Better Equip Launder Center, Inc, 1973-2 Trade Cas (CCH) ¶74,617 (D Mass July 16, 1973), the court held §3 inapplicable in the case of a trademark. This was probably a correct decision, but this has become a nonissue in most cases, for, in virtually any case involving a trademark where the plaintiff sues under §3, §1 of the Sherman Act is included in the pleadings. *See also* Shaeffer v Collins, 1980-81 Trade Cas (CCH) ¶63,666 (ED Pa Dec 9, 1980). In these cases, the courts do not see a need to determine whether the trademark is a commodity under §3 but rather approach the case using traditional §1 per se analysis. *But see* Principe v McDonald's Corp, 631 F2d 303, 304 n 1 (4th Cir 1980), *cert denied,* 451 US 970 (1981). In other instances, the plaintiffs have sued in trademark cases only under §1 of the Sherman Act. This, of course, precludes any need to deal with the commodity question. *See, e.g.,* Krehl v Baskin-Robbins Ice Cream Co, 664 F2d 1348, 1351 (9th Cir 1982).

because they are frequently provided only on the condition that buyer purchase seller's products. Considerable law concerning trademarks and tying has developed, and is dealt with in **§§4.14, 4.26, 4.30, 4.32.**

§4.09 Is it tying to require the purchase of two items that are part of the same product or are related?

In order for there to be illegal tying between item A and item B, they must be two separate items. Therefore, if item A and item B are really integral parts of the same product, such as an automobile and its four tires, the sale of these items as a package is not tying; but where the two items are really separate, even if used together or related, such as an automobile and replacement parts for the automobile, they may be considered two separate items and tying may exist.[52]

§4.10 —When are two items separate items for tying purposes?

To determine whether Seller is selling two separate items or is selling a single multipart item, the courts generally use a real world, common-sense approach. If there is no reason why the two items must be offered together then they are usually found to be separate items for tying purposes.[53] On the other hand, if, for good reason, the products are not considered separate in the trade[54] and are not generally sold separately,[55] they will usually be considered as a single product.

A separate physical product structure,[56] separate charges for each item,[57] or

---

[52] United States v Mercedes-Benz of N Am, Inc, 517 F Supp 1369 1379-81 (ND Cal 1981).

[53] *In re* Data Gen Corp Antitrust Litigation, 490 F Supp 1089, 1104 (ND Cal 1980). (In finding separate products, the court noted that the seller frequently sold software separately from central computer units, had separate prices, and even some separate sales personnel.)

[54] ILC Peripherals Leasing Corp v IBM Corp, 448 F Supp 228, 232-33 (ND Cal 1978), *affd,* 636 F2d 1188 (9th Cir), *cert denied,* 452 US 972 (1979).

[55] Washington Gas Light Co v Virginia Elec & Power Co, 438 F2d 248, 253 (4th Cir 1971); United States v Jerrold Elecs Corp, 187 F Supp 545, 559 (ED Pa 1960), *affd per curiam,* 365 US 567 (1961).

[56] Anderson Foreign Motors, Inc v New England Toyota Distribs, Inc, 475 F Supp 973, 982 (D Mass 1979); United States v Jerrold Elecs Corp, 187 F Supp 545, 559 (ED Pa 1960), *affd per curiam,* 365 US 567 (1961).

[57] *In re* Data Gen Corp Antitrust Litigation, 490 F Supp 1089, 1104-05 (ND Cal 1980); ILC Peripherals Leasing Corp v IBM Corp, 448 F Supp 228, 232-34 (ND Cal 1978), *affd,* 636 F2d 1188 (9th Cir), *cert denied,* 452 US 972 (1979); United States v Jerrold Elecs Corp, 187 F Supp 545, 559 (ED Pa 1960), *affd per curiam,* 365 US 567 (1961)

the ability of item A alone to function properly without item B[58] are also factors which have been used by the courts to find separate products, but reliance on these factors alone may lead to the wrong conclusions. Likewise, the efficiency gained from packaging two items as one product has been cited as a basis for finding that there is a single product,[59] but reliance on this factor would also be misplaced in many instances. As a result of the lack of an accepted test, in some close cases courts have disagreed with one another in essentially identical circumstances—some courts finding two separate products, some courts finding one package. For example, courts are split on whether trademarks and trademarked products,[60] or regular season and exhibition football game tickets[61] are two separate items.

Finally, courts on occasion appear to find a single package rather than two separate items principally as a means of avoiding the per se rule generally applied in tying cases. This is particularly true in cases involving trademarks and franchises, considered separately in **§§4.14** and **4.15,** where the courts appear to first try to decide whether Seller is leveraging control over its trademark to gain control of a distinct second market. If so, the courts are likely to find separate products and tying. If, on the other hand, Seller appears to be offering a package of items that are sought as a unit by Buyers, some courts have found no tying on the ground that Seller was offering only a single package.[62]

---

[58] *Compare In re* Data Gen Corp Antitrust Litigation, 490 F Supp 1089, 1104-05 (ND Cal 1980) *and* United States v Mercedes-Benz of N Am, Inc, 817 F Supp 1369, 1381 (ND Cal 1981); *with* United States v Jerrold Elecs Corp, 187 F Supp 545, 559 (ED Pa 1960), *affd per curiam,* 365 US 567 (1961).

[59] Rosebrough Monument Co v Memorial Park Cemetery Assn, 666 F2d 1130, 1141 (8th Cir 1981); Anderson Foreign Motors, Inc v New England Toyota Distrib, Inc, 475 F Supp 973, 984-85 (D Mass 1979); ILC Peripherals Leasing Corp v IBM Corp, 448 F Supp 228, 232 (ND Cal 1978), *affd,* 636 F2d 1188 (9th Cir), *cert denied,* 452 US 972 (1979).

[60] *Compare* Photovest Corp v Fotomat Corp, 606 F2d 704, 722 (7th Cir 1979), *cert denied,* 445 US 917 (1980), *with* Krehl v Baskin-Robbins Ice Cream Co, 664 F2d 1348, 1352-54 (9th Cir 1982).

[61] *Compare* Coniglio v Highwood Serv Inc, 495 F2d 1286, 1291 (2d Cir), *cert denied,* 419 US 1022 (1974), *with* Pfeiffer v New England Patriots Football Club, Inc, 1973-1 Trade Cas (CCH) ¶74,267 at 93,265 (D Mass July 25, 1972).

[62] *See* Principe v McDonald's Corp, 631 F2d 303 (4th Cir 1980), *cert denied,* 451 US 970 (1981); Krehl v Baskin-Robbins Ice Cream Co, 664 F2d 1348, 1353-54 (9th Cir 1982); Levinson v Maison Grande, Inc, 1981-2 Trade Cas (CCH) ¶64,278 (SD Fla June 10, 1981).

§4.11 —Does it matter if the two items are normally sold as a unit or package in the industry?

In order to determine if there are two separate items the courts often look to whether the two items are normally sold as a unit or package within that industry.[63] However, this fact is not always determinative, and it may represent a double-edged sword in some cases. Industry practice of selling item A and item B as a package may convince a court that they are not separate items where it appears that there are substantial practical reasons for only offering the products as a package.[64] But where such substantial practical reasons do not exist, a court may find that there is tying industry-wide imposed by firms dominant in the market for item A, and the court will be quick to condemn such tying because it has such a substantial anticompetitive effect in the market for item B.[65]

---

[63] In finding a single product encompassing integrated discs and disc drives, the court in ILC Peripherals Leasing Corp, v IBM Corp, 448 F Supp 228 (ND Cal 1978), *affd,* 636 F2d 1188 (9th Cir), *cert denied,* 452 US 972 (1979), noted that "it is clear that the practice in this industry is to sell integrated discs and the drives on which they operate for a single price." 448 F Supp at 232. The court in that case was attempting to apply the standard which the Ninth Circuit set forth in Siegel v Chicken Delight, Inc, 448 F2d 43 (9th Cir 1971), *cert denied,* 405 US 955 (1972). In that case, the Ninth Circuit stated that it would attempt to determine the *function* of the tying of the items together, based on "such questions as whether the amalgamation of products resulted in cost savings apart from those reductions in sales expenses and the like normally attendant upon any tie-in, and whether the items are normally sold or used as a unit with fixed proportions." 448 F2d at 48.

[64] ILC Peripherals Leasing Corp v IBM Corp, 448 F Supp 228, 232-34 (ND Cal 1978), *affd,* 636 F2d 1188 (9th Cir), *cert denied,* 452 US 972 (1979); Washington Gas Light Co v Virginia Elec & Power Co, 438 F2d 248, 254 (4th Cir 1971); Brown v Cameron-Brown Co, 1979-1 Trade Cas (CCH) ¶62,656 (ED Va Mar 23, 1979).

[65] Rosebrough Monument Co v Memorial Park Cemetary Assn, 666 F2d 1130, 1140 (8th Cir 1981); Moore v Jas H Matthews & Co, 473 F2d 328, 333 (9th Cir 1972), *after remand,* 550 F2d 1207 (9th Cir 1977); *after second remand,* 682 F2d 830 (9th Cir 1982). In Anderson Foreign Motors, Inc v New England Toyota Distrib, 475 F Supp 973 (D Mass 1979), the court held that industry practice "although relevant, is by no means conclusive." The court explained: "All firms in an oligopolistic market, for example, might use the same economically inefficient, but financially lucrative, tie-in. If the uniformity of the practice were determinative, a clearly suspect tying arrangement would often be insulated from *per se* scrutiny." 475 F Supp at 983. Industrywide practice also has been found in cases which involve requirements imposed by gasoline manufacturers that their dealers purchase oil, antifreeze, tires, batteries or accessories from the manufacturer or from specified third-party manufacturers for sale at the dealers' stations. Atlantic Ref Co v FTC, 381 US 357, 371 (1965); Osborn v Sinclair Ref Co, 286 F2d 832, 835 n 1 (4th Cir 1960), *cert denied,* 366 US 963 (1961), *and see* the Supreme Court discussion in Standard Oil Co v United States, 221 US 1, 58 (1911).

§4.12 —What are examples of items which have been found to be separate products?

Examples of items that have been found to be two separate products include many easy cases where the issue is not significantly discussed, such as real estate and rail service,[66] and closer cases such as leased copiers and copy paper and supplies,[67] credit and the products purchased with credit,[68] motion pictures put out by the same studio,[69] vacuum cleaners and membership in a buying service,[70] cans and can-closing machines,[71] gravestones and tomb sites,[72] an automobile dealership and replacement parts for those automobiles,[73] a lease for aircraft parking space and aircraft fuel, service and maintenance parts,[74] wholesale automobiles and transportation of those automobiles to dealers,[75] a film development franchise and the film processing work,[76] software and central computers,[77] a fast food franchise and the equipment used by the franchise,[78] and salt tablets and dispensing machines.[79]

§4.13 —What are examples of items which have been found not to be separate products?

Examples of items which have been found not to be separate products, but rather one packaged product, are advertising in the morning and afternoon newspapers put out by the same publisher (the product is readership),[80] electricity and the method of delivering that electricity (electrical service),[81] mort-

---

[66] Northern Pac Ry Co v United States, 356 US 1 (1958).

[67] Advance Business Sys & Supply Co v SCM Corp, 415 F2d 55 (4th Cir 1969), *cert denied,* 397 US 920 (1970).

[68] Fortner Enters Inc v United States Steel Corp, 394 US 495 (1969).

[69] United States v Loew's, Inc, 371 US 38 (1962).

[70] Hill v A-T-O, Inc, 535 F2d 1349, 1354 (2d Cir 1976).

[71] United States v American Can Co, 87 F Supp 18 (ND Cal 1949).

[72] Moore v Jas H Matthews & Co, 473 F2d 328 (9th Cir 1972), *after remand,* 550 F2d 1207 (9th Cir 1977), *after second remand,* 682 F2d 830 (9th Cir 1982); Rosebrough Monument Co v Memorial Park Cemetery Assn, 666 F2d 1130 (8th Cir 1981).

[73] United States v Mercedes-Benz of N Am, Inc, 517 F Supp 1369 (ND Cal 1981).

[74] Bell v Cherokee Aviation Corp, 660 F2d 1123 (6th Cir 1981).

[75] Anderson Foreign Motors, Inc v New England Toyota Distrib, Inc, 475 F Supp 973 (D Mass 1979).

[76] Photovest Corp v Fotomat Corp, 606 F2d 704 (7th Cir 1979), *cert denied,* 445 US 917 (1980).

[77] *In re* Data Gen Corp Antitrust Litigation, 490 F Supp 1089 (ND Cal 1980).

[78] Siegel v Chicken Delight, Inc, 448 F2d 43 (9th Cir 1971), *cert denied,* 405 US 955 (1972).

[79] International Salt Co v United States, 332 US 392 (1947).

[80] Times-Picayune Publishing Co v United States, 345 US 594 (1953).

[81] Washington Gas Light Co v Virginia Elec & Power Co, 438 F2d 248 (4th Cir 1971).

gage loans and escrow for taxes and insurance (a financing program),[82] loans and legal services for the customer (same),[83] a condominium and the lease of an adjoining recreational or garage facility (residential housing package),[84] a franchisor's business system, products, and advertising (franchise package),[85] and certain trademarks and the trademarked products (trademark package).[86]

§4.14 —Is Seller's trademark a separate item from the Seller's products?

Courts have reached different conclusions on whether a trademark is a separate item from the Seller's product,[87] and the determination is often made on the basis of the nature of the trademark, the tied product, and the business. The situation generally arises in the franchise or distributor/dealer context, where Buyer obtains the right to use Seller's trademark or trade name, but seeks to use or offer products other than Seller's products. Although there is no widely accepted standard, the courts usually find that trademarks and the products whose source or nature is directly represented by that trademark—e.g., the *Baskin-Robbins* trademark and ice cream made by Baskin-Robbins[88] or the *Shell* trademark and Shell-manufactured gasoline[89]—are a single item. But

---

[82] Brown v Cameron-Brown Co, 1979-1 Trade Cas (CCH) ¶62,656 (ED Va Mar 23, 1979); *see also* BC Recreational Indus v First Natl Bank, 639 F2d 828 (1st Cir 1981).

[83] Forrest v Capitol Bldg & Loan Assn, 385 F Supp 831 (MD La 1973), *affd,* 504 F2d 891 (5th Cir 1974), *cert denied,* 421 US 978 (1975).

[84] Levinson v Maison Grande, Inc, 1981-2 Trade Cas (CCH) ¶64,278 (SD Fla June 10, 1981); Johnson v Nationwide Indus, 450 F Supp 948 (ND Ill 1978).

[85] Kugler v AAMCO Automatic Transmissions, Inc, 337 F Supp 872 (D Minn 1971), *affd,* 460 F2d 1214 (8th Cir 1972).

[86] See **§4.14.**

[87] Trademark is not a separate item: Hamro v Shell Oil Co, 674 F2d 784 (9th Cir 1982); Krehl v Baskin-Robbins Ice Cream Co, 664 F2d 1348 (9th Cir 1982); Principe v McDonald's Corp, 631 F2d 303 (4th Cir 1980), *cert denied,* 451 US 970 (1981); Kugler v AAMCO Automatic Transmissions, Inc, 337 F Supp 872 (D Minn 1971), *affd,* 460 F2d 1214, 1216 (8th Cir 1972). Trademark is a separate item: Siegel v Chicken Delight, Inc, 448 F2d 43, 47 (9th Cir 1971), *cert denied,* 405 US 955 (1972); Northern v McGraw-Edison Co, 542 F2d 1336, 1345 (8th Cir 1976), *cert denied,* 429 US 1097 (1976); Photovest Corp v Fotomat Corp, 606 F2d 704, 722 (7th Cir 1979), *cert denied,* 445 US 917 (1980).

[88] Krehl v Baskin-Robbins Ice Cream Co, 664 F2d 1348, 1354 (9th Cir 1982).

[89] Redd v Shell Oil Co, 524 F2d 1054, 1057 (10th Cir 1975), *cert denied,* 425 US 912 (1976); *see also* FTC v Sinclair Ref Co, 261 US 463, 474 (1923), and Davidson v Crown Central Petroleum Corp, 1977-1 Trade Cas (CCH) ¶61,277 (D Md Dec 28, 1976). In Hamro v Shell Oil Co, 674 F2d 784 (9th Cir 1982), applying California antitrust laws, the Ninth Circuit stated:

> This Court has held that a trademark may constitute a separate tying item. See *Chicken Delight, Inc.* [448 F.2d 43, at 49] But not all trademarks are treated alike. This Court has suggested that trademarks fall into two distinct functional categories: (1) trademarks that identify the source of a product, and (2) trademarks that warrant a certain method of doing business and certain quality standards. 674 F2d at 787.

products whose source is not directly represented by the trademark—e.g., the *Chicken Delight* trademark and the equipment, ingredients and packaging used to make the product[90] or an oil company's trademark and the tires and batteries sold by its gas station dealers[91]—are usually found to be separate products.

It follows from this *source trademark* distinction that if Buyer is merely reselling Seller's product without alteration, so that Seller is essentially using its Buyers as dealers to distribute its trademarked products, the trademark and the product should be considered one item.[92] The courts in such cases reason that the trademark is as much what Buyer is purchasing and reselling as the product itself. Seller is not using a dominant trademark position to compel the purchase of an undesired product, but is really selling a single item—the trademarked product—which is then resold as the same trademarked product by Buyer. In such a situation, the "desirability of the trademark and the quality of the product it represents are so inextricably interrelated in the mind of the consumer as to preclude any finding that the trademark is a separate item for tie-in purposes."[93]

The court concluded that the circumstances in that case were identical to those in Redd v Shell Oil Co, 524 F2d 1054 (10th Cir 1975), *cert denied,* 425 US 912 (1976), and that "the Shell trademark in the case before us, when used in connection with the sale of gasoline, merely identified the source of the gasoline and did not constitute a separate and distinct product." 674 F2d at 788. *But see* Bogosian v Gulf Oil Corp, 561 F2d 434, 449 (3d Cir 1977), *cert denied,* 434 US 1086 (1978) which held that the Buyer might be able to show that the trademark and gasoline were separate products. Even here, though, the court did not reject the *source trademark* distinction, for it noted that much gasoline was traded back and forth between oil companies.

[90] Siegel v Chicken Delight, Inc, 448 F2d 43 (9th Cir 1971), *cert denied,* 405 US 955 (1972). In this case, the court developed the *function of aggregation* approach, which relied on an analysis of whether the items were normally purchased as a unit with fixed proportions and a separate identity. 448 F2d at 48. The court found that in this situation, "the trade-mark simply reflects the good will and quality standards of the enterprise" and that such good will "does not attach to the multitude of separate articles used in the operation of the licensed system in the production of its end product." 448 F2d at 49. *See also* Carpa, Inc v Ward Foods, Inc, 536 F2d 39, 45 (5th Cir 1976).

[91] Osborn v Sinclair Ref Co, 286 F2d 832, 835-36 (4th Cir 1960), *cert denied,* 366 US 963 (1961).

[92] Krehl v Baskin-Robbins Ice Cream Co, 664 F2d 1348 (9th Cir 1982); Redd v Shell Oil Co, 524 F2d 1054 (10th Cir 1975), *cert denied,* 425 US 912 (1976); Hamro v Shell Oil Co, 674 F2d 784 (9th Cir 1982); Principe v McDonald's Corp, 631 F2d 303 (4th Cir 1980), *cert denied,* 451 US 970 (1981).

[93] Krehl v Baskin-Robbins Ice Cream Co, 664 F2d 1348, 1354 (9th Cir 1982). The court noted in *Baskin-Robbins* that "a determination of whether a trademark may appropriately be regarded as a separate product requires an inquiry into the relationship between the trademark and the products allegedly tied to its sale." 664 F2d at 1353. The court noted that where Buyer, in this case a franchise outlet, is "generally responsible for the production and preparation of the system's end product," there is only "a remote connection between the trademark and the products the franchisees [Buyers] are compelled to purchase." But where the goods "are generally manufactured by the franchisor or, as in the present case, by its licensees," then the "trademark serves a different function . . . as a representation of the end-product marketed by the system."

§4.15 —Is a group of franchise-related items a single package or separate items?

An issue related to the trademark question discussed in **§4.14,** and often considered in the same cases, is whether a franchise package, usually consisting of use of Seller's trade name, business methods, advertising, and certain products or packaging, is one package item or several separate items. Again, there is no agreement among the courts, but some general guidelines can be discerned.

In *Principe v McDonald's Corp,*[94] the court stated that where the package consists of the integral components of a business method that is being franchised and each of the components is "an essential ingredient of the franchised system's formula for success," the arrangement should be treated as the sale of one franchise package and not several tied products. This case, and similar cases,[95] lead to the conclusion that the franchise packaged items will not be considered separate items where (1) the package provides Buyer with special benefits in opening and operating the franchise, and (2) the items in the package are only those reasonably necessary to success of a franchise operation, which may include the trade name, the site preparation, the method of operation, advertising, and special goods or materials not adequately obtainable from other sources.

Conversely, where Seller uses the franchise trademark or leases a franchise site as a lever to require Buyer to purchase equipment, supplies, or other items that are generally available from other suppliers in various markets, these items often will be considered separate products from the franchise lease or trademark. In *Siegel v Chicken Delight, Inc,* the Ninth Circuit developed and applied an "aggregation function" analysis which focused on the purpose of the combination of the tied terms, and the court found that there was no legitimate reason for Chicken Delight to require that certain supplies, including cooking machines and ingredients, be purchased from specified sources.[96] The court held that the "sale of the franchise license, with the attendant rights to operate a business . . . in no way requires the forced sale by the franchisor of some or all of the component articles [and] . . . attempts by tie-in to extend the trademark protection to common articles . . . cannot escape antitrust scrutiny."[97]

Accordingly, "because the prohibition of tying arrangements is designed to strike solely at the use of a dominant *desired* product to compel the purchase of a second *undesired* commodity [cite omitted], the tie-in doctrine can have no application where the trademark serves only to identify the alleged tied product." *Id* at 1353-54 (footnotes omitted). *See also* JBL Enters Inc v Jhirmack Enters, Inc, 509 F Supp 357, 377 (ND Cal 1981); Refrigeration Engg Corp v Frick Co, 370 F Supp 702, 711 (WD Tex 1974).

[94] 631 F2d 303, 309 (4th Cir 1980).

[95] Kugler v AAMCO Automatic Transmissions, Inc, 337 F Supp 872, *affd,* 460 F2d 1214 (8th Cir 1972); *In re* 7-Eleven Franchise Antitrust Litigation, 1974-2 Trade Cas (CCH) ¶75,429 (ND Cal Dec 23, 1974).

[96] 448 F2d 43 (9th Cir 1971), *cert denied,* 405 US 955 (1972).

[97] 448 F2d at 49. The products that the franchisor had attempted to tie with the franchise included cooking equipment, dry-mix food items, and packaging bearing the Chicken Delight trademark. The court held that the determinative factor in whether

The Fourth Circuit in *Principe* suggested that the *Chicken Delight* analysis was outdated and that "[f]ranchising has come a long way since the decision in *Chicken Delight*" but noted that tie-ins continued to be found in franchise cases involving equipment and supplies tie-ins.[98]

§4.16 Does it matter that there was no actual sale or lease from Seller to Buyer?

If a potential Buyer simply refuses to lease or buy from Seller because of a tying condition which Seller seeks to impose, there is no violation of §3 of the Clayton Act, because §3 specifically requires a sale, sales contract, or lease.[99] Nor is there generally found to be a violation of §1 of the Sherman Act, which requires an agreement or combination between the parties, although a violation may be found on the basis of concerted action between Seller and some third party with respect to Buyer.[100] Such an incident is not necessarily free of

---

there were separate products or one amalgamated product was the "function of the aggregation." 448 F2d at 48. The court asked whether there were inherent cost savings in the combination and whether the items were normally sold as a unit with fixed proportions. Absent these factors, the court concluded that the function of the tie-in was simply to extend Seller's power to purchases by Buyer of other items. These items were not even manufactured by Chicken Delight, something which the court pointed to in part for its conclusion that the source of these materials was not crucial to the success of the franchise operation. The court further noted that "undisputed testimony at the trial established that other franchisors in fast food businesses similar to that of Chicken Delight sold their licenses separate from the essential supplies." 448 F2d at 48 n 4. Thus, the question that faced the court was not whether the types of supplies or products were essential to operating a Chicken Delight franchise, but rather whether it was essential that those supplies be purchased from Chicken Delight. The court found that other suppliers could equally well supply the type of product, and that

> as long as the system of operation of the franchisees lives up to those quality standards and remains as represented by the mark so that the public is not misled, neither the protection afforded the trademark by law nor the value of the trademark to the licensee depends upon the source of the components.

448 F2d at 49.

[98] 631 F2d at 309 & n 6.

[99] Ron Tonkin Gran Tourismo, Inc v Fiat Distribs, Inc, 637 F2d 1376, 1389 (9th Cir), *cert denied,* 102 S Ct 128 (1981) (§3); Hunter Douglas Corp v Lando Prods, Inc, 215 F2d 372, 376 (9th Cir 1954) (§3); Allied Equip Co v Webber Engg Prod, Inc, 237 F2d 879 (4th Cir 1956) (§3). *See also* Reisner v General Motors Corp, 1977-2 Trade Cas (CCH) ¶61,728 at 72,981 (SD NY Nov 9, 1977), where the court's early suggestion that no sale was needed appears to have been abandoned at some point in the case. Reisner v General Motors, 1982-1 Trade Cas (CCH) ¶64,542 (Feb 8, 1982) (§1, §3).

[100] It has been suggested that §1 may be violated without an actual sale where there is other concerted activity involved in the attempted tying, but presumably this is not a tying violation as such. *See* Unibrand Tire & Prod Co v Armstrong Rubber Co, 1977-2 Trade Cas (CCH) ¶61,710 at 72,894-96 (WD NY Apr 4, 1977). One lower court held that a requirement that Buyer pay a higher price for item A if Buyer did not purchase item B constituted tying, even where Buyer chose to pay the higher price and not to purchase item B, but that decision was reversed. Stop & Save Food Mkts, Inc v Pneumo Corp, 1982-2 Trade Cas (CCH) ¶64,832 (July 2, 1982).

antitrust impact, however, for it may be cited to show that Seller previously imposed a tying condition on that Buyer or on other buyers (who buy both item A and item B), or to show attempted monopolization under Sherman Act §2 or unfair trade practices under §5 of the Federal Trade Commission Act.[101]

The requirement that there be a sale or lease from Seller to Buyer under §3 also excludes transactions with sales agents or other agents or distributors who do not take title to the products, although this conduct may still constitute a violation of §1 or §5.[102] Consignment contracts are treated in the same manner.[103] Of course, where title does pass to Buyer, the mere fact that Buyer is called an agent will not hide the true nature of the transaction.[104]

§4.17 If two separate items are sold or leased by Seller to Buyer, when are those sales or leases considered to be tied?

It is, of course, not unlawful for Seller to sell or lease two or more separate items to Buyer or to try to convince Buyer to purchase item B as well as item A because item B is superior to products offered by competitors. It is only tying where Seller uses its economic power or leverage over item A to condition the sale or lease of desirable item A on the purchase or lease of undesirable item B.

It is not a defense to tying that Seller only requires Buyer to buy item B when no competing supplier offers item B at a lower price. While the anticompetitive effect of such a tying condition is probably less than that of an unlimited tying condition, Seller has nevertheless used its leverage in market A to influence Buyer's decision in market B. Competitors are prevented from competing on an equal footing, and may be discouraged from competing for that Buyer. In both *Northern Pacific Railway v United States*[105] and *International Salt Co v United States,*[106] the Supreme Court did not distinguish this form of tying condition from other tying arrangements. Similarly, a requirement that Buyer purchase some, but not all, of its needs for item B from Seller may still constitute

---

[101] Attempted monopolization under §2 and unfair trade practices under §5 can be found despite the fact that there has not yet been any substantial injury to competition if the conduct engaged in appears likely to result in a monopoly or have an adverse effect on competition if it is allowed to continue.

[102] CBS Business Equip Corp v Underwood Corp, 240 F Supp 413, 425 (SDNY 1964).

[103] FTC v Curtis Publishing Co, 260 US 568, 581 (1923).

[104] Carter Carburetor Corp v FTC, 112 F2d 722, 731 (8th Cir 1940); Standard Fashion Co v Magrane-Houston Co, 258 US 346, 354 (1922).

[105] 356 US 1 (1958).

[106] 332 US 392 (1947). Damage to the plaintiff's business or property is an element of a private antitrust suit, 15 USC §15, and it may be difficult for a plaintiff to show damage in these circumstances.

tying.[107]

§4.18 —If Seller does not expressly tie the purchase of item A to the purchase or lease of item B, but nevertheless induces Buyer to purchase or lease item B, is there tying?

There is no tying if Seller never suggests that the purchase of item B is related to the purchase of item A, and Buyer independently purchases item B from Seller as a matter of free choice.[108] On the other hand, it is not necessary that the tying condition be written in the sale or lease contract, nor even that Seller explicitly refuse to sell item A without item B. Even absent an explicit tying condition, there may be tying if Seller's course of conduct or business practices in effect force or coerce buyer to purchase item B in order to obtain item A.[109] While many courts have stated that no coercion need be shown, particularly where the tying condition is explicit,[110] generally some evidence of coercion has been held by the courts to be necessary to find tying.[111]

---

[107] Osborn v Sinclair Ref Co, 286 F2d 832, 838-39 (4th Cir 1960), *cert denied,* 366 US 963 (1961).

[108] Such conduct is not prohibited by §3 in that it does not involve a condition imposed by Seller, or a reduction in competition and it is not prohibited by §1 in that it does not involve any restraint in trade.

[109] Davis v Marathon Oil Co, 528 F2d 395, 398 (6th Cir 1975), *cert denied,* 429 US 823 (1976) (holding for Seller); Associated Press v Taft-Ingalls Corp, 340 F2d 753, 756 (6th Cir), *cert denied,* 382 US 820 (1965); Advance Business Sys & Supply Co v SCM Corp, 415 F2d 55, 64 (4th Cir 1969), *cert denied,* 397 US 920 (1970): "The presence of the illegal condition may be inferred from an extrinsic course of conduct supplementing the written contract," even if the written contract does not impose any tying condition. Osborn v Sinclair Ref Co, 286 F2d 832, 837 (4th Cir 1960), *cert denied,* 366 US 963 (1961).

[110] Bell v Cherokee Aviation Corp, 660 F2d 1123, 1131 (6th Cir 1981) ("We do not think that coercion is an element of an illegal tying arrangement."); Ogden Food Serv Corp v Mitchell, 614 F2d 1001 (5th Cir 1980); Photovest Corp v Fotomat Corp, 606 F2d 704, 722 (7th Cir 1979), *cert denied,* 445 US 917 (1980) (Express language is sufficient to find tie-in even where Buyer desired the tie-in); Hi-Co Enters, Inc v Con-Agra, Inc, 75 FRD 628, 632 (D Ga 1976); Bogosian v Gulf Oil Corp, 561 F2d 434, 449 (3d Cir 1977), *cert denied,* 434 US 1086 (1978) (once it is shown that there was a tie-in condition expressly stated, "there is no requirement that [Buyer] prove that his purchase was coerced").

[111] The Supreme Court in Times Picayune Publishing Co v United States, 345 US 594, 605 (1953), stated: "The common core of the adjudicated unlawful tying arrangements is the forced purchase of a second distinct commodity . . . ." *See also* Ungar v Dunkin' Donuts of Am, Inc, 531 F2d 1211, 1218-19 (3d Cir), *cert denied,* 429 US 823 (1976); Bob Maxfield, Inc v American Motors Corp, 637 F2d 1033, 1037 (5th Cir), *cert denied,* 454 US 860 (1981); Ogden Food Serv Corp v Mitchell, 614 F2d 1001, 1002 (5th Cir 1980); Kentucky Fried Chicken Corp v Diversified Packaging Corp, 549 F2d 368, 377 (5th Cir 1977); Electroglas, Inc v Dynatex Corp, 497 F Supp 97 (ND Cal 1980);

§4.19 —When will a court find that Seller coerced rather than convinced Buyer to purchase or lease item B in order to get item A?

Seller is certainly permitted to try to convince Buyer to purchase item B as well as item A, but Seller must do so on the basis of the qualities or price of item B, not by use of its power over the supply of item A. Where Buyer purchases item B, not as a matter of free choice, but because Buyer feels compelled to do so in order to obtain item A, the courts will find coercion and tying. As might be expected, the line between persuasion and coercion is not a clear one.

Mere sales pressure to take both item A and item B does not constitute coercion, no matter how strong or obnoxious or dishonest.[112] Seller is not required to notify its uninformed Buyers that they could buy item B from another manufacturer,[113] nor is Seller required to design item A such that it is equally easy for Buyer to purchase item B from another supplier.[114]

On the other hand, the threat or imposition of economic sanctions by Seller with respect to item A if Buyer decides not to buy item B is sufficient to

---

Krehl v Baskin-Robbins Ice Cream Co, 664 F2d 1348, 1352 n 8 (9th Cir 1982) ("some modicum of coercion"); Yentsch v Texaco, Inc, 630 F2d 46 (2d Cir 1980); Unijax Inc v Champion Intl Inc, 1982-2 Trade Cas (CCH) ¶64,814 (2d Cir June 21, 1982); Sports Form Inc v United Press Intl, Inc, 1982-2 Trade Cas (CCH) ¶64,917 (9th Cir Aug 27, 1982).

[112] A manufacturer may use strong persuasion, encouragement, or cajolery to the point of obnoxiousness to induce his retailer to buy his full line of product. An antitrust violation occurs only if goes beyond persuasion and coerces or forces its customer to buy the tied product to obtain the tying product.

Bob Maxfield, Inc v American Motors Corp, 637 F2d 1033, 1037 (5th Cir), *cert denied,* 454 US 860 (1981). This is true even in the case of a Seller with a dominant position over buyer. Ungar v Dunkin' Donuts of Am, Inc, 531 F2d 1211, 1224-25 (3d Cir), *cert denied,* 429 US 823 (1976). A manufacturer who lies to its customers that item B is not available at a lower price is not thereby guilty of tying. Photovest Corp v Fotomat Corp, 606 F2d 704, 723 (7th Cir 1979), *cert denied,* 445 US 917 (1980); NW Controls, Inc v Outboard Marine Corp, 333 F Supp 493, 511-13 (D Del 1971).

[113] EBE, Inc v Dunkin' Donuts of Am, Inc, 387 F Supp 737, 738 (ED Mich 1971); Photovest Corp v Fotomat Corp, 606 F2d 704, 723-24 (7th Cir 1979), *cert denied,* 445 US 917 (1980). However, failure to inform Buyers that the tied items are available individually from Seller as well as in a package may preclude Seller from relying on this option in defense to a tying charge. *In re* Data Gen Corp Antitrust Litigation, 490 F Supp 1089, 1110-11 (ND Cal 1980).

[114] For example, the failure of an automobile manufacturer to provide knockout panels in the dashboard of its cars ordered without the manufacturer-supplied radio did not constitute tying in a suit brought by an independent radio manufacturer. Automatic Radio Mfg Co v Ford Motor Co, 272 F Supp 744, 749 (D Mass 1967), *affd,* 390 F2d 113 (1st Cir), *cert denied,* 391 US 914 (1968). Similarly, design changes in a new line of item A, incompatible with related items B of other suppliers, does not constitute tying. Foremost Pro Color, Inc v Eastman Kodak Co, 1983-1 Trade Cas (CCH) ¶65,239 (9th Cir Feb 23, 1983).

constitute coercion. Such economic sanctions may include substantially increased prices,[115] noncooperation and inadequate supplies or services,[116] or termination of Buyer as a customer for item A.[117] Moreover, some courts have found that Seller's explicit declaration of a tying requirement may be coercive without more, particularly if Seller has sufficient economic power over item A to enforce the requirement, and this causes a substantial number of Buyers to accede to the tying condition despite the apparent undesirability of item B offered by Seller.[118]

§4.20 —If Seller offers item A at a lower cost when item B is also purchased or leased, is there tying?

While some courts have upheld package discounts when both item A and item B are purchased from Seller,[119] other courts have held that charging higher prices for separate items, resulting in economic penalties when Buyer does not purchase item B, may constitute a tie-in,[120] particularly when item A purchased without item B is so much more expensive than item A purchased

---

[115] Advanced Business Sys & Supply Co v SCM Corp, 415 F2d 55, 61-62 (4th Cir 1969), *cert denied,* 397 US 920 (1970); Carter Carburator Corp v FTC, 112 F2d 722, 732 (8th Cir 1940).

[116] Photovest Corp v Fotomat Corp, 606 F2d 704, 724 (7th Cir 1979), *cert denied,* 445 US 917 (1980); Advance Business Sys & Supply Co v SCM Corp, 415 F2d 55, 65-66 (4th Cir 1969), *cert denied,* 397 US 920 (1970).

[117] Advance Business Sys & Supply Co v SCM Corp, 415 F2d 55, 65-66 (4th Cir 1969), *cert denied,* 397 US 920 (1970); Osborn v Sinclair Ref Co, 286 F2d 832, 836 (4th Cir 1960), *cert denied,* 366 US 963 (1961); Atl Ref Co v FTC, 381 US 357 (1965). *But see* Business Equip Center, Ltd v DeJUR-AMSCO Corp, 465 F Supp 775, 784-86 (DDC 1978).

[118] Photovest Corp v Fotomat Corp, 606 F2d 704, 721-25 (7th Cir 1979), *cert denied,* 445 US 917 (1980); Bogosian v Gulf Oil Corp, 561 F2d 434, 449-50 (3d Cir 1977), *cert denied,* 434 US 1086 (1978); Bell v Cherokee Aviation Corp, 660 F2d 1123, 1130-31 (6th Cir 1981); Bogus v American Speech & Hearing Assn, 582 F2d 277, 287 (3d Cir 1978); Hill v A-T-O Inc, 535 F2d 1349, 1355 (2d Cir 1976); Moore v Jas H Matthews & Co, 550 F2d 1207, 1217 (9th Cir 1977), *after second remand,* 682 F2d 830 (9th Cir 1982).

[119] United States v Westinghouse Elec Corp, 471 F Supp 532, 545 (ND Cal 1978), *affd,* 648 F2d 642 (1981); Smith Kline Corp v Eli Lilly & Co, 427 F Supp 1089, 1114 (ED Pa 1976), *affd,* 575 F2d 1056 (3d Cir), *cert denied,* 439 US 838 (1978); Greenville Publishing Co v Daily Reflector, Inc, 496 F2d 391, 400 (4th Cir 1974); Robert's Waikiki U-Drive, Inc v Budget Rent-A-Car, 491 F Supp 1199 (D Hawaii 1980); *see also* Northern Pac Ry v United States, 356 US 1, 6 n 4 (1958).

[120] American Mfrs Mut Ins Co v American Broadcasting-Paramount Theatres, Inc, 388 F2d 272, 283-84 (2d Cir 1967); Advance Business Sys & Supply Co v SCM Corp, 415 F2d 55, 62 (4th Cir 1969), *cert denied,* 397 US 920 (1970) ("Tie-ins are non-coercive and therefore legal, only if the components are separately available to the customer on a basis as favorable as the tie-in arrangement"); Rex Chainbelt, Inc v Harco Prods, Inc, 512 F2d 993, 1002, n 30 (9th Cir), *cert denied,* 423 US 831 (1975); Carter Carburator Corp v FTC, 112 F2d 722, 732 (8th Cir 1940).

as part of a package that Buyers wanting item A are economically compelled to take the package.[121]

Evidence of the purpose and effect of the package discounts will be considered by a court to determine whether there is a tie-in. If most Buyers take just item A, rejecting the package deal and purchasing item B from another seller, or if the package discount is wholly cost justified and there is no independent evidence that Seller is attempting to use its economic power over item A to gain an advantage in the market for item B, a tie-in is unlikely to be found.[122] If, on the other hand, virtually all Buyers take the low-priced package rather than purchasing item B from a competing supplier, or the lower price is totally unjustified, a tie-in may be found.[123]

§4.21 —If Buyer purchases a tied package because it wants to, not because it is coerced to do so by Seller, is there any antitrust risk?

If Buyer agrees to purchase item B as well as item A because it wants the package, not because it is coerced to do so by Seller's tying condition, the courts usually will find no tying,[124] although in the case of an express condition by a Seller with market power, some courts have nevertheless found tying.[125] Such an agreement may violate §1 or §2 of the Sherman Act, if it is in conjunc-

---

[121] United States v Loew's, Inc, 371 US 38, 52, 54-55 (1962); *In re* Data Gen Corp Antitrust Litigation, 490 F Supp 1089, 1111 (ND Cal 1980). The court found that "Data General's pricing structure chills any potential" for independent purchase of the central computer apart from the memory units because it was less expensive to buy the central unit with memory than to buy an entire package including memory. The court stated: "It is horn book law that differential pricing that makes an unbundled option uneconomical will not save the bundled 'alternative' from antitrust liability." George R Whitten, Jr, Inc v Paddock Pool Builders, Inc, 424 F2d 25, 35 n 10 (1st Cir), *cert denied,* 400 US 850 (1970); American Mfrs Mut Ins Co v American Broadcasting-Paramount Theatres, Inc, 388 F2d 272, 283 (2d Cir 1967).

[122] Ungar v Dunkin' Donuts of Am, Inc, 531 F2d 1211, 1225 (3d Cir), *cert denied,* 429 US 823 (1976); American Mfrs Mut Ins Co v American Broadcasting-Paramount Theatres, Inc, 446 F2d 1131, 1137 (2d Cir 1971), *cert denied,* 404 US 1063 (1972).

[123] Northern Pac Ry v United States, 356 US 1, 7-8.

[124] "[N]o tying arrangement can possibly exist unless the person aggrieved can establish that he has been required to purchase something which he does not want to take." Capital Temporaries, Inc v Olsten Corp, 506 F2d 658, 662 (2d Cir 1974); American Mfrs Mut Ins Co v American Broadcasting-Paramount Theatres, Inc, 446 F2d 1131, 1137 (2d Cir 1971), *cert denied,* 404 US 1063 (1972); Blatt v Lorenz-Schneider Co, 1981-1 Trade Cas (CCH) ¶63,982 (SDNY Apr 28, 1981); Petroleum For Contractors, Inc v Mobil Oil Corp, 493 F Supp 320, 323-26 (EDNY 1980).

[125] Photovest Corp v Fotomat Corp, 606 F2d 704, 725 (7th Cir 1979), *cert denied,* 445 US 917 (1980), holding that the buyers' desire for a complete package of products did not rebut the presence of an illegal tying arrangement; *see also,* United States v Mercedes-Benz of N Am, Inc, 517 F Supp 1369, 1384 (ND Cal 1981);

tion with other activities by Seller designed to have an anticompetitive or monopolizing effect,[126] and, because such an agreement seems contrary to the legitimate business interests of Buyer, it may be subject to particular scrutiny. Even a voluntary agreement to buy item B only from Seller, if over an extended period of time, may constitute exclusive dealing.[127]

§4.22 Must Seller have economic power or leverage over the market in item A to have tying?

The courts have frequently held that Seller must have sufficient economic power or leverage in the market for item A to appreciably restrain free competition in the market for item B in order for the tying to be per se unreasonable or unlawful, particularly under §1.[128] Logically, Seller can require Buyer to purchase item B in order to obtain item A only if Seller has sufficient economic control over the market in item A to make the condition effective. If Seller tries to impose a tying condition, but does not have sufficient economic power to enforce it, Buyer's decision to purchase item B from Seller is not the result of the ineffectual tying condition, but rather is Buyer's free choice.[129]

Arguably, sufficient economic power to impose tying is required only in §1 cases, not in §3 cases. The Supreme Court in *Times-Picayune Publishing Co v United States* held that in order to find that a tying arrangement violates §3 *either* economic power over item A *or* an effect on a substantial volume of commerce in item B is sufficient.[130] Under this standard, a tying condition would violate §3 even if Seller did not have sufficient economic power over item A as long as the tying condition might affect a substantial amount of commerce in the market for item B. The Supreme Court held that both elements—tying power *and* effect on a substantial amount of commerce—are necessary to find a per

---

[126] Greenville Publishing Co v Daily Reflector, Inc, 496 F2d 391, 400 (4th Cir 1974).

[127] See **§4.40.**

[128] United States Steel Corp v Fortner Enters, Inc, 429 US 610 (1977); Foster v Maryland State Savings & Loan Assn, 590 F2d 928, 931 (DC Cir 1978), *cert denied,* 439 US 1071 (1979); Hill v A-T-O, Inc, 535 F2d 1349, 1353 (2d Cir 1976); Northern v McGraw-Edison Co, 542 F2d 1336, 1345 (8th Cir 1976), *cert denied,* 429 US 1097 (1977); Phillips v Crown Central Petroleum Corp, 602 F2d 616 (4th Cir 1979), *cert denied,* 444 US 1074 (1980); Sulmeyer v Coca Cola Co, 515 F2d 835, 844 (5th Cir 1975); Kypta v McDonald's Corp, 671 F2d 1282, 1284 (11th Cir 1982).

[129] Northern Pac Ry v United States, 356 US 1, 7-8. *See* Hill v A-T-O, Inc, 535 F2d 1349, 1353 (2d Cir 1976); Hyde v Jefferson Parish Hosp Dist No 2, 1982-2 Trade Cas (CCH) ¶64,945 (5th Cir Sept 20, 1982).

[130] 345 US 594, 608-09 (1953). This distinction has been noted in several lower court cases, including: Moore v Jas H Matthews & Co, 550 F2d 1207, 1214 (9th Cir 1977), *after second remand,* 682 F2d 830 (9th Cir 1982); Advance Business Sys & Supply Co v SCM Corp, 415 F2d 55, 61 (4th Cir 1969), *cert denied,* 397 US 920 (1970).

se violation of §1.[131]

But, although still arguably viable[132] this supposed distinction between §1 and §3 is usually without any practical effect and is often ignored or said not to exist,[133] for if Seller does not have the power to enforce its tying condition, it will be ineffective. If it is ineffective, it can have no substantial effect on commerce in item B, and Seller can argue *either* lack of tying power or lack of effect on commerce if the suit is brought under §3, or *both* lack of tying power and lack of effect on commerce if the suit is brought under §1. If the tying is widely effective, on the other hand, many courts consider this strong evidence of tying power, again minimizing the distinction between §3 and §1.[134]

§4.23 —What level of power must Seller have in the market for item A in order to have tying power?

It is not necessary for Seller to have a monopoly in the market for item A in order to have tying power. Although the Supreme Court initially indicated that monopoly power was necessary under Sherman Act 1,[135] this standard was overruled in *Northern Pacific Railway v United States.*[136] It is now generally accepted that Seller need not even have dominant power over the market for item A in order to have tying power. It has been held sufficient that Seller have a special or unique power over certain Buyers in the market for item A that permits Seller to impose the tying condition with respect to undesirable item

---

[131] See **§4.03.**

[132] Reisner v General Motors Corp, 511 F Supp 1167, 1176-77 (SDNY 1981), *affd,* 671 F2d 91 (2d Cir), *cert denied,* 103 S Ct 130 (1982); Moore v Jas H Matthews & Co, 550 F2d 1207, 1214 (9th Cir 1977), *after second remand,* 682 F2d 830 (9th Cir 1982); Sargent-Welch Scientific Co v Ventron Corp, 567 F2d 701 708 n 9 (7th Cir 1977).

[133] Many courts simply ignore this difference, stating that the same standards apply for per se determinations under both §3 and §1. The Ninth Circuit has held that the elements for the two statutes are "virtually identical." Moore v Jas H Matthews & Co, 550 F2d 1207, 1214 (9th Cir 1977), *after second remand,* 682 F2d 830 (9th Cir 1982). The Fifth Circuit reached the same conclusion in Spartan Grain & Mill Co v Ayers, 581 F2d 419, 428 (5th Cir 1978). *See also* Colorado Pump & Supply Co v Febco, Inc, 472 F2d 637 (10th Cir 1972), *cert denied,* 411 US 987 (1973); Hirsh v Martindale-Hubbell, Inc, 674 F2d 1343 (9th Cir 1982); Kaiser Aluminum & Chem Sales, Inc v Avondale Shipyards, Inc, 677 F2d 1045 (5th Cir 1982); Susser v Carvel Corp, 332 F2d 505 (2d Cir 1964), *cert dismissed,* 381 US 125 (1965); and Heatransfer Corp v Volkswagenwerk, AG, 553 F2d 964 (5th Cir 1977), *cert denied,* 434 US 1087 (1978); Electroglas, Inc v Dynatex Corp, 497 F Supp 97 (ND Cal 1980); *In re* Data Gen Corp Antitrust Litigation, 490 F Supp 1089 (ND Cal 1980).

[134] Fortner Enters, Inc v United States Steel Corp, 394 US 495, 503-04 (1969); Advance Business Sys & Supply Co v SCM Corp, 415 F2d 55 (4th Cir 1969), *cert denied,* 397 US 920 (1970); Reisner v General Motors Corp, 1977-2 Trade Cas ¶61,728 at 72,980 (SDNY 1977).

[135] Times-Picayune Publishing Co v United States, 345 US 594 (1953).

[136] 356 US 1 (1958).

B. This rejection of automatic tests for tying power and the substitution of tests which require an analysis of Seller's actual power over the market was expressed by the Supreme Court in the two *Fortner* decisions.

The Supreme Court held in *Fortner I*[137] that there is tying power, "even though the power falls far short of dominance," where "the seller has the power to raise prices [for item A], or impose other burdensome terms such as a tie-in [with Item B], with respect to an appreciable number of buyers."[138] The Court stated that tying power exists "whenever the seller can exert some power over some of the buyers in the market, even if his power is not complete over them and over all other buyers in the market."[139]

The Supreme Court in the *Fortner II* decision appeared to limit *Fortner I*, stating that the ability to successfully impose a tying condition would be evidence of tying power only where there was no other explanation for Buyer's decision to purchase item B. The court stressed that there was tying power only where Seller has some special or "unique" advantage within the market for item A "not shared by his competitors."[140] This special advantage in the market for item A would not, according to the Court, include advantages based on a willingness to take a lower profit on item A.[141] Under *Fortner II,* therefore, it appears that tying power exists only where Seller has a position in the item A market that cannot easily be matched by competing suppliers.

Subsequent court decisions have struggled to apply the standards set forth by the Supreme Court in *Fortner I* and *Fortner II.* It has been suggested, in the wake of the *Fortner* decisions, that there are three alternative indicia of tying power: (1) Seller has market dominance, (2) Seller has a product sufficiently unique that it has some advantage not shared by competitors in the market, or (3) a substantial number of customers have accepted the undesirable tie-in product, but only where there is no other explanation for their willingness to do so (e.g., the desirability of item B).[142] With respect to the third indicator, there is no clear rule on what constitutes a sufficient *other explanation* for acceptance of the tie-in. *Fortner II* suggests that if Buyers purchase both item A and item B because of an overall price advantage of doing so, this may be a sufficient other explanation for their willingness to accept the tie-in.

---

137 Fortner Enters, Inc v United States Steel Corp, 394 US 495 (1969).

138 *Id* 504.

139 *Id* 503.

140 United States Steel Corp v Fortner Enters, Inc, 429 US 610, 630 (1977).

141 *Id* 621-22.

142 *See, e.g.,* Hyde v Jefferson Parish Hosp Dist No 2, 1982-2 Trade Cas (CCH) ¶ 64,945 (5th Cir Sept 20, 1982); Metrix Warehouse, Inc v Daimler-Benz, Aktiengesellschaft, 1982-2 Trade Cas (CCH) ¶64,861 (DM June 4, 1982); United States v Mercedes-Benz of N Am, Inc, 517 F Supp 1369 (ND Cal 1981); both cases cite *Fortner II* for these three alternative indicia of tying power (see 429 US at 619 n 7, 620-21). For other post-*Fortner* discussions of tying power, *see* Rosebrough Monument Co v Memorial Park Cemetary Assn, 666 F2d 1130, 1142 (8th Cir 1981); Bell v Cherokee Aviation Corp, 660 F2d 1123, 1127-28 (6th Cir 1981); Kingsport Motors, Inc v Chrysler Motors Corp, 644 F2d 566, 571 (6th Cir 1981).

It should be observed that, whatever standards are used, the courts' rulings on tying power often appear to be result-oriented and at times in direct conflict with one another. Some courts have found tying power without going much beyond the fact that many Buyers accepted the tying condition.[143] Other courts have found lack of tying power, despite substantial Buyer acceptance of tying, apparently as a means of avoiding the harsh per se rule where the tying appears to be justified or have procompetitive results.[144]

§4.24 —What are recent examples of tying power?

Courts have found tying power in cases involving the following tying items (item A): land adjacent to an airport,[145] all cemetery lots in one-quarter of the city's cemeteries;[146] the *Fotomat* trademark and franchise;[147] desirable mobile home sites;[148] the *Mister Softee* trademark;[149] and surgical services offered at a hospital[150]

§4.25 —What are recent examples of no tying power?

Courts have found that tying power does not necessarily exist in cases involving the following tying items (item A): software for computers;[151] Texaco gasoline and stations;[152] the Jhirmack trademark[153] and components for Opel

---

[143] Lessig v Tidewater Oil Co, 327 F2d 459 (9th Cir), *cert denied,* 377 US 993 (1964); Advance Business Sys & Supply Co v SCM Corp, 415 F2d 55, 68-69 (4th Cir 1969), *cert denied,* 397 US 920 (1970). The court in United States v Mercedes-Benz of N Am, Inc, 517 F Supp 1369, 1384-85 (ND Cal 1981) found that this was an insufficient basis for finding tying power.

[144] *See, e.g.,* Yentsch v Texaco Inc, 630 F2d 46, 58-59 (2d Cir 1980); Ungar v Dunkin' Donuts of Am, Inc, 531 F2d 1211, 1222-25 (3d Cir), *cert denied,* 429 US 823 (1976).

[145] Bell v Cherokee Aviation Corp, 660 F2d 1123, 1129-30 (6th Cir 1981).

[146] Rosebrough Monument Co v Memorial Park Cemetary Assn, 666 F2d 1130, 1143 (8th Cir 1981).

[147] Photovest Corp v Fotomat Corp, 606 F2d 704, 725 (7th Cir 1979), *cert denied,* 445 US 917 (1980).

[148] Suburban Mobile Homes, Inc v AMFAC Communities, Inc, 1980-1 Trade Cas (CCH) ¶63,040 (Cal Ct App Jan 30, 1980).

[149] Esposito v Mister Softee, Inc, 1980-1 Trade Cas (CCH) ¶63,089 (EDNY Dec 14, 1979).

[150] Hyde v Jefferson Parish Hosp Dist No 2, 1982-2 Trade Cas (CCH) ¶64,945 (5th Cir Sept 20, 1982).

[151] *In re* Data Gen Corp Antitrust Litigation, 490 F Supp 1089, 1111-16 (ND Cal 1980) (question of fact for the jury).

[152] Yentsch v Texaco, Inc, 630 F2d 46, 58-59 (2d Cir 1980).

[153] JBL Enters, Inc v Jhirmack Enters, Inc, 509 F Supp 357 (ND Cal 1981), *relevant market and defendant's market share determined,* 519 F Supp 1084 (ND Cal 1981), *affd,* 698 F2d 1011 (9th Cir 1983).

automobiles.[154]

§4.26 —Is there tying power if item A is covered by a patent, copyright, or trademark?

The courts have not hesitated to find that products covered by patents or copyrights bestow on Seller tying power, although one court has suggested that this need not always be the case.[155] Several courts have held that the possession of a trademark gives Seller presumed tying power.[156] These courts have stated that the trademark is unique and confers a special power on Seller over an individual Buyer.[157]

However, many decisions have rejected such an automatic test, and instead analyze the true nature of the market and of competition in trademark or franchise cases.[158] Where there are many competing similar trademarks or franchises in the market and there is no strong reason why Buyer need choose one particular trademark or franchise system over another, the courts have generally found a lack of economic power sufficient to force Buyers to purchase unwanted items in other markets.[159] In other cases, such analysis has led

---

[154] Reisner v General Motors Corp, 511 F Supp 1167, 1179 (SDNY 1981).

[155] The Supreme Court has consistently found that patents and copyrights confer tying power on the seller. International Salt Co v United States, 332 US 392 (1947); United States v Loew's, Inc, 371 US 38 (1962); United States v Paramount Pictures, Inc, 334 US 131 (1948). The Northern District of California in *In re* Data Gen Corp Antitrust Litigation, 490 F Supp 1089, 1111-1116 (ND Cal 1980) questioned whether this rule was automatic with respect to copyright patents, suggesting that tying power was a question of fact to be determined by the jury.

[156] Siegel v Chicken Delight, Inc, 448 F2d 43, 50 (9th Cir 1971), *cert denied,* 405 US 955 (1972); *see also* Warriner Hermetics, Inc v Copeland Refrigeration Corp, 463 F2d 1002, 1015 (5th Cir), *cert denied,* 409 US 1086 (1972); Detroit City Dairy, Inc v Kowalski Sausage Co, 393 F Supp 453, 467-70 (D Mich 1975); Falls Church Bratwursthaus, Inc v Bratwursthaus Management Corp, 354 F Supp 1237, 1240 (ED Va 1973).

[157] The court in Siegel v Chicken Delight, Inc, 448 F2d 43, 50 (9th Cir 1971), *cert denied,* 405 US 955 (1972), provided the following reasoning for its conclusion:

> Just as the patent or copyright forecloses competitors from offering the distinctive product on the market, so the registered trade-mark presents a legal barrier against competition. . . . Accordingly we see no reason why the presumption that exists in the case of the patent and copyright does not equally apply to the trade-mark.

[158] Capital Temporaries, Inc v Olsten Corp, 506 F2d 658, 663-64 (2d Cir 1974); Susser v Carvel Corp, 332 F2d 505, 519 (2d Cir 1964), *cert dismissed,* 381 US 125 (1965); Anderson v Home Style Stores, Inc, 58 FRD 125, 129 (ED Pa 1972); *see also* discussion in United States v Mercedes-Benz of N Am, Inc, 517 F Supp 1369, 1386-87 (D Cal 1981); Levinson v Maison Grande, Inc, 1981-2 Trade Cas (CCH) ¶64,278 (SD Fla June 10, 1981); JBL Enters, Inc v Jhirmack Enters, Inc, 509 F Supp 357 (ND Cal 1981), *relevant* market and defendant's market share determined, 519 F Supp 1084 (ND Cal 1981), *affd,* 698 F2d 1011 (9th Cir 1983).

[159] JBL Enters, Inc v Jhirmack Enters, Inc, 509 F Supp 357 (ND Cal 1981); Susser v Carvel Corp, 332 F2d 505, 519 (2d Cir 1964), *cert dismissed,* 381 US 125 (1965); Yentsch v Texaco, Inc, 630 F2d 46, 58-59 (2d Cir 1980).

to a finding of tying power, particularly where the trademark or franchise is so special that Buyers pay a premium or undertake additional burdens in order to obtain it, or where other conditions exist that give Seller a strong bargaining advantage with respect to use of the trademark.[160]

§4.27 If a tying arrangement affects only a small amount of commerce or competition, is it lawful?

Section 3 does not prohibit tying arrangements unless they "may . . . substantially lessen competition" in item B, and §1 prohibits only tying arrangements that unreasonably restrain trade in item B. Under the established per se test, however, the effect on competition question is not reached; the question is simply whether a *not insubstantial* amount of *commerce* in item B is affected.[161] Moreover, virtually any tying arrangement worth litigating may be found to have a sufficient effect on commerce to meet the per se requirement.[162] The Supreme Court in *Fortner I* confirmed prior holdings that as long as the amount of business in item B which is foreclosed to competitors by the tie is not merely de minimis, it is substantial.[163] The Supreme Court held in *United States v Loew's*[164] that $60,000 in foreclosed sales is not insubstantial, and lower courts have found that amounts as low as $50,000 are not insubstantial.[165]

The relevant effect on commerce under the per se test is the total volume of sales subject to the tying policy of Seller, not merely the sales to the particular plaintiff Buyer bringing suit.[166] Thus, the court considers the total volume of purchases of item B foreclosed by the tying practice of Seller.[167] Accordingly, Sellers are rarely able to successfully defend tying on the basis of its limited effect on the market in cases where the court is using a traditional per se analysis.

In some circumstances, such as where only one Buyer is affected,[168] or where

---

[160] Carpa, Inc v Ward Foods, Inc, 536 F2d 39, 48-49 (5th Cir 1976); Esposito v Mister Softee, Inc, 1980-1 Trade Cas (CCH) ¶63,089 (EDNY Dec 14, 1979). *But see* Golden West Insulation, Inc v Stardust Inv Corp, 1980-81 Trade Cas (CCH) ¶63,616 (Or Ct App July 28, 1980).

[161] See **§§4.02, 4.03, 4.22.**

[162] As has been observed above, any distinction between the adverse effect on competition necessary under §1 and that necessary under §3 is often said to have disappeared for most practical purposes. See **§4.03.**

[163] Fortner Enters, Inc v United States Steel Corp, 394 US 495, 501 (1969).

[164] 371 US 38, 49 (1962).

[165] AAMCO Automatic Transmissions, Inc v Tayloe, 407 F Supp 430, 436 (ED Pa 1976).

[166] Fortner Enters, Inc v United States Steel, 394 US 495, 502 (1969).

[167] *Id.*

[168] Reisner v General Motors Corp, 511 F Supp 1167, 1178 (DNY 1981); Beefy Trail Inc v Beefy King Intl, Inc, 348 F Supp 799, 806-07 (MD Fla 1972).

there are no competing sellers of item B,[169] some courts have looked beyond the question whether the tie-in effects a substantial amount of commerce to conclude that there has been no adverse effect on competition and no violation of §1 or §3. Such an analysis was also performed in a few cases where the per se requirements were not met, and the tying was then tested under the rule of reason. A more widespread emphasis on competitive injury is evidenced in recent vertical restraint cases such as *GTE Sylvania*[170] and a few tying cases.[171] Although adverse effect on *competition* is a statutorily required element under §3 and §1, the per se rule ignores this element—presuming that tying will *always* have such an effect where there is tying power and a substantial amount of commerce is affected. This presumption has been questioned, particularly where Seller is new or is struggling,[172] where the market is highly decentralized,[173] or where tying promotes interbrand competition.[174] The courts and authorities are increasingly considering the competitive effect of a tie-in before determining if it is unlawful.[175]

§4.28 Can tying be justified in certain cases?

Although tying is frequently described by the courts as a per se violation of the antitrust laws, in many cases the courts have not in fact applied such a strict standard, holding that there are circumstances under which tying is justified as a reasonable and proper business practice.[176] In these cases, the courts have found that strong legitimate business justifications outweigh the limited or

---

[169] Community Builders, Inc v City of Phoenix, 1981 Trade Cas (CCH) ¶64,207 at 73,780 (9th Cir Aug 3, 1981); Driskell v Dallas Cowboys Football Club, Inc, 498 F2d 321, 323 (8th Cir 1974); Coniglio v Highwood Serv, Inc, 495 F2d 1286, 1289 (2d Cir), *cert denied,* 419 US 1022 (1974).

[170] Continental TV, Inc v GTE Sylvania, 433 US 36 (1977).

[171] *See* Yentsch v Texaco, Inc, 630 F2d 46, 57-58 (2d Cir 1980); *compare* Sandles v Ruben, 89 FRD 635 (SD Fla 1981), *with* Fifth Moorings Condominium, Inc v Shere, 81 FRD 712 (SD Fla 1979). In *Sandles,* the court stated that, in order to have tying, there must be a showing of anticompetitive effects in the tied market. In the earlier case, the court had used the traditional three-step test—tying, economic power, and substantial volume of business affected.

[172] See **§4.31.**

[173] *See, e.g.,* Susser v Carvel Corp, 332 F2d 505, 518-19 (2d Cir 1964), *cert dismissed,* 381 US 125 (1965); Yentsch v Texaco, Inc, 630 F2d 46, 57-59 (2d Cir 1980).

[174] *See, e.g.,* FEL Publications Ltd v Catholic Bishop, 1982-1 Trade Cas (CCH) ¶64,632 (7th Cir Mar 25, 1982).

[175] *See* FEL Publications Ltd v Catholic Bishop, 1982-1 Trade Cas (CCH) ¶64,632 (7th Cir Mar 25, 1982); Metrix Warehouse, Inc v Daimler-Benz, Aktiengesellschaft, 1982-2 Trade Cas (CCH) ¶64,861 (DMd June 4, 1982). This is, in effect, an approach which is consistent with the philosophy expressed in Continental TV, Inc v GTE Sylvania, 433 US 36 (1977). This philosophy has been increasingly adopted with respect to other vertical restraints by the enforcement agencies and the courts.

[176] Susser v Carvel Corp, 332 F2d 505, 519-20 (2d Cir 1964), *cert dismissed,* 381 US 125 (1965).

nonexistent adverse impact on competition in the market for item B, or that the business justification will foster competition. Courts have found that tying is justified because the tying condition is needed to assure the proper or safe use of item A[177] to protect the goodwill of Seller's trademark or tradename[178] or to establish a new competitive company providing consumer benefits[179] or because Seller is offering a franchise package that will result in more competitors in the market.[180] In each instance, however, the tie-in is found justified only if there is no less restrictive alternative adequate to achieve the purpose served by the tie-in.[181]

Because the justification is always balanced against any adverse effect on competition, it is more likely that tying will be found acceptable where the tying is performed by a small Seller, rather than a large, dominant Seller.[182] For the same reason, tying is more likely to be found to be reasonable and justified where the amount of item B tied does not represent a significant portion of the market for products such as item B.[183] Seller may also suggest other reasons why the tying is not likely to have a significant anticompetitive effect, given the nature of the market and Seller's business practices.[184]

In some of those instances where it appears that the tying is justified because it does not have any significant adverse impact on competition or has a procompetitive effect, the courts, rather than overcoming the per se rule by finding the tying justified, have simply found that one of the necessary elements of tying is missing. In some instances, the courts have found that only one package of products was involved, rather than separate tied products;[185] in

---

[177] See **§4.29.**

[178] See **§4.30.**

[179] See **§4.31.**

[180] See **§4.32.**

[181] See **§§4.29-4.32.**

[182] Given that one of the purposes of the prohibition on tying is to prevent a monopolist or dominant Seller in one market from using that power to extend its monopoly or dominance into a second market, it is not surprising or illogical that the courts treat large, dominant Sellers in a different manner, generally, than small, struggling Sellers. A good example of the importance of this difference is presented in United States v Jerrold Elecs Corp, 187 F Supp 545 (ED Pa 1960), *affd per curiam,* 365 US 567 (1961), where the court openly stated that it would apply a different rule during the time period when Jerrold was a new struggling small company in an industry populated by giants such as RCA than it would apply for a later period, when Jerrold had become the leading company in the relevant market and exerted considerable power over that market.

[183] Of course, this factor is often used before the justification stage to find either that Seller does not have sufficient economic power in the market to compel tying or that there is no coercion. See **§§4.19, 4.23;** *see also* JBL Enters, Inc v Jhirmack Enters, Inc, 509 F Supp 357, 377-79 (ND Cal 1981).

[184] See, e.g., Beefy Trail Inc v Beefy King Intl Inc, 348 F Supp 799, 806, 07 (MD Fla 1972); FEL Publications, Ltd v Catholic Bishop, 1982-1 Trade Cas (CCH) ¶64,632 (7th Cir Mar 25, 1982).

[185] See **§4.13.** In United States v Mercedes-Benz of N Am, Inc, 517 F Supp 1369 (ND

other instances the courts have found lack of tying power or coercion.[186]

§4.29 Can tying be justified because use of item B is necessary to the proper functioning of item A, and use of another item might undermine Seller's reputation?

There may be strong and commendable business reasons for Seller to insist that a secondary product (i.e., item B) necessary to the proper functioning of the primary product (i.e., item A) is purchased and used by Buyer. Where it is impossible or impractical to assure that adequate secondary products are used by Buyer without requiring that buyer purchase those items from Seller or a related party, tying may be justified. For example, Seller may require Buyer to purchase special components and services in connection with Buyer's purchase of a new complex community television antenna, [187] or require Buyer to purchase a patented unloading device in connection with a special-design silo.[188] Such tying is particularly justified where use of other secondary products in connection with item A has led to customer dissatisfaction.[189]

The Supreme Court in *Standard Oil Co v United States* held that this justification will not be available, however, where less restrictive alternatives such as product specifications would be sufficient to assure that adequate secondary products are used by Buyer.[190] Therefore, unless specifications for the product

---

Cal 1981), the court noted that "rather than espousing wholesale rejection of a *per se* standard to tying arrangements, courts often reconcile this standard with business reality by finding that two products are not tied, that they are not separate products, or that a business justification exists for a tying arrangement." *Id* 1377-78 n 9.

[186] See **§§4.19, 4.23.**

[187] United States v Jerrold Elecs Corp, 187 F Supp 545 (D Pa 1960), *aff'd per curiam,* 365 US 567 (1961); *see also* Pugh v Mobil Oil Corp, 533 F Supp 169 (SD Tex 1982) (gasoline pumps).

[188] Dehydrating Process Co v AO Smith Corp, 292 F2d 653 (1st Cir), *cert denied,* 368 US 931 (1961).

[189] United States v Jerrold Elecs Corp, 187 F Supp 545, 556-57 (D Pa 1960), *aff'd per curiam,* 365 US 567 (1961); Dehydrating Process Co v AO Smith Corp, 292 F2d 653, 656-57 (1st Cir), *cert denied,* 368 US 931 (1961); *see also* Teleflex Industrial Prods, Inc v Brunswick Corp, 293 F Supp 106, 110 (ED Pa 1968).

[190] The Supreme Court stated:

> "The justification . . . the protection of the good will of the manufacturer of the tying device—fails in the usual situation because specification of the type and quality of the product to be used in connection with the tying device is protection enough. If the manufacturer's brand of the tied product is in fact superior to that of competitors, the buyer will presumably choose it anyway. The only situation, indeed, in which the protection of good will may necessitate the use of tying clauses is where specifications for a substitute would be so detailed that they could not practicably be supplied.

337 US 293, 306 (1949). *See also* IBM v United States, 298 US 131, 138-40 (1936); Moore v Jas H Matthews & Co, 550 F2d 1207, 1217 (9th Cir 1977), *after second remand,* 682 F2d 830 (9th Cir 1982).

would be inadequate[191] or would reveal trade secrets,[192] tying is not permitted. Another less restrictive alternative that may be available is a list of approved suppliers or a certification arrangement for items made by other suppliers.[193] If this alternative would be adequate, a court may rule that it should be used rather than tying.

The justification also fails where use of item B is not really necessary for the proper functioning of item A.[194] The mere claim that Seller is able to produce a higher quality item B than competitors is not a sufficient justification for tying where similar items are offered by competitors and are adequate.[195] Nor is the claim that Seller must install or service its item A in order to maintain uniformity or control a sufficient justification where there is no evidence that others could not do an adequate job.[196]

---

[191] Where specifications would be so detailed or otherwise probably would *not* permit production of adequate products by other suppliers, they would not be considered adequate and tying may be justified. Standard Oil Co v United States, 337 US 293, 306 (1949). Siegel v Chicken Delight, Inc, 448 F2d 43, 51 (9th Cir 1971), *cert denied,* 405 US 955 (1972); Northern v McGraw-Edison Co, 542 F2d 1336, 1347 (8th Cir 1976), *cert denied,* 429 US 1097 (1977). Also, where specifications would be so massive as to be burdensome on Seller, it may not be required to choose this alternative. Susser v Carvel Corp, 332 F2d 505, 519-20 (2d Cir 1964), *cert dismissed,* 381 US 125 (1965). A very good discussion of the adequacy of specifications is contained in United States v Mercedes-Benz of N Am, Inc, 517 F Supp 1369, 1388-90 (ND Cal 1981). There is some question whether specifications would be adequate where they might be ignored by customers. *Compare* United States v Jerrold Elecs Corp, 187 F Supp 545, 556-57 (D Pa 1960), *affd per curiam,* 365 US 567 (1961) *with In re* Data Gen Corp Antitrust Litigation, 490 F Supp 1089, 1122-24 (ND Cal 1980).

[192] *Cf.* Susser v Carvel Corp, 332 F2d 505, 519 n2 (2d Cir 1964), *cert dismissed,* 381 US 125 (1965); Siegel v Chicken Delight, Inc, 448 F2d 43, 51 n9 (9th Cir 1971), *cert denied,* 405 US 955 (1972).

[193] United States v Mercedes-Benz of N Am, Inc, 517 F Supp 1369, 1389 (ND Cal 1981).

[194] For example, in NW Controls, Inc v Outboard Marine Corp, 333 F Supp 493, 505-06 (D Del 1971), the court observed that there was an absence of evidence of any customer dissatisfaction when the defendant's engines were used with control cables manufactured by other suppliers. The court therefore concluded that the tie-in with the defendant's control cables was not justified. The court found that specifications would have been adequate.

[195] Moore v Jas H Matthews & Co, 550 F2d 1207, 1217 (9th Cir 1977), *after second remand,* 682 F2d 830 (9th Cir 1982); United States v Mercedes-Benz of N Am, Inc, 517 F Supp 1369, 1389 (ND Cal 1981); *In re* Data Gen Corp Antitrust Litigation, 490 F Supp 1089, 1122-24 (ND Cal 1980); Standard Oil Co of Cal v United States, 337 US 293 (1949). The Supreme Court stated in *Standard Oil Co* that "if the manufacturer's brand of the tied product is in fact superior to that of competitors, the Buyer will presumably choose it anyway." 337 US at 306.

[196] Moore v Jas H Matthews & Co, 550 F2d 1207 (9th Cir 1977), *after second remand,* 682 F2d 830 (9th Cir 1982); Advance Business Sys Supply Co v SCM Corp, 415 F2d 55, 68-69 (4th Cir 1969), *cert denied,* 397 US 920 (1970).

§4.30 —Can tying be justified because sale of another product in place of item B might undermine Seller's goodwill or reputation?

A Seller has a legitimate business interest in protecting its goodwill, reputation, or trademark, and it is in the interest of consumers to be able to rely on Seller's name or trademark. Such protection of goodwill and the consumer's expectations will often promote full and fair competition. Therefore, despite the supposed per se rule against tying, tying may be justified where Buyer is using Seller's name or trademark to attract customers, and where tying of the trademark and the product is necessary to protect goodwill and avoid the confusion or deception of consumers that might occur if the items or services sold under Seller's name or trademark are not in fact the products represented by that name or trademark.[197]

For example, a Buyer who seeks a license to use the Coca-Cola name may be required by Coca-Cola to also buy the Coca-Cola product.[198] A Buyer who leases a gasoline service station with Seller's brand name on the station's signs and pumps may be required to purchase that Seller's brand of gasoline.[199] A Buyer (motel) that advertises that it uses Seller's mattresses in order to attract customers may be required by Seller to purchase those mattresses.[200] A Buyer that uses the Carvel Ice Cream trademark may be required to purchase that ice cream.[201] In each of these instances, the Sellers have required that those products directly represented by the trademark be purchased.

However, courts have held that if the tied product, item B, is not the specific product identified with the trademark and other suppliers can or do produce an adequate item B, the justification for a tie-in disappears.[202] Thus, if the

---

[197] The need for justification in such cases is often not even reached, for the courts have often found in such cases that the trademark and the trademarked goods are not two separate products, but rather one product, and therefore there can be no tying. See **§4.14.** This type of trademark has often been called a *source* trademark in that it identifies the source of the product and is relied upon by consumers to represent the quality, nature, and manufacture of that particular good.

[198] Coca-Cola Bottling Co v Coca-Cola Co, 269 F Supp 796, 813-14 (D Del 1920).

[199] Hamro v Shell Oil Co, 1982-1 Trade Cas (CCH) ¶64,717 (10th Cir Apr 12, 1982); Redd v Shell Oil Co, 524 F2d 1054 (10th Cir 1975), *cert denied,* 425 US 912 (1976); Davidson v Crown Central Petroleum Corp, 1977-1 Trade Cas (CCH) ¶61,277 (D Md Dec 28, 1976).

[200] Baker v Simmons Co, 307 F2d 458, 468-69 (1st Cir 1962).

[201] Susser v Carvel Corp, 332 F2d 505, 519-21 (2d Cir 1964), *cert dismissed,* 381 US 125 (1965).

[202] Standard Oil Co v United States, 337 US 293, 306 (1949); Siegel v Chicken Delight, Inc, 448 F2d 43, 51 (9th Cir 1971), *cert denied,* 405 US 955 (1972); NW Controls, Inc v Outboard Marine Corp, 333 F Supp 493, 505-06 (D Del 1971). Among the other cases in this line are the *TBA* cases involving requirements by oil companies that their service station dealers handle tires, batteries, and accessories supplied or dictated by the oil companies. *See, e.g.,* Atlantic Ref Co v FTC, 381 US 357, 371 (1965); Texaco, Inc v FTC, 336 F2d 754 (DC Cir 1964).

trademark tie-in requires the purchase of items such as standard types of equipment or ingredients from the Seller, the tie-in is not justified to protect Seller's trademark or goodwill. Also if specifications or recipes would enable Buyer or its supplier to produce an adequate final product for sale under Seller's name, or if standards for and certification of competing items would be adequate to protect Seller's trademark or goodwill, the courts may find that such steps should be used rather than a tie-in.[203] However, courts have suggested that Seller should not be forced to reveal specifications or recipes that are trade secrets, and there may even be a strong justification for tie-ins with respect to trademarked products that can only be properly made by secret formula or methods.[204]

§4.31 —Can tying be justified because Seller is a new competitor trying to enter the market?

The entry of a new competitive supplier into a market is generally a procompetitive occurrence. Therefore, tying may be permitted where it is found to be a necessary or important factor in the viability of a new supplier. For example, in *United States v Jerrold Elec Corp*,[205] the court stated that its conclusion that Jerrold's tying arrangement was not in violation of §1 "is based primarily on the fact that the tie-in was instituted in the launching of a new business with a highly uncertain future" which could be enhanced by the tie-in. It is particularly telling that the court found that the continuation of the tie-in, after Jerrold was well-established and, indeed, dominant, was improper and not justified.[206]

It is important to observe that despite *Jerrold* and other references to the *new competitor* defense, the courts have not established a general rule that new companies can impose tie-ins.[207] Rather, the courts seem to be more willing to find no tying power or to accept other business justifications for tie-ins in the case of new companies. With respect to *Jerrold*, which offered complex community antenna systems, the court found that the tie-in was necessary to prevent breakdown of the initial systems, an occurrence that might have de-

---

[203] *See also In re* Data Gen Corp Antitrust Litigation, 490 F Supp 1089, 1124 (ND Cal 1980); Kentucky Fried Chicken Corp v Diversified Packaging Corp, 376 F Supp 1136 (SD Fla 1974), *affd*, 549 F2d 368 (5th Cir 1977) (condoning an arrangement where item B could be supplied by approved competitors).

[204] Susser v Carvel Corp, 332 F2d 505, 519 n 2 (2d Cir 1964), *cert dismissed*, 381 US 125 (1965).

[205] 187 F Supp 545, 557 (ED Pa 1960), *affd per curiam*, 365 US 567 (1961).

[206] *See also* Northern v McGraw-Edison Co, 542 F2d 1336 (8th Cir 1976), *cert denied*, 429 US 1097 (1977)(dictum).

[207] The new competitor defense appears to have been more often unsuccessful than successful. It was rejected by the court in Siegel v Chicken Delight, Inc, 448 F2d 43, 51 (9th Cir 1971), *cert denied*, 405 US 955 (1972), and similarly rejected in Falls Church Bratwursthaus, Inc v Bratwursthaus Management Corp, 354 F Supp 1237, 1240 (D Va 1973).

stroyed Jerrold's reputation and prevented it from successfully participating in this communications market because it was a new, small company. The court noted that it might not have reached the same result had the tie-in been imposed by a large company "such as R.C.A. and Philco" which had large diversified business to fall back on if the entry into the developing market met with early problems.[208]

§4.32 —Can tying items be justified because Seller is providing an entire franchise or trademark package?

While some courts have treated the franchisor-franchisee relationship like any other Seller/Buyer relationship,[209] the increasing trend is to view franchises as somewhat special Buyer/Seller relationships in tying determinations.[210] On one hand franchisors arguably should be afforded more latitude because their franchise arrangements help individuals get into a business and increase competition; on the other hand, a powerful franchisor may have the power to impose extensive tie-in conditions on such fledgling Buyers.

Cases have often turned not on justification but on the question where there are two separate products or a single franchise package. If Seller/franchisor is selling to Buyer not merely a trademark and items to be used for operations, but, more accurately, an integrated business method or system, all or part of that business method or system may be viewed by the courts as one single package, and therefore not a tie-in.[211] Thus, in the case of franchisors such as AAMCO Transmissions,[212] Baskin Robbins Ice Cream,[213] McDonald's,[214] and 7-Eleven,[215] it has been found that specific items that Buyer was required to buy or lease were part of a single business system or enterprise. In a similar vein, where Buyer is merely a distributor for the trademarked goods of Seller/franchisor, the trademark and the trademarked products will often be consid-

---

[208] 187 F Supp at 557.

[209] Kentucky Fried Chicken Corp v Diversified Packaging Corp, 376 F Supp 1136, 1147 (D Fla 1974), *affd,* 549 F2d 368 (5th Cir 1977); Northern v McGraw-Edison Co, 542 F2d 1336, 1347 (8th Cir 1976), *cert denied,* 429 US 1097 (1977).

[210] Principe v McDonald's Corp, 631 F2d 303, 309-10 (4th Cir 1980), *cert denied,* 451 US 970 (1981); Krehl v Baskin-Robbins Ice Cream Co, 664 F2d 1348, 1354-55 (9th Cir 1982).

[211] Principe v McDonald's Corp, 631 F2d 303, 309-10 (4th Cir 1980), *cert denied,* 451 US 970 (1981); Krehl v Baskin-Robbins Ice Cream Co, 664 F2d 1348, 1353-54 (9th Cir 1982); See also **§4.15.**

[212] Kugler v AAMCO Automatic Transmissions, Inc, 460 F2d 1214, 1215-16 (8th Cir 1972).

[213] Krehl v Baskin-Robbins Ice Cream Co, 664 F2d 1348, 1353-54 (9th Cir 1982).

[214] Principe v McDonald's Corp, 631 F2d 303, 309-10 (4th Cir 1980), *cert denied,* 451 US 970 (1981).

[215] *In re* 7-Eleven Franchise Antitrust Litigation, 1974-2 Trade Cas (CCH) ¶75,429 (ND Cal Dec 23, 1974).

ered the same item.[216]

The courts point out that these are not instances where there is a desired item A and an undesired item B sold to Buyer, but are really sales of a single trademarked item.[217] Buyer is in effect seeking the single combination of what the trademark represents in order to resell that product to its customers. Such a combination does not have an anticompetitive effect on either market, but may in fact promote interbrand competition.[218]

Tied franchise or trademark packages are much less likely to appear justified where the tied products are not directly related to Seller's unique franchise business system or trade name. Franchise or trademark packages that contain items for which there is no legitimate reason to restrict the source of supply, and which are not limited to items central to the franchise system or closely identified with the Seller's trademark are not justified.[219] The franchisor's argument that it is more convenient for franchisees to get all the products as a package is no justification for franchise tying.[220]

§4.33 Does it matter that all tie-in sales are in foreign countries, or within a single state?

In order to violate §3, the sale or lease of item A must be "for use, consumption, or resale within the United States."[221] Therefore, tying arrangements

---

[216] Hamro v Shell Oil Co, 1982-1 Trade Cas (CCH) ¶64,717 (9th Cir Apr 12, 1982). Mid-America ICEE, Inc v John E Mitchell Co, 1973-2 Trade Cas (CCH) ¶74,681 (D Or Aug 7, 1973); Joe Westbrook, Inc v Chrysler Corp, 419 F Supp 824 (ND Ga 1976).

[217] See **§4.14.**

[218] In Principe v McDonald's Corp, 631 F2d 303 (4th Cir 1980), *cert denied,* 451 US 970 (1981), the court noted that McDonald's policies and franchise package arrangement provide special advantages by "broadening the applicant base and opening the door to persons who otherwise could not afford a McDonald's franchise." 631 F2d at 310. The court concluded that: "To characterize the franchise as an unnecessary aggregation of separate products tied to the McDonald's name is to miss the point entirely. Among would be franchisees, the McDonald's name has come to stand for the formula, including all that it entails." *Id* at 311.

[219] Siegel v Chicken Delight, Inc, 448 F2d 43, 51 (9th Cir 1971), *cert denied,* 405 US 955 (1972); Photovest Corp v Fotomat Corp, 606 F2d 704, 725 (7th Cir 1979), *cert denied,* 445 US 917 (1980); Northern v McGraw-Edison Co, 542 F2d 1336, 1347 (8th Cir 1976) *cert denied,* 429 US 1097 (1977); Carpa, Inc v Ward Foods, Inc, 536 F2d 39, 46-47 (5th Cir 1976).

[220] Northern v McGraw-Edison Co, 542 F2d 1336, 1347 (8th Cir 1976), *cert denied,* 429 US 1097 (1977).

[221] The full text of Clayton Act §3 is as follows:

> It shall be unlawful for any person engaged in commerce, in the course of such commerce, to lease or make a sale or contract for sale of goods, wares, merchandise, machinery, supplies, or other commodities, whether patented or unpatented, for use, consumption, or resale within the United States or any Territory thereof or the District of Columbia or any insular possession or other place under the jurisdiction of the United States, or fix a price charged therefor, or discount from, or rebate upon such price, on the condition, agreement, or understanding

involving sales of item A only for use outside the United States do not violate §3. Such sales may, however, violate §1, if the tying condition nevertheless restrains interstate or foreign commerce.[222] Such foreign tying may also be a violation of foreign antitrust laws.

While intrastate sales in the United States with no interstate connection are exempt from the antitrust laws,[223] few significant tying arrangements would be able to qualify as purely intrastate. The test under §3 is different from that under §1. Under §3, Seller must be "a person engaged in commerce" and the tying must be "in the course of such commerce." Therefore, if the tying sale was not by a Seller involved in interstate commerce, or if the tying sale itself was not interstate, §3 should not apply.[224]

Section 1, on the other hand, has a much broader coverage. All that is required is that the tying have a not insubstantial effect on interstate commerce.[225] Therefore, if the goods or parts sold are manufactured out-of-state, if Buyer or Seller compete directly or indirectly with out-of-state competitors, or if the products resold by Buyer move out-of-state, the §1 commerce test is likely to be met. It is difficult to preclude all of these connections with interstate commerce, and the intrastate defense is rarely available under §1. Because a plaintiff can usually resort to §1, and is not limited to §3, the intrastate defense is unlikely to be available for any significant tying arrangement.

> that the lesee or purchaser thereof shall not use or deal in the goods, wares, merchandise, machinery, supplies, or other commodities of a competitor or competitors of the lessor or seller, where the effect of such lease, sale, or contract for sale or such condition, agreement, or understanding may be to substantially lessen competition or tend to create a monopoly in any line of commerce.

15 USC §14.

[222] The relevant text of Sherman Act §1 is as follows: "Every contract, combination in the form of a trust or otherwise, or conspiracy, in restraint of trade or commerce among the several States, or with foreign nations, is declared to be illegal. . . ." 15 USC §1. Some courts have made the broad statement that where conduct does not violate §3, it does not violate §1 (*see, e.g.,* Tampa Elec Co v Nashville Coal Co, 365 US 320, 335 (1961); Mercantile Natl Bank v Quest, Inc, 303 F Supp 926, 935 (ND Ind 1969); but these statements are not true in this context (see **§4.03**).

[223] Joe Westbrook, Inc v Chrysler Corp, 419 F Supp 824 (ND Ga 1976).

[224] In Detroit City Dairy, Inc v Kowalski Sausage Co, 393 F Supp 453, 472-79 (D Mich 1975), the court distinguished the jurisdictional requirements of Sherman Act §1 and Clayton Act §3. It held that the standard for determining Clayton Act jurisdiction was the stream of commerce doctrine. The court nevertheless found no jurisdiction under §3, then found jurisdiction under §1, demonstrating why the limitations on §3 are ultimately of little use to the defendant in avoiding liability for tying. 393 F Supp at 479.

[225] Joe Westbrook, Inc v Chrysler Corp, 419 F Supp 824, 836 (ND Ga 1976). Bob Maxfield, Inc v American Motors Corp, 637 F2d 1033, 1037 (5th Cir), *cert denied,* 454 US 860 (1981); Colorado Pump Supply Co v Febco, Inc, 472 F2d 637 (10th Cir), *cert denied,* 411 US 987 (1973).

§4.34 May the Seller require the Buyer to purchase Seller's full line of a certain type of product?

Often, a Seller of a line of products will wish its distributors to offer the complete line of products. Many courts have analyzed Seller's requirement that Buyer take the full line of products using standards similar to those applied to tying cases, although often referring to the conduct as full-line forcing.[226] One court noted that, "[T]he two theories of liability are substantially synonymous."[227] Other courts have treated full-line forcing arrangements as exclusive dealing agreements[228] under the rule of reason, particularly where Buyer willingly consents to the arrangement. The ultimate question is, of course, the same: whether such full-line forcing unreasonably restrains trade in violation of §1 or may substantially lessen competition or tend to create a monopoly in violation of §3.[229]

Generally, full-line forcing has been upheld as lawful as long as Buyer is not precluded from purchasing other products which compete with the items included in the full-line requirement. For example, the Case farm machinery company required its dealers to keep a full line of Case machinery, but the dealers were not precluded from handling competitors' machinery as well. The court found no antitrust violation because Case did not have sufficient market power over any item sold to foreclose competing manufacturers from also selling to the dealers, and dealers did sell competing brands.[230] The court found that it was in the best interest of the dealers to handle the full line of Case machinery, and so long as there was no competitive restriction imposed, the requirement was lawful.[231] If Seller cannot or does not coerce Buyers to purchase only Seller's products, a court is likely to find no tying power or adverse effect on competition.[232] Mere persuasion to favor Seller's products does not amount to coercion.[233]

---

[226] Pitchford v PEPI, Inc, 531 F2d 92 (3d Cir 1975), *cert denied,* 426 US 935 (1976); Brandeis Mach Co & Supply Corp v Barber Greene Co, 1973-2 Trade Cas (CCH) ¶74,672 (WD Ky July 11, 1973).

[227] Bob Maxfield, Inc v American Motors Corp, 637 F2d 1033, 1037 (5th Cir), *cert denied,* 454 US 860.

[228] Exclusive dealing is covered in **§4.38** *et seq.* United States v JI Case Co, 101 F Supp 856 (D Minn 1951); McElhenny Co v Western Auto Supply Co, 269 F2d 332, 338-339 (4th Cir 1959).

[229] Colorado Pump & Supply Co v Febco, Inc, 472 F2d 637, 640-41 (10th Cir), *cert denied,* 411 US 987 (1973).

[230] United States v JI Case Co, 101 F Supp 856, 867 (D Minn 1951).

[231] *Id.* The court found that Case and its dealer had therefore entered into a "mutual arrangement" to achieve these benefits.

[232] Colorado Pump & Supply Co v Febco, Inc, 472 F2d 637, 641 (10th Cir) *cert denied,* 411 US 987 (1973); McElhenny Co v Western Auto Supply Co, 269 F2d 332, 338 (4th Cir 1959); United States v JI Case Co, 101 F Supp 856, 857 (D Minn 1951).

[233] Bob Maxfield Inc v American Motors Corp, 637 F2d 1033, 1037 (5th Cir), *cert denied,* 454 US 860 (1981).

If, on the other hand, a full-line requirement in effect precludes Buyer from purchasing from competing Sellers, it could be considered a disguised tying arrangement or an exclusive dealing arrangement.[234] The most common example of this is where a Buyer is not only required to purchase the full line of Seller's items, but also to purchase sufficient quantities to meet all its needs for that type of product.

§4.35 May Seller require Buyer to purchase item B from a specified third party or list of third parties?

Generally, a Seller of item A may require that Buyer purchase item B from a third party or from a list of third parties, as long as Seller does not have an economic interest in that third party or in that sale of item B. The Fifth Circuit stated in *Keener v Sizzler Family Steak Houses*:[235] "There is no illegal tying arrangement where a 'tying' company has absolutely no interest in the sales of a third company whose products are favored by the tie-in." This rule has never been stated by the Supreme Court, but has been followed almost universally by the lower courts.[236]

There appear to be two reasons behind the judicial sanction of such an arrangement. First, it does not pose a threat of Seller exploiting its power over the market for item A to give it power over the market for item B, because

---

[234] See **§4.38.**

[235] 597 F2d 453, 456 (5th Cir 1979).

[236] In Esposito v Mr Softee, Inc, 1980-1 Trade Cas (CCH) ¶63,089, (EDNY Dec 14, 1979) the Eastern District of New York observed that none of the Supreme Court cases contains any language that would indicate that the liability imposed upon seller of the tying product is affected by whether or not the party has an economic interest in the sale of the tied products. "However," noted the court,

> where the Seller of the tying product and the Seller of the tied product have been separate entities, the lower federal courts, notwithstanding the absence of any directive from the Supreme Court, have held that '[w]hen the victim of an alleged tie-in is not required to buy a single unit of the tied product from the tying party or from any source in which the tying party has an interest or on whose sales the tying party earns a commission, the arrangement simply does not constitute a tie-in,' Kentucky Fried Chicken Corp v Diversified Packaging Corp, 549 F2d 368 (5th Cir 1977). . . ."

Id at 77, 423. *See also* Imperial Point Collonades Condominium, Inc v Mangurian, 549 F2d 1029, 1043 (5th Cir), *cert denied*, 434 US 859 (1977); Crawford Transp Co v Chrysler Corp, 338 F2d 934, 938-39 (6th Cir 1964), *cert denied*, 380 US 954 (1965); Venzie Corp v United States Mineral Prods Co, 521 F2d 1309, 1317 (3d Cir 1975); Keener v Sizzler Family Steak Houses, 597 F2d 453, 456 (5th Cir 1979); Rodrigue v Chrysler Corp, 421 F Supp 903, 904-05 (D La 1976). Indeed, some courts have suggested that an otherwise unlawful tying condition may be permissible if Buyer is also allowed to purchase from approved suppliers in the alternative. United States v Mercedes-Benz of N Am, Inc, 517 F Supp 1369 (ND Cal 1981). *See also* Anderson Foreign Motors, Inc v New England Toyata Distribs Inc, 475 F Supp 973, 984-85 (D Mass 1979).

Seller does not participate in the market for item B.[237] Inasmuch as this threat is what tying prohibitions are designed to combat, they are not properly applied in such circumstances. The second reason is a more practical: if Seller has no economic interest in the sale of item B, the requirement that Buyer purchase item B from a specific third party in all likelihood has a reasonable and commendable business purpose. Otherwise Seller would not impose the requirement on its sales of item A, for such an additional burden could only cost it sales.

If Seller has *any* interest, direct or indirect, in the designated third-party supplier or sale, this reasoning is no longer valid. The tying arrangement will then be analyzed as if the designated third party were the Seller itself.[238] In this context, it should be observed that even a tenuous interest in the third party, including a desire to gain some business advantage in other business dealings with the third party, may be sufficient to erase Seller's no economic interest exemption.[239] If Seller itself or a third party in which Seller has an economic interest is only one of many suppliers contained on Seller's list of acceptable

---

[237] Crawford Transp Co v Chrysler Corp, *affd,* 338 F2d 934, 938-39 (6th Cir 1964), *cert denied,* 380 US 954 (1965). BBD Transp Co v United States Steel Corp, 1976-2 Trade Cas (CCH) ¶61,079 (ND Cal Aug 25, 1976); *In re* 7-Eleven Franchise Antitrust Litigation, 1974-2 Trade Cas (CCH) ¶75,429 (ND Cal Dec 23, 1974).

[238] In United States Steel v Fortner Enters, 429 US 610, 613 (1977), the Court found that because of common ownership and management, it was proper to regard the credit corporation and the housing materials construction corporation as a single entity. *See also* Ohio-Sealy Mattress Mfg Co v Sealy, Inc, 585 F2d 821, 835 (7th Cir 1978), *cert denied,* 440 US 930 (1979).

[239] In Esposito v Mr Softee, Inc, 1980-1 Trade Cas (CCH) ¶63,089 (EDNY Dec 14, 1979) the court found that the defendant, Mr. Softee, "has been financially involved in the sale of tied products to the members of the plaintiff class." Mr. Softee had argued that it did not have any economic interest in the tied products because the tied products were sold by an independent company. The court noted, however, that Mr. Softee had supplied some of the products to the independent company for resale to the Mr. Softee franchisees. Also, at a later time, Mr. Softee had turned over this supply function to a company owned and controlled by the two principal individuals of Mr. Softee. Finally, the court went even beyond this to find that, under §1, Mr. Softee could be found to have entered into a conspiracy, even with the independent supplier, and that this would be sufficient to meet the requirements of §1, citing Imperial Point Collonades Condominium v Magurian, 549 F2d 1029, 1043 (5th Cir), *cert denied,* 434 US 859 (1977). The court stated:

> Under the circumstances, we believe that even if Mr. Softee itself had no direct financial stake in the sale of the tied products, it would be appropriate to apply the rule that a party 'may be held liable as [a] member[] of a conspiracy to restrain trade by means of the tying agreement' [citing *Imperial Points,* and Perma Life Mufflers, Inc v International Parts Corp, 392 US 134 (1968)]. With the additional evidence of Mr. Softee's pecuniary interest in the success of the tie-in scheme, our conclusion is reinforced."

Id at 77,424. *But see* Roberts v Elaine Powers Figure Salons, Inc, 1981-1 Trade Cas (CCH) ¶63,976 (ED Cal Dec 22, 1980) (holding no economic interest in accounting firm that franchisees were required to use despite considerable business dealings between Seller and the accounting firm).

suppliers of item B, the key question becomes whether the list unjustifiably excludes potential suppliers of item B; if so, the arrangement is likely to be treated as a tie-in.[240]

§4.36 May Seller require Buyer to purchase related items that meet certain quality specifications or are approved by Seller?

Generally, it is permissible for Seller of item A to require that Buyer also purchase an item B of a specific quality or character manufactured by *other* suppliers, where item B is to be used in conjunction with item A and a certain quality level in item B is necessary to maintain the quality or functionability of item A.[241] The underlying judicial rationale for allowing this potentially anticompetitive requirement is the same as that for allowing a requirement that Buyer purchase item B from a particular third party, i.e., Seller cannot thereby extend its power to the item B market and the only reason for Seller to impose such a requirement, since it might cost Seller sales of item A, is that there is a strong and legitimate business reason for the requirement in terms of the proper use of item A.

It follows that where Seller's quality conditions produce some direct or indirect economic return to Seller in the market for item B, the Seller is not so protected. Therefore, if the quality conditions force the purchase of item B from Seller or from a third party in whom Seller has an economic interest,

---

[240] In Kentucky Fried Chicken Corp v Diversified Packaging Corp, 376 F Supp 1136, 1147-48 (SD Fla 1974), *affd,* 549 F2d 368 (5th Cir 1977), the court approved an open-ended list of suppliers which included the Seller. In Susser v Carvel Corp, 332 F2d 505 (2d Cir 1964), *cert dismissed,* 381 US 125 (1965), Carvel required that certain items be purchased from approved suppliers, including on that list itself or a related company. The court observed that the franchise agreement "requires the dealer to purchase from Carvel or approved sources its entire requirement of all items sold as part of the retail product, but permits the dealer to purchase machinery, equipment and paper goods from sources other than Carvel." 332 F2d at 511-12. The court did not even deal with this second type of tying, apparently on the ground that competition was in no sense limited for those products. Similarly, in Photovest Corp v Fotomat Corp, 606 F2d 704, 722 (7th Cir 1979), *cert denied,* 445 US 917 (1980), the court found: "As to the four Photovest franchises which were permitted to purchase processing from Fotomat-approved sources, the tying arrangement was not established sufficiently. Photovest did not show that Fotomat unreasonably withheld approval." These four franchisees had not sought an alternative to Fotomat, even though they were permitted to do so under the agreement. *See also* the discussion of nonexclusive tying arrangements in Osborn v Sinclair Ref Co, 286 F2d 832, 838 (4th Cir 1960), *cert denied,* 366 US 963 (1961).

[241] As in the case of an approved list of suppliers, the courts have frequently suggested that quality standards are a permissible alternative to unlawful tying arrangements. *See, e.g.,* Siegel v Chicken Delight, Inc, 448 F2d 43, 51-52 (9th Cir 1971), *cert denied,* 405 US 955 (1972); Advance Business Sys & Supply Co v SCM Corp, 415 F2d 55, 65 (4th Cir 1969), *cert denied,* 397 US 920 (1970); Moore v Jas H Matthews & Co, 550 F2d 1207, 1217 (9th Cir 1977), *after second remand,* 682 F2d 830 (9th Cir 1982).

and unreasonably exclude suppliers competing with Seller whose products are in fact adequate, the quality conditions may be treated as a tie-in.[242] Such a situation could occur, for example, if the quality condition is unjustifiably restrictive, such that Seller's or a related third party's item meets the requirements but adequate items of some competing suppliers do not.

§4.37 What are the penalties for tying?

There are potential criminal penalties for violation of Sherman Act §1,[243] but they are essentially never imposed in cases where the only antitrust violation is a tie-in. Violation of either Sherman Act §1 or Clayton Act §3 can also result in private action treble damages liability. Under §5 of the Federal Trade Commission Act, tying may be prohibited even if no damage has yet been suffered.

In the case of private litigation, the party suing most often is a Buyer who has been required to purchase item B from Seller, or who has been cut off by Seller for failure to comply with the tying conditions. The damages in cases where the tie-in was accepted may not be large, merely being treble the difference between what Buyer paid and what it can show it would have paid in the absence of the tying condition or cutoff. But if Buyer has been terminated or alleges some permanent damage to its business, damages could be large.[244] Damages suffered by a Buyer class or multiple Buyers suing together would, of course, be some multiple of the loss of individual Buyers.[245]

---

[242] Seligson v Plum Tree, Inc, 361 F Supp 748, 753-54 (D Pa 1973); Ungar v Dunkin' Donuts of Am, Inc, 531 F2d 1211, 1216 (3d Cir), *cert denied,* 429 US 823 (1976). See **§§4.09-4.15** for discussion of when two items may constitute a single product for tying purposes.

[243] Violation of the Sherman Act is a felony, and the maximum fine for each count is $1 million for corporations and $100,000 for others. The maximum jail sentence for individuals is 3 years.

[244] A good discussion of the damages requirement is contained in Gray v Shell Oil Co, 469 F2d 742, 749 (9th Cir 1972), *cert denied,* 412 US 943 (1973).

[245] Generally, class actions are inappropriate unless all of the Buyers are bound by the same express tying clause. Otherwise, there is the question of whether Buyer was coerced to purchase item B in each individual case, and the common questions of fact and law cannot be said to predominate in the case. Cash v Arctic Circle, Inc, 85 FRD. 618 (ED Wash 1979); Ungar v Dunkin' Donuts of Am, Inc, 531 F2d 1211, 1224-25 (3d Cir), *cert denied,* 429 US 823 (1976); Smith v Denny's Restaurant, Inc, 62 FRD 459, 461-62 (ND Cal 1974). Also, where there is a question of whether Seller has tying power over item A, and the answer to this question may differ in different markets or with respect to different individual Buyers, class certification may also be difficult. Cash v Arctic Circle, Inc, 85 FRD 618 (ED Wash 1979). Finally, where the damages suffered by each buyer would be different based on different competitive situations, class treatment may be inappropriate. *Id. But see* Siegel v Chicken Delight, Inc, 271 F Supp 722 (ND Cal 1967) approving class treatment in a tying case.

Suits by competitors of the seller in the market for item B are less frequent, but if sales nationwide have been diminished by the tying condition, the damages may be substantial. These could include lost profits and potential profits over a number of years, lost business value, or lost business opportunities. When trebled, such damages may constitute a severe penalty for the Seller/defendant; in addition, the capacity to obtain reimbursement for costs and attorney's fees, which can be substantial, may be a potent deterrent.

Exclusive Dealing

§4.38 May Seller condition its sale or lease of an item on Buyer's agreement not to obtain that item from anyone else or Buyer's agreement to purchase all its needs for the item from Seller?

Seller may not condition its sale of an item on Buyer's agreement to buy that item in the future from the Seller and not from a competitor, where that arrangement may have a substantial adverse effect on competition. Unlike tying arrangements[246] such *exclusive dealing* arrangements have not traditionally been considered per se unlawful, because the courts have recognized that in many cases an exclusive dealing arrangement may have no adverse effect on competition, or may even be procompetitive.[247] This is particularly the case

---

[246] See **§§4.02-4.37.**

[247] The Supreme Court stated in Standard Oil Co of Cal v United States, 337 US 293, 306 (1949) (*Standard Stations*), that exclusive dealing arrangements, in the form of requirements contracts, "may well be of economic advantage to Buyers as well as to Sellers, and thus indirectly of advantage to the consuming public." The court went on to list the possible advantages stating:

> In the case of the buyer, they may assure supply, afford protection against rises in price, enable long-term planning on the basis of known costs, and obviate the expense and risk of storage in the quantity necessary for a commodity having a fluctuating demand. From the seller's point of view, requirements contracts may make possible the substantial reduction of selling expenses, give protection against price fluctuations, and—of particular advantage to a newcomer to the field to whom it is important to know what capital expenditures are justified—offer the possibility of a predictable market. . . . They may be useful, moreover, to a seller trying to establish a foothold against the counter-attacks of entrenched competitors. *Id* 306-07.

The Court stated that because these advantages might be sufficient to account for use of exclusive dealing arrangements such as requirements contracts, "the coverage by such contracts of a substantial amount of business affords a weaker basis for the inference that the competition may be lessened than with similar coverage by tying clauses. . . ." *Id* 307. Therefore, the Court concluded, exclusive dealing would be treated less strictly than tying.

Subsequent court decisions, consistent with the *Standard Stations* conclusion, have

where the exclusive dealing favors a new or small supplier seeking a foothold in a market dominated by larger established competitors or where the arrangement enhances strong competition between different brands of the product.[248]

Most exclusive dealing cases are brought under §3 of the Clayton Act, which prohibits exclusive dealing where the effect of it "*may* be to substantially lessen competition or tend to create a monopoly in any line of commerce."[249] Because exclusive dealing arrangements involve an agreement or combination between Seller and Buyer, such an arrangement may also violate §1 of the Sherman Act, as a combination which unreasonably restrains trade.[250] Also,

---

applied a less stringent standard to exclusive dealing arrangements than to tying arrangements. These courts sometimes look to the procompetitive advantages of exclusive dealing arrangements in determining whether they violate the antitrust laws. See **§§4.49, 4.51.**

[248] The willingness of courts to allow exclusive dealing arrangements for new, struggling sellers was endorsed by the Supreme Court in its decision in Standard Oil Co v United States, 337 US 293, 307 (1949), where the Court noted that such arrangements "may be useful, moreover, to a Seller trying to establish a foothold against the counterattacks of entrenched competitors." See **§4.51.**

The importance of interbrand competition was identified by the Supreme Court's decision in Continental TV, Inc v GTE Sylvania, Inc, 433 US 36 (1977). While that case did not pertain to exclusive dealing arrangements, the Court, in its decision, spoke in broad language about all nonprice vertical restraints, which would include exclusive dealing arrangements. The Court stressed that vertical restraints in some instances can be used to induce buyers to engage in promotional activities that ultimately enhance competition between brands. For this reason, the Court stated that, as a general rule, a rule of reason standard, that looks to the actual effect on interbrand competition, should be used in analyzing such vertical restraints. In *In re* Beltone Elecs Corp, 3 Trade Reg Rep (CCH) ¶21,934 (July 6, 1982), the FTC refused to condemn exclusive dealing arrangements between Beltone and its distributors of hearing aids on the ground that they would not adversely affect interbrand competition.

[249] The full text of Clayton Act §3 is as follows:

> It shall be unlawful for any person engaged in commerce, in the course of such commerce, to lease or make a sale or contract for sale of goods, wares, merchandise, machinery, supplies, or other commodities, whether patented or unpatented, for use, consumption, or resale within the United States or any Territory thereof or the District of Columbia or any insular possession or other place under the jurisdiction of the United States, or fix a price charged therefor, or discount from, or rebate upon such price, on the condition, agreement, or understanding that the lessee or purchaser thereof shall not use or deal in the goods, wares, merchandise, machinery, supplies, or other commodities of a competitor or competitors of the lessor or seller, where the effect of such lease, sale, or contract for sale or such condition, agreement, or understanding may be to substantially lessen competition or tend to create a monopoly in any line of commerce.

15 USC §14.

[250] The relevant text of Sherman Act §1 is as follows: "Every contract, combination in the form of a trust or otherwise, or conspiracy, in restraint of trade or commerce among the several States, or with foreign nations, is declared to be illegal. . . ." 15 USC §1. Some courts have made the broad statement that where conduct does not violate §3, it does not violate §1 (*see, e.g.,* Tampa Elec Co v Nashville Coal Co, 365 US 320, 335 (1961); Mercantile Natl Bank v Quest, Inc, 303 F Supp 926, 935 (ND Ind 1969); but these statements are almost certainly too broad (see **§4.03**).

§5 FTC

under §5 of the Federal Trade Commission Act, the FTC may challenge such an arrangement as an unfair method of competition even before it has had any significant adverse effect on competition.[251] Also, state antitrust laws would in some cases be violated by an exclusive dealing arrangement.[252]

22? jdle Exclusive dealing cases usually pose two basic questions: (1) whether there was actually a sale conditioned on Buyer's agreement to purchase exclusively from Seller in the future, and (2) whether that agreement foreclosed a significant portion of the market to suppliers competing with Seller or otherwise substantially lessened competition. In determining the second question, the courts earlier relied on the percentage of the market foreclosed as the determinative factor, as endorsed by the Supreme Court in 1949 in the *Standard Stations* case; but that test has largely given way to a broader inquiry into the overall impact on competition established by the Supreme Court in 1961 in the *Tampa Elec Co v Nashville Coal Co* case.[253] Assuming that an exclusive dealing agreement has been implemented, the argument that the arrangement has not had a substantial anticompetitive effect is the principal defense available to Seller.

§4.39 —If Buyer buys or leases the item only from Seller, when is this considered to be an exclusive dealing arrangement?

It is, of course, not unlawful for a Buyer to buy all of a certain type of product from a single Seller. Exclusive dealing occurs only where Buyer loses its usual right to make an independent decision in the future as to which supplier it will use. Where Buyer agrees to make all purchases over a period of time from Seller, there is exclusive dealing, whether Buyer's agreement is voluntary or coerced. Where there is no such agreement, i.e., where Buyer unilaterally of

---

[251] In FTC v Brown Shoe Co, 384 US 316 (1966), the FTC had held that a program of special benefits bestowed by Brown Shoe Company on retail shoe outlets in return for their agreement to handle only Brown shoes was an unfair method of competition under §5 of the FTC Act. The Supreme Court found that it was sufficient to uphold the FTC decision that the Brown Shoe program was contrary to "the central policy of both §1 of the Sherman Act and §3 of the Clayton Act." 384 US at 321. The Court found that it was not necessary that there be a violation of all the elements required by §1 or §3.

[252] There are many state laws similar to §3, and other laws whose general application would appear to encompass exclusive dealing. However, exclusive dealing cases are seldom brought in state court, and are even less often successful.

[253] 365 US 320 (1961). The test developed by the Supreme Court in Standard Oil Co v United States, 337 US 293 (1949) is often called the *quantitative* test, wherein the focus is almost solely upon the percentage of the market foreclosed by the exclusive dealing arrangement. In *Tampa Elec Co* the Supreme Court adopted the *qualitative* test which not only looked at the percentage of the market foreclosed by the exclusive dealing, but also attempted to assess the true impact of this foreclosure on competition in the market. This topic is discussed further in **§4.49.**

its own free will decides to make all future purchases of a product from Seller, there is no exclusive dealing arrangement.

§4.40 —Is a requirements contract exclusive dealing?

A requirements contract is a form of exclusive dealing. Under a requirements contract, Buyer agrees to purchase all of its needs for a certain product from one Seller. In a requirements contract, the competitors of Seller are in practical effect prevented from competing for the business of Buyer because all of Buyer's requirements are met, by prior agreement, by Seller. Contracts for periodic predetermined deliveries designed to meet Buyer's needs, such as installment contracts, are treated similarly.

Most requirements contracts are permitted where they extend only for a short period of time on the ground that there is no substantial adverse effect on competition, but there is no general rule what length of time is too long.[254] Sometimes a year is cited as a generally accepted permissible length of time,[255] but contracts as long as 20 years have been upheld.[256]

In analyzing requirements contracts, a court will take the same approach as with other exclusive dealing arrangements, i.e., the court will assess the impact on competition. A long (e.g., five-year) requirements contract with a Buyer or Buyers who represents a substantial share of the purchases in that market may well be found unlawful, particularly in an industry where there is no rational basis for long-term contracts in terms of capital outlay or delay in obtaining alternative sources.[257] A short (e.g., six-month) requirements contract with a Buyer or Buyers representing only a small portion of the market is relatively

---

[254] Naturally, the duration of a requirements contract, or any other exclusive dealing arrangement, has a direct effect on the amount of competition foreclosed in the relevant market. Thus, if a challenged requirements contract is for less than a year, generally there will be little foreclosure of competition, in the long run, even if the affected Buyer or Buyers represent a significant portion of the market. On the other hand, a standard requirements or exclusive dealing contract covering requirements for 10 years would have a significant foreclosure effect, even if the Buyer or Buyers involved a smaller portion of the market. Twin City Sportservice, Inc v Charles O Finley & Co, 676 F2d 1291, 1305 (9th Cir), *cert denied,* 103 S Ct 364 (1982). Because the exclusive dealing or requirements contracts are tested under the rule of reason, the question posed is whether the effect of the practice is to unreasonably restrain trade. *See, e.g.,* ABC Consolidated Corp, 3 Trade Reg Rep (CCH) ¶17,109 (FTC 1964), in which the FTC agreed to a consent decree allowing seller to use a five-year contract, so long as the affected buyers could terminate at the end of the third and fourth years.

[255] *See, e.g.,* FTC v Motion Picture Advertising Serv Co, 344 US 392, 396 (1953), in which the Supreme Court upheld an FTC order prohibiting contracts of longer than one year.

[256] Tampa Elec Co v Nashville Coal Co, 365 US 320 (1961).

[257] Twin City Sportservice, Inc v Charles O Finley & Co, 676 F2d 1291, 1305 (9th Cir), *cert denied,* 103 S Ct 364 (1982); ABC Consolidiated Corp, 3 Trade Reg Rep (CCH) ¶17,109 (1964).

safe. The tests used by the courts to assess the impact on competition are discussed in **§4.46.**

§4.41 Does it make any difference whether the item is a commodity as opposed to a service or intangible item for exclusive dealing purposes?

As noted in **§4.38,** exclusive dealing may be found unlawful under §1 of the Sherman Act, §3 of the Clayton Act, or §5 of the Federal Trade Commission Act. However, §3 applies only to *commodities,* and therefore, it is not available where the item involved is not a commodity.

The significance of this is that arguably a degree of injury to competition that would not violate §1 might nevertheless violate §3. Under §3, technically it is not necessary to show that the exclusive dealing has yet had a substantial adverse impact on competition, but only that it *may* have such an effect. Under §1, the test is whether there *has* been a restraint of trade. This led the Supreme Court to state in *Tampa Electric Co v Nashville Coal Co,* that if an exclusive dealing arrangement does not fall within the broader proscription of §3, it follows that it is not forbidden by §1.[258]

Thus, where the exclusive dealing does not involve commodities under §3, there is technically less risk of antitrust liability. This distinction between §1 and §3 arguably has caused most cases to be brought under §3, but there is reason to believe that the actual exclusive dealing analysis under §3 has become increasingly equivalent to that under §1.[259] Moreover, exclusive dealing arrangements involving noncommodities may be enjoined under §5 of the FTC Act even in the absence of actual significant anticompetitive effect, when the threat of a significant adverse effect exists.[260]

---

[258] 365 US 320, 335 (1961); *see also* Standard Fashion Co v Magrane-Houston Co, 258 US 346, 355-56 (1922) where the Court stated that §3 is intended to supplement the Sherman Act to catch anticompetitive effects in their incipiency.

[259] In Tampa Elec Co v Nashville Coal Co, the Court stressed that in order to meet the *may* test it must be *probable* that the exclusive dealing will foreclose significant competition. 365 US 320, 327 (1961). In Continental TV Inc v GTE Sylvania, 433 US 36 (1977), the Court overruled the application of *per* se standards to the vertical restraints in that case. The Court went on to suggest that the antitrust laws concerning all nonprice vertical restraints should be found to be violated only where they had a significant adverse effect on competition, and more particularly competition between brands. 433 US at 57-59. The Court made no distinctions between treatment under §3 and that under §1. Thus, the distinction suggested by the Court in Standard Fashion Co v Magrane-Houston Co, 258 US 346, 355-56 (1922) may no longer be of importance. In the tying area, many courts have stated that there is no longer any distinction between the market effect required under §1 and §3 under the per se test.

[260] FTC v Brown Shoe Co, 384 US 316, 321 (1966).

§4.42 —What is a commodity?

A *commodity* is generally held to be a tangible item, other than real property, the value of which is based on its actual physical properties, e.g., an automobile, coal, or food. Where the item is real property or an intangible item whose value is not in its physical properties, such as a service, money, credit, or a license, it is not a commodity. The courts are split on some semitangibles, such as electricity.[261] The definition of a commodity under §3 with respect to exclusive dealing arrangements is identical to that used in analyzing tying arrangements under §3[262] and to that used under the Robinson-Patman Act with respect to price discrimination.

Examples of items that have been found to be commodities under §3 are listed in **§4.06,** and examples of items that have been found not to be commodities under §3 are listed in **§4.07.**

§4.43 Is there exclusive dealing where Buyer refuses to accept the exclusive dealing agreement or Seller refuses to sell without it?

If a potential Buyer refuses to lease or buy from Seller pursuant to an exclusive dealing condition, there should be no violation of §3, because §3 specifically requires a sale, sales contract, or lease.[263] Also, such an event, standing alone, does not constitute a violation of §1, which requires an agreement or combination in restraint of trade, because the two parties have failed to come to terms. In *Amplex, Inc v Outboard Marine Corp,*[264] the court held that Seller's refusal to renew the outboard motor dealership of Buyer because Buyer had previously sold competing goods could not be considered exclusive dealing because §3 applies only to *executed transactions.* Other courts have reached this same result, particularly where the suit is brought by a Buyer who has refused initially to enter into an exclusive dealing arrangement with Seller.[265]

However, other courts have held that, where Seller engages in a pattern of refusing to deal with Buyers who will not accede to Seller's exclusive dealing

---

[261] See **§4.04.**

[262] See **§§4.04-4.08.**

[263] Similarly, where the exclusive arrangement is with an agent of Seller, and there is therefore no true sale by Seller, §3 does not apply. CBS Business Equip Corp v Underwood Corp, 240 F Supp 413 (SDNY 1964).

[264] 380 F2d 112, 115-16 (4th Cir 1967), *cert denied,* 389 US 1036 (1968).

[265] McElhenney Co v Western Auto Supply Co, 269 F2d 332, 338 (4th Cir 1959), (holding that a "mere refusal by a manufacturer to deal with a retailer who will not confine his dealings to the goods of the manufacturer does not run afoul" of the exclusive dealing prohibitions of §3); Leo J Meyberg Co v Eureka Williams Corp, 215 F2d 100 (9th Cir), *cert denied,* 348 US 875 (1954); HL Moore Drug Exch v Eli Lilly & Co, 1977-1 Trade Cas (CCH) ¶61,462 (SDNY June 1, 1977).

requirements, or of threatening such refusal, this may be evidence that Seller is inducing or coercing Buyers into exclusive dealing arrangements.[266] A refusal to deal also may be held an unfair method of competition under §5 of the Federal Trade Commission Act.[267] Under the FTC Act, there is no requirement of an actual sale or an agreement.[268]

§4.44 If Seller does not expressly condition its sale of the item on Buyer's agreement to purchase the product only from Seller, can there be exclusive dealing?

There is no exclusive dealing if Seller never states or implies that Buyer must purchase a product only from Seller. In such an instance, where Buyer purchases as it wishes, even a decision by Buyer to purchase solely from seller will not constitute exclusive dealing.[269]

On the other hand, it is not necessary that the exclusive dealing condition be expressly stated. Where Seller implies or suggests such a condition, or where there is a course of conduct or business practices which result in Buyer implicitly agreeing to purchase the product solely from Seller, there may be exclusive dealing.[270] Thus, where Seller has a policy of terminating Buyers who fail to buy exclusively from Seller and communicates this policy as a threat to Buyers who therefore accede to the condition, this may be exclusive dealing,[271] as may any practices that practically preclude Buyer from purchasing from another supplier.[272]

---

[266] Lessig v Tidewater Oil Co, 327 F2d 459, 467-68 (9th Cir), *cert denied,* 377 US 993 (1964).

[267] Adolph Coors Co v FTC, 497 F2d 1178, 1187 (10th Cir 1974), *cert denied,* 419 US 1105 (1975).

[268] Adolph Coors Co v FTC, 497 F2d 1178, 1187 (10th Cir 1974), *cert denied,* 419 US 1105 (1975).

[269] Dillon Materials Handling, Inc v Albion Indus, 567 F2d 1299, 1302-05 (5th Cir 1978).

[270] Lessig v Tidewater Oil Co, 327 F2d 459, 467-69 (9th Cir), *cert denied,* 377 US 993 (1964); George R Whitten, Inc v Paddock Pool Builders Inc, 424 F2d 25, 35-36 (1st Cir), *cert denied,* 400 US 850 (1970); Alles Corp v Senco Prods, Inc, 329 F2d 567, 570-71 (6th Cir 1964); Advance Business Sys & Supply Co v SCM Corp, 415 F2d 55, 70 (4th Cir 1969), *cert denied,* 397 US 920 (1970).

[271] Lessig v Tidewater Oil Co, 327 F2d 459, 467-68 (9th Cir), *cert denied,* 377 US 993 (1964); Adolph Coors Co v FTC, 497 F2d 1178, 1187 (10th Cir 1974), *cert denied,* 419 US 1105 (1975).

[272] United Shoe Mach Co, v United States, 258 US 451 (1922) (the Court found that the practical effect of interlocking restraints on the buyer, who was operating under a lease from the Seller, was sufficient to constitute a coerced exclusive dealing arrangement).

§4.45 Is there exclusive dealing where Buyer is not forced to purchase exclusively from Seller, but agrees to do so voluntarily?

Certainly, where Seller has market power over a particular product and exercises it to force Buyers to purchase exclusively from the Seller, exclusive dealing exists. But even where Seller does not have the power to impose such a requirement, or does not exercise that power, Buyer sometimes initiates or willingly agrees to an exclusive dealing or requirements agreement with Seller in order to obtain economic benefits connected with the agreement. In such instances, Buyer as well as Seller may be in violation of §1 for participation in an agreement in restraint of trade, and Seller may be in violation of §3 (which is not intended to be used against Buyers).[273] So long as the sale is conditioned on an agreement to purchase exclusively from Seller for a period in the future, there is exclusive dealing, whether the agreement is coerced or voluntary.

The result is the opposite where Buyer simply unilaterally announces its decision to buy exclusively from Seller for an extended period. In such an instance, no condition is imposed, no agreement is reached, and Buyer remains free to change its mind and buy from a competitor of Seller at any time. In such an instance, no matter how sure Buyer is that it will only be purchasing from the Seller in the future, as long as Buyer does not enter into an explicit or implicit agreement with Seller, there is no exclusive dealing.

§4.46 Is there exclusive dealing if Seller offers a significantly better price to Buyer for making all or substantially all of its purchases from Seller?

If Buyer and Seller agree that Buyer will purchase a product only from Seller in exchange for a better price, there is exclusive dealing.[274] The courts are split, however, as to whether a mere offer to sell at a better price if Buyer makes all or substantially all of its purchases from Seller over a period of time is exclusive dealing in the absence of any agreement or commitment by Buyer. In this instance, Buyer would be free at any time to purchase from a competitor, but the price from Seller would be increased.

The determination will turn on the market power of Seller, the conduct of other Buyers, and other market factors. If Buyer is, in effect, coerced by Seller's conduct and by economic realities to limit its purchases to Seller, there is

---

[273] Anchor Serum Co v FTC, 217 F2d 867, 870 (7th Cir 1954) (exclusive dealing arrangements initiated by the buyers).

[274] Standard Fashion Co v Magrane-Houston Co, 258 US 346, 351-52 (1922); United States v Hartford-Empire Co, 46 F Supp 541, 579 (ND Ohio 1942), *affd,* 323 US 386 (1945); Carter Carburetor Corp v FTC, 112 F2d 722, 732-33 (8th Cir 1940).

exclusive dealing.[275] If Buyer is voluntarily taking advantage of the best price for as long as it remains the best price, there is not exclusive dealing.[276]

§4.47 How do the courts determine if the exclusive dealing arrangement restrains a substantial amount of competition?

Once it has been established that there is an exclusive dealing arrangement or a requirements contract that limits Buyer's free choice in purchasing the product in the future, the lawfulness of the arrangement under §1 and §3 will turn principally on whether the arrangement has substantially lessened competition in the market for that product.[277] Because only potential future anticompetitive effect need be shown under §5 of the Federal Trade Commission Act, exclusive dealing could be challenged by the FTC even in the absence of present anticompetitive effect, although the FTC's present attitude toward vertical restraints would appear to diminish this threat.[278] The appropriate market in which to examine the competitive effect is the market for products that compete with or are reasonably interchangeable with the products subject

---

[275] Standard Fashion Co v Magrane-Houston Co, 258 US 346 (1922); Oxford Varnish Corp v Ault & Wiborg Corp, 83 F2d 764, 765 (6th Cir 1936); United States v Hartford-Empire Co, 46 F Supp 541, 579 (ND Ohio 1942), *affd,* 323 US 386 (1945).

[276] In this instance, there is simply no agreement or condition imposed on Buyer. *See, e.g.,* Dillon Materials Handling, Inc v Albion Indus, 567 F2d 1299, 1302-05 (5th Cir 1978).

[277] There is a question of whether §3 requires a less substantial showing of competitive effect than §1. Although the language of §3 requires only that the exclusive deal *may* have a not insignificant effect on competition, the Supreme Court has held that the requirement of §3 is met only where it is "probable that performance of the [exclusive dealing] contract will foreclose competition," indicating that a mere possibility of foreclosure of competition is not sufficient. Tampa Elec Co v Nashville Coal Co, 365 US 320, 327 (1961). In Standard Oil Co v United States, 337 US 293, 314 (1949), the Court had indicated that §3 is violated by exclusive dealing that creates a "potential clog on competition . . . [which], were it to become actual," might foreclose substantial competition. However, the Court had stated just above that §3 is satisfied by proof that "competition has been foreclosed." Thus, while the Court suggested that §3 might be an easier standard for the plaintiff to meet than §1, the Court arguably left little room for practical distinction between the two sections. Most exclusive dealing cases are brought under §3 assumedly on the ground that the cases under §1 require a higher showing of competitive effect—because §1 requires actual injury to competition. In cases involving tying arrangements, many recent court decisions have stated that there is no longer any practical difference between §1 and §3 standards.

[278] The recent decision in Beltone Elecs Corp, 3 Trade Reg Rep (CCH) ¶21,934 (July 6, 1982) indicates that the FTC has altered its position in light of the Supreme Court ruling in Continental TV, Inc v GTE Sylvania, Inc, 433 US 36 (1977). In *Beltone,* the FTC indicated that it would analyze the actual effect on competition, and would not find a violation of §5 unless the exclusive dealing might substantially decrease interbrand competition.

to the exclusive dealing arrangement.[279]

Two principal tests have been applied in the past to determine whether exclusive dealing arrangements have a substantial impact on the market under §1 and §3. The first test was adopted by the Supreme Court in 1949 in *Standard Oil Co v United States,*[280] (*Standard Stations*), where the Court used a percentage-of-the-market test—(the quantitative test). The Court held that §3 is violated whenever exclusive dealing forcloses "a Substantial share of the line of commerce affected."[281] In that case, the Court found that foreclosure of 16 per cent of retail gas stations in the western United States, whose sales accounted for 6.7 per cent of the gasoline sold in that area, was foreclosure of a substantial share of that market. It appears that the Court's decision was spurred somewhat by its conclusion that other major oil companies also had similar requirements and that, in total, these requirements encompassed 65 percent of the market.

In 1961, the Supreme Court adopted a somewhat different test in *Tampa Electric Co v Nashville Coal Co.*[282] Rather than looking purely at the percentage of the market foreclosed, the Court adopted a *qualitative test,* which sought to determine the real effect of the exclusive dealing arrangement on competition within the market. The Court held that it would consider not only the share of the total market foreclosed, but also "the relative strength of the parties" and "the probable immediate and future effects which [foreclosure] of that share of the market might have on competition therein," including any pro-competitive economic effects that justify the exclusive dealing arrangement.[283]

The Court analyzed the particular market (coal), and found that there were many competitors and that there were no artificial barriers to entry.[284] The Court also found that there was a strong need for long-term requirements contracts to assure Buyers of necessary supplies (coal for utilities) and Sellers of consistent demand.[285] For these reasons, the Court concluded that the

---

[279] American Motor Inns, Inc v Holiday Inns, Inc, 521 F2d 1230, 1253 (3d Cir 1975); the market may also be limited to the geographic area in which the Seller competes for the Buyer. Tampa Elec Co v Nashville Coal Co, 365 US 320 (1961).

[280] 337 US 293 (1949).

[281] The Court went on to state that Standard Oil's exclusive dealing program "creates just such a potential clog on competition as it was the purpose of §3 to remove wherever, were it to become actual, it would impede a substantial amount of competitive activity." 337 US at 314.

[282] 365 US 320 (1961).

[283] 365 US at 329, 334-35 It was suggested by the Court in *Tampa Electric* that there might be a threshold percentage of market foreclosure below which there could be no substantial injury to competition, and for which no further analysis was needed. However, because the percentage of the market foreclosed in *Tampa Electric* was so small (0.77%) the level of the threshold is by no means settled. *See, e.g.,* Beltone Elecs Corp, 3 Trade Reg Rep (CCH) ¶21,934 (July 6, 1982).

[284] 365 US at 328.

[285] 365 US at 329-30.

arrangement's net adverse impact on competition in the market would not be significant.

Following these Supreme Court decisions, the courts have looked at various factors to determine whether there has been a significant loss of competition in the market. In general, the foreclosure of a large portion of the market will still create a strong presumption of significant anticompetitive effect. Other evidence that may be considered to determine whether there is a significant anticompetitive effect are the exclusive dealing's effect on potential new entrants competing with Seller or Buyer; the market power of Seller, any increase in the market dominance of Seller, and the period of time covered by an agreement.[286] Weighed against any adverse effects on competition will be any *benefits* to competition or commerce that may result from and justify the exclusive dealing as a reasonable business practice. For example, the percentage of market foreclosure allowed a new firm seeking a foothold in a market dominated by large existing firms probably would be greater than the foreclosure allowed a large existing firm, and legitimate procompetitive business reasons for an exclusive dealing requirement may justify foreclosure of a limited portion of the market.[287] Finally, where the market is highly competitive, with ease of entry by new companies, or for other reasons Sellers have little leverage over Buyers, exclusive dealing is less likely to be found to have a significant anticompetitive effect.[288]

Such judicial analysis of whether the proscribed injury to competition has occurred in exclusive dealing cases is becoming increasingly similar to the competitive injury analysis approach suggested by the Supreme Court generally for nonprice vertical restraints in the *Continental TV Inc v GTE Sylvania* decision.[289] This approach eschews all automatic or fixed standards for a realistic appraisal of the effect of the conduct on competition. There is every reason to believe that this trend will continue.

This trend is also evident in Federal Trade Commission cases. Acting under §5, the FTC in the past has enjoined exclusive dealing arrangements even where there has not been any showing of actual adverse effect on competition, if it appeared that the arrangement had even the *potential* for adversely affecting

---

[286] Tampa Elec Co v Nashville Coal Co, 365 US 320, 329 (1961); Lessig v Tidewater Oil Co, 327 F2d 459, 468 (9th Cir), *cert denied,* 377 US 993 (1964) (preclusion of entrants and dominance of Seller); Bravman v Bassett Furniture Indus, Inc, 552 F2d 90 (3d Cir 1977), *cert denied,* 434 US 823 (1977); Mytinger & Casselberry, Inc v FTC, 301 F2d 534, 539-40 (DC Cir 1962) (dominant position of Seller, and increased dominance of Seller); Bowen v New York News, Inc, 366 F Supp 651, 679-80 (SDNY 1973), *affd,* 522 F2d 1242 (2d Cir 1975), *cert denied,* 425 US 936 (1976) (ease of entry); FTC v Motion Picture Advertising Serv Co, 344 US 392, 395 (1953) (length of time covered by the agreement).

[287] Tampa Elec Co v Nashville Coal Co, 365 US 320, 334-35 (1961); American Motor Inns, Inc v Holiday Inns, Inc, 521 F2d 1230, 1252 (3d Cir 1975).

[288] Refrigeration Engg Corp v Frick Co, 370 F Supp 702, 709 (WD Tex 1974); Bowen v New York News, Inc, 366 F Supp 651, 679-80 (SDNY 1973), *affd,* 522 F2d 1242 (2d Cir 1975), *cert denied,* 425 US 936 (1976).

[289] 433 US 36 (1977).

competition. In *FTC v Brown Shoe Co,*[290] the Supreme Court upheld an FTC order enjoining Brown Shoe from imposing exclusive dealing restrictions on its distributors, even though these distributors represented only 1 per cent of the market. The Court noted that the FTC had broad powers to prevent such arrangements where they were contrary to the policies in §1 and §3, even though they did not actually violate those sections due to lack of actual anticompetitive effect.[291] Courts have frequently cited this holding that no actual anticompetitive effect need be shown in affirming FTC holdings enjoining exclusive dealing arrangements, particularly where the Seller had a substantial share of the market.[292]

A recent FTC decision has signaled a significant change in the commission's approach, however. In *Beltone Electronics Corp,* the FTC conceded that in 1956 it had found a similar arrangement in the same industry unlawful, but found that the law had "undergone considerable evolution" and that rule of reason analysis now should be used for nonprice vertical restraints.[293] Therefore, the FTC undertook an extensive analysis of competition in the market, relying on several factors, and ultimately found that, despite its sizable market share, Beltone's exclusive dealing arrangements with its dealers would not have a significant adverse effect on interbrand competition. The FTC found that analysis of interbrand competition rather than intrabrand competition was mandated by recent Supreme Court decisions, particularly *GTE Sylvania.*

§4.48 Must Seller have sufficient power over the market to impose the exclusive dealing condition in order to find exclusive dealing?

The market power of Seller is a consideration in analysis of exclusive dealing arrangements, but it is not as significant as in the analysis of tying arrangements where it is often held to be a necessary element of a per se offense.[294] Although in a tying arrangement Buyer is unlikely to take the undesirable tied item unless forced to do so by a Seller with market power, there are circumstances in which Buyer may find it desirable to enter into an exclusive dealing or requirements contract with Seller. Because coercion is not necessary to establish exclusive dealing, Seller is not protected from liability simply because

---

[290] 384 US 316 (1966).

[291] The Supreme Court held that the FTC had the power under §5 to enjoin conduct which conflicts with "the basic policies of the Sherman and Clayton Acts even though such practices may not actually violate these laws." 384 US at 321 (footnote omitted).

[292] Luria Bros & Co v FTC, 389 F2d 847, 858-60 (3d Cir), *cert denied,* 393 US 829 (1968); LG Balfour Co v FTC, 442 F2d 1, 19-20 (7th Cir 1971).

[293] 3 Trade Reg Rep (CCH) ¶21,934 (July 6, 1982) Nonprice vertical restraints include exclusive dealing arrangements, exclusive territories or customers, and related restrictions.

[294] See **§4.22.**

it lacked the power to require Buyer to enter such an agreement.[295] Indeed, courts often distinguish exclusive dealing from requirements contracts by using the former to describe coerced agreements, and the latter to describe voluntary agreements.[296]

The possession of market power by Seller does have a major impact in the court's determination of whether the exclusive dealing has a significant anticompetitive effect, however. Many courts, in analyzing the effect of exclusive dealing on competition, have concentrated on the dominance of Seller in the industry, the relative strength of the parties, and the sales structure of the industry.[297] All three of these factors directly reflect of Seller's market power. Thus Seller's market power and the ability to force exclusive dealing arrangements on Buyers may greatly affect the ultimate decision in an exclusive dealing case.

§4.49 Can exclusive dealing be justified where Seller is a new or small competitor seeking to obtain penetration or viability in the market?

Generally, a new, small Seller may enter into limited exclusive dealing arrangements with a high degree of impunity. The creation of a significant new supplier will generally be regarded as procompetitive, and thus not violative of §1 or §3. The Supreme Court in *Standard Oil Co of California v United States* indicated that a Seller seeking to establish a foothold against entrenched competitors would have a legitimate reason to seek an exclusive dealing arrangement.[298] The Court also observed that an exclusive dealing arrangement would give protection to a new or small competitor against price fluctuations, and that a predictable market was of special importance to a new entrant with limited capital.[299] Similarly, an arrangement locking out powerful competitors has been held a valid form of competition for a small established new Seller. One court has held that "[t]o penalize the small manufacturer for competing in this way not only fails to promote the policy of the antitrust laws but defeats it"[300]

---

[295] Anchor Serum Co v FTC, 217 F2d 867 (7th Cir 1954).

[296] Standard Oil Co v United States, 337 US 293, 306-07 (1949); Lessig v Tidewater Oil Co, 327 F2d 459, 469 n 22 (9th Cir), *cert denied,* 377 US 993 (1964).

[297] Tampa Elec Co v Nashville Coal Co, 365 US 320 (1961); Mytinger & Casselberry, Inc v FTC, 301 F2d 534 (DC Cir 1962); Lessig v Tidewater Oil Co, 327 F2d 459, 468 (9th Cir), *cert denied,* 377 US 993 (1964); Fashion Originators' Guild of Am, Inc v FTC, 312 US 457 (1941); Outboard Marine & Mfg Co, 52 FTC 1553 (1956).

[298] 337 US 293, 307-08 (1949).

[299] *Id.*

[300] Packard Motor Car Co v Webster Motor Car Co, 243 F2d 418, 421 (DC Cir), *cert denied,* 355 US 822 (1957).

§4.50 Can exclusive dealing be justified where the condition is necessary to assure proper service, promotion, or viability of the product?

Sellers often try to justify exclusive dealing conditions on the ground that such conditions are necessary because only Buyers who resell Seller's product exclusively will give Seller's product adequate attention with respect to service, promotion, or inventory. Such arrangements are often coupled with exclusive territories for each Buyer as an incentive to Buyer to limit its product line to Seller's product and to promote that product vigorously.[301] This attempted justification has generally been rejected by courts in the past as insufficient by itself to justify exclusive dealing,[302] but this view appears to be changing.

In recent cases, most notably the Supreme Court's decision in *Continental TV, Inc v GTE Sylvania, Inc,* the courts have stressed that vertical restraints may have a procompetitive effect as between competing brands where they are instrumental in establishing or maintaining a strong competitive brand in a market consisting of other strong suppliers and brands.[303] The Federal Trade Commission, in the recent *Beltone Electronics Corp* decision, found that Beltone's exclusive dealing arrangements were important in allowing it to continue as a strong competitive force in the market.[304] Where there are not strong competing products, however, arrangements that foreclose competitors from important Buyers may be prohibited without regard to whether the arrangement improves the promotion, service, or inventory of Seller's product, particularly where Seller is dominant.[305]

---

[301] *See* Dictograph Prods, Inc v FTC, 217 F2d 821 (2d Cir 1954), *cert denied,* 349 US 940 (1955); Continental TV, Inc v GTE Sylvania, Inc, 433 US 36 (1977); *see also* Beltone Elecs, Inc, 3 Trade Reg Rep (CCH) ¶21,934 (July 6, 1982).

[302] Standard Oil Co v United States, 337 US 293 (1949); Fashion Originators' Guild of Am, Inc v FTC, 312 US 457 (1941); Anchor Serum Co v FTC, 217 F2d 867 (7th Cir 1954).

[303] 433 US 36 (1977). *See also* American Motor Inns, Inc v Holiday Inns, Inc, 521 F2d 1230, 1252 (3d Cir 1975); Refrigeration Engg Corp v Frick Co, 370 F Supp 702, 709 (WD Tex 1974); Bowen v New York News, Inc, 366 F Supp 651, 679-80 (SDNY 1973), *affd,* 522 F2d 1242 (2d Cir 1975), *cert denied,* 425 US 936 (1976).

[304] Beltone Elecs, Inc, 3 Trade Reg Rep (CCH) ¶21,934 (July 6, 1982). The FTC appeared to feel that Beltone had chosen a marketing strategy that was unwise and would result in continued loss of market share. Although the FTC based its decision on the lack of effect on interbrand competition, it seemed clear that the FTC was, in the end, willing to let Beltone continue its practices because that created the greatest possibility that Beltone would be able to stay in the market and compete.

[305] LG Balfour Co v FTC, 442 F2d 1, 15 (7th Cir 1971); Anchor Serum Co v FTC, 217 F2d 867 (7th Cir 1954) *See also* Dictograph Prod Inc, 50 FTC 281, 295 (1953), *affd sub nom* Dictograph Prod, Inc v FTC, 217 F2d 821 (2d Cir 1954), *cert denied,* 349 US 940 (1955). This case was in many senses similar to *Beltone,* but was analyzed under pre-*Sylvania* standards. The court of appeals rejected any business justification for the exclusive dealing which involved 22% of the retail outlets for hearing aids.

§4.51 Can exclusive dealing be justified where it does not include all sales or exclude all competitors?

Analysis of a partial exclusive dealing arrangement may differ significantly from analysis of a total exclusive dealing arrangement; indeed, it may not be an *exclusive* dealing arrangement.[306] But if the court finds significant exclusion of competing suppliers as a condition of the sale, the court may find that the arrangement has a sufficiently great adverse effect on competition to violate §1 of the Sherman Act or §3 of the Clayton Act. The arrangement would be less likely to be violative of §1 or §3 if the Seller does not represent a dominant force in the market.[307] In the case of partial exclusive dealing arrangements, §5 of the Federal Trade Commission Act may be particularly important, for such exclusive dealing might be struck down even without a significant effect on competition if the FTC finds that the arrangement was likely to have significant anticompetitive effects.[308]

§4.52 Does it matter that the sales are in foreign countries, or are only made within a single state?

In order to violate §3, the sale or lease must be "for use, consumption, or resale within the United States." Therefore, exclusive dealing arrangements involving sales only for use outside the United States do not violate §3.[309] They may, however, violate §1, if they restrain foreign or interstate commerce. Foreign exclusive dealing arrangements may also violate foreign antitrust law.

While purely intrastate sales with no interstate connection arguably are exempt from the antitrust laws, the defense is not used often. The test under §3 is more narrow than that under §1. Under §3, Seller must be "a person engaged in commerce" and the exclusive dealing must be "in the course of such commerce." Therefore, if the exclusive dealing sale was not by a Seller involved in interstate commerce, or if the exclusive dealing sale was not interstate, §3 does not apply.[310]

Section 1, on the other hand, has a much broader coverage. All that is required is that the exclusive dealing have some effect on interstate commerce.

---

[306] Magnus Petroleum Co v Skelly Oil Co, 599 F2d 196 (7th Cir), *cert denied,* 444 US 916 (1979).

[307] Smith v Scrivner-Boogaart, Inc, 447 F2d 1014 (10th Cir 1971), *cert denied,* 404 US 1059 (1972).

[308] FTC v Brown Shoe Co, 384 US 316, 321 (1966).

[309] However, sales in the United States by foreign companies *are* covered by §3. *See* United States v Volkswagen of Am, Inc, 182 F Supp 405 (DNJ 1960); Reliable Volkswagen Sales & Serv Co v World-Wide Auto Corp, 182 F Supp 412 (DNJ 1960).

[310] Gulf Oil Corp v Copp Paving Co, 419 US 186 (1974); Mailand v Powerine Oil Co, 1973-1 Trade Cas (CCH) ¶74,472 (CD Cal Aug 28, 1972).

Therefore, if the items sold are manufactured out of state, if Buyer or Seller competes directly or indirectly with out-of-state competitors, or if the products resold by Buyer end up out of state, the §1 commerce test is likely to be met.[311] Because it is difficult to prevent all of these connections with interstate commerce, the intrastate only defense is rarely available under §1. Because a plaintiff can usually resort to §1, and is not limited to §3, the intrastate only defense is unlikely to be available for most exclusive dealing arrangements.

§4.53 What are the penalties for exclusive dealing?

Exclusive dealing arrangements that violate either Sherman Act §1 or Clayton Act §3 may result in private treble damage liability.[312] Such exclusive dealing arrangements may also be enjoined in actions brought by the government.[313] Finally, under §5 of the Federal Trade Commission Act, exclusive dealing arrangements may be enjoined by the FTC even in cases where the anticompetitive effect has not fully materialized.[314]

In the case of private litigation, if the party suing is a Buyer who has been required to purchase all of an item from Seller, the damages in many cases may not be significant, merely being treble the difference between what Buyer paid and what it can show it would have paid in the absence of the exclusive dealing condition. In many cases, there may be no damages. Damages suffered by a Buyer class or multiple Buyers suing together could be more significant, though still probably limited.[315]

If the party suing is a competitor of Seller whose sales nationwide have been diminished by the exclusive dealing arrangements, the damages may be significant, representing lost profits and potential profits over a number of years, lost business value, and lost opportunities, which, when trebled, may be significant. A suit brought by such a competitor might well include a §2 monopolization count if Seller is dominant in the market.

---

[311] The commerce covered by §1 is no less broad than the commerce over which the federal government has power under the Commerce Clause of the Constitution.

[312] §4 of the Clayton Act (15 USC §15) provides for treble damages whether the actions brought under §1 or §3.

[313] *See, e.g.,* United Shoe Mach Corp v United States, 258 US 451 (1922); Standard Oil Co v United States, 337 US 293 (1949). Generally, however, the United States Department of Justice will not bring a suit in a simple exclusive dealing case.

[314] *See, e.g.,* Mytinger & Casselberry, Inc v FTC, 301 F2d 534 (DC Cir 1962); Adolph Coors Co v FTC, 497 F2d 1178 (10th Cir 1974), *cert denied,* 419 US 1105 (1975); Anchor Serum Co v FTC, 217 F2d 867 (7th Cir 1954); FTC v Brown Shoe Co, 384 US 316 (1966). The FTC, in these and many other cases, has sought to enjoin exclusive dealing arrangements. However, the Beltone Elecs Corp decision (3 Trade Reg Rep (CCH) ¶21,934 (July 6, 1982)) may signal less FTC exclusive dealing litigation.

[315] Damages are often a difficult element to prove, particularly on a class-wide basis.

Reciprocal Dealing

§4.54 Where Seller purchases item A from Buyer, may Seller condition those purchases on Buyer's agreement to purchase item B from Seller?

In some instances, Seller may be in a position to restrict what Buyer buys not because of Seller's power in the market for the item it sells, but rather because of Seller's power as a purchaser of items from Buyer. Where Seller induces Buyer to agree to purchase Seller's product as a condition of Seller's agreement to purchase Buyer's product, it is known as reciprocal dealing, and it has been condemned often by the courts. Reciprocal dealing is considered anticompetitive and undesirable for essentially the same reasons as tying (discussed in **§4.02**): if Buyer purchases item B from Seller because of a reciprocal dealing agreement, Buyer is not free to purchase the competing product that has the best price or quality.[316] Therefore, competitors of Seller are unfairly foreclosed or disadvantaged, and free competition is restrained.

Reciprocal dealing arrangements do not violate §3 of the Clayton Act, as there is not a "lease . . . sale or contract for sale" by Seller which is conditioned on an agreement not to use a competitor's goods.[317] Instead, it is the *purchase* by Seller that is conditioned. Reciprocal dealing may violate §1 of the Sherman Act where it results in an unreasonable restraint of trade.[318] It may also violate §5 of the Federal Trade Commission Act as an "unfair method of competition."[319] However, most reciprocal dealing cases arise under §7 of the Clayton Act, which is beyond the scope of this chapter. So §7 cases are not considered here except to the extent that they shed light on what is permissible or impermissible under antitrust laws with respect to distribution.[320] Two basic ele-

---

[316] Spartan Grain & Mill v Ayers, 581 F2d 419, 425 (5th Cir 1978) ("The two labels [tying and reciprocal dealing] refer to similar phenomenons.") Betaseed, Inc v U&I, Inc, 1982-2 Trade Cas (CCH) ¶64,878 (9th Cir July 25, 1982) (to the same effect); United States v General Dynamics Corp, 258 F Supp 36 (SDNY 1966); FTC v Consolidated Foods Corp, 380 US 592 (1965).

[317] Spartan Grain & Mill v Ayers, 581 F2d 419, 428 (5th Cir 1978).

[318] Betaseed, Inc v U&I, Inc, 1982-2 Trade Cas (CCH) ¶64,878, at 72,413 (9th Cir July 25, 1982); WL Gore & Assocs, Inc v Carlisle Corp, 381 F Supp 680, 703 (D Del 1974), *affd in part and revd in part,* 529 F2d 614 (3d Cir 1976); Ryals v National Car Rental Sys, Inc, 404 F Supp 481, 485-86 (D Minn 1975); Southern Concrete Co v United States Steel Corp, 535 F2d 313 (5th Cir 1976), *cert denied,* 429 US 1096 (1977); United States v General Dynamics Corp, 258 F Supp 36 (SDNY 1966).

[319] §5 has been used by the FTC to bring actions which have resulted in consent decrees. *See, e.g.,* California Packing Co, 25 FTC 879 (1937). *See also* FTC v Consolidated Foods Corp, 380 US 592 (1965).

[320] Reciprocity is most often considered in relation to *conglomerate mergers,* between companies which are not horizontal competitors. These types of mergers may be challenged under §7 of the Clayton Act on the ground that the merger of the two

ments are essential to a finding of reciprocal dealing in violation of §1: First, Seller must obtain the express or implied agreement of Buyer, that so long as Seller purchases from Buyer, Buyer will also purchase from Seller; and, second, a significant amount of commerce must be foreclosed, although two additional elements—Seller's economic power and coercion—may be necessary to constitute a per se violation.[321] Reciprocal dealing may be in violation of §5 of the FTC Act where there is only potential rather than actual foreclosure of commerce.

With respect to the first element, it is first necessary that Seller have a dual purchaser/supplier role and it is usually the case that Seller is a large company or a multiunit corporation acting in several markets—in some as a purchaser, in others as a supplier. In cases where the exclusive dealing is coerced, Seller generally must be an important customer to Buyer. It is not necessary to show that Buyer was coerced into accepting the reciprocal dealing arrangement.[322] Even if Buyer willingly entered into the agreement, it is still a reciprocal agreement that forecloses other suppliers and therefore may be anticompetitive, but often such voluntary reciprocal dealing arrangements will be tested under the rule of reason, whereas coerced agreements may be treated as per se violations.[323]

It is not necessary that the reciprocal agreement be expressed. It can be an implied or silent understanding on the part of Buyer that, should Buyer fail to purchase from Seller, Seller would cease purchasing from Buyer. Such a message could be conveyed by Seller in many ways: expressly, by a course of conduct or by policy under which Seller stops purchasing from Buyers who do not purchase from Seller, or even by the establishment of internal structures within Seller's company to monitor both purchases to and sales by Buyer with

---

companies will result in reciprocal dealing with other companies or within the newly formed company, either of which will reduce competition in the market. *See, e.g.*, FTC v Consolidated Foods Corp, 380 US 592 (1965).

[321] Spartan Grain & Mill v Ayers, 581 F2d 419, 424 (5th Cir 1978) (relying on tying case precedent and requiring coercion and market power in order to find a per se violation); Betaseed, Inc v U&I, Inc, 1982-2 Trade Cas (CCH) ¶64,878 (9th Cir July 25, 1982) (requiring market power and coercion for a per se violation); United States v General Dynamics Corp, 258 F Supp 36, 58-59 (SDNY 1966); WIXT Television, Inc v Meredith Corp, 506 F Supp 1003, 1007 (NDNY 1980); Southern Concrete v United States Steel Corp, 535 F2d 313, 317 (5th Cir 1976), *cert denied,* 429 US 1096 (1977); United States v Airco, Inc, 386 F Supp 915, 917 (SDNY 1974); Ryals v National Car Rental Sys, 404 F Supp 481, 485-86 (D Minn 1975); United States v Empire Gas Corp, 393 F Supp 903, 915 (SD Mo 1975), *affd,* 537 F2d 296 (1976), *cert denied,* 429 US 1122 (1977).

[322] Betaseed, Inc v U&I, Inc, 1982-2 Trade Cas (CCH) ¶64,878 (9th Cir July 25, 1982); WIXT Television, Inc v Meredith Corp, 506 F Supp 1003, 1018-19 (NDNY 1980); United States v General Dynamics Corp, 258 F Supp 36, 58-59 (SDNY 1966).

[323] Betaseed, Inc v U&I, Inc, 1982-2 Trade Cas (CCH) ¶64,878 at 72,410-23 (9th Cir July 25, 1982); Columbia Nitrogen Corp v Royster Co 451 F2d 3, 13-14 (4th Cir 1971); WIXT Television, Inc v Meredith Corp, 506 F Supp 1003, 1018-19 (NDNY 1980).

the knowledge of Buyer.[324] Numerous consent decrees have been entered requiring Sellers to terminate internal or external business practices that might induce Buyers to participate in reciprocal dealing.[325]

With respect to the second element—the significant foreclosure of competition—it would appear that the standard under §1 is essentially the same as in tying cases, i.e., any amount of commerce that is not de minimis.[326] However, there are so few cases that it is not possible to state with any confidence what amount of reciprocal dealing would be sufficient to meet the test. Furthermore, although in the past coerced reciprocal dealing has been treated essentially as a per se offense where a not insignificant amount of commerce was affected, the developments represented by the Supreme Court's decision in *Continental TV, Inc v GTE Sylvania, Inc* suggest that reciprocal dealing may increasingly be tested under a rule of reason standard, and the actual effect on competition will be assessed by the courts.[327] This trend may also have a

---

[324] Betaseed, Inc v U&I, Inc, 1982-2 Trade Cas (CCH) ¶64,878 (9th Cir July 25, 1982; United States v Inland Steel Co, 1970 Trade Cas (CCH) ¶73,197 (ND Ill July 1, 1970); United States v Ingersoll-Rand Co, 320 F2d 509 (3d Cir 1963); WIXT Television, Inc v Meredith Corp, 506 F Supp 1003 (NDNY 1980).

[325] United States v United States Steel Corp, 1969 Trade Cas (CCH) ¶72,826 (DC Pa Aug 25, 1969); United States v Inland Steel Co, 1970 Trade Cas (CCH) ¶73,197 (ND Ill July 1, 1970); United States v General Tire & Rubber Co, 1970 Trade Cas (CCH) ¶73,303 (ND Ohio Oct 21, 1970).

[326] Betaseed, Inc v U&I, Inc, 1982-2 Trade Cas (CCH) ¶64,878 at 72,414 n 33 (9th Cir July 25, 1982); WIXT Television, Inc v Meredith Corp, 506 F Supp 1003, 1029 (NDNY 1980); Northern Pac RR Co v United States, 356 US 1 (1958); United States v General Dynamics Corp, 258 F Supp 36 (SDNY 1966).

[327] Continental TV, Inc v GTE Sylvania, 433 US 36 (1977); *see also* Metrix Warehouse, Inc v Daimler-Benz Aktiengesellschaft, 1982-2 Trade Cas (CCH) ¶64,861 (DM June 4, 1982).

There is some evidence of this developing attitude on the part of the two antitrust enforcement agencies. For example, in Shop & Save Food Mkts, Inc v Pneumo Corp, 1982-2 Trade Cas (CCH) ¶64,832 (2d Cir 1982), a private action, the Department of Justice filed a brief as amicus curiae in support of reconsideration by the court of its previous decision applying a per se tying analysis. In its conclusion in that case, the court agreed with the Department of Justice and the defendants, finding that it would not invoke the per se rule. The court noted, "[i]n deciding whether to invoke the *per se* rule, we must be cognizant of the teachings of the Supreme Court that 'easy labels do not always supply ready answers' " (citing Broadcast Music Inc v CBS, Inc, 441 US 1, 8 (1979)). 1982-2 Trade Cas (CCH) ¶64,832, at 72,145 (July 2, 1982).

In another example, Assitant Attorney General William F. Baxter, Chief of the Antitrust Division, announced in March 1982 that after a thorough review of the case, the Justice Department was dismissing its suit against Mercedes-Benz of North America, Inc in which the government had alleged that there was tying between the sale of automotive replacement parts and the granting of a franchise to handle Mercedes-Benz automobiles. CCH Trade Reg Rep, No 534 (March 22, 1982). The Justice Department concluded that tying arrangements of this sort did not injure competition or create unreasonable market power.

similar effect on the showing necessary under §5.[328]

[328] FTC Chairman Miller has suggested that vertical restraints, including even price restraints, be challenged only where they have an unreasonable adverse effect on competition. *See, e.g.*, Miller's dissenting opinion in Russell Stover Candies, Inc, 3 Trade Reg Rep (CCH) ¶21,933 at 22,372 (July 1, 1982). The FTC has held that certain restraints, while they may have anticompetitive effects with respect to a certain brand, may in fact enhance interbrand competition, and that the principal focus should be on this interbrand competition.

May Seller Restrict Where or to Whom Buyer Resells?

5

*Irving Scher**

*Mr. Scher is a member of the New York Bar. The author wishes to thank Martin S. Hyman of Weil, Gotshal & Manges for his assistance in the preparation of this chapter.

What is the general rule with regard to restrictions on the customers to whom Buyer may resell?

§5.12 What are vertical customer resale restrictions?
§5.13 What valid business purposes can vertical customer resale restrictions serve?
§5.14 What anticompetitive purposes can vertical customer resale restrictions serve?
§5.15 How is the legality of vertical customer resale restrictions determined?

Has the rule with regard to vertical nonprice resale restrictions always been this way?

§5.16 What rule for analyzing vertical nonprice resale restrictions was first articulated by the Supreme Court?
§5.17 How was this rule changed in 1967?
§5.18 What exceptions to the *Schwinn* rule did the lower courts carve out?
§5.19 Why did the Supreme Court return to the rule of reason in *Sylvania?*

Does it matter whether the goods are distributed on an agency or consignment basis?

§5.20 What is an agency?
§5.21 What is a consignment?
§5.22 Have territorial and customer restrictions in agency and consignment arrangements been treated differently than outright sales under the antitrust laws?

Does it matter whether the party imposing the restrictions is a licensor?

§5.23 How are territorial and customer restrictions in licensing arrangements treated under the antitrust laws?
§5.24 Is the rule any different with regard to restraints imposed on the resale of patented articles?

Does it matter whether a nonprice resale restriction is motivated by Seller or Buyer?

§5.25 Does the source of the restraint affect its legality?
§5.26 What factors do the courts consider in determining whether a restraint is vertical or horizontal?

May Seller arbitrate or settle disputes among its customers concerning territories or customers?

§5.27 Will Seller participation in an arrangement among Buyers be treated as a horizontal or vertical resale restriction?

§5.28 Of what significance is it that Seller is controlled or owned by Buyers?

§5.29 Will Seller involvement in a dispute between Buyers automatically implicate the Seller in an unlawful conspiracy?

What role does purpose play?

§5.30 In its rule of reason analysis does the court consider Seller's purpose in imposing the resale restrictions?

§5.31 Will a valid business purpose save an otherwise unreasonable resale restriction?

§5.32 Is the restraint justified when Seller is attempting to introduce a new product?

§5.33 Is the restraint justified when Seller is attempting to enter a new territory or sell to a new class of customers?

§5.34 Is the restraint justified when Seller is attempting to stop an erosion of its market share?

§5.35 Is the restraint justified when Seller is attempting to encourage Buyers to perform promotional activities or postsale services or to discourage *free riding?*

§5.36 Is the restraint justified when Seller is attempting to promote consumer safety, avoid product liability suits, maintain quality control, and/or fulfill warranty obligations?

§5.37 Is the restraint justified when Seller is attempting to promote distribution of its goods?

§5.38 Does Seller's market share make a difference under the rule of reason?

§5.39 Does the market share of Seller's competitors make a difference under the rule of reason?

Will less restrictive territorial or customer restraints solve the antitrust problem?

§5.40 Is the existence of less restrictive means to achieve the desired end relevant under the rule of reason?

§5.41 What less restrictive alternatives have been upheld by the courts?

Will a primary area of responsibility clause solve the antitrust problem?

§5.42 What is a primary area of responsibility clause?

§5.43 How is the legality of such a restriction tested?

§5.44 Under what circumstances have primary area of responsibility clauses been held unlawful?

Will a profit pass-over clause solve the antitrust problem?

§5.45 What is a profit pass-over clause?

What is the general rule with regard to vertical nonprice resale restrictions?

§5.01 What are vertical nonprice resale restrictions?

Vertical nonprice resale restrictions are Seller-imposed restrictions which limit the geographic territories in which, and/or the customers to whom, the Seller's product(s) may be resold by distributors or dealers. In essence, they are methods by which Sellers attempt to control the marketing of their goods in the chain of distribution.

Although the distinction is not always clear, vertical nonprice resale restrictions are to be distinguished from vertical price restrictions, e.g., arrangements under which Seller restricts the ability of its distributors or dealers independently to determine the prices at which they resell Seller's goods.[1]

Among the more common types of vertical nonprice resale restrictions are the following:

1. *Airtight territorial restrictions* which require distributors or dealers to resell only to customers located within a specified geographic area
2. *Airtight customer restrictions* which require distributors or dealers to resell only to certain customers or certain categories of customers
3. *Location clauses* which require dealers to resell only from Seller-authorized locations
4. *Primary area of responsibility clauses* which obligate distributors or dealers to

---

[1] See **§§5.10, 5.11, 5.27.**

maintain effective distribution of Seller's products in defined geographic areas or to defined categories of customers. Such clauses are generally less restrictive than airtight territorial or customer restrictions because they do not necessarily preclude the distributor or dealer from selling in other geographic areas or to other categories of customers

5. *Profit pass-over clauses* which obligate a distributor or dealer who sells to customers outside an assigned territory or customer category to pay compensation to the distributor or dealer who otherwise would have sold to the customers involved. In theory, a profit pass-over is designed to compensate the nonselling distributor or dealer for expenditures incurred in: (a) developing—through investment, advertising and promotion—the territory or customer category in which the sales were made; and/or (b) performing postsale services on products sold by other distributors or dealers

§5.02 How does a vertical nonprice resale restriction interrelate with an exclusive distributorship?

On occasion, Seller may want only one distributor or dealer to resell its products in a particular territory. Initially, Seller may seek to accomplish this goal by confining its sales to one distributor or dealer in the particular territory. Depending upon such factors as the size of the territory and the practical ability of other distributors to transact business in that territory, such confinement of sales may effectively insulate the exclusive distributor or dealer from intrabrand competition.[2] If the confinement does not adequately insulate the exclusive distributor or dealer, Seller may decide to use vertical nonprice resale restrictions to prohibit or restrict other distributors or dealers from soliciting sales in the exclusive territory.

Exclusive distributorships—whether or not combined with vertical restrictions placed on other distributors or dealers—are tested under the rule of reason.[3] They are generally found to be lawful,[4] at least in cases in which: the

---

[2] See Pitofsky, *The Sylvania Case: Antitrust Analysis of Non-Price Vertical Restrictions,* 78 Colum L Rev 1, 4 (1978). Intrabrand competition has been defined by the Supreme Court as "the competition between the distributors—wholesale or retail—of the products of a particular manufacturer." Continental TV, Inc v GTE Sylvania Inc, 433 US 36, 55 (1977).

[3] *See* Beltone Elecs Corp, 3 Trade Reg Rep (CCH) ¶21,934 (FTC July 6, 1982).

[4] *E.g.,* JBL Enters, Inc v Jhirmack Enters, Inc, 698 F2d 1011, 1018 (9th Cir 1983); Oreck Corp v Whirlpool Corp, 579 F2d 126, 129-30 (2d Cir) (en banc), *cert. denied,* 439 US 946 (1978); Jos E Seagram & Sons v Hawaiian Oke & Liquors Ltd, 416 F2d 71, 78 (9th Cir 1969), *cert denied,* 396 US 1062 (1970); Ace Beer Distribs, Inc v Kohn, 318 F2d 283, 286-87 (6th Cir 1963); Packard Motor Car Co v Webster Motor Car Co, 243 F2d 418, 420 (DC Cir), *cert. denied,* 355 US 822 (1957); Top-All Varieties, Inc v Hallmark Cards, Inc, 301 F Supp 703 (SDNY 1969); Schwing Motor Co v Hudson Sales Corp, 138 F Supp 899 (D Md), *affd,* 239 F2d 176 (4th Cir 1956), *cert. denied,* 355 US 823 (1957).

Seller is not a monopolist; competitive products are readily available; the exclusive is not too broad (temporally or geographically); and the exclusive is not in furtherance of a broader scheme which contravenes the antitrust laws.[5]

§5.03 Are vertical nonprice resale restrictions per se illegal or are they tested by the rule of reason?

In its 1977 decision in *Continental TV, Inc v GTE Sylvania Inc,*[6] the Supreme Court held that vertical nonprice resale restrictions should be tested by the rule of reason, under which "the factfinder weighs all of the circumstances of a case in deciding whether a restrictive practice should be prohibited as imposing an unreasonable restraint on competition."[7] The *Sylvania* Court recog-

---

See generally United States v Arnold, Schwinn & Co, 388 US 365, 376 (1967), *overruled on other grounds,* Continental TV, Inc v GTE Sylvania Inc, 433 US 36 (1977):

> [A] manufacturer of a product other and equivalent brands of which are readily available in the market may select his customers, and for this purpose he may "franchise" certain dealers to whom, alone, he will sell his goods. . . . If the restraint stops at this point—if nothing more is involved than vertical "confinement" of the manufacturer's own sales of the merchandise to selected dealers, and if competitive products are readily available to others, the restrictions, on these facts alone, would not violate the Sherman Act. (Citation omitted.)

[5] *See* Carlson Mach Tools, Inc v American Tool, Inc, 678 F2d 1253, 1259-60 (5th Cir 1982); Quality Mercury, Inc v Ford Motor Co, 542 F2d 466, 469-72 (8th Cir 1976), *cert denied,* 433 US 914 (1977); Elder-Beerman Stores Corp v Federated Dept Stores, Inc, 459 F2d 138 (6th Cir 1972); Bascom Launder Corp v Telecoin Corp, 204 F2d 331, 335 (2d Cir), *cert denied,* 345 US 994 (1953); Hershey Chocolate Corp v FTC, 121 F2d 968, 970-71 (3d Cir 1941); Westman Commn Co v Hobart Corp, 461 F Supp 627 (D Colo 1978); Wisdom Rubber Indus v Johns-Manville Sales Corp, 415 F Supp 363, 365-66 (D Hawaii 1976); United States v Chicago Tribune-NY News Syndicate, Inc, 309 F Supp 1301, 1307-08 (SDNY 1970); United States v American Smelting & Ref Co, 182 F Supp 834 (SDNY 1960).

[6] 433 US 36 (1977).

[7] 433 US at 49 (footnote omitted). The classic formulation of the rule of reason—"the standard traditionally applied for the majority of anticompetitive practices challenged under [Section] 1 of the [Sherman] Act" (433 US at 59)—was articulated by Justice Brandeis in Chicago Bd of Trade v United States, 246 US 231, 238 (1918):

> The true test of legality is whether the restraint imposed is such as merely regulates and perhaps thereby promotes competition or whether it is such as may suppress or even destroy competition. To determine that question the court must ordinarily consider the facts peculiar to the business to which the restraint is applied; its condition before and after the restraint was imposed; the nature of the restraint and its effect, actual or probable. The history of the restraint, the evil believed to exist, the reason for adopting the particular remedy, the purpose or end sought to be attained, are all relevant facts.

See also Broadcast Music, Inc v CBS, Inc, 441 US 1 (1979); National Socy of Professional Engrs v United States, 435 US 679 (1978); Standard Oil Co v United States, 211 US 1 (1911). *See generally* First Beverages, Inc v Royal Crown Cola Co, 612 F2d 1164, 1170-71 (9th Cir), *cert denied,* 447 US 924 (1980); Clairol, Inc v Boston Discount Center, Inc, 608 F2d 1114, 1123-25 (6th Cir 1979).

nized that, unlike trade restraints which are "manifestly anticompetitive" (and thus subject to the rule of per se illegality),[8] vertical nonprice resale restrictions may "promote interbrand competition by allowing the manufacturer to achieve certain efficiencies in the distribution of his products."[9] Finding "no persuasive support for expanding the per se rule,"[10] the Court concluded that "[w]hen anticompetitive effects are shown to result from particular vertical restrictions they can be adequately policed under the rule of reason."[11]

§5.04 What is interbrand competition?

"Interbrand competition is the competition among the manufacturers of the same generic product."[12] For example, manufacturers A, B, and C, all of whom make comparable television sets, engage in interbrand competition in the sale of those television sets.

Vertical nonprice resale restrictions may enhance interbrand competition by enabling a manufacturer "to compete more effectively against other manufacturers."[13] And, as the Supreme Court declared in *Sylvania,* "interbrand competition . . . is the primary concern of antitrust law."[14]

§5.05 What is intrabrand competition?

"[I]ntrabrand competition is the competition between the distributors—wholesale or retail—of the products of a particular manufacturer."[15] For example, distributors X, Y, and Z, all of whom sell television sets made by manufacturer A, may engage in intrabrand competition (depending upon such factors as location, transportation costs, local demand, etc.) in the sale of manufacturer A's televisions.

Vertical nonprice resale restrictions may "reduce intrabrand competition by limiting the number of sellers of a particular product competing for the busi-

---

[8] 433 US at 50-51 (citing Northern Pac Ry v United States, 356 US 1, 5 (1958) (per se rule properly applied only to restrictive agreements which have a "pernicious effect on competition" and lack "any redeeming virtue")). *See also* White Motor Co v United States, 372 US 253, 263 (1963) (per se rule properly applied only to "naked restraints of trade with no purpose except stifling of competition").

[9] 433 US at 54.

[10] *Id* 57.

[11] 433 US at 59. *See also* Rice v Norman Williams Co, 102 S Ct 3294 (1982) (reaffirming *Sylvania*).

[12] Continental TV, Inc v GTE Sylvania Inc, 433 US 36, 52 n 19 (1977).

[13] 433 US at 55. See **§§5.08, 5.13, 5.30, 5.32-5.39.**

[14] 433 US at 52 n 19. *See also* Copy-Data Sys v Toshiba Am, Inc, 663 F2d 405, 411 (2d Cir 1981).

[15] Continental TV, Inc v GTE Sylvania Inc, 433 U.S. 36, 52 n 19 (1977).

ness of a given group of buyers."[16] But, as the Supreme Court acknowledged in *Sylvania,* "when interbrand competition exists, . . . it provides a significant check on the exploitation of intrabrand market power because of the ability of consumers to substitute a different brand of the same product."[17]

§5.06 What factors does the court consider in judging the reasonableness of a vertical nonprice resale restriction?

In determining whether a vertical nonprice resale restriction is reasonable, a court will balance the procompetitive effects of the restriction (e.g., the enhancement of interbrand competition) against its anticompetitive effects (e.g., the reduction in intrabrand competition).[18] In this context, relevant factors may include:

1. *The nature of the restriction*—Is the restriction absolute (airtight) or is it less

---

[16] 433 US at 54.

[17] 433 US at 52 n 19. *See* Muenster Butane, Inc v Stewart Co, 651 F2d 292, 298 (5th Cir 1981) (stiff interbrand competition shields consumers from potential adverse effects of reduced intrabrand competition); *accord* Valley Liquors, Inc v Renfield Importers, Ltd, 678 F2d 742, 745 (7th Cir 1982); Copy-Data Sys v Toshiba Am, Inc, 663 F2d 405, 411 (2d Cir 1981).

[18] Continental TV, Inc v GTE Sylvania Inc, 433 US 36, 51-57 (1977) ("The market impact of vertical restrictions is complex because of their potential for a simultaneous reduction of intrabrand competition and stimulation of interbrand competition"). *See also* Valley Liquors, Inc v Renfield Importers, Ltd, 678 F2d 742, 745 (7th Cir 1982) ("the courts have held that the effects on intrabrand and on interbrand competition must be balanced in deciding whether a challenged restriction on distribution is unreasonable"); Copy-Data Sys v Toshiba Am, Inc, 663 F2d 405, 409-10 n 5 (2d Cir 1981) ("The *Sylvania* decision was based on the recognition that territorial allocations imposed by suppliers or manufacturers, while they may limit intrabrand competition, can be of substantial benefit to interbrand competition"; rule of reason analysis requires "an inquiry into the goals and the effects of the restrictions on both intrabrand and interbrand competition"); Muenster Butane, Inc v Stewart Co, 651 F2d 292, 296 (5th Cir 1981) ("Comparison of the effects of any vertical restriction on intrabrand and interbrand competition is the critical analysis required by [*Sylvania*]"); Eiberger v Sony Corp of Am, 622 F2d 1068, 1076 (2d Cir 1980) ("we must weigh any enhancement of interbrand competition against the restrictive effect on intrabrand competition and determine whether the restraints are, in all the circumstances, reasonable"). *Compare* Schwimmer v Sony Corp of Am, 1980-81 Trade Cas (CCH) ¶63,580, at 77,103-04 (EDNY), *affd on other grounds,* 637 F2d 41 (2d Cir 1980) (restraint upon intrabrand competition without any "offsetting benefits to interbrand competition" would constitute an unreasonable restraint of trade under §1 of the Sherman Act), *and* Eiberger v Sony Corp of Am, 622 F2d 1068, 1081 (2d Cir 1980) (same) *with* Newberry v Washington Post Co, 438 F Supp 470, 473-76 (DDC 1977) (territorial and customer restrictions found reasonable despite "neutral" effect on interbrand competition largely because little intrabrand competition existed), *and* Beltone Elecs Corp, 3 Trade Reg Rep (CCH) ¶21,934 (FTC July 6, 1982) ("a successful challenge to any vertical restraint requires a showing of an adverse effect on interbrand competition").

restrictive (e.g., area of primary responsibility clause, location clause, profit pass-over clause)? Is the restriction strictly enforced?[19]

2. *Seller's market share*—Is Seller a new entrant? A failing company? A company with a small market share? A company with a strong market position? A monopolist or near-monopolist?[20]
3. *The nature of the industry*—Who are Seller's principal competitors? Is the industry characterized by vigorous interbrand competition or is it concentrated? Do Seller's competitors impose resale restrictions on their buyers?[21]
4. *The purpose of the restriction*—Was the restriction intended to increase Seller's market share or to ensure product safety or quality control? Was the restriction the result of concerted action by distributors or dealers? Is there any evidence of price-fixing? Was the restriction designed to induce distributors or dealers to invest in facilities or supplies necessary to resell Seller's products, and/or to engage in advertising and promotional activities or to provide postsale services?[22]
5. *The actual and potential effects of the restriction upon interbrand competition*—To what extent has the restriction assisted distributors or dealers in competing with distributors or dealers of competitive products? Has Seller's market penetration increased since the restriction was imposed? If so, how much? Do the restrictions create barriers to entry?[23]
6. *The actual and potential effects of the restriction upon intrabrand competition*—To what extent has intrabrand competition been reduced since the restriction was imposed? To what extent has the restriction enhanced the ability of distributors or dealers to develop their territories and/or to advertise, promote or service Seller's products more effectively?[24]

Unfortunately, the Supreme Court in *Sylvania* did not indicate how these factors are to be balanced.[25]

---

[19] See **§5.18.**

[20] See **§§5.32, 5.33, 5.34, 5.38, 5.39.**

[21] See *id.*

[22] See **§§5.30-5.37.**

[23] See **§§5.32, 5.33, 5.34, 5.35, 5.37, 5.38, 5.39.**

[24] See **§§5.35, 5.37.**

[25] The balancing approach suggested by the Court in *Sylvania* has been severely criticized. See Posner, *The Next Step in the Antitrust Treatment of Restricted Distribution: Per Se Legality,* 48 U Chi L Rev 6, 8 (1981):

> [T]he Rule of Reason standard lacks content and so does not provide guidance. . . . [T]he idea of balancing the (assumed to be anticompetitive) effects of the restriction on intrabrand competition with the (assumed to be procompetitive) effects of the restriction on interbrand competition—which is the closest thing to a concrete suggestion in *Sylvania* as to how to apply the Rule of Reason in restricted-distribution cases—is infeasible and unsound.

What is the general rule with regard to restrictions on the territories in which Buyer may resell?

§5.07 What are vertical territorial resale restrictions?

Vertical territorial resale restrictions are Seller-imposed restrictions which limit the freedom of distributors or dealers to resell Seller's product(s) to customers located outside specified geographic areas. As previously noted, these restrictions may or may not be absolute.[26]

§5.08 What valid business purposes can vertical territorial resale restrictions serve?

Vertical territorial resale restrictions can serve a number of valid business purposes, most of which relate directly to the generation of market efficiencies. For example, territorial restrictions may enhance Seller's ability to: (1) enter a market; (2) increase market penetration; (3) introduce new products; (4) induce distributors or dealers to invest capital and labor in promoting Seller's products; (5) attract competent and aggressive distributors or dealers; (6) induce distributors or dealers to engage in advertising and promotional activities and to provide efficient postsale service; and (7) maintain control over the quality and safety of the products.[27] Vertical territorial restrictions may also enable *distributors* and *dealers* to achieve higher levels of economic efficiency.[28]

Pitofsky, *The Sylvania Case: Antitrust Analysis of Non-Price Vertical Restrictions,* 78 Colum L Rev 1, 34 (1978):

> There is no existing analytical framework for applying a rule of reason generally, and certainly none for applying it to non-price vertical restraints. The technique of the *Sylvania* majority—quoting a long list of factors without any indication of priority or weight to be accorded to each factor—unfortunately is standard operating procedure.

See also Kestenbaum v Falstaff Brewing Corp, 575 F2d 564, 570 (5th Cir 1978), *cert denied,* 440 US 909 (1979) ("The content of the rule of reason in vertical restraint antitrust cases is not clearly established").

[26] See **§§5.01, 5.06.**

[27] *See, e.g.,* Continental TV, Inc v GTE Sylvania Inc, 433 US 36, 55 (1977); Copy-Data Sys v Toshiba Am, Inc, 663 F2d 405, 409-10 (2d Cir 1981); Abadir & Co v First Miss Corp, 651 F2d 422, 427-28 (5th Cir 1981).

[28] *See, e.g.,* Del Rio Distrib, Inc v Adolph Coors Co, 589 F2d 176, 179 (5th Cir), *cert denied,* 444 US 840 (1979) (territorial restrictions on beer distributors had the "long-term effect of making each distributorship stronger, better able to compete with other brands and provide better service"); New Jersey v Lawn King, Inc, 1979-2 Trade Cas (CCH) ¶62,800, at 78,656 (NJ 1979) ("While [territorial restrictions] may restrict competition among the franchisees, their overall effect may have been to strengthen the franchisees' competitive positions as against rival organizations"). See also Pitofsky, *The*

§5.09 What anticompetitive purposes can vertical territorial resale restrictions serve?

Vertical territorial resale restrictions can serve a number of anticompetitive purposes, such as: reducing or eliminating intrabrand competition among Seller's distributors or dealers; reducing or eliminating competition between Seller and its distributors or dealers;[29] impeding distributor or dealer growth; and disguising or facilitating other forms of anticompetitive conduct (e.g., resale price maintenance).

§5.10 How is the legality of vertical territorial resale restrictions determined?

Since *Sylvania,* the legality of vertical territorial resale restrictions has been tested under the rule of reason.[30] Most recent decisions have found such restrictions to be reasonable (and hence lawful), particularly in cases involving Sellers with small market shares or settings in which interbrand competition has been enhanced.[31] Restrictions have been struck down, however, when

---

Sylvania Case: Antitrust Analysis of Non-Price Vertical Restrictions, 78 Colum L Rev 1, 25-26 (1978). The Supreme Court has also recognized that a Seller who is prevented from using restrictions which the Seller "perceives as important to its successful operation" may instead resort to vertical integration, "thereby eliminating to that extent the role of independent businessmen." Continental TV, Inc v GTE Sylvania Inc, 433 US 36, 57 n 26 (1977). *See also* Red Diamond Supply, Inc v Liquid Carbonic Corp, 637 F2d 1001, 1006-07 (5th Cir), *cert. denied,* 454 US 827 (1981).

[29] See **§§5.51, 5.52.**

[30] See **§5.03.**

[31] *E.g.,* JBL Enters, Inc v Jhirmack Enters, Inc, 698 F2d 1011, 1016-17 (9th Cir 1983) (territorial restrictions did not unreasonably restrain competition; manufacturer's market shares "too small for any restraint or intrabrand competition to have a substantially adverse effect on interbrand competition"); Mendelovitz v Adolph Coors Co, 693 F2d 570, 575-76 (5th Cir 1982) (territorial restrictions lawful in the absence of negative market impact); Davis-Watkins Co v Service Merchandise, 686 F2d 1190 (6th Cir 1982) (territorial restraints designed to enhance interbrand competition); Muenster Butane, Inc v Stewart Co, 651 F2d 292 (5th Cir 1981) (Seller's use of vertical nonprice restrictions to reduce competition between two of its dealers held reasonable in light of Seller's insubstantial market share and the existence of stiff interbrand competition in the relevant market); Red Diamond Supply, Inc v Liquid Carbonic Corp, 637 F2d 1001 (5th Cir), *cert denied,* 454 US 827 (1981) ("Not only does the record not demonstrate that the alleged restrictions harmed interbrand competition; it suggests that they may have improved it"); Donald B Rice Tire Co v Michelin Tire Corp, 638 F2d 15 (4th Cir), *cert denied,* 454 US 864 (1981) (detrimental effects on intrabrand competition resulting from manufacturer's imposition of restrictions were outweighed by beneficial effect on interbrand competition); Cowley v Braden Indus, 613 F2d 751 (9th Cir), *cert denied,* 446 US 965 (1980) (territorial restrictions deemed reasonable in light of Seller's need to ensure marketing efficiency); First Beverages, Inc v Royal Crown Cola Co, 612 F2d 1164 (9th Cir), *cert denied,* 447 US 924 (1980) (vertical restrictions upheld under traditional rule of reason analysis); Del Rio Distrib, Inc v Adolph Coors Co, 589 F2d 176 (5th Cir), *cert denied,* 444 US 840 (1979) (territorial restrictions on beer distributors held

imposed by Sellers with substantial market shares in settings where interbrand competition has been impaired or when a price-fixing or market allocation purpose has been found.[32]

§5.11 May Seller restrict the right of Buyers to resell outside a designated territory except at specified prices?

The *Sylvania* holding was expressly limited to vertical *nonprice* resale restrictions. The Court emphasized that "[t]he *per se* illegality of price restrictions [i.e., resale price maintenance] has been established firmly for many years and involves significantly different questions of analysis and policy."[33] For this reason, serious antitrust problems may arise if Seller seeks to implement a territorial restriction by means of a price restraint, or if a court discerns that a territorial restraint is designed to further a price-fixing arrangement.

---

reasonable in light of manufacturer's need to ensure quality and flavor control in order to compete more aggressively with other brands). *See also* Maykuth v Adolph Coors Co, 1982-83 Trade Cas (CCH) ¶64,996 (9th Cir 1982) (territorial restriction precluding distributor from selling beer into Alabama had no effect on intrabrand competition because brewer did not authorize any distributor to sell into Alabama); Beltone Elecs Corp, 3 Trade Reg Rep (CCH) ¶21,934 (FTC July 6, 1982) (territorial restrictions imposed by hearing aid manufacturer had no adverse effect upon interbrand competition and were justified by manufacturer's desire to prevent *free riding* and ensure efficient presale promotion).

[32] Spray-Rite Serv Corp v Monsanto Co, 684 F2d 1226, 1237 (7th Cir 1982), *cert granted,* __ US __ (1983) (customer and territorial restrictions are per se unlawful when utilized in furtherance of a scheme to fix prices); Carlson Mach Tools, Inc v American Tool, Inc, 678 F2d 1253, 1260 (5th Cir 1982) ("vertical non-price restraint might be open to challenge as per se illegal if it were in furtherance of a per se violation of the antitrust law"); Eiberger v Sony Corp of Am, 622 F2d 1068 (2d Cir 1980) (territorial restrictions imposed by seller with "strong market position" and implemented through sham warranty fee system found unreasonable when the effect (and probable purpose) of such restrictions was to eliminate intrabrand competition and maintain artificially high resale prices); Pitchford Scientific Instruments Corp v PEPI, Inc, 435 F Supp 685 (WD Pa 1977), *affd without opinion,* 582 F2d 1275 (3d Cir 1978), *cert denied,* 440 US 981 (1979) (territorial restrictions unlawful when "part and parcel of a comprehensive price-fixing policy"). *Cf In re* Coca-Cola Co, 91 FTC 517 (1978) (territorial restrictions unlawful under the rule of reason; restraint upon intrabrand competition among Coca-Cola bottlers "ha[d] adverse repercussions throughout the entire soft drink industry"), *vacated as moot,* 642 F2d 1387 (DC Cir 1981) (Congress responded to the FTC's *Coca-Cola* decision by enacting the Soft Drink Interbrand Competition Act, Pub L No 96-308, §2, 94 Stat 939 (1980), which permits soft drink manufacturers to impose exclusive territories on bottlers, provided there is "substantial and effective [interbrand] competition").

[33] Continental TV, Inc v GTE Sylvania Inc, 433 US 36, 51 n 18 (1977). *See also* California Retail Liquor Dealers Assn v Midcal Aluminum, Inc, 445 US 97 (1980); Albrecht v Herald Co, 390 US 145 (1968); United States v Parke Davis & Co, 362 US 29 (1960); Dr Miles Medical Co v John D Park & Sons, 220 US 373 (1911).

For example, in *Eiberger v Sony Corp of America*,[34] the Second Circuit struck down a territorial restraint pursuant to which dealers selling outside their territories were required to remit a profit pass-over to the dealers in whose territories the sales were made. The defendant argued that the payment was intended to compensate nonselling dealers for performing warranty services. However, the payment was required regardless of whether the selling dealer was willing to perform such services, and regardless of whether the nonselling dealer had performed any services. Furthermore, evidence in the record indicated that complaints concerning dealers selling outside their territories often focused on the low prices at which such sales were made. The Second Circuit ruled that the restriction was properly held unlawful because its effect —and probable purpose—were to eliminate a source of price competition.

A different approach was taken in *Eastern Scientific Co v Wild Heerbrugg, Inc*,[35] in which a seller of scientific equipment demanded that its Rhode Island dealer not resell the equipment outside of Rhode Island at less than list price. The First Circuit held that such price restrictions were "not the kind that require *per se* treatment" because they did not have a greater anticompetitive effect upon intrabrand competition than a *pure* territorial restraint.[36]

---

[34] 622 F2d 1068 (2d Cir 1980).

[35] 572 F2d 883 (1st Cir), *cert denied*, 439 US 833 (1978).

[36] The court stated:

> It may be true that defendant's policies here appear in *form* to resemble resale price maintenance agreements. However, we are unable to conceive of how the resale price restrictions used to enforce the assigned territories . . . can possibly have a greater anti-competitive *effect* than a pure policy of territorial restrictions. . . . Thus the resale price restriction in the present case produces the same anti-competitive effect as pure territorial restrictions but to a lesser degree. If the Supreme Court holds that pure territorial restrictions should be analyzed under the rule of reason, we can see no reason based on substantive economic effect why a similar but less anti-competitive scheme should be treated differently.

572 F2d at 885-86 (emphases in original) (footnote omitted). *See also* Whims Appliance Serv v General Motors Corp, 1978-1 Trade Cas (CCH) ¶62,093, at 74,786-87 (ND Ohio 1978). *But cf* Response of Carolina, Inc v Leasco Response, Inc, 537 F2d 1307 (5th Cir 1976) (unlawful to require 70% royalty payment by franchisee on sales to customers outside area of primary responsibility, as compared with 15% on sales to customers within area).

Acknowledging the existence of the per se rule with regard to resale price maintenance, one noted commentator has described the *Eastern Scientific* decision as "an audacious step for a lower court to take." Posner, *The Next Step in the Antitrust Treatment of Restricted Distribution: Per Se Legality*, 48 U Chi L Rev 1, 10 (1981). Professor (now Judge) Posner argues, however, that all vertical restrictions—including price restrictions—should be subject to a rule of per se legality. *Id* 6.

What is the general rule with regard to restrictions on the customers to whom Buyer may resell?

§5.12 What are vertical customer resale restrictions?

Vertical customer resale restrictions are Seller-imposed restrictions which limit the customers or categories of customers to which distributors or dealers may resell Seller's products. For example, Seller may seek to prohibit its authorized dealers from reselling to other dealers,[37] or may seek to reserve certain customers for itself.[38] As with territorial restrictions, customer restrictions may or may not be absolute.[39]

§5.13 What valid business purposes can vertical customer resale restrictions serve?

Vertical customer resale restrictions can serve the same valid business purposes as vertical territorial resale restrictions. For example, customer restrictions may enhance Seller's ability to: (1) enter a new market; (2) increase market penetration; (3) introduce new products; (4) induce distributors or dealers to invest capital and labor in promoting Seller's products; (5) attract competent and aggressive distributors or dealers; (6) induce distributors or dealers to engage in advertising and promotional activities, and to provide efficient postsale service; and (7) maintain control over the quality and safety of the products.

§5.14 What anticompetitive purposes can vertical customer resale restrictions serve?

Vertical customer resale restrictions can serve the same anticompetitive purposes as vertical territorial resale restrictions. Customer restrictions can: reduce or eliminate intrabrand competition among distributors or dealers; reduce or eliminate competition between Seller and its distributors or dealers; impede distributor or dealer growth; and disguise or facilitate other forms of anticompetitive conduct.

---

[37] *See, e.g.,* Sports Center, Inc v Riddell, Inc, 673 F2d 786 (5th Cir 1982).

[38] *See, e.g.,* White Motor Co v United States, 372 US 253 (1963) (reservation of national accounts, fleet accounts, and government accounts); Bostick Oil Co v Michelin Tire Corp, 1983-1 Trade Cas (CCH) ¶65,271 (4th Cir 1983) (national accounts); Snap-On Tools Corp v FTC, 321 F2d 825, 835-36 (7th Cir 1963).

[39] See **§§5.01, 5.06.**

§5.15 How is the legality of vertical customer resale restrictions determined?

Since *Sylvania,* the legality of vertical customer resale restrictions has been tested by the rule of reason.[40] Most recent decisions have found such restrictions to be reasonable.[41]

Has the rule with regard to vertical nonprice resale restrictions always been this way?

§5.16 What rule for analyzing vertical nonprice resale restrictions was first articulated by the Supreme Court?

In *White Motor Co v United States,*[42] decided in 1963, the Supreme Court first considered the legality of vertical nonprice resale restrictions. The Court at that time refused to endorse a per se rule for vertical territorial and customer restrictions, acknowledging that it knew "too little of the actual impact of [territorial and customer restrictions] to reach a conclusion. . . ."[43] The Court stressed:

> We do not know enough of the economic and business stuff out of which these arrangements emerge to be certain. They may be too dangerous to sanction or they may be allowable protections against aggressive competitors or the only practicable means a small company has for breaking into or staying in business . . . and within the "rule of reason." We need to know more than we do about the actual impact of these arrangements

---

[40] *See* Continental TV, Inc v GTE Sylvania Inc, 433 US 36, 46 (1977) (distinctions between territorial and customer restrictions are "irrelevant to functional antitrust analysis").

[41] *E.g.,* JBL Enters, Inc v Jhirmack Enters, Inc, 698 F2d 1011 (9th Cir 1983); Davis-Watkins Co v Service Merchandise, 686 F2d 1190 (6th Cir 1982); Sports Center, Inc v Riddell, Inc, 673 F2d 786 (5th Cir 1982); Red Diamond Supply, Inc v Liquid Carbonic Corp, 637 F2d 1001 (5th Cir), *cert denied,* 454 US 827 (1981); Donald B Rice Tire Co v Michelin Tire Corp, 483 F Supp 750 (D Md 1980), *affd per curiam,* 583 F2d 15 (4th Cir), *cert denied,* 454 US 864 (1981); Clairol, Inc v Boston Discount Center, Inc, 608 F2d 1114 (6th Cir 1979); Newberry v Washington Post Co, 438 F Supp 470, 476 (DDC 1977). *See also* US Pioneer Elecs Corp, 3 Trade Reg Rep (CCH) ¶21,973 (FTC Nov 5, 1982); Hammermill Paper Co, 3 Trade Reg Rep (CCH) ¶21,950 (FTC Aug 9, 1982); Lenox, Inc, 3 Trade Reg Rep (CCH) ¶21,938 (FTC July 12, 1982). *But cf* United States v Parke Davis & Co, 372 US 29 (1960) (per se unlawful for manufacturer to secure retailer adherence to suggested minimum prices by refusing to deal with wholesalers who resold manufacturer's products to discounters).

[42] 372 US 253 (1963).

[43] *Id* 261.

> on competition to decide whether they . . . should be classified as *per se* violations of the Sherman Act.[44]

From 1963 to 1967, vertical nonprice resale restrictions were analyzed under the rule of reason.[45]

§5.17 How was this rule changed in 1967?

In 1967, in *United States v Arnold, Schwinn & Co*,[46] the Supreme Court considered vertical territorial and customer resale restrictions for the second time, and ruled that they were per se illegal. Relying upon the "ancient rule against restraints on alienation," Justice Fortas declared that

> where a manufacturer *sells* products to his distributor subject to territorial restrictions upon resale, a *per se* violation of the Sherman Act results. And . . . the same principle applies to restrictions of outlets with which the distributors may deal and to restraints upon retailers to whom the goods are sold. Under the Sherman Act, it is unreasonable without more for a manufacturer to seek to restrict and confine areas or persons with whom an article may be traded after the manufacturer has parted with dominion over it. . . . Such restraints are so obviously destructive of competition that their mere existence is enough. If the manufacturer parts with dominion over his product or transfers risk of loss to another, he may not reserve control over its destiny or the conditions of its resale. . . .[47] Once the manufacturer has parted with title and risk [of loss], he has parted with dominion over the product, and his efforts thereafter to restrict territory or persons to whom the product may be transferred—whether by agreement or by silent combination or understanding with his vendee —is a *per se* violation of §1 of the Sherman Act.[48]

The *Schwinn* decision, described by one distinguished commentator as a "mischievious precedent which rested on a nonexistent principle of property law,"[49] became a frequent subject of academic and judicial criticism.[50]

---

[44] *Id* 263 (citations omitted).

[45] *See* Sandura Co v FTC, 339 F2d 847 (6th Cir 1964) (rule of reason applied to territorial restrictions imposed by a faltering manufacturer seeking to attract and keep dealers who would aggressively promote and properly service its products); Snap-On Tools Corp v FTC, 321 F2d 825 (7th Cir 1963) (enhancement of interbrand competition through vertical territorial and customer restrictions justifies a "minimal curtailment of intrabrand competition").

[46] 388 US 365 (1967).

[47] *Id* 379 (emphasis in original) (citations and footnote omitted).

[48] *Id* 382.

[49] Handler, *Changing Trends in Antitrust Doctrines: An Unprecedented Supreme Court Term—1977*, 77 Colum L Rev 979, 980-81 (1977) (footnotes omitted).

[50] *See* Continental TV, Inc v GTE Sylvania Inc, 433 US 36, 47-48 n 13 (1977); ABA

§5.18 What exceptions to the *Schwinn* rule did the lower courts carve out?

From 1967 to 1977, some courts interpreted *Schwinn* as establishing a broad per se rule for all vertical territorial and customer resale restrictions.[51] Other courts sought to limit the application of the per se rule to cases, such as *Schwinn,* in which the restrictions were firmly and resolutely enforced (e.g., by threat of termination).[52] Still other courts, drawing upon *Schwinn's* statement that vertical territorial and customer restrictions are unreasonable "without more," interpreted that statement to allow an exception to the per se rule when a manufacturer could show more—e.g., that the restrictions were imposed for bona fide health or safety reasons.[53]

Section on Antitrust, Vertical Restrictions Limiting Intrabrand Competition 9-10 n 24 (Monograph No 2 1977).

[51] *E.g.,* Adolph Coors Co v FTC, 497 F2d 1178 (10th Cir 1974), *cert denied,* 419 US 1105 (1975) (reluctantly applying per se rule to territorial restrictions imposed by brewer upon its distributors, despite contention that purpose of restrictions was to ensure proper refrigeration and quality maintenance); United States v Revlon, Inc, 1975-1 Trade Cas (CCH) ¶60,202 (SDNY 1975) (rejecting manufacturer's health and safety justifications for territorial and customer restrictions, and applying per se rule); United States v Glaxo Group, Ltd, 302 F Supp 1, 7-11 (DDC 1969), *revd on other grounds,* 410 US 52 (1973) (manufacturer's restraint upon distributors' right to sell antibiotic without manufacturer's consent per se unlawful despite claim that restraint necessary to ensure uniform health and safety standards in preparation of drug). See generally ABA Section on Antitrust, Vertical Restrictions Limiting Intrabrand Competition 10 n 26 (Monograph No 2 1977) (citing numerous cases).

[52] *See* United States v Arnold, Schwinn & Co, 388 US 365, 372 (1967) (Seller had been "firm and resolute" in enforcing restrictions; "firmness" grounded upon the "communicated danger of termination"); World of Sleep, Inc v Stearns & Foster Co, 525 F2d 40, 44-45 (10th Cir 1975); Good Investment Promotions, Inc v Corning Glass Works, 493 F2d 891, 893 (6th Cir 1974); Colorado Pump & Supply Co v Febco, Inc, 472 F2d 637, 639 (10th Cir), *cert denied,* 441 US 987 (1973); Beverage Distribs, Inc v Olympia Brewing Co, 440 F2d 21 (9th Cir), *cert denied,* 403 US 906 (1971); *cf* Carter-Wallace, Inc v United States, 449 F2d 1374 (Ct Cl 1971) (per se rule inapplicable when purchaser can avoid restraints by electing to purchase product at a higher price). *Compare* Janel Sales Corp v Lanvin Parfums, Inc, 396 F2d 398, 406 (2d Cir), *cert denied,* 393 US 938 (1968) (existence of contractual clause imposing vertical restrictions "does not necessarily imply a *per se* violation"; jury must determine whether Seller had a policy of *enforcing* the clause), *with* Response of Carolina, Inc v Leasco Response, Inc, 537 F2d 1307 (5th Cir 1976) (existence of contractual clause imposing territorial restriction constitutes per se violation "whether or not the restriction has been enforced, much less firmly and resolutely enforced . . .").

[53] Tripoli, Co v Wella Corp, 425 F2d 932 (3d Cir), *cert denied,* 400 US 831 (1970) (under *Schwinn,* vertical restraints are unreasonable "without more"; court found *more* when restraints were imposed for health and safety reasons); Clairol, Inc v Boston Discount Center, 1976-2 Trade Cas (CCH) ¶61,108 (ED Mich 1976) (customer restrictions allowed for safety reasons); Mitchell v United States Surgical Corp, 1976-1 Trade Cas (CCH) ¶60,879 (SD Ohio 1976) (territorial restrictions on sales of surgical staplers to ensure prompt service and to protect consumer-patients tested under rule of reason); Clairol, Inc v Asaro, 1975-1 Trade Cas (CCH) ¶60,350 (ED Mich 1975). See generally Posner, *The Rule of Reason and the Economic Approach: Reflections on the Sylvania Decision,*

§5.19 Why did the Supreme Court return to the rule of reason in *Sylvania?*

As previously noted, the *Schwinn* decision evoked a flood of scholarly criticism and a considerable amount of judicial resistance. Finally, in 1977, the Supreme Court expressly overruled *Schwinn,* stating in *Sylvania:*

> we are convinced that the need for clarification of the law in this area justifies reconsideration [of *Schwinn*]. *Schwinn* itself was an abrupt and largely unexplained departure from *White Motor Co. v. United States* . . . , where only four years earlier the Court had refused to endorse a *per se* rule for vertical restrictions.[54]

Rejecting the "ancient rule" of property law adopted in *Schwinn,*[55] and relying instead upon economic analyses of the "ways in which manufacturers can use [vertical non-price resale] restrictions to compete more effectively against other manufacturers,"[56] the *Sylvania* Court declared that "departure from the rule-of-reason standard must be based upon demonstrable economic effect rather than . . . upon formalistic line drawing."[57] Indeed, "the experience of the past 10 years [since *Schwinn*]" had revealed that vertical nonprice resale restrictions were not "manifestly anticompetitive."[58] The Supreme Court returned to the rule of reason as the standard by which the legality of vertical nonprice restrictions was to be judged.[59] Thereafter, several cases decided under *Schwinn's* per se rule were reconsidered and vacated.[60]

---

45 U Chi L Rev 1, 3 (1977) ("The lower federal courts were plainly unhappy with the per se rule of *Schwinn* and exercised their ingenuity to find exceptions to the rule"); Robinson, *Recent Antitrust Developments: 1974,* 75 Colum L Rev 243, 270-75 (1975).

[54] Continental TV, Inc v GTE Sylvania Inc, 433 US 36, 47 (1977) (citation omitted).

[55] *Id* 53 n 21 ("an antitrust policy divorced from market considerations would lack any objective benchmarks").

[56] *Id* 54-55.

[57] *Id* 58-59.

[58] *Id* 49-51. *See* Broadcast Music, Inc v CBS, Inc, 441 US 1 (1979) (court must examine an industry before applying per se rule); National Socy of Professional Engrs v United States, 435 US 679, 692 (1978) (per se rule applies only to "agreements whose nature and necessary effect are so plainly anticompetitive that no elaborate study of the industry is needed to establish their illegality"); United States v Topco Assocs, 405 US 596, 607-08 (1972) ("It is only after considerable experience with certain business relationships that courts classify them as *per se* violations"). *See also* White Motor Co v United States, 372 US 253, 265 (1963) (Brennan J, concurring) (per se rule properly applied only when experience and analysis establish that the challenged practice utterly lacks justification and constitutes an "inherent threat to competition").

[59] Continental TV, Inc v GTE Sylvania Inc, 433 US 36, 59 (1977). Although the Supreme Court returned to the rule of reason, it did not "foreclose the possibility that particular applications of vertical [non-price] restrictions might justify *per se* prohibition." *Id* 58. What those "particular applications" are, however, remains unclear.

[60] United States v Arnold, Schwinn & Co, 1977-2 Trade Cas (CCH) ¶61,776 (ND Ill 1977) (vacating final judgment in view of *Sylvania;* vertical restraints in the revised

Does it matter whether the goods are distributed on an agency or consignment basis?

§5.20 What is an agency?

An agency arrangement is one in which a manufacturer markets its products through an intermediary, but retains the indicia of ownership (e.g., title, dominion, risk of loss). The most common form of agency relationship arises when a manufacturer utilizes the services of a sales representative.

§5.21 What is a consignment?

A consignment is an arrangement in which a manufacturer markets its products through a distributor or dealer, relinquishing possession of the goods, but typically retaining title, dominion, and risk of loss.

§5.22 Have territorial and customer restrictions in agency and consignment arrangements been treated differently than outright sales under the antitrust laws?

In *Schwinn,* the Supreme Court held that it was per se unlawful for a manufacturer to impose territorial or customer restrictions upon a distributor or dealer after the manufacturer had parted with ownership of the goods. The Court distinguished outright sales from agency and consignment arrangements, holding that territorial and customer restrictions placed upon agents and consignees would be subject to a rule of reason analysis:

> The Government does not here contend for a *per se* rule as to agency [or] consignment . . . transactions even though these may be used—as they are here—to implement a scheme of confining distribution outlets. . . . Where the manufacturer retains title, dominion, and risk with respect to the product and the position and function of the dealer in question are, in fact, indistinguishable from those of an agent or salesman of the manufacturer, it is only if the impact of the confinement is "unreasonably" restrictive of competition that a violation of §1 results from such

---

Schwinn Authorized Dealer Agreement "are reasonable restraints under the 'rule of reason,' and do not violate Section 1 of the Sherman Act"); General Beverage Sales Co v East-Side Winery, 568 F2d 1147 (7th Cir 1978) (reversing damage judgment and remanding); Florida Harvestore, Inc v AO Smith Harvestore Prods, Inc, 561 F2d 631 (5th Cir 1977), *cert denied,* 436 US 919 (1978) (vacating damage judgment on a territorial restriction claim in light of *Sylvania*); McClatchy Newspapers v Noble, 433 US 904 (1977) (vacating judgment of per se illegality of territorial restriction in light of *Sylvania*).

confinement, unencumbered by culpable price fixing.[61]

This distinction was flatly rejected in *Sylvania,* in which the Court concluded that "the distinction drawn in *Schwinn* between sale and non-sale transactions is not sufficient to justify the application of the *per se* rule in one situation and a rule of reason in the other."[62] In short, the passage of title was deemed irrelevant to the issue of whether a vertical restraint was pro- or anticompetitive.

Territorial and customer restrictions imposed by principals upon bona fide agents and consignees continue to be analyzed under the rule of reason. More serious problems may arise, however, if the principal imposes both nonprice and price restrictions upon an agent or consignee.[63]

Does it matter whether the party imposing the restrictions is a licensor?

§5.23 How are territorial and customer restrictions in licensing arrangements treated under the antitrust laws?

Territorial and customer restrictions in licensing arrangements have always been tested under the rule of reason, and have been found to be reasonable in cases in which the restrictions were ancillary to the licensor's primary purpose of lawfully exploiting and protecting its trademarks, trade names or

---

[61] United States v Arnold, Schwinn & Co, 388 US 365, 380 (1967). *See also* Williams & Co v Williams & Co-East, 542 F2d 1053 (9th Cir 1976); American Oil Co v McMullin, 508 F2d 1345 (10th Cir 1974). *Cf* Bravman v Bassett Furniture Indus, Inc, 552 F2d 90 (3d Cir), *cert. denied,* 434 US 823 (1977) (territorial restrictions imposed upon sales representative may be unlawful if unsupported by legitimate business purpose and anticompetitive in effect).

[62] Continental TV, Inc v GTE Sylvania Inc, 433 US 36, 57 (1977). See also Pitofsky, *The Sylvania Case: Antitrust Analysis of Non-Price Vertical Restrictions,* 78 Colum L Rev 1, 10 n 39, 17 (1978) ("the agency-sale distinction is exceedingly difficult to defend on practical or theoretical grounds, and the *Sylvania* majority performed a useful service in sending it to its demise").

[63] *Compare* Simpson v Union Oil Co, 377 US 13 (1964) (consignment may not be used to cloak a pervasive price-fixing scheme) *and* Greene v General Foods Corp, 517 F2d 635 (5th Cir), *cert denied,* 424 US 942 (1975), *with* Mesirow v Pepperidge Farm, Inc, 1982-83 Trade Cas (CCH) ¶65,164 (9th Cir 1983) (bona fide consignment arrangements not per se unlawful, particularly where distributors were free to solicit customers to be their own) *and* Hardwick v Nu-Way Oil Co, 589 F2d 806 (5th Cir), *cert denied,* 444 US 836 (1979) (consignment arrangement between supplier of gasoline and gas station operator did not constitute an unlawful resale price-fixing scheme where operator was essentially an employee of the supplier).

copyrights.[64]

§5.24 Is the rule any different with regard to restraints imposed on the resale of patented articles?

In *Schwinn,* the Supreme Court did not have occasion to consider the legality of territorial restrictions imposed by patentees.[65] Several cases decided prior to *Schwinn* adopted the view that "the sale of [a patented article] exhausts the monopoly in that article and the patentee may not thereafter, by virtue of his patent, control the use or disposition of the article."[66] However, in a post-*Sylvania* decision involving process patents, one circuit court applied the rule of reason.[67]

Does it matter whether a nonprice resale restriction is motivated by Seller or Buyer?

§5.25 Does the source of the restraint affect its legality?

As previously discussed, *vertical* nonprice restrictions—restrictions imposed by agreement between Seller and its distributor or dealer[68]—are tested under

---

[64] Williams & Co v Williams & Co-East, 542 F2d 1053 (9th Cir 1976); Mid-America ICEE, Inc v John E Mitchell Co, 1972 Trade Cas (CCH) ¶73,833 (D Or 1971); Walt Disney Prods v American Broadcasting Paramount Theatres, 180 F Supp 113, 117 (SDNY 1960). *See also* Siegel v Chicken Delight, Inc, 448 F2d 43, 51 (9th Cir 1971), *cert denied,* 405 US 955 (1972) (trade name licensor must maintain control over the quality of goods sold by its licensees).

[65] United States v Arnold, Schwinn & Co, 388 US 365, 379 n 6 (1967).

[66] United States v Univis Lens Co, 316 US 241, 249-52 (1942). *See also* Hensley Equip Co v Esco Corp, 383 F2d 252, 263 (5th Cir 1967); United States v Glaxo Group, Ltd, 302 F Supp 1, 8-11 (DDC 1969), *revd on other grounds,* 410 US 52 (1973); Baldwin Lima-Hamilton v Tatnall Measuring Sys, 169 F Supp 1, 28-31 (ED Pa 1958), *affd per curiam,* 268 F2d 395 (3d Cir), *cert denied,* 361 US 894 (1959).

[67] In United States v Studiengesellschaft Kohle, mbH, 670 F2d 1122 (DC Cir 1981), the District of Columbia Circuit held that it was not per se illegal for the owner of a patented process to impose restrictions on the disposition by a licensee of products produced under that process. The court rejected the district court's application of the per se rule and held that, under the rule of reason, a restriction prohibiting sales of such products by all but one of the involved licensees was *not* unduly restrictive of competition. The court reasoned that, since the favored licensee could properly have been granted an exclusive license under the process patent, the restriction limiting other licensees to internal use of the products made under the process was not unreasonable.

[68] *See* Muenster Butane, Inc v Stewart Co, 651 F2d 292, 295 (5th Cir 1981) ("Vertical restraints are imposed by persons or firms further up the chain of distribution of a specific product . . . than the enterprise restrained"); Oreck Corp v Whirlpool Corp,

the rule of reason.[69] In sharp contrast, horizontal restrictions—restrictions arising from agreements among competitors[70]—are generally subject to per se condemnation.[71]

Occasionally, problems may arise "in differentiating vertical restrictions from horizontal restrictions originating in agreements among the [distributors or dealers]."[72] And, since most vertical nonprice resale restrictions have been upheld under the rule of reason,[73] the classification of a restraint as vertical or horizontal may often predetermine the outcome of the litigation.

§5.26 What factors do the courts consider in determining whether a restraint is vertical or horizontal?

The courts have not established any rules for determining whether a resale restraint is vertical or horizontal. Recent decisions indicate that, in close cases, courts will determine the true source of a restriction by looking to substance and purpose, rather than to form.

Thus, in *Donald B Rice Tire Co v Michelin Tire Corp*,[74] the Fourth Circuit rejected the "implication . . . that a restraint may always be regarded as vertical

---

579 F2d 126, 131 (2d Cir) (en banc), *cert denied,* 439 US 946 (1978) (vertical restraints are "combinations of persons at different levels of the market structure, such as manufacturers and distributors").

69 See **§5.03.**

70 *See* Muenster Butane, Inc v Stewart Co, 651 F2d 292, 295 (5th Cir 1981) ("Horizontal combinations are cartels or agreements among competitors which restrain competition among enterprises at the same level of distribution"). *See also* White Motor Co v United States, 372 US 253, 263 (1963) (horizontal restraints are "naked restraints of trade with no purpose except stifling of competition"); Davis-Watkins Co v Service Merchandise, 686 F2d 1190, 1196 (6th Cir 1982).

71 *See, e.g.,* United States v Topco Assocs, 405 US 596 (1972); United States v Sealy, Inc, 388 US 350 (1967); United States v General Motors Corp, 384 US 127 (1966); American Motor Inns, Inc v Holiday Inns, Inc, 521 F2d 1230 (3d Cir 1975).

72 Continental TV, Inc v GTE Sylvania, Inc, 433 US 36, 58 n 28 (1977). *See* United States v Arnold, Schwinn & Co, 388 US 365, 372 (1967) (distinguishing restraints originating with the manufacturer from "horizontal restraints in which the actors are distributors with or without the manufacturer's participation"); White Motor Co v United States, 372 US 253, 267 (1963) (Brennan, J concurring) (if territorial restrictions were "induced solely or even primarily" by dealers or distributors, it would make no difference that the restrictions were formally imposed by the manufacturer); Red Diamond Supply, Inc v Liquid Carbonic Corp, 637 F2d 1001 (5th Cir), *cert denied,* 454 US 827 (1981) (acknowledging that a "nominally vertical arrangement may in fact be a horizontal one in disguise"); H&B Equip Co v International Harvester Co, 577 F2d 239 (5th Cir 1978) (restraint imposed by Seller upon its distributors is vertical and judged under the rule of reason unless "the source of the conspiracy is a combination of the [independent] distributors").

73 See **§§5.10, 5.15.**

74 638 F2d 15 (4th Cir), *cert denied,* 454 US 864 (1981).

if it is imposed by the manufacturer,"[75] and concluded that a restraint should be deemed vertical if it "redound[s] primarily to the benefit of the manufacturer as a result of increased interbrand competition."[76] The court held that if the restriction were implemented by Seller "for the purpose of promoting interbrand competition," it should be deemed vertical.[77] If, however, the restriction were the product of "a conspiracy among dealers and their supplying manufacturer for the purpose of resale price maintenance," it should be deemed horizontal.[78]

In *Abadir & Co v First Mississippi Corp*,[79] the Fifth Circuit also declared that the determination of verticality or horizontality would depend upon the *substance* of the arrangement:

> While horizontal market-distributing agreements have no significant potential advantages to the participants other than a reduction in competition, vertical market-distributing agreements do have significant potential economic advantages which are legitimate. . . . [V]ertical market-distributing agreements must *truly* be imposed by a supplier, *in fact.* Market-distributing agreements which are initiated by distributors are horizontal, even if the supplier is nominally a party to the contract.[80]

In short, if it appears that the Seller imposing nonprice restrictions was motivated primarily by a desire to: increase its market penetration; attract competent and aggressive distributors or dealers; induce distributors or dealers to engage in promotional activities; and/or maintain control over the quality or safety of its products,[81] the restrictions are likely to be deemed vertical and subject to the rule of reason even though numerous distributors or dealers support, or otherwise acquiesce in, their enforcement.[82] On the

---

[75] 638 F2d at 16.

[76] *Id*

[77] *Id* 16-17.

[78] *Id* 16. *See also* Bostick Oil Co v Michelin Tire Corp, 1983-1 Trade Cas (CCH) ¶65,271 (4th Cir 1983); Eiberger v Sony Corp of Am, 459 F Supp 1276 (SDNY 1978), *affd in part & revd in part on other grounds*, 622 F2d 1068 (2d Cir 1980).

[79] 651 F2d 422 (5th Cir 1981).

[80] *Id* 427 n 5 (emphasis added). *See also* Dougherty v Continental Oil Co, 579 F2d 954 (5th Cir 1978); Rubbermaid, Inc v FTC, 575 F2d 1169 (6th Cir 1978).

[81] See **§§5.08, 5.13.**

[82] *See* Davis-Watkins Co v Service Merchandise, 686 F2d 1190, 1199-1201 (6th Cir 1982) (territorial, customer and location restrictions were vertically imposed, notwithstanding evidence of complaints by distributors and dealers; manufacturer's actions were consistent with its marketing strategy); Sports Center, Inc v Riddell, Inc, 673 F2d 786, 791 (5th Cir 1982) (restriction which "emanated" from manufacturer was vertical, even though manufacturer asked its dealers to report infractions); Overhead Door Corp v Nordpal Corp, 1979-1 Trade Cas (CCH) ¶62,594, at 77,427 (D Minn 1978) ("Where the manufacturer is the 'dominant partner' or the chief motivating force behind the restraints, they retain their vertical character even if distributors acquiesce in their enforcement"); Newberry v Washington Post Co, 438 F Supp 470, 474 n 5 (DDC 1977)

other hand, if the restrictions appear to be the result of a conspiracy among distributors or dealers seeking insulation from intrabrand competition, they are likely to be deemed horizontal.[83]

May Seller arbitrate or settle disputes among its customers concerning territories or customers?

§5.27 Will Seller participation in an arrangement among Buyers be treated as a horizontal or vertical resale restriction?

Seller participation in an unlawful arrangement among Buyers may implicate Seller in a horizontal conspiracy. For example, in *United States v General Motors Corp*,[84] a group of Chevrolet dealers (and their trade association) collectively complained to their supplier about certain other dealers who sold automobiles to or through discounters. In response to these complaints, the supplier (in collaboration with the complaining dealers and their trade association) undertook to put an end to this practice by enforcing a location clause contained in the supplier's uniform dealer selling agreement. The Supreme Court found such conduct to constitute a per se violation of the Sherman Act:

> We need not reach these questions concerning the meaning, effect, or validity of the "location clause" or of any other provision in the Dealer Selling Agreement, and we do not. We do not decide whether the "location clause" may be construed to prohibit a dealer, party to it, from selling through discounters, or whether [the manufacturer] could by unilateral action enforce the clause, so construed. We have here a classic conspiracy in restraint of trade: joint, collaborative action by dealers, the [dealer] associations, and [a manufacturer] to eliminate a class of competitors by terminating business dealings between them and a minority of Chevrolet dealers and to deprive franchised dealers of their freedom to deal through discounters if they so choose. Against this fact of unlawful combination, the "location clause" is of no avail. Whatever [the manufacturer] might or might not lawfully have done to enforce individual Dealer Selling Agreements by action within the borders of those agreements and the relationship which each defines, is beside the point. And, because the action taken constitutes a combination or conspiracy, it is not necessary to consider what might be the legitimate interest of a dealer in securing compliance by others with the "location clause," or the lawfulness of

---

("Notwithstanding the dealers' willing participation . . . the scheme was initiated and orchestrated by the [Seller], and thus was vertical in effect as well as appearance").

[83] See **§5.27.** For a brief discussion of the problems concerning the classification of territorial and customer restrictions in *dual distribution* systems, see **§§5.51-5.52.**

[84] 384 US 127 (1966).

action a dealer might individually take to vindicate this interest.[85]

Thus, a Seller who participates in an unlawful arrangement among its dealers runs a serious risk of being found to have committed a per se violation of the Sherman Act.[86]

§5.28 Of what significance is it that Seller is controlled or owned by Buyers?

Territorial restrictions imposed by entities which are controlled or owned by their Buyers have been found to constitute horizontal restraints.[87] Since the Seller in such cases is, in essence, a combination of actual or potential competi-

---

[85] *Id* 139-40. *See also* Spray-Rite Corp v Monsanto Co, 684 F2d 1226, 1237 (7th Cir 1982), *cert granted*, __ US __ (1983) (manufacturer may not "utilize customer or territorial restrictions as part of a comprehensive price-fixing plan or boycott"); Eiberger v Sony Corp of Am, 459 F Supp 1276, 1284 (SDNY 1978), *affd in part & revd in part on other grounds*, 622 F2d 1068 (2d Cir 1980) (district court found, inter alia, that dealers conspired to divide territories and that Seller joined in this conspiracy and furthered its aims through implementation of a sham warranty fee system); Posner, *The Next Step in the Antitrust Treatment of Restricted Distribution: Per Se Legality*, 48 U Chi L Rev 6, 23 n 63 (1981) ("A manufacturer that agreed to enforce a dealer's cartel would, of course, be liable along with the dealers as a coconspirator"). *Compare* Davis-Watkins Co v Service Merchandise, 686 F2d 1190, 1198-99 (6th Cir 1982) (no evidence that dealers or distributors joined together to exclude plaintiff or that manufacturer "acted other than in its own economic interest"); Valley Liquors, Inc v Renfield Importers, Ltd, 678 F2d 742, 744 (7th Cir 1982) (termination of price-cutting distributor not per se unlawful absent evidence of manufacturer participation in an unlawful agreement between two remaining distributors); Sandura Co v FTC, 339 F2d 847, 857-58 (6th Cir 1964) (mere fact that distributors would not handle Seller's product without territorial protection "is not sufficient basis for finding a horizontal conspiracy among them").

[86] In Com-Tel, Inc v DuKane Corp, 669 F2d 404 (6th Cir 1982), the Sixth Circuit held that a manufacturer of sound systems equipment and its franchised distributor engaged in a per se illegal boycott of a nonfranchised distributor. The evidence indicated that the franchised distributor had induced the manufacturer to pressure two other franchised distributors to abandon commitments to sell DuKane products to the nonfranchised distributor, even though the manufacturer's franchise agreement did not prohibit such sales. (The franchise agreement permitted franchised distributors to sell outside their areas of primary responsibility, provided that they paid a 10% commission to the distributor in whose territory the sale was made.) The court applied the per se rule, rejecting the argument that the manufacturer had imposed a legitimate vertical restraint designed to prevent free riding problems.

[87] *E.g.*, United States v Topco Assocs, 405 US 596 (1972) (territorial restrictions imposed by buying association upon members deemed horizontal when members collectively owned the association); United States v Sealy, Inc, 388 US 350 (1967) (territorial restrictions imposed by licensor deemed horizontal when licensees owned and controlled licensor); Ohio-Sealy Mattress Mfg Co v Sealy, Inc, 585 F2d 821 (7th Cir 1978), *cert denied*, 440 US 930 (1979) (territorial restrictions which severely restricted licensees' ability to sell outside their assigned territories perpetuated horizontal market division scheme).

tors, courts have not been reluctant to apply the rule of per se illegality to such arrangements.

§5.29 Will Seller involvement in a dispute between Buyers automatically implicate the Seller in an unlawful conspiracy?

Seller's efforts to reduce intrabrand rivalry between its dealers by enforcing nonprice resale restrictions will not necessarily implicate seller in an unlawful conspiracy. Illustratively, in *Muenster Butane, Inc v Stewart Co*,[88] a television distributor tried to reduce bitter intrabrand competition between two of its dealers by, inter alia, enforcing territorial restrictions against (and, ultimately, by terminating) one of the dealers. Describing this as "a classic vertical restraint case,"[89] the Fifth Circuit held that Seller's conduct did not constitute an unreasonable restraint of trade in light of its insubstantial market share and the existence of stiff interbrand competition.[90] The principal distinction between *Muenster Butane* and the Supreme Court's *General Motors* decision is that in *Muenster Butane* the court discerned no concerted action among the dealers, whereas in *General Motors* a Seller participated in a horizontal conspiracy in which its dealers were engaged.

What role does purpose play?

§5.30 In its rule of reason analysis does the court consider Seller's purpose in imposing the resale restrictions?

Purpose has always been an important factor in a rule of reason analysis.[91] Courts invariably inquire into Seller's purpose for imposing resale restrictions

---

[88] 651 F2d 292 (5th Cir 1981).

[89] *Id* 295.

[90] *Id* 298. *Compare* Battle v Lubrizol Corp, 673 F2d 984 (8th Cir 1982) (termination of distributor following price-related complaints by another distributor may be per se unlawful), *and* Cernuto, Inc v United Cabinet Corp, 595 F2d 164 (3d Cir 1979) (same), *with* Valley Liquors, Inc v Renfield Importers, Ltd, 678 F2d 742, 744 (7th Cir 1982) (termination of price-cutting distributor not *per se* unlawful absent evidence that manufacturer had "knuckl[ed] under to [remaining] distributors' desire for less price competition"), *and* Roesch, Inc v Star Cooler Corp, 671 F2d 1168 (8th Cir 1982) (termination of distributor following price-related complaints by two other distributors did not, in and of itself, constitute sufficient evidence of a price-fixing conspiracy).

[91] Continental TV, Inc v GTE Sylvania Inc, 433 US 36, 54-56 (1977); United States v Topco Assoc, 405 US 596, 607 (1972); Chicago Bd of Trade v United States, 246 US 231, 238 (1918); Mendelovitz v Adolph Coors Co, 693 F2d 570, 576 (5th Cir 1982); Davis-Watkins Co v Service Merchandise, 686 F2d 1190 (6th Cir 1982); Copy-Data Sys v Toshiba Am, Inc, 663 F2d 405, 409-10 (2d Cir 1981); Abadir & Co v First Miss Corp,

in determining whether the restrictions constitute an unreasonable restraint of trade.

§5.31 Will a valid business purpose save an otherwise unreasonable resale restriction?

A valid business purpose will not necessarily save an otherwise unreasonable resale restriction, although it will be a factor considered by the court in determining whether the restraint is unreasonable.[92] In *Eiberger v Sony Corp of America*,[93] the Second Circuit rejected Seller's argument that a territorial restriction must pass the rule of reason test if it is supported by a valid business purpose. The court stated:

> This contention is analytically, as well as factually, unsound. That a practice is not *per se* unlawful does not mean it is *per se* lawful. Thus, the fact that adequate provision of warranty services is a worthwhile goal which may increase the competitiveness of a brand and thus justify the manufacturer's imposition of vertical restraints is not . . . the end of our inquiry. It is just the beginning, for we must weigh any enhancement of interbrand competition against the restrictive effect on intrabrand competition, and determine whether the restraints are, in all the circumstances, reasonable. In so doing we look to the history of the restraint itself, to the problem perceived by the manufacturer and the goal sought to be achieved, and to the actual effect of the restraint.[94]

§5.32 Is the restraint justified when Seller is attempting to introduce a new product?

The Supreme Court has recognized that a Seller who attempts to introduce a new product into a market must establish an efficient distribution system, and that such a Seller "can use [vertical non-price resale] restrictions in order to induce competent and aggressive retailers to make the kind of investment of

---

651 F2d 422 (5th Cir 1981); Kaplan v Burroughs Corp, 611 F2d 286 (9th Cir 1979), *cert denied,* 447 US 924 (1980); Overhead Door Corp v Nordpal Corp, 1979-1 Trade Cas (CCH) ¶62,694 (D Minn 1978); Newberry v Washington Post Co, 438 F Supp 470, 475 (DDC 1977).

As previously noted, purpose can also be a major factor in determining whether a restraint is vertical or horizontal. See **§§5.25, 5.26.**

92 Chicago Bd of Trade v United States, 246 US 231, 238 (1918) (a good intention will not save an "otherwise objectionable regulation," but "knowledge of intent may help the court to interpret facts and to predict consequences"). *Cf* Borger v Yamaha Intl Corp, 625 F2d 390, 398 n 4 (2d Cir 1980) (absent anticompetitive effect, evidence of anticompetitive intent will not render vertical restraint unlawful).

93 622 F2d 1068 (2d Cir 1980).

94 *Id* 1076.

capital and labor that is often required in the distribution of products unknown to the consumer."[95] To the extent that the new product requires servicing (e.g., automobiles, household appliances)[96] or raises health and safety concerns (e.g., drugs, cosmetics),[97] vertical restrictions may also provide Seller with the degree of control necessary to avoid problems which could result in lawsuits or could otherwise adversely affect goodwill.[98]

§5.33 Is the restraint justified when Seller is attempting to enter a new territory or sell to a new class of customers?

A Seller who attempts to enter a new geographic or customer market is likely to encounter many of the same problems as a Seller who attempts to introduce a new product. To the extent that vertical nonprice resale restrictions enable the Seller to expand into—and compete effectively in—new markets, interbrand competition will be enhanced. And, as previously noted, interbrand competition is "the primary concern of antitrust law."[99]

---

[95] Continental TV, Inc v GTE Sylvania Inc, 433 US 36, 55 (1977); *see also* United States v Topco Assocs, 319 F Supp 1031, 1043 (ND Ill 1970), *revd on other grounds,* 405 US 596 (1972). *Compare* United States v Jerrold Elecs Corp, 187 F Supp 545 (ED Pa 1960), *affd per curiam,* 365 US 567 (1961) (Seller's status as *new entrant* may justify what might otherwise be an unlawful tying arrangement) *with* Eiberger v Sony Corp of Am, 622 F2d 1068, 1080 (2d Cir 1980) (rejecting new entrant argument asserted by Seller whose "fast-growing" market share was 12%); Donald B Rice Tire Co v Michelin Tire Corp, 483 F Supp 750, 757 (D Md 1980), *affd per curiam on other grounds,* 638 F2d 15 (4th Cir), *cert denied,* 454 US 864 (1981) (expressing skepticism concerning the validity of the new entrant rationale when Seller had "no difficulties finding dealers for its products").

[96] *See* Copy-Data Sys v Toshiba Am, Inc, 663 F2d 405, 410 (2d Cir 1981):

> In this case, TAI was an insignificant force in the American market for copiers hoping to increase its market share primarily on the strength of a newly developed plain paper copier. To be successful in this quest, TAI not only had to develop a product the quality of which rivaled the offerings of industry giants Xerox and IBM, but also had to assure the availability of prompt and skillful after-sale service on this technically sophisticated machine. The ability of distributors to handle the difficult servicing and maintenance problems associated with plain paper copiers would be of utmost concern to all competent management personnel in companies in TAI's position. In these circumstances, TAI might well have had legitimate reasons, consistent with antitrust law and policy, to restrict Copy-Data's freedom to market Toshiba products. (Footnote omitted.)

[97] *E.g.,* Tripoli Co v Wella Corp, 425 F2d 932 (3d Cir), *cert denied,* 400 US 831 (1970); Clairol, Inc v Boston Discount Center, 1976-2 Trade Cas (CCH) ¶61,108 (ED Mich 1976); Mitchell v United States Surgical Corp, 1976-1 Trade Cas (CCH) ¶60,879 (SD Ohio 1976).

[98] *See, e.g.,* Sports Center, Inc v Riddell, Inc, 673 F2d 786, 788, 791 (5th Cir 1982).

[99] Continental TV, Inc v GTE Sylvania Inc, 433 US 36, 52 n 19 (1977).

§5.34 Is the restraint justified when Seller is attempting to stop an erosion of its market share?

Faltering manufacturers frequently resort to nonprice resale restrictions to strengthen their distribution systems. In *White Motor Co v United States,*[100] the Supreme Court acknowledged that vertical territorial restrictions "may be allowable protections against aggressive competitors or the only practicable means a small company has for breaking into or staying in business."[101] And in *Sandura Co v FTC,*[102] the Sixth Circuit held that the imposition of "closed" territories by a struggling manufacturer might well have been essential to the manufacturer's existence. "Given the dependence of Sandura on its distributors for much of its advertising program, and given the distributors' unwillingness to cooperate without the quid pro quo of closed territories, we believe justification has been made out."[103]

In *United States v Arnold, Schwinn & Co,*[104] the Supreme Court was less sympathetic to the manufacturer. Schwinn, a leading producer of bicycles, assigned territories and imposed territorial restrictions upon its customers. Between 1951 and 1961, Schwinn's dollar and unit sales volumes rose substantially, but its market share declined from 22.5 per cent to 12.8 per cent.[105] Schwinn argued, inter alia, that the decline in its market share justified the imposition of territorial restrictions. The Court disagreed, noting that Schwinn had adopted the challenged practices prior to the erosion of its market share:

> We first observe that the facts of this case do not come within the specific illustrations which the Court in *White Motor* articulated as possible factors relevant to a showing that the challenged vertical restraint is sheltered by the rule of reason because it is not anticompetitive. Schwinn was not a newcomer, seeking to break into or stay in the bicycle business. It was not a "failing company." On the contrary, at the initiation of these practices, it was the leading bicycle producer in the Nation.[106]

Unlike Schwinn, GTE Sylvania established its distribution system (which included location restrictions upon dealers) in direct response to a decline in its market share. Prior to 1962, Sylvania sold television sets to company-owned and independent distributors. After its market share decreased from 2 per cent to 1 per cent, Sylvania phased out its distributors and began selling to a select group of dealers, each of whom was required to sell Sylvania products only

---

[100] 372 US 253 (1963).

[101] *Id* 263.

[102] 339 F2d 847 (6th Cir 1964).

[103] *Id* 857.

[104] 388 US 365 (1967).

[105] *Id* 367.

[106] *Id* 374.

from the location(s) at which it was franchised.[107] As a result of this change in policy, Sylvania's market share rose to approximately 5 per cent by 1965, and Sylvania became the eighth largest color television manufacturer in the country.[108] The change in Sylvania's distribution system may have contributed to the enhancement of interbrand competition by enabling Sylvania to "achieve certain efficiencies in the distribution of [its] products,"[109] and the Supreme Court declared unequivocally that a manufacturer may be justified in using vertical restrictions to prevent an erosion of its market share, regardless of whether the manufacturer could be classified as a failing firm: "Sylvania was faltering, if not failing, and we think it would be unduly artificial to deny it the use of valuable competitive tools."[110] On remand, the district court granted Sylvania's motion for summary judgment, holding that the challenged restraint "had an overall pro-competitive effect" in that it enabled Sylvania to increase its market share and thereby become "an effective interbrand competitor."[111]

§5.35 Is the restraint justified when Seller is attempting to encourage Buyers to perform promotional activities or postsale services or to discourage *Free Riding?*

Vertical nonprice resale restrictions have been described as "a form of compensation to distributors to induce them to represent the manufacturer fully and adequately (often through investments in showroom facilities, salesperson salaries, etc.), and to undertake promotional activities such as advertising and post-sale service and repair."[112] As the Supreme Court observed in *Sylvania:*

> Established manufacturers can use [non-price resale restrictions] to induce retailers to engage in promotional activities or to provide service

---

[107] Continental TV, Inc v GTE Sylvania Inc, 433 US 36, 38 (1977).

[108] *Id* 38-39.

[109] *Id* 54.

[110] *Id* 58 n 29.

[111] Continental TV, Inc v GTE Sylvania Inc 461 F Supp 1046, 1052 (ND Cal 1978), *affd,* 694 F2d 1132 (9th Cir 1982). *Compare* In re Coca-Cola Co, 91 FTC 517 (1978) (capital investment considerations may justify territorial restrictions imposed by a new entrant, a failing firm, or a faltering firm, but they should not be allowed to reduce entrepreneurial risk in perpetuity); In re Pepsico, Inc, 91 FTC 680 (1978) (territorial restrictions which may have been justifiable when Pepsico was a new entrant no longer justifiable after Pepsico had become an effective interbrand competitor), *with* Beltone Elecs Corp, 3 Trade Reg Rep (CCH) ¶21,934 (FTC July 6, 1982) (territorial restrictions imposed by established manufacturer had no adverse effect upon interbrand competition and were justified by manufacturer's desire to prevent free riding and ensure efficient promotion).

[112] Pitofsky, *The Sylvania Case: Antitrust Analysis of Non-Price Vertical Restrictions,* 78 Colum L Rev 1, 20 (1978).

> and repair facilities necessary to the efficient marketing of their products. Service and repair are vital for many products, such as automobiles and major household appliances. The availability and quality of such services affect a manufacturer's goodwill and the competitiveness of his product. Because of market imperfections such as the so-called "free rider" effect, these services might not be provided by retailers in a purely competitive situation. . . .[113]

The *free rider* effect to which the Supreme Court specifically referred in *Sylvania* occurs when one distributor or dealer obtains the benefits of another distributor or dealer's promotional or service efforts without incurring commensurate costs. For example, assume that dealer A effectively promotes the sale of a product in its territory by implementing an advertising campaign and establishing excellent service facilities, while dealer B, who is located in another geographic territory and who does not advertise or service the product (and therefore does not incur any of the expenses associated with such activities), undersells dealer A on sales to customers in dealer A's geographic area. The effect of dealer B's free riding may be to discourage dealer A from advertising or providing postsale services in its geographic area, to the detriment of the manufacturer and, very possibly, the consumer.

Vertical nonprice restrictions such as territorial and customer restraints, location clauses, and profit pass-over clauses can minimize or eliminate the free rider problem. For example, in *Donald B Rice Tire Co v Michelin Tire Corp*,[114] the district court found that customer restrictions which prohibited authorized dealers from selling to unauthorized dealers were reasonable methods by which a manufacturer could prevent free riding:

> [Unauthorized] dealers, unlike those operating under a [dealer agreement] were not contractually obligated to "vigorously and aggressively promote the retail sale of Michelin Products." Rather, they were free to reap the benefits of increased demand for Michelin tires generated by the promotion efforts of authorized dealers. Michelin could have reasonably concluded that its authorized dealers would be unwilling to engage in the efficient amount of promotion lest they be undersold by unauthorized dealers, as evidenced by the fact that Michelin's advantage in the radial market stemming from its pioneering role and reputation for quality was apparently declining as other major tire manufacturers developed radial tires of comparable quality and price that were rapidly gaining acceptance. . . . Defendant [also] introduced evidence concerning the important role of service in marketing Michelin tires. . . . Several cases have recognized the manufacturer's legitimate interest in ensuring the provision of point-of-sale services. . . . The economic argument, as outlined [by

---

[113] Continental TV, Inc v GTE Sylvania Inc, 433 US 36, 55 (1977).

[114] 483 F Supp 750 (D Md 1980), *affd per curiam*, 638 F2d 15 (4th Cir), *cert denied*, 454 US 864 (1981).

Professor Posner] is that if manufacturers are not permitted to impose vertical restraints which have the effect of stimulating point-of-sales services, dealers will not provide these services lest they be undercut by dealers not providing services. The problem is particularly acute in markets wherein it is difficult to prevent customers from obtaining services at one location while purchasing products from another outlet that does not offer the services but does offer lower prices.

The evidence at trial established that plaintiff's sales to unauthorized dealers were creating such problems. . . .

As the [dealer agreement] indicates, Michelin dealers are obligated to service Michelin tires. Customers who bought Michelin tires from unauthorized dealers who were not so obligated presumably went to authorized dealers to obtain service. [A former Baltimore district manager] testified that dealers resent having to service tires that they did not sell. This fact was conceded by a number of tire dealers and suggests that the free-rider problem set out earlier existed and that Michelin reasonably could have determined that nonrenewal of major wholesalers was necessary to ensure provision of point-of-sale services.[115]

§5.36 Is the restraint justified when Seller is attempting to promote consumer safety, avoid product liability suits, maintain quality control, and/or fulfill warranty obligations?

In *Sylvania,* the Supreme Court acknowledged that vertical nonprice resale restrictions enable Sellers to compete more effectively against other Sellers of comparable goods. The Court also stated that:

> Market efficiency is not the only legitimate reason for a manufacturer's desire to exert control over the manner in which his products are sold and serviced. As a result of statutory and common-law developments, society increasingly demands that manufacturers assume direct responsibility for the safety and quality of their products.[116]

---

[115] 483 F Supp at 757-59 (citations omitted). For other recent cases discussing the free rider effect, *see* Bostick Oil Co v Michelin Tire Corp, 1983-1 Trade Cas (CCH) ¶65,271 (4th Cir 1983); Davis-Watkins Co v Service Merchandise, 686 F2d 1190, 1199-1201 (6th Cir 1982); Com-Tel, Inc v DuKane Corp, 669 F2d 404, 409 n 7 (6th Cir 1982); Muenster Butane, Inc v Stewart Co, 651 F2d 292, 297 (5th Cir 1981); Eiberger v Sony Corp of Am, 622 F2d 1068, 1075-81 (2d Cir 1980); Beltone Elecs Corp, 3 Trade Reg Rep (CCH) ¶21,934 (FTC July 6, 1982).

[116] Continental TV, Inc v GTE Sylvania Inc, 433 US 36, 55 n 23 (1977). *Cf* National Socy of Professional Engrs v United States, 435 US 679, 696 n 22 (1978) (restrictions related to product safety are permissible, "provided that they have no anticompetitive effect").

Health, safety, and quality control factors are therefore relevant to a rule of reason analysis of nonprice vertical restrictions.[117]

§5.37 Is the restraint justified when Seller is attempting to promote distribution of its goods?

Sellers who impose nonprice resale restrictions upon their Buyers are very often motivated by the desire to achieve a more efficient distribution of their goods. Although the restraints may reduce or eliminate competition among Seller's distributors or dealers, they may also promote interbrand competition by enabling Seller to attract competent and aggressive distributors or dealers, induce such distributors or dealers to invest capital and labor in developing and promoting Seller's products against those of competing Sellers, provide for better controls over the quality and safety of Seller's products, and increase Seller's market penetration. This was recognized by the Supreme Court in *Sylvania*[118] and has been recognized by lower courts since that decision.

In *Newberry v Washington Post Co,*[119] the court considered the legality of a *dual dealer* system in which a newspaper authorized one group of dealers to serve home subscribers, while authorizing another group of dealers to serve single sales outlets. The system also had the effect of limiting each dealer's sales to a designated territory. The court upheld the restrictions, noting that the system was designed to ensure efficient distribution and that, for economic reasons, dealers generally did not compete with one another:

> Both the Post and its dealers shared an interest in the widest possible circulation of the newspaper and thus in prompt, reliable, consistent delivery at the lowest possible cost. Both would have confronted many troublesome operating problems if dealers sought to invade each other's territories. Competition would interrupt smooth delivery to subscribers. Difficulties would also be encountered in handling subscriber complaints, new subscriptions, stop orders, billing, and the like because of

---

[117] *E.g.,* Sports Center, Inc v Riddell, Inc, 673 F2d 786, 788, 791 (5th Cir 1982); Clairol, Inc v Boston Discount Center, Inc, 608 F2d 1114, 1125 (6th Cir 1979); Del Rio Distrib, Inc v Adolph Coors Co, 589 F2d 176, 179 (5th Cir 1979); Adolph Coors Co v A&S Wholesalers, Inc, 561 F2d 807, 813 (10th Cir 1977); Tripoli Co v Wella Corp, 425 F2d 932 (3d Cir), *cert denied,* 400 US 831 (1970); Mitchell v United States Surgical Corp, 1976-1 Trade Cas (CCH) ¶60,879 (SD Ohio 1976). *Compare* Donald B Rice Tire Co v Michelin Tire Corp, 483 F Supp 750 (D Md 1980), *affd per curiam,* 638 F2d 15 (4th Cir), *cert denied,* 454 US 864 (1981) (acknowledging a safety justification for vertical restrictions, but concluding that the manufacturer failed to establish the justification); In re Coca-Cola Co, 91 FTC 517 (1978) (although territorial restrictions did facilitate product source identification to some extent, they were more restrictive than necessary to maintain quality control standards).

[118] Continental TV, Inc v GTE Sylvania Inc, 433 US 36, 54-57 (1977).

[119] 438 F Supp 470 (DDC 1977).

uncertainty as to which dealer was serving or planning to serve which subscriber.

In addition, competition simply would not have been profitable for the dealers. In areas in which subscribers are widely scattered, the costs of service are very high in relation to the profit to be gained. . . . [T]he territories specified in the dealer contracts were tailored with efficient delivery in mind. . . .[120]

In *Cowley v Braden Indus, Inc*,[121] a manufacturer of windmills and pumps marketed its products, in part, through independent distributors. Each distributor was assigned a particular geographic area and was prohibited from "actively soliciting business outside [its] assigned territory." Distributors were permitted to sell outside their territories only if the goods first came into their territories and were placed in stock.[122] The Ninth Circuit held these restrictions to be reasonable, relying, inter alia, upon the district court's finding that "the requirement that a distributor take goods into his trade area before selling them improved the efficiency in marketing since it ensured the distributor's maintenance of a proper stock of goods and its intense promotion of sales in the assigned area."[123]

§5.38 Does Seller's market share make a difference under the rule of reason?

Under the rule of reason, a plaintiff must demonstrate that the challenged conduct unreasonably restrained competition. This, in turn, requires proof of the relevant market, defendant's power in that market, and the impact of the challenged conduct on that market.[124] The market share of the Seller imposing resale restrictions is an important factor in a rule of reason analysis because it reflects the Seller's power in the relevant market. The imposition of nonprice

---

120 *Id* 474.

121 613 F2d 751 (9th Cir 1980).

122 *Id* 753.

123 *Id* 755. *See also* Davis-Watkins Co v Service Merchandise, 686 F2d 1190, 1200-01 (6th Cir 1982) (manufacturer demonstrated "the need to eliminate the free rider problem within its chain of distribution in order to be more efficient and thereby more competitive"); Muenster Butane, Inc v Stewart Co, 651 F2d 292, 298 (5th Cir 1981) (Seller "merely tried to improve its distribution efficiency by reducing intrabrand competition"); Abadir & Co v First Miss Corp, 651 F2d 422, 427 (5th Cir 1981) ("market-distribution efficiency" is among the legitimate potential economic advantages available to a seller who imposes nonprice resale restrictions).

124 *See, e.g.*, National Socy of Professional Engrs v United States, 435 US 679, 690-91 (1978); Times-Picayune Publishing Co v United States, 345 US 594, 614-22 (1953); Muenster Butane, Inc v Stewart Co, 651 F2d 292, 295 (5th Cir 1981) (plaintiff in a rule of reason case "must prove that the restraint had an anticompetitive effect in the relevant market in order to prevail"); Kaplan v Burroughs Corp, 611 F2d 286, 291 (9th Cir 1979), *cert denied*, 447 US 924 (1980); Oreck Corp v Whirlpool Corp, 579 F2d 126, 133-34 (2d Cir) (en banc), *cert denied*, 439 US 946 (1978).

resale restrictions by a Seller with a small market share is unlikely to impair interbrand competition, and has a greater potential for enhancing interbrand competition than the imposition of such restrictions by a Seller with a large market share.

Although Seller's market share may significantly influence the outcome of the rule of reason inquiry, it is generally not dispositive.[125] Territorial and customer restrictions imposed by a monopolist have been upheld under the rule of reason upon a showing of minimal impact on intrabrand competition and enhancement of marketing efficiencies,[126] while territorial restrictions imposed by a Seller with only a 12 per cent market share were held unreasonable when the Seller was unable to persuade the court that it had valid business reasons for the restrictions.[127] Nevertheless, many decisions upholding vertical restrictions under the rule of reason have emphasized Seller's lack of market power.[128]

---

[125] As the Third Circuit stated in Friedman, Inc v Thorofare Mkts, Inc, 587 F2d 127, 141 (3d Cir 1978):

> The reasonableness of any anticompetitive conduct may be judged only after careful consideration of the effect it will have on competition. The purpose of such activity, the structure of the industry, and the strength of competition in the relevant geographic and product markets are among the factors that generally mold the outcome of such analysis. Of course, no single aspect is dispositive. Also, conclusions reached by courts in one context are not necessarily applicable in another. (Footnote omitted.)

[126] Newberry v Washington Post Co, 438 F Supp 470 (DDC 1977). *See also* Cowley v Braden Indus, 613 F2d 751 (9th Cir 1980) (territorial restrictions imposed by Seller which controlled 70-80% of the market found reasonable; distributor failed to adduce evidence of harm to interbrand competition, and Seller demonstrated that restraints were necessary to enhance marketing efficiency).

[127] Eiberger v Sony Corp of Am, 622 F2d 1068 (2d Cir 1980).

[128] *E.g.,* JBL Enters, Inc v Jhirmack Enters, Inc, 698 F2d 1011, 1017 (9th Cir 1983) (market share of 2.3%-4.2% "too small for any restraint on intrabrand competition to have a substantially adverse effect on interbrand competition"); Carlson Mach Tools, Inc v American Tool, Inc, 678 F2d 1253, 1259 (5th Cir 1982) (supplier's market share never exceeded 10%); Sports Center, Inc v Riddell, Inc, 673 F2d 786, 788, 791 (5th Cir 1982) (sporting goods manufacturer was a "small company"; no evidence that customer restriction had any anticompetitive effect in the relevant product or geographic market); Muenster Butane, Inc v Stewart Co, 651 F2d 292, 298 (5th Cir 1981) (television Seller "had no market power in Gainesville"; therefore, vertical restraints upon dealers could not have the effect of raising the price consumers paid for television sets); Donald B Rice Tire Co v Michelin Tire Corp, 483 F Supp 750, 761 (D Md 1980), *affd per curiam,* 638 F2d 15 (4th Cir), *cert denied,* 454 US 864 (1981) (evidence that manufacturer's share of radial passenger tire market was 7.9% supported conclusion that manufacturer "lacked the requisite market power to restrain competition"); Continental TV, Inc v GTE Sylvania, Inc, 461 F Supp 1046, 1052 (ND Cal 1978) (1 or 2% market share "relatively insignificant"), *affd,* 694 F2d 1132 (9th Cir 1982). *See also* Davis-Watkins Co v Service Merchandise, 686 F2d 1190, 1202 (6th Cir 1982) (jury properly instructed to consider manufacturer's market power; "[w]ithout market power, a firm cannot have an adverse effect on competition"); Valley Liquors, Inc v Renfield Importers, Ltd, 678 F2d 742, 745 (7th Cir 1982) ("A firm that has no market power is unlikely to adopt policies that disserve its consumers; it cannot afford to"). See

§5.39 Does the market share of Seller's competitors make a difference under the rule of reason?

In determining whether vertical nonprice resale restrictions are reasonable, courts must consider the impact of such restrictions upon competition in the relevant market. The market shares of Seller's competitors are unquestionably relevant to such an inquiry. Vertical restrictions are more likely to be upheld in industries in which vigorous interbrand competition exists or in which a relatively small Seller is attempting to compete effectively against large competitors than in highly concentrated industries.[129]

---

generally Posner, *The Next Step in the Antitrust Treatment of Restricted Distribution: Per Se Legality,* 48 U Chi L Rev 6, 16-18 (1981) (arguing that a plaintiff in a rule of reason case should always be required to prove that the Seller possesses substantial market power).

[129] *E.g.,* Continental TV, Inc v GTE Sylvania Inc, 433 US 36, 53 n 18 (1977); Mendelovitz v Adolph Coors Co, 693 F2d 570, 576 n 10 (5th Cir 1982) ("the record indicates that interbrand competition in beer is significant"); Sports Center, Inc v Riddell, Inc, 673 F2d 786, 788, 791 (5th Cir 1982) ("anti-bootlegging" policy enabled small manufacturer "to remain reasonably competitive with much larger manufacturers"); Copy-Data Sys v Toshiba Am, Inc, 663 F2d 405, 410 (2d Cir 1981) (territorial restrictions in part justified by manufacturer's need to develop products which rivaled products of "industry giants"); Muenster Butane, Inc v Stewart Co, 651 F2d 292, 297-98 (5th Cir 1981) (restrictions did not have an anticompetitive effect within a relevant market characterized by stiff interbrand competition); Red Diamond Supply, Inc v Liquid Carbonic Corp, 637 F2d 1001, 1005-06 (5th Cir), *cert denied,* 454 US 827 (1981) (record suggested "significant interbrand competition" among seven Sellers; plaintiff did not produce market share data to support claim of market concentration); Donald B Rice Tire Co v Michelin Tire Corp, 483 F Supp 750, 761 (D Md 1980), *affd per curiam,* 638 F2d 15 (4th Cir), *cert denied,* 454 US 864 (1981) (noting the presence of large competitors and fierce interbrand competition in the industry); Continental TV, Inc v GTE Sylvania, Inc, 461 F Supp 1046, 1052 (ND Cal 1978) ("Sylvania was not part of an oligopolistic industry, but rather, was one of more than 100 television manufacturers in a competitive industry"), *affd,* 694 F2d 1132 (9th Cir 1982) (noting further that neither Sylvania nor any of its competitors prevented its customers from handling competing products); Beltone Elecs Corp, 3 Trade Reg Rep (CCH) ¶21,934 (FTC July 6, 1982) (noting that manufacturer's market share dropped from 21% to 16% and that "other firms have recently entered the market or grown vigorously"). *See also* Sandura Co v FTC, 339 F2d 847 (6th Cir 1964). *Cf* Newberry v Washington Post Co, 438 F Supp 470, 475 (DDC 1977) (upholding territorial and customer restrictions imposed by dominant Seller, but noting that such restrictions "are likely to be more pernicious when instituted by a monopolist or near monopolist").

Will less restrictive territorial or customer restraints solve the antitrust problem?

§5.40 Is the existence of less restrictive means to achieve the desired end relevant under the rule of reason?

A Seller who imposes a nonprice resale restriction upon Buyers is not required under the rule of reason to demonstrate that the restriction is the least restrictive means to achieve a desired end. In *Sylvania,* the Supreme Court recognized the economic utility of a location restriction, even though it "was neither the least nor the most restrictive provision that [the manufacturer] could have used."[130] And, as the Third Circuit stated in *American Motor Inns, Inc v Holiday Inns, Inc:*

> In its descriptions of the rule of reason inquiry, the Supreme Court has never indicated that, regardless of the other circumstances present, the availability of an alternative means of achieving the asserted business purpose renders the existing arrangement unlawful if that alternative would be less restrictive of competition no matter to how small a degree. . . .
>
> Application of the rigid "no less restrictive alternative" test . . . would place an undue burden on the ordinary conduct of business. Entrepreneurs . . . would then be made guarantors that the imaginations of lawyers could not conjure up some method of achieving the business purpose in question which would result in a somewhat lesser restriction of trade. And courts would be placed in the position of second-guessing business judgments as to what arrangements would or would not provide "adequate" protection for legitimate commercial interests.[131]

However, Seller is generally required to demonstrate that the restriction is a "reasonably necessary" means to achieve a legitimate commercial objective.[132]

---

[130] Continental TV, Inc v GTE Sylvania Inc, 433 US 36, 58 n 29 (1977).

[131] 521 F2d 1230, 1249 (3d Cir 1975). *Accord* Newberry v Washington Post Co, 438 F Supp 470, 475 (DDC 1977); Continental TV, Inc v GTE Sylvania Inc, 694 F2d 1132, 1138 n 11 (9th Cir 1982). *See also* Beltone Elecs Corp, 3 Trade Reg Rep (CCH) ¶21,934 (FTC July 6, 1982) ("In evaluating the competitive benefits of vertical restraints, we do not suggest that the search should focus on whether a less restrictive method of distribution is available. *Sylvania* clearly does not contemplate such an approach and it undoubtedly would prove elusive in any event"). *But cf* Cowley v Braden Indus, 613 F2d 751, 755 (9th Cir 1980) (affirming trial court's finding of reasonableness of territorial restrictions because, inter alia, distributor made "no showing . . . of any effective, alternate means [for Seller] to maintain an efficient distributor system").

[132] Donald B Rice Tire Co v Michelin Tire Corp, 483 F Supp 750, 758 (D Md 1980), *affd per curiam,* 638 F2d 15 (4th Cir), *cert denied,* 454 US 864 (1981). *See also* American

Thus, the extent and nature of the restraint will be a factor considered by a court analyzing a vertical nonprice restriction under the rule of reason.

§5.41 What less restrictive alternatives have been upheld by the courts?

Seller may, of course, be able to achieve legitimate business objectives by imposing resale restraints which are less restrictive than absolute (*airtight*) territorial and customer restrictions. Various less restrictive means of regulating distribution, including primary area of responsibility clauses, profit pass-over clauses, and location clauses, have been upheld by the courts.[133]

Will a primary area of responsibility clause solve the antitrust problem?

§5.42 What is a primary area of responsibility clause?

Primary area of responsibility clauses obligate a distributor or dealer to maintain effective distribution in a defined geographic area or to a defined class of customers.[134] In many cases, such clauses obligate the distributor or dealer to do nothing more than devote its *best efforts* (as defined in the distribution agreement) to develop its sales area.[135] The distributor or dealer is free to sell anywhere or to anyone, provided it fulfills its commitments in its assigned territory.[136]

§5.43 How is the legality of such a restriction tested?

Primary area of responsibility clauses are tested under the rule of reason,

---

Motor Inns, Inc v Holiday Inns, Inc, 521 F2d 1230, 1249 (3d Cir 1975); United States v Columbia Pictures Corp, 189 F Supp 153, 178 (SDNY 1960); Pitofsky, *The Sylvania Case: Antitrust Analysis of Non-Price Vertical Restrictions,* 78 Colum L Rev 1, 36-37 (1978).

133 See **§§5.01, 5.42-5.50.**

134 See **§5.01.**

135 See Pitofsky, *The Sylvania Case: Antitrust Analysis of Non-Price Vertical Restrictions,* 78 Colum L Rev 1, 4 n 12 (1978) (since dealers naturally devote their best sales efforts to promoting local sales, a primary area of responsibility clause "is little more than an assurance to the supplier of the kind of marketwide coverage that probably would occur anyway").

136 In the event that a primary area of responsibility clause expresses nothing more than Seller's expectations with regard to a particular territory, the clause might not even rise to the level of an agreement between Seller and Buyer, and would therefore not fall within the scope of §1 of the Sherman Act.

and are generally upheld.[137]

§5.44 Under what circumstances have primary area of responsibility clauses been held unlawful?

Prior to *Sylvania,*[138] the Fifth Circuit held that when a primary area of responsibility clause effectively precluded a franchisee from selling outside of its assigned territory, such a clause could constitute a per se unlawful territorial restriction under *Schwinn.*[139] Vertical territorial resale restrictions are no longer per se unlawful. However, a primary area of responsibility clause, even if lawful in and of itself, may not be used to implement broader anticompetitive schemes such as resale price maintenance or horizontal market allocation.[140]

Will a profit pass-over clause solve the antitrust problem?

§5.45 What is a profit pass-over clause?

A profit pass-over clause obligates a distributor or dealer which makes sales to customers outside its assigned territory to pay compensation to the distributor or dealer in whose territory the sale was made.[141] Bona fide profit pass-overs compensate the local dealer for costs incurred in developing the territory (or in providing post-sale services), thereby avoiding *free rider* problems.

---

[137] Knutson v Daily Review, Inc, 548 F2d 795, 808-09 (9th Cir 1976), *cert denied,* 433 US 910 (1977); Colorado Pump & Supply Co v Febco, Inc, 472 F2d 637 (10th Cir), *cert denied,* 411 US 987 (1973); Kaiser v General Motors Corp, 396 F Supp 33, 39-41 (ED Pa 1975), *affd without opinion,* 530 F2d 964 (3d Cir 1976); AP Hopkins Corp v Studebaker Corp, 355 F Supp 816 (ED Mich 1972), *affd,* 496 F2d 969 (6th Cir 1974); Superior Bedding Co v Serta Assocs, 353 F Supp 1143, 1148-49 (ND Ill 1972); Plastic Packaging Materials, Inc v Dow Chem Co, 327 F Supp 213, 225 (ED Pa 1971).

[138] Continental TV, Inc v GTE Sylvania Inc, 433 US 36 (1977).

[139] Response of Carolina, Inc v Leasco Response, Inc, 537 F2d 1307, 1319-20 (5th Cir 1976) (citing United States v Arnold, Schwinn & Co, 388 US 365 (1967)) (franchise agreement required 70% royalty payment by franchisee on sales to customers outside of area of primary responsibility as compared with 15% royalty on sales to customers within area).

[140] *See* Ohio-Sealy Mfg Co v Sealy, Inc, 585 F2d 821 (7th Cir 1978), *cert denied,* 440 US 930 (1979) (primary area of responsibility clause, imposed in conjunction with other restraints, perpetuated a horizontal market division scheme).

[141] See **§5.01.**

§5.46 How is the legality of such a restriction tested?

Profit pass-over clauses are tested under the rule of reason, and are generally found to be lawful.[142]

§5.47 Under what circumstances have profit pass-over clauses been held unlawful?

A profit pass-over clause may be held unlawful when it is found to be punitive (rather than compensatory) and unreasonably restrictive of competition. For example, in *Eiberger v Sony Corp of America,*[143] a Seller of dictation machines imposed a warranty fee upon dealers who sold outside of their assigned territories. The manufacturer argued that the fee system was designed to improve warranty service to equipment users by ensuring that nonselling dealers were compensated for performing such services. However, the Second Circuit affirmed the district court's finding that the warranty fee bore no reasonable relationship to services actually performed by nonselling dealers. The fee was imposed regardless of whether the selling dealer was willing to perform the required services and regardless of whether the nonselling dealer had actually performed such services. Under these circumstances, the court ruled that the fee was merely a mechanism by which the Seller discouraged extraterritorial sales, eliminated intrabrand competition, and maintained artificially high resale prices.[144]

Will a location clause solve the antitrust problem?

§5.48 What is a location clause?

A location clause permits a dealer to resell anywhere and to anyone, but only from Seller-authorized locations.[145]

---

[142] Superior Bedding Co v Serta Assocs, Inc, 353 F Supp 1143 (ND Ill 1972) (pass-over profit arrangement obligating licensee to pay 7% of gross receipts on sales outside its area of primary responsibility found reasonable); *see also* United States v Topco Assocs, 1973-1 Trade Cas (CCH) ¶74,391 (ND Ill 1973) (profit pass-over permitted so long as not "used to achieve or maintain territorial exclusivity for any member firm").

[143] 622 F2d 1068 (2d Cir 1980).

[144] *Id* 1076-81.

[145] See **§5.01.**

§5.49 How is the legality of such a restriction tested?

Location clauses are tested under the rule of reason and have traditionally been upheld—even during the *Schwinn* era.[146]

§5.50 Under what circumstances have location clauses been held unlawful?

Location clauses, even if lawful in and of themselves, may not be used to implement broader anticompetitive schemes such as resale price maintenance, group boycotts, or horizontal market divisions.[147]

---

[146] *E.g.,* Muenster Butane, Inc v Stewart Co, 651 F2d 292 (5th Cir 1981); Cowley v Braden Indus, 613 F2d 751 (9th Cir 1980); Golden Gate Acceptance Corp v General Motors Corp, 597 F2d 676, 678 n 4 (9th Cir 1979); Salco Corp v General Motors Corp, 517 F2d 567 (10th Cir 1975); Boro Hall Corp v General Motors Corp, 122 F2d 822 (2d Cir 1942); Donald B Rice Tire Co v Michelin Tire Corp, 483 F Supp 750 (D Md 1980), *affd per curiam,* 638 F2d 15 (4th Cir), *cert denied,* 454 US 864 (1981); Whims Appliance Serv, Inc v General Motors Corp, 1978-1 Trade Cas (CCH) ¶62,093 (ND Ohio 1978); Continental TV, Inc v GTE Sylvania Inc, 461 F Supp 1046 (ND Cal 1978); Sheldon Pontiac v Pontiac Motor Div, 418 F Supp 1024 (DNJ 1976); Kaiser v General Motors Corp, 396 F Supp 33 (ED Pa 1975), *affd without opinion,* 530 F2d 964 (3d Cir 1976). *See also* GTE Sylvania Inc v Continental TV, Inc, 537 F2d 980, 997-98 (9th Cir 1976) (en banc), *affd,* 433 US 36 (1977), in which Judge Ely observed that it would be illogical to permit a manufacturer to grant an exclusive dealership, while denying the manufacturer the right to enforce a location clause against those who seek to open unauthorized outlets in the exclusive dealer's territory.

> The clearly established legality of exclusive dealerships logically compels the conclusion that location clauses cannot be *per se* illegal. If it is legal for a manufacturer to promise one dealer that he will have the exclusive right to sell the manufacturer's products within a designated territory, then obviously it is legal for that manufacturer to keep his promise of exclusivity by denying other dealers like Continental the power to sell from retail outlets at unauthorized locations within the first dealer's exclusive territory. The accepted principle that a manufacturer may legally grant an exclusive dealership is rendered meaningless if he cannot legally use a location clause to prevent his other dealers from opening their own retail outlets in the same area. If a manufacturer cannot include a location restriction in a franchise agreement, he cannot do what the exclusive dealership cases hold is legal, *i.e.,* promise that "I will not franchise another dealer in your area." If a location restriction cannot legally be enforced, and, for example, a franchisee is established in San Francisco, California, who then opens a store in Los Angeles, California, the manufacturer cannot fulfill his promise to his original Los Angeles franchisee that he will not recognize another dealer in Los Angeles. Therefore, we conclude that the rule of *per se* illegality applied below is logically inconsistent and irreconcilable with our decision in *Hawaiian Oke* and the many other cases upholding the right of manufacturers to establish exclusive dealerships.

[147] *See, e.g.,* United States v General Motors Corp, 384 US 127 (1966); Ohio-Sealy Mfg Co v Sealy Inc, 585 F2d 821 (7th Cir 1978), *cert denied,* 440 US 930 (1979).

May Seller who also distributes in competition with Buyers place resale restrictions on Buyers?

§5.51 What is a dual distributor?

A *dual distributor* sells to purchasers at different levels of the distribution chain, and thereby places itself in actual or potential competition with some of its customers. For example, a Seller which sells to both wholesalers and retailers (and competes with its wholesaler customers for the business of retailers) is a dual distributor.

§5.52 Are resale restrictions imposed by dual distributors deemed vertical or horizontal?

As previously indicated, the classification of resale restrictions as *vertical* or *horizontal* is very important.[148] Problems of classification are exacerbated in the context of dual distribution.

Some courts (mostly pre-*Sylvania*) have held that the imposition of territorial or customer restrictions by a dual distributor constitutes a horizontal allocation of markets.[149] However, recent decisions have held that nonprice restrictions which are designed to enhance market efficiency and promote interbrand competition are vertical, notwithstanding the fact that the Seller imposing the restrictions is a dual distributor.[150] But the courts have also indicated that when the customers are the motivating parties, the restraint will be considered horizontal and hence subject to the rule of per se illegality.[151]

---

[148] See **§5.25.**

[149] *E.g.*, Pitchford v PEPI, Inc, 531 F2d 92, 103-04 (3d Cir), *cert denied*, 426 US 935 (1976), *on remand*, 435 F Supp 685 (WD Pa 1977), *affd without opinion*, 582 F2d 1275 (3d Cir 1978), *cert denied*, 440 US 981 (1979); Hobart Bros v Malcolm T Gilliland, Inc, 471 F2d 894, 899 (5th Cir), *cert denied*, 412 US 923 (1973); Interphoto Corp v Minolta Corp, 295 F Supp 711, 719-20 (SDNY), *affd per curiam*, 417 F2d 621 (2d Cir 1969); United States v CIBA-GEIGY Corp, 1976-1 Trade Cas (CCH) ¶60,908 (DNJ 1976).

[150] *E.g.*, Copy-Data Sys v Toshiba Am, Inc, 663 F2d 405 (2d Cir 1981); Abadir & Co v First Miss Corp, 651 F2d 422 (5th Cir 1981); Donald B Rice Tire Co v Michelin Tire Corp, 638 F2d 15 (4th Cir), *cert denied*, 454 US 864 (1981); Red Diamond Supply, Inc v Liquid Carbonic Corp, 637 F2d 1001, 1004-07 (5th Cir), *cert denied*, 454 US 827 (1981); Cowley v Braden Indus, 613 F2d 751, 754-56 (9th Cir 1980); Clairol, Inc v Boston Discount Center, Inc, 608 F2d 1114, 1121-25 (6th Cir 1979); Blake Assocs v Omni Spectra, Inc, 1982-83 Trade Cas (CCH) ¶65,155, at 71,499-54 n 1 (D Mass 1982), Westpoint Pepperell, Inc v Rea, 1980-2 Trade Cas (CCH) ¶63,341, at 75,742-45 (ND Cal 1980); Krehl v Baskin-Robbins Ice Cream Co, 1979-2 Trade Cas (CCH) ¶62,806, at 78,704 (CD Cal 1979), *affd*, 664 F2d 1348 (9th Cir 1982); In re Coca-Cola Co, 91 FTC 517, 610-16 (FTC 1978).

[151] *E.g.*, H&B Equip Co v International Harvester Co, 577 F2d 239, 245-46 (5th Cir 1978) (restraint imposed by dual distributor is vertical unless "the source of the conspiracy is a combination of the [independent] distributors").

May Seller Restrict the Prices at which Buyer Resells?

*Jay Greenfield**

6

---

*Mr. Greenfield is a member of the New York Bar. The author wishes to thank Professor Aryeh S. Friedman of the Wharton School, University of Pennsylvania, and James Rubinger of Paul, Weiss, Rifkind, Wharton & Garrison for their assistance in the preparation of this chapter.

§6.01 May Seller control the prices at which Buyer resells its products?

The Seller cannot control the prices at which Buyer resells its products. Such vertical control of pricing, commonly referred to as *resale price maintenance,* has been consistently held to constitute vertical price-fixing. Like horizontal price-fixing, it is per se illegal.[1] It has been condemned under §1 of the Sherman

---

[1] United States v Socony-Vacuum Oil Co, 310 US 150, 223 (1940). The Supreme Court applied a per se analysis to vertical price-fixing in its 1980 decision in California Retail Liquor Dealers' Assoc v Midcal Aluminum, Inc, 445 US 97 (1980). See generally ABA Section on Antitrust, Vertical Restrictions Limiting Intrabrand Competition 71-72 (Monograph No 2 1977).

Act,[2] §5 of the Federal Trade Commission Act,[3] and various state antitrust laws.[4]

Senior Justice Department officials have recently stated that, in their views, vertical price-fixing should not be per se unlawful but, as with other vertical restraints (for example, territorial restraints),[5] should be judged by the rule of reason.[6] Similar views have been put forward by the Director of the Federal Trade Commission's Bureau of Competition[7] and by prominent commentators.[8] Nevertheless, the per se rule has been applied, without exception, in

---

[2] 15 USC §1. Until 1975 a statutory exemption from this blanket condemnation was provided by two amendments to the Sherman Act—the Miller-Tydings Amendment, ch 690 50 Stat, 693 (1937), and the McGuire Act, ch 745, 66 Stat 632 (1952). These amendments exempted resale price maintenance agreements permitted under state fair trade laws. This exemption was repealed by the Consumer Goods Pricing Act, Pub L No 94-145 89 Stat 801, in 1975.

[3] 15 USC §45.

[4] *See, e.g.*, the California Cartwright Act, Cal Bus & Prof Code §§16,700-760 (West 1964 & Supp 1981) (*see* Mailand v Burckle, 20 Cal 3d 367, 572 P2d 1142, 143 Cal Rptr 1 (1978)); the Illinois Antitrust Act, Ill Ann Stat ch 38, §60-3(1) *et seq* (Smith-Hurd 1977) (*see* People *ex rel* Scott v Convenient Food Mart, Inc, 21 Ill App 3d 97, 315 NE2d 124 (1974)); the Maryland Antitrust Act, Md Com Law Code Ann §§11-201 to -213 (1975 & Supp 1980) (*see* Quality Discount Tires, Inc v Firestone Tire & Rubber Co, 282 Md 7, 382 A2d 867 (Ct App 1978)); the Missouri Antitrust Act, Mo Rev Stat §416.141 (1974) (*see* Battle v Lubrizol Corp, 513 F Supp 995 (ED Mo 1981), *revd on other grounds,* 673 F2d 984 (8th Cir 1982)); the New Jersey Antitrust Act, NJ Stat Ann 56:9-1 et seq (West Supp 1981-1982) (see State v Lawn King, Inc, 150 NJ Super 204, 375 A2d 295 (1977), *revd,* 169 NJ Super 346, 404 A2d 1215 (App Div 1979), *affd,* 84 NJ 179, 417 A2d 1025 (1980)); and the New York Donnelly Act, NY Gen Bus L §340 *et seq* (McKinney 1968 & Supp 1980-1981) (*see* Uniroyal, Inc v Jetco Auto Serv Inc, 461 F Supp 350, 357 (SDNY 1978)).

[5] *See* Continental TV, Inc v GTE Sylvania, Inc, 433 US 36 (1977).

[6] Attorney General Smith, Antitrust & Trade Reg Rep (BNA) slip no 1021, at A-3 (July 2, 1981):

> Vertical arrangements between a manufacturer . . . and its distributors—such as . . . resale price maintenance—are not necessarily anti-competitive. To the contrary, these types of arrangements often are procompetitive by promoting cost-saving efficiencies along the chain of distribution. In analyzing any specific vertical arrangement, one must ask whether it has an anticompetitive effect at any identifiable horizontal level.

Assistant Attorney General William Baxter, Head of the Justice Department's Antitrust Division, Antitrust & Trade Reg Rep (BNA) slip no 1022, at A-8 (July 9, 1981) ("Vertical pricing arrangements, in and of themselves, do not impair the efficiency of markets or lessen the welfare of consumer"); Ronald G Carr, Deputy Assistant Attorney General, Antitrust Division, Trade Reg Rep (CCH) slip no 516, at 4 (Nov. 8, 1981).

[7] *See* 43 Antitrust & Trade Reg Rep (BNA) 238 (July 22, 1982).

[8] Posner, *The Next Step in the Antitrust Treatment of Restricted Distribution: Per Se Legality,* 48 U Chi L Rev 6, 8-14 (1981); Posner, *The Rule of Reason and the Economic Approach: Reflections on the Sylvania Decision,* 45 U Chi L Rev 1 (1977); Bork, *The Rule of Reason and the Per Se Concept: Price Fixing and Market Division,* 75 Yale LJ 373 (1966).

vertical price-fixing cases.[9]

Although Seller may not control the resale prices of Buyer, Seller may take certain steps which may have an effect on resale prices. In particular, Seller may suggest the resale prices of its products.[10] The question of whether particular conduct by Seller constitutes unlawful *price control* or lawful *price suggesting* is frequently a difficult one, and the judicial response to a particular pricing program cannot always be safely predicted.[11]

§6.02 —When is a resale price fixed?

Resale prices are *fixed* when Seller and Buyer agree upon what the resale prices should be. Price-fixing is also likely to be found, however, if there is any restraint upon Buyer's pricing discretion—

> if the range within which purchases or sales will be made is agreed upon, if the prices paid or charged are to be at a certain level or on ascending or descending scales, if they are to be uniform, or if by various formulae they are related to the market prices.[12]

Thus, establishing percent markup formulas or regulating Buyer's discount from list has been found to constitute vertical price-fixing.[13]

---

[9] California Retail Liquor Dealers' Assn v Midcal Aluminum, Inc, 445 US 97 (1980); Yentsch v Texaco, Inc, 630 F2d 46, 51 (2d Cir 1980) ("Vertical resale price maintenance is, so far as it still appears, per se illegal under §1 of the Sherman Act" (citing *Midcal*)); Arnott v American Oil Co, 609 F2d 873, 885 (8th Cir 1979), *cert denied,* 446 US 918 (1980); Knutson v Daily Review, Inc, 548 F2d 795, 806 n12 (9th Cir 1976), *cert denied,* 433 US 910 (1977). *See also* Continental TV, Inc v GTE Sylvania, Inc, 433 US 36, 51 n 18 (1977) (applying rule of reason to geographic restrictions; Court noted, however, that "[t]he *per se* illegality of *price* restrictions has been established firmly for many years and involves significantly different questions of analysis and policy." (emphasis added); *but see,* Eastern Scientific Co v Wild Heerbrugg Instruments, Inc, 572 F2d 883 (1st Cir), *cert denied,* 439 US 833 (1978).

[10] See **§6.06.**

[11] L. Sullivan, Handbook of the Law of Antitrust §139, at 395 (1977).

[12] United States v Socony-Vacuum Oil Co, 310 US 150, 222 (1939).

[13] Swettlen v Wagoner Gas & Oil, Inc, 373 F Supp 1022 (WD Pa), *affd,* 511 F2d 1395 (3d Cir 1975); Burton Supply Co v Wheel Horse Prods, Inc, 1974-2 Trade Cases (CCH) ¶75,224, (ND Ohio 1974). In *Yentsch v Texaco, Inc,* 630 F2d 46, 53 n 7 (2d Cir 1980), the plaintiff alleged that the seller's requirement that it give trading stamps to customers constituted a forced discount and, thus, vertical price-fixing; the court found vertical price-fixing on other grounds and did not decide this issue. See **§6.13.**

§6.03 —Does it make any difference if the prices in question are maximum prices, rather than minimum prices?

The Supreme Court has held, unequivocally, that it makes no difference whether Seller seeks to control the maximum or minimum resale prices charged by Buyer.[14]

Since maximum prices are in the interests of consumers while minimum prices are not, it has been argued by dissenting judges and commentators that the fixing of maximum prices should not be unlawful per se but should be judged by the rule of reason.[15] Indeed, judges have sometimes demonstrated a reluctance to find injury or impose more than nominal damages when Seller has sought only to control the maximum resale prices of Buyer.[16] But, unless the Supreme Court reverses its express condemnation of maximum price-fixing, such conduct remains per se unlawful.

---

[14] Albrecht v Herald Co, 390 US 145, 153 (1968):

> Maximum price fixing may channel distribution through a few large or specifically advantaged dealers who otherwise would be subject to significant non-price competition. Moreover, if the actual price charged under a maximum price scheme is nearly always the fixed maximum price, which is increasingly likely as the maximum price approaches the actual cost of the dealer, the scheme tends to acquire all the attributes of an arrangement fixing minimum prices.

Auburn News Co v Providence Journal Co, 659 F2d 273 (1st Cir 1981), *cert denied,* 455 US 921 (1982).

[15] Albrecht v Herald Co, 390 US 145, 156-59 (1968) (Harlan, J., dissenting):

> Price ceilings are a different matter . . . they drive prices toward the level that would be set by intense competition. . . . Since price ceilings reflect the manufacturer's view that there is insufficient competition to drive prices down to a competitive level, they have the arguable justification that they prevent retailers or wholesalers from reaping monpoly or supercompetitive profits. . . .

Id 159; Yentsch v Texaco, Inc 630 F2d 46, 51 n 3 (2d Cir 1980); Arnott v American Oil Co, 609 F2d 873, 891 n 6 (8th Cir 1979) (Bright J., concurring and dissenting), *cert denied,* 446 US 918 (1980); Quinn v Mobil Oil Co, 375 F2d 273, 276-78 (1st Cir) (Coffin, J., concurring), *cert dismissed,* 389 US 801 (1967). See also 3 P. Areeda & D. Turner, Antitrust Law §734e (1978); Posner, *The Rule of Reason and the Economic Approach: Reflections on the Sylvania Decision,* 45 U Chi L Rev 1, 12 (1977); Halligan, *GTE Sylvania: The Case for Overruling Albrecht v. Herald Co.,* 39 Ohio St LJ 496 (1978); Pitofsky, *The Sylvania Case: Antitrust Analysis of Non-Price Vertical Restrictions,* 78 Colum L Rev 1, 16 n 59 (1978).

[16] Kestenbaum v Falstaff Brewing Corp, 514 F2d 690 (5th Cir 1975), *cert denied,* 424 US 943 (1976), *appeal after remand,* 575 F2d 564 (1978), *cert denied,* 440 US 909 (1979) (no injury); Newberry v Washington Post Co, 438 F Supp 470 (DDC 1977) (nominal damages); Knutson v Daily Review, Inc, 383 F Supp 1346 (ND Cal 1974), *modified,* 401 F Supp 1374 (ND Cal 1975), *affd in part, revd in part on other grounds,* 548 F2d 795 (9th Cir 1976), *cert denied,* 433 US 910 (1977), *on remand,* 468 F Supp 226 (ND Cal 1979), *affd,* 664 F2d 1120 (9th Cir 1981) (nominal damages).

§6.04 —Does it make a difference if the product is an alcoholic beverage?

Because the Twenty-First Amendment to the United States Constitution grants the states special power to regulate the sale of alcoholic beverages,[17] the freedom of Buyers of such products to determine independently their resale prices may be curtailed more than the freedom of Buyers of other products. For example, the Second Circuit recently held that states may require Buyers of alcoholic beverages to charge resale prices that are at least a specified amount above the prices charged by their Seller.[18] This effectively gives Seller some control over Buyer's resale pricing.

A number of states presently have statutes which might fall within this possible exception to the otherwise absolute ban on resale price maintenance. The law concerning any such exception is unsettled.[19]

§6.05 —May Seller control the prices charged for servicing its products?

Seller's products may require servicing by Buyer after their resale to the end user. This is common with mechanical products, such as equipment, automobiles, and appliances.

Very often Seller furnishes Buyer's customers with a warranty for the

---

[17] The amendment at §2 provides: "The transportation or importation into any State, Territory, or possession of the United States for delivery or use therein of intoxicating liquors, in violation of the laws thereof, is hereby prohibited." The Supreme Court has also enunciated a *state immunity* doctrine in Parker v Brown, 317 US 341 (1943), in which the Court held that federal antitrust laws did not prohibit a state, "as sovereign," from imposing certain anticompetitive restraints "as an act of government." *See also* Community Communications Co v City of Boulder, 455 US 40 (1982).

[18] Serlin Wine & Spirit Merchants, Inc v Healy, 512 F Supp 936 (D Conn), *affd sub nom,* Morgan v Division of Liquor Control, 664 F2d 353 (2d Cir 1981). The Connecticut law was repealed by Conn Gen Ass Pub L No 81-294 effective January 1, 1982. *See generally* California Liquor Dealers' Assn v Midcal Aluminum, Inc, 445 US 97 (1980) (the Supreme Court decision striking down a California statute that required sellers to establish resale prices—distinguished in *Morgan*). *Compare* Lewis-Westco & Co v Alcoholic Beverage Control Appeals Bd, 136 Cal App 3d 829, 186 Cal Rptr 552 (1982) (statutes requiring wholesalers to file price and discount schedules with state agency and to adhere to the schedules for 30 days violates the Sherman Act) *with* Enrico's Inc v Rice, 551 F Supp 511 (ND Cal 1982) (same statutes do not violate the Sherman Act, as they require only unilateral conduct by each wholesaler and require only the wholesalers, not the retailers, to maintain prices) *and* Schnapps Shops, Inc v HW Wright & Co, 377 F Supp 570, 584 (D Md 1973):

> Whatever the potential breadth of state powers under the Twenty-First Amendment, the powers themselves provide no shelter for federal antitrust violators in a case in which the state . . . has enacted no law which in any way has required, encouraged or suggested any acts in violation of the strong federal antitrust prohibition against price fixing.

[19] For a discussion of such state statutes, see Annot, 96 ALR3d 639.

products. When this happens, Buyer may, for a period of time, be required to service the product under Seller's warranty. Seller typically pays Buyer for the repair work done under the warranty. Seller may set the prices for such warranty services because it is doing no more than establishing the terms under which it will purchase from Buyer services to be performed for a third party.[20]

On the other hand, where Buyer agrees with its customer to service Seller's products, Seller may not control the prices to be charged by Buyer.[21] Under the antitrust laws, agreements concerning the price for services are treated no differently than agreements concerning the price for goods.[22]

§6.06 —May Seller suggest the prices at which the Buyer should resell its products?

As noted above,[23] Seller may suggest the prices at which Buyer should resell its products. This well-established principle, known as the *Colgate doctrine,* derives from the Supreme Court's decision in *United States v Colgate & Co.*[24]

In *Colgate,* the government brought a criminal indictment which, as construed by the district court, charged that the Seller unilaterally specified resale prices and then refused to deal with anyone who failed to maintain those prices. The Supreme Court affirmed the district court's dismissal of the indictment, holding that it did not charge an illegal combination to fix prices. Its holding—the *Colgate* doctrine—is as follows:

> In the absence of any purpose to create or maintain a monopoly, [the Sherman Act] does not restrict the long recognized right of trader or manufacturer engaged in an entirely private business, freely to exercise his own independent discretion as to parties with whom he will deal. And, of course, he may announce in advance the circumstances under which he will refuse to sell.[25]

The demise of this doctrine has been frequently predicted and, on occasion,

---

[20] Morrison v Nissan Co, 601 F2d 139 (4th Cir 1979); *see also* Quality Auto Body, Inc v Allstate Ins Co, 1980-2 Trade Cases (CCH) ¶63,507 (ND Ill 1980), *affd,* 660 F2d 1195 (7th Cir 1981), *cert denied,* 455 US 1020 (1982); Brown, Franchising, Realities & Remedies 294 (1978).

[21] Morrison v Nissan Co, 601 F2d 139 (4th Cir 1979).

[22] *Id* 143.

[23] See **§6.01.**

[24] 250 US 300 (1919).

[25] *Id* 307.

even proclaimed.[26] The doctrine has, however, been recently cited with approval by the United States Supreme Court and several circuit courts.[27] The doctrine's rationale—that in a free economy Sellers should normally be able to select their customers—is regularly applied in judicial decisions which find terminations lawful even though Seller has attempted to influence Buyer's resale prices.[28]

The doctrine, of course, has limits and, on occasion, has been read narrowly.[29] The Federal Trade Commission read it particularly narrowly in *Russell Stover Candies, Inc,*[30] when it held that Russell Stover's announced policy of termination of retailers for refusal to adhere to designated prices, coupled with actual compliance by retailers, did not fall within the *Colgate* doctrine, but violated the Sherman Act. The FTC recognized the continued, though limited, validity of the doctrine. In effect, the commission limited the *Colgate* doctrine to the first of the two sentences quoted above. It noted that the *Colgate* doctrine permits Sellers to determine with whom they will deal initially, as long as they do not condition future dealing, after initial selection, on the charging of particular prices.[31] The FTC reaffirmed, however, that mere suggestion of prices, with no steps taken to enforce the suggestion, does not lead to a finding of an improper agreement.[32]

No court has gone as far as the FTC did in *Russell Stover.* Most of the vertical price-fixing cases deal with attempts to define the *Colgate* doctrine's limits in a broader fashion. Stated differently, most of the cases involve the general question: How do you determine whether Seller is engaging in lawful price suggestion or unlawful vertical price-fixing?

---

[26] See, e.g., Pitofsky & Dam, *Is the Colgate Doctrine Dead?,* 37 ABA Antitrust LJ 772 (1968); see generally ABA Section on Antitrust, Vertical Restrictions Limiting Intrabrand Competiton 72-74 (Monograph No 2 1977).

[27] Reeves Inc v Stake, 447 US 429, 438-39 (1980); Continental TV, Inc v GTE Sylvania, Inc, 433 US 36, 67-69 (1977) (White, J., concurring); Dart Indus v Plunkett Co, 1983-1 Trade Cas (CCH) ¶65,314 (10th Cir 1983); Spray-Rite Serv Corp v Monsanto Co, 684 F2d 1226, 1234 (7th Cir 1982), *cert granted,* __ US __, 75 L Ed 2d 479, 103 S Ct 1249 (1983); Yentsch v Texaco Inc, 630 F2d 46, 51 (2d Cir 1980); Edward J Sweeney & Sons v Texaco, Inc, 637 F2d 105, 110-11 (3d Cir 1980), *cert denied,* 455 US 911 (1981).

[28] *See, e.g.,* Garrett's Inc v Farah Mfg Co, 412 F Supp 656, 665 (DSC 1976); Belk-Avery, Inc v Henry I Siegel Co, 457 F Supp 1330, 1334 (MD Ala 1978).

[29] *See, e.g.,* Garrett's Inc v Farah Mfg Co, 412 F Supp 656, 665 (DSC 1976), quoting Osborne v Sinclair Refg Co, 324 F2d 566 (4th Cir 1963); Greene v General Foods Corp, 517 F2d 635 (5th Cir 1975), *cert denied,* 424 US 942 (1976); Interphoto Corp v Minolta Corp, 295 F Supp 711 (SDNY), *affd,* 417 F2d 621 (2d Cir 1969).

[30] 3 Trade Reg Rep (CCH) ¶21,933 (FTC July 1, 1982).

[31] *Id* at 22,369.

[32] *Id* at 22,370. The FTC's decision has been appealed to the Eighth Circuit.

§6.07 Is there any general rule which can be applied in determining whether there is lawful price suggestion or unlawful price-fixing?

Except for extreme cases—for example, where Seller does nothing more than make a mere unilateral suggestion[33] or where there is an express price-fixing agreement between Seller and Buyer[34]—there is no simple test which can be universally applied to determine whether Seller is engaging in price control or price suggestion. If there is more than a unilateral suggestion, there is a risk that price-fixing may ultimately be found. The degree of risk will depend upon various factors which are discussed in subsequent sections.

§6.08 —What are the outer limits of Seller's right to suggest prices?

The Supreme Court has stated, in its 1960 *Parke, Davis* decision[35] that an illegal combination to fix vertical prices will be found "if the [Seller] secures adherence to his suggested prices by means which go beyond his mere declination to sell to a customer who will not observe his announced policy."[36]

The lower courts appear to have defined this limitation in different ways. In *Interphoto Corp v Minolta Corp*,[37] for example, a district court wrote:

> Today, a manufacturer can avail himself of the *Colgate* doctrine only where he suggests a resale price and does not make any attempts to enforce his suggestion, and he then refuses to sell to dissident distributors. Anything beyond this act of 'Doric simplicity' is more than a unilateral refusal to deal and constitutes a *per se* violation of the antitrust laws.[38]

On the other hand, the Ninth Circuit has stated in *Hanson v Shell Oil*

---

[33] Paul v Pulitzer Publishing Co, 1974 Trade Cases (CCH) ¶75,116 (ED Mo) (publishing a suggested resale price on the upper righthand corner of newspaper—no violation); Bailey's Bakery, Ltd v Continental Baking Co, 235 F Supp 705 (D Hawaii 1964), *affd*, 401 F2d 182 (9th Cir 1968), *cert denied*, 393 US 1086 (1969).

[34] Sahm v V-1 Oil Co, 402 F2d 69 (10th Cir 1968); Knutson v Daily Review, Inc, 383 F Supp 1346, 1357 (ND Cal 1974), *modified*, 401 F Supp 1374 (ND Cal 1975), *affd in part, revd in part on other grounds*, 548 F2d 795 (9th Cir 1976), *cert denied*, 433 US 910 (1977).

[35] United States v Parke, Davis & Co, 362 US 29 (1960).

[36] *Id* 42.

[37] 295 F Supp 711 (SDNY), *affd*, 417 F2d 621 (2d Cir 1969).

[38] 295 F Supp at 719. Similar language is found in Schnapps Shops, Inc v HW Wright & Co, 377 F Supp 570, 577 (D Md 1973) (referring to "the precarious safety area established by *Colgate*"). *Accord* Russell Stover Candies, Inc, 3 Trade Reg Rep (CCH) ¶21,933, at 22,369-70 (FTC July 1, 1982) (see discussion in **§6.06**).

Corp[39]

> [I]t [is] clear that a supplier may suggest retail prices to its dealers and use 'persuasion' to get them to adopt the suggested prices. No violation is made out unless [the aggrieved dealers] can show that the supplier's conduct rose to the level of coercion sufficient to deprive the dealers of their free choices.[40]

The phraseology used by the courts, however, may not always be helpful in predicting how a particular pricing practice will be treated if and when it is judicially examined. In construing the decisions, the conduct at issue may be as instructive as the courts' generally phrased principles. In many cases where the *Colgate* doctrine's[41] limits have been narrowly defined—for example, *Parke, Davis* and *Interphoto*—there was clear coercion, if not an express price-fixing agreement.[42] Where the doctrine has not been so narrowly defined—for example, in *Hanson*—there was generally no evidence of coercion or agreement.[43]

Accordingly, when advice is sought concerning a particular pricing program, counsel should compare the details of that program with those of programs which have already been reviewed by the courts. Subsequent sections deal with

---

[39] 541 F2d 1352 (9th Cir 1976), *cert denied,* 429 US 1074 (1977).

[40] 541 F2d at 1357 n 4; *see also* Gray v Shell Oil Co, 469 F2d 742 (9th Cir 1971), *cert denied,* 412 US 943 (1973); Dunn v Phoenix Newspapers, Inc, No Civ 81-723 PHX CAM, slip op at 27-28 (D Ariz Jan 3, 1983). Similar language appears in Dart Indus v Plunkett Co, 1983-1 Trade Cas (CCH) ¶65,314 (10th Cir 1983) and in Yentsch v Texaco, Inc, 630 F2d 46, 53 (2d Cir 1980).

[41] See **§6.06** for a discussion of the *Colgate* doctrine.

[42] In United States v Parke, Davis & Co, 362 US 29 (1960), the seller, discovering that some of the buyer's customers were discounting, implemented a program of refusing to deal with buyers who sold to discounters, and using the assurance of one buyer's customer not to discount to obtain similar assurances from the other customers. In *Interphoto Corp v Minolta Corp, 295 F Supp 711 (SDNY), affd,* 417 F2d 621 (2d Cir 1969), the seller policed the pricing activities of its buyers and their customers and wrote to its buyers, "In accordance with our sales agreement the [suggested prices] must be adhered to by your respective companies." *See also* Arnott v American Oil Co, 609 F2d 873 (8th Cir 1979), *cert denied,* 446 US 918 (1980); Greene v General Foods Corp, 517 F2d 635 (5th Cir 1975), *cert denied,* 424 US 942 (1976); Burton Supply Co v Wheel Horse Prods, Inc, 1974-2 Trade Cases (CCH) ¶75,224 (ND Ohio 1974); Russell Stover Candies, Inc, 3 Trade Reg Rep (CCH) ¶21,933 (FTC July 1, 1982).

[43] In Hanson v Shell Oil Co, 541 F2d 1352 (9th Cir 1976), *cert denied,* 429 US 1074 (1977), the court, in its statement of the facts, outlined plaintiff Hanson's inability to run his businesses profitably and concluded: "Like many another loser in the competitive endeavor, he decided to try the antitrust laws as a means of shifting his losses to someone else." 541 F2d at 1355. *See also* Santa Clara Valley Distrib Co v Pabst Brewing Co, 556 F2d 942 (9th Cir 1977); Umphres v Shell Oil Co, 512 F2d 420 (5th Cir), *cert denied,* 423 US 929 (1975); Dunn v Phoenix Newspapers, Inc, No Civ 81-723 PHX CAM, slip op at 27-28 (D Ariz Jan 3, 1983). Belk-Avery, Inc v Henry I Siegel Co, 457 F Supp 1330 (MD Ala 1978); World-Wide Volkswagen Corp v Autobahn Motors Co, 1980-81 Trade Cases (CCH) ¶63,601 (SDNY 1980).

particular programs that have been considered by the courts.[44]

§6.09 —When does Seller go beyond the outer limits of its right to suggest prices?

Two criteria have been generally applied in determining whether particular conduct falls outside of the *Colgate* doctrine: First, whether Seller, in announcing its suggested resale prices, had "any purpose to create or maintain a monopoly"; and second, whether Seller was acting pursuant to an agreement or combination concerning prices.[45]

The first criterion, whether Seller had any purpose to create or maintain a monopoly, deals with issues relating to §2 of the Sherman Act, and is beyond the scope of this chapter. This should be of no concern unless Seller has, or is in the process of obtaining, a large market share.[46]

As to the second criterion, §1 of the Sherman Act, by its very terms, requires that there be an unlawful agreement—a "contract, combination . . . or conspiracy" in restraint of trade. The courts have noted that "the statutory language presents a single concept about common action, not three separate ones: 'contract, combination . . . or conspiracy' becomes an alliterative compound noun, roughly translated to mean concerted action."[47]

An unlawful agreement may be found between Seller and those Buyers who willingly accept Seller's suggested resale prices, or between Seller and the complaining Buyer if that Buyer unwillingly adhered to Seller's suggestions.[48] In addition, where Buyer's customers resell the goods (as opposed to using them), an agreement may be found between Seller and Buyer to control the prices charged by Buyer's customers.[49] However, no matter what type of agreement may be alleged, no violation can be found unless the evidence is sufficient to establish a meeting of the minds to fix prices.[50]

Where Seller employs coercion to require Buyer to comply with its suggest-

---

[44] See **§§6.13-6.21.**

[45] United States v Colgate & Co, 250 US 300, 307 (1919); Carbon Steel Prods Corp v Alan Wood Steel Co, 289 F Supp 584, 587 (SDNY 1968).

[46] See generally ABA, Antitrust Law Developments 26-32 (3d ed 1980).

[47] Edward J Sweeney & Sons v Texaco, Inc, 637 F2d 105, 111 (3d Cir 1980), *cert denied,* 451 US 911 (1981); Dart Drug Corp v Parke Davis & Co, 344 F2d 173, 182-83 (DC Cir 1965).

[48] Albrecht v Herald Co, 390 US 145, 149 n 6 (1968); Lepore v New York News, 346 F Supp 755 (SDNY 1972); Russell Stover Candies, Inc, 3 Trade Reg Rep (CCH) ¶21,933, at 22,366 (FTC July 1, 1982).

[49] United States v Parke, Davis & Co, 362 US 29 (1960); Blankenship v Hearst Corp, 519 F2d 418 (9th Cir 1975).

[50] If Buyer simply adheres to the suggested resale prices because it knows that compliance is expected by seller, such "conscious parallelism" does not constitute a "combination." Klein v American Luggage Works, Inc, 323 F2d 787, 791 (3d Cir 1963). See also Turner, *The Definition of Agreement Under the Sherman Act: Conscious Parallelism and Refusals to Deal,* 75 Harv L Rev 655, 684-91 (1962).

ed prices, the coercion may itself support a finding of an agreement or combination. Some decisions seem to treat coercion as a separate requirement[51] while others view it only as circumstantial evidence of agreement or combination.[52] In either event, if there is genuine coercion, court or jury findings of price-fixing are likely to be upheld on either rationale.[53]

The courts have held that, under the *Colgate* doctrine, coercion is not established merely because Seller announces that it will not deal with Buyers who do not adhere to the suggested prices; however, the Federal Trade Commission's recent decision in *Russell Stover* appears to depart from this proposition.[54] But both the courts and the FTC appear to agree that the critical question is whether Seller has circumscribed Buyer's pricing discretion—whether Buyer's ability "to sell in accordance with its own judgment" has been limited.[55]

For example, the Tenth Circuit recently held that when a Buyer initiates a discount program to promote interbrand competition, and successfully seeks reimbursement from Seller in the amount of the discount, Seller's conditioning of that reimbursement on the Buyer's passing on the price break and maintaining the discount price does not violate the Sherman Act. The court reasoned that the Buyer retained its control over its own prices; despite the incentives provided by the Seller to encourage price reductions, the Buyer was neither coerced into charging a particular price, nor punished for failing to do so.[56]

Stated slightly differently, in evaluating any pricing program, the most meaningful question to ask is: Does Buyer, in fact, have the freedom to determine its own resale prices? If the answer to that question is not clearly in the

---

[51] *See, e.g.,* Auburn News Co v Providence Journal Co, 504 F Supp 292 (DRI 1980), *revd on other grounds,* 659 F2d 273 (1st Cir 1981), *cert denied,* 455 US 921 (1982); Knutson v Daily Review, Inc, 548 F2d 795 (9th Cir 1976), *cert denied,* 433 US 910 (1977).

[52] *See, e.g.,* Blankenship v Hearst Corp, 519 F2d 418 (9th Cir 1975); Russell Stover Candies, Inc, 3 Trade Reg Rep (CCH) ¶21,933 (FTC July 1, 1982).

[53] *See* United States v Parke, Davis & Co, 362 US 29 (1960); Arnott v American Oil Co, 609 F2d 873 (8th Cir 1979), *cert denied,* 446 US 918 (1980); Greene v General Foods Corp, 517 F2d 635 (5th Cir 1975), *cert denied,* 424 US 942 (1976); Burton Supply Co v Wheel Horse Prods, Inc, 1974-2 Trade Cases (CCH) ¶75,224 (ND Ohio 1974); Interphoto Corp v Minolta Corp, 295 F Supp 711 (SDNY), *affd,* 417 F2d 621 (2d Cir 1969); Russell Stover Candies, Inc, 3 Trade Reg Rep (CCH) ¶21,933 (FTC July 1, 1982).

[54] *Compare* Adolph Coors Co v FTC, 497 F2d 1178 (10th Cir 1974) *and* Pearl Brewing Co v Anheuser-Busch, Inc, 339 F Supp 945, 952 (SD Tex 1972) *with* Russell Stover Candies, Inc, 3 Trade Reg Rep (CCH) ¶21,933, at 22,366, 22,369-70 (FTC July 1, 1982).

[55] Adolph Coors Co v FTC, 497 F2d 1178, 1184 (10th Cir 1974), *cert denied,* 419 US 1105 (1975); Pearl Brewing Co v Anheuser-Busch, Inc, 339 F Supp 945, 952 (SD Tex 1972); Russell Stover Candies, Inc, 3 Trade Reg Rep (CCH) ¶21,933 (FTC July 1, 1982).

[56] AAA Liquors, Inc v Joseph E Seagram & Sons, 1982-83 Trade Cases (CCH) ¶65,075 at 71,018 (10th Cir 1982), *cert denied,* 51 USLW 3790 (May 3, 1983).

affirmative, there is a genuine risk that price-fixing may be found. If the answer is in the negative, that risk will be substantial and Seller's freedom to terminate that Buyer may be, as noted below, severely limited.[57]

§6.10 Under what circumstances may Seller refuse to deal with those Buyers that do not adhere to its suggested retail prices?

The courts have held that, if Seller suggests prices and Buyer does not follow those suggestions, Seller is free, under the antitrust laws, to terminate that Buyer so long as the termination: is not for a monopolistic purpose; is not in furtherance of a price-fixing agreement or combination; or is not in furtherance of any other anticompetitive arrangement (for example, an unreasonable territorial restriction).[58] As noted elsewhere, the Federal Trade Commission appears to have departed from these principles.[59]

In litigation arising out of a termination, the central issue is frequently the reason for the termination. If the reason is found to be Buyer's nonadherence to prices and there is either a monopolistic purpose or a price-fixing agreement or combination, the termination should be held unlawful.[60] Terminations have been condemned on this ground where they were designed to warn other Buyers against noncompliance,[61] as well as where they followed threats which went beyond a mere announcement of a policy not to sell to nonadhering Buyers.[62]

A contractual right to terminate will not protect Seller if the termination otherwise violates the antitrust laws.[63] Indeed, reservation of the right to terminate a relationship on short notice, where termination can effectively preclude Buyer from continuing in its business, has been found to be itself a

---

[57] Overseas Motors, Inc v Import Motors Ltd, Inc, 375 F Supp 499, 539 (ED Mich 1974) ("restriction of the dealer's pricing freedom is the essence of the offense"), *affd,* 519 F2d 119 (6th Cir), *cert denied,* 423 US 987 (1975). See **§§6.10, 6.11.**

[58] United States v Colgate & Co, 250 US 300, 307 (1919). As to termination of discounters in furtherance of any other anticompetitive arrangement, *compare* Eiberger v Sony Corp of Am, 622 F2d 1068 (2d Cir 1980) *with* Donald B Rice Tire Co v Michelin Tire Co, 638 F2d 15 (4th Cir), *cert denied,* 454 US 864 (1981). For a discussion on Seller's termination of independent Buyers in the course of shifting to a direct sales system, see **§6.26.**

[59] See discussion of *Russell Stover* **§6.06.**

[60] See generally Annot, 41 ALR Fed 175, §§17-20.

[61] *See, e.g.,* Burton Supply Co v Wheel Horse Prods, Inc, 1974-2 Trade Cases (CCH) ¶75,224 (ND Ohio 1974).

[62] Yentsch v Texaco, Inc, 630 F2d 46 (2d Cir 1980); Arnott v American Oil Co, 609 F2d 873 (8th Cir 1979), *cert denied,* 446 US 918 (1980); *see also* World Wide Volkswagen Corp v Autobahn Motors Co, 1980-81 Trade Cases (CCH) ¶63,601 (SDNY 1980).

[63] Interphoto Corp v Minolta Corp, 295 F Supp 711, 723 (SDNY), *affd,* 417 F2d 621 (2d Cir 1969).

coercive attempt to enforce resale prices.[64]

On the other hand, if the termination is found to be for a legitimate reason—for example, Buyer's poor sales or poor credit—nonadherence to suggested prices will not make it unlawful.[65] If it is found that the termination is for both a legitimate purpose and an illegitimate purpose, there is a significant risk that the termination will be held unlawful.[66]

§6.11 —May Seller refuse to deal with a discounting Buyer in response to complaints from other Buyers?

Discounting or price-cutting by one Buyer will frequently cause other Buyers to complain to Seller about the low prices. Very often, Seller will be asked to do something about it. Such complaints may occur even if Seller does not suggest prices.

Where such complaints are followed by termination, the critical question in ensuing litigation is frequently whether this sequence of events (complaints and termination) is, without more, sufficient to support an inference of an unlawful vertical price-fixing agreement. This question remains unsettled.

Decisions from the First, Second, and Third Circuits hold that more than this mere sequence of events is required,[67] while decisions from the Fourth and Seventh Circuits would appear to permit a finding of liability solely because of the sequence.[68] Two panels of the Eighth Circuit differed on the question.[69]

---

[64] Phillips v Crown Central Petroleum Corp, 376 F Supp 1250, 1256 (D Md 1973), *as supplemented by,* 395 F Supp 735 (D Md 1975) and 426 F Supp 1156 (D Md) (short-term leases between seller and buyer are by their very nature coercive), *revd & remanded on other grounds,* 556 F2d 702 (4th Cir 1977); Perry v Amerada Hess Corp, 427 F Supp 667 (ND Ga 1977).

[65] *See, e.g.,* Malcolm v Marathon Oil Co, 642 F2d 845, 860 (5th Cir), *cert denied,* 454 US 1125 (1981); Belk-Avery, Inc v Henry I Siegel Co, 457 F Supp 1330 (MD Ala 1978).

[66] *See, e.g.,* Lessig v Tidewater Oil Co, 327 F2d 459, 475-76 (9th Cir) (Madden, J., dissenting), *cert denied,* 377 US 993 (1964); Burton Supply Co v Wheel Horse Prods, Inc, 1974-2 Trade Cases (CCH) ¶75,224 (ND Ohio 1974); *see also* United States v Wohl Shoe Co, 369 F Supp 386, 392-93 (DNM 1974). *But see* Olympic Distribs Inc v Perkins Co, No 80 C 1602 (ND Ill Sept 14, 1982) (independent business reasons for termination enough to rebut inference of collusion).

[67] Bruce Drug, Inc v Hollister Inc, 688 F2d 853, 856 (1st Cir 1982); Schwimmer v Sony Corp of Am, 677 F2d 946, 953 (2d Cir), *cert denied,* 103 S Ct 362 (1982); HL Moore Drug Exch v Eli Lilly & Co, 662 F2d 935 (2d Cir 1981), *cert denied,* 103 S Ct 176 (1982); Edward J Sweeney & Sons v Texaco, Inc, 637 F2d 105 (3d Cir 1980), *cert denied,* 451 US 911 (1981). *See also* Blake Assocs v Omni Spectra, Inc, 1982-83 Trade Cases (CCH) ¶65,155 (D Mass 1982); Belk-Avery, Inc v Henry I Siegel Co, 457 F Supp 1330 (MD Ala 1978); Interphoto Corp v Minolta Corp, 295 F Supp 711 (SDNY), *affd,* 417 F2d 621 (2d Cir 1969).

[68] Bostick Oil Co v Michelin Tire Corp, 1983-1 Trade Cas (CCH) ¶65,271 (4th Cir 1983); Spray-Rite Serv Corp v Monsanto Co, 684 F2d 1226 (7th Cir 1982), *cert granted,* __ US __, 75 L Ed 2d 479, 103 S Ct 1249 (1983).

[69] *Compare* Battle v Lubrizol Corp, 673 F2d 984 (8th Cir 1982) (a complaint followed

(Certiorari has been granted in the Seventh Circuit decision.)

Risks can be minimized if Seller's employees are instructed to refuse to discuss with one Buyer the prices charged by another Buyer. In certain industries such instructions simply may not be feasible. At a minimum, however, Seller's employees should be instructed that they should make it clear to the complaining Buyer that each Buyer has a right to determine its own prices, and that, as a matter of company policy, they will not convey the complaints to the price-cutter. Seller's employees should, of course, be instructed to carry out these policies.

Whenever Seller talks to one Buyer about prices of another Buyer, the talks may also be cited as evidence of a horizontal conspiracy.[70] Sellers' employees who deal with Buyers should also be made aware of the very serious risks which this presents.

§6.12 Aside from suggesting prices, what may Seller do to influence the prices charged by Buyer?

Price-suggesting by Seller can take various forms, and never takes place in a vacuum. The suggestions can be oral or written; they can be in the form of price lists or preticketing; they can be accompanied by advertising; they can be related in various ways to special prices charged by Seller; and they can be accompanied by different types of policing to determine whether there is Buyer compliance. The following sections deal with the legality of specific techniques employed by Sellers, short of termination, to influence Buyers' resale prices.

As indicated above,[71] it is difficult to state a meaningful general principle. Nevertheless, courts, in practice, seem to permit conduct by Seller which does not, in fact, interfere with Buyer's freedom to determine, by itself, its own retail prices.[72] If Buyer does not, in fact, have such freedom, vertical price-fixing is

---

by termination is enough to raise an inference of unlawful concerted action) *with* Roesch, Inc v Star Cooler Corp, 671 F2d 1168 (8th Cir 1982) (mere complaints followed by termination insufficient to imply a conspiracy in violation of §1). The Eighth Circuit has granted rehearing en banc in both cases.

[70] United States v General Motors Corp, 384 US 127 (1966). *See also* Donald B Rice Tire Co v Michelin Tire Corp, 638 F2d 15 (4th Cir), *cert denied,* 454 US 864 (1981). One court has described this as "the vertical expression of a horizontal desire." Valley Liquors, Inc v Renfield Importers, Ltd, 678 F2d 742, 744 (7th Cir 1982).

[71] See **§6.07.**

[72] *See, e.g.,* Chisholm Bros Farm Equip v International Harvester Co, 498 F2d 1137 (9th Cir), *cert denied,* 419 US 1023 (1974); Susser v Carvel Corp, 332 F2d 505, 510 (2d Cir 1964), *cert dismissed,* 381 US 125 (1965); Paul v Pulitzer Publishing Co, 1974 Trade Cases (CCH) ¶75,116 (ED Mo 1974); Peter v Union Oil Co, 328 F Supp 998 (CD Cal 1971). *But see* Russell Stover Candies, Inc, 3 Trade Reg Rep (CCH) ¶21,933 (FTC July 1, 1982).

likely to be found.[73]

§6.13 —May Seller employ persuasion, argument or pressure?

Opinions in the Second, Fifth, and Ninth Circuits have stated that, in addition to suggesting prices, announcing a policy of refusing to deal with noncompliers, and carrying out that policy, Seller: "is free to effectuate such policies through 'exposition, persuasion and argument' directed at those of its customers reluctant to agree to prices suggested."[74] Such exposition, persuasion and argument, however, may not amount to "threats of termination" which "secure adherence" to the suggested price.[75]

While no bright line test can be uniformly applied in determining whether there is permissible persuasion or unlawful threats, the following conduct has been found to be unobjectionable persuasion:

1. Seller informing Buyer on one occasion that they could enter a "period of better cooperation" if the Buyer would follow the Seller's recommended prices[76]
2. Seller's "suggestion—even pressure—" that its Buyer set prices low enough to facilitate the depletion of Buyer's inventory of Seller's goods[77]

On the other hand, vertical price-fixing was found where Seller told its Buyer to lower its prices so that it could sell more of Seller's product, and warned that if sales did not increase, Seller "could find somebody else."[78]

In an opinion which appears to depart from judicial holdings, the Federal Trade Commission implied, in *Russell Stover Candies Inc,* that any pressure may

---

[73] *See, e.g.,* Greene v General Foods Corp, 517 F2d 635 (5th Cir), *cert denied,* 424 US 942 (1976); Adolph Coors Co v FTC, 497 F2d 1178 (10th Cir 1974), *cert denied,* 419 US 1105 (1975); Pearl Brewing Co v Anheuser Busch, Inc, 339 F Supp 945 (SD Tex 1972); Interphoto Corp v Minolta Corp, 295 F Supp 711 (SDNY), *affd,* 417 F2d 621 (2d Cir 1969). *See* Russell Stover Candies, Inc, 3 Trade Reg Rep (CCH) ¶21,933, at 22,363-64 (FTC July 1, 1982) (see discussion at **§6.06**).

[74] Levi Strauss & Co v Federal Pants Co, 1979-2 Trade Cases (CCH) ¶62,727, at 78,082-83 (CD Cal 1979); *see also* Carlson Mach Tools, Inc v American Tool, Inc, 678 F2d 1253 (5th Cir 1982); Yentsch v Texaco, 630 F2d 46, 53 (2d Cir 1980); Hanson v Shell Oil Co, 541 F2d 1352, 1347 n 4 (9th Cir 1976), *cert denied,* 429 US 1074 (1977); Gray v Shell Oil Co, 469 F2d 742 (9th Cir 1971); Krehl v Baskin-Robbins Ice Cream Co, 78 FRD 108, 122 (CD Cal 1978).

[75] Yentsch v Texaco, Inc, 630 F2d 46, 53 (2d Cir 1980); Russell Stover Candies, Inc, 3 Trade Reg Rep (CCH) ¶21,933 (FTC July 1, 1982); *see also* Arnott v American Oil Co, 609 F2d 873 (8th Cir 1979), *cert denied,* 446 US 918 (1980).

[76] Hanson v Shell Oil Co, 541 F2d 1352 (9th Cir 1976), *cert denied,* 429 US 1074 (1977).

[77] Chisholm Bros Farm Equip v International Harvester Co, 498 F2d 1137 (9th Cir), *cert denied,* 419 US 1023 (1974).

[78] Yentsch v Texaco, Inc, 630 F2d 46 (2d Cir 1980).

be improper. The commission seemed to hold that Seller may do no more than suggest prices—any steps to encourage compliance, if effective, would give rise to an inference of unlawful concerted activity.[79]

§6.14 —May Seller's prices to Buyer be dependent upon Buyer's adherence to Seller's suggested resale prices?

If Seller's price to Buyer is dependent upon Buyer's adherence to Seller's suggested resale prices, vertical price-fixing is likely to be found.[80] (*AAA Liquors Inc v Joseph E Seagram & Sons*,[81] which may take a different position, is discussed in **§6.15**). When Seller's price to Buyer is raised or lowered, depending upon Buyer's adherence to the suggested price, Buyer's margin of profit is effectively controlled by Seller. Buyer then has less, if any, incentive to price independently—and it is this lack of independence which is generally condemned as vertical price-fixing.[82]

This technique for influencing resale prices has been condemned when

---

[79] Russell Stover Candies, Inc, 3 Trade Reg Rep (CCH) ¶21,933, at 22,370 (FTC July 1, 1982) ("compliance with suggested prices entirely based on the dealer's own preferences and without influence of a threat of termination or other sanctions, does not lead to a finding of combination between the dealer and the manufacturer").

[80] Newberry v Washington Post Co, 438 F Supp 470 (DDC 1977); Phillips v Crown Central Petroleum, 395 F Supp 735 (D Md 1975), *revd & remanded on other grounds,* 556 F2d 702 (4th Cir 1977), *affd after remand,* 602 F2d 616 (4th Cir 1979), *cert denied,* 444 US 1074 (1980). *See also* Kestenbaum v Falstaff Brewing Co, 514 F2d 690 (5th Cir 1975), *cert denied,* 424 US 943 (1976).

[81] 1982-83 Trade Cases (CCH) ¶65,075 (10th Cir 1982), *cert denied,* 57 USLW 3790 (May 3, 1983).

[82] The following cases discuss the importance of Buyer's pricing independence as a factor in determining the existence, or not, of vertical price-fixing: Greene v General Foods Corp, 517 F2d 635 (5th Cir), *cert denied,* 424 US 942 (1976); Chisholm Bros Farm Equip v International Harvester Co, 498 F2d 1137 (9th Cir), *cert denied,* 419 US 1023 (1974); Adolph Coors Co v FTC, 497 F2d 1178 (10th Cir 1974), *cert denied,* 419 US 1105 (1975); Susser v Carvel Corp, 332 F2d 505, 510 (2d Cir 1964), *cert dismissed,* 381 US 125 (1965); Paul v Pulitzer Publishing Co, 1974 Trade Cases (CCH) ¶75,116 (ED Mo 1974); Pearl Brewing Co v Anheuser Busch, Inc, 339 F Supp 945 (SD Tex 1972); Peter v Union Oil Co, 328 F Supp 998 (CD Cal 1971); Interphoto Corp v Minolta Corp, 295 F Supp 711 (SDNY), *affd,* 417 F2d 621 (2d Cir 1969); Russell Stover Candies, Inc, 3 Trade Reg Rep (CCH) ¶21,933, at 22,363-64 (FTC July 1, 1982) (see discussion at **§6.06**). In General Cinema Corp v Buena Vista Distrib Co, 681 F2d 594 (9th Cir 1982), the Buyer had to pay the Seller the greater of a stated percentage of the resale price or the same percentage of a stated minimum per resale amount; the court found no price-fixing because this pricing system had "no elements of coercion that might encourage exhibitors to set any price other than a competitive price." 681 F2d at 597. In Westgo Indus, Inc v WJ King Co, 1981-1 Trade Cases ¶63,984 (DND 1981), where the Seller's price to the Buyer was computed as a percentage of a minimum Buyer's resale price, vertical price-fixing was not found; the Buyer was, in fact, free to set any price it desired.

expressly provided for by contract.[83] It has also been condemned when the Seller did not announce it beforehand. In *Newberry v Washington Post Co*,[84] where vertical price-fixing was found, the Seller raised the price to a single Buyer that was charging more than the suggested resale price, "knowing that [its actions] would become immediately known to all dealers and would serve to deter those who might be contemplating a price increase."[85]

§6.15 —May Seller use a competitive allowance or other form of price support to influence resale prices?

Competitive allowances (sometimes called price supports) are regional or local reductions of Seller's prices designed to allow Buyer to meet regional or local competition; they may be direct or indirect and may take the form of rebates.[86] Such allowances have been used extensively in gasoline marketing, and could be used for other products as well.

So long as Buyer remains free to determine its prices, the use of price supports should not be held to be illegal resale price maintenance.[87] However, where the availability of price supports is dependent upon Buyer's adherence to the suggested resale prices, vertical price-fixing has generally been found.[88] Thus, Seller's withdrawal of price supports from a discounting Buyer was held illegal where it was designed to secure the discounter's adherence to the suggested resale price and to demonstrate to other Buyers that they should not discount.[89]

The Tenth Circuit's recent decision in *AAA Liquors, Inc v Joseph E Seagram & Sons*, appears to depart from earlier cases addressing this subject. There, the court found no price fixing when price supports furnished at Buyer's request for the maintenance of discount prices to promote competition with other

---

[83] Phillips v Crown Central Petroleum, 395 F Supp 735 (D Md 1975), *revd & remanded on other grounds*, 556 F2d 702 (4th Cir 1977), *affd after remand*, 602 F2d 616 (4th Cir 1979), *cert denied*, 444 US 1074 (1980).

[84] 438 F Supp 470 (DDC 1977).

[85] *Id* 481. Only nominal damages were awarded here (see **§6.03** regarding reluctance of some courts to impose more than nominal damages where maximum resale price-fixing is involved). Seller's right to terminate could also be limited (see **§6.29**).

[86] Swettlen v Wagoner Gas & Oil, Inc, 373 F Supp 1022 (WD Pa 1974), *affd*, 511 F2d 1395 (3d Cir 1975); Lehrman v Gulf Oil Corp, 464 F2d 26 (5th Cir), *cert denied*, 409 US 1077 (1972); OM Droney Beverage Co v Miller Brewing Co, 365 F Supp 1067, 1070 (D Minn 1973).

[87] Peter v Union Oil Co, 328 F Supp 998 (CD Cal 1971).

[88] Hanson v Shell Oil Co, 541 F2d 1352, 1356 (9th Cir 1976), *cert denied*, 429 US 1074 (1977); Lehrman v Gulf Oil Corp, 464 F2d 26 (5th Cir), *cert denied*, 409 US 1077 (1972); Lessig v Tidewater Oil Co, 327 F2d 459 (9th Cir), *cert denied*, 377 US 993 (1964).

[89] Lehrman v Gulf Oil Corp, 464 F2d 26 (5th Cir), *cert denied*, 409 US 1077 (1972).

brands was conditioned on Buyer's actual maintenance of these prices.[90]

In any event price supports, however, need not be completely unqualified. Their purpose is to support Buyer during periods of intense competition and, accordingly, they may be made available only for goods resold at particular times.[91]

§6.16 —May Seller use price promotions?

Price promotions—or special price reductions—are, as such, unobjectionable.[92] They may be accompanied by a suggestion that Buyer have a special reduction in its resale prices. However, if Buyer's right to receive the lower price is conditioned upon Buyer's adherence to a suggested resale price, there is a strong probability of unlawful resale price maintenance being found.[93]

It is not uncommon for a Seller and its Buyer to discuss a special price promotion in advance of Seller's price reduction. While such discussions are not, in and of themselves, unlawful, they may subsequently be cited as evidence of an unlawful resale price maintenance agreement or unlawful coercion.[94] If there are any discussions between Buyers—or even if Seller notifies one Buyer of what another Buyer said—horizontal price-fixing may be charged.[95]

Accordingly, it would be prudent to advise sellers not to discuss price promotions beforehand where there is no strong business need to do so. When such discussions do take place, Seller may be taking a substantial risk if it does not make clear that its special price to Buyer is unrelated to Buyer's resale price.

§6.17 —May Seller use preticketing or price lists?

Seller may send suggested resale price lists to its Buyers,[96] or preticket its

---

[90] AAA Liquors, Inc, v Joseph E Seagram & Sons, 1982-83 Trade Cases (CCH) ¶65,075 (10th Cir 1982), *cert denied,* 51 USLW 3790 (May 3, 1983).

[91] Butera v Sun Oil Co, 496 F2d 434 (1st Cir 1974). This same rationale would seem to make it lawful to limit price supports to goods resold at particular places. This, however, would raise the additional questions of whether Seller is attempting to restrict territories in which Buyer can resell, and if so, whether such a restriction violates the rule of reason. Robinson-Patman questions might also be raised.

[92] Santa Clara Valley Distrib v Pabst Brewing Co, 556 F2d 942 (9th Cir 1977); OM Droney Beverage Co v Miller Brewing Co, 365 F Supp 1067 (D Minn 1973).

[93] Kestenbaum v Falstaff Brewing Co, 514 F2d 690 (5th Cir 1975), *cert denied,* 424 US 943 (1976); Newberry v Washington Post Co, 438 F Supp 470 (DDC 1977); Pearl Brewing Co v Anheuser-Busch, Inc, 339 F Supp 945 (SD Tex 1972). *But see* AAA Liquors Inc v Joseph Seagram & Sons, 1982-83 Trade Cases (CCH) ¶65,075 (10th Cir 1982), *cert denied,* 51 USLW 3790 (May 3, 1983) (disapproving *Pearl Brewing Co*).

[94] Pearl Brewing Co v Anheuser-Busch, Inc, 339 F Supp 945 (SD Tex 1972).

[95] *See, e.g.,* United States v General Motors Corp, 384 US 127 (1966); Donald B Rice Tire Co v Michelin Tire Corp, 638 F2d 15 (4th Cir), *cert denied,* 454 US 864 (1981).

[96] Abrams v Interco, Inc, 93 FRD 331, 332 (SDNY 1981) (the allegations that suggest-

products,[97] so long as Buyers are left free to determine their own prices.

When this technique is used, it may, of course, be alleged that there has been more than suggesting and that steps were taken to insure that resale will be made at the listed or preticketed prices. The risk of such a claim being upheld may be increased if price lists are sent to Buyer's customers since this could constitute evidence of combination or coercion.[98] The risk should be decreased if the listed or preticketed price is expressly referred to as a *suggested price.*

The use of preticketing may deter Buyers from reselling at more than the suggested price since Buyer's customers may conclude that the higher price is excessive. On the other hand, this technique may encourage, rather than discourage, price-cutting, since a discounter's slashed price may be viewed as a bargain price.

§6.18 —To what extent may Seller control or influence price advertising by Buyer?

Since control of resale price advertising obviously limits Buyer's freedom to price Seller's product independently, Seller can no more control Buyer's advertising of resale prices than it can control Buyer's actual resale price.[99]

Attempts by Sellers to control Buyers' resale prices or resale price advertising indirectly, through cooperative advertising programs, advertising allowances, or reimbursements have been condemned.[100] Vertical price-fixing has also been found where Seller contributed to Buyer's price advertising only if the advertised price was the suggested price, or only if Buyer's advertisements

---

ed price lists were sent to Buyers "is barely a start at making out the alleged claim of antitrust violation").

[97] Mesirow v Pepperidge Farms, Inc, 1981-2 Trade Cases (CCH) ¶64,292 (ND Cal 1981), *affd,* 1982-83 Trade Cases (CCH) ¶65,164 (9th Cir 1983); Belk-Avery Inc v Henry I Siegel Co, 457 F Supp 1330 (MD Ala 1978). *See also* Klein v American Luggage Works, Inc, 323 F2d 787, 790-91 (3d Cir 1963) (no violation where "[a]ll that the evidence established was that prospective retailers were 'advised' of [the seller's] price maintenance policy, and its expectation that those to whom it sold its line would not sell below preticketed prices").

[98] Burton Supply Co v Wheel Horse Prods, Inc, 1974-2 Trade Cases (CCH) ¶75,224 (ND Ohio 1974); Mesirow v Pepperidge Farm, Inc, 1981-2 Trade Cases (CCH) ¶64,292 (ND Cal 1981), *affd,* 1982-83 Trade Cases (CCH) ¶65,164 (9th Cir 1983).

[99] Schnapps Shops, Inc v HW Wright & Co, 377 F Supp 570 (D Md 1973).

[100] *E.g.,* Mt Vernon Datsun, Inc v Nissan Motors Corp, 1976-1 Trade Cases (CCH) ¶60,842 (ED Va 1975); Burton Supply Co v Wheel Horse Prods, Inc, 1974-2 Trade Cases (CCH) ¶75,224 (ND Ohio 1974); United States v EI duPont de Nemours & Co, 1980-81 Trade Cases (CCH) ¶63,570 (ND Ohio 1980) (consent decree); *In re* Clinique Laboratories Inc, 96 FTC 51, 55 (1980) (consent decree); *In re* Advertising Checking Bureau, Inc, 93 FTC 4 (1979) (consent decree); Quality Discount Tires, Inc v Firestone Tire & Rubber Co, 1978-1 Trade Cases (CCH) ¶61,848 (Md 1978) (Maryland Antitrust Act).

avoided any language which indicated that there was intrabrand price competition.[101]

This does not mean, however, that Sellers may not set up or participate in cooperative advertising programs. But when they do (and if the advertisement mentions price) Buyer's advertised resale price must be determined by Buyer; Seller's financial contribution cannot be conditioned upon Buyer's advertising of Seller's suggested price.

Seller is free to suggest price advertising by Buyer so long as there is no combination or coercion—that is, so long as Buyer remains free to advertise its own prices.[102]

§6.19 —May Seller advertise its suggested resale prices?

Seller's direct price advertising is treated no differently than Seller's preticketing or sending suggested price lists to the end user. Thus, Seller may advertise so long as the Buyers are left free to set, and to advertise, their own prices.[103] There is, of course, a risk that such conduct might be pointed to as evidence of coercion, but Seller could lower this risk using such terms as *suggested* or *sticker price* in its advertisements.

§6.20 —To what degree may Seller police Buyer's resale prices?

If Seller uses certain of its Buyers to police the prices charged by other Buyers, there is a strong likelihood that vertical price-fixing will be found.[104] Policing by Seller itself should not, without more, establish vertical price-fixing; however, if as a result of Seller's policing activities Buyers are induced to comply with the suggested prices, vertical price-fixing is likely to be

---

[101] Mt Vernon Datsun, Inc v Nissan Motors Corp, 1976-1 Trade Cases (CCH) ¶60,842 (ED Va 1975); *but see In re* Nissan Antitrust Litigation, 577 F2d 910 (5th Cir 1978), *cert denied,* 439 US 1079 (1979).

[102] United Shoppers Exclusive v Broadway-Hale Stores, Inc, 1966 Trade Cases (CCH) ¶71,727 (ND Cal 1965).

[103] United States v OM Scott & Sons, 303 F Supp 141, 153 (DDC 1969); United States v Uniroyal, Inc, 300 F Supp 84, 94 (SDNY 1969); Engbrecht v Dairy Queen Co, 203 F Supp 714, 719 (D Kan 1962).

[104] United States v Parke, Davis & Co, 362 US 29 (1960); FTC v Beech-Nut Packing Co, 257 US 441 (1922); Kobi Co v FTC, 23 F2d 41 (2d Cir 1927); Hills Bros v FTC, 9 F2d 481 (9th Cir), *cert denied,* 270 US 662 (1926). *See also* the recent consent orders in *In re* Clinique Laboratories, Inc, 96 FTC 51, 55 (1980); *In re* Towle Mfg Co, 96 FTC 83, 85, 87-88 (1980); *In re* Darvel, Inc, 96 FTC 145, 148-49 (1980); *In re* Jonathan Logan, Inc, 94 FTC 159, 164 (1979); *In re* Pendleton Woolen Mills, Inc, 94 FTC 229, 233 (1979); *In re* Jaymar-Ruby, Inc, 94 FTC 1162, 1165-66 (1979); *In re* Huk-A-Poo Sportswear, Inc, 93 FTC 545, 550 (1979).

found.[105]

Seller's employee's practice of reading a Buyer's newspaper advertisements, and, when visiting Buyer's resale outlet, looking at the prices posted for Seller's product, has been held, in and of itself, to be lawful.[106] The following types of policing have, however, been held to be unlawful:

1. Seller's use of special agents (including detectives) or its own Buyers to report the names of Buyers who did not comply with Seller's suggested resale price[107]
2. Seller's use of symbols or certificates attached to its product to trace price cutters and their suppliers, where Seller, upon discovering their identity, refused to deal with either unless and until Seller received assurances of compliance[108]
3. Requiring Buyer to use a billing form that is returned to Seller[109]

§6.21 May Seller give rebates to the customers of Buyer?

Seller may give rebates, not contingent upon Buyer's resale price, directly to Buyer's customers. This practice, which is used extensively in the sale of automobiles and appliances, has been expressly approved by the Second Circuit on the ground that it does not involve any resale price understanding between Seller and Buyer.[110] Indeed, it need not involve price suggestions at all.

§6.22 May Seller control prices by utilizing agents or consignees?

Under the antitrust laws, Seller can set its prices to *its* customers[111] and may do so directly. It may also do so through sales agents or consignees because the latter are not Buyers and the price being charged to the end user is Seller's

---

[105] United States v Bausch & Lomb Optical Co, 321 US 707 (1944); FTC v Beech Nut Packing Co, 257 US 441 (1922); Russell Stover Candies, Inc, 3 Trade Reg Rep (CCH) ¶21,933, at 22,368 (FTC July 1, 1982).

[106] Schnapps Shop, Inc v HW Wright & Co, 377 F Supp 570 (D Md 1973).

[107] FTC v Beech Nut Packing Co, 257 US 441 (1922); United States v House of Seagram, Inc, 1965 Trade Cases (CCH) ¶71,517 (SD Fla 1965).

[108] United States v Bausch & Lomb Optical Co, 321 US 707 (1944).

[109] Greene v General Foods Corp, 517 F2d 635 (5th Cir 1975), *cert denied,* 424 US 942 (1976).

[110] Checker Motors Corp v Chrysler Corp, 408 F2d 319 (2d Cir), *cert denied,* 394 US 999 (1969). *See also* Knuth v Erie-Crawford Dairy Coop Assn, 326 F Supp 48, 52 (WD Pa 1971), *modified on other grounds,* 463 F2d 470, 476 (3d Cir 1972), *cert denied,* 410 US 913 (1973).

[111] *See, e.g.,* Fagan v Sunbeam Lighting Co, 303 F Supp 356, 360-61 (SD Ill 1969).

own price for its own goods; that price is unilaterally determined by the owner and is not being fixed in combination with a subsequent owner.[112]

The mere use of a consignment or agency arrangement, however, will not necessarily immunize Seller from price-fixing liability. Should litigation arise, courts will address the question of whether there is a *true consignment* or a *sham* which is designed to camouflage unlawful resale price maintenance.[113] If the latter is found, antitrust liability will be imposed.

§6.23 —What criteria are relevant in determining whether a consignment or agency program is an improper attempt to control resale prices?

In determining whether a consignment or agency program is an improper attempt to control resale prices (a *sham*) the lower courts, following the Supreme Court's decision in *Simpson v Union Oil,*[114] have identified two general criteria. The first is whether the consignees or agents have "all or most of the indicia of entrepreneurs, except for price fixing"; the second is whether the consignment or agency is used as part of a vast distribution system.[115]

Under the first criterion, the *indicia of entrepreneurship,* the courts review the relationship between the parties under the terms of the contract and in actual operation. The question asked is whether Seller "retains title, dominion and risk with respect to the product."[116] In these arrangements, formal title invariably remains with Seller, and this fact is given little weight.[117]

Other aspects of title and dominion, such as the rights and responsibilities of ownership, and the actual physical control of Seller's product, are given greater weight. On this issue, the courts consider such factors as the place where the product is stored pending sale to the end user; the ownership of equipment, if any, needed for sale of the product; tax liability; and responsibility for obtaining and maintaining any necessary permits and licenses.[118]

The most important indicia of entrepreneurship are those that relate to risk.

---

[112] United States v General Elec Co, 272 US 476 (1926); Knuth v Erie-Crawford Dairy Coop Assn, 326 F Supp 48, 52 (WD Pa 1971), *modified on other grounds,* 463 F2d 470 (3d Cir 1972), *cert denied,* 410 US 913 (1973).

[113] Stan Togut Corp v Hobart Mfg Co, 398 F Supp 1323 (SDNY 1974).

[114] 377 US 13 (1964).

[115] *Id* 20-22. *See* Hardwick v Nu-Way Oil Co, 589 F2d 806, 809 (5th Cir), *cert denied,* 444 US 836 (1979); Stan Togut Corp v Hobart Mfg Co, 398 F Supp 1323, 1326 (SDNY 1974); United States v General Elec Co, 358 F Supp 731 (SDNY 1973).

[116] Stan Togut Corp v Hobart Mfg Co, 398 F Supp 1323, 1325 (SDNY 1974).

[117] *See, e.g.,* Simpson v Union Oil Co, 377 US 13 (1964); Roberts v Exxon Corp, 427 F Supp 389 (WD La 1977).

[118] *See, e.g.,* Hardwick v Nu-Way Oil Co, 443 F Supp 940 (SD Tex 1978), *affd,* 589 F2d 806 (5th Cir), *cert denied,* 444 US 836 (1979); Pogue v International Indus, 524 F2d 342 (6th Cir 1975).

Here, the courts ask which party bears the risk of economic loss (the loss or destruction of the goods) and which bears the risk of market loss (a decrease in price or demand).[119] The risk of market loss will probably be found to be the middleman's where the middleman's compensation is based on total dollar sales.[120]

Where the risk of loss is not clearly Seller's or where the more important aspects of dominion (such as tax liability) are not retained by Seller, there is a very strong likelihood that, notwithstanding Seller's retention of title, the consignment will be found to be price-fixing.[121]

The second criterion articulated by the courts—the vastness of the distribution system—has apparently never been determinative. In those cases which mention it the courts also found that the middlemen had indicia of entrepreneurship.[122] We mention this second criterion because if the leading decisions are read literally, it remains theoretically possible to find a consignment a sham simply because it covers a vast distribution system.[123]

§6.24 Under what circumstances may Seller control the prices charged to national accounts?

Seller may find it desirable, or necessary, when dealing with large accounts (often national in scope) to negotiate prices directly with those accounts. Under such a national accounts program Seller's products are generally delivered by an intermediary which also purchases products from Seller for resale to non-national accounts—the *intermediate Buyer.*[124] As part of the national accounts program, the intermediate Buyer may be called upon to perform various services in addition to product delivery. These may include promoting sales, soliciting orders, warehousing, installation, billing, collection, maintenance, training, and supplying related material.

National account programs may or may not involve a formal transfer of title

---

[119] Hardwick v Nu-Way Oil Co, 589 F2d 806, 809 (5th Cir), *cert denied,* 444 US 836 (1979); Goldinger v Boron Oil Co, 375 F Supp 400 (WD Pa 1974), *affd,* 511 F2d 1393 (3d Cir), *cert denied,* 423 US 834 (1975).

[120] Simpson v Union Oil Co, 377 US 13 (1964); Roberts v Exxon Corp, 427 F Supp 389 (WD La 1977).

[121] Simpson v Union Oil Co, 377 US 13 (1964); Roberts v Exxon Corp, 427 F Supp 389 (WD La 1977); United States v General Elec, 358 F Supp 731 (SDNY 1973).

[122] *See, e.g.,* United States v General Elec Co, 358 F Supp 731 (SDNY 1973). *Compare* Hardwick v Nu-Way Oil Co, 589 F2d 806, 809 n 6 (5th Cir), *cert denied,* 444 US 836 (1979).

[123] In Simpson v Union Oil Co, 377 US 13, 22 (1964) the Court wrote:

> When, however, a "consignment" device is used to cover a vast gasoline distribution system, fixing prices through many retail outlets, the antitrust laws prevent calling the "consignment" an agency, for then the end result of *United States* v *Socony-Vacuum Oil Co.* would be avoided merely by clever manipulation of words, not by differences in substance.

See also Stan Togut Corp v Hobart Mfg Co, 398 F Supp 1323 (SDNY 1974). *Compare* Stanton v Texaco, Inc, 289 F Supp 884 (DRI 1968).

[124] Such national accounts programs are a form of dual distribution, which is discussed in **ch 8.**

in Seller's product to the intermediate buyer. In either event, if litigation arises, the courts are likely to look to the substance of the relationships between the parties, not to their form. If the intermediate Buyer does little more than deliver Seller's products, vertical price-fixing should not be found. If, on the other hand, the intermediate buyer performs services for the national account essentially identical with those it performs for its own accounts, there is a substantial likelihood that, for the reasons applied in piercing sham consignment arrangements,[125] vertical price-fixing will be found.

Since there is little case law (and no Supreme Court decisions) on the subject, no reliable general principles can be formulated concerning national accounts programs in which the intermediate Buyer does more than deliver, but significantly less than it does for its own customers. In counseling on the vertical price-fixing risks raised by such in-between programs, the attorney can do little more than compare the program under review with the national accounts programs that have been the subject of reported decisions. There are four such decisions.

In one of these decisions, the Fifth Circuit upheld a finding of vertical price-fixing where the intermediate Buyer was required to assume all sales activity up to the point of billing and collection, where Buyer held title to the product, and where Buyer was not free to solicit its own orders from national accounts.[126] In the remaining three cases, the courts found no price-fixing. The factors considered in these three cases were that: participation in the program was wholly voluntary; Buyers acted merely as suppliers; Sellers played a more dominant role in promoting sales and soliciting orders; title or the risk of loss remained with Sellers; and Buyers were free to compete with Sellers in soliciting sales from national accounts customers.[127]

§6.25 Are there circumstances under which Seller may determine the prices to the end user even though title may first pass from Seller to an intermediary?

In at least one circuit court decision, *Marty's Floor Covering Co v GAF*,[128] the Seller was found to have properly determined the price to the end user even though title was first transferred to an intermediary. The court held that while "there was perhaps a technical transfer of title" to the intermediary, the Seller

---

[125] Greene v General Foods Corp, 517 F2d 635, 656-57 (5th Cir 1975), *cert denied*, 424 US 942 (1976). For a discussion on piercing sham consignment arrangements see **§§6.22, 6.23.**

[126] Greene v General Foods Corp, 517 F2d 635 (5th Cir 1975), *cert denied*, 424 US 942 (1976).

[127] Ohio-Sealy Mattress Mfg Co v Sealy, Inc, 585 F2d 821, 836-38 (7th Cir 1978); Mesirow v Pepperidge Farms, Inc, 1981-2 Trade Cases (CCH) ¶64,292 (ND Cal 1981), *affd*, 1982-83 Trade Cases (CCH) ¶65,164 (9th Cir 1983); Overhead Door Corp v Nordpal Corp 1979-1 Trade Cases (CCH) ¶62,959 (D Minn 1978).

[128] 604 F2d 266 (4th Cir 1979), *cert denied*, 444 US 1017 (1980).

negotiated with, and shipped to, the end user directly.[129] The intermediary—whose function was described as "merely that of a factor or discounter"—apparently did little more than bill and collect.

No general conclusion should be drawn from this case. It does demonstrate, however, that it may be possible to structure a marketing system in which an intermediary receives title without Seller necessarily losing control over the price paid by the end user. For such a system to achieve this result, Seller, like the Seller in *Marty's,* probably has to have extensive direct dealings with the end user, and the intermediary's role has to be clearly minor.

§6.26 May Seller eliminate the intermediate Buyer and shift to a direct distribution system in order to control the price to the end user?

As noted above, there can be no resale price maintenance where Seller sells directly to the end user.[130] Under the antitrust laws Seller may shift to such a direct sales system from a system which utilizes independent intermediate Buyers in order to control the price paid by the end user, so long as there is no ulterior anticompetitive purpose.[131] As a general antitrust proposition, consistent with the *Colgate* doctrine, Seller is allowed to structure or restructure its marketing system in the manner it deems most effective.[132] However, any restructuring and, in particular, any termination may raise contract questions as well as questions under state franchise laws.[133]

The shift can take various forms. All or some Buyers can be terminated; all, some, or none of the terminated Buyers can be offered positions as sales employees;[134] Buyers can also be acquired by Seller and their operations

---

[129] 604 F2d at 269.

[130] See **§6.22.**

[131] Auburn News Co v Providence Journal Co, 659 F2d 273 (1st Cir 1981), *cert denied,* 455 US 921 (1982); Naify v McClatchy Newspapers, 599 F2d 335 (9th Cir 1979); Call Carl, Inc v BP Oil Corp, 554 F2d 623 (4th Cir), *cert denied,* 434 US 923 (1977); Hardin v Houston Chronicle Publishing Co, 434 F Supp 54 (SD Tex 1977), *affd,* 572 F2d 1106 (5th Cir 1978); Knutson v Daily Review, Inc, 383 F Supp 1346 (ND Cal 1974), *modified,* 401 F Supp 1374 (ND Cal 1975), *affd in part, revd in part on other grounds,* 548 F2d 795 (9th Cir 1976), *cert denied,* 433 US 910 (1977); Newberry v Washington Post Co, 438 F Supp 470 (DDC 1971).

[132] Newberry v Washington Post Co, 438 F Supp 470, 484 (DDC 1977). For a discussion of the *Colgate* doctrine see **§6.06.**

[133] *See, e.g.,* HL Moore Drug Exch v Eli Lilly & Co, 662 F2d 935 (2d Cir 1981) (alleging breach of contract and violation of §2 of Connecticut's Fairness in Franchising Act, Conn Gen Stat Ann §42.133f (West Supp 1980)), *cert denied,* 103 S Ct 176 (1982); Call Carl, Inc v BP Oil Corp, 554 F2d 623 (4th Cir), *cert denied,* 434 US 923 (1977) (alleging breach of contract); Martin Ice Cream Co v Chipwich, Inc, 1982-83 Trade Cases (CCH) ¶65,142 (SDNY 1983) (alleging breach of contract); Mt Vernon Datsun, Inc v Nissan Motor Corp, 1976-1 Trade Cases (CCH) ¶60,842 (ED Va 1975) (Automobile Dealers' Day in Court Act, 15 USC §§1221-1225).

[134] See **Ch 7** and **§§6.10, 6.11** for a more complete discussion of terminations.

eliminated or vertically integrated with those of Seller. When there is such *downstream vertical integration,* there is a risk of someone alleging a parent-subsidiary vertical price-fixing conspiracy.[135] In addition, Seller can terminate some Buyers, acquire others, and continue to deal with still others.

The terminated Buyers may claim that the shift is an unlawful attempt to control resale prices. If there has been a selective termination of only those Buyers who have failed to adhere to Seller's suggested resale prices, Buyers may argue that the shift was an attempt to fix prices by punishing those who did not follow suggested prices and by warning the remaining Buyers. Seller will probably contend that the shift took place because it unilaterally determined that it could market its products more effectively by a direct marketing system rather than through independent intermediary Buyers. If the finder of fact accepts Seller's contention, antitrust liability should not be found.[136]

The likelihood of Seller prevailing will be greater if all Buyers are treated exactly the same.[137] This, however, may not be commercially feasible. Thus, Seller may not have the resources to integrate vertically in every area where it markets; moreover, in particular geographic markets, direct selling may not be efficient because of population density or the strength of individual independent Buyers. But where Buyers have to be treated differently, there is a substantial risk of antitrust liability when there is no rational basis for distinguishing between terminated and nonterminated buyers other than adherence to suggested prices.[138]

There are at least two circumstances in which even a nondiscriminatory shift in marketing systems might violate the antitrust laws. First, if the new system is primarily a change in form and not substance (for example, if the sales employee who was previously a Buyer still has many of the indicia and risks of entrepreneurship), vertical price-fixing may be found.[139] The rationale for the finding would be similar to that employed in cases holding that particular consignments are *sham* attempts to control prices.[140]

---

[135] *See, e.g.,* Auburn News Co v Providence Journal Co, 659 F2d 273 (1st Cir 1981), *cert denied,* 455 US 921 (1982).

[136] *E.g.,* Hardin v Houston Chronicle Publishing Co, 434 F Supp 54 (SD Tex 1977), *affd,* 572 F2d 1106 (5th Cir 1978); Knutson v Daily Review, Inc, 383 F Supp 1346 (ND Cal 1974), *modified,* 401 F Supp 1374 (ND Cal 1975), *affd in part, revd in part on other grounds,* 548 F2d 795 (9th Cir 1976), *cert denied,* 433 US 910 (1977). *Cf* Martin Ice Cream Co v Chipwich, Inc, 554 F Supp 933 (SDNY 1983) (summary judgment for Seller denied where terminated Buyer alleged that Seller's shift to direct sales was done to punish Buyer for discounting and to discourage others from discounting.

[137] *See, e.g.,* Hardin v Houston Chronicle Publishing Co, 434 F Supp 54 (SD Tex 1977), *affd,* 572 F2d 1106 (5th Cir 1978).

[138] This is suggested by the court's language in Naify v McClatchy Newspapers, 599 F2d 335 (9th Cir 1979); *see also,* Martin Ice Cream Co v Chipwich, Inc, 554 F Supp 933 (SDNY 1983); Knutson v Daily Review, Inc, 383 F Supp 1346, 1367 (ND Cal 1974), *modified,* 401 F Supp 1374 (ND Cal 1975), *affd in part, revd in part on other grounds,* 548 F2d 795 (9th Cir 1976), *cert denied,* 433 US 910 (1977).

[139] This is suggested by the rationale of Newberry v Washington Post Co, 438 F Supp 470 (DDC 1977) and Hardin v Houston Chronicle Publishing Co, 434 F Supp 54 (SD Tex 1977), *affd,* 572 F2d 1106 (5th Cir 1978).

[140] See **§§6.22, 6.23** for a discussion of sham consignments.

Second, if Seller has a large market share, its attempts to expand its distribution activities could be challenged under §2 of the Sherman Act as an unlawful monopolization or attempt to monopolize.[141] If Seller acquires its independent Buyers, the acquisition might also be attacked under §7 of the Clayton Act which prohibits acquisitions "where in any line of commerce or in any activity affecting commerce in any section of the country, the effect of such acquisition may be substantially to lessen competition, or to tend to create a monopoly."[142]

It appears, however, that no shift in marketing systems has been found to be a sham or a violation of either §2 of the Sherman Act or §7 of the Clayton Act. Moreover, the merger guidelines recently issued by the Department of Justice and statements by the Assistant Attorney General in charge of the antitrust division reveal that such attacks are unlikely to be mounted by the department in the near future.[143] Nevertheless, given the likelihood and consequences of private litigation, Sellers might still be taking significant risks if they utilize sham systems or if they possess very large market shares.

§6.27 Does the Seller of patented products have any greater rights to influence Buyer's resale prices?

The principles discussed in this chapter apply equally to both patented and unpatented products. The patent owner has the exclusive right to sell the patented product[144] but once having made the sale, it has no special rights concerning resale price.[145] The presence of a patent neither expands nor restricts Seller's rights to suggest prices or unilaterally to terminate Buyers who do not follow those suggestions.

Although there are some cases which might be construed otherwise,[146] it

---

[141] Such challenges were made in Auburn News Co, Inc v Providence Journal Co, 659 F2d 273 (1st Cir 1981), *cert denied,* 455 US 921 (1982), and Knutson v Daily Review, Inc, 383 F Supp 1346 (ND Cal 1974), *modified,* 401 F Supp 1374 (ND Cal 1975), *affd in part, revd in part on other grounds,* 548 F2d 795 (9th Cir 1976), *cert denied,* 433 US 910 (1977). In both cases the claims were entertained but the court found that the plaintiffs had failed to meet their burden of proof.

[142] 15 USC §18.

[143] The merger guidelines and accompanying press release indicate that vertical mergers will be challenged only when there would be real or potential horizontal effects. Trade Reg Rep (CCH) ¶¶4500-4505, at 6881-4, 6881-15 to -19 (June 14, 1982). *See also* Assistant Attorney General William Baxter's remarks reported in Antitrust and Trade Reg Rep (BNA) slip no 1036, at A-3, (Oct 11, 1981): "[Baxter] would expect the Division to bring vertical actions 'seldom to almost never.' Although he acknowledged that vertical price fixing could be a facilitating device for horizontal activity, Baxter noted that 'one must be quite imaginative,' to contrive a vertical situation that would be challenged by the Division."

[144] 35 USC §154.

[145] Bauer & Cie v O'Donnell, 229 US 1 (1913); Agrashell, Inc v Hammons Prods Co, 479 F2d 269, 279 (8th Cir), *cert denied,* 414 US 1022 (1973). See generally Nordhaus, Patent-Antitrust Law §83 (3d ed 1977).

[146] In Simpson v Union Oil Co, 377 US 13 (1964), the Court distinguished the

would be imprudent for Seller to seek to control the resale prices of patented goods through a patent licensing arrangement or through a consignment arrangement which would be found to be a sham under the criteria discussed in **§6.23.**[147] The rationale of the cases condemning vertical price-fixing and stressing the need to look to substance instead of form applies fully to the resale of patented products.[148]

Indeed, if the patent owner tries to use the patent as a means of securing adherence to suggested prices, patent misuse may be found. If it is found, enforcement of the patent will be banned until the misuse is purged and the effects of the improper pricing have been dissipated.[149]

§6.28 What control does Seller have over copyrighted or trademarked products?

The discussion concerning patented products in the preceding section applies equally to copyrighted products. Seller is afforded no greater control over resale prices by virtue of its copyright.[150]

Trademarks, particularly important in the context of a franchise relationship, similarly do not afford Seller any greater right to control resale prices.[151] Thus franchisors and other trademark owners have been treated like any other Seller by the courts which, in their decisions, often do not even note the presence of a trademark.[152]

§6.29 What are the penalties for unlawful resale price maintenance?

The full panoply of civil and criminal penalties imposed by the antitrust laws can be levied against a Seller or Buyer found to have engaged in resale price maintenance.

Vertical price-fixing was the subject of a criminal action commenced by the

---

consignment arrangement in United States v General Elec Co, 272 US 476 (1926), on the narrow ground that the consignment agreement there involved patented articles; *see also* Agrashell, Inc v Hammons Prod Co, 479 F2d 269, 279 (8th Cir), *cert denied,* 414 US 1022 (1973).

[147] Straus v Victor Talking Mach Co, 243 US 490 (1917) (sham licensing); United States v Masonite Corp, 316 US 265, 279 (1942) (sham agency or consignment); see generally Nordhaus, Patent-Antitrust Law §§33-35 (3d ed 1977).

[148] See **§§6.22, 6.23,** for a discussion of the cases stressing the need to look to the substance of the relationships rather than to their form.

[149] Ansul Co v Uniroyal, Inc, 448 F2d 872 (2d Cir 1971), *cert denied,* 404 US 1018 (1972). See generally Nordhaus, Patent-Antitrust Law §83B (3d ed 1977).

[150] Straus v American Publishers' Assn, 231 US 222 (1913); Bobbs-Merrill Co v Straus, 210 US 339 (1907). *See also In re* Doubleday & Co, 52 FTC 169 (1955).

[151] United States v Sealy, Inc, 388 US 350 (1967); Susser v Carvel Corp, 332 F2d 505 (2d Cir 1964), *cert dismissed,* 381 US 125 (1965); Denison Mattress Factory v Spring-Air Co, 308 F2d 403 (5th Cir 1962); Engbrecht v Dairy Queen Co, 203 F Supp 714 (D Kan 1962); Sunbeam Corp v Payless Drug Stores, 113 F Supp 31, 44 (ND Cal 1953); *In re* Amway Corp, 93 FTC 618, 695-98 (1979).

[152] *See, e.g.,* Pogue v International Indus, 524 F2d 342 (6th Cir 1975).

Department of Justice in 1980.[153] Present senior Justice Department officials have stated that vertical price-fixing is not necessarily anticompetitive and should be governed by the rule of reason.[154] Thus, it seems unlikely that federal criminal prosecutions for such conduct will be brought in the near future. Nevertheless, there can be no assurances, and it would be imprudent to assume that a vertical price-fixer faces civil penalties only. At least one state has brought a criminal action for vertical price-fixing.[155]

In the private civil context, where litigation is typically instituted by an aggrieved (and often terminated) buyer, Seller faces an exposure to treble damages,[156] attorney's fees,[157] and injunctive relief.[158]

Whether Seller fixes minimum or maximum prices, the usual measure of damages is Buyer's lost profits.[159] In practice, Buyers who complain of maximum resale price maintenance may find it difficult to prove substantial damages. They would have to establish that, despite the loss of volume resulting from the increased price, " 'their net profit would have been higher in some amount' had there been no price restraint."[160] They would also have to establish this difficult proposition before a judge or jury which might be sympathetic toward the Seller who seeks to "help the consumer" by preventing "price gouging."

Even in minimum resale price maintenance cases, damages are often difficult to prove. Damages have been limited to lost profits in the product line directly affected by the pricing policy, and not extended to plaintiff's lost profits generally.[161] However, if the plaintiff can show that its entire business was destroyed by an unlawful termination, it may be able to recover the full amount of the loss. Applying this principle, the Seventh Circuit recently affirmed a treble damages award of $10 million, plus attorney's fees.[162]

Suits on behalf of Buyer's customers for minimum resale price-fixing have been successfully maintained against Seller and Buyer by states under the

---

[153] *In re* Grand Jury Investigation of Cuisinarts, Inc, 516 F.Supp 1008, 1009 (D Conn 1981).

[154] See **§6.01.**

[155] State v Lawn King, Inc, 150 NJ Super 204, 375 A2d 295 (1977), *revd,* 169 NJ Super 346, 404 A2d 1215 (App Div 1979), *affd,* 84 NJ 1979, 417 A2d 1025 (1980).

[156] §4 of the Clayton Act, 15 USC §15.

[157] *Id.*

[158] §16 of the Clayton Act, 15 USC §26.

[159] *See, e.g.,* Trabert & Hoeffer, Inc v Piaget Watch Corp, 633 F2d 477 (7th Cir 1980); Arnott v American Oil Co, 609 F2d 873 (8th Cir 1979), *cert denied,* 446 US 918 (1980); Greene v General Foods Corp, 517 F2d 635 (5th Cir 1975), *cert denied,* 424 US 942 (1976).

[160] Knutson v Daily Review, Inc, 468 F Supp 226, 230 (ND Cal 1979), *affd,* 644 F2d 1120 (9th Cir 1981); *see also* Kestenbaum v Falstaff Brewing Corp, 575 F2d 564, 569 (5th Cir 1978), *cert denied,* 440 US 909 (1979); Newberry v Washington Post Co, 438 F Supp 470 (DDC 1977).

[161] Trabert & Hoeffer, Inc v Piaget Watch Corp, 633 F2d 477 (7th Cir 1980).

[162] Spray-Rite Serv Corp v Monsanto Co, 684 F2d 1226 (7th Cir 1982), *cert granted,* __ US __, 75 L Ed 2d 479, 103 S Ct 1249 (1983).

parens patriae doctrine[163] and by the customers directly.[164] Because of the *Illinois Brick* doctrine,[165] which denies price-fixing damages to *indirect purchasers,* plaintiffs in such suits may have to establish that both Seller and Buyer actively participated in the price maintenance program.[166]

Damages are not the only serious problem faced by a Seller found liable for vertical price-fixing. In *Russell Stover,*[167] the Federal Trade Commission ordered the Seller to cease and desist from its policy of threatening terminations for price-cutting; to offer to reinstate dealers terminated in whole or in part because of price-cutting; to advertise the terms of the order in trade publications; to bear the expense of a market survey after two years to determine the percentage of dealers selling at or above Russell Stover's designated prices; and, if the survey showed that there was not a decrease of at least 10 per cent in the percentage of such dealers, to stop suggesting resale prices for three years.[168] This harsh remedy, which was stipulated to by the parties, goes beyond anything that courts have ordered.

In a private antitrust action, a finding of vertical price-fixing could freeze Seller's relationships with unsatisfactory Buyers. If a terminated Buyer can prove that Seller engaged in vertical price-fixing, the finder of fact is likely to conclude that the termination was related to the price-fixing. In that event, Buyer may be able to obtain injunctive relief requiring the Seller to continue dealing with it and restricting Seller's rights to terminate it later for cause.[169]

---

[163] New Mexico v Scott & Fetzer Co, 1981-2 Trade Cases (CCH) ¶64,439 (DNM 1981); *In re* Mid-Atlantic Toyota Antitrust Litigation, 516 F Supp 1287 (D Md 1981); State v Russell Stover Candies, Inc, 541 F Supp 143 (D Mass 1981). Parens patriae suits are provided for in 15 USC §15c. See generally Scher, *Emerging Issues under the Antitrust Improvement Act of 1976,* 77 Colum L Rev 679, 701-40 (1977); Handler & Blechman, *Antitrust and the Consumer Interest: The Fallacy of Parens Patriae and a Suggested New Approach,* 85 Yale LJ 626 (1976).

[164] Morrison v Nissan Motor Co, Ltd, 601 F2d 139 (4th Cir 1979).

[165] This doctrine was enunciated by the Supreme Court in Illinois Brick Co v Illinois, 432 US 720 (1977). The *Illinois Brick* doctrine derives from a case involving horizontal price-fixing, is beyond the scope of this chapter and is discussed in ch 3. The doctrine's implications should be considered by anyone facing or contemplating a vertical price-fixing suit by Buyer's customers. See generally Landes & Posner, *Should Indirect Purchasers Have Standing to Sue Under the Antitrust Laws? An Economic Analysis of the Rule of Illinois Brick,* 46 U Chi L Rev 602 (1979); Note, *Scaling the Illinois Brick Wall: The Future of Indirect Purchases in Antitrust Litigation,* 63 Cornell L Rev 309 (1978).

[166] *In re* Mid-Atlantic Toyota Antitrust Litigation, 516 F Supp 1287 (D Md 1981).

[167] Russell Stover Candies, Inc, 3 Trade Reg Rep (CCH) ¶21,933 (FTC July 1, 1982).

[168] *Id* at 22,370-71.

[169] Trabert & Hoeffer, Inc v Piaget Watch Corp, 633 F2d 477 (7th Cir 1980); Phillips v Crown Central Petroleum Corp, 602 F2d 616, 629-31 (4th Cir 1979), *cert denied,* 444 US 1074 (1980); Interphoto Corp v Minolta Corp, 295 F Supp 711 (SDNY), *affd,* 417 F2d 621 (2d Cir 1969).

May Seller Cease Selling to Buyer?

*Arthur I. Cantor**

7

---

*Mr. Cantor is a member of the District of Columbia Bar. The author wishes to thank Anita K. Blair of Brownstein Zeidman and Schomer for her assistance in the preparation of this chapter.

§7.47 What remedies are available to a wrongfully terminated Buyer?

§7.01 What are the sources of law regarding termination of Buyer by Seller?

In seller-buyer relationships, Seller always encounters two fundamental questions: First, on what terms and conditions will I deal with my customers generally? Second, must I deal, or continue to deal, with a particular customer at all? Most of this book is concerned with the first of these questions: What obligations and restrictions may Seller impose upon Buyer in the course of the relationship? But few such relationships are perpetual; at some time, for some reason, most come to an end. It is the termination of the relationship that is the concern of this chapter.

The termination of a seller-buyer relationship may, of course, raise antitrust issues, as may a Seller's refusal to begin dealing with a prospective Buyer; the antitrust analysis of these two kinds of refusal to deal is largely the same, and is set out in Chapter 2. However, when Seller wishes to cease dealing with a Buyer, matters other than antitrust issues must also be considered.

When a Seller decides to terminate its relationship with a particular Buyer, several bodies of law may apply. The parties are bound by the lawful terms of their own agreement. The common law of contracts applies to termination, as do certain provisions of the Uniform Commercial Code (UCC).[1] As noted above, antitrust laws, both federal and state, may govern Seller's action insofar as it affects competition.[2] In addition, there are several federal and state statutes which specifically address terminations of certain categories of Buyers.[3]

The Seller wishing to terminate a Buyer will consider five basic questions:

1. May I terminate under the terms of my contract with Buyer?
2. Would termination raise antitrust questions?
3. Do any nonantitrust laws affect my right to terminate?
4. Assuming I may terminate Buyer, what procedures must I follow?
5. If I choose to terminate, will Buyer be likely to assert other claims against me?

A more elaborate checklist is suggested in **§7.40.**

---

[1] See **§§7.04, 7.12, 7.13.**

[2] See generally **ch 2,** concerning federal antitrust law as it applies in terminations and refusals to deal.

[3] See **§§7.05, 7.14.**

§7.02 —What is termination?

As used in this chapter, *termination* refers to the decision by one party to no longer sell to—or buy from—another party. Unlike a mere refusal to deal, termination only occurs when the parties have had previous dealings with each other on more than a casual, sporadic basis.[4] The parties must have had an express or implied agreement to continue dealing with each other. The agreement need not be written, and it may be indefinite in duration. If the agreement does have a definite duration, merely allowing it to expire may constitute termination if the other party has a right, and desires, to be renewed.[5]

Under UCC §2-106, termination is distinguished from cancellation. As used in the UCC, *termination* occurs when a party exercises its right under the agreement or under law to end the contract for a reason other than breach by the other party. All executory obligations are discharged, and only rights based on prior breach or performance survive the termination.[6] *Cancellation* is termination by one party because of the other's breach, and rights based on the entire contract, including the unperformed balance, survive the cancellation.[7]

Throughout this chapter, the term termination is used in its ordinary sense, to signify the ending of the contract by one party (usually Seller) either because of breach by the other or through exercise of a contractual or other legal power. The nature of the rights which survive such termination will vary according to the subject matter and the terms of the agreement, the reason for termination, and the requirements of applicable statutes.

§7.03 —May Seller and Buyer agree on the grounds and procedures for termination?

In general, parties to a contract may specify the grounds and procedures for termination. Unless the provisions are illegal, they generally will be enforced.[8] Some statutes may supersede the parties' own provisions, particularly with respect to procedures for advance notice and cure periods.[9] In addition, some statutes may prohibit termination except on certain grounds. Under such statutes, if one or more of those grounds are not present, the termination may be unlawful, even if the contract would permit termination.[10] A termination for any different reasons, even if originally agreed to by Buyer, may be unlawful.

---

[4] See generally Goetz & Scott, *Principles of Relational Contracts*, 67 Va L Rev 1089 (1981).

[5] See **§7.36.**

[6] UCC §2-106(3).

[7] *Id* §2-106(4).

[8] *See* Restatement (Second) of Contracts §178 (1981). *Cf* KFC Corp v Darsam Corp, 543 F Supp 222 (WD Ky 1982) (agreement to terminate enforced in summary proceeding despite Buyer's claim that contrary oral promises were made).

[9] See **§§7.14, 7.31.**

[10] See **§§7.14-7.25.**

§7.04 —When does the UCC govern the terms of the agreement?

Article 2 of the UCC, concerning sales, applies whenever a contract is for the purchase and sale of goods.[11] There are two provisions of the UCC which may affect termination of a continuing relationship. Section 2-306 concerns output, requirements, and exclusive dealing contracts. Section 2-306 requires good faith on the part of parties to output and requirements contracts, and best efforts on the part of parties to exclusive dealing contracts. It does not, however, specifically address termination of such contracts.[12]

Section 2-309 governs performance and termination of continuing agreements which lack specific time provisions. A contract which calls for successive performances but which is of indefinite duration is presumed to be valid for a reasonable time, and is then terminable at any time by either party.[13] Unless otherwise agreed, Seller must give reasonable notice of termination.[14] An agreement to dispense with notice may be deemed invalid if termination without notice would be unconscionable.[15]

The UCC also imposes a general obligation of good faith[16] and prohibits any unconscionable provision.[17] These standards apply whether or not the parties have specifically agreed on grounds and procedures for termination.

§7.05 —When do special industry laws govern the terms of the agreement?

Both federal and state laws may govern termination if Seller and Buyer are members of certain industries or use certain methods of distribution. In particular, federal laws apply to terminations of motor vehicle dealers[18] and petroleum dealers.[19] State laws may apply in a variety of cases: motor vehicle dealers, petroleum dealers, beer and wine distributors, farm implement dealers, construction equipment dealers, and franchisees.[20] In general, these laws

---

[11] UCC §2-102.

[12] See T. Quinn, Uniform Commercial Code Commentary and Law Digest §2-306[A][4] (1978).

[13] UCC §2-309(2).

[14] *Id* §2-309(3).

[15] The test of unconscionability is applied as of the time the contract was entered, not as of the time of termination. Thus, a court enforced a provision for termination without notice where both parties originally found it beneficial, even though one suffered damage at the time of termination. Sinkoff Beverage Co v Jos Schlitz Brewing Co, 51 Misc 2d 446, 273 NYS2d 364 (Sup Ct 1966).

[16] UCC §1-203.

[17] *Id* §2-302.

[18] See **§7.06.**

[19] See **§7.07.**

[20] See **§7.08.**

impose a requirement of good faith or good cause in the termination of such buyers. Usually the statutes apply notwithstanding the terms of any contract between the parties. Some statutes impose procedural requirements for termination,[21] and some afford special remedies to terminated buyers, such as required repurchase of their inventory by the seller.[22]

§7.06 —What if Buyer is a motor vehicle dealer?

The Automobile Dealer's Day in Court Act[23] permits an automobile dealer to sue in federal court for damages caused by an automobile manufacturer's failure to act in good faith in terminating, canceling, or not renewing the dealer. *Good faith* is defined in the statute as "the duty of each party . . . to act in a fair and equitable manner toward each other so as to guarantee the one party freedom from coercion, intimidation, or threats of coercion or intimidation from the other party."[24] Since the enactment of this law in 1956, scores of cases have been brought under it.[25]

In addition to the federal statute, there are approximately forty state laws governing termination, cancellation, or nonrenewal of motor vehicle dealers.[26] In general, these laws prohibit terminations which are *arbitrary and unreasonable* or *without due cause.* Many states impose notice requirements prior to termination.[27] In several states, a terminated motor vehicle dealer may seek administrative review by a state motor vehicle board or commission.[28]

§7.07 —What if Buyer is a petroleum dealer?

The federal Petroleum Marketing Practices Act (PMPA)[29] prohibits termina-

---

[21] See **§7.31.**

[22] See **§7.46.**

[23] 15 USC §§1221-1225. This law is also known as the Automobile Dealer's Franchise Act.

[24] 15 USC §1221(e).

[25] See generally Note, *Hope Yet for the Automobile Dealers' Day in Court Act: Marquis v Chrysler Corp,* 1979 Duke LJ 1185. This note chronicles the "tradition of strict construction" of the act by numerous courts. *Id* 1213. Several elements are necessary to make out a violation of the act. Courts have focused particularly on the element of coercion: whether the franchisor made a wrongful demand coupled with a threat of sanctions. See Donovan, *Federal Laws Affecting the Right of a Franchisor to Terminate or Not Renew a Franchise: Automobile Dealers Day in Court Act,* 49 Antitrust LJ 1353 (1981).

[26] See **app L.**

[27] Alabama, Arizona, California, Connecticut, Florida, Georgia, Illinois, Iowa, Kansas, Kentucky, Louisiana, Maine, Maryland, Massachusetts, Michigan, Minnesota, Nebraska, New Hampshire, North Carolina, Ohio, Pennsylvania, Rhode Island, South Dakota, Texas, Vermont, Virginia, West Virginia. (**App L.**)

[28] See generally Note, *State Motor Vehicle Franchise Legislation: A Survey and Due Process Challenge to Board Composition,* 33 Vand L Rev 385, 399-405 (1980).

[29] 15 USC §§2801-2806.

tion of petroleum dealers by their oil company suppliers except on certain grounds:

1. Dealer's failure to comply with provisions of the agreement which are both reasonable and of material significance to the relationship
2. Dealer's failure to use good faith efforts
3. Occurrence of an event which relates to the relationship which makes termination reasonable
4. Mutual agreement to terminate
5. Supplier's withdrawal from the market area[30]

Nonrenewals may be based only on any of the above grounds or any of the following grounds:

1. Failure to agree on changes or additions to the contract suggested in good faith
2. Customer complaints
3. Repeated failure to operate dealership in a clean, safe, healthful manner
4. Supplier's good faith decision to convert, alter, or sell leased premises of the dealership[31]

The law also requires prior notice to the dealer of intention to terminate or not renew the agreement.[32]

The PMPA prohibits the states from enforcing any state law provision unless it is the same as the applicable provision of the PMPA.[33] In effect, although other provisions of the thirty-odd state laws affecting petroleum dealers[34] may differ, all states are bound to the federal standards for termination.[35]

§7.08 —What if Buyer is a franchisee?

Sixteen states prohibit termination of a franchisee unless good cause or a similar basis for termination can be shown.[36] Each state has its own definition of *franchisee* or *franchise,* but in general three elements are necessary: (1) sub-

---

[30] *Id* §2802(b)(2).

[31] *Id* §2802(b)(3).

[32] *Id* §2804.

[33] *Id* §2806.

[34] See **app M.**

[35] *Compare* Westfield Centre Serv Inc v Cities Serv Oil Co, 86 NJ 453, 432 A2d 48 (1981) (pre-PMPA case, state law applied) *with* Malone v Crown Cent Petroleum Corp, 474 F Supp 306 (D Md 1979) (PMPA applied). *See also* Ted's Tire Serv Inc v Chevron USA Inc, 470 F Supp 163 (D Conn 1979) (nonrenewal judged under PMPA and nonconflicting provisions of state law).

[36] See **app K.**

stantial association of the business with a trademark, service mark, or trade name of the Seller; (2) a required payment; and (3) either a marketing plan or system prescribed by Seller or a community of interest between Seller and Buyer.[37]

Likewise, definitions of good cause vary, but, in general, good cause for termination exists if the franchisee has failed substantially to comply with the reasonable terms of the agreement.[38] Most states which regulate franchise terminations require prior notice and an opportunity to cure before a termination may take effect.[39] Some states specify certain defaults for which termination may be automatic.[40] Examples of such defaults are abandonment or loss of the franchised premises, bankruptcy or criminal conviction of the franchisee, misrepresentation by the franchisee, and repeated default after notice.

Thirteen states make it unlawful to refuse to renew a franchisee unless certain conditions exist.[41] Nine states require that the franchisor-Seller compensate the franchisee-Buyer or repurchase certain goods from Buyer upon termination or nonrenewal.[42]

§7.09 —Suppose Seller and Buyer have no explicit agreement regarding termination?

If the contract of the parties contains no provision regarding termination, then common law rules as well as any applicable statute will govern. Statutory provisions that may affect Seller's power to terminate buyer include the Uniform Commercial Code,[43] special industry[44] and franchise[45] laws, antitrust laws,[46] and unfair trade practices laws.[47]

If the common law alone governs the agreement, the general rule is that,

---

[37] See generally **ch 9;** Fern, *The Overbroad Scope of Franchise Regulation: A Definitional Dilemma,* 34 Bus Law 1387 (1979).

[38] See **§7.16.**

[39] Arkansas, California, Connecticut, Delaware, Hawaii, Illinois, Indiana, Michigan, Minnesota, Mississippi, Missouri, Nebraska, New Jersey, Washington, Wisconsin. (**App K.**)

[40] See **§7.16.**

[41] Connecticut, Delaware, New Jersey, and Wisconsin impose a good cause standard for nonrenewal. Arkansas, Hawaii, Indiana, and Nebraska require renewal if and as provided in the franchise agreement. California and Minnesota require prior notice of nonrenewal. Illinois, Michigan, and Washington impose a repurchase requirement upon nonrenewal, in addition to prior notice. (**App K.**)

[42] Arkansas, California, Connecticut, Hawaii, Illinois, Michigan, Mississippi, Washington, Wisconsin. (**App K.**)

[43] *See, e.g.,* UCC §2-309.

[44] See **§§7.05-7.07.**

[45] See **§§7.08-7.14.**

[46] See generally **ch 2.**

[47] See generally Stadfeld, *Survey of State Little FTC Acts and Consumer Protection Statutes,* in ABA Forum Committee on Franchising Fourth Annual Forum (Oct 15-16, 1981).

unless the parties intended otherwise, the agreement may be terminated by either party at any time without cause, subject to the implied duty of good faith.[48] Where a termination appears to work an undue hardship on Buyer, however, courts at times have invoked additional common law theories[49] and equitable principles[50] in order to limit Seller's discretion in terminating Buyer.

§7.10 —When does antitrust law apply in termination situations?

A termination may constitute an unlawful refusal to deal under the antitrust laws in a wide range of settings—for example, if it is based on Buyer's noncompliance with a contractual obligation which itself violates the antitrust laws (such as resale price maintenance) or upon complaints from Buyer's competitors.[51] Because of the scope of antitrust law and the severity of potential civil and criminal penalties for its violation, prudence dictates that Seller always consider antitrust aspects before effecting a termination. However, antitrust law will rarely bar a termination for common Buyer derelictions, such as nonpayment for goods or services.

§7.11 May Seller terminate Buyer without cause?

This part of the chapter focuses on Seller's right to terminate its relationship with Buyer without cause. Various principles of common law, the Uniform Commercial Code and other state laws, and the agreement between Buyer and Seller are determinative in this area. This part also deals with how the law varies depending on whether the parties have provided for termination in their agreement.

A termination is without cause if it occurs without a breach by Buyer. Seller will not ordinarily terminate Buyer if Seller is completely satisfied with Buyer's performance.[52] Nevertheless, in certain circumstances Seller may terminate

---

[48] A leading case, Atlantic Richfield Co v Razumic, 480 Pa 366, 390 A2d 736 (1978), held that in a petroleum franchise, the franchisor's right to terminate the lease (on which the agreement was silent) was subject to a good cause requirement because to terminate without good cause would violate the franchisor's duty of good faith. Other cases, however, have upheld termination without cause where the agreement so provided, notwithstanding good faith arguments. *See, e.g.,* Witmer v Exxon Corp, 260 Pa Super 537, 394 A2d 1276 (1978) *affd,* 495 Pa 540, 434 A2d 1222 (1981).

[49] *See, e.g.,* Arnott v American Oil Co, 609 F2d 873 (8th Cir 1979), *cert denied,* 446 US 918 (1980) (fiduciary duty to franchisee); Call Carl, Inc v BP Oil Corp, 554 F2d 623 (4th Cir), *cert denied,* 434 US 923 (1977) (fraud); Ashland Oil, Inc v Donahue, 223 SE2d 433 (W Va 1976) (unconscionability); Shell Oil Co v Marinello, 63 NJ 402, 307 A2d 598 (1973), *cert denied,* 415 US 920 (1974) (public policy).

[50] *See, e.g.,* Straup v Times Herald, 283 Pa Super 58, 423 A2d 713 (1980).

[51] These and many other situations are discussed in detail in **ch 2.**

[52] *See* Corenswet, Inc v Amana Refrigeration, Inc, 594 F2d 129, 132 (5th Cir), *cert denied,* 444 US 938 (1979) (termination clause of little interest to parties as long as business relationship going well).

Buyer without cause. If Seller desires and the law permits it to terminate Buyer without cause, Seller need not justify its action by any reason, good or bad.[53] Under principles of contract law, Seller's motives for termination are irrelevant.[54] although if other factors are present, Seller may be liable for a business tort[55] or an antitrust violation.[56] Many state laws, however, require good cause for termination of certain classes of Buyers.[57] Moreover, the parties' own agreement may limit Seller's ability to terminate.[58]

§7.12 —Suppose the agreement provides for termination without cause?

An agreement that provides expressly for termination without cause is usually of indefinite duration because the parties intend to deal with each other for as long as both are satisfied with their business relationship.[59] If an agreement contains a definite termination date and an express power to terminate without cause, a court will most likely apply rules of construction to determine whether the parties intended one clause to take precedence over the other.[60]

In *Corenswet, Inc v Amana Refrigeration, Inc,*[61] Buyer sued to prevent Seller from terminating its exclusive distributorship.[62] Their agreement was of indefinite duration, terminable by either party "with or without cause" upon 10

---

[53] *See* Amoco Oil Co v Burns, 496 Pa 336, 437 A2d 381 (1981) (franchise contract authorizing termination without cause allows Seller to terminate without justification). The *Burns* court distinguished Atlantic Richfield Co v Razumic, 480 Pa 366, 390 A2d 736 (1978), on the basis that Razumic's contract permitted Arco, the franchisor, to terminate for limited business reasons rather than without any reason.

[54] In *Burns,* for example, the court looked no further than the written agreement providing for termination without cause. The court believed that only where the parties do not provide for termination rights will the court look to other factors. 437 A2d at 384.

[55] See generally Restatement (Second) of Torts §§762-774A (1977) (refusal to deal, intentional interference with contractual relations).

[56] See generally **ch 2.**

[57] See **§7.14.**

[58] *See* CF Bard, Inc v Medical Elec Corp, 529 F Supp 1382, 1385 (D Mass 1982) (allowing Seller to terminate upon default in payment according to terms); Atlantic Richfield Co v Razumic, 480 Pa 366, 390 A2d 736, 741 (1978) (limiting Seller's ability to terminate to situations in which Buyer abandons or closes premises, causes damages to premises, fails to pay rent, or dies, or where government takes property).

[59] See Goetz & Scott, *Principles of Relational Contracts,* 67 Va L Rev 1089, 1135 (1981) (in the absence of a specific duration term parties are presumed to intend termination at will).

[60] See S. Williston, Treatise on the Law of Contracts §624 (3d ed 1961) (where contract clauses conflict, courts should give effect to more important clause).

[61] 594 F2d 129 (5th Cir), *cert denied,* 444 US 938 (1979).

[62] 594 F2d at 131.

days' notice.[63] A later modification allowed termination by either party "at any time for any reason" upon 10 days' notice.[64]

Buyer argued that "for any reason" implied a good cause limitation on termination. The Court of Appeals for the Fifth Circuit disagreed, and reasoned that parties ordinarily use such language not to limit their powers to terminate but to free them from implied constraints.[65] Thus, the language meant that any reason, good or bad, was sufficient for Seller to terminate.[66]

The court also examined Buyer's arguments based on the Uniform Commercial Code. It first determined that the course of dealing[67] and course of performance[68] between the parties as well as the usage of trade[69] were irreconcilably in conflict with the express contract terms that literally permitted arbitrary termination.[70] Thus, applying the UCC, the court ruled that the express terms prevailed.[71]

Second, the court decided not to read a good faith[72] limitation into the termination clause. In doing so, the court specifically chose not to override UCC §2-309(2), which provides: "Where the contract provides for successive performances but is indefinite in duration, it is valid for a reasonable time but unless otherwise agreed may be terminated at any time by either party."[73]

---

[63] *Id.*

[64] *Id* 132.

[65] *Id* 135.

[66] *Id.* The court added that the language "at any time" indicated further the parties' intent to keep the agreement free from termination restrictions. *Id.*

[67] A course of dealing consists of previous dealings by the parties to a particular transaction that form a common basis for interpreting their conduct. UCC §1-205(1).

[68] A course of performance involves repeated occasions for performance by either party under one contract that form an understanding of the meaning of the contract. UCC §2-208(1).

[69] A usage of trade is a regularly observed practice within a trade, vocation, or place that establishes an expectation that parties to a particular transaction will observe such practice. UCC §1-205(3).

[70] 594 F2d at 136. The court noted that the only law on this issue in Iowa was pre-UCC. In Des Moines Blue Ribbon Distrib v Drewrys Ltd, 256 Iowa 899, 129 NW2d 731 (1964), the Iowa Supreme Court held that the only limitation applicable to an exclusive distributorship contract of indefinite duration was that the terminating party give reasonable notice, not that reasonable cause exist to terminate. The *Corenswet* court believed that Iowa state courts would follow that rule and choose not to interpret the UCC to forbid arbitrary terminations.

[71] Express terms of an agreement are controlling over course of performance, UCC §2-208(2), as well as course of dealing and usage of trade. *Id* §1-205(4).

[72] Good faith is defined as "honesty in fact in the conduct or transaction concerned." *Id* §1-201(19).

[73] *Id* §2-309(2). *See* Rockwell Engg Co v Automatic Timing & Controls Co, 559 F2d 460 (7th Cir 1977) (agency contract of indefinite duration terminable by either party without cause under Indiana law); Aaron E Levine & Co v Calkraft Paper Co, 429 F Supp 1039 (ED Mich 1976) (distributorship agreement of indefinite duration terminable by either party without cause under Michigan law). *See also* Zapatha v Dairy Mart, Inc, 408 NE2d 1370 (Mass 1980) (termination provision did not violate UCC implied

Although a provision for termination without cause may appear valid under *Corenswet,* such a provision may be unconscionable[74] under the UCC or common law if unreasonably favorable to Seller and if Seller imposes it with no meaningful choice to Buyer.[75] One example of an unconscionable provision might be a clause permitting termination without notice if lack of notice would impose an excessive, undue hardship upon Buyer.[76]

---

good faith obligation); *but see* Baker v Ratzlaff, 1 Kan App 2d 285, 564 P2d 153 (1977) (termination prohibited by UCC implied good faith obligation).

Other states, not relying on the UCC, have read a good faith obligation into unrestricted termination clauses of distributorship contracts. This is not the equivalent, however, of implying a reasonable cause limitation. *See* Randolph v New England Mut Life Ins Co, 526 F2d 1383, 1386 (6th Cir 1975) (Ohio law permits termination without cause but not without good faith); De Treville v Outboard Marine Corp, 439 F2d 1099 (4th Cir 1971) (South Carolina law limits unilateral termination power if manner of termination "contrary to equity and good conscience"); Tele-Controls, Inc v Ford Indus, 388 F2d 48, 51 (7th Cir 1967) (Oregon law requires terminations of dealership contracts to be in good faith).

[74] §2-302 permits a court to refuse to enforce a contract if it is unconscionable at the time the parties entered into it. The official comment to §2-302 states generally the test of unconscionability as "whether, in the light of the general commercial background and the commercial needs of the particular trade or case, the clauses involved are so one-sided as to be unconscionable under the circumstances existing at the time of the making of the contract." The comment adds that §2-302 is designed to prevent oppression and unfair surprise but not to disturb allocations of risk resulting from superior bargaining power. See also Goetz & Scott, *Principles of Relational Contracts,* 67 Va L Rev 1089, 1136 (1981) (discussing unconscionability doctrine as limitation on termination).

[75] *See* Zapatha v Dairy Mart, Inc 408 NE2d 1370 (Mass 1980) (termination provision not unconscionable where risks and benefits not allocated in unreasonably disproportionate manner); Corenswet, Inc v Amana Refrigeration, Inc, 594 F2d 129, 139, n 12 (5th Cir), *cert denied,* 444 US 938 (1979) (agreement unconscionable if distributor has no meaningful choice but to deal with seller and to accept offered contract including termination clause which is unreasonably favorable to seller); Ashland Oil, Inc v Donahue, 223 SE2d 433 (W Va 1976) (termination clause giving unilateral right to terminate and sole discretion to one party unconscionable); Central Ohio Co-op Milk Producers, Inc v Rowland, 29 Ohio App 2d 236, 281 NE2d 42 (1972) (termination clause unconscionable where terms onerous, oppressive, or one-sided and bear no reasonable relation to business risks); Shell Oil Co v Marinello, 63 NJ 402, 307 A2d 598 (1973), *cert denied,* 415 US 920 (1974) (termination clause giving franchisor effectively unilateral right to terminate result of disproportionate bargaining position and thus void). For a general discussion of the unconscionability doctrine, *see* Williams v Walker-Thomas Furniture Co, 350 F2d 445 (DC Cir 1965).

[76] Zapatha v Dairy Mart, Inc, 408 NE2d 1370 (Mass 1980). In *Zapatha,* the court determined that a 90-day notice provision was reasonable and thus not unconscionable. *Id.* The court concluded that because the clause was not obscurely worded or hidden, *id,* and the provision did not operate in an oppressive manner, no unfair surprise would result from termination.

§7.13 —Suppose the agreement is silent about termination?

If the agreement is for an indefinite duration, the common law rule that requires performance within a reasonable time applies.[77] If the parties make no provision regarding permitted grounds for termination, either party may terminate the agreement upon reasonable notification and after a reasonable time.[78] In cases involving a potentially long-term relationship, courts imply a reasonable notice period to allow recoupment of initial expenses.[79] This requirement is derived from agency law, which requires that a principal (Seller) who terminates without cause must afford the agent (Buyer) a reasonable opportunity to recoup expenditures made in preparation for performance.[80] The actual length of the notice period depends on several factors: amount of preliminary expenses, length of time the agreement has been in effect, current profits, and prospects for future profits.[81] Seller is not required to pay damages (unless Seller is otherwise in breach), or to wait until Buyer actually recoups its expenses, but only to give Buyer a fair opportunity to do so.[82]

If the agreement has a definite termination date but does not provide specific grounds for termination, a court would most likely interpret the agreement as prohibiting termination without cause. In such a case, the parties apparently intend to deal with each other until the end of the contract term or until cause for termination arises.[83] One example of cause for termination, of course, is

---

[77] S. Williston, Treatise on the Law of Contracts §38 (3d ed 1961); *cf* UCC §2-309(2) (contract indefinite in duration valid for reasonable time but terminable at any time by either party); UCC §2-309(2) comment 7 (where arrangement carried on for years, contract not terminable until notice given).

[78] Goetz & Scott, *Principles of Relational Contracts,* 67 Va L Rev 1089, 1135 (1981). *See, e.g.,* Consolidated Theatres, Inc v Theatrical Stage Employees Local 16, 69 Cal 2d 713, 447 P2d 325, 73 Cal Rptr 213 (1968); Des Moines Blue Ribbon Distrib v Drewrys Ltd, USA, 256 Iowa 899, 129 NW2d 731 (1964).

[79] Ag-Chem Equip Co v Hahn, Inc, 480 F2d 482, 486 (8th Cir 1973). *Cf* Lockewill, Inc v United States Shoe Corp, 547 F2d 1024, 1020 (8th Cir 1976), *cert denied,* 431 US 956 (1977) (purpose of notice is to allow distributor reasonable opportunity to arrange affairs). Note that recoupment is available only where the term of the agreement is indefinite. Schultz v Onan Corp, Bus Fran Guide (CCH) ¶7849 (3d Cir May 28, 1982). If the agreement fails to provide a definite duration term but does contain procedures for termination, it may be construed as prohibiting termination at will. Lichnovsky v Ziebart Intl Corp, Bus Fran Guide (CCH) ¶7904 (Mich Sept 28, 1982).

[80] *See* Jack's Cookie Co v Brooks, 227 F2d 935, 938-39 (4th Cir 1955), *cert denied,* 351 US 908 (1956) (where agent furnishes consideration to distribute manufacturer's goods, manufacturer must retain agent for reasonable period of time); S. Williston, Treatise on the Laws of Contracts §1027(a) (3d ed 1961).

[81] General Tire & Rubber Co v Distribs Inc, 253 NC 459, 117 SE2d 479, 489 (1960).

[82] *Id.*

[83] A court would be unlikely to allow termination without cause because such an interpretation would effectively nullify the specified termination date. See Restatement (Second) of Contracts §204 (1981) (meaning of words, as well as probability that term would have been included if issue had been raised, are factors in determining reasonable construction).

material breach of an agreement.[84]

Seller's duty to perform may be executed or discharged by anticipatory repudiation,[85] waiver,[86] impossibility,[87] commercial impracticability,[88] or frustration,[89] or by operation of law.[90] In addition, Seller and Buyer may agree to rescind, modify, or cancel their agreement.[91]

§7.14 If Seller may not terminate Buyer without cause, what reasons are sufficient to justify termination?

Seller may be prohibited from terminating Buyer without cause when either the agreement itself or a statute requires cause for termination. If no statute applies, the parties may agree to terminate the agreement for any reason at all, whether or not it is related to their own conduct or performance. Further, the parties may provide, if they wish, for notice and cure periods, for automatic termination, or for any other procedure for termination. In general, the parties are free to agree upon any remedies, such as liquidated damages, in connection

---

[84] *See* Suburban Beverages, Inc v Pabst Brewing Co, 462 F Supp 1301, 1312 (ED Wis 1978) (Buyer's sales of Seller's product outside area specified in contract material breach and grounds for termination by Seller); *cf* Burger King Corp v Family Dining, Inc, 426 F Supp 485, 494 (ED Pa), *affd,* 566 F2d 1168 (3d Cir 1977) (provision in agreement limiting number of franchisees in specified area not critical).

[85] The UCC permits Seller to suspend performance when Buyer repudiates causing substantial impairment of the value of the contract to Seller. UCC §2-610(c). The official comment defines substantial impairment as whether material inconvenience will result if the aggrieved party must wait and receive tender without the part repudiated. *Id* comment 3. Seller is similarly discharged from performance under the common law. See Restatement (Second) of Contracts §253(2) (1981) (one party's repudiation discharges other party's remaining duty to perform); Restatement, *supra,* at §250 (statement by party that it will not perform may impair value of contract to other party).

[86] *See* UCC §1-107 (party may waive rights arising out of alleged breach); S. Williston, Treatise on the Law of Contracts §690 (3d ed 1961) (parties may excuse liability on obligation and performance). *Cf* 33 Flavors of Greater Del Valley, Inc v Bresler's 33 Flavors, Inc, 475 F Supp 217, 229 (D Del 1979) (when party to contract learns of breach by other party, but fails to exercise right to terminate, termination right is waived).

[87] See S. Williston, Treatise on the Law of Contracts §§1931-1979 (3d ed 1961) (discussing principles of impossibility defense to liability).

[88] *See* UCC §2-615(a) (nonperformance not breach where performance made impracticable by a contingency which the parties assumed would not occur); Restatement (Second) of Contracts §261 (1981) (same).

[89] See Restatement (Second) of Contracts §265 (1981) (discharge of obligations where "after a contract is made, a party's principal purpose is substantially frustrated without his fault by the occurrence of an event the nonoccurrence of which was a basic assumption on which the contract was made").

[90] S. Williston, Treatise on the Law of Contracts §1793 (3d ed 1961).

[91] *Id.*

with the termination of the agreement.[92]

If a special statute relating to termination does apply, then the parties are somewhat circumscribed in their power to determine the reasons and procedures for ending their relationship. Most statutes which govern termination require *good cause* (or a similar standard) for Seller to terminate Buyer.[93] (Some laws also require good cause for Seller to refuse to renew Buyer.[94]) Some statutes define good cause rather explicitly, while others refer more more generally to Buyer's failure to comply substantially with the terms of the agreement.[95] Many states impose specific requirements for notice and cure periods,[96] and many laws set forth the measure of damages or other appropriate relief for an unlawful termination.[97]

§7.15 —What statutes require good cause for termination?

Both federal and state statutes may require good cause for Seller to terminate Buyer. On the federal level, the Automobile Dealer's Day in Court Act[98] and the Petroleum Marketing Practices Act[99] govern termination of automobile and petroleum dealers, respectively. Although bills have been introduced in Congress in recent years to require good cause for termination of other classes of Buyers,[100] no other federal legislation has yet been enacted.

On the state level, numerous laws apply in various industries: motor vehicle dealer laws (generally more restrictive than the federal law);[101] petroleum wholesaler and dealer laws (preempted to the extent they exceed federal requirements);[102] laws relating to dealers in farm implements, industrial equipment, construction equipment and parts;[103] and laws for alcohol, beer, and wine distributors and dealers.[104] Finally, many states regulate franchise terminations, a category which encompasses many types of distribution arrange-

---

92 See Restatement (Second) of Contracts §361 comment b (1981).

93 See **§7.15.**

94 See **§7.36.**

95 See **§7.16.**

96 See **§7.31.**

97 See **§7.46.**

98 See **§7.06.**

99 See **§7.07.**

100 *See, e.g.,* S1256, 97th Cong, 1st Sess (1981) (Office Machinery and Equipment Retail Dealers' Agreement Act); HR 460, 97th Cong, 1st Sess (1981) (a bill to require good cause for termination of franchise relationships generally; often referred to as a *Mikva Bill,* after the congressman who sponsored this type of legislation in the mid-1970s).

101 See **§7.06, app L.**

102 See **§7.07, app M.**

103 See **app I.**

104 See **app F.**

ments for both products and services.[105]

§7.16 —What is *good cause* under the statutes?

The definitions of *good cause* and related terms range from broad descriptions of a duty of good faith to specific enumerations of acceptable reasons for termination. For the purposes of this chapter, good cause will be treated as synonymous with other terms such as *good faith, due cause,* or *just cause,* and with prohibitions against terminations that are *unfair* or *without due regard to the equities of the dealer.* Although these terms are not identical, they are treated as such in practical effect. Courts apply virtually the same analysis regardless of the specific term used to denote the general standard.[106]

Several statutes specify examples of good cause for termination.[107] A few such examples are: willful abandonment of the business by Buyer, or loss of the business;[108] criminal conviction of Buyer;[109] bankruptcy of Buyer;[110] impairment of Seller's trademark by Buyer;[111] Buyer's failure to pay money owed to Seller;[112] misrepresentation or fraud by Buyer in entering the agreement;[113] Buyer's failure to comply with laws and regulations applicable to business;[114] repeated instances of default by Buyer.[115]

In many of the situations listed above, Seller may be permitted to terminate Buyer immediately upon notice, without an opportunity to cure. For other types of default by Buyer, most statutes require a notice and cure period.[116] A number of states do not distinguish between more serious and less serious types of default. Instead, many states define good cause without reference to

---

[105] See **§7.08, app K.** See also **ch 9.**

[106] Note, however, that *good faith* under termination laws may be viewed as a different concept from the implied obligation of good faith described in **§§7.09** and **7.12.** *See* Brattleboro Auto Sales, Inc v Subaru of New England, Inc, 633 F2d 649 (2d Cir 1980).

[107] All references in notes 108-16 below are to provisions of franchise termination laws listed in **app K.** Certain other states, included in **app G,** prohibit misrepresentation by Seller concerning termination.

[108] Arkansas, California, Connecticut, Illinois, Minnesota, Mississippi, Missouri, New Jersey, Washington. (**App K.**)

[109] Arkansas, California, Connecticut, Illinois, Minnesota, Mississippi, Missouri, Nebraska, New Jersey, Washington. (**App K.**) See also **§7.24.**

[110] Arkansas, California, Illinois, Minnesota, Mississippi, Missouri, Nebraska, Washington, Wisconsin. (**App K.**) See also **§7.18.**

[111] Arkansas, Illinois, Minnesota. (**App K.**)

[112] Arkansas, California, Mississippi, Missouri, Nebraska. (**App K.**) See Also **§7.17.**

[113] California, Mississippi, Missouri, Nebraska. (**App K.**)

[114] California, Minnesota. (**App K.**) See also **§7.24.**

[115] California, Illinois, Washington. (**App K.**) See also **§7.25.**

[116] Arkansas, California, Connecticut, Delaware, Hawaii, Illinois, Indiana, Michigan, Minnesota, Mississippi, Missouri, Nebraska, New Jersey, Washington, Wisconsin. (**App K.**)

specific examples.[117] A typical definition provides that good cause "shall include, but not be limited to, the failure of [Buyer] to comply with any lawful, material provision of the franchise agreement after having been given written notice thereof and an opportunity to cure the failure within a reasonable period of time."[118]

§7.17 —Suppose Buyer fails to pay its debts to Seller?

Failure to pay money owed is probably the most common, and the least vulnerable, ground for termination.[119] Unless the amount in dispute is truly minimal, or unless Buyer is withholding payment because of a legitimate claim against Seller,[120] Seller most likely has good cause to terminate Buyer when Buyer refuses to pay.[121] Note that where a statute applies, Seller often must give notice and an opportunity to cure prior to termination for failure to pay money owed.[122]

§7.18 —Suppose Seller is apprehensive about Buyer's ability to pay?

Under the doctrine of repudiation, if Buyer appears to be prospectively unwilling or unable to perform,[123] Seller can demand assurance of performance.[124] If Buyer fails to give adequate assurance, Seller may treat Buyer's repudiation as a breach and may terminate the agreement. Whether repudia-

---

117 Delaware, Hawaii, Indiana, Michigan, Nebraska, New Jersey, Virginia. (**App K.**) South Dakota prohibits unfair and inequitable practices by franchisors, not limited to termination. (**App J.**)

118 Hawaii Rev Stat § 482E-6(2)(H) (Supp 1978).

119 According to the United States Department of Commerce, 6,756 franchises were terminated in 1980. Of that number, 2,780 (or 40%) were terminated by the franchisor, and of that total, 1,597 (or 57%) were terminated for failure to pay money owed. United States Dept of Commerce, Franchising in the Economy 1980-1982, at 11 (1982).

120 *See, e.g.*, Span-Deck, Inc v Fab-Con, Inc, 677 F2d 1237 (8th Cir 1982) (royalty payments rightfully suspended while franchisee challenged validity of franchisor's patent). *But see* Arthur Treacher's Fish & Chips, Inc v A&B Management Corp, 519 F Supp 739 (ED Pa 1981) (franchisees ordered to pay royalties to near-bankrupt franchisor pending trial on franchisees' claim of breach).

121 *See, e.g.*, Cycleway, Inc v Kawasaki Motors Corp, 77 Misc 2d 829, 354 NYS2d 812 (1974). *But see* Tappan Motors, Inc v Volvo of Am Corp, 85 AD2d 624, 444 NYS2d 938 (1981), *appeal dismissed*, 56 NY2d 632, 435 NE2d 1098, 450 NYS2d 483 (1982).

122 *See* White Hen Pantry v Buttke, 98 Wis 2d 119, 295 NW2d 763 (Ct App 1981) (statute requires at least 90 days' notice for termination; 10-day statutory cure period for nonpayment is not a substitute for full notice period).

123 Buyer's repudiation must be manifested by a statement or a voluntary affirmative act indicating that Buyer will not perform. UCC §2-610 comment 1.

124 See Restatement (Second) of Contracts §§250-257 (1981); UCC §2-609.

tion is sufficient to establish good cause for termination depends on the nature and severity of the underlying problem. One case has held that "mere insecurity" on Seller's part about Buyer's future performance is not sufficient to establish good cause for termination.[125] On the other hand, a pattern of conduct, such as continual late payments, may furnish good cause for termination.[126]

Several state franchise laws specifically recognize Buyer's bankruptcy as good cause for termination.[127] Under current bankruptcy laws, however, Seller must terminate Buyer prior to Buyer's filing for bankruptcy; otherwise, the agreement may be treated as an executory contract which the trustee or debtor may assume.[128] In order to assume the agreement, the trustee or debtor must give adequate assurance of curing existing defaults and performing in the future.[129] Federal bankruptcy courts may use their broad powers to enjoin termination by Seller so long as Buyer or its trustee is complying with a rehabilitation plan.[130]

§7.19 —Suppose Buyer fails to meet sales quotas?

If a definite sales quota is set forth in the agreement, then Buyer's failure to meet the quota ordinarily constitutes a default.[131] Whether such a default provides good cause for termination depends on the facts and circumstances. Courts may examine the reasonableness of the quota[132] and the amount of Buyer's shortfall.[133] Market conditions at the time of the default, rather than at the time of contracting, determine the reasonableness of the termi-

---

[125] Al Bishop Agency, Inc v Lithonia-Div of Natl Serv Indus, 474 F Supp 828 (ED Wis 1979).

[126] *See* Excello Wine Co v Monsieur Henri Wines, Ltd, 474 F Supp 203 (SD Ohio 1979).

[127] Nine states list bankruptcy among permissible grounds for termination. See **§7.17.**

[128] *See, e.g., In re* Chavez, 18 Bankr 530 (DNM 1982) (no termination even though Seller gave notice of default prior to Buyer's reorganization); *In re* Varisco, Bus Fran Guide (CCH) ¶7769 (MD Fla Dec 4, 1981); *In re* Dan Hixson Chevrolet Co, 12 Bankr 917 (ND Tex 1981).

[129] 11 USC §365(b)(1)(A) & (C). *See, e.g., In re* Sapolin Paints, Inc, 5 Bankr 412 (EDNY 1980) (adequacy determined on a case-by-case basis).

[130] *See, e.g., In re* Frank Meador Buick, Inc, 13 Bankr 841 (WD Va 1981). *See also In re* Bronx-Westchester Mack Corp, 20 Bankr 139 (SDNY 1982) (termination enjoined even though Buyer's business was transferred).

[131] *See, e.g.,* Al Bishop Agency, Inc v Lithonia-Div of Natl Serv Indus, 474 F Supp 828 (ED Wis 1979).

[132] *See, e.g.,* Chrysler Motors Corp v Nebraska Motor Vehicle Indus Licensing Bd, 202 Neb 230, 274 NW2d 862 (1979) (no good cause to terminate when no other dealer met its quota).

[133] *See, e.g.,* State-Wide Lighting, Inc v Globe Illum Co, Bus Fran Guide (CCH) ¶825.35 (ED Wis 1979).

nation.[134] For example, if a number of buyers fail to meet their sales quotas and Seller accepts a lesser degree of performance from them, Seller may be prevented from strictly enforcing the quota against a particular Buyer if that Buyer's failure to meet the quota is the only reason for termination.[135] If Buyer actually attains the minimum quota provided in the agreement, Seller may not terminate on the ground that with additional effort, Buyer could have sold more.[136]

§7.20 —Suppose Buyer fails to exercise its best efforts on behalf of Seller?

If Buyer is required under the agreement to exercise its best efforts to promote sales, a mere decline in sales will not constitute good cause for termination.[137] Additional proof that sales were unreasonably low and that Buyer's conduct led to the decreased sales would be required in order to establish good cause.[138]

Seller would have great difficulty in proving good cause for termination if sales actually increased, no matter how inadequate Seller believed the increase to be.[139] Likewise, Seller would encounter problems in attempting to terminate Buyer on the ground that Buyer did not implement Seller's sales suggestions and thus did not achieve the sales increase Seller expected.[140]

§7.21 —Suppose Buyer acquires interests in other businesses?

Seller may have good cause to terminate Buyer if Buyer dissipates its promotional or selling efforts,[141] but the mere fact that Buyer deals with Seller's

---

[134] R&R Assocs, Inc v Deltona Corp, Bus Fran Guide (CCH) ¶7526 (D Conn May 21, 1980).

[135] Madsen v Chrysler Corp, 261 F Supp 488 (ND Ill 1966), *vacated as moot,* 375 F2d 773 (7th Cir 1967).

[136] Executive Business Sys v Philips Business Sys, Bus Fran Guide (CCH) ¶7703 (EDNY July 24, 1981).

[137] Reinders Bros v Rain Bird E Sales Corp, 627 F2d 44 (7th Cir 1980).

[138] *See* Bloor v Falstaff Brewing Corp, 601 F2d 609 (2d Cir 1979) (*best efforts* requires more than good faith compliance; Buyer must show that no other significant steps could have been taken to improve sales).

[139] Wilburn v Jack Cartwright, Inc, 514 F Supp 493 (ED Wis 1979) *revd & remanded,* 676 F2d 698 (7th Cir 1982). On remand, the issue was whether the relationship constituted a franchise under state law. The district court reaffirmed its original decision. Bus Fran Guide (CCH) ¶7874 (ED Wis May 28, 1982).

[140] *See* Al Bishop Agency, Inc v Lithonia-Div of Natl Serv Indus, 474 F Supp 828 (ED Wis 1979).

[141] *See, e.g.,* Day Enters, Inc v Crown Cent Petroleum Corp, 529 F Supp 1291 (D Md 1982) (dealer failed to devote "substantial full time" to business, as required in agreement).

competitors does not constitute good cause.[142] However, if Buyer deals with seller's competitors to such an extent that, as a practical matter, Buyer cannot properly promote Seller's product, such conduct may furnish good cause for termination.[143]

§7.22 —Suppose Buyer transfers part or all of its interest in its own business?

Some state statutes may prohibit Seller from unreasonably withholding permission for Buyer to transfer part or all of its business.[144] Seller may refuse permission, however, if the proposed transferee is unqualified because of lack of capital, lack of adequate experience, or other such reasons.[145] Seller has broad discretion to disapprove a proposed transferee;[146] however, under the statutes governing transfers, Seller must act reasonably, and Seller's decision is measured by an objective standard.[147]

If a statute governing transfer applies and if Buyer failed to observe the statute by not seeking Seller's approval of a transfer, or by transferring to a person whom Seller had reasonably disapproved, then Seller would have good cause to terminate Buyer.[148] If no transfer statute applies, Buyer and Seller are bound by the terms of their agreement. If the agreement forbids transfer by Buyer, any unauthorized transfer by Buyer probably would furnish good cause for Seller to terminate the agreement.[149]

§7.23 —Suppose Buyer fails to meet standards set by Seller?

Agreements often contain provisions requiring Buyer to meet certain standards of service, operation, sanitation, etc. Whether Buyer's failure to meet

---

[142] *See* Reinders Bros v Rain Bird E Sales Corp, 627 F2d 44 (7th Cir 1980).

[143] Brattleboro Auto Sales, Inc v Subaru of New England, Inc, 633 F2d 649 (2d Cir 1980).

[144] Arkansas, Hawaii, Minnesota, Nebraska, New Jersey. (**App K.**) *See also* Florida. (**App G.**)

[145] For example, the franchise relations law in Hawaii allows a franchisor to refuse permission to transfer if the proposed transferee fails to meet reasonable standards or refuses to sign the current form of agreement; if the proposed transferee is a competitor of the franchisor; or if the franchisee or the proposed transferee fails to pay money owed or to have cured existing defaults by the time of the proposed transfer. Hawaii Rev Stat §482E-6(2)(I) (Supp 1978).

[146] Hamro v Shell Oil Co, 674 F2d 784 (9th Cir 1982).

[147] Richter v Dairy Queen, Inc, 131 Ariz 595, 643 P2d 508 (Ct App 1982).

[148] Simmons v General Motors Corp, 180 NJ Super 522, 435 A2d 1167 (1981).

[149] Hamro v Shell Oil Co, 674 F2d 784 (9th Cir 1982) (tortious interference claim by dealer failed because Seller did not employ wrongful means and acted to protect its own interest).

such standards constitutes good cause for termination depends on the seriousness of Buyer's default.[150] An occasional small lapse by buyer probably would not be good cause for termination, but persistent failure to comply with Seller's standards might be good cause, as might a single instance of a very egregious noncompliance. If Buyer's conduct has drawn significant consumer complaints, Seller may be found to be justified in terminating Buyer. This might occur, for example, if Buyer's location is kept in an unsanitary condition or if Buyer permits rude and abusive treatment of customers.[151]

§7.24 —Suppose Buyer violates the law?

Some statutes provide that Seller has good cause to terminate Buyer if Buyer is found guilty of any criminal conduct related to Buyer's business.[152] In addition, Seller probably would be justified in terminating Buyer for certain other kinds of crimes if they brought the business into disrepute. Courts have readily permitted terminations in cases where the Buyer was found guilty of price-gouging,[153] misbranding,[154] and consumer fraud.[155]

§7.25 —Suppose Buyer and Seller are continually at odds with each other?

Seller may desire to terminate Buyer not because of a particular breach but because Seller and Buyer have differences with each other which impede their business relationship. If seller is unable to persuade Buyer to agree to terminate their agreement,[156] it is unlikely that dissension alone would furnish good cause for Seller to terminate Buyer. If Seller and Buyer have irreconcilable differences, coupled with a pattern of uncooperative conduct by Buyer, then

---

[150] *See, e.g.,* Walters v Chevron USA, Inc, 476 F Supp 353 (ND Ga 1979) *affd,* 615 F2d 1135 (5th Cir 1980); Frisard v Texaco, Inc, 460 F Supp 1094 (ED La 1978). *But see* Lewis v Exxon Corp, Bus Fran Guide (CCH) ¶7914 (DDC Nov 10, 1982) (termination enjoined pending Buyer's appeal of conviction of felony involving moral turpitude); Tappan Motors, Inc v Volvo of Am Corp, 85 AD2d 624, 444 NYS2d 938 (1981), *appeal dismissed,* 56 NY2d 632, 435 NE2d 1098, 450 NYS2d 483 (1982) (although Buyer failed to meet reasonable standards imposed by Seller, termination was enjoined because of hardship to Buyer).

[151] *See, e.g.,* Dayan v McDonald's Corp, No 70 CH 2258 (Ill Cir Ct Sept 9, 1982); Orr v Texaco, Inc, Bus Fran Guide (CCH) ¶7589 (ND Ga Dec 5, 1980); Aselta v Radio Shack Div of Tandy Corp, Bus Fran Guide (CCH) ¶825.22 (DNJ 1977).

[152] Arkansas, California, Connecticut, Illinois, Minnesota, Mississippi, Missouri, Nebraska, New Jersey, Washington. (**App K.**)

[153] Palombi v Getty Oil Co, 501 F Supp 158 (ED Pa 1980).

[154] Stewart v Shell Oil Co, 518 F Supp 6 (D Nev 1980); Haynes v Exxon Co, USA, 512 F Supp 543 (ED Tenn 1981).

[155] AAMCO Indus v DeWolf, 312 Minn 95, 250 NW2d 835 (1977).

[156] California recognizes mutual agreement to terminate as good cause for termination. Cal Bus & Prof Code §20021(c) (West 1981).

Seller may be able to show that good cause for termination exists.[157] But if Seller's true motive is retaliation against Buyer for political and legal activities, for example, then good cause probably will not be found.[158]

Some statutes permit termination if Buyer engages in a series of defaults, the cumulative effect of which amounts to good cause for termination.[159]

§7.26 May Seller terminate Buyer for reasons unrelated to Buyer's performance?

Ordinarily, if Buyer is performing satisfactorily, Seller will not be prompted to terminate their relationship. There may be situations, however, in which Seller has other reasons for desiring to terminate Buyer: Seller may be losing money, or may want to change its marketing strategy. If Seller for some reason is not able to terminate Buyer without cause and if Buyer is not in breach of the agreement, Seller may nevertheless be permitted to terminate Buyer in certain circumstances. The parties may specify in their agreement any (otherwise lawful) grounds for termination, whether related to their own dealings or not.[160] If a special termination statute applies, however, Seller may need *good cause* to terminate Buyer. Reasons for termination which are not related to Buyer's performance usually will not suffice as good cause.[161] In addition, general principles of good faith and unconscionability may limit Seller's ability to terminate when Buyer is not in breach.[162]

---

157 *See* Excello Wine Co v Monsieur Henri Wines, Ltd, 474 F Supp 203 (SD Ohio 1979).

158 *See* Graves v Texaco, Inc, Bus Fran Guide (CCH) ¶7637 (D Mass Mar 6, 1981) (dealer claimed termination was retaliation for two lawsuits he brought against Seller and for his outspoken support of prodealer legislation). Termination based on race, sex, or other suspect classifications is prohibited by the California Fair Dealership Law, Cal Civ Code, §§80-86 (West 1980). A buyer who is terminated for such reasons also might have a federal cause of action under 42 USC §1981. *See* Sud v Import Motors Ltd, 379 F Supp 1064 (WD Mich 1974) (denial of dealership, allegedly based on race, states a claim under §1981).

159 California, Illinois, Washington. (App K) *But cf* Baal v McDonald's Corp, 97 Ill App 3d 495, 422 NE2d 1166 (1981) (franchisee's prior misconduct does not trigger *unclean hands* doctrine; franchisee not barred from obtaining an equitable remedy under a different agreement with same franchisor).

160 In that case, the common law contract rules would apply. Seller might be able to terminate the agreement on grounds of impossibility, impracticability, or frustration; or the agreement may be terminated by operation of law. See **§7.13.**

161 See **§7.14.**

162 *See, e.g.,* Baker v Ratzlaff, 1 Kan App 2d 285, 564 P2d 153 (1977) (Seller terminated output contract in rising market, based on Buyer's failure to pay on delivery as agreed; court found Seller's failure to demand payment was bad faith and ordered Seller to pay damages based on difference between market price and contract price at time of termination).

§7.27 —Suppose Seller is losing money in its dealings with Buyer?

Seller may not lawfully terminate Buyer merely because of increased expenses unless the increase is hugely disproportionate to the normal cost of performing such an agreement.[163] In the case of a contract for the sale of goods, Buyer's remedy for Seller's refusal to sell in a rising market would be the difference between the contract price and either the market price or the cost of replacement goods, plus incidental and consequential damages, and less expenses saved.[164] In the case of a contract for services, Buyer could recover similar damages or possibly demand and receive specific performance.[165]

§7.28 —Suppose Seller wants to change its marketing strategy?

Some cases and statutes recognize that Seller may, in good faith and for good reasons, desire to terminate Buyer in order to implement a different marketing strategy. Under certain state franchise laws, termination because of a change in marketing strategy does not constitute good cause, and a franchisor terminating for that reason alone may be liable to its franchisee for damages.[166] Under the federal Petroleum Marketing Practices Act, termination on the ground of withdrawal from the relevant geographical market area is permitted, subject to certain conditions. Among those conditions are that the dealer must be given a right of first refusal on the sale of the leased premises and that the termination must not be for the purpose of vertical integration by Seller.[167]

---

[163] See Restatement (Second) of Contracts §261 (1981).

> Performance may be impracticable because extreme and unreasonable difficulty, expense, injury, or loss to one of the parties will be involved. . . . However, "impracticability" means more than "impracticality." A mere change in the degree of difficulty or expense due to such causes as increased wages, prices of raw materials, or costs of construction, unless well beyond the normal range, does not amount to impracticability since it is this sort of risk that a fixed-price contract is intended to cover.

Id comment d. *See, e.g.*, Eastern Air Lines, Inc v Gulf Oil Corp, 415 F Supp 429 (SD Fla 1975); Northern Corp v Chugach Elec Assn, 563 P2d 883 (Alaska 1977).

[164] UCC §2-712(2).

[165] See Restatement (Second) of Contracts §§345, 347 (1981).

[166] *See, e.g.*, Kealey Pharmacy & Home Care Servs, Inc v Walgreen Co, Bus Fran Guide (CCH) ¶7841 (WD Wis June 3, 1982); Designs in Medicine, Inc v Xomed, Inc, 522 F Supp 1054 (ED Wis 1981); Westfield Centre Serv, Inc v Cities Serv Oil Co, 86 NJ 453, 432 A2d 48 (1981). *But see* St. Joseph Equip v Massey-Ferguson, Inc, Bus Fran Guide (CCH) ¶7895 (WD Wis Sept 13, 1982).

[167] 15 USC §2802(b)(2)(E). *Cf* Amoco Oil Co v Burns, 496 Pa 336, 437 A2d 381 (1981) (Seller's good faith decision to divest itself of unprofitable property was good cause for nonrenewal).

Even if a termination is lawful under applicable statutes, it may violate the terms of the agreement between Seller and Buyer. In the case of withdrawal from a market or a line of business, Seller would not be required to continue the relationship, but Seller might be liable to Buyer for damages caused by the termination.[168] In addition, even if the contract does not prohibit such termination, a court might find that under rules of equity, Seller must purchase Buyer's interest in the agreement.[169]

§7.29 —Suppose Seller wants to enter the market itself?

If Seller wants to terminate Buyer so that Seller can enter the market itself, the principles discussed above[170] generally apply. In addition, some special problems may arise in the context of a full or partial vertical integration. These problems generally pertain to antitrust and unfair competition law, which are covered in other chapters of this volume.[171]

§7.30 Suppose a third party is involved in Seller's decision to terminate Buyer?

Under general contract law, it makes no difference whether Seller terminates on its own initiative or at the request or urging of another. Seller's most significant potential liability in this situation is under the antitrust laws.[172] In addition, there may be a cause of action under tort law for wrongful interference in the contractual relations of another.[173]

§7.31 Must Seller give Buyer notice and an opportunity to cure before termination?

If the parties have provided in their agreement for notice and/or opportunity to cure prior to termination, generally they are bound by the terms of their agreement.[174] Note, however, that in some states, a termination statute may

---

[168] J&S Home Realty, Inc v Anaconda Co, 172 Mont 236, 563 P2d 566 (1977).

[169] Straup v Times Herald, 283 Pa Super 58, 423 A2d 713 (1980).

[170] See **§§7.26-7.28.**

[171] See generally **ch 8.**

[172] See generally **§§2.30, 2.40.**

[173] See Restatement (Second) of Torts §766 (1977); Hamro v Shell Oil Co, 674 F2d 784 (9th Cir 1982); Frank Coulson, Inc Buick v Gen Motors Corp, 488 F2d 202 (5th Cir 1974); Diehl & Sons v International Harvester Co, 445 F Supp 282 (EDNY 1978).

[174] Division of Triple T Serv Inc v Mobil Oil Corp, 60 Misc 2d 270, 304 NYS2d 191 (1969), *affd,* 34 AD2d 618, 311 NYS2d 961 (1970).

override the terms of the contract.[175]

If the parties have not provided for notice and/or opportunity to cure prior to termination, either statutory or common law may apply. The common law rule is reflected in Uniform Commercial Code §2-309, which requires reasonable notice unless otherwise agreed by the parties, and notice in any event if lack of notice would be unconscionable.[176] Neither common law nor the UCC requires that an opportunity to cure be given, unless the agreement so provides.[177]

§7.32 —What is a reasonable time for notice?

Assuming that there is no applicable statute setting the time for notice, the parties may set their own time limit, provided that it is not unconscionable in operation. A notice period might be found unconscionable if Seller had imposed the requirement without giving Buyer any opportunity to negotiate, and if the short notice period worked to the extreme detriment of Buyer.[178]

If the parties did not specify a time for notice in their agreement, a reasonable time period is implied.[179] Reasonableness depends on the circumstances of each case, including the general commercial needs of each party. Termination virtually immediately upon notice may be reasonable if, for example, Buyer is bankrupt or has committed a crime related to the business.[180] On the other hand, a longer notice period is required in most situations.[181]

---

[175] Arkansas, California, Connecticut, Delaware, Illinois, Michigan, Minnesota, Mississippi, Missouri, Nebraska, New Jersey, Washington, Wisconsin. (App K) In addition, Hawaii requires reasonable prior notice, and Indiana requires 90 days' notice unless the parties provide otherwise. Snihurowycz v AAMCO Transmissions, Inc, 418 NE2d 1190 (Ind Ct App 1981). A number of statutes permit automatic termination upon the occurrence of specified defaults. See **§7.16.** Some motor vehicle dealer statutes provide for a shorter notice period in some cases, *e.g.*, unlawful transfer by dealer, Simmons v General Motors Corp, 180 NJ Super 522, 435 A2d 1167 (1981); poor financial condition of dealer, Annapolis Motors, Inc v Motor Vehicle Admin, Bus Fran Guide (CCH) ¶7831 (Md Cir Ct Mar 16, 1982).

[176] The test for unconscionability is applied as of the time the agreement was entered, not as of the time of termination. Sinkoff Beverage Co v Jos Schlitz Brewing Co, 51 Misc 2d 446, 273 NYS2d 364 (1966).

[177] Generally each party is obliged to perform exactly according to the contract terms under both common law and UCC law. See Restatement (Second) of Contracts §235 (1981); UCC §§2-601, 2-703. If the breach is not material, however, it may be treated as not affecting the other party's duty to perform. See Restatement (Second) of Contracts §241 (1981); UCC §2-608.

[178] *See, e.g.*, Ashland Oil Inc v Donahue, 223 SE2d 433 (W Va 1976) (10-day notice period found unconscionable).

[179] UCC §2-309(3).

[180] See **§7.16.**

[181] *See, e.g.*, AR Dervaes Co v Houdaille Indus, Bus Fran Guide (CCH) ¶7803 (Del Ch Ct Sept 29, 1981) (5 weeks is reasonable notice); Cycleway, Inc v Kawasaki Motors Corp, 77 Misc 2d 829, 354 NYS2d 812 (1974) (30 days' notice "not contrary to public policy").

Where a statutory notice period applies, it is normally strictly enforced. If Seller attempts to terminate in a shorter time period than that permitted by the statute, the usual remedy is to enjoin termination for at least the statutory period.[182] Some courts, however, have enjoined such termination beyond that time, until the propriety of the termination has been decided at trial.[183]

§7.33 —Must formal notice be given?

Unless a statute requires otherwise, the parties may adopt any form of notice, and they are bound by their agreement. If they fail to provide a formal notice procedure, the Uniform Commercial Code or common law may apply. In that case, notice may be either actual or constructive. If notice is not actual, Buyer must have reason to know the substance of the notice, based on all the facts and circumstances known to Buyer at the time in question.[184] Seller "gives" notice by "taking such steps as may be reasonably required to inform the other in ordinary course whether or not such other actually comes to know of it."[185] Buyer "receives" notice when it is duly delivered at the designated place of business or when it "comes to [Buyer's] attention."[186]

If a termination statute applies, it may provide special procedures for notice,[187] and it also may govern the content of the notice.[188] Seller may be obliged to state reasons for termination[189] or to advise Buyer of any rights Buyer may have with respect to cure.[190] In addition, some motor vehicle dealer laws require that Seller also notify a state agency at the same time notice is sent

---

182 Paul Reilly Co v Dynaforce Corp, 449 F Supp 1033 (ED Wis 1978). *Cf* United States Surgical Corp v Oregon Medical & Surgical Specialties, Inc, 497 F Supp 68 (SDNY 1980) (sales arrangement found to be a franchise, but since contractual notice period exceeded notice required by statute, termination was permitted).

183 *See, e.g.,* Burn-Valley Drug, Inc v Walgreen Co, Bus Fran Guide (CCH) ¶7740 (Minn Dist Ct Sept 12, 1980) (termination enjoined pending determination of whether arrangement was a franchise).

184 UCC §1-201(25).

185 *Id* §1-201(26).

186 *Id.*

187 For example, notice must usually be in writing. Graves v Texaco, Inc, Bus Fran Guide (CCH) ¶7637 (D Mass Mar 6, 1981).

188 Notice may be required in circumstances other than termination or nonrenewal. For example, a market withdrawal, Designs in Medicine, Inc v Xomed, Inc, 522 F Supp 1054 (ED Wis 1981), or a new form of agreement, Executive Business Sys v Philips Business Sys, Bus Fran Guide (CCH) ¶7703 (EDNY July 24, 1981), may require formal notice.

189 *See, e.g.,* Mobil Oil Corp v Clark, 652 F2d 2 (8th Cir 1981).

190 If a cure period is required and if Seller intends to terminate upon Buyer's failure to cure, then the notice must refer to both the cure period and the termination notice period. *See* White Hen Pantry v Buttke, 98 Wis 2d 119, 295 NW2d 763 (Ct App 1981). The notice probably need not specify that Buyer failed to cure, so long as it does state a reason for termination. Orr v Texaco Inc, Bus Fran Guide (CCH) ¶7589 (ND Ga Dec 5, 1980).

to Buyer.[191]

§7.34 —When must Buyer be afforded an opportunity to cure?

If Buyer is afforded an opportunity to correct a breach on which termination is grounded, Buyer may effect a proper cure to avoid termination. A proper cure consists of performance that brings Buyer into substantial compliance with its obligations.[192] What constitutes substantial compliance is a factual question which may vary according to the circumstances.[193]

Buyer usually is bound by a definite time limit in effecting a cure. Periods for cure usually are short,[194] but a court might extend the period if cure would be impracticable in the time allowed.[195] A court also might extend the period for cure where a special statute applies.[196]

---

[191] *See, e.g.,* Fiat Motors of N Am, Inc v Calvin, 356 So 2d 908 (Fla Dist Ct App), *cert denied,* 360 So 2d 1247 (Fla 1978); Mazda Motors of Am, Inc v Southwestern Motors, Inc, 36 NC App 1, 243 SE2d 793 (1978), *affd in part & revd in part,* 296 NC 357, 250 SE2d 250 (1979).

[192] *See* Wash Rev Code §19.100.180(2)(j) (1981) (after franchisee fails to comply with material provisions of agreement and to cure or initiate substantial action to cure, franchisor may terminate franchisee).

Under the UCC, if Buyer rejects nonconforming goods, Seller may cure so long as the time for performance has not expired, Seller notifies Buyer of its intention to cure, and Seller cures within the contract time. UCC §2-508(1). Seller may have time to cure beyond the contract period if it had reasonable grounds to believe that the nonconforming tender would be acceptable. *Id* §2-508(2).

[193] The degree of performance required for substantial compliance is not exact. Factors which must be considered include the ratio between the work left unperformed to that completed, the ratio of the dollar value of the work left unperformed to that completed, the character of performance, the extent to which nonperformance defeats the purposes of the work, and the degree to which a party can correct errors and omissions without tearing down and starting over again. See Corbin on Contracts §§704-706 (1952) (discussing factors that courts use in determining substantial performance); Tolstoy Constr Co v Minter, 78 Cal App 3d 665, 143 Cal Rptr 570 (1978) (substantial performance is matter of degree determined relative to all other factors).

[194] *See* Wash Rev Code Ann §19.100.180(2)(j) (1981) (30-day cure period); Al Bishop Agency, Inc v Lithonia-Div of Natl Serv Indus, 474 F Supp 828 (ED Wis 1979) (contract providing for 60-day cure period); Paul Reilly Co v Dynaforce Corp, 449 F Supp 1033, 1036 (ED Wis 1978) (discussing 60-day cure provision under Wisconsin law).

[195] *See* 33 Flavors of Greater Del Valley, Inc v Bresler's 33 Flavors, Inc, 475 F Supp 217, 230 (D Del 1979) (30 days in which to cure by meeting quota unreasonable); Al Bishop Agency, Inc v Lithonia-Div of Natl Serv Indus, 474 F Supp 828, 836 (ED Wis 1979) (granting dealer over 6 months extra to cure defects); *cf* Jorgensen v Pressnall, 274 Or 285, 545 P2d 1382 (1976) (party effecting cure does not have unlimited amount of time to cure defects). Notice and an opportunity to cure may not be required where it would be futile to do so. *See* AAMCO Indus v DeWolf, 312 Minn 95, 250 NW2d 835 (1977) (cause for termination was conviction for fraud).

[196] *See* Paul Reilly Co v Dynaforce Cop, 449 F Supp 1033, 1036 (ED Wis 1978) (imposing 60-day cure period under Wisconsin law despite absence of cure provision in agreement).

Generally, Seller has no obligation to afford Buyer an opportunity to cure unless a statute or the agreement requires it. If the agreement provides for cure, certain conditions may apply. For example, Seller may require accelerated performance in the event of default.[197] Acceleration clauses are not prohibited as long as their terms are reasonable. Some courts, however, may examine Seller's good faith in invoking the clause.[198]

§7.35 —Suppose Buyer has been in default before?

If Buyer has previously been in default but has not yet been terminated, Seller's current right to terminate may be affected. If Seller ignored or waived previous instances of default, Seller may be estopped from strictly enforcing the agreement later.[199] But if Seller had no reason to know of prior defaults, or if Seller knew and complained to Buyer about them, then Seller will not be considered to have waived its right to terminate for past or present defaults.[200]

Seller may be able to terminate Buyer if Buyer continually engages in defaults, even though Buyer cures each default within the proper time limit. Some state statutes specify that this situation constitutes good cause for termination.[201]

---

[197] *See* Brown v Avemco Inv Corp, 603 F2d 1367, 1369 (9th Cir 1979) (discussing acceleration clause providing that upon default on note, principal and interest immediately due); Sheppard Fed Credit Union v Palmer, 408 F2d 1369, 1371 (5th Cir 1969) (discussing broad acceleration clause that allowed mortgagee to collect entire amount owed if he felt insecure).

[198] *See* Brown v Avemco Inv Corp, 603 F2d at 1376 (evaluating fairness of invoking acceleration clause under equitable principles); *see also* Vaughan v Crown Plumbing & Sewer Serv, Inc, 523 SW2d 72 (Tex Civ App 1975) (acceleration clause invalid where facts make its use unjust or oppressive); Sheppard Fed Credit Union v Palmer, 408 F2d at 1371 (clauses permitting acceleration at will or when insecure are operative only when good faith belief exists that prospect of payment or performance impaired).

[199] See Restatement (Second) of Contracts §84 (1981).

[200] Seller's failure to object operates as a promise to continue performance "to the extent that it justifies [Buyer] in believing that subsequent performances will be accepted" despite Buyer's previous defaults. Restatement (Second) of Contracts §247 (1981). If Seller consistently complained of Buyer's defaults, then Buyer may not be justified in such a belief. *Id* comment a.

[201] California, Illinois, Washington. (**App K.**) Under an appropriate fact situation, a Seller could be negligent for failing to terminate a Buyer which is continually in default. *See* Cullen v BMW of N Am, Inc Bus Fran Guide (CCH) ¶7888 (2d Cir Oct 13, 1982) (trial court's finding of negligence by Seller overturned on ground that Seller could not have reasonably foreseen criminal activity of Buyer which was subject of consumer's complaint).

§7.36 May Seller refuse to renew its agreement with Buyer?

Unless a statute requires it, Seller is not obligated to give Buyer a right to renew their agreement when its term expires. The parties may agree to provide for renewal and they may set conditions for renewal. Generally, the parties are bound by the terms of their agreement. If the agreement is silent on the question of renewal, it is presumed that no right to renew exists, and the contract expires according to its terms.

Some statutes restrict Seller's ability to refuse to renew.[202] A number of statutes require prior notice to Buyer of Seller's decision not to renew,[203] and a few statutes require good cause for nonrenewal.[204] In most cases, good cause for nonrenewal is the same as good cause for termination. The federal Petroleum Marketing Practices Act requires Seller to offer Buyer the opportunity to renew; however, a permissible ground for nonrenewal under that act is failure to agree on changes to the agreement which are proposed in good faith.[205]

§7.37 What circumstances may be deemed the equivalent of a termination or a nonrenewal by Seller even though they are not described as such?

Sometimes Seller's conduct toward Buyer may be considered to be the equivalent of an unlawful termination even though Seller did not formally terminate Buyer. A Seller which wants to end its relationship with Buyer may be tempted to take actions designed to cause Buyer to default, to force Buyer to withdraw from the agreement, or to reduce significantly the value of Buyer's investment. These types of situations are discussed below. Very few statutes specifically address such conduct, but courts may rely on several sources of law to proscribe such conduct, including general contract and tort law, and antitrust and unfair competition laws.

---

[202] The statutes which govern nonrenewal typically require either notice, or notice and good cause, or notice and repurchase. A few statutes operate simply to enforce the terms of the agreement, if any, concerning renewal. In the motor vehicle and petroleum industries, where dealers' capital investments are very large, nonrenewal often is treated as virtually equivalent to termination.

[203] Arkansas, California, Hawaii, Illinois, Indiana, Michigan, Minnesota, Mississippi, Missouri, Nebraska, Washington. (**App K.**)

[204] Connecticut, New Jersey, Wisconsin. In addition, Delaware forbids unjustly failing to renew. (**App K.**)

[205] 15 USC §2802(b)(3)(A). *See, e.g.*, Thompson v Kerr-McGee Ref Corp, 660 F2d 1380 (10th Cir 1981), *cert denied,* 102 S Ct 1716 (1982).

§7.38 —Is there any limitation on the right of Seller to enforce the terms of the agreement strictly?

Parties to an agreement are generally bound by its express terms. Thus, Seller generally may enforce the agreement strictly according to its terms. In some cases, however, a court might find that the provisions Seller seeks to enforce are unreasonable; for example, a sales quota might be unreasonably high.[206] In that event, the court might forbid Seller to terminate so long as Buyer has reasonably complied with the lawful terms of the agreement.

The agreement may contain an acceleration clause which permits Seller to demand faster or additional performance if Buyer defaults.[207] Such a clause in itself is lawful; however, Seller must exercise its power in good faith.[208] As noted above, if Seller has waived previous defaults by Buyer, Seller may be deemed to waive future strict compliance as well.[209]

Seller should exercise care in attempting to impose new conditions for performance by Buyer. In making such changes, especially if not all Buyers are affected, Seller may risk violating the Robinson-Patman Act[210] or other laws which forbid certain kinds of discrimination among Buyers.[211]

§7.39 —May Seller increase competition in Buyer's market by adding other outlets or dealers?

In a classic case of encroachment, Seller had granted Buyer an area franchise under which Buyer was entitled to develop 15 outlets in a particular area. After Buyer had fulfilled its development obligation, Seller decided to cut back on its sales of franchises, repurchase its most successful franchises, and preempt desirable locations. Seller carried out this plan by, among other things, saturating its buyers' markets with outlets of its own. Buyer sued Seller and won on a number of claims, including antitrust and breach of contract. The court also awarded punitive damages to Buyer, because of Seller's blatant bad faith.[212]

Most encroachment situations involve far less extreme conduct, yet Seller

---

[206] See **§7.19.** *See also* Carlo C Gelardi Corp v Miller Brewing Co, 502 F Supp 637 (DNJ 1980).

[207] *See* UCC §3-109(1) (acceleration in context of commercial paper).

[208] *See* Brown v Avemco Inv Corp, 603 F2d 1367 (9th Cir 1979).

[209] See **§7.35.**

[210] See **ch 3.**

[211] Some state laws (Hawaii, Illinois, Indiana, Minnesota, Washington) prohibit discrimination between franchisees. Justifiable and nonarbitrary differences in treatment, however, are generally permitted. (**App K.**)

[212] Photovest Corp v Fotomat Corp, 606 F2d 704 (7th Cir 1979), *cert denied,* 445 US 917 (1980).

may be liable under antitrust[213] or contract law,[214] as in the case above, or under special statutes. In particular, several motor vehicle dealer laws prescribe procedures and standards for the award of additional dealerships of the same line-make in a particular market area.[215] A few states also have laws designed to curb encroachment by franchisors. Generally, these laws operate only where an exclusive territory has been granted.[216]

§7.40 What issues should Seller consider when deciding whether to terminate Buyer?

The following checklist suggests some issues which Seller should consider when considering termination of Buyer.

A. The Agreement
  1. Is there a written agreement?
  2. Has the agreement been modified
     a. formally?
     b. informally by course of dealing or waiver?
  3. Is the duration of the agreement
     a. indefinite?
     b. definite?
     c. definite, with a right to renew?
  4. Does the agreement provide for termination
     a. at will?
     b. for specified causes?
     c. for good cause?
  5. Does the agreement provide for
     a. notice prior to termination?
     b. opportunity to cure?
  6. Does the agreement provide for

---

[213] See also **ch 8.**

[214] A likely claim would be breach of the obligation of good faith; however, if Seller did not promise that it would not compete with Buyer, then ordinary expansion by Seller is not prohibited. *See, e.g.,* New York Motel Enter, Inc v Holiday Inns, Inc, 1980-1 Trade Cas ¶63,167 (Sup Ct NY 1980); McAlpine v AAMCO Automatic Transmissions, Inc, 461 F Supp 1232 (ED Mich 1978).

[215] *See generally* New Motor Vehicle Bd v Orrin W Fox Co, 439 US 96 (1978).

[216] Hawaii, Michigan, Minnesota, Washington. In addition, Indiana prohibits "competing unfairly within a reasonable area" whether or not the arrangement is termed "exclusive." Also, Wisconsin prohibits a franchisor from changing the competitive circumstances of its franchisees—a broad prohibition which could include encroachment and other conduct as well. (**App K.**) See also Florida. (**App G.**)

a. repurchase of inventory?

b. liquidated damages?

c. other

B. The Governing Law

1. What law governs the agreement

a. under express choice-of-law clause?

b. under choice-of-law principles?

c. under applicable statutes?

2. Do special termination statutes apply?

a. motor vehicle dealership

b. petroleum dealership

c. franchise

d. farm implements, construction equipment, etc., dealerships

e. liquor, beer, or wine dealerships

3. If a special statute applies, does it require

a. prior notice?

b. opportunity for cure?

c. good cause?

d. repurchase?

e. state administrative hearing?

4. If a special statute applies, does it operate in case of nonrenewal?

C. Questions for Seller

1. If Buyer is wrongfully terminated, what is Seller's potential exposure

a. under agreement?

b. under special statutes?

c. under antitrust, tort, or other laws?

2. Do documents or other evidence exist which

a. show default by Buyer?

b. show default by Seller?

c. show other conduct by Seller which could lead to liability?

3. Is Seller's motive for terminating Buyer

a. acceptable as good cause under applicable law?

b. acceptable under antitrust laws?

4. Can Seller persuade Buyer to agree to termination?

5. Is Buyer likely to terminate the agreement on its own?

6. Does Buyer have other claims against Seller which Buyer will proba-

bly assert in the event of termination? Would the claims be asserted otherwise?

7. Has Seller allowed other Buyers to do the same thing without objection?
8. Where do the equities lie?

§7.41 May Buyer cease purchasing from Seller?

Buyer may cease purchasing from Seller for essentially the same reasons for which Seller could terminate Buyer, e.g., material breach by Seller; mistake, impossibility, illegality, or other factors rendering the agreement void or voidable; and exercise of a contractual right to terminate, either with or without cause.[217] The special termination statutes do not govern termination of Seller by Buyer; hence, Seller generally must rely on contract, tort, Uniform Commercial Code or antitrust law to obtain relief from an unlawful termination by Buyer.[218]

§7.42 —May Buyer assign its contractual rights and obligations to another party?

If the agreement prohibits assignment by Buyer, then an attempt by Buyer to assign its interest is a breach. If the agreement permits assignment, Buyer may assign subject to the conditions therein. If the agreement is silent, Buyer probably would be permitted to assign its interest unless Buyer is uniquely qualified to perform its duties under the agreement (e.g., a personal service contract).[219]

Some franchise statutes prevent Seller from imposing unreasonable restrictions on the transfer of Buyer's interest.[220] Some motor vehicle dealer laws

---

[217] Cf **§7.11** (termination by Seller under UCC and general contract law).

[218] *See, e.g.,* McAlpine v AAMCO Automatic Transmissions, Inc, 461 F Supp 1232 (ED Mich 1978).

[219] See generally Restatement (Second) of Contracts §§318-319 (1981); UCC §2-210(2). An agreement may not be assignable if (1) assignment would materially change the obligations of the other party, (2) it would materially increase the burden or risk placed on the other party, or (3) it would materially impair the likelihood that the other party will receive performance. J Calamari & J Perillo, Contracts §18-7, at 640 (2d ed 1977).

[220] Arkansas, Hawaii, Minnesota, Nebraska, New Jersey. (**App K.**) See also Florida. (**App G.**) Note, however, that it is generally agreed that where a special relationship such as a franchise exists, Seller is within its rights to reserve the power to approve the transferee based on considerations such as business ability, reputation, etc. *See, e.g.,* Seligson v Plum Tree, Inc, 361 F Supp 748 (ED Pa 1970). Seller may refuse consent to a franchise transfer if Seller is persuaded that the transferee will not be able to conduct the business successfully. *See, e.g.,* Kestenbaum v Falstaff Brewing Corp, 575 F2d 574 (5th Cir 1978), *cert denied,* 440 US 909 (1979) (sale price of business was so high that transferee would not be able to sustain profit-making business).

establish a period for notice and specify permissible reasons for denying transfer.[221]

§7.43 —May Buyer act in concert with other Buyers in ceasing to purchase from Seller?

If a group of Buyers acts in concert to refuse to deal with Seller, their action may constitute an unlawful boycott under the antitrust laws, especially if the action is designed to exact concessions from Seller.[222] Likewise, Seller might have a cause of action for tortious interference against one or more of the Buyers.[223] As a matter of contract law, however, Seller's claim against the Buyers would depend on the individual agreements Seller had with each Buyer.

§7.44 Do Seller and Buyer owe obligations to each other after termination?

Seller and Buyer may provide in their agreement that certain obligations survive termination or expiration of the contract. If the parties fail to provide for postterm obligations, it is very unlikely that any will be implied.[224] However, the intent of the parties may be a determinative factor; if, in the circumstances, the court concludes that certain provisions were contemplated to survive termination or expiration, they are likely to be enforced. The obligation to pay damages for breach always survives termination.[225] As noted above, under the Uniform Commercial Code rights based on the unperformed balance of an agreement survive *cancellation,* but not *termination.*[226]

§7.45 —What postterm obligations may be imposed on Buyer?

The parties are generally free to agree on what obligations will be imposed on either party after termination or expiration of the agreement. If the obliga-

---

[221] *See, e.g,* Simmons v General Motors Corp, 180 NJ Super 522, 435 A2d 1167 (1981).

[222] *See, e.g.,* United States v General Motors Corp, 384 US 127 (1966). See generally **ch 2.**

[223] See generally Restatement (Second) of Torts §766 (1974).

[224] *See* Witt v Union Oil Co, 99 Cal App3d 435, 160 Cal Rptr 285 (1979) (covenants will not be implied against express terms of agreement or where agreement was intentionally left silent). *See also* WL May Co v Philco-Ford Corp, 273 Or 701, 543 P2d 283 (1975) (repurchase option provision not unconscionable; Seller permitted to refuse to exercise option to repurchase).

[225] See UCC §2-720.

[226] See **§7.02.**

tions relate to noncompetition by Buyer, they are subject to statutory and common law restrictions.[227] In general, covenants against competition must be reasonable as to time, place, and scope of activity covered. Besides any federal antitrust considerations, each jurisdiction has its own rules concerning these elements. Some states refuse to enforce an entire covenant if any part of it is unreasonable,[228] while others will enforce the covenant to the extent that is reasonable and lawful.[229]

§7.46 —What postterm obligations may be imposed on Seller?

Besides any postterm obligations which the parties may provide in their agreement, Seller may also be subject to statutory requirements. Several state franchise laws require that certain Sellers must repurchase certain goods and equipment from Buyer upon termination or nonrenewal.[230] Many such statutes also prescribe at what price (e.g., fair market value, purchase price) such items must be repurchased.[231]

§7.47 What remedies are available to a wrongfully terminated Buyer?

If Seller has wrongfully terminated Buyer, both legal and equitable remedies may be available to Buyer. Initially, Buyer may sue for money damages, which can be calculated in various ways. The usual measure of damages is the loss incurred by Buyer as a result of Seller's action, plus incidental and consequen-

---

[227] Covenants not to compete may be examined as restraints of trade under the antitrust laws, *see, e.g.,* Lektro-Vend Corp v Vendo Co, 660 F2d 255 (7th Cir 1981), *cert denied,* 455 US 921 (1982); American Motor Inns, Inc v Holiday Inns, Inc, 521 F2d 1230 (3d Cir 1975). Covenants also may be examined under the common law of contracts, *see, e.g.,* Armstrong v Taco Time Intl, Inc, 30 Wash App 538, 635 P2d 1114 (1981). One state, Florida, has enacted a statute expressly permitting covenants against competition in the context of franchising, Fla Stat Ann §542.33(2)(b) (West 1980). Several states have statutory restrictions concerning such covenants, e.g., Minnesota; Indiana (time and area restrictions); Michigan; Washington (repurchase obligations). (**App K.**) See generally Klarfeld & Kennedy, *Covenants Against Competition in Franchise Agreements,* J of the Forum Committee on Franchising 3 (Summer/Fall 1982).

[228] *See, e.g.,* Richard P Rita Personnel Servs Intl, Inc v Kot, 229 Ga 314, 191 SE2d 79 (1972).

[229] *See, e.g.,* Wilkinson v Manpower, Inc, 531 F2d 712 (5th Cir 1976).

[230] Arkansas, Mississippi and Wisconsin require repurchase upon termination only. California, Connecticut, Hawaii, and Washington require repurchase upon termination or nonrenewal. Illinois and Michigan require repurchase unless proper notice of non-renewal was given. (**App K.**)

[231] In addition, some states, e.g., California and Washington, specifically provide for setoff of amounts owed by the franchisee to the franchisor. (**App K.**)

tial losses, less expenses saved by Buyer in not having to perform.[232] For example, Buyer might recover the profits it would have made for the unexpired portion of the term.[233] An alternative measure of damages is Buyer's expenditures in preparation for performance, less losses Buyer would have suffered if the contract had been performed.[234] In that case, Buyer might recover, for example, expenditures for advertising, salaries, rent, etc.[235] The latter measure of damages might be chosen if Buyer could not prove its profits with reasonable certainty or if Buyer was in a losing contract. Under either measure of damages, Buyer must mitigate its damages by exercising reasonable efforts to make substitute arrangements.[236] As a rule, there are no punitive damages in contract cases,[237] but Seller may be liable for punitive damages under tort claims by Buyer,[238] and for treble damages under antitrust claims.[239]

If a termination statute applies, Buyer may be permitted to seek damages as provided in the statute.[240] Most such laws adopt the usual measure of damages (direct and indirect losses, minus expenses saved), but some states provide a nonexclusive remedy requiring repurchase of Buyer's assets or other specified compensation.[241] Several statutes permit Buyer to recover costs and reasonable attorney's fees.[242] A few laws provide for civil penalties in addition to

---

[232] See Restatement (Second) of Contracts §347 (1981); UCC §2-711.

[233] *See. e.g.*, Thompson v Kerr-McGee Ref Corp, 660 F2d 1380 (10th Cir 1981), *cert denied*, 102 S Ct 1716 (1982) (jury verdict of damages equal to 6 years' profits of Buyer was not excessive); Esch v Yazoo Mfg Co, 510 F Supp 53 (ED Wis 1981) (award of 10 years' profits not reduced by liquidation value of business).

[234] See Restatement (Second) of Contracts §349 (1981). *See also* CA May Marine Supply Co v Brunswick Corp, 649 F2d 1049 (5th Cir), *cert denied*, 102 S Ct 974 (1981) (contrasting two methods of calculating damages).

[235] *See* Lichnovsky v Ziebart Intl Corp, 93 Mich App 60, 285 NW2d 795 (1979), *revd*, Bus Fran Guide (CCH) ¶7904 (Mich Sept 28, 1982) (describing *Missouri Rule*, under which Buyer may recover costs of preparing to perform).

[236] *See, e.g.*, CA May Marine Supply Co v Brunswick Corp, 649 F2d 1049 (5th Cir), *cert denied*, 102 S Ct 974 (1981). Buyer need not accept an offer of reinstatement, even if to do so would mitigate its damages. Esch v Yazoo Mfg Co, 510 F Supp 53 (ED Wis 1981). *Cf* McAlpine v AAMCO Automatic Transmissions, Inc, 461 F Supp 1232, 1275 (ED Mich 1978) (wrongfully terminated Seller may recover lost profits, reduced by the amount of actual profits received).

[237] *See, e.g.*, Benlo Chems, Inc v Buckman Labs, Inc., 520 F Supp 160 (ED Wis 1981).

[238] *See, e.g.*, Walker v KFC Corp, 515 F Supp 612 (SD Cal 1981) (misrepresentation and emotional distress claims).

[239] *See, e.g.*, Spray-Rite Serv Corp v Monsanto Co, 1982-2 Trade Cas (CCH) ¶64,808 (7th Cir 1982) (Buyer may recover aggregated sum of damages—even value of entire business—attributable to boycott and refusal to deal).

[240] Arkansas, Connecticut, Delaware, Illinois, Indiana, Mississippi, Missouri, Nebraska, New Jersey, Virginia, Wisconsin. In Arkansas and New Jersey, the statutory remedy is the exclusive remedy. (**App K.**) See also Puerto Rico, Virgin Islands. (**App G.**)

[241] *E.g.*, California, Delaware, Hawaii, Michigan, Wisconsin. (**App K.**) See also Puerto Rico. (**App G.**)

[242] Arkansas, Connecticut, Delaware, Illinois, Mississippi, Missouri, Nebraska, New Jersey, Virginia, Wisconsin. (**App K.**) See also Virgin Islands. (**App G.**).

private remedies.[243]

Many termination statutes also provide for equitable relief for a terminated Buyer, usually through an injunction.[244] Courts sometimes enjoin franchise terminations;[245] but in many cases, and especially if the relationship is not a franchise or another arrangement protected by statute, an injunction against termination may be more difficult to obtain. For example, Buyer may be unable to prove one or more of the elements necessary to obtain an injunction and thus may be relegated to seeking another remedy.[246]

---

[243] Michigan, Minnesota, Mississippi, Missouri. In addition, Washington provides for treble damages. (**App K.**)

[244] Arkansas, Connecticut, Delaware, Mississippi, Missouri, Nebraska, New Jersey, Wisconsin. Indiana law permits reformation of the contract, and Illinois requires that an offer of rescission be made. (**App K.**) see also Puerto Rico. (**App G.**)

[245] *See e.g.,* Humboldt Oil Co, Inc v Exxon Co, USA, 532 F Supp 896 (D Nev 1982) (injunction pending outcome of Buyer's appeal of felony conviction); Bender v Southland Corp, Bus Fran Guide (CCH) ¶7777 (ED Mich Jan 6, 1982) (injunction pending outcome of antitrust suit); Burn-Valley Drug, Inc v Walgreen Co, Bus Fran Guide (CCH) ¶7740 (Minn Dist Ct Sept 12, 1980) (injunction pending determination whether arrangement was a franchise). *But see* Pugh v Mobil Oil Corp, 533 F Supp 169 (SD Tex 1982) (since Seller had sufficient cause to terminate and gave proper notice, no injunction against termination issued).

[246] *See, e.g.,* Jack Kahn Music Co v Baldwin Piano & Organ Co, 604 F2d 755 (2d Cir 1979) (injunction denied where Buyer failed to show irreparable harm); Kealey Pharmacy & Home Care Serv, Inc v Walgreen Co, Bus Fran Guide (CCH) ¶7841 (WD Wis June 3, 1982) (injunction denied where legal remedy would be adequate); AR Dervaes Co v Houdaille Indus, Bus Fran Guide (CCH) ¶7803 (Del Ch Ct Sept 29, 1981) (since agreement provided for termination at will, Buyer could not show probable success on merits). In evaluating the balance of hardships, however, courts may conclude that Seller is better able to withstand an injunction than Buyer is able to withstand termination. *See, e.g.,* Designs in Medicine, Inc v Xomed, Inc, 522 F Supp 1054 (ED Wis 1981).

Will the Answers Be Different if the Seller is Also Competing with the Buyer?

8

*Stephen S. Mayne**

---

*Mr. Mayne is a member of the California Bar and the District of Columbia Bar. The author wishes to thank Barry W. Lee for his assistance in the preparation of this chapter.

§8.01 What is dual distribution?

The term *dual distribution* refers primarily to situations in which Seller competes with its own Buyers in the resale of its products. For the purposes of this chapter, the term *dual distribution* is also used to describe a situation in which Seller converts its distribution system in whole or in part from independent distributors to direct selling by its own employees or wholly owned subsidiaries.

§8.02 What antitrust issues may arise in the context of dual distribution?

The antitrust statutes which may apply to the variety of dual distribution contexts are §§1 and 2 of the Sherman Act[1] and the Robinson-Patman Price Discrimination Act.[2] Although the Supreme Court has not yet squarely ruled whether dual distribution systems fall within the rule of per se illegality,[3] the

---

[1] 15 USC §§1, 2.

[2] *Id* §13(a).

[3] Krehl v Baskin-Robbins Ice Cream Co, 78 FRD 108 (CD Cal 1978), *affd,* 664 F2d 1348 (9th Cir 1982). The court noted, however, that both times the Supreme Court has faced this issue, it has not squarely ruled whether dual distribution systems fall within the rule of per se illegality. See **§8.04.** Both times it has faced the issue, the Supreme Court has, sub silentio, treated dual distribution systems as imposing only vertical restraints which are now subject to the rule of reason. *See* United States v Arnold Schwinn & Co, 388 US 365 (1967), 1977-2 Trade Cas (CCH) ¶61,776 (ND Ill 1977); White Motor Co v United States, 372 US 253 (1963). Because the Court's silence was regarded as an unsteady foundation upon which to base a decision, the Ninth Circuit

consensus of the courts is that "there is nothing inherently evil in a dual distribution system" whereby a manufacturer sells its own products to customers directly in competition with its own distributors.[4] Similarly, as a general rule, there is nothing inherently unlawful under §1 of the Sherman Act either in a manufacturer's decision to terminate an independent distributor and thereafter sell directly through its own outlets, or in the conversion of its entire distribution system from independent dealers to wholly owned dealers.[5]

There are, of course, a broad range of circumstances under which antitrust violations may occur in the context of Seller competing with Buyer in the resale of its products or of Seller converting its distribution system to one utilizing its own employees or wholly owned subsidiaries. The applicable legal principles and the variety of dual distribution-related restraints that generate antitrust inquiry are reviewed in this chapter.

Among the questions that arise in these various dual distribution contexts are: (1) the means by which Seller may compete with its Buyers in the resale of the Seller's products; (2) the extent to which a dual distributor may limit either the resale territories or the Buyers to whom its Buyers may resell; (3) the circumstances under which Seller may either terminate some or all of the Buyers with whom it also competes in the resale of Seller's products or convert its entire distribution system to one utilizing its own employees or subsidiaries; and (4) the prices at which Seller may sell its products.

§8.03 Does §1 of the Sherman Act require a plurality of actors?

The traditional framework of analysis under §1 of the Sherman Act has been explored in Chapter 1 and does not require extended discussion. It is important to remember, however, that §1 of the Sherman Act, which prohibits

---

undertook its own inquiry into the appropriate standard under which to measure the legality of dual distribution systems.

[4] Accordingly, "in the absence of proof of anti-competitive purpose or effect, dual distribution systems must be evaluated under the traditional rule of reason standard." Krehl v Baskin-Robbins Ice Cream Co, 664 F2d at 1357.

[5] White v Hearst Corp, 669 F2d 14, 19 (1st Cir 1982); Auburn News Co v Providence Journal Co, 659 F2d 273, 278 (1st Cir 1981), *cert denied,* 455 US 921 (1982); Associated Radio Serv Co v Page Airways, Inc, 624 F2d 1342 (5th Cir 1980), *cert denied,* 450 US 1030 (1981); Knutson v Daily Review, Inc, 383 F Supp 1346 (ND Cal 1974), *affd in part & revd in part,* 548 F2d 795, 804-05 (9th Cir 1976), *cert denied,* 433 US 910 (1977); Bowen v New York News Inc, 522 F2d 1242 (2d Cir 1975), *cert denied,* 425 US 936 (1976); Bushie v Stenocord Corp, 460 F2d 116 (9th Cir 1972); Ark Dental Supply Co v Cavitron Corp, 461 F2d 1093 (3d Cir 1972); Clarke v Amerada Hess Corp, 1980-2 Trade Cas (CCH) ¶63,452 (SDNY 1980); Castoe v Amerada Hess Corp; 1976-2 Trade Cas (CCH) ¶61,054 (SDNY 1976). *Cf* Beltronics, Inc v Eberline Instrument Corp, 509 F2d 1316 (10th Cir 1974). See 3 Areeda & Turner, Antitrust Law §§725-727, §828c (1978). *See also* Fuchs Sugars & Syrups, Inc v Amstar Corp, 602 F2d 1025 (2d Cir), *cert denied,* 444 US 917 (1979). *Compare* Indus Bldg Materials, Inc v Inter-chemical Corp, 437 F2d 1336 (9th Cir 1970).

"[e]very contract, combination . . . or conspiracy, in restraint of trade or commerce," requires "a plurality of actors combining their efforts towards a common goal;"[6] it does not proscribe single-firm conduct.[7]

It is important for dual distribution purposes, however, to remember that a parent corporation is legally capable of conspiring with its wholly owned subsidiaries and that a parent's subsidiaries are legally capable of conspiring among themselves (commonly known as a *bathtub* or *intra-enterprise* conspiracy) in violation of §1.[8] In general, the courts have held that separate incorporation, albeit an important factor, is alone not conclusive proof of the requisite two actors for a §1 conspiracy.[9] Although some courts are reluctant to impose any limitations on the intra-enterprise corporate conspiracy doctrine,[10] it would appear that most courts are of the view that affiliated corporations cannot conspire with each other where they function as an integrated enterprise or a single economic unit.[11] Whether the two related actors constitute distinct economic entities must be determined by the economic realities of their rela-

---

[6] Mutual Fund Investors, Inc v Putnam Management Co, 553 F2d 620, 625 (9th Cir 1977). 15 USC §1.

[7] *See, e.g.*, Barnosky Oils, Inc v Union Oil Co, 665 F2d 74,79 (6th Cir 1981). *See also* American Motor Inns, Inc v Holiday Inns, Inc, 521 F2d 1230,1253 (3d Cir 1975).

[8] *See* Perma Life Mufflers, Inc v Intl Parts Corp, 392 US 134 (1968); Timken Roller Bearing Co v United States, 341 US 593, 598 (1951); Kiefer-Stewart Co v Joseph E Seagram & Sons, 340 US 211 (1951); Schine Chain Theatres Inc v United States, 334 US 110, 116 (1948); United States v Yellow Cab Co, 332 US 218 (1947).

[9] *See, e.g.*, Harvey v Fearless Farris Wholesale, Inc, 589 F2d 451, 456 (9th Cir 1979); Las Vegas Sun, Inc v Summa Corp, 610 F2d 614 (9th Cir 1979), *cert denied*, 447 US 906 (1980).

[10] This view is held by the Third Circuit. *See, e.g.*, Columbia Metal Culvert Co, v Kaiser Aluminum & Chem Corp, 579 F2d 20, 33-34 n 49 (3d Cir 1978); Glauser Dodge v Chrysler Corp, 570 F2d 72, 81 (3d Cir 1977), *cert denied*, 436 US 913 (1978). *See* Cromar Co v Nuclear Materials & Equip Corp, 543 F2d 501, 511-12 (3d Cir 1976); Coleman Motor Co v Chrysler Corp, 525 F2d 1338 (3d Cir 1975), *cert denied*, 419 US 869 (1975); Bravman v Bassett Furniture Indus, 552 F2d 90, 101 n 32 (3d Cir 1977). See generally Sullivan, Handbook of the Law of Antitrust (1977); Report of Attorney General's National Committee to Study the Antitrust Laws 34 (1955) (no violation occurs if the "conspiracy" restrains no trade other than that of the parent and its subsidiaries).

[11] *See, e.g.*, Murray v Toyota Motor Distribs, Inc, 664 F2d 1377 (9th Cir 1982), *cert denied*, __ US __, 102 S Ct 2905 (1982); Hunt Wesson Foods, Inc v Ragu Foods, Inc, 627 F2d 919, 927 n 5 (9th Cir 1980), *cert denied*, 450 US 921 (1981); Call Carl, Inc v BP Oil Corp, 403 FSupp 568 (DMd 1975), *affd on this issue*, 554 F2d 623, 628 (4th Cir), *cert denied*, 434 US 923 (1977); Janush v U-Haul Co of Detroit, 1981-1 Trade Cas (CCH) ¶64,070, at 76,475 (ED Mich 1981) (the U-Haul System, consisting of a parent company, 94 rental companies and 5000 dealers, was found to be a "nationally integrated system for the marketing of equipment, which is centrally controlled, and the various subparts do not in any way hold themselves out as competing with one another," with the result that there was found to be no basis for a conspiracy). See Note, *Intra-Enterprise Conspiracy under Section 1 of the Sherman Act: A Suggested Standard*, 75 U Mich L Rev 717 (1977).

tionship.[12] Some courts have gone so far as to refuse to find a conspiracy between a parent and its subsidiaries in the absence of predatory conduct.[13] The courts have not gone so far as to hold that a corporation can conspire for §1 purposes with its wholly owned, unincorporated sales division.[14]

Thus, in a *dual distribution* context, Seller's scheme to force independent dealers out of business pursuant to a plan of vertical integration, or a vertically integrated Seller's actions designed to preclude competition with it by its Buyers in the resale of its products, both of which would be immune from §1 attack if carried out by a single entity,[15] could be a violation of §1 if effected through a combination or conspiracy with Seller's subsidiaries.[16] Indeed, the case of vertically related operating companies, such as a manufacturer and distributor, a wholesaler and retailer, or a Seller and Buyer, in which the power of one is used to restrain trade between the other and its competitors, has been cited as an example of the type of situation in which the *bathtub conspiracy* would be found to exist.[17] A different standard may be applied with respect to the bathtub conspiracy issue, however, where the Seller merely converts its distribution system from one using independents to one using a wholly owned subsidiary.[18]

§8.04 What is the distinction between the rule of reason and the per se rule?

Since the early years of this century, a judicial gloss on §1's statutory language has established the *rule of reason*[19] as the prevailing standard of analysis

---

[12] *See, e.g.*, Knutson v Daily Review, Inc, 548 F2d 795, 801-02 (9th Cir 1976), *cert denied*, 433 US 910 (1977).

[13] *See, e.g.*, *In re* Western Liquid Asphalt, 478 F Supp 785 (ND Cal 1979).

[14] *See, e.g.*, H&B Equip Co v International Harvestor Co, 577 F2d 239, 244 (5th Cir 1978); Ark Dental Supply Co v Cavitron Corp, 461 F2d 1093, 1094-95 n1 (3d Cir 1972). *But cf* Poller v Columbia Broadcasting Sys, 368 US 464, 469 n4 (1962).

[15] *See* Barnosky Oils, Inc v Union Oil Co, 665 F2d 74 (6th Cir 1981).

[16] *See, e.g.*, Columbia Metal Culvert Co v Kaiser Aluminum & Chem Corp, 579 F2d 20, 34-35 (3d Cir 1978); Coleman Motor Co v Chrysler Corp, 525 F2d 1338 (3d Cir 1975), *cert denied*, 419 US 869 (1975); American Motor Inns, Inc v Holiday Inns, Inc, 521 F2d 1230 (3d Cir 1975). *See also* City of Kirkwood v Union Elec Co, 671 F2d 1173 (8th Cir 1982). *But cf* Photovest Corp v Fotomat Corp, 606 F2d 704 (7th Cir 1979), *cert denied*, 445 US 917 (1980).

[17] William Inglis & Sons Baking Co, 668 F2d 1014 (9th Cir 1981) *cert denied*, 103 S Ct 57 (1982) (No 81-2083) (ITT), *cert denied*, 103 S Ct 58 (1982) (No 81-2289) (Inglis). *See* Columbia Metal Culvert Co v Kaiser Aluminum & Chem Corp, 579 F2d 20, 34-35 (3d Cir 1978); Perma Life Mufflers, Inc v International Parts Corp, 392 US 134 (1968); United States v Yellow Cab Co, 332 US 218 (1947).

[18] White v Hearst Corp, 669 F2d 14 (1st Cir 1982).

[19] The elements of the rule of reason and the per se rule, and the critical distinctions between them, are examined in depth in **ch 1.**

under §1.[20] Under this rule, the restrictive practice is reviewed to determine whether it imposes an unreasonable restraint on competition. That analysis involves considerations of the purpose of the restraint, the market power of the participants in the restraint, and the effect of the restraint. Some restraints have come to be regarded as so "manifestly anticompetitive," however, as to be per se unreasonable[21] and, therefore, illegal "without elaborate inquiry as to the precise harm they have caused or the business excuse for their use."[22] Thus, the per se rule dispenses with the frequently complicated analysis required under the rule of reason.[23] In order to be unreasonable per se, restrictive agreements must have a "pernicious effect on competition and lack . . . any redeeming virtue."[24] While restrictive agreements among independent business entities at the same level of the market, i.e., *horizontal* agreements, are illegal per se,[25] restraints imposed by a manufacturer or supplier upon its distributor or retailer customers, i.e., *vertical* restraints, are permissible (with the exception of resale price-fixing which remains per se illegal) unless they violate the rule of reason.[26] Thus, "[w]hile the per se approach is commendable for the certainty which it offers, the rule creates great urgency in the art of characterization as the label applied to a restraint will, in many instances, determine its legality."[27]

---

[20] Standard Oil Co v United States, 221 US 1 (1911).

[21] Continental TV, Inc v GTE Sylvania, Inc, 433 US 36, 49-50 (1977) (footnote omitted). The per se rule was first adopted by the Supreme Court in United States v Socony-Vacuum Oil Co, 310 US 150 (1940).

[22] Northern Pac Ry Co v United States, 356 US 1 (1958). The Court added:

> This principle of per se unreasonableness not only makes the type of restraints which are proscribed by the Sherman Act more certain to the benefit of everyone concerned, but it also avoids the necessity for an incredibly complicated and prolonged economic investigation into the entire history of the industry involved, as well as related industries, in an effort to determine at large whether a particular restraint has been unreasonable—an inquiry so often wholly fruitless when undertaken.

Id 5.

[23] As noted in **ch 1** however, even in some classes of cases which fall within the per se rule, market power is relevant to a finding of violation. *See, e.g.,* United States Steel Corp v Fortner Enters Inc, 429 US 610, 619-22 (1977) (tying requires market power); Continental TV Inc v GTE Sylvania, Inc, 433 US 36, 65-66 (1977) (White, J concurring); Columbia Metal Culvert Co v Kaiser Aluminum & Chem Corp, 579 F2d 20, 26 n9 (3d Cir 1978).

[24] Northern Pac Ry Co v United States, 356 US 1, 5 (1958). Most courts recognize four categories of competitive restraints which have been held unreasonable per se: (1) horizontal and vertical price fixing; (2) horizontal market division; (3) group boycotts and concerted refusals to deal; and (4) tie-in sales. *See, e.g.,* Gough v Rossmoor Corp, 585 F2d 381, 386 (9th Cir 1978), *cert denied,* 440 US 936 (1979).

[25] United States v Topco Assocs, 405 US 596 (1972).

[26] Continental TV, Inc v GTE Sylvania, Inc, 433 US 36 (1977).

[27] Town of Massena v Niagara Mohawk Power Corp, 1980-2 Trade Cas (CCH) ¶63,526 (NDNY 1980). For example, in United States v Sealy, Inc, 388 US 350 (1967), a territorial agreement between a trademark licensor and its licensees was classified as

§8.05 What is the distinction between interbrand and intrabrand competition?

The "primary concern of antitrust law" is with *interbrand* competition.[28] Although vertical restraints inevitably have some effect on *intraband* competition, they do not necessarily have an adverse effect on interbrand competition.[29] Indeed, in removing vertical customer and territorial distribution restraints from coverage by the per se rule established in *United States v Arnold Schwinn & Co*,[30] the Supreme Court stated in *Continental TV, Inc v GTE Sylvania, Inc*, that "[v]ertical restrictions promote interbrand competition by allowing the manufacturer to achieve certain efficiencies in the distribution of his products."[31] The Court further observed that "when interbrand competition exists . . . it provides a significant check on the exploitation of intrabrand market power. . . ."[32] Accordingly, the Court ruled that the antitrust legality of vertical distribution, i.e., nonprice, restrictions must be assessed under the rule of reason.[33] Many recent decisions have followed the Supreme Court's lead in *GTE Sylvania* in applying the rule of reason test under §1 and have focused almost exclusively on the effects which the challenged conduct has had on interbrand, as opposed to intrabrand, competition.[34] Intrabrand competition is, however, still a concern of the antitrust laws, especially where there is no benefit in the form of increased interbrand competition.[35]

---

vertical and reasonable by the trial court, but as horizontal and therefore per se illegal by the Supreme Court.

[28] Continental TV, Inc v GTE Sylvania, Inc, 433 US 36, 52 n 19 (1977). Interbrand competition is defined as "competition among the manufacturers of the same generic product." *Id.*

[29] Borger v Yamaha Intl Corp, 625 F2d 390 (2d Cir 1980).

[30] 388 US 365 (1967).

[31] 433 US 36, 54 (1977).

[32] *Id.*

[33] *Id.*

[34] *See, e.g.*, Borger v Yamaha Intl Corp, 625 F2d 390 (2d Cir 1980) (reversible error to instruct jury only on the basis of intraband competition; jury must be instructed that it had to find "either a purpose or effect related to interbrand competition"); Cowley v Braden Indus, 613 F2d 751 (9th Cir), *cert denied*, 446 US 965 (1980); Oreck Corp v Whirlpool Corp, 579 F2d 126 (2d Cir) (*en banc*), *cert denied*, 439 US 946 (1978). *But see* Com-Tel, Inc v DuKane Corp, 669 F2d 404 (6th Cir 1982) ("Although the primary concern of the antitrust laws is with interbrand competition, intrabrand competition is still a concern, especially in cases such as this where no benefits from increased interbrand competition may or did result from the vertical restrictions" (footnotes omitted)); H&B Equip Co v Intl Harvester Co, 577 F2d 239, 242 (5th Cir 1978) ("The first step in establishing an unreasonable restraint of trade is to show anticompetitive effect either in the intrabrand or interbrand markets"); Glauser Dodge Co v Chrysler Corp, 570 F2d 72, 82 n 20 (3d Cir 1977), *cert denied*, 436 US 913 (1978) (court rejected contention that Continental TV, Inc v GTE Sylvania, Inc, 433 US 36 (1977) altered the weights to be given to interbrand and intrabrand competition within the rule of reason test).

[35] *See, e.g.*, Com-Tel, Inc v DuKane Corp, 669 F2d 404 (6th Cir 1982).

§8.06 What is the distinction between horizontal and vertical restraints?

As we have seen, the distinction between horizontal and vertical restraints in the context of §1 analysis is important. *Horizontal* restraints are uniformly condemned through a *per se* prohibition that forecloses inquiry into their economic or business justification, i.e., they are conclusively presumed to serve no purpose other than stifling competition.[36] *vertical* restraints, on the other hand, are not so dogmatically circumscribed. Rather, the courts have recognized that, although some vertical restraints inevitably may reduce *intrabrand* competition, they may also promote *interbrand* rivalry by allowing a manufacturer to achieve certain efficiencies in the distribution of its products[37] and to improve the quality of service and profits.[38] As a result, vertical restraints (except resale price-fixing) are examined under the *rule of reason* analysis and may be justified if it can be shown that the limitations are based on sound economic or business considerations and that they merely regulate competition as opposed to destroying it.[39]

As can be anticipated, when a restraint involves both horizontal and vertical aspects the courts frequently encounter difficulties in differentiating those which are vertical from those which are horizontal[40] and deciding "which, if any, substantive pigeonhole [provides] the proper framework" for analyzing a particular restraint or agreement.[41] Nevertheless, when a restraint involves both horizontal and vertical aspects, some distinctions must be drawn because of the sharp differences in the results for the two categories, i.e., rule of reason analysis for a vertical restraint and per se classification for a horizontal restraint.[42]

The label applied by a court will, of course, frequently control the outcome

---

[36] White Motor Co v United States, 372 US 253, 263 (1963). *See* United States v Topco Assocs, 405 US 596, 608 (1972); Gough v Rossmoor Copr, 585 F2d 381 (9th Cir 1978), *cert denied,* 440 US 936 (1979); Oreck Corp v Whirlpool Corp, 579 F2d 126 (2d Cir) (*en banc*), *cert denied,* 439 US 946 (1978).

[37] Oreck Corp v Whirlpool Corp, 579 F2d 126 (2d Cir), *cert denied,* 439 US 946 (1978).

[38] *See* Continental TV, Inc v GTE Sylvania, Inc, 433 US 36, 50, 54 (1977).

[39] *Id* 49 n 15, citing Chicago Bd of Trade v United States, 246 US 231, 238 (1918).

[40] Continental TV, Inc v GTE Sylvania, 433 US at 58 n 28.

[41] Dougherty v Continental Oil Co, 579 F2d 954, 958-59 (5th Cir 1978), *vacated on other grounds,* 591 F2d 1206 (5th Cir 1979). *See, e.g.,* Hobart Bros v Malcolm T Gilliland, Inc, 471 F2d 894 (5th Cir), *cert denied,* 412 US 923 (1973); *In re* Coca-Cola Co, 91 S Ct 517 (1978), *vacated as moot,* 642 F2d 1387 (DC Cir 1981). *Cf* Ambook Enters v Time, Inc, 612 F2d 604, 618 n 23 (2d Cir 1979), *cert dismissed,* 448 US 914 (1980).

[42] Com-Tel, Inc v DuKane Corp, 669 F2d 404 (6th Cir 1982). It has been suggested that this sharp difference in approach be eliminated in favor of a uniform rule of reason analysis, at least with respect to all non-price restraints, "since the legality of some arrangements may turn upon a possibly arbitrary and inconsistent characterization as vertical rather than horizontal [and] [v]aluable resources are spent by the courts . . . in making these ultimately irrelevant classifications." Note, *A Uniform Rule of Reason for Vertical and Horizontal Nonprice Restraints,* 55 US Cal L Rev 441, 443-44 (1981).

of the case. Thus, what may appear to be a vertical restraint could be treated as a per se violation of §1 if its effect is primarily horizontal,[43] or if it redounds primarily to the benefit of the Buyer-dealers,[44] or if the desired impact of the restraint was horizontal on the dealer level.[45] And this may be true even where no two members of the conspiracy operate at the same level of competition[46]

---

[43] *See* United States v General Motors Corp, 384 US 127 (1966); Red Diamond Supply, Inc v Liquid Carbonic Corp, 637 F2d 1001, 1005 (5th Cir), *cert denied sub nom,* Red Diamond Supply, Inc v Acme Welding, 454 US 827, (1981); American Motor Inns, Inc v Holiday Inns, Inc, 521 F2d 1230 (3d Cir 1975). *See also* AH Cox & Co v Star Mach Co, 653 F2d 1302, 1305 n 3 (9th Cir 1981), where the court concluded that "vertical agreements to exclude competition may in some instances require application of the *per se* rule."

[44] Donald B Rice Tire Co v Michelin Tire Corp, 638 F2d 15, 16 (4th Cir) (*affd per curiam*), *cert denied,* 454 US 864, (1981).

[45] Cernuto, Inc v United Cabinet Corp, 595 F2d 164 (3d Cir 1979). In applying the per se rule to a dealer termination by a supplier at the urging of another dealer, the court in *Cernuto* reasoned:

> When a manufacturer acts on its own, in purusing its own market strategy, it is seeking to compete with other manufacturers by imposing what may be defended as reasonable vertical restraints. This would appear to be the rationale of the *GTE Sylvania* decision. However, if the action of a manufacturer or other supplier is taken at the direction of its customer, the restraint becomes primarily horizontal in nature in that one customer is seeking to suppress its competition by utilizing the power of a common supplier. Therefore, although the termination in such a situation is, itself, a vertical restraint, the *desired impact is horizontal* and on the dealer, not the manufacturer, level.

Id 168 (emphasis added). *See also* Westman Commn Co v Hobart Corp, 461 F Supp 627 (D Colo 1978) (dealer termination by a supplier at the urging of a competing dealer is an antitrust violation); Eiberger v Sony Corp of Am, 459 F Supp 1276 (SDNY 1978), *affd,* 622 F2d 1068 (2d Cir 1980); Evanston Motor Co v Mid-Southern Toyota Distribs, Inc, 436 F Supp 1370 (ND Ill 1977) (involvement of other dealers in supplier's boycott of dealer added a horizontal element to the combination); Jinkinson & Foster, *Commentary: Per Se Rules Against Vertical Restraints: Down But Not Out,* 58 Wash ULQ 795, 799-800 (1980).

[46] *See, e.g.,* Com-Tel, Inc v DuKane Corp, 669 F2d 404 (6th Cir 1982); Cernuto, Inc v United Cabinet Corp, 595 F2d 164 (3d Cir 1979); Sport Shoe, Inc v Ralph Libonati Co, 1981-2 Trade Cas (CCH) ¶64,230 (D Del 1981); Westman Commn Co v Hobart Corp, 461 F Supp 627 (D Colo 1978); Copperstone v Griswold Sporting Goods Co, 1977-2 Trade Cas (CCH) ¶61,623 (ED Mich 1977). *See also* AH Cox & Co v Star Mach Co, 653 F2d 1302, 1305 n 3 (9th Cir 1981). See generally Bauer, *Per Se Illegality of Concerted Refusals to Deal; A Rule Ripe for Reexamination,* 79 Colum L Rev 689, 713 (1979). In *Com-Tel* although the coercive pressure was applied vertically—one dealer induced its supplier to abandon its commitments to sell to a competing dealer—the pressure was initiated at the behest of a horizontal competitor and was intended to affect on the dealer, not the supplier, level. Thus, the court ruled that the arrangement constituted a classic per se illegal group boycott. *Contra* Gough v Rossmoor Corp., 585 F2d 381, 387 (9th Cir 1978), *cert denied,* 440 US 936 (1979); Oreck Corp v Whirlpool Corp, 579 F2d 126, 131 (2d Cir) (*en banc*), *cert denied,* 439 US 946 (1978); Sitkin Smelting & Ref Co v FMC Corp, 575 F2d 440, 446 (3d Cir), *cert denied,* 439 US 866 (1978); Mutual Fund Investors, Inc v Putnam Management Co, 553 F2d 620, 626-27 (9th Cir 1977).

or where only one member of the conspiracy competes with the injured party.[47]

These distinctions, between interbrand competition and intrabrand competition, vertical restraints and horizontal restraints, and the corollary distinction between the rule of reason and the per se rule, are of critical importance in the dual distribution context, even to the point of determining whether the challenged conduct is criminal.[48] If Seller imposes a restraint upon Buyer with whom Seller competes, is that restraint to be viewed as horizontal and thus probably per se illegal, or is it to be viewed as vertical and thus subject to the rule of reason? Even if viewed as horizontal, to what extent does the fact that the restraint affects intraband, not interbrand, competition call for application of the rule of reason?

§8.07 Why is the horizontal-vertical characterization often so difficult in a dual distribution context?

Since the characterization of the restraint either as horizontal or vertical frequently will preordain the result in a suit attacking its legality, it is often the central issue in an antitrust challenge to a dual distribution system.[49] The

---

[47] Klor's, Inc v Broadway-Hale Stores, Inc, 359 US 207 (1959); Com-Tel, Inc v DuKane Corp, 669 F2d 404 (6th Cir 1982).

[48] The characterization of the restraint may have criminal, as well as civil, implications to a dual distributor. In United States v Koppers Co, Inc, 652 F2d 290 (2d Cir), *cert denied,* 454 US 1083 (1981), the defendant, who was found guilty of a felony violation of §1 for engaging in a conspiracy to rig bids and allocate territories in the sale of road tar, argued on appeal that it supplied its co-conspirator with all of its road tar and that therefore the relationship between the two was a vertical one, subject to the rule of reason. In rejecting this claim, the court stated:

> The decision in *Continental T.V.* not to impose a *per se* rule was based on the Court's determination that the kind of vertical restraint under consideration there held out at least some possibility of increased competition, both intraband and interbrand. No such possibility exists here. Koppers' obvious and only motive for maintaining Dosch-King as a supplier and bidder . . . was not to promote competition but to raise prices and deceive state and local officials into the belief that Koppers and Dosch-King were bona fide competitors when in fact, as the evidence conclusively showed, they were not. The sole purpose of the allocation was to enable Koppers and Dosch-King to fix higher prices while maintaining the pretense of price-based competition. For a relationship to qualify for rule-of-reason treatment under *Continental T.V.*, it is not enough that it be shown to be vertical; there must also be some "redeeming virtue," some possibility that the terms of the relationship hold out the prospect for being pro-competitive. Since the scheme entered into by Koppers and Dosch-King could not have had any effect except an anti-competitive one, *Northern Pacific Railway Co. v. United States, supra,* 356 U.S. at 5, the rule laid down in *Continental T.V.* is not applicable.

652 F2d at 296-97.

[49] The central antitrust issue in a dual distribution system, with the manufacturer functioning at the same level of the market as its dealers, is whether the relationship between the manufacturer and the independent dealers should automatically be viewed as a horizontal one—and thus subject to *per se* rules—or as a vertical one [subject to the rule of reason].

answer to the question of whether a restraint should be viewed as vertical or horizontal is of critical importance for a Seller who competes with its Buyers. For example, one who imposes restraints in its capacity as Seller on the unwitting assumption that they are legal under the rule of reason standard applicable in a purely vertical context may, by virtue of the fact that it has some competitive relationship with its Buyers, find those practices transformed into horizontal restraints which are illegal per se.

Unfortunately, nowhere does there exist greater confusion as to the proper label to apply (i.e., horizontal or vertical) or indeed, whether any label should be applied at all,[50] than a situation involving a dual distributor.[51] When Seller sells a product to Buyer, the parties are vertically related. When Seller competes with Buyer, the parties are horizontally related. Thus, a dual distributorship can generate agreements which at once appear horizontal and unredeemably illegal under *United States v Topco Assocs*,[52] and vertical and conditionally approved under *Continental TV, Inc v GTE Sylvania Inc.*[53]

The origin of the confusion, which frequently has gone unrecognized by the courts, is seemingly conflicting Supreme Court mandates regarding horizontal restraints which are per se unlawful, on the one hand, and intrabrand restraints which are generally subject to the rule of reason, on the other. Since horizontal restraints in a dual distribution context affect only competitors who resell the same product, i.e., intrabrand competition, which standard should be applied? This question has brought the differences between "formalistic line drawing" and "demonstrable economic effect"[54] into sharp focus in the dual distribution context.

Predictably, because of this conflict between the primacy of interbrand competition over intrabrand competition on the one hand, and the dichotomy in the treatment of horizontal restraints and vertical restraints on the other, the courts have failed to adopt a uniform approach on the question of whether restrictions imposed by a dual distributor are subject to per se or rule of reason analysis. While some courts have held that the rule of reason is the proper

---

Vertical Restraints and Other Current Distribution Issues in the Wake of Sylvania, Address by Richard J. Favretto, Deputy Director of Operations, Antitrust Division, Department of Justice, before the Southwestern Legal Foundation Symposium on Antitrust Law, Dallas, Texas (May 12, 1978), *reported in* 5 Trade Reg Rep (CCH 1979) ¶50,370.

[50] One court expressed its frustration with this labeling process and its distorting effect on the the analytical process as follows: "Whether nonprice distribution restrictions in such a dual distribution system are to be examined under the rule of reason or under the per se doctrine should not turn on whether the restrictions are pigeonholed as horizontal or vertical. This is the type of formalistic line drawing condemned in *Sylvania.*" Guild Wineries & Distilleries v J Sosnick & Son, 102 Cal App 3d 627, 162 Cal Rptr 87 (1980) (dissenting opinion) (footnote omitted).

[51] See generally ABA Section on Antitrust, *Vertical Restraints Limiting Intrabrand Competition,* 2 n 3 (Monograph No 2 1977).

[52] 405 US 596 (1972).

[53] 433 US 36 (1977).

[54] *Id* 58-50.

standard by which to judge such restrictions,[55] other courts have held that the horizontal element of a dual distributorship renders restrictive agreements emanating therefrom illegal per se.[56]

In grappling with the horizontal-vertical overlap in the dual distribution context, one approach has been to determine whether the relationship and restraint are primarily horizontal or primarily vertical, applying the per se rule to the former and the rule of reason to the latter.[57]

Another approach has been to look for the source of the restraint or the capacity in which the dual distributor was acting.[58] In reaching this conclusion, the courts have frequently relied on *United States v Arnold Schwinn & Co,* in which the Supreme Court stated that in a dual distribution system where the Seller competes with its Buyers "the source of the restriction is the manufacturer,"

---

[55] *See, e.g.,* Copy-Data Sys, Inc v Toshiba Am, Inc, 663 F2d 405 (2d Cir 1981); Abadir & Co v First Miss Corp, 651 F2d 422 (5th Cir 1981); Donald B Rice Tire Co v Michelin Tire Corp, 638 F2d 15 (4th Cir) (*affd per curiam*), cert denied, 454 US 864, (1981); Red Diamond Supply, Inc v Liquid Carbonic Corp, 637 F2d 1001 (5th Cir) *cert denied sub nom* Red Diamond Supply, Inc v Acme Welding, 454 US 827, (1981); Cowley v Braden Indus, 613 F2d 751 (9th Cir), *cert denied,* 446 US 965 (1980); H&B Equip Co v Intl Harvester Co, 577 F2d 239 (5th Cir 1978); Krehl v Baskin-Robbins Ice Cream Co, 78 FRD 108 (CD Cal 1978), *affd,* 664 F2d 1348 (9th Cir 1982).

[56] *See, e.g.,* Dougherty v Continental Oil Co, 579 F2d 954 (5th Cir 1978), *vacated on other grounds,* 591 F2d 1206 (5th Cir 1979); Pitchford v Pepi, Inc, 531 F2d 92 (3d Cir), *cert denied,* 426 US 935 (1976); American Motor Inns, Inc v Holiday Inns, Inc, 521 F2d 1230 (3d Cir 1975); Hobart Bros v Malcolm T Gilliland, Inc, 471 F2d 894 (5th Cir), *cert denied,* 412 US 923 (1973); Crime Check & Communications Corp of Am v Novar Elec Corp, No HM 75-1680 (DMd Sept 19, 1978]; Interphoto Corp v Minolta Corp, 295 F Supp 711 (SDNY 1969), *affd on other grounds,* 417 F2d 621 (2d Cir 1969); Guild Wineries & Distilleries v J Sosnick & Son, 102 Cal App 3d 627, 162 Cal Rptr 87 (1980).

[57] *See, e.g.,* Hobart Bros v Malcolm T Gilliland, Inc, 471 F2d 894 (5th Cir), *cert denied,* 412 US 923 (1973); *In re* Coca Cola Co, Trade Reg Rep (CCH) No 330, at 1 (1978), 91 FTC 517 (1978), *vacated as moot,* 642 F2d 1387 (DC Cir 1981).

[58] *See, e.g.,* Abadir & Co v First Miss Corp, 651 F2d 422, 427 n 5 (5th Cir 1981) (market-dividing agreement between supplier and customers with whom it competed held to be vertical); Red Diamond Supply, Inc v Liquid Carbonic Corp, 637 F2d 1001, 1004-05 (5th Cir), *cert denied sub nom* Red Diamond Supply, Inc v Acme Welding, 454 US 827, (1981) (since the supplier imposed a territorial and customer agreement on its distributor, the restrictions imposed are vertical; the fact that the supplier "distributed some of its own goods does not alter the situation"). *See also* H&B Equip Co v Intl Harvester Co, 577 F2d 239, 245 (5th Cir 1978):

> Conspiracies between a manufacturer and its distributors are only treated as horizontal . . . when the *source* of the conspiracy is a combination of the distributors. *United States v. Arnold, Schwinn & Co.,* 388 U.S. 365, 372-73 (1967), 1977-2 Trade Cas (CCH) ¶61,776 (ND Ill 1977); cf. Posner, *The Rule of Reason and the Economic Approach: Reflections on the Sylvania Decision,* 45 U. Chi. L. Rev. 1, 17 (1977) (condemning distributor cartels). (Emphasis added.)

Krehl v Baskin-Robbins Ice Cream Co, 78 FRD 108 (CD Cal 1979), *affd,* 664 F2d 1348 (9th Cir 1982) (territorial allocation dictated from the top of the system, not induced by concerted action among competitors); Westpoint Pepperell, Inc v Rea, 1980-2 Trade Cas (CCH) ¶63,341 (ND Cal 1980) (court concluded that defendant was acting vertically, not as a competitor of its distributor).

and thus the restraints imposed are "not horizontal" but rather are to be evaluated as "vertical."[59]

Some courts have altogether ignored the vertical-horizontol characterization question and applied the rule of reason to vertical restraints occurring in the context of dual distribution.[60]

A few courts have recognized the horizontal-vertical characterization problem but have refused to be drawn into the labelling process with which most courts struggle. Instead, these courts have asked whether the market restraints emanating from a dual distributorship are so plainly anticompetitive that they should be declared illegal "without elaborate inquiry as to the precise harm they have caused or the business excuse for their use."[61] The courts have focused upon the purpose of the per se rule and on the actual competitive impact of the dual distribution system, not on whether the vertical or horizontal aspects of the system predominate.[62] For example, in determining whether the rule of per se illegality should be extended to a business practice not theretofore afforded per se treatment, the court in *Krehl v Baskin-Robbins Ice Cream Co*[63] applied the test set forth by the Supreme Court in *Broadcast Music, Inc v CBS,* namely: "Whether the practice facially appears to be one that would always or almost always tend to restrict competition and decrease output . . . or instead one designed to 'increase economic efficiency and render markets more, rather than less, competitive' " (citations omitted).[64] Applying this test to the system at issue, the *Krehl* court concluded that application of the rule of per se illegality to restraints imposed in a dual distribution context would be both inappropriate and anti-competitive.

It would appear that this approach is the most appropriate course for the courts to follow—to apply the rule of reason to dual distribution arrangements, except in those situations in which the vertical aspect of the restraint is subject to the per se rule (i.e., resale price maintenance).[65]

---

[59] 388 US 365, 372 (1967), *overruled on other grounds,* Continental TV, Inc v GTE Sylvania, Inc, 433 US 36 (1977).

[60] *See, e.g.,* Jack Kahn Music Co v Baldwin Piano & Organ Co, 604 F2d 755 (2d Cir 1979) (location clause); Roesch, Inc v Star Cooler Corp, 671 F2d 1168 (8th Cir 1982) (termination of dealer pursuant to alleged price fixing scheme).

[61] Northern Pac Ry Co v United States, 356 US 1, 5 (1958).

[62] *See, e.g.,* Krehl v Baskin-Robbins Ice Cream Co, 78 FRD 108 (CD Cal 1979), *affd,* 664 F2d 1348 (9th Cir 1982); Donald B Rice Tire Co v Michelin Tire Corp, 683 F2d 15 (4th Cir) (*per curiam*), *cert denied,* 454 US 864 (1981); Copy-Data Sys, Inc v Toshiba Am, Inc, 663 F2d 405 (2d Cir 1981).

[63] 664 F2d 1348 (9th Cir 1982).

[64] 441 US 1 (1980).

[65] *See* Continental TV, Inc v GTE Sylvania, Inc, 433 US 36, 51 n 18 (1977); Albrecht v Herold Co, 390 US 145 (1968). Such an approach would be consistent with the Supreme Court's admonition in Continental TV, Inc 433 US at 58-59 that "[d]eparture from the rule of reason standard must be based upon demonstrable economic effect rather than—as in *Schwinn*—upon formalistic line drawing," and its admonition in *White Motor Co v United States,* 372 US 253 (1963), that "[w]e need to know more than we do about the actual impact of these arrangements on competition to decide whether they

§8.08 What actions by seller competing with its buyer may give rise to an unreasonable restraint of trade?

The potential quality of the character of a trade restraint in a dual distribution context can occur in a variety of contexts, including where Seller provides suggested retail prices to its independent Buyers, when Seller imposes territorial and customer restraints on its dealers, and when Seller terminates or refuses to deal with dealers. Beyond those specific categories of trade restraints, a dual distributor must be aware of the antitrust issues that may arise out of the means by which Seller competes with its Buyer. We now turn initially to this broader question of competition between a dual distributor Seller and its Buyer, followed by an examination of the more specific forms of trade restraints.

Assuming that the per se rule does not apply to a particular trade restraint, the legality of such trade restraint, if any, arising out of a dual distribution context must be determined under the rule of reason[66] trilogy: purpose, power, and effect. Specifically, in analyzing a §1 claim, the courts look generally to the defendant's *purpose* in engaging in the challenged conduct, its *power* to restrain competition in the relevant market, and the anticompetitive *effect* of its conduct.

---

have such a 'pernicious effect on competition and lack . . . any redeeming virtue' [citation omitted] so as to warrant application of the *per se* rule." Any other result would cause a focus upon "formalistic line drawing," rather than upon "demonstratable [sic] economic effect," an approach which the Supreme Court criticized in Continental TV, 433 US at 58-59. Somewhat similar is a proposal to equate the legal concept of "verticality" with the business or economic concept of *intrabrand* arrangements and the legal concept of "horizontality" with *interbrand* arrangements. C. Hills, Antitrust Advisor, 89-90 (2d ed Supp 1981). Under this approach, the rule of reason would apply to intrabrand restraints, even if horizontal.

[66] In his well-known formulation of the rule of reason, Justice Brandeis stated in Chicago Bd of Trade v United States, 246 US 231, 238 (1918):

> The true test of legality is whether the restraint imposed is such as merely regulates and perhaps thereby promotes competition or whether it is such as may suppress or even destroy competition. To determine that question the court must ordinarily consider the facts peculiar to the business to which the restraint is applied; its condition before and after the restraint was imposed; the nature of the restraint and its effect, actual or probable. The history of the restraint, the evil believed to exist, the reason for adopting the particular remedy, the purpose or end sought to be attained, are all relevant facts. This is not because a good intention will save an otherwise objectionable regulation or the reverse; but because knowledge of intent may help the court to interpret facts and to predict consequences.

§8.09 What is the purpose of the challenged conduct?

It has been argued that Seller's mere recklessness and disregard of the likely effects of its conduct on its Buyer-competitors is sufficient to show a violation of §1. In *England v Chrysler Corp*,[67] for example, the court held that the plaintiff must show that the defendant's "conduct was deliberate." Such deliberateness or intent can be proved by showing that the defendant has determined a course of conduct which in turn is likely to have an anticompetitive effect. Thus, said the court: "It may well be that the predominant emphasis on market penetration which results in the deliberately reckless operation of a subsidized retailer and which has the inevitable effect of forcing competing and non-subsidized dealers to function at an unprofitable level, could, if proved, constitute an unreasonable restraint of trade."[68]

Seller's attempts to drive out of business its independent distributors who are actual or potential competitors rather than terminate them and leave them free to sell another line, or its attempts to intentionally reduce Buyer's profits with the ultimate goal of acquiring Buyer at a modest cost, have been held to justify the conclusion that the complained-of activity has an anticompetitive purpose.[69]

Seller's decision to raise its prices to its independent distributors, with the intent of driving them out of business and replacing them with its wholly owned distributors, has been held predatory and unlawful under §1.[70] Similarly, a conspiracy to eliminate independent franchises and replace them with company operations could violate §1 where there is no independent business need, economic justification, or direct profit motive.[71]

Operation of retail outlets without regard for retail profits in order to maximize market penetration and resulting wholesale profits may indicate a purpose inconsistent with free retail competition.[72] Evidence of such disregard can

---

[67] 493 F2d 269, 273 (9th Cir 1974).

[68] *Id* 273, citing Rea v Ford Motor Co, 355 F Supp 842, 863-71 (WD Pa 1973) *revd on other grounds,* 497 F2d 577 (3d Cir), *cert denied,* 419 US 868 (1974); Industrial Bldg Materials, Inc v Interchemical Corp, 437 F2d 1336, 1341-43 (9th Cir 1970). *Accord* Glauser Dodge Co v Chrysler Corp, 570 F2d 72, 84 (3d Cir 1977), *cert denied,* 436 US 913 (1978).

[69] *See* Photovest Corp v Fotomat Corp, 606 F2d 704 (7th Cir 1979), *cert denied,* 445 US 917 (1980) (a §2 case); Coleman Motor Co v Chrysler Corp, 525 F2d 1338, 1345, 1347 (3d Cir 1975), *cert denied,* 419 US 869 (1975); Indus Bldg Materials, Inc v Interchemical Corp, 437 F2d 1336, 1341 (9th Cir 1970); Rea v Ford Motor Co, 355 F Supp 842, 865 (WD Pa 1973), *revd on other grounds,* 497 F2d 577 (3d Cir), *cert denied,* 419 US 868 (1974). *Cf* Poller v Columbia Broadcasting Sys, Inc, 368 US 464 (1962).

[70] Castoe v Amerada Hess Corp, 1976-2 Trade Cas (CCH) ¶61,054, at 69,759 (SDNY 1976).

[71] Suburban Car Rentals, Inc v IT&T Corp, 1973-1 Trade Cas (CCH) ¶74,552, at 94,431 (SDNY 1973).

[72] *See* Coleman Motor Co v Chrysler Corp, 525 F2d 1338, 1343 (3d Cir 1975), *cert denied,* 419 US 869 (1975); England v. Chrysler Corp, 493 F2d 269, 273-74 (9th Cir 1974); Rea 355 F Supp at 842.

be derived from a variety of factors: sales at unusually low prices;[73] excessive expenditures on advertising;[74] statements by the manufacturer to the effect that retail losses are unimportant;[75] statements by the manufacturer indicating it intended to take over retail distribution in certain areas.[76]

It has been held, however, that the switching of business to an affiliated company with the intent to favor that affiliated company, without more, is not the equivalent of an intent to impose an unreasonable restraint of trade.[77] Similarly, the payment of subsidies (e.g., capital investments, absorption of start-up expenses, favorable credit arrangements) by Seller to its wholly owned sales subsidiaries for the purpose of increasing market penetration has been recognized as procompetitive and as not establishing a recoverable injury to a competing Buyer,[78] at least in the absence of vertical integration whose purpose or actual effect is to consolidate or concentrate the sales of Seller's products in the hands of its wholly or partially owned dealers.[79] Moreover, standing alone, the fact that a terminated dealer provided good service to the manufacturer does not support the conclusion that the manufacturer had an anticompetitive purpose.[80]

It should be noted, however, that the existence of less anticompetitive alternatives supports a finding of an anticompetitive purpose. Thus, a manufacturer's extension of certain financial and other assistance to distributors it partially owns and its failure to extend similar assistance to its independent distributors may, under some circumstances, support a finding of an anticompetitive purpose.[81]

In conjunction with assessing the foregoing indications of an anticompetitive intent the courts will take account of business justifications for the challenged course of conduct.[82] The various business justifications accepted by the courts suggest that: a manufacturer's need to have a distributor at a particular loca-

---

[73] *See* England 493 F2d at 274 n 7; Rea 497 F2d at 589 n 26.

[74] *See* Coleman Motor Co, 525 F2d at 1344; *England,* 493 F2d at 274.

[75] *See* Coleman Motor Co, 525 F2d at 1344.

[76] *See* Rea, 355 F Supp at 865-66.

[77] DeVoto v Pacific Fidelity Life Ins Co, 618 F2d 1340 (9th Cir), *cert denied,* 449 US 869 (1980). *See* American Motor Inns, Inc v Holiday Inns, Inc, 521 F2d 1230, 1246-48 (3d Cir 1975).

[78] *See* Rea, 497 F2d 577 (1974).

[79] Glauser Dodge Co v Chrysler Corp, 570 F2d 72, 84, 86 (3d Cir 1977), *cert denied,* 436 US 913 (1978).

[80] *See* Glauser Dodge Co v Chrysler Corp, 1976-2 Trade Cas (CCH) ¶61,093, at 69,972 (DNJ 1976), *revd,* 570 F2d 72 (3d Cir 1977) (financial assistance was a temporary and supplemental means of bolstering a defective dealer network), *cert denied,* 436 US 913 (1978).

[81] Bushie v Stenocord Corp., 460 F2d 116, 119-20 (9th Cir 1972); V&L Cicione, Inc v C Schmidt & Sons, 403 F Supp 643, 650 (ED Pa 1975), *affd,* 656 F2d 154 (3d Cir 1977).

[82] Joseph E Seagram & Sons v Hawaiian Oke & Liquors, Ltd, 416 F2d 71 (9th Cir 1969); Glauser Dodge Co v Chrysler Corp, 570 F2d 72, 82-83 (3d Cir 1977), *cert denied,* 436 US 913 (1978).

tion may justify subsidizing a dealership at that location;[83] a manufacturer's need to give junior personnel greater sales experience may justify the decision to substitute direct distribution for independent distributors;[84] Seller's desire to maintain both full compliance with the antitrust laws and the greatest degree of influence which the law will allow over all aspects of the distribution of its products, including resale prices and territorial restraints, is a justification for conversion;[85] and the desire to achieve operating efficiencies and thereby reduce the price of a product or to exercise greater control over the quality of the product or service are valid business reasons for conversion.[86] Moreover, a parent corporation's decision to have its partially owned dealer move its overage of new and used goods, "regardless of price" in order to avoid excessive interest charges on such inventory and loss attributable to depreciation, is an exercise of sound business judgment.[87]

§8.10 How much power does Seller have in the relevant market?

Seller's market power, primarily a function of the market share commanded by its product in the interbrand market, is important in determining the reasonableness of a given course of conduct and the likelihood of that conduct having an anticompetitive effect. Seller's possession of market power tends to "raise the likelihood of a restraint of trade."[88] Indeed, a showing of "dramatic market power" (i.e., a market share of 50 per cent or more) on the part of Seller may allow a jury to draw an inference of an anticompetitive effect.[89] Moreover, it has been said that "action tending to strengthen that position [of market power] would be an unreasonable restraint of trade."[90]

---

83 *See* England 493 F2d at 271.

84 Trixler Brokerage Co v Ralston Purina Co, 505 F2d 1045, 1047 (9th Cir 1974).

85 *See* McGuire v Times Mirror Co, 405 F Supp 57 (CD Cal 1975); Knutson v Daily Review, Inc, 383 F Supp 1346, 1060-61 (ND Cal 1974), *modified,* 401 F Supp 1374 (ND Cal 1975), *affd in part & revd in part, on other grounds,* 548 F2d 795 (9th Cir 1976), *cert denied,* 433 US 910 (1977); Call Carl, Inc v BP Oil Corp, 403 F Supp 568, 575-76 (D Md 1975), *revd on other grounds,* 554 F2d 623, 628 (4th Cir), *cert denied,* 434 US 923 (1977); Lamarca v Miami Herald Publishing Co, 395 F Supp 324, 327 (SD Fla 1975), *affd,* 524 F2d 1230 (5th Cir 1975). *See also* Bowen v New York News, Inc, 522 F2d 1242 (2d Cir 1975), *cert denied,* 425 US 936 (1976).

86 *See* Lamarca 395 F Supp at 327; Varney v Coleman Co, 385 F Supp 1339, 1342-43 (DNH 1974).

87 Chisholm Bros Farm Equip v Intl Harvester Co, 498 F2d 1137, 1142 (9th Cir), *cert denied,* 419 US 1023 (1974).

88 Indus Bldg Materials v Interchemical Corp, 437 F2d 1336, 1342 (9th Cir 1970).

89 Associated Radio Serv Co v Page Airways, Inc, 624 F2d 1342, 1353 (5th Cir 1980), *cert denied,* 450 US 1030 (1981). *Accord* Northwest Power Prods, Inc v Omark Indus, 576 F2d 83, 89 (5th Cir 1978), *cert denied,* 439 US 1116 (1979).

90 Indus Bldg Materials, 437 F2d at 1343. *See* Knutson v Daily Review, Inc, 383 F Supp 1346 (ND Cal 1974), *modified,* 401 F Supp 1374 (ND Cal 1975), *affd in part & revd in part,* 548 F2d 795 (9th Cir 1976), *cert denied,* 433 US 910 (1977).

§8.11 What is the effect of the challenged conduct in the relevant market?

It is essential to a §1 claim not based on a per se violation that the plaintiff demonstrate that the challenged conduct had an anticompetitive effect in the marketplace; economic injury to the plaintiff is not sufficient. In order to make out a prima facie case under the rule of reason, an antitrust plaintiff generally must prove a well-defined market upon which the challenged anticompetitive actions could have had a substantial impact.[91]

Where the independent distributor goes out of business and no distributor takes its place, there may be an anticompetitive effect.[92] The plaintiff must demonstrate, however, that the challenged conduct (and not other factors) actually caused the diminution of competition in the retail market. If, for example, plaintiff's failure does not appear to be related to the challenged conduct, there is no standing to make a claim based upon that conduct.[93] Standing may exist, however, if plaintiff establishes that its proportion of the market steadily diminished and the proportion held by the company outlet steadily increased.[94]

It should also be noted that in dual distribution cases involving injunctive relief courts generally will consider the economic hardship to which the independent distributor is subjected by its supplier's competition or termination and whether the supplier has acted unfairly.[95] Even where the availability of injunctive relief is not directly in issue, the use of unfair tactics against a Buyer who is a competitor in an effort to take over that Buyer's customers may give rise to a §1 violation if the resulting market effect would have been prohibited under the law of mergers and if the conduct threatens "Sherman Act values."[96] Thus, where the defendant used unfair tactics including bribing away employees, theft of trade secrets, filing spurious lawsuits, and suspicious payments to actual or potential customers of the competitor to induce them to do business directly with the defendant supplier, a §1 violation was established.[97]

---

[91] Dougherty v Continental Oil Co, 579 F2d 954, 962-64 (5th Cir 1978), *vacated on other grounds,* 591 F2d 1206 (5th Cir 1979); Knutson v Daily Review, Inc, 383 F Supp 1346 (ND Cal 1974), *modified,* 401 F Supp 1374 (ND Cal 1975) *affd in part & revd in part,* 548 F2d 795, 803 (9th Cir 1976), *cert denied,* 433 US 910 (1977); Coleman Motor Co v Chrysler Corp, 525 F2d 1338, 1346 (3d Cir 1975), *cert denied,* 419 US 869 (1975).

[92] Indus Bldg Materials, Inc 437 F2d at 1342.

[93] *See* Rea 497 F2d at 588-89.

[94] *See* Coleman Motor Co 525 F2d at 1345.

[95] *See* Semmes Motors, Inc v Ford Motor Co, 429 F2d 1197, 1205 (2d Cir 1970); Crown High Corp v IT&T Corp, 1974-2 Trade Cas (CCH) ¶75,154 (D Conn 1974). *See also* Madsen v Chrysler Corp., 261 F Supp 488, 507 (ND Ill 1966), *vacated as moot,* 375 F2d 773 (7th Cir 1967).

[96] Associated Radio Serv Co v Page Airways, Inc, 624 F2d 1342, 1351 (5th Cir 1980), *cert denied,* 450 US 1030 (1981). *Accord* Northwest Power Prods, Inc v Omark Indus, 576 F2d 83, 89 (5th Cir, 1978), *cert denied,* 439 US 1116 (1979). *See also* Industrial Bldg Materials, Inc, v Interchemical Corp, 437 F2d 1336 (9th Cir 1970).

[97] Associated Radio Serv Co v Page Airways, Inc, 624 F2d 1342.

§8.12 May Seller suggest resale prices to Buyer with whom it also competes?

The suggestion of prices by a horizontal competitor followed by adherence to that suggestion may evidence an illegal price-fixing agreement.[98] Accordingly, a dual distributor must be sensitive to the possibility that its use of suggested resale prices under circumstances which would be lawful in a purely vertical context could be the basis for a finding of a horizontal price-fixing conspiracy which is per se unlawful.[99] A dual distributor must be sensitive, also, to the risk created by complaints to it by its wholly owned subsidiary Buyer regarding the pricing practices of Seller's independent Buyer with whom the subsidiary competes, since any subsequent action taken against the independent Buyer, such as termination, could give rise to a claim of price-fixing.[100]

Similarly, the use of Seller-owned retail outlets to put competitive pressure on Seller's independent customer-retailer—e.g., by cutting retail prices and thereby achieving control over the independent's retail price—could also vio-

---

[98] *See* United States v Masonite Corp, 316 US 265 (1942); Interstate Circuit, Inc v United States, 306 US 208 (1939); Esco Corp v United States, 340 F2d 1000 (9th Cir 1965).

[99] *See In re* Folding Carton Antitrust Litigation, 1980-2 Trade Cas (CCH) ¶63,458 (ND Ill 1980). *See also* Roesch, Inc v Star Cooler Corp, 671 F2d 1168 (8th Cir 1982). The horizontal price fixing implications of a dual distributor's use of suggested resale prices first arose in the context of the Fair Trade Laws. The authorizing Federal legislation prohibited agreements to maintain prices between competing entities. In United States v McKesson & Robbins, Inc 351 US 305 (1956), companies engaged in dual distributorships were held to be competitors of their distributors and thus prohibited from fixing the resale prices of their products in Fair Trade states. *Cf* Schwegmann Bros v Calvert Distillers Corp, 341 US 384 (1951).

[100] *See* Davis-Watkins Co v Serv Merchandise, 686 F2d 1190 (6th Cir 1982); Roesch, Inc, v Star Cooler Corp, 671 F2d 1168 (8th Cir 1982). In *Roesch,* the court affirmed summary judgment for the defendant because of insufficient evidence of conspiracy, stating:

> Although there is limited authority to the contrary, see *Giradi v. Gates Rubber Co. Sales Division,* 325 F.2d 196 (9th Cir. 1963), the majority view, which we adopt, is that mere complaints by customers of a manufacturer that distributors and dealers engage in price-cutting are not enough to imply a conspiracy in violation of section 1. Such complaints arise in the normal course of business and do not indicate illegal concerted action. See *Oreck Corp. v. Whirlpool Corp., supra,* 639 F.2d at 80; *Edward J. Sweeney & Son, Inc. v. Texaco, Inc., supra,* 637 F.2d at 111; *Borger v. Yamaha International Corp.,* 625 F.2d 390, 395 (2d Cir. 1980); *Oreck Corp. v. Whirlpool Corp., supra,* 579 F.2d at 133; *Westinghouse Electric Corp. v. CX Processing Laboratories, Inc.,* 523 F.2d 668, 675 (9th Cir. 1975); *Carr Electronics Corp. v. Sony Corp. of America,* 472 F.Supp. 9, 13 (N.D. Cal. 1979); *Interphoto Corp. v. Minolta Corp.,* 295 F. Supp. 711, 719 n.3 (S.D.N.Y. 1969), *aff'd per curiam,* 417 F.2d 621 (2d Cir. 1969); *Carbon Steel Products Corp. v. Alan Wood Steel Co.,* 289 F.Supp. 584, 588 (S.D.N.Y. 1968).

Roesch, 671 F2d at 1172.

late the Sherman Act.[101]

§8.13 May Seller impose customer or territorial restraints upon Buyers with whom it also competes?

Without question, the antitrust issue that has arisen most frequently in the dual distribution context is the legality of territorial or customer restraints. As previously discussed, horizontal market divisions are per se illegal.[102] Entities in a seemingly vertical relationship may be deemed capable of horizontal restraints subject to the per se rule if they are actual or potential competitors.[103] On the other hand, many courts have applied the rule of reason to territorial and customer restraints, notwithstanding the presence of horizontal relationships between Seller and its Buyers.[104]

A thorough consideration of dual distributorships and territorial restraints is found in several recent cases.[105] Most of those courts rejected the assertion that the per se rule applied to the territorial or customer restraints at issue because of the presence of a horizontal relationship between the dual distribu-

---

[101] Hanson v Shell Oil Co, 541 F2d 1352 (9th Cir 1976), *cert denied,* 429 US 1074 (1977).

[102] Timken Roller Bearing Co v United States, 341 US 593 (1951).

[103] *See, e.g.,* United States v Topco Assocs, 405 US 596 (1972); United States v Sealy, Inc, 388 US 350 (1967); Ohio-Sealy Mattress Mfg Co v Sealy, Inc, 585 F2d 821 (7th Cir 1978), *cert denied,* 440 US 930 (1979); American Motor Inns, Inc v Holiday Inns, Inc, 521 F2d 1230 (3d Cir 1975); Hobart Bros v Malcolm T Gilliland, Inc, 471 F2d 894 (5th Cir), *cert denied,* 412 US 923 (1973); Ohio-Sealy Mattress Mfg Co v Duncan, 1980-2 Trade Cas (CCH) ¶63,307 (ND Ill 1980); United States v CIBA GIEGY Corp, 1976-1 Trade Cas (CCH) ¶60,908 (DNJ 1976). *Cf* Pitchford v Pepi, Inc, 531 F2d 92 (3d Cir), *cert denied,* 426 US 935 (1976); Rubbermaid, Inc v FTC, 575 F2d 1169 (6th Cir 1978).

[104] *See, e.g.,* Dougherty v Continental Oil Co, 579 F2d 954 (5th Cir 1978), *vacated on other grounds,* 591 F2d 1206 (1979); H&B Equip Co v International Harvester Co, 577 F2d 239 (5th Cir 1978); Westpoint Pepperell, Inc, v Rea, 1980-2 Trade Cas (CCH) ¶63,341 (ND Cal 1980); Krehl v Baskin-Robbins Ice Cream Co, 78 FRD 108 (CD Cal 1979) *affd,* 664 F2d 1348 (9th Cir 1982); Donald B Rice Tire Co v Michelin Tire Corp, 483 F Supp 750 (D Md 1980), *affd per curiam,* 638 F2d 15 (4th Cir), *cert denied,* 454 US 864, (1981); *In re* Coca Cola Co, Dkt 8855, Trade Reg Rep (CCH) No 330, at 1 (1978) 91 FTC 517 (1978), *vacated as moot,* 642 F2d 1387 (DC Cir 1981). *See also* Williams & Co v Williams & Co-East, 542 F2d 1053 (9th Cir 1976), *cert denied,* 433 US 908 (1977).

[105] Davis-Watkins Co v Service Merchandise, 1982-2 Trade Cas (CCH) ¶64,901 (6th Cir 1982); Red Diamond Supply, Inc v Liquid Carbonic Corp, 637 F2d 1001 (5th Cir), *cert denied, sub nom,* Red Diamond Supply, Inc v Acme Welding, 454 US 827 (1981); Abadir & Co v First Miss Corp, 651 F2d 422 (5th Cir 1981); Copy-Data Sys, Inc v Toshiba Am, Inc 663 F2d 405 (2d Cir 1981); Donald B Rice Tire Co v Michelin Tire Corp, 483 F Supp 750 (D Md 1980), *affd per curiam,* 638 F2d 15 (4th Cir), *cert denied,* 454 US 864 (1981); Krehl v Baskin-Robbins Ice Cream Co, 78 FRD 108 (CD Cal 1979), *affd,* 664 F2d 1348 (9th Cir 1982); Cowley v Braden Indus, 613 F2d 751 (9th Cir), *cert denied,* 446 US 965 (1980); Guild Wineries & Distilleries v Sosnick, 1980-1 Trade Cas (CCH) ¶63,258, 102 Cal App 3d 627, 162 Cal Rptr 87 (1980).

tor supplier and its customers. For example, in *Red Diamond Supply, Inc v Liquid Carbonic Corp,*[106] plaintiff had claimed that a market-dividing agreement between Liquid Carbonic and Liquid Carbonic's distributors was a horizontal agreement, and thus per se unlawful, because Liquid Carbonic also distributed some of its own goods. In rejecting the horizontal label, the court reasoned:

> Since the allegation here is that Liquid imposed an agreement upon its distributors to abide by territorial and customer restrictions, that agreement is a vertical one, and the restrictions imposed are vertical restrictions.
>
> That Liquid also distributed some of its own goods does not alter the situation. [Citations omitted.] When a producer elects to market its goods through distributors, the latter are not, in an economic sense, competitors of the producer even though the producer also markets some of its goods itself; rather, the distributors are agents of the producer, employed because the producer has determined that it can supply its goods to consumers more efficiently by using distributors than it can by marketing them entirely by itself. [Citation omitted.] While it is possible that a nominally vertical arrangement may in fact be a horizontal one in disguise [citations omitted], such is not the case here.[107]

Applying the rule of reason, the court concluded that the defendant's conduct had not had the requisite adverse effect on competition. There was no basis for inferring either a lack of interbrand competition or an adverse effect on interbrand competition. Moreover, although the court was willing to presume a reduction in intraband competition, the reduction was ruled insufficient to constitute injury to competition.[108]

---

[106] 637 F2d 1001 (5th Cir), *cert denied sub nom* Red Diamond Supply, Inc v Acme Welding, 454 US 827 (1981).

[107] 637 F2d at 1004-05.

[108] The court's reasoning on this point, emphasizing as it does the right of the defendant to vertically integrate downward and thereby achieve total control over the resale of its products, is of interest:

> [G]iven the apparent nature of the market and Liquid's relative place in it, Liquid most probably could have chosen, consistent with the antitrust laws, to do all of its own distributing in the New Orleans area, either by cancelling its distributors and expanding internally or by simply acquiring the distributors themselves. If Liquid had thus vertically integrated into distributing, it clearly could have instructed its employees to abide by territorial and customer restrictions. And since Liquid could have accomplished these ends by either internal expansion or merger, either of which would have had an even greater impact on intrabrand competition, we fail to see why it would have been unreasonable for Liquid to accomplish the same ends by contract. See *Northwest Power Products, Inc. v. Omark Industries, Inc.*, 576 F.2d 83, 89 (5th Cir. 1978) (If a defendant could achieve a desired result either by lawful merger or by engaging in unfair competition, the choice of the unfair competition route alone should not give rise to an antitrust violation.), *cert. denied,* 439 U.S. 1116 (1979); *Associated Radio Service Co. v. Page Airways, Inc.*, 624 F. 2d 1342, 1351 (5th Cir. 1980) (the defendant in

Following *Red Diamond,* the Fifth Circuit undertook a more thorough consideration of a territorial restraint in a dual distribution context in *Abadir & Co v First Mississippi Corp.*[109] First Mississippi was a producer of fertilizers and chemicals which sold its products directly to users and to independent dealers or brokers who resold to users. Abadir was a dealer which purchased fertilizer from First Mississippi for resale. Abadir alleged that First Mississippi forced it to agree to resell the fertilizer only for consumption in Asia. The trial court ruled that this restriction was horizontal and therefore per se illegal. On appeal, the Fifth Circuit reversed. Noting the dearth of rule of reason cases analyzing the economic effects of dual distributorships and the Supreme Court's dictate that "departure from the rule-of-reason standard must be based upon demonstrable economic effect rather than . . . upon formalistic line drawing,"[110] the court held that the rule of reason was the proper standard to apply. It rejected the contention that a per se rule should apply to the territorial restraint imposed by the dual distributor because horizontal elements were present, stating that "a *per se* rule is applicable to a particular case if and only if the economic analysis which justifies the rule applies to the particular case."[111] It was the court's view that because the potential competitive benefits which might have motivated the dual distributor's actions were those of a vertical market-distributing agreement, the per se rule was not appropriate notwithstanding the horizontal aspects of the parties' relationship.

> *Northwest Power Products* "probably could have eliminated all distributors of its products by vertical integration (i.e., by beginning distribution of its own products) without running afoul of the antitrust laws), *cert. denied,* __ U.S. __, 102 S.Ct. 1277 (1982). To hold otherwise would in general simply create an incentive for vertical integration into the distribution system, thereby eliminating to that extent the role of independent businessmen. *Continental T.V.*, 433 U.S. at 57 n. 26, 97 S. Ct. at 2561 n. 26.

637 F2d at 1006-7.

[109] 651 F2d 422 (5th Cir 1981).

[110] Continental TV, Inc v GTE Sylvania Inc, 433 US 36, 58-59 (1977).

[111] 651 F2d at 426. In an extensive discussion of the bases for its rejection of the per se rule, the court stated:

> In the application of a recognized *per se* test, the Supreme Court has warned, 'Literalness is overly simplistic and often overbroad.' *Broadcast Music, Inc. v. Columbia Broadcasting Systems, Inc.*, 441 U.S. 1, 9, 99 S Ct 1551, 1557, 60 L.Ed.2d 1 (1979). And this Court has previously warned that 'courts must be careful not to extend the *per se* treatment to a type of restraint literally falling within a *per se* category where the rationale of the generalization is not applicable.' " *United States v. Realty Multi-List, Inc.*, 629 F.2d 1351 (5th Cir. 1980).
>
> Neither should literalness stand in the way of applying a *per se* rule where the rationale for the *per se* rule applies. For example, competitors are not allowed to make an otherwise horizontal agreement vertical by merely setting up a licensing corporation to 'impose' market-dividing agreements on its license-stockholders. 'We seek the central substance of the situation, not its periphery; and in this pursuit, we are moved by the identity of the persons who act, rather than the label of their hats.' *United States v. Sealy, Inc.*, 388 U.S. 350, 353, 87 S Ct 1847, 1850, 18 L Ed 2d 1238 (1967) (footnotes omitted).

Id 426.

The *Abadir* decision was cited with approval in *Copy-Data Systems v Toshiba America, Inc,*[112] a case arising out of a Seller's takeover of the distribution of its own products in areas in which its Buyer had had the exclusive distribution rights and its imposition of territorial restraints on the Buyer.[113] In reversing a jury verdict for the plaintiff which had been premised on the per se rule, the court stated that the expansion of that rule should be approached with great caution. It held that the mere presence of the horizontal territorial elements, which the district court had viewed as protecting Seller's profits rather than enhancing interbrand competition,[114] did not justify application of the per se rule because those restraints affected only intrabrand competition.[115]

An assertion that the per se rule applied to a dual distributor's allocation of exclusive territories among wholly owned and independent franchises similarly

---

[112] 663 F2d 405 (2d Cir 1981).

[113] Copy-Data had the exclusive distribution rights for 11 states and Chicago. Shortly after Copy-Data began to develop the Chicago market, Toshiba, which the court characterized as an "insignificant" force in a copier market in which there was stiff competition, decided to distribute directly and asked for and received without compensation Copy-Data's Chicago customer information. Not wishing to offend, Copy-Data complied with this request. Thereafter, Toshiba asked Copy-Data for its complete customer list. Copy-Data finally acquiesced upon Toshiba's assurance that it would use the lists for the distribution of new product announcements and price lists. Subsequently, Toshiba expressed dissatisfaction with Copy-Data at which point Copy-Data's problems began to accelerate: In succession, Toshiba took over the distribution of its products in Copy-Data's exclusive regions, extracted Copy-Data's records, persuaded Copy-Data to accept unneeded equipment, reneged on its promise not to count such purchases against Copy-Data's credit line, reduced Copy-Data's credit line, limited Copy-Data's "primary area of responsibility" to one state, required Copy-Data's credit line to be paid off in full and refused (contrary to industry practice and its own practice with other distributors) to accept returns or give credit on defective copiers for which Copy-Data had paid in advance. Not surprisingly, Copy-Data was driven into bankruptcy. Thereafter, it instituted suit, claiming that Toshiba's tactics, along with Copy-Data's coerced withdrawal from most of its market areas, constituted a horizontal market division which was per se illegal under §1 of the Sherman Act. 663 F2d at 408.

[114] *Id* 408. The court also rejected the contention that Toshiba's coercive and unfair tactics somehow justified the imposition of the per se rule in this context, stating that they added nothing in the absence of a showing of an anticompetitive effect. *Id* 410.

[115] The court specifically acknowledged that the nature of its inquiry would have been substantially different had Toshiba's conduct been challenged under the rule of reason, stating:

> We need not speculate as to the precise goals of [Toshiba's] restrictions on Copy-Data. Had Copy-Data pursued a rule of reason theory, an inquiry into the goals and the effects of the restrictions on both intrabrand and interbrand competition would have been appropriate. [Citations omitted.] However, in determining that the *per se* rule does not apply, we need only recognize that the restrictions had sufficient potential to enhance competition, and hence should not be 'conclusively presumed to be unreasonable and therefore illegal without elaborate inquiry as to the precise harm they have caused or the business excuse for their use". [Citations omitted.]

663 F2d at 410 n 5.

was rejected in *Krehl v Baskin-Robbins Ice Cream Co.*[116] The court found that rather than being a horizontal market allocation, the restraint came from the top, that is, the Seller was acting not as a competitor of the independent franchisees, but as an entity at the apex of the market structure concerned with expanding the market for its products.[117] In the absence of concerted activities among entities acting as competitors, the court applied the rule of reason and concluded that the restraints were lawful since they enhanced interbrand competition.[118]

§8.14 May Seller Terminate or Refuse to deal with Buyer who is an actual or potential competitor in the resale of Seller's own products?

As discussed in Chapters 2 and 7, it is well established that a manufacturer or producer has the right to deal with whom it pleases and to select customers at will, so long as there is no purpose or resultant effect to create or maintain a monopoly or otherwise to violate the antitrust laws.[119] Thus, "a manufacturer may discontinue a relationship or refuse to open a new relationship for business reasons which are sufficient to the manufacturer, and an adverse effect on the business of the distributor is immaterial in the absence of any arrangement restraining trade or competition."[120] A manufacturer's refusal to deal with a distributor can, however, under certain circumstances be so inherently anticompetitive in purpose or effect, or both, as to be a combination in unreason-

---

[116] 664 F2d 1348 (9th Cir 1982).

[117] *Id* 1355.

[118] *Accord* Davis-Watkins Co v Service Merchandise, 686 F2d 1190 (6th Cir 1982), where territorial and customer restraints were held subject to the rule of reason. The fact that the supplier was a dual distributor made no apparent difference to the court. Rather, citing *Krehl, Copy-Data, Abadir,* and *Red Diamond,* it applied the same analysis as it would to a nondual distributor case to determine whether the restrictions imposed should be subject to the per se rule. Accordingly, if the territorial/customer restrictions originated as unilateral action from the supplier, rather than from agreement or concerted action among distributors, the restraints were subject to the rule of reason. *Id* at 1201-02. In short, the source of the restraint (*i.e.,* supplier or customer) controlled its characterization as "vertical" or "horizontal" and thus whether the rule of reason or the per se rule applied. See generally Posner, *The Next Step in the Antitrust Treatment of Restricted Distribution: Per Se Legality,* 48 U Chi L Rev 6, 21 (1981).

[119] United States v Colgate & Co, 250 US 300, 309 (1919).

[120] Ricchetti v Meister Brau, Inc, 431 F2d 1211, 1215 (9th Cir 1970), *cert denied,* 401 US 939 (1971), citing United States v Arnold Schwinn & Co, 388 US 365 (1967), *overruled on other grounds,* Continental TV, Inc v GTE Sylvania, Inc, 433 US 36 (1977); Joseph E Seagram & Sons v Hawaiian Oke & Liquors, Ltd, 416 F2d 71 (9th Cir 1969), *cert denied,* 396 US 1062 (1970). *See also* Mogul v General Motors Corp, 391 F Supp 1305 (ED Pa 1975), *affd,* 527 F2d 645 (3d Cir 1976), and numerous cases cited therein at 1311.

able restraint of trade.[121]

As with refusals to deal generally, assuming the requisite plurality of actors, a dual distributor's refusal to deal is subject to §1 if it is accompanied by anticompetitive acts or purpose.[122] Thus, for example, a complaint to Seller's independent Buyers with whom the subsidiary competed, followed by a termination of the independent, could be the basis for a concerted refusal to deal claim.[123] Similarly, as discussed in Chapter 2, a refusal to deal in aid of some other form of unlawful restraint, such as an unreasonable territorial or customer limitation, will result in the refusal to deal itself being held unlawful. In this regard, it should be noted that one of the consequences of territorial and customer restrictions in a dual distribution context being characterized as horizontal restraints, and thus subject to per se treatment, is that a dual distributor's refusal to deal with or termination of one of its independent dealers as a result of or in aid of such restraints will result in the termination or refusal to deal itself being treated as per se unlawful.[124]

§8.15 Under what circumstances will Seller's decision to integrate vertically or to refuse to deal with actual or potential competitors run afoul of §1 of the Sherman Act?

With the emergence of vertical integration[125] as an alternative method of distribution, it is important to consider the circumstances in which a Seller's termination of or refusal to deal with a Buyer as part of that process may run afoul of §1 of the Sherman Act.

As a general rule, it is "clear . . . that vertical integration, as such without more, cannot be held violative of the Sherman Act. . . . [T]he extent of permissible integration must be governed, as other factors in Sherman Act violations,

---

[121] Trixler Brokerage Co v Ralston Purina Co 505 F2d 1045, 1052 (9th Cir 1974); Bushie v Stenocord Corp, 460 F2d 116 (9th Cir 1972); V&L Cicione, Inc v C Schmidt & Sons, 403 F Supp 643, 648 (ED Pa 1975), *affd,* 656 F2d 154 (3d Cir 1977).

[122] California Steel & Tube v Kaiser Steel Corp, 650 F2d 1001 (9th Cir 1981).

[123] *See* Roesch, Inc v Star Cooler Corp, 671 F2d 1168 (8th Cir 1982).

[124] *See* Hobart Bros v. Malcolm T Gilliland, Inc, 471 F2d 894 (5th Cir), *cert denied,* 412 US 923 (1973); Interphoto Corp v Minolta Corp, 295 F Supp 711 (SDNY), *affd per curiam,* 417 F2d 621 (2d Cir 1969); Guild Wineries & Distilleries v J Sosnick & Son, 1980-1 Trade Cas (CCH) ¶63,258 102 Cal App 3d 627, 162 Cal Rptr 87 (1980). *See also* American Motor Inns, Inc v Holiday Inns, Inc, 521 F2d 1230 (3d Cir 1975); McAlpine v AAMCO Automatic Transmissions, Inc, 461 F Supp 1232 (ED Mich 1978).

[125] To vertically integrate downstream is to undertake the distribution of one's own products which had been and could be sold to independent producers or distributors. 3 P. Areeda & D. Turner, Antitrust Law ¶724, at 195 (1978). For an overview of vertical integration, see Kaserman, *Theories of Vertical Integration: Implications for Antitrust Policy,* 23 Antitrust Bull 483 (1978).

by the other circumstance of individual cases."[126] Thus, Seller's termination of its relationships with independent distributors for the purpose of converting to a direct selling system using its own employees is legitimate, absent a purpose to restrain trade or monopolize.[127] This is true because such vertical integration into distribution, absent substantial market power at any one product or distribution level, will "not have an anticompetitive effect."[128] Such a rule is consistent with Seller's right to seek greater control of its product by changing its distribution structure.[129] The fact that there is some adverse effect on the distributor's business is not equated with an unlawful restraint of trade.[130] In short, a supplier's freedom under §1 of the Sherman Act to switch distributors is not impaired by the fact that the switch was effected by or was part of a plan of vertical integration.[131]

It is important to consider the purpose of the vertical integration. For example, Seller's termination of its wholesalers and assumption of the wholesaling function itself, in order to counteract *free-riding* by dealers that had not borne their fair share of the costs of promotion and service, has been upheld as reasonable.[132] Similarly, a desire to increase profits is a legitimate motive.[133]

Where Seller has substantial market power or where there is significant consumer loyalty to a particular brand of product, some courts have suggested

---

[126] United States v Columbia Steel Co, 334 US 495, 525-26 (1948).

[127] Millcarek v Miami Herald Publishing Co, 388 F Supp 1002, 1005-06 (SD Fla 1975); McGuire v Times Mirror Co, 405 F Supp 57, 67 (CD Cal 1975).

[128] Auburn News Co v Providence Journal Co, 659 F2d 273 (1st Cir 1981), *cert denied,* 455 US 921 (1982), vacating a preliminary injunction forbidding the defendant from terminating the newspaper's independent distributors. *See* Gilbuilt Homes, Inc v Continental Homes, 667 F2d 209 (1st Cir 1982).

[129] *See, e.g.,* Auburn News Co v Providence Journal Co, 659 F2d 273 (1st Cir 1981), *cert denied,* 455 US 921 (1982); Naify v McClatchy Newspapers, 599 F2d 335, 336 (9th Cir 1979); Knutson v Daily Review, Inc, 548 F2d 795, 805 (9th Cir 1976), *cert denied,* 433 US 910 (1977).

[130] White v Hearst Corp, 669 F2d 14 (1st Cir 1982); Knutson v Daily Review, Inc, 548 F2d 795, 803 (9th Cir 1976), *cert denied,* 433 US 910 (1977). *But see* Foremost Intl Tours, Inc v Qantas Airways Ltd, 379 F Supp 88 (D Hawaii 1974), *affd,* 525 F2d 281 (9th Cir 1975), *cert denied,* 429 US 816 (1976), in which a preliminary injunction was issued against Qantas following its termination of an air transportation contract with the plaintiff tour operator and subsequent entry into the field of producing and selling integrated tour packages. The court found that the actions taken by Qantas in its vertical-conglomerate expansion into the tour business established a prima facie violation of the antitrust laws. 379 F Supp at 97.

[131] Crown Beverage Co, v Cerveceria Moctezuma, *SA,* 663 F2d 886, 888 (9th Cir 1981) (*per curiam*) (citing Bushie v Stenocord Corp, 460 F2d 116 (9th Cir 1972)).

[132] Donald B Rice Tire Co v Michelin Tire Corp, 483 F Supp 750 (D Md 1980), *affd per curiam,* 638 F2d 15 (4th Cir), *cert denied,* 454 US 864, (1981).

[133] *See generally* Fuchs Sugars & Syrups, Inc v Amstar Corp, 602 F2d 1025 (2d Cir), *cert denied,* 444 US 917 (1979), in which the conversion of a sales force from independent general brokers (who simultaneously acted on behalf of several competing suppliers) to direct brokers (who worked only on behalf of one supplier) for the purpose, in part, of increasing the price (and profit margin) of the supplier's product was held lawful.

that the focal point of inquiry is whether Seller's implementation of a vertically integrated distribution system has the effect of reducing intrabrand competition.[134] Thus, in some dual distribution cases involving oligopolistic industries such as automobile manufacturing, where intrabrand competition among dealers of a single brand may be highly significant to the consumer,[135] more stringent standards of conduct may be imposed with the result that "restraints designed to achieve vertical integration may be found to be unreasonable."[136] Similarly, the manufacturer's possession of market power may make anticompetitive effects arising from termination of independent distributors in favor of direct sales more likely because independent distributors would be less likely to have other options available to them and the supplier might end up with more power to control resale prices, including those charged by the remaining distributors.[137] Thus, the possibility exists that a company with substantial market power could be foreclosed from ever replacing a system of independent distributors with its own system of direct sales.[138]

The elimination of intrabrand competition, resulting from the termination of independent distributors in favor of direct distribution by the manufacturer, might constitute enough of an anticompetitive effect to give rise to a §1 violation in some circumstances. However, where competition among manufacturers itself guarantees that a reduction in intrabrand retail competition will not give any manufacturer greater power to control prices, the anticompetitive effect of such a reduction in intrabrand retail competition should not give rise to a §1 violation.[139]

---

[134] *See* Coleman Motor Co v Chrysler Corp, 525 F2d 1338, 1358 (3d Cir 1975), *cert denied,* 419 US 869 (1975); Castoe v Amerada Hess Corp, 1976-2 Trade Cas (CCH) ¶ 61,054 (SDNY 1976) at 69,759, and cases cited therein. *See also* Glauser Dodge Co v Chrysler Corp, 570 F2d 72, 81-82 n 17 (3d Cir 1977), *cert denied,* 435 US 913 (1978), where the court noted without deciding Glauser's contention in conjunction with its focus on intrabrand competitive effects that the wholesale Dodge market was the relevant market (citing Joe Westbrook, Inc v Chrysler Corp, 419 F Supp 824 (ND Ga 1976)) and that the retail market similarly should be limited to new Dodge automobiles.

[135] See Note, *Vertical Integration as a Restraint on Intrabrand Competition: the Automobile Industry,* 17 BC Indus & Com LR 871, 875-76 (1976).

[136] Glauser Dodge Co v Chrysler Corp, 570 F2d 72 (3d Cir 1977), *cert denied,* 436 US 913 (1978).

[137] *See* Industrial Bldg Materials, Inc v Interchemical Corp, 437 F2d 1336, 1342 (9th Cir 1970). *Cf* Venzie Corp v United States Mineral Prod Co, 382 F Supp 939, 952-54 (ED Pa 1974), *affd,* 521 F2d 1309 (3d Cir 1975).

[138] *See* Industrial Bldg Materials, Inc 437 F2d at 1342-43.

[139] Knutson v Daily Review, Inc, 383 F Supp 1346, 1365 (ND Cal 1974), *modified,* 401 F Supp 1374 (ND Cal 1975), *affd in part, revd in part,* 548 F2d 795 (9th Cir 1976), *cert denied,* 433 US 910 (1977), *on remand,* 468 F Supp 226 (ND Cal 1979), *affd,* 664 F2d 1120 (9th Cir 1981).

§8.16 —What is the relevant market in which to assess the anticompetitive effect of the refusal to deal?

When Seller's method of competing with its Buyers or its conversion from independent distributors to direct selling by its own employees or subsidiaries is challenged under §2,[140] the key issue frequently is whether the relevant product market[141] is made up of all products of the same or similar type, or

---

[140] In brief summary, there are three types of §2 violations: monopolizing, attempts to monopolize, and conspiracies to monopolize. In order to prove monopolization in violation of Section 2 of the Sherman Act, a plaintiff must establish: "(1) the possession of monopoly power in the relevant market and (2) the willful acquisition or maintenance of that power as distinguished from growth or development as a consequence of a superior product, business acumen, or historic accident." United States v Grinnell Corp, 384 US 563, 570-71 (1966). While it is required that the monopolist have engaged in "willful" acts directed at establishing or retaining its monopoly, *id* 571, plaintiff need not show that such acts were of a kind that would be unlawful for an ordinary enterprise. Greyhound Computer Corp v IBM Corp, 559 F2d 488, 498 (9th Cir 1977), *cert denied,* 434 US 1040 (1978). In the last analysis a defendant's acts, otherwise lawful, must not be unreasonably restrictive of competition. *See* Gough v Rossmoor Corp, 487 F2d 373, 376 (9th Cir 1973), *cert denied,* 429 US 857 (1976). *See generally* Sherman v British Leyland Motors, Ltd, 601 F2d 429 (9th Cir 1979); Purex Corp v Proctor & Gamble Co, 596 F2d 881 (9th Cir 1979). Proof of an attempt to monopolize in violation of Section 2 requires three elements: "(1) specific intent to control prices or destroy competition with respect to a part of commerce, (2) predatory or anticompetitive conduct directed to accomplishing the unlawful purpose, and (3) a dangerous probability of success." Gough v Rossmoor Corp, 585 F2d at 390; Janich Bros v American Distilling Co, 570 F2d 848, 853 (9th Cir 1977), *cert denied,* 439 US 829 (1978). Both intent and probability of success may be inferred from predatory conduct if such conduct "can serve as the basis for a substantial claim of restraint of trade." 439 US at 854; Marquis v Chrysler Corp, 577 F2d 624, 641 (9th Cir 1978). Market power is relevant to determining whether such an inference is proper; but where a §1 violation "clearly exists," proof of market power is unnecessary to support an inference of specific intent. Hallmark Indus v Reynolds Metals Co, 489 F2d 8, 12-13 (9th Cir 1973), *cert denied,* 417 US 932 (1974).

[141] Where conduct is challenged under §2, a key issue may be the relevant market in which to assess the conduct in question. A definition of the relevant market, which is defined in terms of product and geography, United States v EI DuPont de Nemours, 351 US 377 (1956), is generally regarded as essential because "without a definition . . . there is no way to measure [the defendant's] ability to lessen or destroy competition." Walker Process Equip, Inc v Ford Mach & Chem Corp, 382 US 172, 177 (1965). The broader the relevant market, the smaller the supplier's share of that market and the less likely that he has or may be able to achieve monopoly power. United States v Grinnell Corp, 384 US 563, 570 (1966). The market definition process has been described as follows:

> In sum, defining a relevant product market is a process of describing those groups of producers which, because of the similarity of their products, have the ability—actual or potential—to take significant amounts of business away from each other. A market definition must look at all relevant sources of supply, either actual rivals or eager potential entrants to the market. A market definition must provide the numerator and denominator in the fraction labelled market share.

Smith-Kline Corp v Eli Lilly & Co, 575 F2d 1056, 1063 (3d Cir), *cert denied,* 439 US 838 (1978).

whether it consists solely of the products of the Seller in question. Although §2 violations have been found in a dual distribution context where the Seller has monopolized or is likely (*dangerous probability*) to acquire monopoly power in a relevant product market which includes more than its own products,[142] the burden of establishing a §2 claim becomes lighter if the relevant product market is shown to be Seller's product.

Most courts, however, have rejected contentions that the product of a particular Seller constituted the relevant product market for §2 purposes. For example, in *Mogul v General Motors Corp,*[143] the court rejected plaintiff's contention that Cadillacs constituted a definable submarket by taking judicial notice that "[t]he Cadillac is interchangeable with other luxury automobiles on the market."[144] Even where Buyer is without other sources of the product as a result of a shortage of the product, the courts have generally refused to treat Seller's product as the relevant product market.[145]

Some courts have been willing, however, to consider the possibility that one manufacturer's products may be the relevant market, notwithstanding the fact that other products of the same generic type are readily available, where they "are so unique or so dominant in the market in which they compete that any action by the manufacturer to increase his control over his product virtually assures that competition in the market will be destroyed."[146] In *Rea v Ford*

---

[142] *See, e.g.,* Photovest Corp v Fotomat Corp, 606 F2d 704 (7th Cir 1979), *cert denied,* 445 US 917 (1980).

[143] 391 F Supp 1305, 1313 (ED Pa 1975), *affd,* 527 F2d 645 (3d Cir 1976).

[144] For similar holdings, *see* Edward J Sweeney & Sons v Texaco, Inc, 637 F2d 105 (3d Cir 1980), *cert denied,* 451 US 911 (1981); Kaplan v Burroughs Corp, 611 F2d 286, (9th Cir 1979), *cert denied,* 447 US 924 (1980); Sherman v British Leyland Motors, Ltd, 601 F2d 429 (9th Cir 1979); Coleman Motor Co v Chrysler Corp, 525 F2d 1338, 1349 (3d Cir), *cert denied,* 419 US 869 (1975); Kresl Power Equip, Inc v Acco Indus, 1980-2 Trade Cas (CCH) ¶63,554 (ND Ill 1980); McDaniel v General Motors Corp, 1980-1 Trade Cas (CCH) ¶63,043 (EDNY 1979); Speed Auto Sales, Inc v American Motors Corp, 1979-2 Trade Cas (CCH) ¶62,981 (EDNY 1979); Neugebauer v AS Abell Co, 1979-2 Trade Cas (CCH) ¶62,933 (D Md 1979). *See also* Newberry v Washington Post Co, 438 F Supp 470 (DDC 1977).

[145] *See, e.g.,* Mullis v Arco Petroleum Corp, 502 F2d 290 (7th Cir 1974); White Bag Co v Intl Paper Co, 502 F2d 1164 (4th Cir 1974); Consumers Oil Co v Continental Oil Co, 1979-1 Trade Cas (CCH) ¶62,596 (D Minn 1978); Levine & Co v Calkraft Paper Co, 429 F Supp 1039 (ED Mich 1976). *See also* Harvey v Fearless Farris Wholesale, Inc, 589 F2d 451 (9th Cir 1979).

[146] Bushie v Stenocord Corp, 460 F2d 116, 121 (9th Cir 1972). *See* Coleman Motor Co, 525 F2d 1338, 1349 (3d Cir 1975); Indus Bldg Materials Inc v Interchemical Corp, 437 F2d 1336, 1337 (9th Cir 1970); Paschall v Kansas City Star Co, 1978-2 Trade Cas (CCH) ¶62,261, 1979-1 Trade Cas (CCH) ¶62,464 (WD Mo 1979), *interlocutory review denied,* 605 F2d 403 (8th Cir 1979); Castoe v Amerada Hess Corp, 1976-2 Trade Cas (CCH) ¶61,054, at 69,759 (SDNY 1976); Joe Westbrook, Inc v Chrysler Corp, 419 F Supp 824 (ND Ga 1976); Tire Sales Corp v Cities Serv Oil Co, 1976-1 Trade Cas (CCH) ¶60,827, at 68,612 (ND Ill 1976); Rea v Ford Motor Co, 355 F Supp 842, 876-78 (WD Pa), *revd on other grounds,* 497 F2d 577 (3d Cir), *cert denied,* 419 US 868 (1974); Mt Lebanon Motors, Inc v Chrysler Corp, 283 F Supp 453, 460 (WD Pa 1968), *affd on other*

Motor Co, for example, the court noted that "Ford is the only source of Ford-Lincoln-Mercury motor vehicles,"[147] and held that Ford automobiles constituted a relevant submarket for a §2 claim based upon a showing that the brand loyalty of Ford customers approached 90 per cent. The court observed that the average automobile dealer must make a substantial investment in the branch from which it sells and is therefore inhibited from looking to another manufacturer to supply its needs.[148]

§8.17 —What are the rules by which to assess the legality of the refusal to deal under §2 of the Sherman Act?

It has been said that the most conceptually difficult context in which to evaluate the legality of refusals to deal occurs when a monopolist seeks to vertically integrate or refuses to deal with actual or potential competitors of its vertically integrated enterprise.[149] Although it is generally recognized that

---

grounds, 417 F2d 622 (3d Cir 1969). *Cf* Perington Wholesale, Inc v Burger King Corp, 631 F2d 1369 (10th Cir 1979) (allegation that market consisted of supplies for particular fast food franchises). *See also* Glauser Dodge Co v Chrysler Corp, 570 F2d 72, 81 n 16 (3d Cir 1977), *cert denied,* 436 US 913 (1978) (court expressed no opinion on contentions that wholesale Dodges and retail Dodges were separate product markets for §1 purposes); Ovitron Corp v General Motors Corp, 364 F Supp 944 (SDNY 1973), *affd,* 512 F2d 442 (2d Cir 1975).

147 355 F Supp at 842.

148 *Id* 877.

149 *See* Byars v Bluff City News Co, 609 F2d 843 (6th Cir 1979). Subsequent opinion following remand, 1982-2 Trade Cas (CCH) ¶64,838 (8th Cir 1982). To summarize briefly the refusal to deal law under §2, unilateral refusals to deal when a customer has no other sources for the products sold by the supplier come within the stated exception to the *Colgate* doctrine (United States v Colgate & Co, 250 US 300 (1919)). *See* Otter Tail Power Co v United States, 410 US 366 (1973); Lorain Journal Co v United States, 342 US 143 (1951); Eastman Kodak Co v Southern Photo Materials Co, 273 US 359 (1927); Sargent-Welch Scientific Co v Ventron Corp, 567 F2d 701 (7th Cir 1977), *cert denied,* 439 US 822 (1978); Burdett Sound, Inc v Altec Corp, 515 F2d 1245, 1248 (5th Cir 1975); Packaged Program, Inc v Westinghouse Broadcasting Co, 255 F2d 708 (3d Cir 1958). *See also* Midland Telecasting Co v Midessa Telecasting Co, 617 F2d 1141 (5th Cir), *cert denied,* 449 US 954 (1980); Hershey Chocolate Corp v FTC, 121 F2d 968 (3d Cir 1941). *Cf* Local 1330, United States Steel Workers of Am v United States Steel Corp, 631 F2d 1264 (6th Cir 1980); Cascade Broadcasting Corp v KPDQ, Inc, 1976-1 Trade Cas (CCH) ¶60,719 (D Ore 1976). There exist two conceptually similar lines of cases which impose upon a monopolist a duty to deal. The first is a straightforward intent test which originated from *dicta* in *Colgate.* 250 US at 307 (the Court stated that a business is free to deal with whomever it pleases so long as it has no "purpose to create or maintain a monopoly"). *See also* Poller v Columbia Broadcasting Sys, 368 US 464, 468-60 (1962). The second involves a related line of cases styled as promulgating the "bottleneck theory of antitrust law." Under this approach, a business or group of businesses which control a scarce facility has an obligation to give competitors reasonable access to it. The seminal case is United States v Terminal *RR,* 244 US 383 (1912), where a group of railroads acquired ownership over a facility which constituted the only

"a refusal to deal to accomplish vertical integration, without more, should not be a basis for imposing liability" under §2,[150] vertical integration combined with a refusal to deal will, under some circumstances, give rise to §2 liability.[151]

While the courts are willing to accord a monopolist the right to vertically integrate (and to terminate existing customers in the process), it is also recognized that vertical integration by a monopolist can have adverse consequences for competition because monopoly at one level of the production-distribution process may carry with it the ability to affect adversely competition on other levels.[152] Such a view is consistent with the well-established §2 principle that a firm may not employ its market power in one market as a lever to create—or attempt to create—a monopoly in another market.[153] As we shall see, it is Seller's motive and intent in carrying out its plan of vertical integration that are the critical factors in an inquiry as to the legality of its conduct.

The definitive judicial analysis of the §2 issues arising out of a dual distributor monopolist's refusal to deal in the context of vertical integration can be found in the Sixth Circuit's opinion in *Byars v Bluff City News Co.*[154] *Byars* arose out of a claim by a small independent distributor of periodicals to small retail outlets that the refusal by a large regional distributor of such periodicals to continue to deal with the plaintiff and subsequent direct sales to plaintiff's customers violated §2 of the Sherman Act. Because of the structure of the wholesale publication distribution business, plaintiff was unable to obtain the same periodicals from other sources. In addition to the termination of Byars, there were allegations that the defendant had played dirty tricks when he tried to stay in business after the parties' relationship ended.

---

feasible terminal for rail traffic coming to the city of St. Louis from the West. The court ruled that the terminal owners had to make the facility equally accessible to all users. See A. Neale, The Antitrust Laws of the United States of America 66-69, 127-33 (2d ed 1970); Note, *Refusals to Deal by Vertically Integrated Monopolists,* 87 Harv L Rev 1720, 1740-52 (1974).

[150] Byars v Bluff City News Co, 609 F2d at 861. See *Areeda & Turner,* at ¶725; Sullivan, Handbook on Antitrust Law 129-30 (1976). *See also* Sargent-Welch Scientific Co v Ventron Corp, 567 F2d 701, 712 (7th Cir 1977), *cert denied,* 439 US 822 (1978); Pure Water Resources v Consolidated Foods Corp, 1980-1 Trade Cas (CCH) ¶63,064 (ND Cal 1979); Foremost Intl Tours, Inc v Qantas Airways, Ltd, 1980-1 Trade Cas (CCH) ¶63,004 (D Hawaii 1979).

[151] *See, e.g.,* Otter Tail Power Co v United States, 410 US 366 (1973); Eastman Kodak Co v Southern Photo Materials Co, 273 US 359 (1927); Poster Exchange v National Screen Serv Corp, 431 F2d 334 (5th Cir 1970), *cert denied,* 401 US 912 (1971). *See also* Paschall v Kansas City Star Co, 605 F2d 403 (8th Cir 1979).

[152] *See, e.g.* Auburn News Co v Providence Journal Co, 659 F2d 273 (1st Cir 1981), *cert denied,* 455 US 921, (1982).

[153] *See, e.g.,* United States v Griffith, 334 US 100 (1948); Smith-Kline Corp v Eli Lilly & Co, 575 F2d 1056 (3d Cir), *cert denied,* 439 US 838 (1978); Berkey Photo, Inc v Eastman Kodak Co, 603 F2d 263 (2d Cir 1979), *cert denied,* 444 US 1093 (1980) ("There is no reason to allow the exercise of such power to the detriment of competition, in either the controlled market or any other. That the competition in the leveraged market may not be destroyed but merely distorted does not make it more palatable").

[154] 609 F2d 843 (6th Cir 1979).

The court first analyzed the most significant §2 vertical integration-refusal to deal cases: *Eastman Kodak Co v Southern Photo Materials Co,*[155] *Otter Tail Power Co v United States,*[156] and *Poster Exchange, Inc v National Screen Service Corp.*[157] In *Eastman Kodak,* the Court affirmed a finding of illegal monopolization where Kodak had monopoly power over the national wholesale market for certain photographic supplies and cut off a distributor in furtherance of its desire to vertically integrate and take over retail distribution as well. In *Otter Tail,* a private utility which had monopoly power in a wholesale power market and which also was responsible for providing power at retail to the inhabitants of certain small towns was held to have wrongfully refused to sell power at wholesale prices or to *wheel* power to municipalities who proposed to replace Otter Tail in the local retail market with their own power companies.[158] In *Poster Exchange,* the defendant, National Screen, had a monopoly in the sale of certain movie posters and other related materials. For several years, Poster had bought these materials from National at wholesale prices and competed with it in the retail distribution market. National was found to have violated §2 because of its termination of Poster. Although the court's ruling was based upon a specific intent by National to exclude Poster from the retail market, in dicta, the court indicated that the evidence might otherwise have been sufficient to find that an unlawful monopoly would result from National's refusal to deal.[159]

Following its extensive analysis of the applicable legal precedent, the court concluded that "[a]lthough a general intent to monopolize is all that is generally required to find a §2 violation, cases discussing a monopolist's duty to deal have effectively required a finding of a *specific* intent to monopolize."[160] In the court's view, however, what matters most is not the monopolist's state of mind, but the overall impact of its practices.[161] It reasoned that since preservation of competition is at the heart of the antitrust laws, "a practice should be deemed 'unfair' or 'predatory' only if it is unreasonably anticompetitive," a determination that can only be made following a thorough analysis of each fact on a case-by-case basis.[162] The court then identified the factual situations in which a vertical integration scheme would be found to be anticompetitive: (1) where integration facilitates price discrimination so that the monopolist can reap the

---

[155] 273 US 359 (1927).

[156] 410 US 366 (1973).

[157] 431 F2d 334 (5th Cir 1970), *cert denied,* 401 US 912 (1971).

[158] *But see* Almeda Mall, Inc v Houston Lighting & Power, 615 F2d 343 (5th Cir), *cert denied,* 449 US 870 (1980). *Cf* City of Mishawaka v American Elec Power Co, 616 F2d 976 (7th Cir 1980), *cert denied,* 449 US 1096 (1981) (instead of refusing to deal, the power company sold electricity to municipalities at higher rates than the power charged its direct retail customers, for whom the power companies and municipalities competed, resulting in a §2 violation).

[159] 431 F2d at 388 n 12.

[160] Byars v Bluff City News Co, 609 F2d at 859 (6th Cir 1979) (emphasis in original).

[161] *Id* 860.

[162] *Id.*

maximum monopoly profit from different consumers; (2) where integration increases first-level entry barriers so that potential competitors are stymied; and (3) where integration facilitates evasion of regulation of monopoly profits.[163]

In remanding the case, the court specifically directed the district court to examine carefully the defendant's alleged dirty tricks since such predatory conduct "would go a long way toward establishing a section 2 violation."[164] It also recognized the problem of forming a final decree which would not enmesh the court in the difficult process of price regulation, advising the lower court that "the difficulty of setting a price at which a monopolist must deal might well justify withholding relief altogether."[165]

§8.18 May Seller discriminate in prices in favor of its own subsidiaries?

A Seller engaged in dual distribution who discriminates in prices, allowances or services in favor of its wholly owned distributors or affiliated companies against its independent distributors, or who sells directly to retailers at prices lower than it sells to its independent distributors, may violate the Sherman Act.[166] But Seller's intent to favor its affiliate or subsidiary, without more, does not amount to an unreasonable restraint of trade.[167]

Such discrimination may also give rise to Robinson-Patman Act[168] viola-

---

[163] *Id* 861 (citations omitted).

[164] *Id* 863, citing Otter Tail Power Co v United States, 410 US 366 (1973).

[165] 609 F2d at 864. (footnote omitted).

[166] *See* Glauser v Chrysler Corp, 418 F Supp 1009, 1013-15 (DNJ 1976), *revd,* 570, F2d 72 (3rd Cir 1977), *cert denied,* 436 US 913 (1978); Coleman Motor Co v Chrysler Corp, 525 F2d 1338, 1358 (3d Cir 1975); England v Chrysler Corp, 493 F2d 269, 271 (9th Cir 1974); Industrial Bldg Materials, Inc v Interchemical Corp, 437 F2d 1336, 1341 (9th Cir 1970) ; Mt Lebanon Motors, Inc v Chrysler Corp, 283 F Supp 453 (WD Pa 1968), *affd on other grounds,* 417 F2d 622 (3d Cir 1969). *See also* City of Mishawaka v American Elec Power Co, 616 F2d 976 (7th Cir 1980), *cert denied,* 449 US 1096 (1981) (a §2 case).

[167] *See* DeVoto v Pacific Fidelity Ins Co, 618 F2d 1340 (9th Cir), *cert denied,* 449 US 869 (1980).

[168] For the purposes of this discussion, we consider only §2(a), the portion of the act prohibiting price discrimination, which provides:

> It shall be unlawful for any person engaged in commerce, in the course of such commerce, either directly or indirectly, to discriminate in price between different purchasers of commodities of like grade and quality . . . where the effect of such discrimination may be substantially to lessen competition or tend to create a monopoly in any line of commerce, or to injure, destroy, or prevent competition with any person who either grants or knowingly receives the benefit of such discrimination, or with customers of either of them. . . .

15 USC §13(a)

tions.[169] In *Baim & Blank Inc v Philco Co,* for example, the defendant was charged with violating §2(a) by selling its products to a direct buying retailer at prices lower than those paid by competing retailers who purchased Seller's products from its wholly owned sales subsidiary.[170] In order to satisfy §2(a)'s requirement that the discriminatory sales be by the "same seller," plaintiff contended that the Seller so dominated and regulated its subsidiary as to cause the two corporations to be treated as one. The court rejected this contention, finding instead that the subsidiary controlled its own resale prices and sales policies and that therefore it was a separate seller.[171]

If sales by a wholly owned subsidiary of Seller are to be treated as legally distinct from sales by its parent, however, it follows that sales by the parent to its subsidiary may constitute a *sale* within the meaning of the Robinson-Patman Act, and some courts have so held,[172] at least where the subsidiary is operated independently of the dominion and control of the parent.[173] Accordingly, such sales at prices more favorable than the prices at which Seller sells to independent resellers could give rise to §2(a) liability. Although the viability of this theory has been recognized by some courts,[174] other courts have held that *transfers* by a parent corporation to its wholly owned subsidiary could never be considered *sales* to a separate purchaser within the meaning of the Robinson-Patman Act.[175]

§8.19 What other Robinson-Patman Act issues may arise in the dual distribution context?

If a dual distributor sells its products to its wholly owned wholesaler subsidi-

---

169 *See* Baim & Blank, Inc v Philco Co, 148 F Supp 541 (EDNY 1957).

170 *Id.*

171 *Id* 543-44.

172 *See* Perkins v Standard Oil, 395 US 642 (1969); Mississippi Petroleum, Inc v Vermont Gas Sys, Inc, 1972 Trade Cas (CCH) ¶73,843 (SD Miss 1972); Danko v Shell Oil Co, 115 F Supp 886 (EDNY 1953).

173 *See* Parrish v Cox, 586 F2d 9 (6th Cir 1978); Brewer v Uniroyal Tire, Inc, 498 F2d 973, 977 n 2 (6th Cir 1974); Reines Distribs, Inc v Admiral Corp, 256 F Supp 581 (SDNY 1966). *See also* Emil J Lauter Co v Brunswick Corp, 532 F Supp 983 (ND Ill 1982).

174 *See, e.g.,* Schaben v Samuel Moore & Co, 606 F2d 831 (8th Cir 1979) (product exchanges between supplier and its sales subsidiary were found to be intracompany *transfers* rather than *sales* with the result that no §2(a) claim could be made); Parrish v Cox, 586 F2d 9 (6th Cir 1978) (§2(a) claim was rejected on the ground that there was no *sale* within the meaning of the act because the subsidiary was not operated independently from its parent). *See also* Ivan's Tire Serv Store, Inc v Goodyear Tire & Rubber Co, 1976-1 Trade Cas (CCH) ¶60,797, 86 Wash 2d 513 (Wash Sup Ct 1976) (state law).

175 Security Tire & Rubber Co v Gates Rubber Co, 598 F2d 962, 965 (5th Cir.), *cert denied,* 444 US 942 (1979). See P. Areeda, Antitrust Analysis ¶701, at 845 n 13 (2d ed 1974). *See also* Emil J Lauter Co v Brunswick Corp, 532 F Supp 983 (ND Ill 1982).

ary at the same prices that it sells to direct buying retailers,[176] it would appear that no §2(a) violation has occurred since a party alleging price discrimination under the Robinson-Patman Act must, among other things, prove that the same seller charged different prices to different customers. Under the *indirect purchaser doctrine,* however, if Seller ignores the separate economic status of its wholesaler subsidiary and controls the terms upon which the subsidiary's retail Buyers purchase Seller's products, then those Buyers will be regarded as dealing directly with Seller for §2(a) purposes.[177] In that event, if the prices at which the wholesaler subsidiary resells Seller's products are different than those charged by Seller to the direct buying retailer, the requisite price discrimination exists.[178]

The critical question in determining whether a Buyer once removed has become Seller's customer for Robinson-Patman Act purposes is the degree of control exercised by Seller over its immediate Buyer—its wholesaler subsidiary.[179] In determining the degree of control necessary to invoke the indirect purchaser doctrine, it must be remembered that its purpose is to prevent Seller from insulating itself from Robinson-Patman liability by using a dummy wholesaler to make sales at terms actually controlled by Seller.[180] Thus the mere existence of repeated contacts between Seller and retail Buyers of its wholesaler subsidiary to provide training and advertising materials or to promote the sale of Seller's products does not establish the requisite degree of control; the solicitation and taking of purchase orders by Seller would, however, establish

---

[176] Not considered here is the more obvious form of price discrimination that arises when a dual distributor supplier sells to a direct buying retailer at prices below the prices at which it sells to independent wholesalers with whom it competes in the resale of its products. *See, e.g.,* City of Kirkwood v Union Elec Co, 671 F2d 1173, 1176 (8th Cir 1982); Industrial Bldg Materials, Inc v Interchemical Corp, 437 F2d 1336, 1345 (9th Cir 1970). Such discrimination may be the basis for a *price squeeze* claim in violation of the Sherman Act. *See, e.g.,* City of Kirkwood, 671 F2d at 1177 n 8.

[177] The indirect purchaser doctrine was described in Purolator Prods, Inc v FTC, 352 F2d 874 (7th Cir 1965), *cert denied,* 389 US 1045 (1968), as follows:

> To ensure fair competition among purchasers from the same seller, the Robinson-Patman Act amendments to the Clayton Act forbade sellers to make price discriminations between purchasers except when justified by economies to the seller. If a seller can control the terms upon which a buyer once removed may purchase the seller's product from the seller's immediate buyer, the buyer once removed is for all practical, economic purposes dealing directly with the seller. If the seller controls the sale, he is responsible for the discrimination in the sale price, if there is such discrimination. If the seller cannot in some manner control the sale between his immediate buyer and a buyer once removed, then he has not power by his own action to prevent an injury to competition [citation omitted].

Id 883.

[178] *See* Barnosky Oils, Inc v Union Oil Co 665 F2d 74 (6th Cir 1981); Purolator Prods, Inc v FTC, 352 F2d 874 (7th Cir 1965), *cert denied,* 389 US 1045 (1968).

[179] Brewer v Uniroyal Tire, Inc, 498 F2d 973, 977 n 2 (6th Cir 1974).

[180] American News Co v FTC, 300 F2d 104, 109-10 (2d Cir), *cert denied,* 371 US 824 (1962).

such control.[181]

The indirect purchaser doctrine does not represent the only circumstance in which a Buyer from a wholesaler subsidiary could assert a §2(a) claim against the parent Seller. Although there is a point in the distribution chain at which the injury from price discrimination becomes too remote to permit an indirect purchaser to recover damages, the courts will "guard against a situation in which a seller interposes a middleman as a shield against antitrust liability, especially where the middleman is a subsidiary of the seller."[182] Such liability may exist if the indirect buyer can prove that it was the *target* of Seller's price discrimination or that the discrimination was *aimed at* the indirect purchaser.[183] Seller's purpose in discriminating in prices is a relevant factor to consider in this connection.[184]

§8.20 May Seller raise its prices to its wholesale Buyers to the point that they will be unable to compete against it in the retail market?

A vertically integrated company which has dominant power at the wholesale level but faces competition at the retail level and which sets its wholesale prices so high in comparison to its retail prices that its wholesale customers will be unable to compete with it in the retail market may have engaged in a *price squeeze* in violation of both §§1 and 2 of the Sherman Act.[185] A price squeeze may arise not only when Seller sells directly to retail Buyers at discounts lower than or equal to the discounts it offers to a wholesaler with whom it competes in the

---

[181] *See* Barnosky Oils, Inc v Union Oil, 665 F2d 74 (6th Cir 1981); Hiram Walker, Inc v A&S Tropical, Inc, 407 F2d 4, 7 (5th Cir), *cert denied,* 396 US 901 (1969).

[182] Schwimmer v Sony Corp of Am, 637 F2d 41, 48-49 (2d Cir 1980).

[183] *Id* 48.

[184] *See, e.g.,* FLM Collision Parts, Inc v Ford Motor Co, 406 F Supp 224 (SDNY 1975), *affd in part on other grounds, revd in part on other grounds,* 543 F2d 1019 (2d Cir 1976), *cert denied,* 429 US 1097 (1977).

[185] *See, e.g.,* California Steel & Tube v Kaiser Steel Corp, 650 F2d 1001 (9th Cir 1981); Columbia Metal Culvert Co v Kaiser Aluminum & Chem Corp, 579 F2d 20 (9th Cir 1978); United States v Aluminum Co of Am, 148 F2d 416, 436-48 (2d Cir 1945). Many of the recent price squeeze cases have involved claims by municipalities that dual distributing electric power companies have raised wholesale, but not retail, rates, thereby putting the municipalities at a competitive disadvantage in the retail market. Generally, it has been held that such price squeeze claims are cognizable under the antitrust laws. *See, e.g.* City of Kirkwood v Union Elec Co 671 F2d 1173 (8th Cir 1982); City of Groton v Connecticut Light & Power Co, 662 F2d 921 (2d Cir 1981); City of Mishawaka v Indiana & Mich Elec Co, 560 F2d 1314 (7th Cir 1977), *cert denied,* 436 US 922 (1978); City of Mishawaka v American Elec Power Co, 616 F2d 976 (7th Cir 1980), *cert denied,* 449 US 1096 (1981); Borough of Ellwood City Pa v Pennsylvania Power Co, 462 F Supp 1343 (WD Pa 1979). *Contra* City of Newark v Delmarva Power & Light Co, 467 F Supp 763 (D Del 1979).

resale of its products;[186] it may also arise where the price to the wholesaler is lower than the price to retailers but not low enough to allow the wholesaler to compete with Seller.[187]

An unlawful price squeeze may also arise where Seller provides raw materials to its fabrication subsidiary at prices significantly lower than those charged to independent fabricators. As a result of such conduct, the subsidiary is able to make a profit on sales of its finished product at prices too low to be matched by the independents who had to buy their raw materials at market prices.[188] Such action may violate §2 if it results in the elimination of independents from the market, particularly where the raw material prices are only selectively reduced to those subsidiaries that compete with independent fabricators.[189] Moreover, such action could violate §1, particularly if elimination of an independent competitor of the subsidiary was brought about by concerted action to which a dominant company was a party.[190] Similarly, it may be unlawful for an integrated Seller with a dominant market position to exert a vertical price squeeze on competition of its fabricating operation by raising the prices of the raw materials which it sells to fabricators while holding down the prices of the finished product charged by Seller's fabricating operation.[191]

A price squeeze can also be effected through elimination of discounts. Thus, a dual distributing Seller's elimination of discounts to existing distributors, which has the purpose or effect of sharply reducing or eliminating altogether the ability of those distributors to compete with Seller in the resale of its

---

[186] *See* Industrial Bldg Materials, Inc v Interchemical Corp, 437 F2d 1336 (9th Cir 1970).

[187] *See* City of Kirkwood v Union Elec Co, 671 F2d 1173 (8th Cir 1982).

[188] *See* Columbia Metal Culvert Co v Kaiser Aluminum & Chem Corp, 579 F2d 20 (3d Cir 1978).

[189] *Id* 31-32.

[190] *Id* 32-33 n 47, citing Coleman Motor Co v Chrysler Corp, 525 F2d 1338, 1347 (3d Cir 1975), *cert denied,* 419 US 869 (1975); American Motor Inns, Inc v Holiday Inns, Inc, 521 F2d 1230, 1248 (3d Cir 1975); Fount-Wip v Reddi-Wip, Inc, 568 F2d 1296 (9th Cir 1978); Taxi Weekly v Metropolitan Taxicab Bd of Trade, 539 F2d 907 (2d Cir 1976).

Because the supplier in *Columbia Metal* had 80% of the relevant market, the court did not decide "whether a conspiracy to eliminate a competitor would be a violation of § 1 in the absence of such a market position on the part of one of the conspirators." *Id.* The *Columbia Metal* court acknowledged, however, that " 'A contract, regardless of actual effect, contravenes the Act if it was intended as part of a scheme to . . . drive a competitor out of the market.' American Motor Inns, Inc. v. Holiday Inns, Inc., 521 F2d 1230, 1248 (3d Cir 1975)." *Id.*

Even where a supplier has sufficient market dominance to subject its activities to §2 scrutiny, the possible applicability of §1 (assuming the requisite conspiracy exists) should not be overlooked since, as the court in *Columbia Metal* stated, "the inquiries into the scope of competition under §1 and §2 are not precisely the same." *Id* 27 n 11 (citations omitted). Those differences could produce different results on the issue of liability.

[191] California Steel & Tube v Kaiser Steel Corp, 650 F2d 1001 (9th Cir 1981).

products, may give rise to both §1 and §2 violations.[192] In *Eastman Kodak Co v Southern Photo Material Co,*[193] for example, the defendant manufacturer vertically integrated into the retail sale of its products by purchasing distributorships and opening its own retail outlets. The defendant also purchased competing producers. The government's challenge of these actions as monopolistic in violation of §2 was upheld by one district court. Thereafter, defendant eliminated dealer discounts previously given to its former distributors. The Supreme Court held that this latter action was unlawful because it was in futherance of an intent to monopolize.[194]

Even in the absence of monopoly power, such a pattern of conduct may be found anticompetitive, at least where a dominant line of products is involved.[195] Thus, the elimination of discounts to a distributor (or direct sales by Seller at prices at or below those charged the distributor) may have a sufficiently adverse effect on competition in the distribution of Seller's products as to constitute a restraint of trade in violation of §1.[196]

---

[192] *See,* Eastman Kodak Co v Southern Photo Materials Co, 273 US 359 (1927); Industrial Bldg Materials, Inc v Interchemical Corp, 437 F2d 1336 (9th Cir 1970).

[193] 273 US 359 (1927).

[194] *Id* 375.

[195] The court in *Industrial Building Materials, Inc* specifically offered no opinion as to the result if the "same actions were taken by a less powerful member of the industry" (footnote omitted). 437 F2d at 1343.

[196] The court summarized the adverse effects on competition as follows:

> First, the general public is damaged by being deprived of an independent distributor, who may handle competing products, thus giving the customer a ready comparison and a less biased assessment of each product. Second, elimination of the major independent distributor would give Presstite even more power to control prices, including those charged by the few remaining small distributors. Third, elimination of Industrial was apparently so effective as to leave it without the ability to continue business in distribution of other lines of sealants, a result constituting a direct restraint on trade. See *Poller v. Columbia Broadcasting System, Inc.,* 109 U.S. App. D.C. 170, 284 F.2d 599, 607 (1960) (Washington, J., dissenting).

437 F2d at 1342.

Will the Answers Be Different if the Seller-Buyer Relationship is a Franchise?

*Philip F. Zeidman and Perry C. Ausbrook**

9

* Both Mr. Zeidman and Mr. Ausbrook are members of the District of Columbia Bar. The authors wish to thank Andrew A. Caffey and Rosemary Sarka of Brownstein Zeidman and Schomer for their assistance in the preparation of this chapter.

What is a franchise?

§9.01 What kind of relationships are franchises?

A relationship is a franchise only if it is defined by statute or federal regulation as such. Accordingly, the name the parties give to the relationship is not determinative of whether the relationship is a franchise.[1] Because of a variety

---

[1] 16 CFR §436 (1982) as interpreted in *Final Guides to the Franchising and Business Opportunity Ventures Trade Regulation Rule,* 44 Fed Reg 49966 (1979) at IA.

of applicable statutes and regulations, a number of different relationships may be classified as franchises. Some are known as *package franchises,* others as *product franchises,* still others as *business opportunity franchises.* In order to determine whether a relationship is a franchise, it is necessary to determine first which laws are applicable and then examine the definition of each applicable law.

§9.02 —What laws define the term franchise?

The Federal Trade Commission's Trade Regulation Rule, Disclosure Requirements and Prohibitions Concerning Franchising and Business Opportunity Ventures (the *FTC rule*),[2] defines franchises for purposes of federal regulation of the sale of franchises. The FTC rule, promulgated pursuant to §5 of the Federal Trade Commission Act,[3] applies to the sale of franchises in all states. In addition, many states have laws which define franchises.[4] Some of these are for the purpose of regulating the sale of franchises[5] and others regulate the substantive aspects of the franchisor/franchisee relationship.[6] More than one state law may apply to a particular relationship.[7] States which have franchise registration laws may also have laws which apply to business opportunities.[8] The definition of a *business opportunity* typically overlaps with definitions of a *franchise* but the laws generally exempt, in various ways, relationships covered by franchise laws. In the absence of state franchise laws, however, the sale of franchises may well be covered by state business opportunity laws.[9]

§9.03 —Where can guidance be obtained regarding the applicability of state law or the Federal Trade Commission rule?

There are published guidelines which assist in interpreting as well as complying with the FTC rule (Final Guides to the Franchising and Business Opportunity Ventures Trade Regulation Rule, hereinafter, *guidelines*).[10] Guidance is

---

2 16 CFR §436 (1982).

3 15 USC §45.

4 Regarding the relationship of the FTC rule to state laws, see **§9.76.**

5 See **app J** for citations.

6 See **app K** for citations.

7 See **§9.68.**

8 See **app H** for citations.

9 See **§9.27.**

10 *Final Guides to the Franchising and Business Opportunity Ventures Trade Regulation Rule,* 44 Fed Reg 49966 (1979).

also available to assist in complying with the disclosure requirements of state law generally,[11] but little has been published concerning other aspects of the state franchise laws. Regarding both state law and federal regulations, however, not all questions are covered in published materials. Advisory opinions may be obtained from the staff of the Federal Trade Commission; however, delays in receiving responses may be substantial. State administrative agencies will accept applications for interpretation of state statutes and rules. In some cases, a request for interpretation must be accompanied by a filing fee.

§9.04 What is the Federal Trade Commission rule definition of franchise?

The Federal Trade Commission (FTC) rule applies to three types of *continuing commercial relationships* which are either *package franchises, product franchises,* or *business opportunity ventures.*[12] If the conduct of a relationship satisfies the elements of the definition of a franchise under the FTC rule, it is covered by the FTC rule whether or not it is described by the parties as a franchise. Further, it will be covered by the FTC rule if the agreement contains characteristics specified in the FTC rule definition of a franchise without regard to whether the parties abide by their obligations or enforce their rights.[13] Conversely, a relationship will not be covered by the FTC rule unless it meets the definitional characteristics, regardless of how it is characterized by the parties.

§9.05 —What is a package franchise under the Federal Trade Commission rule definition?

A package franchise is one in which the franchisee adopts the business format established by the franchisor and identified by the franchisor's trademark.[14] The franchisor requires the franchisee to pay money and promises to render significant assistance to the franchisee in the operation of its business or subjects the franchisee's method of operation in producing goods and

---

[11] The Midwest Securities Commissioners Association (MSCA) adopted the Uniform Franchise Offering Circular (UFOC) on September 2, 1975. The MSCA was dissolved in 1980 and its responsibilities were undertaken by the North American Securities Administrators Association which adopted the UFOC and Guidelines for its preparation on April 28, 1981. The UFOC is reprinted in Bus Fran Guide (CCH) ¶5700 *et seq* (1980).

[12] 16 CFR §436, §436.2(a) (1982); *Final Guides to the Franchising and Business Opportunity Ventures Trade Regulation Rule,* 44 Fed Reg 49,966, 49,966 (1979) [hereinafter cited as Guidelines].

[13] *Guidelines, supra* note 12, at 49966.

[14] *Final Guides to the Franchising and Business Opportunity Ventures Trade Regulation Rule,* 44 Fed Reg 49,966, 49,966 (1979). See also **§9.07.**

services to significant controls.[15]

§9.06 —What is a product franchise under the FTC rule definition?

A *product franchise* is created when goods produced by the franchisor (or under its control or direction) bear the franchisor's trademark and are distributed by the franchisee.[16] As in a package franchise,[17] the franchisor either exercises significant control or promises significant assistance in the franchisee's method of operation. The franchisor requires the franchisee to pay for the right to sell the trademarked goods, either by required purchases of equipment or supplies, or by paying an initial fee for the right to sell goods, or both.

Three elements common to package and product franchises covered by the FTC rule are:

1. Distribution of goods or services associated with the franchisor's trademark[18]
2. Significant control of, or significant assistance to, the franchisee's method of operation[19]
3. Required payments by the franchisee to the franchisor[20]

§9.07 —What is necessary to satisfy the trademark element in the Federal Trade Commission rule definition?

The guidelines to the Federal Trade Commission (FTC) rule state[21] that this element will be satisfied when the franchisee is granted the right to distribute goods and services which bear the franchisor's trademark, service mark, trade name, advertising, or other commercial symbol. The most common instances in which this element will be satisfied occur when the goods or services being distributed by the franchisee are associated with the franchisor's mark or when the franchisee must conform quality standards with respect to the goods and services being distributed and the franchisee operates under a name which includes, in whole or in part, the franchisor's mark. Essentially, this element will be met by any relationship in which a franchisee is given the benefit of the

---

15 See **§9.08.**

16 *Final Guides to the Franchising and Business Opportunity Ventures Trade Regulation Rule,* 44 Fed Reg 49,966, 49,966 (1979).

17 See **§9.05.**

18 See **§9.07.**

19 See **§9.08.**

20 See **§9.10.**

21 *Final Guides to the Franchising and Business Opportunity Ventures Trade Regulation Rule,* 44 Fed Reg 49966, 49966 (1979).

franchisor's reputation.[22]

§9.08 —What is necessary to satisfy the element of significant control/assistance in the Federal Trade Commission rule definition?

The term *significant* in either case relates to the degree to which the franchisee is dependent upon the franchisor's superior business expertise, which is made available to the franchisee by virtue of its association with the franchisor.[23] This expertise may be conveyed either by the exercise of control over the franchisee's method of operation or by furnishing assistance to the franchisee in its business operations.

Whether the assistance or control is significant is interpreted by the Federal Trade Commission staff according to certain somewhat subjective characteristics,[24] as, for example, whether the franchisee is relatively inexperienced in the business represented by the franchisor, the relative financial risk assumed by the franchisee in relation to the total business, and whether controls or promised assistance are unique to one specific franchisor as opposed to practices employed by all businesses in the same industry.

§9.09 —What types of assistance or control will be considered significant?

Three categories of assistance or control are described in the Guidelines.[25] In the first category are activities which will be considered significant in and of themselves. The second set of examples are those which are not of themselves significant but in combination with other activities may be considered to be so. A third category lists certain activities which, as a matter of policy, will not be considered significant by the staff of the Federal Trade Commission (FTC).

In the first category are such activities as furnishing formal sales, repair, or business training programs; establishing accounting systems; furnishing management, marketing, or personnel advice; selecting sites; and furnishing a detailed operating manual. However, requiring a franchisee to service or repair a product (except a product under warranty), exercising controls over inventory, requiring a franchisee to display goods, or furnishing on-the-job

---

22 43 Fed Reg 59621 (1978) at 59700-01.

23 *Final Guides to the Franchising and Business Opportunity Ventures Trade Regulation Rule,* 44 Fed Reg 49966, 49966-67 (1979) [hereinafter cited as Guidelines].

24 *Guidelines, supra* note 23, at 49967. See also **§9.09.**

25 *Final Guides to the Franchising and Business Opportunity Ventures Trade Regulation Rule,* 44 Fed Reg 49966, 49967 (1979).

assistance in sales or repairs will not, according to the Guidelines, be considered significant per se.

Promotional activities, in order to be considered significant, must be provided in conjunction with additional forms of assistance, such as furnishing a distributor with point-of-sales advertising displays, sales kits, product samples, and other promotional materials intended to assist the distributor in making sales. Promotional activities may also be considered significant if they include assistance in connection with advertising in the media, whether provided solely by the franchisor or on a cooperative basis with the franchisee.

Controls or assistance will not be classified as significant, without more, if the franchisee is experienced in the business, if the risk assumed by the franchisee is modest in relation to its total business, or if the controls or types of assistance offered are typical of the practices of the industry.

Items or activities which will not, as a matter of policy, be considered by the FTC staff in determining whether significant control or assistance exists[26] include trademark controls designed solely to protect legal ownership in the mark, health or safety restrictions required by federal or state laws or regulations, agreements between a retailer and a trading stamp company providing for the distribution of trading stamps in connection with retail sales, agreements between a bank credit interchange organization and retailers or member banks which provide credit cards and credit services, and assistance to distributors in obtaining financing to enable them to transact business.

§9.10 —What is a required payment for purposes of the Federal Trade Commission rule definition?

The staff of the Federal Trade Commission (FTC) considers that significant financial risk on the part of the franchisee is a necessary element of a franchise. Accordingly, if a franchisee pays less than $500 from any time before, to within six months after, commencing operations, such a relationship will be exempt from the FTC rule.[27] The giving of a note on which neither interest nor principal is payable in this period of time is not considered a *payment* if it meets certain additional conditions.[28]

A payment may fit the classification of a *required payment* if it is required by the franchise agreement, or any companion contract, such as a real estate lease, or if it is required by practical necessity, including circumstances in which equipment can be obtained, in fact, only from the franchisor or its affiliate.[29]

---

[26] *Id.*

[27] *Final Guides to the Franchising and Business Opportunity Ventures Trade Regulation Rule,* 44 Fed Reg 49966, 49967 (1979) [hereinafter cited as Guidelines].

[28] See **§9.12.**

[29] *Guidelines, supra* note 27, at 49967.

§9.11 What are the principal means of avoiding the definition of a franchise under the Federal Trade Commission rule?

Since all three elements must be met, it is possible to avoid the franchise definition by avoiding any one element. For example, if a mark is not essential to the package sold or the product being distributed, and a supplier or manufacturer expressly prohibits the use of its marks by the distributor,[30] the presence of other elements is irrelevant. But an advisory opinion[31] has further amplified this exclusion by requiring that the Seller place purchasers on notice of an express prohibition of the use of the marks; and, even if the Seller does so, this relationship will not be excluded if the marks are in fact displayed on products sold by dealers or used in connection with the sale or products or services. A *commercial symbol* might be a trademark in the broadest sense, such as the design of the building, display rack, or any other item which brings the feature to the attention of the franchisee's customers to such an extent that they would regard the franchisee's establishment as one in a chain identified with the franchisor.[32]

§9.12 —How may the required payment element of the Federal Trade Commission rule definition be avoided?

The Federal Trade Commission (FTC) has stated that it will not construe as a required payment any payment made by a person at a bona fide wholesale price for reasonable amounts of merchandise to be used for resale.[33] The practical effect of the bona fide wholesale price exemption is to exempt many distributorship relationships which would otherwise be covered. However, the FTC staff considers the question of what constitutes a bona fide wholesale price to be a question of fact and will not render advisory opinions on this point.[34] There is some utility for this exemption: although the terms *bona fide wholesale price* and *reasonable amounts* raise questions of fact, the criterion for

---

[30] FTC Advisory Opinion to US Marble, Inc, Oct 9, 1980, *reprinted in* Bus Fran Guide (CCH) ¶6424 (1980).

[31] *Id.*

[32] *Id.*

[33] *Final Guides to the Franchising and Business Opportunity Ventures Trade Regulation Rule,* 44 Fed Reg 49966, 49967 (1979).

[34] Typically, when the staff of the FTC issues an opinion, it accepts as fact the statement in the request that the price charged is a bona fide wholesale price. For example: FTC Advisory Opinion to Schwinn Bicycle Co, Aug 3, 1979, *reprinted in* Bus Fran Guide (CCH) ¶6381 (1980). FTC Advisory Opinion to General Motors Corp, Aug 17, 1979, *reprinted in* Bus Fran Guide (CCH) ¶6384 (1980). FTC Advisory Opinion to Marathon Oil Co, Oct 5, 1979, *reprinted in* Bus Fran Guide (CCH) ¶6393 (1980).

determination is that of a reasonable standard.[35]

The *required payment* element can also be avoided by structuring the relationship so that payment is deferred to a time beyond the coverage of the rule. The FTC staff, in an advisory opinion,[36] states that the waiting period of six months will satisfy the rationale of the FTC rule and will serve in lieu of disclosure, since the franchisee has six months of business dealings with the franchisor before being required to make a payment. It should be noted that the six-month period is measured from the time of commencement of operations and not the time of execution of the agreement. The opinion further states that the required payment can be avoided even if a promissory note is required to be executed at the commencement of the relationship, but is not payable until after the relevant waiting period, because under those circumstances, the franchisor's ability to enforce payment of the note in court would be subject to the franchisee's ability to defend the suit on the grounds that the franchisor failed to perform under the agreement.[37] Accordingly, the note held by the franchisor must either be specifically nonnegotiable, or, by its terms, it may be negotiable only under circumstances which preserve the defenses of the franchisee/payor.

It is also possible for a franchisor to structure a relationship so that payments for such items as equipment, tools, real estate, signs, or other items will not be required. These payments will be considered optional if the buyer has the option to buy these items from third parties who are not affiliates of the franchisor and if the option is genuine and realistic in the context of the industry and community in which the dealer chooses to conduct business.[38] The third party source of supply must be equivalent and competitive as a practical matter and the choice for each dealer must be real, legitimate, and practical.[39] The third party which offers such an option may not be either an affiliate of the franchisor nor may he make any payments to the franchisor or any affiliate of the franchisor as a result of the dealer's purchases.[40] Such payments will also be considered optional if the dealer has a genuine and realistic alternative to do without and operate its business successfully without the purchase of goods or services from the franchisor.[41]

While the relationship may be purposely structured to avoid the FTC rule application, the staff of the FTC has said that it will not accept otherwise valid

---

[35] *Id.*

[36] FTC Advisory Opinion to Automobile Importers of America, Inc, Aug 9, 1979, *reprinted in* Bus Fran Guide (CCH) ¶6382 (1980).

[37] *Id.*

[38] FTC Advisory Opinion to Chrysler Corp, Aug 10, 1979, *reprinted in* Bus Fran Guide (CCH) ¶6383 (1980).

[39] *Id.*

[40] FTC Advisory Opinion to General Motors Corp, Aug 17, 1979, *reprinted in* Bus Fran Guide (CCH) ¶6384 (1980).

[41] FTC Advisory Opinion to American Motors Corp, Aug 22, 1979, *reprinted in* Bus Fran Guide (CCH) ¶6385 (1980).

payment devices if the effect is to circumvent the protections afforded by the FTC rule or impose substantial financial risks on prospective franchisees.[42]

§9.13 —If the relationship is a franchise as defined by the Federal Trade Commission (FTC) rule, what exemptions are available from coverage by the FTC rule?

The Federal Trade Commission (FTC) rule specifically exempts[43] fractional franchises, leased departments, minimal investments, and purely oral agreements. The FTC rule also excludes[44] employer-employee relationships and general business partnerships as well as relationships created by membership in a *retailer-owned cooperative,* relationships for testing or certification service, and *single* license relationships.

§9.14 —What is a fractional franchise?

When an established business adds a franchised product line to its existing line of goods or services, a *fractional franchise* is created.[45] This relationship is exempt under the Federal Trade Commission FTC rule if the franchisee or any of its current directors or executive officers have had more than two years of prior management experience at any time in the past in the business represented by the franchise. These individuals may have two years of management experience if they have been with a competitor of the franchisor, or if the franchisee has been in a business which would have been expected to sell goods similar to the franchised goods.[46] The Guidelines illustrate this by the example of a service station dealer who obtains a franchise to sell tires, batteries, and accessories. This would be viewed as the requisite type of experience. A service station dealer would not be considered to have the requisite experience for obtaining a franchise to offer truck rental services.[47]

A fractional franchise also requires that the parties must have, or should have, anticipated in good faith at the time of entering into the franchise agreement that the sales arising from the proposed relationship would represent no more than 20 percent of the dollar volume of the franchisee's projected gross

---

[42] FTC Advisory Opinion to Automobile Importers of America, Inc, Aug 9, 1979, *reprinted in* Bus Fran Guide (CCH) ¶6382 (1980).

[43] *Final Guides to the Franchising and Business Opportunity Ventures Trade Regulation Rule,* 44 Fed Reg 49966, 49968 (1979).

[44] *Id.*

[45] *Final Guides to the Franchising And Business Opportunity Ventures Trade Regulation Rule,* 44 Fed Reg 49966, 49968 (1979).

[46] *Id.*

[47] *Id.*

sales within the franchisee's first year of business.[48]

§9.15 —What is a leased department?

The term *leased department* is used to describe an arrangement in which an independent retailer sells its own goods and services from premises leased from a large retailer in the latter's store, such as the independent retail outlets for optometry or jewelry within a department store.[49] This exemption is only available if the independent retailer is not required to purchase its goods or services, either directly or indirectly, from the large retailer or from suppliers required or approved by the large retailer.[50]

§9.16 —What is a minimal investment exemption?

The *minimal investment exemption,* provided by the Federal Trade Commission rule itself,[51] exempts from coverage a relationship in which the franchisee is required to pay less than $500 from any time before to within six months after commencement of business.[52]

§9.17 —Which oral agreements are exempt?

As a matter of policy, to avoid problems with proof and enforcement, the Federal Trade Commission rule exempts from coverage purely oral relationships which lack any written evidence of a material term.[53] This exemption will not apply, however, if there is written evidence of any material term, such as a purchase invoice for goods or services, even if the writing is unexecuted.[54]

As a practical matter, it is a rare case in which there will be no written acknowledgment of an agreement.

---

[48] *Id.*

[49] *Final Guides to the Franchising and Business Opportunity Ventures Trade Regulation Rule,* 44 Fed Reg 49966, 49968 (1979).

[50] *Id.*

[51] 16 CFR §436, §436.2(a)(3)(iii) (1982).

[52] *Final Guides to the Franchising and Business Opportunity Ventures Trade Regulation Rule,* 44 Fed Reg 49966, 49968 (1979). See also **§9.10.**

[53] *Final Guides to the Franchising and Business Opportunity Ventures Trade Regulation Rule,* 44 Fed Reg 49966, 49968 (1979).

[54] *Id.*

§9.18 —How are employer-employee and general partnership relationships excluded from the Federal Trade Commission rule?

The Federal Trade Commission (FTC) staff will apply the traditional test of *right of control* in determining whether an employment relationship exists.[55] For example, the staff of the FTC will ascertain whether a salary or a definite sum of money is given as consideration for the work, or whether the employee can be discharged or his employment terminated without liability on the part of the principal, as well as whether the employee must invest money in the business before being hired.[56]

The FTC rule excludes only general partners.[57] If an employment or partnership arrangement is structured to shield the franchisor as an employer or limited partner to the disadvantage of an employee or a general partner, these relationships will be carefully scrutinized.[58]

§9.19 —When will the cooperative association exclusion be applicable?

A cooperative association will be excluded if it is either (1) an agriculture cooperative authorized by federal legislation[59] or (2) a retailer-owned cooperative chain.[60] The latter must be operated by and for independent retailers on a cooperative basis. The members must be independent retailers, and goods or services must be furnished by the organization primarily to its members.[61]

§9.20 —What is a certification or testing service exclusion?

These relationships are distinguished from franchises because the latter involve distribution of goods or services through selected outlets whereas certification or testing services authorize use of their trademark by all parties meeting their standards and willing to pay their fee, such as the certification offered by Underwriters Laboratory.[62]

---

[55] *Final Guides to the Franchising and Business Opportunity Ventures Trade Regulation Rule,* 44 Fed Reg 49966, 49968 (1979).

[56] *Id.*

[57] *Id.*

[58] *Id.*

[59] Capper-Volstead Act, 7 USC §291.

[60] *Final Guides to the Franchising and Business Opportunity Ventures Trade Regulation Rule,* 44 Fed Reg 49966, 49968 (1979).

[61] *Id.*

[62] *Final Guides to the Franchising and Business Opportunity Ventures Trade Regulation Rule,* 44 Fed Reg 49966, 49968-69 (1979).

§9.21 —What is a single trademark license?

The *single* trademark license exclusion is applicable when only a single license is granted for the right to use the trademark or a *one-on-one* licensing arrangement is created in which a single licensee manufactures the trademarked goods according to the licensor's specifications.[63] This exclusion also includes *collateral product* licensing, such as the practice of licensing a trademark which is well-known in one context (*e.g.*, a soft drink) for use in another (*e.g.*, clothing or decorative items embossed with the soft drink logo).[64] This exclusion also includes all licensing agreements which might be entered into in the course of settlement negotiations in trademark infringement litigation, where the licensor will grant the infringing party a license to use the trademark for a specified period of time.[65]

§9.22 —Are there other possible exemptions from the Federal Trade Commission rule?

The Federal Trade Commission Act[66] provides that any person may petition the Federal Trade Commission (FTC) for a personal exemption or an exemption on behalf of a class if the FTC rule is not necessary to prevent the unfairness or deceptive practice to which the FTC rule relates. Grounds for exemption include the unlikelihood of unfair or deceptive practices because of the business sophistication of the franchisee, absence of proof of significant abuse, and duplication of other regulation.[67]

§9.23 What is necessary to satisfy the business opportunity venture definition in the Federal Trade Commission rule?

A business opportunity venture includes, by way of example, distributorships,[68] rack jobbing opportunities,[69] and vending machine routes.[70] The fol-

---

[63] *Final Guides to the Franchising and Business Opportunity Ventures Trade Regulation Rule,* 44 Fed Reg 49966, 49969 (1979).

[64] *Id.*

[65] *Id.*

[66] 15 USC §§41-58.

[67] In the Matter of Petitions for Exemption from Trade Regulation Rule entitled *Disclosure Requirements and Prohibitions Concerning Franchising and Business Opportunity Ventures* filed by Automobile Importers of America, Inc and American Motors Corp, July 18, 1980, *reprinted in* Bus Fran Guide (CCH) ¶7540 (1980). In the Matter of Petitions for Exemption from Trade Regulation Rule entitled *Disclosure Requirements and Prohibitions Concerning Franchising and Business Opportunity Ventures* filed by Shell Oil Co, *et al,* July 18, 1980, *reprinted in* Bus Fran Guide (CCH) ¶7539 (1980).

[68] *Final Guides to the Franchising and Business Opportunity Ventures Trade Regulation Rule,* 44 Fed Reg 49966, 49968 (1979) [hereinafter cited as Guidelines]. See also FTC Advisory Opinion to Garcia Marketing, May 29, 1980, *reprinted in* Bus Fran Guide (CCH) ¶6415 (1980).

lowing three elements[71] are necessary if the venture is to be considered a business opportunity:

1. The franchisee sells goods or services supplied by the franchisor or its affiliate, or by suppliers with which it is required by the franchisor to do business
2. The franchisor secures retail outlets or accounts for the goods or services, or secures locations for vending devices or racks, or provides the services of a person to do either
3. The franchisee is required to pay the franchisor or an affiliated person in order to obtain or commence the franchised business

§9.24 —What is necessary to satisfy the supplied goods or services element in the Federal Trade Commission rule definition of a business opportunity?

This element of the Federal Trade Commission rule definition will be met if either the franchisor or an affiliate provides goods or services to a franchisee or suggests a third party supplier to the franchisee. Advisory opinions,[72] however, have principally discussed direct requirements by the franchisor.

§9.25 —What is necessary to satisfy the outlet/account/location element in the Federal Trade Commission rule definition of a business opportunity?

The franchisor is supplying location assistance if it secures retail outlets or accounts for the goods or services to be sold by the franchisee; secures locations or sites for devices to dispense goods such as vending machines or rack displays; or provides the services of a person able to secure the accounts,

---

[69] *Guidelines, supra* note 68, at 49,968. See also FTC Advisory Opinion to Roman Enters, Inc, July 18, 1980, *reprinted in* Bus Fran Guide (CCH) ¶6422 (1980).

[70] *Guidelines, supra* note 68, at 49,968. See also FTC Advisory Opinion to Coin-Op Sales Co, Inc, Oct 19, 1979, *reprinted in* Bus Fran Guide (CCH) ¶6394 (1980).

[71] 16 CFR §436, §§436.2(a)(1)(ii)(A)-(B) (1982). *Guidelines, supra* note 68, at 49,968.

[72] FTC Advisory Opinion to Coin-Op Sales Co, Inc, Oct 19, 1979, *reprinted in* Bus Fran Guide (CCH) ¶6394 (1980). FTC Advisory Opinion to Yasmin Enters, Inc, Mar 27, 1980, *reprinted in* Bus Fran Guide (CCH) ¶6406 (1980). FTC Advisory Opinion to Langlois, Jan 24, 1980, *reprinted in* Bus Fran Guide (CCH) ¶6402 (1980). FTC Advisory Opinion to Interstate Vending Servs, July 1, 1980, *reprinted in* Bus Fran Guide (CCH) ¶6418 (1980). FTC Advisory Opinion to Sells Enters, Inc, Aug 28, 1980, *reprinted in* Bus Fran Guide (CCH) ¶6423 (1980).

outlets, locations, or sites.[73]

§9.26 —What is necessary to satisfy the required payment element in the Federal Trade Commission rule definition of a business opportunity?

The required payment element in the business opportunity definition is the same as that of the product or package franchise.[74]

§9.27 —How do state business opportunity laws relate to franchises?

Typically, state business opportunity laws[75] attempt to discourage irresponsible advertising and sales schemes which purport to promise a high return on a modest investment, guarantee profit, or promise that the Seller will buy back any of the Buyer's product which is not sold on the open market. The regulation may consist of a registration procedure and or requirement that the Seller post a bond to cover potential liabilities.

States which have franchise laws as well as business opportunity laws commonly exempt relationships covered by the franchise law from the business opportunity law.[76] Others exempt business opportunities marketed under a trademark, a necessary element of most definitions of a franchise.[77] There are a few jurisdictions in which business opportunity laws may encompass a franchise by definition and require compliance with business opportunity laws either because a franchisor may not have a federal trademark effectively registered[78] or because a franchisor makes representations in the sale of franchises similar to those regulated by business opportunity laws.[79]

---

[73] *Final Guides to the Franchising and Business Opportunity Ventures Trade Regulation Rule,* 44 Fed Reg 49966, 49968 (1979).

[74] See **§9.10.**

[75] See **app H** for citations.

[76] Cal Civ Code §1812.201(b)(2) (West Supp 1982); Md Ann Code art 56, §404(3) (Supp 1981); Va Code §59.1-263.B.2 (1982); Wash Rev Code Ann §19.110.040(2) (Supp 1982).

[77] Fla Stat Ann §559.801(1)(d) (West Supp 1982); Ga Code Ann §10-1-410(a)(4) (1981); Iowa Code Ann §523B.1.b(3) (West Supp 1982-83); Me Rev Stat Ann tit 32, §4691.3.A(5) (Supp 1982-83); Md Ann Code art 56, §401(b)(4) (Supp 1981); SC Code Ann §39-57-20(4) (Law Co-op Supp 1981). See also **§§9.07, 9.31.**

[78] Conn Gen Stat Ann §36-504(6) (West 1981 & Supp 1982); NC Gen Stat §66-94(4) (1981 & Supp 1981).

[79] See, e.g., NC Gen Stat §66-94(4) (1981 & Supp 1981).

§9.28 How do state laws define the term franchise?

There are fifteen states which define *franchise* for the purpose of regulating the sale of franchises.[80] Other states define franchise for the purpose of regulating the substantive relationship.[81] The definitions for the purpose of regulating the substantive relationship are substantially similar, although not necessarily identical, to the definitions of franchise for the purpose of regulating sales.

There are two principal definitions[82] of franchise: the *marketing plan or system* definition[83] and the *community of interest* definition.[84] Each of these definitions contains three elements. The first element is distinguishing; the second and third elements are common to both definitions.

The marketing plan or system definition includes (1) a marketing plan or system prescribed in substantial part by the franchisor, (2) substantial association of the business with the franchisor's trademark, and (3) payment of a fee by the franchisee for the use of the system and the mark.

The community of interest definition includes the following elements: (1) a community of interest, (2) use of the franchisor's trademark, and (3) payment of a fee by the franchisee for the use of the system and the mark.

§9.29 —What is meant by a marketing plan or system in state law definitions?

A definitive answer requires recourse to an individual state's regulations and such interpretative opinions, rulings, or releases offered by the state's administrative authority as are available. A marketing plan or system may be evidenced by either requirements or suggestions, and not only the agreement between the parties, but also the provisions of the law and customs in the trade or industry, may be examined to determine whether a marketing plan or system exists.

A marketing plan or system must be *prescribed in substantial part.* California

---

[80] See **app J** for citations.

[81] See **app K** for citations.

[82] Michigan and New York utilize a definition of *franchise* which is a variation of the *marketing plan or system* definition. Mich Comp Laws Ann §445.1502(3) (Supp 1982-83); NY Gen Bus Law §681.3 (McKinney Supp 1981-82).

[83] Cal Corp Code §31005 (Deering 1979 & Supp 1982); Ill Ann Stat ch 121 1/2 §703(1) (Smith-Hurd Supp 1982-83); Ind Code Ann §23-2-2.5-1(a) (Burns Supp 1982); Md Ann Code art 56, §345(d) (1979 & Supp 1982); ND Cent Code §51-19-02.5 (1981); Or Rev Stat §650.005(4) (1977); RI Gen Laws §19-28-3(c) (Supp 1980); Wis Stat Ann §553.03(4) (West Supp 1982).

[84] Hawaii Rev Stat §482E-2 (1976 & Supp 1980); Minn Stat Ann §80C.01.4 (West Supp 1982); SD Codified Laws Ann §37-5A-1 (1977 & Supp 1982); Wash Rev Code Ann §19.100.010(4) (1978 & Supp 1982).

administrators have offered interpretative guidelines[85] which may be helpful in determining whether a plan or system is prescribed in substantial part since many state statutes use a definition which is the same as or similar to the California definition. These guidelines list the following provisions as significant evidence of a marketing plan or system prescribed in substantial part:

1. Advertising claims that a successful marketing plan is available
2. Provisions granting an exclusive territory
3. Suggestions, provisions, or controls over site selection
4. Uniformity of the premises as indicated by requirements for construction, offers of architectural designs, requirements pertaining to identifying characteristics and signage
5. Required training, provision of training materials and personnel
6. Uniform administrative procedures, control over hours of operation, trade name usage, and prices
7. Requirements pertaining to business standards, dress codes, credit practices, limitations on persons to whom goods and services may be sold by the dealer
8. Restrictions on quality and uniformity of goods and services or obligations to service products in accordance with the Seller's request for instruction
9. Controls over, or assistance in preparation of, advertisements or promotional materials
10. Mandated compliance with uniform standards enforced by provisions allowing for termination, buy-back, or nonrenewal

§9.30 —What is meant by community of interest in state law definitions?

This definition, utilized in four states,[86] is broad and requires recourse to judicial opinion and the few interpretations which have been issued by state authorities. The community of interest referred to is financial,[87] and the financial interest need not be substantial. However the financial interest is required to be continuing; and, in one case, was measured by the extent to which the manufacturer's fortunes rose or fell with the sales of the distributor.[88] Where a manufacturer's representative made promotional efforts to substantially in-

---

[85] *Guidelines for Determining Whether an Agreement Constitutes a 'Franchise,' reprinted in* Bus Fran Guide (CCH) ¶7558 (1980).

[86] Hawaii Rev Stat §482E-1 - §482E-12 (1976 & Supp 1980); Minn Stat Ann §80C.01 - §80C.22 (West Supp 1982); SD Codified Laws Ann §37-5A-1 - §37-5A-87 (1977 & Supp 1982); Wash Rev Code Ann §19.100.010 - §19.100.940 (1978 & Supp 1982).

[87] Martin Investors, Inc v Vander Bie, 269 NW2d 868 (Minn 1978).

[88] H Phillips Co v Brown-Forman Distillers Corp, 483 F Supp 1289 (WD Wis 1980).

crease sales in a specific territory so that the representative was more than a "commissioned salesman" for the manufacturer, a community of interest has been found.[89]

§9.31 —What is necessary to satisfy the trademark element in state law definitions?

Typically, the *marketing plan or system*[90] statutes require *substantial association* of the franchisee's business with the franchisor's commercial symbol or mark, whereas *community of interest*[91] statutes require mere *use* of the franchisor's symbol or mark. In practice, however, substantial association may well be found where the franchisor's mark contributes substantially to the success of the franchisee's enterprise. For example, in California, the determinative factor is the communication of the commercial symbol to the customers of the franchisee.[92] The trademark element will be satisfied if the public associates the dealer with the supplier's mark to a greater extent than with marks of other suppliers, the mark is likely to convey that the business is an outlet of the supplier, or the dealer's customers regard the dealer's establishment as one in a chain identified with the supplier.[93]

§9.32 —What is meant by the franchise fee in state law definitions?

All state definitions of *franchise*[94] (with the exception of Virginia) include a requirement that the franchisee pay a fee, either directly or indirectly, to the

---

[89] Wilburn v Jack Cartwright, Inc, Bus Fran Guide (CCH) ¶7645 (ED Wis 1979), *affd,* 514 F Supp 493 (ED Wis 1981), *revd & remanded,* 676 F2d 698 (7th Cir 1982), *revd,* Bus Fran Guide (CCH) ¶7874 (ED Wis, May 28, 1982).

[90] See **§9.29.**

[91] See **§9.30.**

[92] *Guidelines for Determining Whether an Agreement Constitutes a 'Franchise,' reprinted in* Bus Fran Guide (CCH) ¶7558 (1980) at 12,350-51.

[93] *Id.*

[94] Cal Corp Code §31005, §31011 (Deering 1979 & Supp 1982); Hawaii Rev Stat §482E-2 (1976 & Supp 1980); Ill Ann Stat ch 121 1/2 §§703(1)(c) and (14) (Smith-Hurd Supp 1982-83); Ind Code Ann §§23-2-2.5-1(a)(3) and (i) (Burns Supp 1982); Md Ann Code art 56, §§345(d)(3) and (j) (1979 & Supp 1982); Mich Comp Laws Ann §445.1502(3) and §445-1503(1) (Supp 1982-83); Minn Stat Ann §§80C.01.4(3) and .9 (West Supp 1982); NY Gen Bus Law §§681(3) and (7) (McKinney Supp 1981-82); ND Cent Code §§51-19-02.5.a(3) and .6 (1981); Or Rev Stat §650.005(4)(c) (1977) (valuable consideration); RI Gen Laws §§19-28-3(c)(3) and (i) (Supp 1980); SD Codified Laws Ann §37-5A-1(3) and §37-5A-3 (1977 & Supp 1982); Wash Rev Code Ann §§19.100.010(4) and (11) (1978 & Supp 1982); Wis Stat Ann §§553.03(4)(a)3 and (b)(7) (West Supp 1982).

franchisor. This element is referred to as a *required payment*[95] in the Federal Trade Commission rule definition.

A *franchise fee,* as defined, is very broad; and, any monies paid to the franchisor should be analyzed to determine whether a franchise fee is involved, since a franchise fee has been found, notwithstanding that:

1. The amount was indefinite[96] or the relationship was not characterized as a franchise
2. The fee was reflected in the price of goods, services, equipment, or inventory[97]
3. The amount was paid either by lump sum, installment, periodic royalties, profits, or cash flow[98]
4. The fee was wholly or partially contingent on other factors[99]
5. Rent was charged by the Seller, an affiliate of the Seller, or an unaffiliated company which paid consideration to the Seller or its affiliates[100]
6. Payment was made for the lease of real estate to the extent that the payment exceeds fair rental or market value[101]

A few state statutes specifically describe certain payments that are *not* franchise fees, such as payments which are optional in fact[102] or are below a minimum.[103] Since definitions of franchise fees tend to be inclusive, however, it is advisable to seek an opinion from state administrators if the question is close.

§9.33 Are there variations on state franchise registration/disclosure statute definitions?

Two states, Michigan[104] and New York,[105] use the same three elements as the *marketing plan or system* definition; however, rather than require all three elements of that definition, these states will determine that a franchise exists if *either* a marketing plan *or* the trademark element is present *together with* the

[95] 16 CFR §436, §436.2(a)(2) (1982). See also **§9.10.**

[96] Illinois Regulations, *reprinted in* Bus Fran Guide (CCH) ¶5130.05 (1980).

[97] Maryland Regulations, *reprinted in* Bus Fran Guide (CCH) ¶5200.01 (1980).

[98] *Id.*

[99] Illinois Regulations, *reprinted in* Bus Fran Guide (CCH) ¶5130.05 (1980).

[100] Michigan Regulations, *reprinted in* Bus Fran Guide (CCH) ¶5220.01 (1980).

[101] *Id.*

[102] *Guidelines for Determining Whether an Agreement Constitutes a 'Franchise,' reprinted in* Bus Fran Guide (CCH) ¶7558 (1980) at 12,352-53.

[103] Va Code §13.1-559 (1978 & Supp 1982); Minn Stat Ann §80C.01(4)(e) (West Supp 1982). See also **§9.36.**

[104] Mich Comp Laws Ann §445.1502(3) (Supp 1982-83).

[105] NY Gen Bus Law §681.3 (McKinney Supp 1981-82).

payment of a franchise fee. Another state, Virginia, omits the payment of a franchise fee as a required element.[106]

§9.34 —Are there other variations in state law definitions of a franchise?

Those states which do not require franchise registration but have statutes governing some substantive aspects of the franchise relationship[107] (typically, termination and nonrenewal[108]) define franchise in a similar way to those states which regulate the sale of franchises.

The statutes of some jurisdictions[109] define franchise principally to proscribe fraud in the franchisor/franchisee relationship. There are variations among these definitions and, for example, the definition of franchise of the Florida statute is quite broad.

§9.35 What is the principal means of avoiding state franchise definitions?

Since all elements of the definition must be met, it is possible to avoid the definition by avoiding any one element. Thirteen states provide for a bona fide wholesale price exemption[110] analogous to the Federal Trade Commission (FTC) rule exemption.[111] As under the FTC rule, however, the finding of whether a price charged is a *bona fide wholesale price* is ordinarily a question of fact. State administrators in some states have developed guides as to what is not a bona fide wholesale price. For example, a state administrator may take the position that a bona fide wholesale price applies only to amounts paid for purchases of inventory,[112] or a state administrator may require a "well-estab-

---

[106] Va Code §13.1-559(b) (1978 & Supp 1982).

[107] Conn Gen Stat Ann §§42-133e to 42-133i (West Supp 1982); Miss Code Ann §75-24-53 (Supp 1982); Mo Ann Stat §§407.400-.420 (Vernon 1979); Neb Rev Stat §§87-401 to 87-410 (Supp 1980); NJ Stat Ann §§56:10-1 to 56:10-12 (Supp 1982-83).

[108] See **ch 7.**

[109] See **app G** for citations.

[110] Cal Corp Code §31011(a) (Deering 1979 & Supp 1982); Hawaii Rev Stat §482E-2 (1976 & Supp 1980); Ill Ann Stat ch 121 1/2 §703(14)(c) (Smith-Hurd Supp 1982-83); Ind Code Ann §23-2-2.5-1(i)(3) (Burns Supp 1982); Md Ann Code art 56, §345(j)(4) (1979 & Supp 1982); Mich Comp Laws Ann §445.1503(1)(a) (Supp 1982-83); Minn Stat Ann §80C.01.9(a) (West Supp 1982); NY Gen Bus Law §681.7(a) (McKinney Supp 1981-82); ND Cent Code §51-19-02.6.a (1981); RI Gen Laws §19-28-3(i)(1) (Supp 1980); SD Codified Laws Ann §37-5A-4(1) (1977 & Supp 1982); Wash Rev Code Ann §19.100.010(11)(a) (1978 & Supp 1982); Wis Stat Ann §553.03(7)(a) (West Supp 1982).

[111] See **§9.12.**

[112] Illinois Regulations, *reprinted in* Bus Fran Guide (CCH) ¶ 5130.07 (1980).

lished market" to be demonstrated by the franchisor.[113] Rarely, however, will a state administrator opine that the bona fide wholesale price exemption is available.

§9.36 —Besides the bona fide wholesale price exemption, are there other ways of avoiding the franchise fee element of state law definitions?

Some states have other exceptions for payments made to the franchisor which are not considered to constitute a *franchise fee.* These exceptions include the following:

1. Payments made for goods on consignment[114]
2. Payments with respect to a bona fide loan to the franchisee from the franchisor[115]
3. The purchase or agreement to purchase supplies or fixtures at their fair market value which are necessary to enter into the business or to continue the business under the franchise agreement[116]
4. The purchase or agreement to purchase goods for which there is an established market at a bona fide retail price subject to a bona fide commission or compensation plan[117]
5. Payments for the purchase of sales demonstration material or equipment for use in making the sale, not intended for resale, and sold with no profit to the Seller[118]
6. Payments which do not exceed $500 on an annual basis, for which the

---

[113] Mich Comp Laws Ann §445.1503(1)(a) (Supp 1982-83).

[114] Hawaii Rev Stat §482E-2 (1976 & Supp 1980); Md Ann Code art 56, §345(j)(4) (1979 & Supp 1982); Minn Stat Ann §80C.01.9(b) (West Supp 1982); SD Codified Laws Ann §37-5A-4(2) (1977 & Supp 1982); Wash Rev Code Ann §19.100.010(11)(b) (1978 & Supp 1982).

[115] Hawaii Rev Stat §482E-2 (1976 & Supp 1980); Md Ann Code art 56, §345(j)(5) (1979 & Supp 1982); Minn Stat Ann §80C.01.9(c) (West Supp 1982); SD Codified Laws Ann §37-5A-4(3) (1977 & Supp 1982); Wash Rev Code Ann §19.100.010(11)(c) (1978 & Supp 1982).

[116] Hawaii Rev Stat §482E-2 (1976 & Supp 1980); Md Ann Code art 56, §345(j)(7) (1979 & Supp 1982); Minn Stat Ann §80C.01.9(e) (West Supp 1982); SD Codified Laws Ann §37-5A-4(5) (1977 & Supp 1982); Wash Rev Code Ann §19.100.010(11)(e) (1978 & Supp 1982).

[117] Hawaii Rev Stat §482E-2 (1976 & Supp 1980); Md Ann Code art 56, §345(j)(6) (1979 & Supp 1982); Minn Stat Ann §80C.01.9(d) (West Supp 1982); SD Codified Laws Ann §37-5A-4(4) (1977 & Supp 1982); Wash Rev Code Ann §19.100.010(11)(d) (1978 & Supp 1982).

[118] Md Ann Code art 56, §345(j)(9) (1979 & Supp 1982); NY Gen Bus Law §681.7(f) (McKinney Supp 1981-82).

Buyer receives sales material of an equivalent, or greater, value than the payment[119]

7. Payments made to lease, or agreement to lease, a business to be operated by the franchisee on the premises of the franchisor or subfranchisor, if the franchised business is incidental to the business conducted by the franchisor or subfranchisor, at those premises[120] (This is analogous to a leased department under the Federal Trade Commission rule.[121])
8. An agreement by a retailer permitting another person to offer, sell, or distribute goods or services on or about the premises occupied by the retailer[122]
9. Payments of $100 or less[123]
10. Payments for the purchase or rental of property to be utilized in, and which is necessary for, the operation of the franchised business, provided the price or rental charge does not exceed the cost of acquiring items for other persons or on the public market, and provided the payments do not exceed $1000[124]

§9.37 —What exemptions from state statutes are available?

All the states which have registration requirements have provisions which exempt certain franchisors from registration. These exemptions are, however, limited to a particular state and sometimes require the franchisor to apply for an exemption which, in some cases, may be as onerous as registration.[125] Since the Federal Trade Commission rule applies to offers in all states, an exemption under state laws will not relieve a franchisor from its disclosure obligation to prospective franchisees.[126]

However, in the circumstances in which a state exemption may be valuable (for example, a franchisor may already have a disclosure document prepared and may be able to avoid the time required for administrative procedures

---

[119] NY Gen Bus Law §681.7(e) (McKinney Supp 1981-82).

[120] Ill Ann Stat ch 121 1/2 §703(1) (Smith-Hurd Supp 1982-83); Mich Comp Laws Ann §445.1503(1)(d) (Supp 1982-83).

[121] See **§9.15.**

[122] NY Gen Bus Law §681.7(g) (McKinney Supp 1981-82).

[123] Cal Bus & Prof Code §20007(d) (West Supp 1982); Ill Ann Stat ch 121 1/2 §703(1)(c) (Smith-Hurd Supp 1982-83); Md Ann Code art 56, §345(d)(3) (1979 & Supp 1982); Mich Comp Laws Ann §445.1506(2)(e) (Supp 1982-83); Or Rev Stat §650.005(6) (1977); RI Gen Laws §19-28-3(c)(3) (Supp 1980).

[124] Cal Bus & Prof Code §20007(e) (West Supp 1982).

[125] See **§§9.67, 9.75.**

[126] See **§9.65.**

necessary for registration in a particular state),[127] the following exemptions may be helpful.

Large Franchisor/Experience Exemption

Franchisors with a large net worth and/or with significant franchising experience are exempt in several states.[128] The qualifications for this exemption differ from state to state, commonly requiring from $1,000,000 (if a franchisor is 80 percent controlled by a corporation with a net worth of $10,000,000) to $5,000,000 in net worth, and/or that the franchisor has conducted the business which is the subject of the franchise for at least five years, or the franchisor has from 10 to 25 franchises or, in some cases, company-owned businesses which have operated for a period of from 5 to 25 years.

Substantial Initial Investment Exemption

The franchisee is required by the franchisor to invest at least $100,000, not including intangible assets, the proceeds of any loan or the projected reinvestment of operating income.[129]

Transactions With an Existing Franchisee

If an existing franchisee wishes to extend or renew its franchise, many state statutes exempt this transaction from definitions of *offer* or *sale.*[130] Some states carry this further, and exempt from registration and disclosure the offer of a modified or amended franchise agreement or the transfer of a franchisee's location where there is no interruption in the operation of the franchised business and no material change in the relationship between the franchisee and the franchisor.[131] The requirement of no material change[132] makes this exemption of limited utility, however, since new financial statements from a current fiscal year will, for example, be considered a material change.

Six states exempt from registration and/or disclosure the sale of additional

---

[127] See **§§9.67, 9.75.**

[128] Cal Corp Code §§31101(a) and (b) (Deering 1979 & Supp 1982); Ind Code Ann §§23-2-2.5-3(a) and (b) (Burns Supp 1982); Mich Comp Laws Ann §445.1506(2)(a) (Supp 1982-83); NY Gen Bus Law §§684.2, 684.3 (McKinney Supp 1981-82); ND Cent Code §51-19-04.1 (1981); RI Gen Laws §19-28-4(b) (Supp 1980); SD Codified Laws Ann §37-5A-12 (1977 & Supp 1982); Wash Rev Code Ann §19.100.030(4)(b)(i) (1978 & Supp 1982); Wis Stat Ann §§553.22(1), 553.22(2) (West Supp 1982).

[129] Michigan Regulations, *reprinted in* Bus Fran Guide (CCH) ¶5220.18 (1980).

[130] Some examples are to found in: Cal Corp Code §31018(c) (Deering 1979 & Supp 1982); Ind Code Ann §23-2-2.5-1(g) (Burns Supp 1982); Md Ann Code art 56, §345(m) (1979 & Supp 1982); ND Cent Code §51-19-02.14.a(2) (1981); Wis Stat Ann §553.03(11)(b) (West Supp 1982).

[131] Hawaii Rev Stat §482E-4(5) (1976 & Supp 1980); Ill Ann Stat ch 121 1/2 §712 (Smith-Hurd Supp 1982-83).

[132] See **§9.66.**

franchises to an existing franchisee.[133] Of these six, two states require that the new franchise be *substantially similar* to the existing franchise;[134] and one state exempts sales to existing franchisees if it is the same franchisor who grants the franchise.[135]

The New York statute has an exemption for transactions with existing franchisees which applies only where the existing franchisee has actively operated a franchise of the selling franchisor for at least the previous 18 months; the existing franchisee purchases the additional franchise to operate it, and not for resale; and the franchisor reports the sale to the state administrator within 15 days of the sale.[136] Michigan statute imposes the same three requirements, and also requires that the franchisor provide the franchisee with current balance sheets not less than 15 days prior to the sale.[137]

The Minnesota statute exempts sales to an existing franchisee provided the franchisee is not required to conform to provisions in the franchise agreement which are "unfair and inequitable."[138] Oregon requires that a disclosure document have been provided to the franchisee in a prior sale, and that there is no material adverse change in the information in that document.[139]

Advisory opinions have clarified this exemption in certain states. In California, where the exemption is applicable only in the absence of any material change, *material changes* in the franchise agreement have been held to include the insertion of a conditional right of renewal; an administrative charge, increased charges for rent, taxes, and other expenses; a reduction in royalty payment; increased insurance coverage; mandatory participation and contributions to a regional advertising cooperative; and a reduction in accounting services performed by the franchisor.[140] A recent case in the United States Court of Appeals for the Seventh Circuit construing the Illinois statute suggests that a change in location, without any other changes, is, nevertheless, a material change.[141]

---

[133] Hawaii Rev Stat §482E-4(6) (1976 & Supp 1980); Md Ann Code art 56, §348(3) (1979 & Supp 1982); Mich Comp Laws Ann §1506(2)(j) (Supp 1982-83); Minnesota Regulations, *reprinted in* Bus Fran Guide (CCH) ¶5230, ¶5230.02(c) (1980) [hereinafter cited as Minn Regs]; NY Gen Bus Law §684.3(d) (McKinney Supp 1981-82); Oregon Regulations, *reprinted in* Bus Fran Guide (CCH) ¶5370, ¶5370.06 (1980) [hereinafter cited as Or Regs].

[134] Md Ann Code art 56, §348(3) (1979 & Supp 1982); Minn Regs, *supra* note 133, at ¶5230.02(c).

[135] Hawaii Rev Stat §482E-4(6) (1976 & Supp 1980).

[136] NY Gen Bus Law §684.3(d) (McKinney Supp 1981-82).

[137] Mich Comp Laws Ann §1506(2)(j) (Supp 1982-83).

[138] Minn Regs, *supra* note 133, at ¶5230.02(c).

[139] Or Regs, *supra* note 133, at ¶5370.06.

[140] Love's Enters, Inc (Cal Op 76/2F, Mar 30, 1976).

[141] My Pie Intl, Inc v Debould, Inc, 687 F2d 919 (7th Cir 1982).

Franchisee's Sale for Its Own Account

All states, except Virginia, exempt from registration/disclosure the offer or sale of a franchise by a franchisee or a subfranchisor for its own account.[142] Even though the franchise agreement may require that the franchisor approve of the sale, the sale is not considered to be effected by or through the franchisor. There are, however, certain additional requirements imposed by certain states for this exemption. For example, the South Dakota[143] and Minnesota[144] statutes make the exemption available for instances of only one sale during a 12-month period. Illinois[145] and North Dakota[146] statutes have limited this exemption by requring disclosure by the selling franchisee; and North Dakota imposes an additional requirement that the franchise administrator approve the exemption. New York statutes[147] requires that the franchisor remain registered if its franchisees sell a franchise, since the franchisees are required, by state law, to provide a prospective purchaser with a copy of the franchisor's currently registered offering circular.

Michigan statute allows this exemption provided that the following conditions are met:

1) The sale is an isolated sale and not part of a distribution of franchises;
2) The franchisee provides such information to the prospective purchaser concerning the franchisor as the state requires; and
3) The franchisor files a notification with the state administrator, together with such other disclosure information as the Department of Commerce may require, ten days prior to the completion of the sale.[148]

While regulations and advisory opinions have attempted to clarify the degree of permissible franchisor involvement without the loss of the exemption, this issue is still evolving.

---

[142] Cal Corp Code §31102 (Deering 1979 & Supp 1982); Hawaii Rev Stat §482E-4(7) (1976 & Supp 1980); Ill Ann Stat ch 121 1/2 §717 (Smith-Hurd Supp 1982-83); Ind Code Ann §23-2-2.5-4 (Burns Supp 1982); Md Ann Code art 56, §348(1) (1979 & Supp 1982); Mich Comp Laws Ann §445.1506(2)(h) (Supp 1982-83); Minn Stat Ann §80C.03(a) (West Supp 1982); NY Gen Bus Law §684.5 (McKinney Supp 1981-82); ND Cent Code §51-19-04.2 (1981); Or Regs, *supra* note 133, at ¶5370.05; RI Gen Laws §19-28-4(c) (Supp 1980); SD Codified Laws Ann §37-5A-13 (1977 & Supp 1982); Wash Rev Code Ann §19.100.030(1) (1978 & Supp 1982); Wis Stat Ann §553.23 (West Supp 1982).

[143] SD Codified Laws Ann §37-5A-13 (1977 & Supp 1982).

[144] Minn Stat Ann §80C.03(a) (West Supp 1982).

[145] Ill Ann Stat ch 121 1/2 §717 (Smith-Hurd Supp 1982-83).

[146] ND Cent Code §51-19-04.2 (1981).

[147] NY Gen Bus Law §684.5(c) (McKinney Supp 1981-82).

[148] Mich Comp Laws Ann §445.1506(2)(h) (Supp 1982-83).

Sales by Judicial Officers and Financial Institutions, and Sales of Registered Securities

Several states[149] exempt from registration, as well as from disclosure, the sale or transfer of a franchise by an executor, administrator, sheriff, receiver, trustee in bankruptcy, guardian, or conservator. In addition, if a transaction meets the definition of franchise but is also required to be registered under the state Blue Sky Laws as a sale of securities, it is exempt from registration and disclosure requirements in some states.[150]

Miscellaneous Exemptions

Some states exempt from the franchise laws relationships which would be franchises if they existed within industries that are otherwise specifically regulated, such as motor vehicle dealerships;[151] petroleum corporations, or wholesale distributors of petroleum;[152] farm machinery, and recreational vehicle franchises;[153] contracts or agreements for the right to transport freight which are otherwise regulated by the Interstate Commerce Commission;[154] contracts for the sale of gasoline and other motor fuels;[155] the rental or lease of motor vehicles which otherwise meet the "large franchisor exemption";[156] transactions regulated by a state insurance commissioner;[157] and offers and sales by governmental entitites of certain franchises for cable telecommunications.[158]

The states of Michigan, New York, Washington, and Minnesota[159] exempt franchise sales which are few in number (ten in Washington and not more than two in each of the others) subject to certain other conditions.

Other miscellaneous exemptions include the following:

---

[149] Hawaii Rev Stat §482E-4(a)(1) (1976 & Supp 1980); Md Ann Code art 56, §348(2) (1979 & Supp 1982); Mich Comp Laws Ann §445.1506(2)(c) (Supp 1982-83); Minn Stat Ann §80C.03(b) (West Supp 1982); SD Codified Laws Ann §37-5A-14(1) (1977 & Supp 1982); Wash Rev Code Ann §19.100.030(2) (1978 & Supp 1982).

[150] Minn Stat Ann §80C.03(d) (West Supp 1982); SD Codified Laws Ann §37-5A-14(3) (1977 & Supp 1982).

[151] Hawaii Rev Stat §482E-4(a)(3) (1976 & Supp 1980); SD Codified Laws Ann §37-5A-11 (1977 & Supp 1982); Wash Rev Code Ann §19.100.030(5) (1978 & Supp 1982).

[152] Cal Corp Code §31104(a) (Deering 1979 & Supp 1982).

[153] SD Codified Laws Ann §37-5A-11 (1977 & Supp 1982).

[154] Minn Regs, *supra* note 133, at ¶5230.01(e).

[155] NY Gen Bus Law §681.3 (McKinney Supp 1981-82).

[156] Wash Rev Code Ann §19.100.030(5) (1978 & Supp 1982).

[157] *Id.*

[158] Wisconsin Regulations, *reprinted in* Bus Fran Guide (CCH) ¶5490, ¶5490.07 (1980) [hereinafter cited as Wis Regs].

[159] Mich Comp Laws Ann §445.1506(2)(k) (Supp 1982-83); Minn Stat Ann §80C.03(e) (West Supp 1982); NY Gen Bus Law §684.3(c) (McKinney Supp 1981-82); Wash Rev Code Ann §19.100.030(4)(b)(ii)(A) (1978 & Supp 1982).

1. Transactions relating to bank credit card plans[160]
2. Franchisors who do not charge a franchise fee in excess of $1500; do not advertise through any media originating in the states of Washington and Oregon; and during the past 7 years have not been found in violation of the Washington Franchise Investment Law, the Washington Unfair Business Practices Law, or any similar federal law[161]
3. Sales to franchisees who will be required to pay less than $100 on an annual basis[162]
4. An agreement by which a retailer of goods or services is granted the right to utilize a marketing plan or system to promote the sale of goods or services which are deemed "incidental and ancillary" to the principal business of the retailer, *i.e.*, sales accounting for less than 20 per cent of the retailer's gross sales[163] (This is analogous to a *fractional franchise* under the Federal Trade Commission (FTC) rule.)[164]
5. Franchised businesses operating on the franchisor's premises which are incidental to the franchisor's business, *e.g.*, leased departments and concessions[165] (This is analogous to a *leased department* under the FTC rule.)[166]
6. Offers and sales of an interest in a franchise.[167] Presumably, this would include, for example, a partnership interest or equity interest in a corporate franchisee

§9.38 —Is it possible to obtain an exemption which does not fit into any of these categories?

Most states which regulate the sale of franchises provide their franchise administrator with the power to exempt transactions if the administrator finds that the imposition of registration or disclosure requirements as applied in a particular case are not necessary in the public interest and are not necessary

---

[160] Cal Corp Code §31103 (Deering 1979 & Supp 1982); NY Gen Bus Law §684.6 (McKinney Supp 1981-82); RI Gen Laws §19-28-4(d) (Supp 1980); Wash Rev Code Ann §§19.100.010(4)(a) and (5) (1978 & Supp 1982).

[161] Wash Rev Code Ann §19.100.030(4)(b)(iii) (1978 & Supp 1982).

[162] Minn Stat Ann §80C.01(4)(e) (West Supp 1982).

[163] Minn Stat Ann §80C.03(f) (West Supp 1982).

[164] See **§9.14.**

[165] Ill Ann Stat ch 121 1/2 §703(1) (Smith-Hurd Supp 1982-83); Minn Stat Ann §80C.01(4)(d) (West Supp 1982); SD Codified Laws Ann §37-5A-2 (1977 & Supp 1982); Va Code §13.1-559 (1978 & Supp 1982).

[166] See **§9.15.**

[167] Wis Regs, *supra* note 158, at ¶5490.07(1)(c).

to protect investors.[168] Frequently, this exemption requires formal rule making procedures before it may be granted, and such a finding may be limited to a case-by-case basis. The Michigan administrator has used this power to provide certain exemptions[169] for any franchisor meeting the following qualifications:

1. Sales to franchisees who are not required to pay more than $500 at any time prior to six months after commencing business
2. Sales to businesses which have a net income in excess of $100,000 during the previous fiscal year or latest 12-month period; or have a net worth in excess of $1,000,000 and less than 10 per cent of those assets invested in the franchise
3. Sales to individuals who will invest more than $50,000 in the franchise, have a personal income in excess of $100,000 during the previous fiscal year or latest 12-month period, or a net worth in excess of $500,000; and have had experience in financial and business matters or the advice of an attorney or accountant
4. Sales by federal, state, or local governments and governmental agencies

Will the answers in chapters 2 through 7 change in the case of a franchise?

§9.39 Does the franchise relationship enjoy any special or distinctive treatment under antitrust principles?

Although the principles of antitrust law discussed in the Buyer-Seller context have full application to the commercial activity of franchisors and franchisees, the characteristic features of the franchise relationship, and the policy questions which arise when franchising is the subject of antitrust analysis, have lent a distinctive flavor to antitrust cases involving franchises. Many of the major developments in antitrust law in recent years have emerged from decisions reviewing franchised methods of distribution. A leading example, of course, is the standard of review of vertical restraints articulated in *United States v Arnold Schwinn & Co*,[170] and subsequently reversed in *Continental TV, Inc v GTE Syl-*

---

[168] Cal Corp Code §31100 (Deering 1979 & Supp 1982); Ill Ann Stat ch 121 1/2 §712 (Smith-Hurd Supp 1982-83); Ind Code Ann §23-2-2.5-5 (Burns Supp 1982); Md Ann Code art 56, §348(4) (1979 & Supp 1982); Mich Comp Laws Ann §445.1506(4) (Supp 1982-83); Minn Stat Ann §80C.03(g) (West Supp 1982); NY Gen Bus Law §684.1 (McKinney Supp 1981-82); ND Cent Code §51-19-04.3 (1981); RI Gen Laws §19-28-4(a) (1981); Wis Stat Ann §553.25 (West Supp 1982).

[169] Michigan Regulations, *reprinted in* Bus Fran Guide (CCH) ¶7694 (1980).

[170] 388 US 365 (1967).

vania, Inc,[171] both franchising decisions. These cases, which have had a major impact on the regulation of commercial activity under the federal antitrust laws generally, involved basic marketing restraints imposed in a franchising context.

Recent decisions have recognized the unique economic underpinnings of the franchise relationship, and have applied special standards that often have little application to the usual Buyer-Seller relationship. For instance, an analysis of illegal tying arrangements in the franchising context may well turn on whether the franchisor's trademark constitutes a *tying product,* or whether the trademark is separate and distinct from the allegedly *tied product*—neither is likely to arise very often in a nonfranchising context.[172] Certain marketing restrictions may be justified as legitimate features of a franchisor's marketing concept.[173]

In considering franchise terminations and disapproval of franchisee transfers, both species of *refusals to deal,* courts have been sensitive to the competing interests of franchisor and franchisee: the high level of the franchisee's investment and its often exclusive dependence on the franchisor balanced against the franchisor's need to protect the integrity of its trademarks and the franchise system.[174] Similar considerations are weighed when evaluating covenants against competition imposed on franchisees during and after the term of the franchise.[175] Again, there is a qualitative difference in the nature of the courts' approach when compared to a traditional Buyer-Seller context.

Territorial restraints are common in franchising and raise a number of complex antitrust issues. The rule of reason standard applies to such nonprice vertical restraints, weighing the beneficial effects of the restraint against its anticompetitive impact.[176] Franchisors often have legitimate business reasons for imposing territorial and customer restrictions—such as the need to encourage franchisee investment in the assets of the franchised business and in promotion within a certain market by protecting the franchisee against competition from other franchisees—which may not be applicable to other Sellers.[177]

The issues become even more complex when a franchisor engages in *dual distribution,* offering goods or services in competition with its own franchisees. In a dual distribution system, it is often unclear whether a particular restraint should be considered a *horizontal* agreement among competitors or a *vertical* restraint involving two levels of the distribution chain.[178]

Many of these issues rarely arise in a coventional Buyer-Seller relationship. In this sense, if not in any larger sense, franchising enjoys distinctive treatment

---

[171] 433 US 36 (1977). For a discussion of the impact of *Sylvania,* see **ch 1** and **§5.03.**

[172] See **§§9.50-9.56.**

[173] See **§9.46.**

[174] See **§§9.43-9.45, 9.59, 9.60.**

[175] See **§9.61.**

[176] See **§9.46.**

[177] *Id.*

[178] See **§9.47.**

under antitrust principles. It remains to be seen whether the distinctions elaborated on in the discussion which follows will develop into a broader doctrine, recognized by the courts as one which, with a degree of predictability, will lead to different results in franchising and nonfranchising cases.[179]

§9.40 Must the franchisor sell a franchise to a prospective franchisee?

The general principle applicable to franchisors/franchisees as well as to Sellers/Buyers is discussed in detail in Chapter 2: under the *Colgate* doctrine a Seller/franchisor may, in the absence of monopoly, unilaterally select with whom it chooses to deal.[180] As pointed out in Chapter 2, a number of factual situations, such as communications with competitors[181] or prior agreement between Seller and Buyer,[182] may satisfy the joint action element of an antitrust violation, change the purpose or effect of an otherwise unilateral decision, and, therefore, affect the legality of a refusal to sell.

In the franchise setting, there may be additional considerations affecting the legality of a refusal to sell a franchise to a prospective franchisee. For instance, in *American Motor Inns, Inc v Holiday Inns, Inc,*[183] the court held illegal a hotel franchisor's simultaneous policies that (1) certain markets were company towns in which no franchises would be offered and (2) franchisees were prevented by contract from owning nonfranchised hotels. The court further ruled that the combined effect of the two policies constituted an unlawful division of territories among competitors.

Other cases, involving the disapproval of a proposed transfer of a franchisee, are analogous to the decision not to sell to a prospective franchisee in the first instance.[184] Those cases have upheld a franchisor's right to refuse a proposed transfer where the franchisor was dissatisfied with the transferee's prior business performance,[185] or personal characteristics.[186] The courts have also upheld a franchisor's refusal of one proposed transfer because another trans-

---

[179] See, generally Zeidman, *The Rule of Reason in Franchisor - Franchisee Relationships,* 47 Antitrust LJ 873 (1978).

[180] United States v Colgate & Co, 250 US 300 (1919). See **§2.17.**

[181] See **§§2.30-2.40** (Seller's communications with competing Buyers) and **§§2.41-2.45.** (Seller's communications with competing Sellers).

[182] See **§§2.15-2.29.**

[183] American Motor Inns, Inc v Holiday Inns, Inc, 521 F2d 1230 (3rd Cir 1975).

[184] See generally **§§9.43, 9.44, 9.45.**

[185] *See* Hamro v Shell Oil Co, 674 F2d 784 (9th Cir 1982).

[186] *See* Carrozza v Webber Chevrolet Co, 1978-1 Trade Cas (CCH) ¶61,982 (DRI 1978) (criminal record); McDaniel v General Motors Corp, 480 F Supp 666 (EDNY 1979); *affd mem,* 628 F2d 1345 (2d Cir 1980) (consumer complaints filed against the proposed transferee); Seligson v Plum Tree, Inc, 361 F Supp 748 (ED Pa 1973) (disreputable character).

feree was preferred;[187] and where the price negotiated for the proposed transfer was considered too high and might jeopardize the viability of the business, a court has upheld a franchisor's refusal to approve the transfer.[188]

State franchise law may also apply to a refusal to sell to a prospective franchisee. California law, for instance, prohibits a grantor of a dealership from refusing to grant a dealership on the basis of race, color, religion, national origin, ancestry, or sex of the purchaser.[189] A number of industry-specific state statutes, primarily in the automobile industry, may limit the sale of a franchise for a location within a certain radius of an established franchisee.[190] Finally, state franchise laws may prohibit a franchisor from competing unfairly with the franchisee by selling a franchise within the exclusive territory granted to another franchisee; or, if no exclusive territory is granted, within a reasonable area.[191]

The question to be considered in the context of a franchise relationship is thus different from the typical question which arises in the Seller-Buyer context. In the case of a franchisor/franchisee, the question is likely to be broader and more fundamental than whether the Seller has an obligation to sell goods. Instead, it is likely to be whether the franchisor has an obligation to permit the franchisee (or the proposed transferee of a franchise) to engage in business at all, typically a decision with far broader ramifications than whether the Buyer may buy goods: the Buyer is usually able to buy the same or similar goods elsewhere, whereas the franchisee is, by definition, seeking to acquire a unique bundle of rights. Notwithstanding the greater equity which a franchisee can assert in such a case, the courts have, in the absence of state statutes or other considerations, recognized and given weight to the franchisor's interest in the identity of the franchisee—an interest which generally exceeds the interest of a Seller in the identity and character of its Buyer.[192]

---

[187] *See* Mogul v General Motors Corp, 391 F Supp 1305 (ED Pa 1975), *affd mem,* 527 F2d 645 (3rd Cir 1976).

[188] *See* Kestenbaum v Falstaff Brewing Corp, 575 F2d 564 (5th Cir 1978), *cert denied,* 440 US 909 (1979).

[189] California Fair Dealership Law, Cal Civ Code §§80-86 (Deering Supp 1982). *Dealership* is defined at §81 of the California Fair Dealership Law to mean:

> a contract or agreement, either express or implied, whether oral or written, between two or more persons, by which a person is granted the right to sell or distribute goods or services, to use a trade name, trademark, service mark, logotype, or advertising or other commercial symbol, in which there is a community of interest in the business of offering, selling or distributing goods or services at wholesale or at retail by lease, agreement, or otherwise.

[190] See, e.g., Automobile Franchise Act, Cal Veh Codes §§3060—3069 (West Supp 1982). *See also* New Motor Vehicle Bd of Cal v Orrin W Fox Co, 439 US 96 (1978) (upholding constitutionality of California Automobile Franchise Act).

[191] See discussion at **§§9.48, 9.49** and the cases cited therein.

[192] See **§9.43.**

§9.41 —What if other franchisees urge the franchisor to refuse a proposed sale?

Complaints by franchisees, as with the complaints of competing Buyers,[193] heighten the risk that a court will find a subsequent decision not to sell the franchise to be the result of concerted action among competitors and therefore repugnant to §1 of the Sherman Act.

The presence or absence of the *joint action* element of a Sherman Act violation, discussed in detail in Chapter 2,[194] is a controversial point of antitrust analysis on which the courts have differed in their approach. The question of joint action more frequently arises in franchise termination situations, but the antitrust analysis of a refusal to sell in the first instance is essentially the same.[195] The critical question of fact is whether the decision not to sell is the result of urging by other franchisees. Some courts have been willing to infer a causal link where the circumstances suggest the decision resulted from the communications.[196] Other courts have ruled that franchisee complaints do not, standing alone, transform a franchisor's unilateral decision into illegal concerted action.[197]

For the purposes of joint action analysis, franchising systems differ from other Buyer-Seller relationships in two important practical respects. Franchisors are in constant communications with their franchisees while providing support services, marketing and advertising information, and other business services required under the franchise agreement—communications which provide increased opportunity for the franchisor to receive comments and complaints about selling or terminating franchises. Second, franchisees are linked to one another through their common business identity, informal communication, and a variety of franchisor-sponsored seminars and meetings—a linkage which certainly affords more opportunities than typical Buyers would have to exchange sensitive information.

For antitrust purposes the joint action of more than one competing franchisee or Buyer is subjected to a stricter standard of review than if only one

---

[193] See **§§2.30-.40.**

[194] See **§§2.30-2.45.**

[195] See **§§2.32, 9.59, 9.60.** As in the Seller-Buyer context, most of the refusal to deal cases in franchising address termination situations. As a practical matter, franchisees are more likely to complain to the franchisor about the marketing activities of another franchisee than about a proposed sale to a prospective purchaser.

[196] *See* Cernuto, Inc v United Cabinet Corp, 595 F2d 164 (3d Cir 1979); Spray-Rite Serv Corp v Monsanto Co, 684 F2d 1226 (7th Cir 1982), *cert granted,* __ US __, 75 L Ed 2d 479, 103 S Ct 1249 (1983); *accord* Battle v Lubrizol, 673 F2d 984 (8th Cir 1982). *See also* Alloy Intern Co v Hoover-NSK Bearing Co, 635 F2d 1222 (7th Cir 1980).

[197] *See* Bruce Drug, Inc v Hollister Inc, 688 F2d 853 (1st Cir 1982); Valley Liquors, Inc v Renfield Importers Ltd, 678 F2d 742 (7th Cir 1982); Schwimmer v Sony Corp of Am, 678 F2d 946 (2d Cir 1982); Roesch, Inc v Star Cooler Corp, 671 F2d 1168 (8th Cir 1982); Edward J Sweeney & Sons v Texaco, Inc, 637 F2d 105 (3d Cir 1980), *cert denied,* 451 US 911 (1981). *See also* the discussion at **§§2.30-2.40.**

complainant is involved.[198] And although the thrust of an antitrust violation may be the horizontal conspiracy among franchisees, the franchisor may also be liable if it participates in the concerted activity in any way.[199]

Potential antitrust liability underscores the importance of caution in handling with care all franchisee complaints, in making business decisions regarding franchise sales and terminations which are based solely on the franchisor's independent business discretion, and in establishing a system of record retention which can demonstrate the unilateral nature of the ultimate decision.

§9.42 —What if other franchisees can veto the franchisor's decision to sell the franchise?

The courts have condemned such a veto practice as a per se illegal combination or conspiracy among competitors to allocate markets. In *American Motor Inns, Inc v Holiday Inns, Inc, (AMI)*[200] the defendant hotel franchisor maintained a *radius letter* procedure: upon receiving an application for a franchise, it would notify in writing the franchisees nearest the proposed location, soliciting their written comments. The court found that objections registered by the existing franchisees were treated as a veto by the franchisor: in many cases proposed sales were refused as a result of franchisee objections. The plaintiff, who unsuccessfully sought to establish a location in the face of such objections, argued that this policy enabled existing franchisees to determine whether a potential competitor would be allowed to enter the market, thereby precluding intrabrand competition, and the court agreed.

The court in *AMI* relied heavily on the Supreme Court's reasoning in regard to a similar practice in *United States v Topco Associate.*[201] In that case, the licensor defendant was an association of grocery chains formed to market private label grocery products. Member grocers were assigned exclusive territories in which they could market the private label products and, when membership applications were received, the existing member whose territory was closest to the proposed territory had a right to register an objection. The member objection was found to operate as "a veto of sorts" over the application,[202] and the Court found that the procedure constituted a per se violation of §1 of the Sherman Act.

---

[198] Courts have applied the per se standard to such horizontal collaboration. *See* United States v General Motors Corp, 384 US 127, 140 (1966) (joint, collaborative action by dealers and auto manufacturer to eliminate discounting dealer from market is per se illegal); Com-Tel, Inc v DuKane Corp, 669 F2d 404 (6th Cir 1982); American Motor Inns, Inc v Holiday Inns, Inc, 521 F2d 1230 (3d Cir 1975).

[199] *See* United States v General Motors Corp, 384 US 127, 140 (1966); Com-Tel, Inc v Dukane Corp, 669 F2d 404 (6th Cir 1982); American Motor Inns, Inc v Holiday Inns, Inc, 521 F2d 1230 (3d Cir 1975).

[200] American Motor Inns, Inc v Holiday Inns, Inc, 521 F2d 1230 (3d Cir 1975).

[201] United States v Topco Assoc, 405 US 596 (1972).

[202] *Id* 602.

Business decisions in the sale of franchises cannot be controlled by the would-be competitors of prospective franchisees without risking antitrust liability. Solicitation of franchisee comments about franchise sales raises the risk of a finding that a refused franchise sale is the result of a conspiracy to restrain trade and not the result of a unilateral business decision of the franchisor. The procedures recommended in the case of franchisee *urging* are thus even more clearly applicable in the case of franchisee *vetoes*.[203]

§9.43 —When and under what circumstances may a franchisor refuse to deal with a proposed transferee of an existing franchisee?

Franchisors have an interest in ensuring that the franchises within the system are owned and operated by qualified individuals, and that the quality of goods and services offered through the franchised businesses is maintained. To achieve these objectives, franchisors typically restrict a franchisee's ability to transfer its interests in the franchised business. So as not to restrict unduly a franchisee's right to sell its business (and thus to maintain the marketability of the franchise) franchise agreements typically do not flatly prohibit transfers but, rather, reserve to the franchisor the right to approve or disapprove of any transfers.[204] The standards for approval or disapproval of transfers[205] are usually enunciated in greater or lesser detail in the franchise agreement, but, as discussed below, may be superseded by state statute or antitrust prohibitions.

Courts have long recognized that franchisors have a legitimate interest in requiring their franchisees to seek prior consent to all transfers.[206] In *Seligson v Plum Tree, Inc*,[207] the court stated that a franchisor "has a perfect right to consider the character, stability, reputation, business ability, etc. of those to whom it will entrust its own good name, its mark and its products."

Many franchise agreements include a requirement that the franchisor act *reasonably* in exercising its power of prior consent,[208] and the courts have found

---

[203] For a discussion of the principles of law governing a unilateral refusal to sell, see **ch 2.**

[204] In one study, 74.1% of the franchise agreements surveyed required the franchisee to obtain the franchisor's approval of a proposed transfer. G Udell, *The Franchise Agreement Handbook*, Research Bull No 889, Purdue Univ (May 1973).

[205] See **§§9.44-9.45.**

[206] See Seligson v Plum Tree, Inc, 361 F Supp 748, 753 (ED Pa 1973) ("We see nothing invidious in a franchisor taking precautions against the indiscriminate use of its own reputation and the intrusion of perhaps unsavory strangers.").

[207] 361 F Supp 748, 753 (ED Pa 1973).

[208] Where the franchise agreement includes such a limitation, it has been held that the action must be objectively reasonable. *See* Richter v Dairy Queen, 643 P2d 508 (Ariz App 1982).

an implied duty to act reasonably where there is no such limitation in the franchise agreement.[209]

The grounds for a franchisor's disapproval of a proposed transfer, discussed in the following section, have generally been upheld where the franchisor has demonstrated that it was protecting its legitimate interests.

§9.44 —What grounds for disapproval have been upheld or rejected by the courts?

Franchisor disapprovals have generally been upheld where the franchisor has made a unilateral business decision and has acted reasonably to protect its legitimate interests in the franchise system.

Disapprovals have been upheld on a variety of grounds. When the basis of the franchisor's action was its dissatisfaction with the terms of the proposed transfer, the court in *Kestenbaum v Falstaff Brewing Corp*[210] found the franchisor was justified in withholding its consent. In that case, the proposed purchase price was so high the franchisor determined that the financial stability of the business would be jeopardized.[211] On the other hand, it has been held that an automobile manufacturer may not condition its approval on a purchase price that is unreasonably low.[212] Disapprovals have also been upheld where the franchisor was dissatisfied with the proposed transferee's business qualifications,[213] other business activities,[214] or criminal record.[215] However, if the franchisor's dissatisfaction is deemed irrelevant to its legitimate interests, a court may substitute its own judgment for that of the franchisor.[216]

Franchisors may also be justified in favoring one proposed transferee over another,[217] or in assigning a right of first refusal to a preferred transferee.[218]

---

209 *See* Richter v Dairy Queen, 643 P2d 508 (Ariz App 1982).

210 575 F2d 574 (5th Cir 1978), *cert denied,* 440 US 909 (1979).

211 *See also* Pierce Ford Sales v Ford Motor Co, 299 F2d 425 (2d Cir 1962); Walner v Baskin-Robbins Ice Cream Co, 514 F Supp 1029 (ND Tex 1981).

212 *See* Frank Coulson, Inc-Buick v General Motors Corp, 488 F2d 202 (5th Cir 1974).

213 *See* Hamro v Shell Oil Co, 674 F2d 784 (9th Cir 1982). In Hamro, the court found there had been no tortious interference with a prospective sales agreement where the franchisor disapproved a proposed transfer to an existing licensee who had generated a level of business return well below the system average.

214 *See* Hawkins v Holiday Inns, Inc, 634 F2d 342 (6th Cir 1980), *cert denied,* 451 US 987 (1981).

215 *See* Carrozza v Webber Chevrolet Co, 1978-1 Trade Cas (CCH) ¶61,982 (DRI 1978). Other cases have found a franchisor justified in disapproving a transfer where the proposed transferee had been the subject of numerous consumer complaints, McDaniel v General Motors Corp, 480 F Supp 666 (EDNY 1979), *affd mem,* 628 F2d 1345 (2d Cir 1980); or because it had a disreputable character, Seligson v Plum Tree, Inc, 361 F Supp 748 (ED Pa 1973).

216 Richter v Dairy Queen, 643 P2d 508 (Ariz App 1982).

217 Mogul v General Motors Corp, 391 F Supp 1305 (ED Pa 1975), *affd mem,* 527 F2d 645 (3rd Cir 1976).

In both of these situations franchisors have overcome antitrust challenges. In *Aladdin Oil Co v Texaco*,[219] even though the preferred transferee was a competitor of the disapproved plaintiff, the court upheld the franchisor's selection on the basis of the *Colgate* doctrine.[220]

The exercise of transfer approval rights may not be upheld where it would operate to prevent competition. In *Ohio-Sealy Mattress Mfg Co v Sealy, Inc*,[221] the licensor, which was actually a group of independent manufacturers of mattresses, repeatedly exercised its contractual right of first refusal when the plaintiff attempted to purchase the businesses of licensee members. The jury found that the licensor's real reason for this pattern of activity was a desire to impede the plaintiff from engaging in intrabrand competition and the practice was held to constitute a violation of the Sherman Act.

§9.45 —How do the state franchise laws regulate transfers?

A number of state statutes impose limitations on a franchisor's right to restrict franchise transfers. All of the laws, however, recognize the franchisor's right to review and either approve or disapprove a proposed transfer.

A few states impose procedural requirements on the approval process. In Arkansas,[222] Nebraska,[223] and New Jersey[224] a franchisee must provide written notice of a proposed transfer and certain information regarding the proposed transferee. The franchisor must then respond within 60 days; if the transferee is not acceptable, the franchisor must include in its response a recitation of the material reasons for the disapproval. If the franchisor fails to respond in the 60-day period, the transfer will be deemed approved.

Other states impose different standards which must be met by franchisors if their transfer restrictions are to be upheld. Hawaii law prohibits a disapproval by a franchisor except for *good cause*, which is defined to include a failure by the proposed transferee to meet reasonable qualifications or the current standards for a franchisee.[225] Similarly, Minnesota law allows a franchisor to withhold consent where the proposed transferee fails to meet the qualifications and standards required of the franchisor's franchisees.[226]

Finally, special industry statutes may apply to a transfer restriction. Such

---

[218] 603 F2d 1107 (5th Cir 1979).

[219] *Id.*

[220] United States v Colgate & Co, 250 US 300 (1919). See **§2.17.**

[221] 585 F2d 821 (7th Cir 1978), *cert denied*, 440 US 930 (1979). *Compare with* Alladin Oil Co v Texaco, 603 F2d 1107 (5th Cir 1979).

[222] Ark Stat Ann §70-813 (1979).

[223] Neb Rev Stat §87-406 (Supp 1978).

[224] NJ Stat Ann §56:10-7 (West Supp 1982).

[225] Hawaii Rev Stat §482E-6(2)(I) (Supp 1981).

[226] Minn Stat Ann §80C.14(h) (West Supp 1983).

laws are quite common in both the automobile and petroleum industries; and, as discussed in Chapter 7, either the federal Automobile Dealer's Day in Court Act or the Petroleum Marketing Practices Act may apply.[227]

§9.46 May the franchisor restrict where or to whom the franchisee resells?

In some franchise systems, franchisors limit competition among franchisees by imposing territorial and/or customer restrictions in their franchise agreements. The general principles governing territorial and customer restrictions are discussed in detail in Chapter 5.

The types of territorial restrictions often imposed in the franchise relationship are several. A *location clause*[228] restricts the franchisee to conducting the business only from a certain location.[229] Location clauses tend as a practical matter to restrict the area serviced by the franchisee. Often location clauses are imposed in conjunction with a grant of exclusivity within a certain territory surrounding the particular location. A franchisee may be granted a primary area of responsibility,[230] in which it must exercise its best efforts and, typically, meet an agreed-upon sales quota. While these types of territorial restraints limit intrabrand competition among franchisees, they do not completely eliminate the ability of franchisees to compete for business outside of their assigned market areas.

Other territorial provisions may be more restrictive. A *profit passover* clause permits a franchisee to sell outside of its assigned territory but requires that a fee be paid to other franchisees in whose territories sales are made.[231] Such provisions are designed to compensate the other franchisees for promotional efforts in their territories as well as encourage the franchisee to develop its territory and thus engage more effectively in interbrand competition. Finally, an *air-tight* territorial restriction would prohibit a franchisee from conducting business outside of the perimeter of its assigned territory and at the same time prohibit other franchisees from conducting business within the territory.[232]

There are also a number of different types of customer restrictions used in the franchise context. In some systems, franchisees may be permitted to sell only at retail, and prohibited from selling at wholesale; or, if wholesale transactions are allowed, they may be restricted to sell only to other franchised dealers. Franchisees may be limited to direct, door-to-door selling and prohib-

---

[227] 15 USC §§1221-1225 ("Automotive Dealer's Day in Court Act"); 15 USC §§2801-2806 ("Petroleum Marketing Practices Act"). See **§§7.06, 7.07.**

[228] See **§§5.48-5.50.**

[229] It was a location clause restriction reviewed and upheld by the Supreme Court in Continental TV, Inc v GTE Sylvania, Inc, 433 US 36 (1977). See **chs 1, 5.**

[230] See **§§5.42-5.44.**

[231] See **§§5.45-.47.**

[232] See **§5.01.**

ited from selling to retailers.[233] Other customer restrictions may be narrower where, for instance, a franchisor reserves to itself the right to sell to particular national accounts, or reserves to itself, or certain qualified franchisees, the handling of specific accounts which may need special service. Customer restrictions may be combined with territorial restrictions by prohibiting or imposing passover payments or other conditions on sales made to a class of customers, i.e., customers from outside of a given territory.

As discussed in Chapters 1 and 5, the Supreme Court ruled in *Continental TV Inc v GTE Sylvania Inc,*[234] a case involving a location clause restriction imposed by Sylvania upon its franchised dealers, that vertical territorial and customer restraints are to be reviewed by the courts under the rule of reason.[235] The rule of reason, articulated in *Sylvania,* requires a case-by-case inquiry into the purpose and effect of the particular restriction in question in order to determine whether it should be prohibited as imposing an unreasonable restraint on competition.[236] A number of factors must be considered in order to make such a determination, including: the purpose of the restraint, the availability of less restrictive alternatives, the effects upon intrabrand and interbrand competition in the products involved, the market share of the firm imposing the restraint, and the existence of any business justifications for the restraint.

A number of legitimate business purposes for territorial and customer restraints have been asserted by franchisors and approved by the courts in upholding the legality of the restraints. These include increasing the market share of a particular brand;[237] inducing better service and warranties by distributors;[238] and preventing the unfair *free rider* practice of some franchisees that exploit the marketing efforts of other franchisees.[239] The actual impact on competition of the restriction in question is, of course, given greater weight than the business purpose advanced by the franchisor or manufacturer. In *Eiberger v Sony Corp of America,*[240] a manufacturer imposed a warranty program under which its dealers were automatically assessed a *warranty fee* for each item sold outside of the dealer's territory. The Second Circuit found that in actual

---

[233] See *In re* Amway Corp [1976-1979 Transfer Binder] Trade Reg Rep (CCH) ¶21,574 (FTC 1979).

[234] 433 US 36 (1977).

[235] Under certain circumstances territorial restrictions may be deemed *horizontal* (an agreement between competitors to allocate markets) rather than *vertical* and would thus be illegal per se. *See generally* United States v Topco Assocs, 405 US 596 (1972). See also discussion at **chs 1, 5.**

[236] The rule of reason standard is discussed in detail in **ch 1.**

[237] *See, e.g.,* Newberry v Washington Post Co, 438 F Supp 470 (DDC 1977).

[238] *See, e.g.,* Donald B Rice Tire Co v Michelin Tire Corp, 483 F Supp 750 (D Md 1980), *affd,* 638 F2d 15 (4th Cir), *cert denied,* 454 US 864 (1981). *But see* Eiberger v Sony Corp of Am, 622 F2d 1068 (2d Cir 1980) (warranty program held a "sham" designed to impose an illegal restraint).

[239] *See, e.g.,* Continental TV, Inc v GTE Sylvania, Inc, 433 US 36 (1977). *But see* Coca Cola Co [1976-1979 Transfer Binder] Trade Reg Rep (CCH) ¶21,420 (FTC 1978).

[240] 622 F2d 1068 (2d Cir 1980).

practice the program was not used to assure customers of adequate service, since the passover was paid without regard to any service provided by the recipient, but served to eliminate extraterritorial competition.

Antitrust concerns also arise when territorial or customer restrictions operate to fix or otherwise influence the price at which the franchisee resells.[241] The ruling in *Sylvania* extended only to *nonprice* vertical restrictions; the Supreme Court expressly noted that price restrictions will continue to be condemned under the antitrust laws as per se illegal.[242] Thus, vertical restraints which directly affect prices have been ruled per se illegal;[243] however, the cases have suggested that a vertical restraint which has an indirect effect on pricing may not be condemned.[244]

Customer restrictions in particular are susceptible to antitrust attack as being in furtherance of an illegal price-fixing scheme. In his concurring opinion in the *Sylvania* decision, Justice White suggested that customer restraints pose a potentially greater threat to intrabrand competition than territorial restraints because they operate to keep the product out of the hands of discounters and other price cutters, and thus may act to eliminate intrabrand price competition.[245] This position has not been adopted by lower courts, but does suggest that customer restrictions be reviewed by counsel with increased caution and awareness of the restraint's impact on prices.

The few post-*Sylvania* cases which have reviewed vertical customer restrictions have indicated that certain types of restrictions may be upheld under a rule of reason analysis.[246] In *Ohio-Sealy Mattress Manufacturing Co v Sealy, Inc,*[247] the Seventh Circuit reviewed and upheld a program in which the licensor, Sealy, negotiated the terms of supplying a national purchasing account and invited its licensees to service the local needs of the national account within their respective assigned areas of primary responsibility on the terms negotiated by the licensor. In upholding the legality of the program under a rule of reason analysis, the court emphasized that (1) each Sealy licensee was given an opportunity to take part in the program on a *voluntary* basis and (2) there were no restrictions imposed on a nonparticipating licensee to prevent the licensee from selling directly to national accounts on its own negotiated terms.

---

[241] *See* **§§5.12-5.15.**

[242] *See* Continental TV, Inc v GTE Sylvania, Inc, 433 US 36, 52 n 18 (1977).

[243] *See, e.g.,* National Socy of Professional Engrs v United States, 435 US 679 (1978).

[244] *See, e.g.,* Muenster Butane, Inc v Steward Co, 651 Fd 292 (5th Cir 1981); Eastern Scientific v Wild Heerburg Instruments, 572 F2d 883 (1st Cir), *cert denied,* 439 US 833 (1978).

[245] *See* Continental TV, Inc v GTE Sylvania, Inc, 433 US 36, 59 (1977) (concurring opinion); *see also* Eiberger v Sony Corp of Am, 622 F2d 1068 (2d Cir 1980). *See generally In re* Levi Strauss, & Co, [1976-1979 Transfer Binder] Trade Reg Rep (CCH) ¶21,400 (FTC Consent Order 1978).

[246] *See, e.g.,* Ohio-Sealy Mattress Mfg Co v Sealy, Inc, 585 F2d 821 (7th Cir 1978), *cert denied,* 440 US 930 (1979); Newberry v Washington Post Co, 438 F Supp 470 (DDC 1977).

[247] 585 F2d 821 (7th Cir 1978), *cert denied,* 440 US 930 (1979).

In another case involving a customer restriction, *In re Amway Corp.*,[248] the Federal Trade Commission ruled that a sales policy which prevented Amway distributors from selling to retailers did not violate the antitrust laws. The commission found that the restriction was necessary to implement Amway's unique marketing plan of door-to-door sales.

§9.47 —What if the franchisor is also competing with the franchisee?

Continental TV Inc v GTE Sylvania Inc, did not alter the per se illegality of horizontal restrictions among competitors.[249] In *Sylvania,* the Court stated:

> There may be occasional problems in differentiating vertical restrictions from horizontal restrictions originating in agreements among retailers. There is no doubt that restrictions in the latter category would be illegal per se . . ., but we do not regard the problems of proof as sufficiently great to justify a per se rule.[250] [citations omitted]

As discussed in Chapter 8, the distinction between *vertical* and *horizontal* restrictions is often difficult to discern, particularly where the Seller engages in *dual distribution.*

In the franchise context, dual distribution issues arise where the franchisor operates at the wholesale or retail level in competition with its franchisees. In a number of cases, most of them pre-*Sylvania,* courts have held that restrictions imposed by a dual distributor should be viewed as horizontal and therefore per se illegal.[251] However, other courts have found that restrictions imposed in a dual distribution system are not necessarily horizontal, and not always an unlawful practice violating the antitrust laws.[252] In addition, recent decisions have indicated a trend toward evaluating the territorial restraints of a dual distributor under the rule of reason where a close analysis reveals that the restraint is not the result of a horizontal combination or conspiracy.[253] In *Red*

---

[248] [1976-1979 Transfer Binder] Trade Reg Rep (CCH) ¶21,574 (FTC 1979).

[249] 433 US 36 (1977). *See, e.g.,* United States v Topco Assocs, Inc, 405 US 596 (1972).

[250] 433 US 36, 57 n 28 (1977).

[251] *See, e.g.,* Hobart Bros Co v Malcolm T Gilliard, Inc, 471 F2d 894 (5th Cir), *cert denied,* 412 US 923 (1973); Interphoto Corp v Minolta Corp, 295 F Supp 711 (SDNY), *affd per curiam,* 417 F2d 621 (2nd Cir 1969); Pitchford Scientific Instruments Corp v PEPI, Inc, 435 F Supp 685 (WD Pa 1977); Guild Wineries & Distillations v J Sosnick & Son, 1980-1 Trade Cas (CCH) ¶62,258 (Cal Ct App 1980).

[252] *See* Rea v Ford Motor Corp, 355 F Supp 842 (WD Pa 1972); *revd on other grounds,* 497 F2d 577 (3d Cir), *cert denied,* 419 US 868 (1974); *see also* Joseph E Seagram & Son v Hawaiian Oke & Liquors Ltd, 416 F2d 71 (9th Cir), *cert denied,* 396 US 1962 (1969); Mogul v General Motors Corp, 391 F Supp 1305 (ED Pa 1975); Carlo Gelardi Corp v Miller Brewing Co, 421 F Supp 237 (DNJ 1976).

[253] 637 F2d 1001 (5th Cir 1981); *see also* Copy-Data Sys v Toshita Am, Inc, 663 F2d 405 (2nd Cir 1981); Abadir & Co v First Miss Corp, 651 F2d 422 (5th Cir 1981); Krehl v Baskin-Robbins Ice Cream Co, 664 F2d 1348 (9th Cir 1982).

Diamond Supply, Inc v Liquid Carbonic Corp,[254] the plaintiff distributor alleged, and the lower court found, that the territorial and customer restrictions imposed by the manufacturer constituted a horizontal conspiracy because it sold some of its products directly to customers in competition with its distributors. The Fifth Circuit disagreed, holding that a restraint is horizontal where the source of the conspiracy is a combination of the distributors; and vertical where the manufacturer is the source, as was the case in *Red Diamond.* The Ninth Circuit Court of Appeals reached a similar conclusion in *Krehl v Baskin-Robbins Ice Cream Co.*[255] In that case, the court refused to extend the rule of per se illegality to dual distribution systems such as Baskin-Robbins. The plaintiff franchisees failed to demonstrate an anticompetitive purpose or effect in the dual distribution system, and, in the absence of such proof, the court concluded, "dual distribution systems must be evaluated under the traditional rule of reason standard."[256]

§9.48 May the franchisor grant a franchise within the market area of an existing franchisee?

In the absence of a contractual grant of exclusive territorial rights, franchisors are generally free to determine where their franchisees are to be located. The courts have been reluctant either to expand limited exclusivity rights when contained in the franchise agreement, or to find an implied right of exclusivity where the franchise agreement contains no express provisions.[257]

Of course, where the franchisor places a new franchise or a company owned unit in proximity with an existing franchise as part of an anticompetitive attack designed to drive the franchisee out of business, the courts will protect the franchisee's legitimate interests. This exception to the general rule was discussed in the rather extreme fact pattern presented in *Photovest Corp v Fotomat Corp.*[258] In *Photovest,* the franchisor's illegal predatory conduct included the placement of company-owned stores in the market areas of franchisees.[259] The cases have also suggested that implied covenants of good faith and fair dealing may apply to situations where a franchise is established within the market area

---

[254] 637 F2d 1001 (5th Cir 1981).

[255] 664 F2d 1348 (9th Cir 1982).

[256] *Id* 1357.

[257] *See* Dayton Motels, Inc v Holiday Inns, Inc, CA No 74-1150 (CP Montgomery County, Ohio, July 29, 1977) (unreported). *See also* New York Motel Enters v Holiday Inns, Inc, 1980-1 Trade Cas (CCH) ¶63,167 (Sup Ct NY 1980); Newark Motor Inn Corp v Holiday Inns, Inc, 472 F Supp 1143 (DNJ 1979). *Cf* So Good Potato Chip Co v Frito-Lay, Inc, 462 F2d 239 (8th Cir 1982).

[258] 606 F2d 704 (7th Cir 1979).

[259] The court found that the franchisor had set out to drive its franchisees out of business by, among other actions, building company-owned units within the franchisee's market area despite oral representations that there would be no overlap of the roughly 2-mile radius surrounding each franchised location. *See* Photovest Corp v Fotomat Corp, 606 F2d 704, 716.

of another franchisee.[260]

Certain state franchise laws may also restrict encroachment on the franchisee's market area.[261] Indiana law, for instance, prohibits "establishing a franchisor-owned outlet engaged in a substantially identical business to that of the franchisee within the exclusive territory granted the franchisee by the franchise agreement; or, if no exclusive territory is designated, competing unfairly with the franchisee within a reasonable area . . ."[262] Industry specific statutes, primarily in the automobile industry, may also restrict the placement of a franchisee within a certain radius of an existing franchised business.[263]

In short, franchisors are generally free, in the absence of contractual restrictions, to locate franchises even if within the market area of another franchisee —much as Sellers are free to select their Buyers. In the franchising context, an oppressive franchise placement may be unlawful, and a few state franchise statutes may be applicable. Another common feature in franchising involves the granting of exclusive territorial rights. This is discussed in **§9.49.**

§9.49 What if the franchise agreement grants exclusive rights?

If the franchisor has promised not to place another franchise within a certain territory, or not to grant any portion of an area of primary responsibility to another, and then violates that promise by establishing another franchise, a clear claim of breach of contract will be available to the existing franchisee.[264]

State franchise law may also apply to such a contractual breach. Several state franchise statutes prohibit a franchisor from establishing a competing business

---

[260] 606 F2d 704, 728 (7th Cir 1979); So Good Potato Chip Co v Frito-Lay, Inc, 462 F2d 239 (8th Cir 1972). Many courts have found an implied covenant of good faith and fair dealing in a franchise agreement. *See generally* Arnott v American Oil Co, 609 F2d 873 (8th Cir 1979), *cert denied,* 446 US 918 (1980); UCC §1-203. See also the discussion of "fiduciary duty of good faith and fair dealing in the franchisor-franchisee relationship at **§9.63.**

[261] See Fla Admin Code §2-17.04(10); Hawaii Rev Stat §482E-6(2)(E) (Supp 1981); Ind Code Ann §23-2-2.7-2(4) (Burns Supp 1982); Mich Stat Ann §19.854(27)(c) (Callaghan 1981); Minn Stat Ann §80C.14(c) (West Supp 1983); Wash Rev Code Ann §19.100.180(2)(f) (1978 & Supp 1982).

[262] Ind Code Ann §23-2-2.7-2(4) (Burns Supp 1982).

[263] *See, e.g.,* The California Automobile Franchise Act, which requires an automobile manufacturer to obtain approval of the California New Motor Vehicle Board before opening or relocating a franchised dealership within the market area of an existing franchisee, if the franchisee protests. *See* New Motor Vehicle Bd of Cal v Orrin Fox Co, 439 US 96 (1978) (upholding constitutionality of the California Automobile Franchise Act). *Compare with* American Motor Inns, Inc, v Holiday Inns, Inc, 521 F2d 1230 (3d Cir 1975).

[264] Photovest Corp v Fotomat Corp, 606 F2d 704, 727 (7th Cir 1979). *Cf* So Good Potato Chip Co v Frito-Lay, Inc, 462 F2d 239 (8th Cir 1972).

in violation of a contractual exclusivity provision.[265]

The types of *exclusive rights* granted in the franchise context vary considerably and, depending on the specific provision in question, may or may not limit a franchisor's ability to place another franchise within the market area of an existing franchisee. For example, the franchise agreement may restrict the franchisor's right to establish another franchise located in the franchisee's territory; it may restrict the franchisor's right to license another area of primary responsibility which overlaps the area granted to the franchisee; or, as is often the case where a simple location clause restriction is imposed, it may grant no exclusive rights at all.

§9.50 May the franchisee be required to purchase the products of the franchisor?

The law of tying, discussed generally at Chapter 4, prohibits arrangements in which a Seller agrees to sell one product (the *tying* product) only on the condition that the Buyer also purchase a second product (the *tied* product).[266] Where the Seller has sufficient *economic power* in the tying product,[267] and the arrangement affects a *not insubstantial* amount of interstate commerce,[268] the courts have consistently ruled that the tie-in constitutes a per se violation of §1 of the Sherman Act,[269] §3 of the Clayton Act,[270] or §5 of the Federal Trade Commission (FTC) Act.[271] Traditional tying analysis focuses on the underlying market impact of a tie-in arrangement: from the point of view of competing Sellers, foreclosure of competition in the market for the tied product, and from the point of view of the Buyer, restriction on its ability to shop for competing products. The courts have concluded that this foreclosure of competition is inherent in each tying arrangement, and sufficiently pernicious to warrant application of the per se illegality standard.[272]

The prohibition against tying arrangements applies fully in the franchise context, and may prohibit the imposition of restrictive purchasing requirements by a franchisor. However, application of tying analysis to the franchise relationship has given rise to special considerations which set franchising cases

---

[265] See Fla Admin Code §§2-17.04(7), (10); Hawaii Rev Stat §482E-6(2)(E) (Supp 1981); Ind Code Ann §23-2-2.7-2(4) (Burns Supp 1982); Mich Stat Ann §19.854(27)(c) (Callaghan 1981); Minn Stat Ann §80C.14(c) (West Supp 1983); Wash Rev Code Ann §19.100.180(2)(f) (1978 & Supp 1982).

[266] See **§§4.07-4.37.** *See also* Northern Pac Ry v United States, 356 US 1 (1958).

[267] See **§§4.22-4.26, 9.53.**

[268] See **§4.27.**

[269] 15 USC §1.

[270] 15 USC §14.

[271] 15 USC §45.

[272] See **§4.02.** As discussed in **§4.02,** tying is generally found to be per se unlawful, but the analysis applied by the courts in tying cases does not usually follow a purely per se approach. See the discussions of tying justifications at **§§4.28, 9.54.**

apart from usual Buyer-Seller transactions. The courts have shown a growing sensitivity to the economic realities of franchising, weighing the high level of investment by both franchisor and franchisee, the mutual economic interests of both parties in the success of the franchisee's business, and the often beneficial effect on competition of many of the controls and restrictions imposed in the franchisor-franchisee relationship. As noted by the Fifth Circuit Court of Appeals: "Although in the archetypal case '[t]ying arrangements serve hardly any purpose beyond the suppression of competition . . .,' in the franchising context ties may well serve legitimate purposes."[273]

Tie-in arrangements in the franchising context may be attacked not only under the antitrust laws but also under §5 of the FTC Act, which prohibits unfair methods of competition.[274] In addition, several state franchise statutes prohibit a franchisor from requiring that goods or services be purchased or leased from the franchisor unless it can prove that the restrictive purchasing arrangement is reasonably necessary for a lawful purpose, justified on business grounds, and does not substantially affect competition.[275]

In short, any requirement that a franchisee purchase equipment, products or other goods or services from its franchisor raises the question of an illegal tying arrangement. While tying prohibitions are fully applicable in the franchise context, policy considerations and a sensitivity to the particular economic realities of franchising have led to a special set of tying rules that may not apply to the typical Seller-Buyer transaction.

§9.51 —When is the franchisor's trademark considered a tying item?

Unlike the usual Buyer-Seller tying case involving tangible goods, tying cases in the franchising context typically involve an allegation that the franchisor's trademark, or the franchise itself (the *tying item*), is sold on the condition that the franchisee purchase equipment or supplies (the *tied item*) from the

---

[273] Kentucky Fried Chicken Corp v Diversified Packaging Corp, 549 F2d 368, 375 (1975).

[274] *See, e.g.*, Times-Picayune Publishing Co v United States, 345 US 594 (1953). See also discussion at **§4.02**.

[275] *See, e.g.*, Hawaii Rev Stat §482E-6(2)(B) (1976 & Supp 1981) and Wash Rev Code Ann §§19.100.180(2)(b), (d) (1978 & Supp 1982) (excludes initial inventory of the franchisee). See also Ind Code Ann §23-2-2.7-1(1) (Burns Supp 1982) (prohibiting purchasing requirements where goods/services of comparable quality are available from sources other than those designated by the franchisor; specific exclusion for approved supplier programs and the "principal goods, supplies, inventories or service manufactured or trademarked by the franchisor"); and Mich Stat Ann §19.854(27)(b) (Callaghan 1981) (state may prohibit registration where the franchise agreement requires purchasing from designated sources "unless the goods or services are an integral part of the franchised business or the restrictive purchasing arrangements are necessary for the protection of a trade or service mark").

franchisor.[276] As discussed in Chapter 4, ties have been held to violate both §1 of the Sherman Act and §3 of the Clayton Act. Since §3 of the Clayton Act applies only to tangible goods, tying charges in the franchise context are most often brought under the Sherman Act.[277]

Since the Second Circuit's 1964 ruling in *Susser v. Carvel Corp*,[278] the courts have generally accepted the proposition that a trademark can serve as a tying item for the purposes of antitrust tying analysis.[279] In *Carvel*, the court concluded that the franchisor's trademark, the motivating force behind the franchise arrangement, could serve as a tying item.

While it seems clear that a trademark may constitute a tying item, questions have arisen whether it may be presumed to possess economic power, and whether there are circumstances in which the trademark and the tied item should be treated not as two distinct items tied together but as a single product. These questions are addressed in **§§9.52** and **9.53.**

§9.52 —When is a franchisor's trademark considered a separate tying item?

Where a trademark or a franchise license is alleged to be the tying item, the courts have focused on the role of the trademark license in the franchised business and the relationship of the mark to the allegedly tied item. Indeed, in many tying cases in the franchise context the two-product test may become the central issue in tying analysis. For tying purposes the cases have treated differently a trademark which represents the origin of the alleged tied product and a trademark which represents a standard of product quality and uniformity.[280] Where the trademark serves as an emblem of origin, it may be indistinguishable from the product it represents. Where it represents a standard of quality, a trademark may indeed be separate and distinct, and may serve as a *tying item.* Thus, in *Krehl v Baskin-Robbins Ice Cream Co*,[281] the Ninth Circuit held that the trademark licensed to the franchisee of a specialty ice cream shop "lacked sufficient independent existence apart from the ice cream products" allegedly tied to the trademark to justify the finding of an unlawful tie.[282]

---

[276] *See, e.g.*, Carpa, Inc v Ward Foods, Inc, 536 F2d 39 (5th Cir 1976); Susser v Carvel Corp, 332 F2d 505 (2d Cir 1964), *cert dismissed*, 381 US 125 (1965); Siegel v Chicken Delight, Inc, 448 F2d 43 (9th Cir 1971), *cert denied*, 405 US 955 (1972).

[277] *See* Shaeffer v Collins, 1980-81 Trade Cas (CCH) ¶63,666 (ED Pa 1980). See generally **§§4.02, 4.03.**

[278] 332 F2d 505 (2d Cir 1964), *cert dismissed*, 381 US 125 (1965).

[279] See **§4.14** and the cases cited therein.

[280] *See, e.g.*, Krehl v Baskin-Robbins Ice Cream Co, 664 F2d 1348 (9th Cir 1982); Hamro v Shell Oil Co, 674 F2d 784 (9th Cir 1982).

[281] 664 F2d 1348 (9th Cir 1982).

[282] *Id* 1354.

Similarly, in *Hamro v Shell Oil Co,*[283] the court ruled that the trademark licensed to a service station franchisee identified the source of the gasoline sold at the station and that the nexus between trademark and gasoline was sufficiently close to treat them as a single product.[284] In addition, the Federal Trade Commission has suggested that a trademark may not constitute a separate tying item if its use is merely ancillary to the sale of the underlying product.[285]

Several recent decisions have concluded that under certain circumstances an allegedly tied item may be an integral and essential element of the franchise package, and that the franchise itself constitutes a single product rather than distinct products unlawfully tied together.[286] In *Principe v McDonald's Corp,*[287] for instance, the court held that the required lease of real estate from the franchisor was not *tied* to the purchase of the McDonald's franchise, but, rather, that the McDonald's franchise was a single set of related products, all contributing to a formula for success that is uniquely attractive to prospective franchisees.[288] Franchisors should not conclude from these cases, however, that all purchasing requirements may be justifiable on the *Principe* theory of an inseparable franchise package. Rather, where the franchisor's trademark and a product or service of which the franchisor is the source are inextricably intertwined in the franchise operation or in the mind of the public, the single package rationale may apply.[289]

---

[283] 674 F2d 784 (9th Cir 1982).

[284] *Id* 788.

[285] *See* Chock Full O' Nuts [1973-76 Transfer Binder] 3 Trade Reg Rep (CCH) ¶20,441 (FTC 1973).

[286] *See* Principe v McDonald's Corp, 631 F2d 303 (4th Cir 1980), *cert denied,* 451 US 970 (1981). *See also* Kugler v AAMCO Automatic Transmissions, Inc, 337 F Supp 872 (D Minn 1971), *affd,* 460 F2d 1214 (8th Cir 1972); Kypta v McDonald's Corp, 1979-2 Trade Cas (CCH) ¶62,827 (SD Fla 1979), *affd,* 671 F2d 1282 (11th Cir), *cert denied,* 103 S Ct 127 (1982).

[287] 631 F2d 303 (4th Cir 1980), *cert denied,* 451 US 970 (1981).

[288] The court stated:

> All of these factors contribute significantly to the overall success of the McDonald's system. The formula that produced system-wide success, the formula that promises to make each new McDonald's store successful, that formula is what McDonald's sells its franchisees. To characterize the franchise as an unnecessary aggregate of separate products tied to the McDonald's name is to miss the point entirely. Among would be franchisees, the McDonald's name has come to stand for the formula, including all that it entails. We decline to find that it is an illegal tie in.

631 F2d at 311.

[289] In several cases franchisors have been unsuccessful in arguing the existence of a single package theory. *See, e.g.,* Northern v McGraw-Edison, Co, 542 F2d 1336 (8th Cir 1976), *cert denied,* 429 US 1097 (1977); Carpa, Inc v Ward Foods, Inc, 536 F2d 39 (5th Cir 1976). See generally **§4.15.**

§9.53 —When is proof of market power and coercion required?

The *market power* and *coercion* elements of a tie also may raise different questions when tying is alleged in the franchise context. In *Siegel v Chicken Delight, Inc,*[290] the court concluded that the owner of a unique trademark had sufficient market power through his natural monopoly in the mark to support a per se analysis, much in the same way as a patent or copyright owner has a monopoly in the rights to an invention or written material.[291] Some later cases have distinguished this point, rejecting the notion that a legally unique name alone should demand the presumption of economic power.[292] Rather, it has been held, the existence vel non of sufficient economic power to appreciably restrain competition in the tied market is more appropriately a question for determination by the fact finder.[293]

A plaintiff franchisee, like any Buyer, to establish a tying claim, must usually show that it was required or coerced to buy the tied product.[294] However, where there is an express agreement to purchase the tied item, perhaps embodied in the franchise license itself, it has been held that there is no need to inquire into the franchisee's motives for purchasing.[295]

The issue is more difficult where there is no express agreement. In *Ungar v Dunkin Donuts of America, Inc,*[296] the Third Circuit, reversing a lower court

---

[290] 448 F2d 43 (9th Cir 1971), *cert denied,* 405 US 955 (1972).

[291] See **§4.26.** Other cases in the franchise context in which courts have presumed sufficient economic power because of the existence of the trademark include Photovest Corp v Fotomat Corp, 606 F2d 704 (7th Cir 1979); Martino v McDonald's Sys, 81 FRD 81, 90 (ND Ill 1979); McAlpine v AAMCO Automatic Transmissions, Inc, 461 F Supp 1232 (ED Mich 1978); AAMCO Automatic Transmissions, Inc v Taylor, 407 F Supp 430 (ED Pa 1976). *See also* Susser v Carvel Corp, 332 F2d 505 (2d Cir 1964), *cert dismissed,* 381 US 125 (1965).

[292] *See* Carpa, Inc v Ward Foods, Inc, 536 F2d 39, 49 (5th Cir 1976); Cash v Arctic Circle, Inc, 85 FRD 618 (ED Wash 1979); Esposito v Mister Softee, Inc, 1976-2 Trade Cas (CCH) ¶61,202 (EDNY 1976).

[293] Carpa, Inc v Ward Foods, Inc, 536 F2d 39, 49 (5th Cir 1976); Esposito v Mister Softee, Inc, 1980-1 Trade Cas (CCH) ¶63,089 (EDNY 1979). *Cf* Fortner Enters v United States Steel Corp, 394 US 495 (1969), in which the Court stated: "[T]he proper focus of concern is whether the seller has the power to raise prices, or impose other burdensome terms such as a tie-in, with respect to any appreciable number of buyers within the market." 394 US at 504.

[294] *See* Bob Maxfield, Inc v American Motors, Corp, 637 F2d 1033 (5th Cir 1981); Ogden Food Serv Corp v Mitchell, 614 F2d 1001 (5th Cir 1980); Ungar v Dunkin Donuts of Am, Inc, 531 F2d 1211 (3d Cir), *cert denied,* 429 US 823 (1976); Response of Carolina, Inc v Leasco Response, Inc, 537 F2d 1307 (5th Cir 1976); Capital Temporaries, Inc v Olsten Corp, 506 F2d 658 (2d Cir 1974); Esposito v Mister Softee, Inc, 1980-1 Trade Cas (CCH) ¶63,089 (EDNY 1979).

[295] *See* Bell v Cherokee Aviation, Corp, 660 F2d 1123 (6th Cir 1981); Bogosian v Gulf Oil Corp, 561 F2d 434 (3d Cir 1977), *cert denied,* 434 US 1086 (1978). *But see* Plekowski v Ralston Purina Co, 68 FRD 443 (MD Ga 1975).

[296] Ungar v Dunkin Donuts of Am, Inc, 531 F2d 211 (3d Cir), *cert denied,* 429 US 823 (1976).

class certification, ruled that, in the absence of an express contractual tie, the plaintiff franchisees must prove that each of them was coerced into purchasing the allegedly tied items. The plaintiffs failed to persuade the court that coercion could be demonstrated by proving merely (1) that the franchisor had a policy of persuading franchisees to buy from it and (2) that a large number of franchisees in fact bought from the franchisor.[297] Hence, class certification was improper, since individual, rather than common, questions would predominate.[298]

§9.54 —What other justifications have been argued by franchisors?

Despite its per se characterization, the courts have considered a variety of justifications for a tying arrangement in the franchising context which would usually not be available to nonfranchising Buyers and Sellers.[299] In one case, a franchisor successfully argued that a new franchise sale constituted the sale of a packaged, going business.[300] Another case suggested that a tie may be justified when it is necessary to aid the franchisor and franchisee in breaking into the market.[301] The arguments have also been raised that a tie-in is justifiable when necessary to protect a trade secret[302] or to maintain product quality and the goodwill of trademarks.[303] There are, however, very few cases in which these arguments have prevailed. In addition, the Federal Trade Commission

---

[297] *See also* Bogosian v Gulf Oil Corp, 561 F2d 434 (3d Cir 1977), *cert denied,* 434 US 1086 (1978) (interpreting Ungar).

[298] The courts have been generally reluctant to extend coercion analysis in the franchise context to the *inherent coercion* findings of the *TBA* (tires, batteries and accessories) cases brought under the Federal Trade Commission (FTC) Act. *See* FTC v Texaco, Inc, 393 US 223 (1968); Atlantic Ref Co v FTC, 381 US 357 (1965); and Shell Oil Co v FTC, 360 F2d 470 (5th Cir 1966), *cert denied,* 385 US 1002 (1967). In those cases, the courts upheld the commission's contention that coercion was inherent in the relationship between the national oil company franchisor and the service station franchisee. Not only were the TBA cases brought under §5 of the FTC Act, which courts have interpreted to be broader in scope than the Sherman and Clayton Acts, but the level of implicit coercion in the business format system is typically lower than in the oil company dealership systems. *See* Kentucky Fried Chicken Corp v Diversified Packaging Corp, 549 F2d 368, 377 n 10 (5th Cir 1977).

[299] See **§4.28.**

[300] *See* Beefy Trail, Inc v Beefy King Intl, Inc, 348 F Supp 799 (MD Fla 1972). *But see* Carpa, Inc, v Ward Foods, Inc, 536 F2d 39, 46 (5th Cir 1976).

[301] *See* United States v Jerrold Elecs Corp, 187 F Supp 545, 556-57 (ED Pa 1960), *affd,* 365 US 567 (1961). *But see* Siegel v Chicken Delight, Inc, 448 F2d 43, 51 (9th Cir 1971), *cert denied,* 405 US 955 (1972).

[302] *See* Krehl v Baskin-Robbins Ice Cream Co, 664 F2d 1348 (9th Cir 1982); Siegel v Chicken Delight, Inc, 448 F2d 43, 51 n 9 (9th Cir 1971), *cert denied,* 405 US 955 (1972).

[303] *See* Susser v Carvel Corp, 332 F2d 505 (2d Cir 1964), *cert dismissed,* 381 US 125 (1965). *But see* Siegel v Chicken Delight, Inc, 448 F2d 43, 51 (9th Cir 1971), *cert denied,* 405 US 955 (1972).

and the courts have ruled that otherwise illegal ties will not be justifiable as protecting trade secrets or product quality if there is some less restrictive way to afford the same protection.[304]

§9.55 —May the franchisee be required to purchase products from approved suppliers?

The answer to the question is generally, yes. Approved supplier programs allow a franchisor to protect its legitimate interest in controlling the quality of goods and services offered under its trademarks while not unreasonably restricting product purchasing by its franchisees. Through an approved supplier program, a franchisor requires its franchisees to purchase equipment and/or supplies only from sources it approves. Properly administered, such a program features uniform procedures and product quality standards for evaluating those who apply to become approved suppliers.

The courts have upheld the legality of approved supplier arrangements in the face of antitrust challenges. It has been noted, however, that "franchisors must walk a narrow path when including in their franchise agreements clauses requiring franchisees to buy supplies from approved sources."[305] In *Kentucky Fried Chicken Corp v Diversified Packaging Corp*,[306] the Fifth Circuit ruled that the approved source program established by Kentucky Fried Chicken Corporation was not a per se illegal tying arrangement, and, in addition, did not violate the law under a rule of reason analysis. In that case, the court acknowledged the legitimate interests of Kentucky Fried Chicken (KFC) Corporation in the quality of the chicken product and in the product's packaging. The court also found that the administration of the program in no way restricted competition among suppliers who would sell to KFC franchisees, did not restrict supplier entry into the franchisee market, and did not exert influence over the terms on which KFC franchisees purchased from approved suppliers.[307]

Franchisors must exercise caution that the operation of the approved supplier program does not violate §2(c) of the Robinson-Patman Act, which prohibits payment of *brokerage* to a buyer's agent. Thus, if the approved supplier pays a rebate to the franchisor in any form, it may violate §2(c).[308]

---

[304] *See, e.g.*, Chock Full O'Nuts [1973-76 Transfer Binder] 3 Trade Reg Rep (CCH) ¶20,441 (FTC 1973); Siegel v Chicken Delight, Inc, 448 F2d 43, 51 (9th Cir 1971), *cert denied*, 405 US 955 (1972).

[305] Kentucky Fried Chicken Corp v Diversified Packaging Corp, 549 F2d 368, 372 (5th Cir 1977).

[306] 549 F2d 368 (5th Cir 1977).

[307] *Id* 380.

[308] 15 USC §13(c). See **§§3.16-3.17.** Other antitrust issues may also arise when a franchisor forms a franchisee *buying group* and negotiates terms with suppliers on behalf of franchisees. For example, a franchisor's receipt of payments from suppliers as a condition for negotiating with those suppliers on behalf of franchisees could be found to violate §2(c) of the Robinson-Patman Act (see **ch 3**), or to constitute an unlawful

In addition, the state franchise laws may apply to the payment of rebates or kickbacks to a franchisor by a supplier. Those laws prohibit the franchisor from obtaining "money, goods, services, anything of value, or any other benefit from any other person with whom the franchisee does business" unless the benefit is "disclosed to the franchisee,"[309] or "promptly accounted for and transmitted to the franchisee."[310]

§9.56 —May the franchisor have a financial interest in its approved suppliers?

The courts have found sufficient grounds to establish an illegal tie in when an approved supplier program operates to force the franchisee to purchase from the franchisor itself or from an affiliate of the franchisor.[311] In *Carpa, Inc v Ward Foods, Inc,*[312] for instance, an illegal tie was found where the franchise agreement for a restaurant required the plaintiff franchisee to purchase all food, supplies, and equipment from the franchisor or its affiliated company.[313]

The cases indicate, however, that a franchisor may require its franchisee to purchase from an approved supplier in which the franchisor has no financial interest.[314] In *Keener v Sizzler Family Steak House,*[315] the plaintiff franchisee was required to use a building contractor designated by the franchisor to construct the franchised restaurant. The court rejected plaintiff's tying claim, stating:

> The franchisor had no financial interest in or connection with the building contractor whom it had designated to erect the new building. It had no stake in that contractor's business, it derived no income from his sales, and it would receive no rental income from the building. There is no illegal tying arrangement where a "tying" company has absolutely no interest in the sales of a third company whose products are favored by

---

tie-in arrangement under §1 of the Sherman Act (see generally **ch 4**). Section 2(c) would not, however, prevent a franchisor from charging franchisees participating in a buying group reasonable fees to compensate the franchisor for negotiating with suppliers on behalf of franchisees, provided that franchisee participation in the buying group is voluntary.

[309] Wash Rev Code Ann §19.100.180(2)(e) (1978 & Supp 1982). See also Hawaii Rev Stat §482E-6(2)(D) (Supp 1981).

[310] See Ind Code Ann §§23-2-2.7-2(4), (6) (Burns Supp 1982).

[311] *See, e.g.,* Carpa Inc v Ward Foods, Inc, 536 F2d 39 (5th Cir 1976); *see also* Kentucky Fried Chicken Corp v Diversified Packaging Corp, 549 F2d 368, 377 n 9 (5th Cir 1977).

[312] Carpa, Inc v Ward Foods, Inc, 536 F2d 39 (5th Cir 1976).

[313] *Id* 43.

[314] *See* Kentucky Fried Chicken Corp v Diversified Packaging Corp, 549 F2d 368, 377 n 9 (5th Cir 1977); Crawford Transp Co v Chrysler Corp, 338 F2d 934 (6th Cir 1964); *cert denied,* 380 US 954 (1965); Shaeffer v Collins, 1980-1 Trade Cas (CCH) ¶63,666 (ED Pa 1980).

[315] Keener v Sizzler Family Steak House, 597 F2d 453 (5th Cir 1979).

the tie-in.[316]

The question of the existence of a financial interest, however, is often not as clear. In *Roberts v Elaine Powers Figure Salons, Inc*,[317] the court found no direct financial interest in the designated supplier of bookkeeping services, even though plaintiffs demonstrated the existence of a substantial loan and other payments and services provided by the supplier to the franchisor. Other cases have suggested that a franchisor's "financial interest" in a designated supplier will be broadly construed.[318]

§9.57 May the franchisor discriminate among its franchisees?

A franchisor's sale of products, if made to different franchisees on different terms, is subject to scrutiny under the Robinson-Patman Act.[319] As discussed in Chapter 3, the Robinson-Patman Act prohibits a Seller from discriminating among its customers in price, terms of sale, or in the provision of promotional allowances or services, where the effect of such discrimination is to reduce competition among the Seller's customers. The franchise relationship affords no protection from enforcement under the act.[320]

In some franchise systems franchisors eliminate or reduce competition among franchisees by imposing territorial and/or customer restraints in their franchise agreements.[321] In these franchise systems, a franchisor's sale of a product to different franchisees at different prices would not reduce competition among franchisees, and hence would not run afoul of the Robinson-Patman Act.[322]

The Robinson-Patman Act by its terms only applies to discrimination in the sale of commodities.[323] Courts have uniformly held that services and grants of intangible rights, such as trademark or franchise licenses, do not constitute commodities. This category includes trademark and franchise licenses;[324] therefore the Robinson-Patman Act would not prevent a franchisor from charging different franchisees different franchise or license fees.

Other federal and state statutes, however, may condemn discriminatory

---

[316] *Id* 456.

[317] 1981-1 Trade Cas (CCH) ¶63,976 (ED Cal 1980).

[318] *See* Martino v McDonald's, 81 FRD 81 (ND Ill 1979).

[319] 15 USC §§13-13c, 21a.

[320] *See* FLM Collision Parts, Inc v Ford Motor Co, 543 F2d 1019 (2d Cir 1976), *cert denied*, 429 US 1097 (1977).

[321] See **§9.46.**

[322] See **§3.13.**

[323] See **§3.06.**

[324] *See, e.g.*, Record Club of Am, Inc v Columbia Broadcasting Sys, 310 F Supp 1241 (ED Pa 1970); General Shale Prods v Struck Constr Co, 132 F2d 425 (6th Cir 1942), *cert denied*, 318 US 780 (1943).

treatment of franchisees not involving the sale of commodities. Discrimination among franchisees may fall under the purview of the Federal Trade Commission Act and state *Little FTC Acts* which condemn unfair trade practices.[325] A number of states have enacted statutes tracking the Robinson-Patman Act, but which condemn discrimination in the provision of services as well as the sale of commodities.[326]

Finally, a number of state franchise laws prohibit discrimination "in the charges offered or made for royalties, goods, services, equipment, rentals, advertising services or in any other business dealing."[327] Such restrictions go well beyond the strict application of the Robinson-Patman Act to the sale of commodities, and apply to virtually all aspects of the franchisor-franchisee business relationship. Indiana generally prohibits "unfair" discrimination be-

---

[325] 15 USC §§41-46, 47-58; 1981 Ala Acts No 355 §§1-17; Alaska Stat §§45-50.471 to .561 (1980 & Supp 1981); Ariz Rev Stat Ann §§44-1521 to -1534 (1956 & Supp 1982-1983); Ark Stat Ann §§70-901 to -913 (1979 & Supp 1981); Cal Civ Code §§1750-1757 (West 1973 & Supp 1982), Cal Bus & Prof Code §§17500-17505 (West 1964 & Supp 1982); Colo Rev Stat §§6-1-101 to -114 (1973 & Supp 1982); Conn Gen Stat Ann §§42-110a to -110q (West Supp 1982); Del Code Ann tit 6, §§2511-2526, 2531-2536 (1974 & Supp 1982); DC Code Ann §§28-1 to -10 (1981 & Supp 1982); Fla Stat Ann §§501.201-.213 (Harrison 1979 & Supp 1982); Ga Code Ann tit 10, §§10-1-390 to -407 (1982 & Supp 1982); Hawaii Rev Stat §§480-1 to -37 (1976 & Supp 1981); Idaho Code §§48-601 to -619 (1977 & Supp 1982); Ill Ann Stat ch 121 1/2, §§261-272 (Smith-Hurd Supp 1982-1983); Ind Code Ann §§24-5-0.5-1 to -9 (Burns 1982 & Supp 1982); Iowa Code Ann §§714.16-.22 (West 1979 & Supp 1982-1983); Kan Stat Ann §§50-623 to -643 (1976); Ky Rev Stat §§367.110-.360 (Supp 1982); La Rev Stat Ann §§51-1401 to -1418 (West Supp 1983); Me Rev Stat Ann tit 5, §§206-214 (1964 & Supp 1982-1983); Md Ann Code §§13-101 to -501 (1975 & Supp 1982); Mass Ann Laws ch 93A, §§1-11 (Michie/Law Co-op 1975 & Supp 1982); Mich Stat Ann §§19.418(1) - (22) (Callaghan 1981); Minn Stat Ann §§325F.68-.70, 8.31 (West 1981); Miss Code Ann §§75-24-1 to -23 (Supp 1982); Mo Ann Stat §§407.010 - .200 (Vernon 1979 Supp 1983); Mont Code Ann §§30-14-101 to -142 (1981); Neb Rev Stat §§59-1601 to -1623 (1978); Nev Rev Stat §§598.360 - 598.640 (1979); NH Rev Stat Ann §§358-A:1 to 13 (Supp 1981-1983); NJ Stat Ann §§56:8-1 to 8-25 (West Supp 1982-1983); NM Stat Ann §§57-12-1 to 12-20 (1978); NY Exec Law §63 (McKinney 1982), NY Gen Bus Law §§349-349a (McKinney Supp 1982-1983); NC Gen Stat §§75-1 to -49 (1981 & Supp 1981); ND Cent Code §§51-15-01 to -11 (1982); Ohio Rev Code Ann §§1345.01 - .13 (Page 1979 & Supp 1983); Okla Stat Ann tit 15, §§751-763 (West Supp 1982-1983); Or Rev Stat §§646.605 - 646.656 (1981); Pa Cons Stat Ann §§201-1 to -9 (Purdon Supp 1982-1983); RI Gen Laws §§6-13.1-1 to .1-11 (1969 & Supp 1980); SC Code Ann §§39-5-10 to 5-160 (Law Co-op 1976 & Supp 1982); SD Comp Laws Ann §§37-24-1 to 24-35 (1977 & Supp 1982); Tenn Code Ann §§47-18-101 to 18-116 (1979 & Supp 1982); Tex Bus & Com Code Ann §§17.41 - 17.63 (Vernon Supp 1982-1983); Utah Code Ann §§13-11-1 to 11-23 (Supp 1981); Vt Stat Ann tit 9, §§2451-2462 (1970); Va Code §§59.1-196 to -207 (1982); Wash Rev Code Ann §§19.86.010 - .86.920 (1978 & Supp 1982); W Va Code §§46A-6-101 to -108 (1980 & Supp 1982); Wis Stat Ann §§100.18-.20 (1973 & Supp 1982-1983); Wyo Stat §§40-12-101 to -112 (1977 & Supp 1982).

[326] See, e.g., Md Ann Code §§11-204 (1975 & Supp 1982).

[327] Hawaii Rev Stat §482E-6(2)(c) (1976 & Supp 1981); Ill Ann Stat ch 121 1/2 §704.12 (Smith-Hurd Supp 1982-1983); Ind Code Ann §23-2-2.7-2(5); Minn Stat Ann §80C.14(b) (West Supp 1983); Wash Rev Code Ann §19.100.180(2)(c) (1978 & Supp 1982).

tween franchisees; and Illinois prohibits a franchisor from "unreasonably and materially" discriminating among franchisees.[328] Some state statutes provide specific exemptions for discrimination between franchisees based on franchises granted at materially different times; making franchises available to persons with insufficient capital, training or experience; product testing, curing deficiencies in the business operations; the justifications provided under the Robinson-Patman Act; or other reasonable distinctions that are not arbitrary.[329]

§9.58 —May the franchisor, engaged in the sale of products, discriminate in favor of its franchisees?

A franchisor engaged in the sale of products may seek to sell those products to its franchisees at lower prices than it makes them available to independent dealers. This sales strategy places the franchisees in a competitively advantageous position. The result may be increased franchisee profits, increased franchisor royalty revenue, and establishment of an efficient, cost-effective distribution system.

The Robinson-Patman Act, discussed in Chapter 3, directly applies to this sales strategy, notwithstanding the fact that discounts are granted solely to franchisees. The law regards franchisees in this context simply as customers of the franchisor; and prohibits discrimination in favor of one class of customers, franchisees, relative to a second class of customers, independent dealers.[330]

A key element of a Robinson-Patman Act violation is that the discriminatory conduct reduces competition between competing customers.[331] In the franchise context, a court would focus on whether the favored customers, franchisees, actually competed against the disfavored customers, independent dealers. If the two classes of customers operated in different territories and/or catered to nonoverlapping clienteles, the requisite element of competitive effect would not be present.

A franchisor risks Robinson-Patman Act liability not only by selling products to franchisees at lower prices but, in addition, by granting franchisees preferential terms on sales, including favorable credit terms, rebate allowances, repurchase guarantees, or wholesale compensation allowances.[332] The act also prohibits a franchisor from granting to franchisees promotional allowances or

---

[328] Ill Ann Stat ch 121 1/2 §704.12 (Smith-Hurd Supp 1982-1983); Ind Code Ann §23-2-2.7-2(5) (Burns Supp 1982).

[329] Hawaii Rev Stat §482E-6(2)(C) (1976 & Supp 1981); Ill Ann Stat ch 121 1/2, §704.12 (Smith-Hurd Supp 1982-1983); Minn Stat Ann §80C.14(b) (West Supp 1983); Wash Rev Code Ann §19.100.180(2)(c) (1978 & Supp 1982).

[330] See generally **§3.02.**

[331] See **§3.13.**

[332] See **§3.03.**

services to be used for the resale of the franchisor's products, on more favorable terms than to independent dealers.[333]

One distribution option available to franchisors engaged in the sale of a product, according to a recent FTC decision, is for the franchisor simply to refuse to sell to parties outside of its franchise system.[334] This is true even if a franchisor is the dominant seller of a particular product. If the franchisor sells only to franchisees, and sells to all franchisees on the same terms, the franchisor has not discriminated in price and is not subject to attack under the Robinson-Patman Act.

A franchisor may grant concessions to franchisees, which are not made available to nonfranchised purchasers, where such concessions are not connected with the sale of the product to franchisees, and are not connected with the franchisee's resale of the product to consumers. These concessions are, by definition, outside of the scope of the Robinson-Patman Act.[335]

§9.59 When may the franchisor terminate or fail to renew the franchise relationship?

As may be expected where the parties to an agreement have so much at stake, franchise terminations provide fruitful grounds for litigation, often involving claims under applicable contract law or state franchise law. A franchisor may incur significant liability for a wrongful termination or nonrenewal under these laws. Buyer terminations are discussed in detail in Chapter 7.

Unlike most Seller-Buyer arrangements, the typical franchise agreement provides for a long-term business relationship, often 10 to 20 years in duration, and addresses in detail the conditions for renewal and the grounds for termination of the relationship.[336] The enforceability of the termination and renewal provisions, however, may depend on applicable state and federal law.

In recognition of a perceived disparity in bargaining power between franchisors and franchisees, and in an effort to curb alleged abuses in franchisor termination and renewal practices, state and federal legislation has been enacted to regulate termination and renewal practices in specific industries, chiefly the liquor,[337] petroleum,[338] and automobile industries.[339] In addition, sixteen

---

333 See **§§3.19, 3.20.**

334 General Motors Corp, Docket No 9077, June 25, 1982 (FTC).

335 See generally **§3.03.**

336 In 1981, over 42% of operating business format franchising companies used franchise agreements with terms of twenty years or more; and over 75% used franchise agreements with terms of 10 years or more. See Bureau of Industrial Economics, US Dept of Commerce, Franchising in the Economy 1981-1983, 10 (1983).

337 See **§7.05, app F.**

338 See **§7.07, app M.**

339 See **§7.06, app L.**

states[340] have franchise relationship statutes of general applicability which prohibit termination, and, in some cases, nonrenewal of a franchisee[341] unless *good cause* or a similar basis for termination can be demonstrated by the franchisor.

The state franchise relationship laws, in addition to imposing a good cause standard for terminations, also provide that the franchisee be given prior written notice setting forth the reasons for the termination or nonrenewal. Advance notice requirements range from 60 to 90 days;[342] in two states, 180 days' advance notice of nonrenewal is required.[343] In other states, written notice must be provided sufficiently in advance to allow the franchisee an opportunity to cure the default, usually 30 days.[344] The cure period may be as short as 10 days for repeated nonpayment of fees.[345] Many state statutes allow exceptions to the notice and cure requirements to permit the franchisor to take immediate action; these include situations where the franchisee is adjudicated bankrupt,[346] abandons the business,[347] is convicted of a crime,[348] makes any material misrepresentation,[349] or loses the right to occupy the franchised busi-

---

340 See **§7.08, app K.**

341 Ark Stat Ann §70-810 (1979); Cal Bus & Prof Code §20025 (West Supp 1982); Conn Gen Stat Ann §42-133f (West Supp 1982); Del Code Ann tit 6, §2552 (1974 & Supp 1982); 1980 Fla Laws ch 80-217; Hawaii Rev Stat §482E-6(2)(H) (Supp 1981); Ill Ann Stat ch 121 1/2, §704.4 (Smith-Hurd Supp 1982-1983); Mich Stat Ann §19.854(27)(f) (Callaghan 1981); Minn Stat Ann §80C.14(c) (West Supp 1983); Neb Rev Stat §87-404 (Supp 1980); NJ Stat Ann §56:10-5 (West Supp 1982-1983); Wis Stat Ann §135.04 (West 1974 & Supp 1982-1983). See also **§7.08.**

342 See, e.g., Ark Stat Ann §70-811(5) (1979); Conn Gen Stat Ann §42-133f(a) (West Supp 1982).

343 Cal Bus & Prof Code §20025 (West Supp 1982); Ill Ann Stat ch 121 1/2, §704.2 (Smith Hurd Supp 1982-1983).

344 See e.g., Hawaii Rev Stat §482E-6(2)(H) (Supp 1981); Ill Ann Stat ch 121 1/2 §704.3(b) (Smith-Hurd Supp 1982-1983); Mich Stat Ann §19.854(27)(e) (Callaghan 1981).

345 See, e.g., Wis Stat Ann §135.04 (West 1974 & Supp 1982-1983); Ark Stat Ann §70-811 (1979).

346 See, e.g., Ark Stat Ann §70-808 (1979); Cal Bus & Prof Code §20021(a) (West Supp 1982); Ill Ann Stat ch 121 1/2 §704.3(c)(1) (Smith-Hurd 1982-1983); Neb Rev Stat §87-404(2)(b) (Supp 1980); Wash Rev Code Ann §19.100.180(2)(j) (1978 & Supp 1982); Wis Stat Ann §135.04 (West 1974 & Supp 1982-1983).

347 See e.g., Ark Stat Ann §70-808 (1979); Cal Bus & Prof Code §20021(b) (West Supp 1982); Conn Gen Stat Ann §42-133f(a) (West Supp 1982); Ill Ann Stat ch 121 1/2 §704.3(c)(3) (Smith-Hurd 1982-1983); Minn Stat Ann §80C.14(a)(i) (West Supp 1983); Wash Rev Code Ann §19.100.180(2)(j) (1978 & Supp 1982).

348 See e.g., Ark Stat Ann §70-808 (1979); Conn Gen Stat Ann §42-133f(a) (West Supp 1982); Ill Ann Stat ch 121 1/2 §704.3(c)(4) (Smith-Hurd Supp 1982-1983); Minn Stat Ann §80C.14(a)(2) (West Supp 1983); Neb Rev Stat §87-404(2)(a) (Supp 1980); NJ Stat Ann §56:10-5(2) (West Supp 1982-1983); Wash Rev Code Ann §19.100.180(2)(j) (1978 & Supp 1982).

349 See, e.g., Cal Bus & Prof Code §20021(d) (West Supp 1982); Neb Rev Stat §87-404(2)(d) (Supp 1980) (falsification of records or reports required by the franchisor).

ness premises.[350]

The statutory definitions of *good cause,* and the similar standards of *just cause* and *reasonable cause,* vary from one state to the next. Typically, they refer to the franchisee's failure to comply substantially with the requirements of the franchise;[351] the franchisee's failure to act in good faith and in a commercially reasonable manner;[352] the franchisee's voluntary abandonment of the franchised business;[353] the franchisee's conviction of a crime;[354] impairment by the franchisee of the franchisor's trademarks;[355] the institution of insolvency or bankruptcy proceedings;[356] and failure by the franchisee to pay the franchisor monies owed.[357] In addition to these statutory definitions, state courts have found a variety of grounds for termination to constitute good cause under state franchise laws.[358]

---

[350] See, e.g., Ark Stat Ann §70-808 (1979); Cal Bus & Prof Code §20021(h) (West Supp 1982); Neb Rev Stat §87-404(2)(f) (Supp 1980).

[351] See, e.g., Hawaii Rev Stat §482E-6(2)(H) (Supp 1981); Mich Stat Ann §19.854(27)(e) (Callaghan 1981); NJ Stat Ann §56:10-5 (West Supp 1982-1983); Wis Stat Ann §135.02(6)(a) (West 1974 & Supp 1982-1983).

[352] See, e.g., Cal Bus & Prof Code §20021(d) (West Supp 1982); Wis Stat Ann §135.02(6)(b) (West 1974 & Supp 1982-1983).

[353] See, e.g., Conn Gen Stat Ann §42-133f(a)(1) (West Supp 1982); Ill Ann Stat ch 121 1/2 §704.3(c)(3) (Smith-Hurd Supp 1982-1983); Minn Stat Ann §80C.14(b)(3) (West Supp 1983); Wash Rev Code Ann §19.100.180(2)(j) (1978 & Supp 1982).

[354] See, e.g., Conn Gen Stat Ann §42-133f(a)(2) (West Supp 1982); Ill App Stat ch 121 1/2 §704.3(c)(4) (Smith-Hurd Supp 1982-1983); Wash Rev Code Ann §19.100.180(2)(j) (1978) & Supp 1982).

[355] See, e.g., Ark Stat Ann §70-808(g)(5) (1979); Minn Stat Ann §80C.14(b)(5) (West Supp 1983).

[356] See, e.g., Ill Ann Stat ch 121 1/2 §704.3(c)(1) (Smith-Hurd Supp 1982-1983); Minn Stat Ann §80C.14(f)(1) (West Supp 1983); Wash Rev Code Ann §19.100.180(2)(j) (1978 & Supp 1982).

[357] See, e.g., Ark Stat Ann §70-808(g)(8) (1979); Cal Bus & Prof Code §20021(j) (West Supp 1982).

[358] See, e.g., State Wide Lighting Inc v Globe Illumination Co, Civ No 77-C-716 (ED Wis 1979) (failure to achieve sales quotas); Al Bishop Agency, Inc v Lithonia-Div of Natl Serv Indus, Inc, 474 F Supp 828 (ED Wis 1979) (failure to meet market penetration goals); Amoco Oil Co v Burns, 437 A2d 381 (Pa Sup Ct 1981) (dealership unprofitable); Amoco Oil Co v Dickson, 389 NE2d 406 (Mass Supp Ind Ct 1979) (franchisor's good faith decision to cease operations at dealer's location plus inadequate return on investment); Exxon Corp v Wilson, 394 A2d 1288 (Pa Super Ct 1978) (failure to agree on terms of renewal where parties negotiated in good faith); Tulowitzki v Atlantic Richfield Co, 396 A2d 956 (Del Sup Ct 1978) (failure to agree to a lease requiring a reasonable rent increase); Aselta v Radio Shack Div of Tandy Corp, No 76-2396 (DCNJ 1977) (abusive language employed by franchisee in dealing with customers); AAMCO Indus v DeWolff, 250 NW2d 835 (Minn Sup Ct 1977) (consumer deception); Amerada Hess Corp v Quinn, 362 A2d 1258 (NJ Super Ct Law Div 1976) (willful overcharging of customers in violation of federal pricing regulations). *See also* Atlantic Richfield Co v Razumic, 390 A2d 736 (Pa Sup Ct 1978) (where franchise agreement did not provide for nonrenewal, franchisor must renew where franchisee had reasonable expectations of continuing contractual relationship).

Many states require that a franchisor compensate a terminated or non-renewed franchisee for certain assets of the franchised business.[359] It is common for state law to provide for private actions by injured franchisees for damages, rescission and attorney's fees. State authorities are empowered to seek civil penalties, injunctive relief, cease and desist orders, and to suspend, deny or revoke franchise sales registrations; and willful violations are usually subject to felony or misdemeanor penalties.[360]

Franchisees have successfully sued to prevent a wrongful termination or to seek damages for a wrongful termination in state courts under a number of common law theories, including breach of fiduciary duty,[361] and breach of implied covenants.[362] However, many courts have been reluctant to follow such common law precedent where the express terms of the franchise agreement are to the contrary.[363]

§9.60 —Does such conduct violate the antitrust laws?

The legal principles that apply to a Seller's refusal to deal with a Buyer, discussed in detail in Chapters 2 and 7, are equally applicable to franchise terminations and nonrenewals. Generally, joint action by two or more parties for the purpose or with the effect of unreasonably restraining trade violates §1 of the Sherman Act.

In franchise termination situations, the question often becomes: Was the franchisor conspiring with other franchisees to terminate for anticompetitive reasons?[364] It has been argued that the joint action element of an alleged violation should be inferred where the Seller receives complaints from competing Buyers and, with no more showing of an agreement or conspiracy, the Seller then refuses to deal with the Buyer.[365] As discussed in Chapter 2, the courts have disagreed as to whether the joint action element of a Sherman Act

---

[359] See, e.g., Ark Stat Ann §70-810 (1979); Cal Bus & Prof Code §20035 (West Supp 1982); Conn Gen Stat Ann §42-133f(b) (West Supp 1982); Hawaii Rev Stat §482E-6(3) (Supp 1981); Ill Ann Stat ch 121 1/2 §704.4 (Smith-Hurd Supp 1982-1983); Mich Stat Ann §19.854(27)(f) (Callaghan 1981); Wash Rev Code Ann §19.100.180(2)(i) (West Supp 1982); Wis Stat Ann §135.045 (West Supp 1982-1983).

[360] See generally **app K.**

[361] See **§9.63.**

[362] *See, e.g.,* Photovest Corp v Fotomat, 606 F2d 704 (7th Cir 1979), *cert denied,* 445 US 917 (1980).

[363] *See, e.g.,* Zapatha v Dairy Mart, Inc, 408 NE2d 1370 (Mass 1980).

[364] A similar question of conspiracy arises where the franchisor's decision to sell a franchise is influenced by communications with existing franchisees. *See* **§§9.41-9.42.** *See, also,* American Motor Inns, Inc v Holiday Inns, Inc, 521 F2d 1230 (3d Cir 1975).

[365] *See, e.g.,* Spray-Rite Serv Corp v Monsanto Co, 684 F2d 1226 (7th Cir 1982), *cert granted,* __ US __, 75 L Ed 2d 479, 103 S Ct 1249 (1983).

violation is met in this situation.[366] The nonrenewal of a franchise may also have antitrust implications if the primary purpose of the nonrenewal is anticompetitive. As with terminations, however, a failure to renew a franchise agreement will not be actionable under the antitrust laws unless the plaintiff can demonstrate joint action, a harm to competition, and a causal connection between the alleged illegal nonrenewal and the plaintiff's injury.[367] Franchise nonrenewals have been upheld where the franchisor had unilaterally decided to reduce the number of franchises in an area,[368] or itself to operate certain stores.[369]

What tends to set franchising apart from other Seller-Buyer relationships in termination and nonrenewal situations is the greater degree of business communication between a franchisor and its franchisees. It is not at all uncommon for a franchisor to receive complaints in the course of its dealings with a franchisee about another franchisee; indeed, franchisee complaints can be useful and legitimate. This increases the likelihood that a franchisor who terminates one of its franchisees may be accused of having conspired with the complaining franchisees to eliminate one of their competitors. Whether or not a sufficient causal link can be established between the complaints and the termination may depend on the franchisor's ability to demonstrate that a termination decision was for legitimate business reasons, and not simply the result of franchisee complaints. Consequently, franchisee complaints, particularly complaints relating to termination decisions, and franchise terminations must be handled with special caution.

§9.61 May the franchisor impose covenants against competition?

la cl. anti-cc du franchiseur

Covenants restricting a franchisee from competing with its own franchised unit or other units in the franchise system are common provisions in franchise agreements. The covenants may apply during or after the term of the franchise, or both; may restrict competition at the location of the franchise; and may also seek to restrict competition within a certain radius around the franchise location or other unit locations (in existence at the time of execution of the contract or sometimes established later) in the franchisor's system. These restrictions are usually designed to prevent a franchisee from operating similar businesses in direct competition with the franchisee's own franchised business, or with

---

366 See **§2.33** and the cases cited therein.

367 *See, e.g.*, Hugh O Grandstaff v Mobil Oil Corp, 1979-1 Trade Cas (CCH) ¶62,421 (ED Va 1978).

368 *See, e.g.*, Copy-Data Sys v Toshiba Am, Inc, 663 F2d 405 (2d Cir 1981); Call Carl v BP Oil Corp, 554 F2d 623 (4th Cir 1977).

369 *See, e.g.*, Schwing Motor Co v Hudson Sales Corp, 138 F Supp 899 (D Md), *affd*, 239 F2d 176 (4th Cir 1956), *cert denied*, 355 US 823 (1957).

other businesses in the same franchise system.[370] In many ways, covenants against competition in the franchise setting are analagous to similar restrictions between an employee and an employer, and between the buyer and seller of a business. The courts have looked to the legal principles surrounding employment contracts[371] and contracts for the sale of businesses[372] in analyzing franchise covenants, but have not consistently ruled on which analogy, if either, is more appropriate.

Covenants against competition are enforceable if "ancillary" to a lawful agreement and if in furtherance of the lawful goals of that agreement.[373] The courts have held that a covenant is enforceable if it is "reasonable"[374] in view of the interests to be protected; and no broader in scope of activities, area, and time than is reasonably necessary to protect those interests. The key to the enforceability of a covenant against competition, then, is the nature of the franchisor's business and the particular aspects of the business that make the covenant reasonably necessary.

Franchisors can usually demonstrate a number of legitimate *protectable* interests, although such interests will vary from system to system in both degree and kind.[375] It should be noted for the purposes of this section that the types of franchisor interests which have been held to support a covenant against competition are typically not present in simpler Seller-Buyer transactions. For

---

[370] See, generally, Klarfeld and Kennedy, *Covenants Against Competition in Franchise Agreements,* 2 J ABA Forum Comm on Franchising, No 2 (Summer/Fall 1982).

[371] *See, e.g.,* Mansfield v B&W Gas, Inc, 222 Ga 259, 149 SE2d 482 (1966); H&R Block, Inc v Lovelace, 208 Kan 538, 493 P2d 205, 212 (1972); *see also* Armstrong v Taco Time Intl, Inc, 30 Wash App 538, 635 P2d 1114, 1117 (1981) ("Courts agree a franchise agreement is akin to an employment contract."). *Cf* Budget Rent-A-Car Corp of Am v Fein, 342 F2d 509, 516 (5th Cir 1965) (in which the court declined to categorize the restraint on a prospective franchisee as either an employee restraint or a restraint ancillary to the sale of a business.)

[372] *See, e.g.,* Wilkinson v Manpower, Inc, 531 F2d 712 (5th Cir 1976); Williams v Shrimp Boats, Inc, 229 Ga 330, 191 SE2d 50 (1972).

[373] This rule was best articulated by the Sixth Circuit in United States v Addyston Pipe & Steel Co, 85 F 271, 282 (6th Cir 1898), *modified and affd,* 175 US 211 (1899):

> [N]o conventional restraint of trade can be enforced unless the covenant embodying it is merely ancillary to the main purpose of a lawful contract, and necessary to protect the covenantee in the enjoyment of the legitimate fruits of the contract, or to protect him from the dangers of an unjust use of those fruits by the other party . . .
>
> The main purpose of the contract suggests the measure of protection needed, and furnishes a sufficiently uniform standard by which the validity of such restraints may be judicially determined.

[374] See Restatement of Contracts, §514 (1932).

[375] There have not been many cases in which the protectable interests of a franchisor are specifically analyzed. *See, e.g.,* Williams v Shrimp Boats, Inc, 229 Ga 300, 191 SE2d 50 (1972); Shakey's, Inc v Martin, 91 Idaho 758, 430 P2d 504 (1967); McDonald's Sys v Sandy's, Inc, 45 Ill App 2d 57, 195 NE2d 22 (1963); Piercing Pagoda, Inc v Hoffner, 465 Pa 500, 351 A2d 207 (1976); Armstrong v Taco Time Intl, Inc, 30 Wash App 538, 635 P2d 1114 (1981).

example, in contrast to such a relationship entailing the pure sale of goods, franchisors usually impart a great deal of confidential business information, including detailed management, marketing, and operational information, and trade secrets. From the franchisor's economic point of view, this information, often comprising the essence of the franchised business system, represents a significant investment in the franchisee which the franchisor anticipates recouping in the form of franchise fees over the full term of the franchise. A covenant which, in a reasonable fashion, prevents a franchisee from competing with the franchise provides added incentive for the franchisee to stay in the franchised business for the term of the agreement, and helps ensure a franchisor's return on its investment as contemplated in the agreement.[376] In addition, a franchisor has a protectable interest in the integrity of its franchise system and the marketability of its franchises. This interest might be threatened without some form of protection against a franchisee itself exploiting the business concept in a market where the franchisor has established, or is selling, franchises.

No one type of protectable interest will determine enforceability. A court will balance all aspects of the restriction, including the potential harm to the franchisee and the public interest if a covenant is upheld. In consideration of the more severe impact on the franchisee's livelihood, some courts have shown a greater willingness to enforce in-term covenants, restricting a franchisee during the term of the franchise agreement, than postterm restraints.[377]

Postterm covenants restricting competition at or near the formerly franchised location which have been upheld as reasonable are usually of short duration. The franchisor's protectable interests in the confidential information imparted to the franchisee or the publicly perceived association of the franchisee with the franchise system diminish rather quickly over time. In the franchise context, postterm covenants of six months to three years have been upheld as reasonable; however, peculiar circumstances could lengthen or shorten what a court might consider a reasonable period of time.[378] As with

---

[376] A recent economic analysis of employment contract covenants has suggested that the employer's investment in the relationship takes the form of general training and specific training of the employee. The analysis may also be applied to the franchise relationship. See Rubin & Shedd, *Human Capital and Covenants Not to Compete,* 10 J Legal Stud 93 (1981).

[377] *See, e.g.,* McDonald's Sys v Sandy's Inc, 45 Ill App 2d 57, 195 NW2d 22 (1963). *Cf* Armstrong v Taco Time Intl, Inc, 30 Wash App 538, 635 P2d 1114 (1981).

[378] The courts have upheld as reasonable a number of limited postterm covenants not to compete at the former location. *See, e.g.,* Wilkinson v Manpower, Inc, 531 F2d 712 (5th Cir 1976) (within licensed area for two years); Meineke Discount Muffler Shops, Inc v Bleier, Civ Act No H-80-2495 (SD Tex 1981) (within a 25-mile radius of former shop for one year); Shakey's, Inc v White, No 77-106, Slip Op (ED Mo Mar 31, 1977) (within 30 miles of franchised location for one year); Snelling & Snelling, Inc v Dupay Enters, 125 Ariz 362, 609 P2d 1062 (1980) (within 35 miles of franchised location for three years); Williams v Shrimp Boats, Inc, 229 Ga 300, 191 SE2d 50 (1972) (at location for one year); Shakey's, Inc v Martin, 91 Idaho 758, 430 P2d 504 (1967) (within 30 miles of franchised location for one year); Simpson v Kelly Servs, Inc, 339 So2d 490 (La Ct

in-term covenants, the area and scope of activities covered by the postterm covenant may be unenforceable if not reasonably related to the franchisor's protectable interests.

The courts have split on whether it is reasonable for a franchisor to restrict a franchisee from competing near other franchised locations owned by other franchisees.[379] Courts are often reluctant to find that a national franchisor has a protectable interest in preventing one franchisee's direct competition with other franchisees anywhere in the country.[380]

The enforceability of covenants against competition can change substantially from state to state. In a few states, courts will render void an entire provision if it is found to be overbroad in any respect.[381] Most state courts will reshape the covenant and enforce it to the extent that it is found to be reasonable.[382]

App 1976), *cert denied,* 341 So2d 1121 (1977) (within 50 miles of franchised location for six months); Welcome Wagon Intl Inc v Pender, 255 NC 244, 120 SE2d 739 (1961) (within city where employed for five years); Piercing Pagoda, Inc v Hoffner, 465 Pa 500, 351 A2d 207 (1976) (where the business was operated and terminated for one year); Pelton's Spudnuts, Inc v Doane, 120 Utah 366, 234 P2d 852 (1951) (within the territory in which the business was operated for one year); Armstrong v Taco Time Intl, Inc, 30 Wash App 538, 635 P2d 1114 (1981) (within franchised area for two and one-half years).

[379] Cases in which the courts have upheld as reasonable covenants restricting competition at other franchised locations include: Piercing Pagoda, Inc v Hoffner, 465 Pa 500, 351 A2d 207 (1976) (within 30 miles of any Piercing Pagoda for three years); Armstrong v Taco Time Intl, Inc, 30 Wash App 538, 635 P2d 1114 (1981) (for two and one-half years after termination in the area covered by any then existing system franchise agreement). Cases in which such covenants have been held unreasonable include: Interstate Automatic Transmission Co v WR McAlpine Co, 1982-1 Trade Cas (CCH) ¶64,538 (ND Ohio 1981) (within ten miles of any business operated by an Interstate licensee for one year); Snelling & Snelling, Inc v Dupay Enters, 125 Ariz 362, 609 P2d 1062 (1980) (within 35 miles of any other Snelling office or franchised area for eighteen months); Manpower, Inc v Olsten Permanent Agency, 309 So2d 57, 1975 Trade Cas (CCH) ¶60,170 (Fla Dist Ct App 1975) (former branch manager enjoined from competing within a 200-mile radius of any city where there is a Manpower office or licensed business for two years); TE McCutcheon Enters v Snelling & Snelling, Inc, 232 Ga 609, 212 SE2d 319 (1974) (within five miles of the perimeter of any other Snelling office or franchised area for one year); Richard P Rita Personnel Servs Intl, Inc v Kot, 229 Ga 314, 191 SE2d 79 (1972) (within any territorial areas in which a franchise had been granted by Rita for two years); Welcome Wagon Intl v Pender, 255 NC 244, 120 SE2d 739 (1961) (in any city of the United States outside of North Carolina where a Welcome Wagon is doing business or intends to do business).

[380] Piercing Pagoda, Inc v Hoffner, 465 Pa 500, 351 A2d 207 (1976); Armstrong v Taco Time Intl, Inc, 30 Wash App 538, 635 P2d 1114 (1981); Interstate Automatic Transmission Co v WH McAlpine Co, 1982-1 Trade Cas (CCH) ¶64,538 (ND Ohio 1981); Snelling & Snelling, Inc v Dupay Enters, 125 Ariz 362, 609 P2d 1062 (1980); Manpower, Inc v Olsten Permanent Agency, 309 So2d 57, 1975 Trade Cas (CCH) ¶60,170 (Fla Dist Ct App 1975); TE McCutcheon Enters v Snelling & Snelling, Inc, 232 Ga 609, 212 SE2d 319 (1974); Richard P Rita Personnel Servs Intl, Inc v Kot, 229 Ga 314, 191 SE2d 79 (1972); Welcome Wagon Intl v Pender 255 NC 244, 120 SE2d 739 (1961).

[381] *See, e.g.,* Richard P Rita Personnel Servs Intl, Inc v Kot, 229 Ga 314, 191 SE2d 79 (1972).

[382] *See, e.g.,* Three Phoenix Co v Pace Indus, Inc, No 1 CA-CIV 4773, Slip Op (Ariz

The great bulk of the state standards of enforceability are dictated by state common law; however, some state statutes prohibit or limit postterm covenants against competition in franchise agreements.[383]

The state franchise investment laws generally require disclosure of the terms of any covenant against competition, and, in Michigan[384] and California,[385] the administrators of the franchise investment laws require that the franchisor include disclaimers regarding the enforceability of covenants against competition under their state laws.

Finally, covenants against competition generally do not, by themselves, violate the rule of reason standard applied to such vertical restraints for the purposes of antitrust analysis.[386] However, where the covenant is shown to have the purpose or effect of eliminating competition, rather than protecting the legitimate interests of the franchisor, it may be in violation of the antitrust laws.[387]

Franchisors usually impose a variety of other postterm obligations that arise from the special relationship with the franchisee and, as with postterm covenants against competition, protect the interests of a franchisor after termination of the relationship. A terminated franchisee is usually prohibited from continuing to use the franchisor's proprietary marks, using the trade dress associated with the franchise system, or holding itself out as a former franchisee. The agreement usually requires that the franchisee return all confidential information, operating manuals, and customer lists, and transfer the telephone numbers of the business, to the franchisor. Some franchise agreements also provide the franchisor a right to purchase certain assets of the business, and, at its option, to take over the lease for the premises in order to continue the operation at that location.

§9.62 Does the franchisor owe any special duty to its franchisee?

In one important sense, the relationship between franchisor and franchisee is similar to that of Seller and Buyer: franchisees, like Buyers, are not em-

---

Ct App Nov 19, 1981); *see, also,* Cockerill v Wilson, 51 Ill 2d 179, 281 NE2d 648 (1972); House of Vision, Inc v Hiyane, 37 Ill 2d 32, 225 NE2d 21 (1967).

[383] See Mich Stat Ann §28.61 (Callaghan 1981); Ind Code Ann §23-3-2.7-1(9) (Burns 1982). See, also, Fla Stat Ann §2.33(2)(b) (Harrisons 1981), expressly allowing covenants in the franchise context.

[384] Mich Comp Laws Ann §§445.1501 - .1545 (Supp 1982-1983).

[385] Cal Corp Code §§31000-31516 (Deering 1979 & Supp 1982).

[386] *See* Lektro-Vend Corp v Vendo Co, 660 F2d 255 (7th Cir 1981), *cert denied,* 455 US 921 (1982); American Motor Inns, Inc v Holiday Inns, Inc, 521 F2d 1230 (3rd Cir 1975); Bradford v New York Times Co, 501 F2d 51 (2d Cir 1974); Interstate Automatic Transmission Co v WR McAlpine Co, 1982-1 Trade Cas (CCH) ¶64,538 (ND Ohio 1981).

[387] *See* American Motor Inns, Inc v Holiday Inns, Inc, 521 F2d 1230 (3rd Cir 1975).

ployees, but independent businessmen; and the rights, duties, and obligations of each party to the transaction are set forth in an agreement or imposed through general standards of commercial fair dealing. As is true in all commercial transactions, however, the application of product liability law, tort law, and agency law may limit a business's ability to insulate itself by contract from liability for the conduct of others.

Buyers are generally not controlled in any sense by Sellers. Distribution and supply agreements set forth the terms of sales transactions, and the Seller has little interest in details of the Buyer's business operation beyond its ability to comply with the terms of the transaction. In contrast, franchisees typically operate under the detailed operational controls, standards, and procedures imposed through the franchise agreement and operating manuals. Franchise agreements, as a rule, expressly define the franchisee as an independent contractor of the franchisor, disclaim any obligations not specified in the agreement, and often require full indemnification of the franchisor against claims which may arise from the operation of the franchise.

Although the courts have traditionally enforced such provisions, a significant number of recent cases have held that, on the basis of the close contractual and operational ties in the relationship, the franchisor may be vicariously liable for the conduct of its *agent* franchisees. Other cases have considered whether and under what circumstances a franchisor should be held to a standard of fiduciary care in business dealings with its franchisee. These areas are addressed in **§§9.63-9.64.**

§9.63 —Is there a fiduciary duty owed by a franchisor to its franchisee?

A fiduciary duty is generally that standard of scrupulous care, candor and good faith which must be exercised by a trustee, or one placed in a position of trust or confidence, regarding the matters entrusted. It is the highest standard of care; and one traditionally not imposed in Seller-Buyer or franchisor-franchisee relationships.

As a general rule there is no fiduciary duty owed by a franchisor to its franchisee. However, several recent decisions have considered the argument that there is a fiduciary duty owed by a franchisor and in at least one case a court has concluded that a fiduciary duty is "inherent" in the franchise relationship. In that case, *Arnott v. American Oil Co.*,[388] the Eighth Circuit upheld a jury award based in large part on a finding that a "fiduciary duty of good faith and fair dealing" was breached when a petroleum company terminated without good cause the plaintiff's one-year service station lease.

Other circuits have not followed the Eighth Circuit's holding.[389] In *Carter v.*

---

[388] 609 F2d 873 (8th Cir 1979), *cert denied,* 446 US 918 (1980). See also Brown, *Franchising—A Fiduciary Relationship,* 49 Tex L Rev 650 (1971).

[389] *See* Carter Equip Co v John Deere Indus Co, 681 F2d 386 (5th Cir 1982); Picture Lake Campground, Inc v Holiday Inns, Inc, 497 F Supp 858 (ED Va 1980); Shaeffer

John Deere Industrial Equipment Co.,[390] the Fifth Circuit declined to follow the holding in *Arnott* but stressed that a fiduciary relationship may arise if appropriate factors are present. The court in *Carter* included among the factors to be considered in determining the existence of a fiduciary relationship the parties' "mutual or shared intentions"; whether the parties "repose trust or confidence in one another"; and the nature of the power and control exercised through the franchise agreement. The court stated: "If the franchisor has the power to control the franchisee, there is an increased likelihood that a fiduciary relationship exists, since trust or confidence necessarily must flow from the controlled or dominated party."[391]

Other decisions have flatly rejected the application of a fiduciary duty to a franchisee-franchisor relationship as "inappropriate."[392] In *Picture Lake Campground, Inc v Holiday Inns, Inc*,[393] a federal district court in Virginia found more persuasive *Arnott's* dissenting opinion, and concluded that a "franchise relationship is inherently a business relationship, not a fiduciary relationship."[394]

The Eighth Circuit itself has distinguished and significantly limited its ruling in *Arnott*. In *Bain v Champlin Petroleum Co*,[395] the court rejected a contention that the defendant petroleum company breached a fiduciary duty by alleged improprieties in its gasoline marketing practices. The court distinguished *Arnott* on its facts, and stated: "Inasmuch as the duty of 'good faith and fair dealing' is inherent in every business relationship, it was unnecessary to the [*Arnott*] decision to label that duty as 'fiduciary.' "[396]

Given this narrow reading, *Arnott* becomes roughly consistent with prior rulings on the general duty of good faith owed a franchisee,[397] and with the

---

v Collins, Bus Fran Guide (CCH) ¶7578 (ED Pa 1980); Murphy v White Hen Pantry, Bus Fran Guide (CCH) ¶7716 (ED Wis 1981).

390 Carter v John Deere Indus Equip Co, 681 F2d 386 (5th Cir 1982).

391 *Id* 391.

392 *See, e.g.*, Picture Lake Campground, Inc v Holiday Inns, Inc, 497 F Supp 858 (ED Pa 1980); *see also* Newark Motor Inn Corp v Holiday Inns, Inc, 472 F Supp 1143, 1151-53 (DNJ 1979); Weight Watchers of Quebec Ltd v Weight Watchers Intl, Inc, 398 F Supp 1047, 1053-54 (EDNY 1975); *In Re* 7-11 Franchise Antitrust Litigation, 1974-2 Trade Cas (CCH) ¶75,429 at 98,428 (ND Cal 1974); Eaton, Yale & Towne, Inc v Sherman Indus Equip Co, 316 F Supp 435, 445 (ED Mo 1970); Mobil Oil v Rubenfeld, 48 AD2d 428, 370 NYS2d 943, 947 (1975); Texaco, Inc v AA Gold, Inc, 78 Misc 2d 1050, 357 NYS2d 951, 954-56, *affd* 45 AD2d 1054, 358 NYS2d 973 (1974); Noel Holding Corp v Carvel Dari-Freeze, 140 NYS2d 640, 641 (1955); William C Cornitius, Inc v Dayton Wheeler, 276 Or 747, 556 P2d 666, 670 (1976).

393 Picture Lake Campground, Inc v Holiday Inns, Inc, 497 F Supp 858 (ED Va 1980).

394 *Id* 869.

395 Bain v Champlin Petroleum Co, 692 F2d 43 (8th Cir 1982).

396 *Id* 48.

397 Many courts have found an implied common law duty of good faith and fair dealing in the franchise relationship, especially in regard to franchise termination cases. *See generally* Arnott v American Oil Co, 609 F2d 873 (7th Cir 1979), *cert denied*, 446 US 918 (1980) (fiduciary duty breached); Atlantic Richfield Co v Rasumic, 480 Pa 366, 390 A2d 736 (1978) (breach of implied good faith covenant); Ashland Oil Co v Donahue,

general standard of commercial fair dealing articulated in the Uniform Commercial Code.[398] In any event, the cases suggesting that the duty owed is a fudiciary duty are in the distinct minority.

§9.64 —Is a franchisor vicariously liable for the acts of its franchisee?

In light of relatively recent case law developments, the likelihood of finding a franchisor vicariously liable is not clear. Prior to the 1970s, very few cases considered the question, but recent cases have suggested that franchisors may be vicariously liable for the conduct of their franchisees on a variety of legal theories.

The doctrine of vicarious liability[399] imposes on a principal liability for the wrongful conduct of its agent. Decisions holding against franchisors have applied the vicarious liability doctrine under two different theories of agency law: *actual authority* and *apparent authority.* Under the theory of actual authority, vicarious liability will be imposed where the principal actually exercises authority and control over its agent. In the franchise context, courts have measured the extent of the franchisor's control over the day-to-day operations of the franchised business. There is no clear demarcation of controls that may lead a court to find a franchisor vicariously liable. Certain controls are necessary to protect the licensed trademarks and accompanying goodwill, and thus a franchisor is often caught in the quandary of at once protecting its trademarks while avoiding excessive controls which might lead to an unwelcome finding of vicarious liability.[400]

---

223 SE2d 433 (W Va 1976) (unconscionability); Shell Oil v Marinello, 63 NJ 402, 307 A2d 598 (NJ Sup Ct 1972), *cert denied,* 415 US 920 (1974) (public policy). *See also* Randolf v New England Mutual Life Ins, 526 F2d 1383 (6th Cir 1975); deTreville v Outboard Marine Corp, 439 F2d 1099 (4th Cir 1971); Tile-Controls, Inc v Ford Indus, Inc, 388 F2d 48 (7th Cir 1967).

398 See UCC §1-203. *But see* Corenswet, Inc v Amana Refrigeration, Inc, 594 F2d 129, (5th Cir), *cert denied,* 444 US 938 (1979), which held that the *good faith* principle of the Uniform Commercial Code cannot properly be used to override or strike express contract terms.

399 *Vicarious liability,* also referred to as respondeat superior, stands for the proposition that a principal may under certain circumstances be held liable for the wrongful or tortious conduct of an agent. The doctrine bases liability not on any actual participation in the agent's wrongful acts but solely on the existence of the principal-agent relationship. The wrongful deeds, for which the courts may find a principal vicariously liable, may arise in either a tortious or a contractual setting.

400 This legal quandary is a classic one in franchising, and the source of legitimate frustration for both franchisors and their counsel. The requirements of the federal trademark law, the Lanham Act, 15 USC §§1051-1072, 1091-1096, 1111-1121, 1123-1127, impose an affirmative duty on a trademark owner to exercise adequate control over the quality of the goods and services sold under the mark; if inadequate control is exercised, the owner risks a finding that the mark has been "abandoned." *See* 15 USC §1127. On the other hand, as discussed further in **§9.64,** excessive controls over the

Courts have identified a number of contractual powers that might indicate actual authority over a franchised business. These include the control over the franchisee's employees;[401] the imposition of uniform accounting and reporting procedures;[402] prescribed hours of operation;[403] restricted sources of supply;[404] restricted product lines;[405] a minutely detailed operating manual;[406] the right of unilateral termination;[407] the right to inspect the business premises;[408]

---

day-to-day operation of the franchised business may threaten the legal independence of the franchisee, raising the risk of the franchisor being held vicariously liable for its franchisee's actions. Thus, franchisors must carefully consider the controls to be exercised over their franchisees. *See* Singleton v Intl Dairy Queen, Inc, 332 A2d 160, 162-63 (Del 1975); Nichols v Arthur Murray, Inc, 248 Cal App 2d 610, 56 Cal Rptr 728, 732 (1967); and Porter v Arthur Murray, Inc, 249 Cal App 2d 410, 57 Cal Rptr 554, 560 (1967). See generally Annot: *Vicarious Liability of Private Franchisor,* 81 ALR3d 764 (1977).

[401] One court has stressed the absence of control over the performance of the franchisee's employees, and the absence of the franchisor's ability to hire and fire, as evidence that it "did not retain any day-to-day supervisory control." Coty v US Slicing Mach Co, 15 Ill App 3d 237, 373 NE2d 1371, 1375 (1978); *see, also,* Nichols v Arthur Murray, Inc, 248 Cal App 2d 610, 56 Cal Rptr 728, 730 (1967); Slates v Intl House of Pancakes, Inc, 413 NE2d 427, 464 (Ill App 1980). Other courts have viewed employee controls as tending to show day-to-day control. *See* Porter v Arthur Murray, Inc, 249 Cal App 2d 410, 57 Cal Rptr 554, 558 (1967) (ability to hire and fire); Drexel v Union Prescription Centers, Inc, 582 F2d 781, 788 (3d Cir 1978) (ability to supervise employee actions); and Weil v Arthur Murray, Inc, 67 Misc 2d 417, 324 NYS2d 381, 387 (1971).

[402] Other factors related to accounting procedures have also been considered by the courts. *See* Drexel v Union Prescription Centers, Inc, 582 F2d 781, 787 n 3 (retention of right to audit books a factor suggesting control); Murphy v Holiday Inns, Inc, 216 Va 490, 219 SE2d 874, 878 (1975) (inability to control franchisee's business expenses a factor suggesting lack of control); *see also* Beck v Arthur Murray, 245 Cal App 2d 976, 54 Cal Rptr 328, 329 (1966). Other cases have suggested that required reporting procedures are indicative of control over daily operations. *See* Weil v Arthur Murray, Inc, 67 Misc 2d 417, 324 NYS2d 381, 387 (1971) (weekly sales reports); Aweida v Kientz, 536 P2d 1138, 1140 (Colo App 1975) (daily sales reports); and Billops v Magness Constr Co, 391 A2d 196, 198 (Del 1978).

[403] *See* Dorsic v Kurtin, 19 Cal App 3d 226, 96 Cal Rptr 528 (1971); Aweida v Kientz, 536 P2d 1138, 1140 (Col App 1975); Chevron Oil Co v Sutton, 85 NM 679, 515 P2d 1283, 1286 (1973); and Beckham v Exxon Corp, 539 SW2d 217 (Tex Civ App 1976).

[404] *See* McLaughlin v Chicken Delight, Inc, 164 Conn 317, 321 A2d 456, 458 (1973).

[405] *See* Coe v Esau, 377 P2d 815, 818 (Okla 1963); Aweida v Kientz, 536 P2d 1138, 1140 (Colo App 1975); and Singleton v International Intl Dairy Queen, Inc, 332 A2d 160, 162 (Del 1975).

[406] *See* Wood v Holiday Inns, Inc, 508 F2d 167, 175 (5th Cir 1975); Billops v Magness Constr, Co, 391 A2d 196, 198 (Del 1978); and Lamb v Wedgewood Corp, 286 SE2d 876, 881 (NC App 1982).

[407] *See* Dorsic v Kurtin, 19 Cal App 3d 226, 96 Cal Rptr 528, 537 (1971); Wood v Holiday Inns, Inc, 508 F2d 167, 175 (5th Cir 1975); Porter v Arthur Murray, Inc, 249 Cal App 2d 410, 57 Cal Rptr 554, 558 (1967); Billops v Magness Constr Co, 391 A2d 196, 198 (Del 1978). At least one court has viewed a franchisor's ability to terminate unilaterally as an in terrorem clause which alone is sufficient to control all activities of the franchisee since any variation may lead to a swift end of the franchisee's business.

the promotion of uniform franchisee marketing activities;[409] and payment by the franchisor of the franchisee's taxes.[410] Many of these provisions, or similar provisions, are commonly included in franchise agreements.

The theory of apparent authority, on the other hand, bases vicarious liability on (1) the *representation* that an agency relationship exists, and (2) the plaintiff's reasonable reliance on the representation to his or her detriment.[411] Apparent authority cases in franchising have cited a number of representations—most of which are quite common franchise practices—to support a finding of vicarious liability. These include uniform appearance and architecture;[412] advertising in the name of the franchisor;[413] telephone listings in the name of the franchisor only;[414] letterhead stationery bearing the franchisor's name only;[415] and answering the telephone with the franchisor's name.[416] Thus, the very indicia of belonging to the same system, so important to a franchise system, can lead to franchisor liability under the theory of apparent authority.

Other theories of franchisor vicarious liability have been suggested including breach of a legal duty owed,[417] and strict liability and implied warranty

---

Aweida v Keintz, 536 P2d 1138, 1140 (Colo App 1975).

[408] *See* Drexel v Union Prescription Centers, Inc, 582 F2d 781, 787 (3d Cir 1978); Wood v Holiday Inns, Inc, 508 F2d 167, 175 (5th Cir 1975), Dorsic v Kurtin, 19 Cal App 3d 226, 96 Cal Rptr 528, 537 (1971); Lamb v Wedgewood Corp, 286 SE2d 876, 881 (NC App 1982). *See also* Singleton v International Dairy Queen, Inc, 332 A2d 160, 161 (Del 1975).

[409] *See* Whitfield v Century 21 Real Estate Corp, 484 F Supp 984 (SD Tex 1979).

[410] *See* BP Oil Co v Mabe, 279 Md 632, 370 A2d 554, 557 (1977); and Beckham v Exxon Corp, 539 SW2d 217, 218-19 (Tex Civ App 1976).

[411] *See* BP Oil Co v Mabe, 279 Md 632, 370 A2d 554, 561 (1977); *see generally* Restatement (Second) of Agency §267 (1957).

[412] *See* Drexel v Union Prescription Centers, Inc, 582 F2d 781, 787, 795 (3d Cir 1978); Wood v Holiday Inns, Inc, 508 F2d 167, 176 (5th Cir 1975); Jordan v Robert Half Personnel Agencies, 615 SW2d 574, 582 (Mo App 1981); *see also* de Carvalho v Holiday Inns, Inc, Bus Fran Guide (CCH) ¶7559 at 12,355 (DDC 1980).

[413] *See* Johnston v American Oil Co, 51 Mich App 646, 215 NW2d 719, 721 (1974); Billops v Magness Constr Co, 391 A2d 196, 198 (Del 1978); *but see* Ortega v General Motors Corp, 392 SE2d 40, 44 (1980).

[414] *See* Duluth Herald & News Tribune v Plymoth Optical Co, 286 Minn 455, 176 NW2d 552, 554 (1970); Buchanan v Canada Dry Corp, 138 Ga App 588, 226 SE2d 613, 616 (1976).

[415] *See* Vowels v Arthur Murray Studios, Inc, 12 Mich App 359, 163 NW3d 35, 37 (1968); Beck v Arthur Murray, Inc, 245 Cal App 2d 976, 54 Cal Rptr 328, 330 (1966).

[416] *See* Beck v Arthur Murray, Inc, 245 Cal App 2d 976, 54 Cal Rptr 328, 330 (1966).

[417] *See* O'Boyle v Avis Rent-A-Car Sys, Inc, Bus Fran Guide (CCH) ¶7604 (NY App Div 1981). In O'Boyle, the court apparently assumed that an agency relationship existed between the franchisor and its franchisee and found the franchisor, who failed to control the day-to-day operations of the franchised car rental business, liable for tortious negligence of one of its franchisees. The decision does not make it clear whether the franchisor was directly or vicariously liable for its negligence in failing properly to train, supervise, or control its agent-franchisee or its employees. *See also* Wise v Kentucky Fried Chicken Corp, Civ No 82-427-D, Slip Op (DCNH Feb 1, 1983). *Compare with* Cullen v BMW of N Am, 691 F2d 1097 (2d Cir 1982).

theories.[418]

The cases are not at all consistent. Often a decision of vicarious liability seems hinged to a compelling set of facts; or the *deep pocket* theory of including as liable all parties who benefit from a particular commercial relationship—particularly those in a financial position to pay the injured victim. Franchisors are well-advised to remove unnecessary controls on day-to-day operations; to require public notice of the franchise relationship through use of signs and stationery; and to assure that adequate levels of liability insurance are maintained.

How must companies offering and selling a franchise comply with the various state and federal laws and regulations?

§9.65 What does the Federal Trade Commission rule require?

Essentially, the Federal Trade Commission (FTC) rule requires specified, timely disclosure to prospective franchisees.[419] Such disclosure must be complete and accurate in its entirety according to either the format provided by the FTC rule itself, or a format developed by state administrators and approved by a national association of state security administrators. This latter format is known as the Uniform Franchise Offering Circular[420] (UFOC). The choice of format is made by the franchisor.[421]

The FTC rule also requires that earnings claims which are made must be substantiated by an "earnings claims document,"[422] the format and standards for which are provided by the FTC rule. As with other items of disclosure under the FTC rule, the UFOC format and standards may also be used to

---

[418] Strict liability and implied warranty theories have not been applied directly in a franchise context; however, they have arisen in product liability cases and may be applied in many Seller-Buyer transactions. See generally Restatement (Second) of Torts, §402A (1965). Of particular relevance to franchising are cases in which the courts have found liability on the basis of trademark ownership. *See generally* Kosters v Seven-Up Co, 595 F2d 347 (6th Cir 1979); Germain, *Tort Liability of Trademark Licensors in an Era of 'Accountability': A Tale of Three Cases,* 69 Trademark Rep 128 (1979); Goldstein, *Products Liability and the Trademark Owner: When a Trademark is a Warranty,* 67 Trademark Rep 587 (1977).

[419] 16 CFR §436, §436.1(a) (1982).

[420] The Midwest Commissioners Association (MSCA) adopted the Uniform Franchise Offering Circular (UFOC) on September 2, 1975. The MSCA was dissolved in 1980 and its responsibilities were undertaken by the North American Securities Administrators Association which adopted the UFOC and guidelines for its preparation on April 28, 1981. The UFOC is reprinted in Bus Fran Guide (CCH) ¶5700 *et seq* (1980).

[421] See **§9.71.**

[422] See **§9.72.**

present and substantiate earnings claims except when media claims are made. If media claims are made, the UFOC format may not be used and the franchisor must prepare an earnings claims document, as prescribed by the FTC rule.[423] Disclosure must be made to prospective franchisees by a required time before the franchise agreement is executed.[424]

§9.66 —How current must disclosures be?

Under the Federal Trade Commission (FTC) rule, the offering circular must be revised within 90 days after the end of the franchisor's fiscal year, and at least quarterly if there has been any *material change.* A material fact or change is defined by the FTC rule as "any fact, circumstance, or set of conditions which has a substantial likelihood of influencing a reasonable franchisee or a reasonable prospective franchisee in the making of a significant decision relating to a named franchise business or which has any significant financial impact on a franchisee or prospective franchisee."[425] If a Uniform Franchise Offering Circular (UFOC) format is used to comply with the FTC rule, however, and the franchisor is registered in any registration state, the FTC rule must be satisfied by renewal and amendment of the offering circular as required by state law.[426] Generally, state law provides that an amendment is required upon the occurrence of any material change in the information disclosed (in practice, state administrators define a material change in the same manner as it is defined by the FTC rule), and an updated document is required to be registered either on each anniversary of the initial effective date or 90 to 120 days from the conclusion of the franchisor's fiscal year.

§9.67 What do state registration/disclosure laws require?

Typically, state laws require that, prior to the offer of a franchise, the franchisor file with state administrators a disclosure document (also called an *offering circular* or *prospectus*) and certain collateral documents such as a consent to service of process, a verification of disclosure, and a salesman disclosure form. Before any sale, disclosure must be made to prospective franchisees by presentation of an offering circular.[427]

---

[423] See §9.72.

[424] See §9.75.

[425] 16 CFR §436, §436.2(n) (1982); *Final Guides to the Franchising and Business Opportunity Ventures Trade Regulation Rule,* 44 Fed Reg 49966, 49971-72 (1979) [hereinafter cited as Guidelines].

[426] Guidelines, *supra* note 425, at 49970.

[427] Cal Corp Code §31119 (Deering 1976 & Supp 1982); Hawaii Rev Stat §482E-5(d) (1976 & Supp 1980); Ill Ann Stat ch 121 1/2 §704(2) (Smith-Hurd Supp 1982-83); Ind Code Ann §23-2-2.5-9 (Burns Supp 1982); Md Ann Code art 56, §357 (1979 & Supp Supp 1982); Mich Comp Laws Ann §445.1516 (Supp 1982-83); Minn Stat Ann

§9.68 —When does a state have jurisdiction over the sale of a franchise?

State statutes are generally applicable when an offer to sell is made in the state. An offer to sell is considered to be made in a state when either: (1) the offer originates from the state; or (2) the offer is directed by the franchisor to a prospective franchisee within a particular state.

The states of California,[428] Illinois,[429] Maryland,[430] Minnesota,[431] and Wisconsin[432] exempt certain *out of state* offers and sales.[433] Out of state is, however, variously defined and may apply to offers made to one who is not a resident of the state, or not domiciled in the state, or not present in the state when the offer is made. Out of state may also mean that the franchised business is not to be operated in the state.

Illinois law provides for an exemption from disclosure for nonresidents who are otherwise covered by state disclosure law of another state but registration in Illinois is still required.[434]

§9.69 —What does the Uniform Franchise Offering Circular format require?

Information concerning the following matters must be disclosed;[435] those items with an asterick are of particular importance, and a more detailed discussion of disclosure requirements follows:

1. The franchisor and any predecessor
2. Identity and business experience of persons affiliated with the franchisor; franchise brokers
3. Litigation
4. Bankruptcy
5. Franchisee's initial franchise fee or other initial payment

---

§80C.06.5 (West Supp 1982); NY Gen Bus Law §683.8 (McKinney Supp 1981-82); ND Cent Code §51-19-08.6 (1981); Or Rev Stat §650.020(6)(a) (1977); RI Gen Laws §19-28-5.I (Supp 1980); SD Codified Laws Ann §37-5A-47 (1977 & Supp 1982); Va Code §13.1-565(c) (1978 & Supp 1982); Wash Rev Code Ann §19.100.080 (1978 & Supp 1982); Wis Stat Ann §553.27(4) (West Supp 1982). See also **§9.75.**

[428] California, Bus Fran Guide (CCH) ¶5050.07 (1980).

[429] Ill Ann Stat ch 121 1/2 §713 (Smith-Hurd Supp 1982-83).

[430] Maryland, Bus Fran Guide (CCH) ¶5200.04.A (1980).

[431] Minnesota, Minn Stat Ann §80C.03(h) (West Supp 1982).

[432] Wisconsin, Bus Fran Guide (CCH) ¶5490.01(5) (1980).

[433] See **§9.37.**

[434] Illinois, Bus Fran Guide (CCH) ¶5130.23 (1980).

[435] *Uniform Franchise Offering Circular Guidelines,* Bus Fran Guide (CCH) ¶5700 *et seq,* ¶5790 (1980).

6. Other fees
7. Franchisee's initial investment
8. Obligations of franchisee to purchase or lease from designated sources*
9. Obligations of franchisee to purchase or lease in accordance with specifications or from approved suppliers*
10. Financing arrangements
11. Obligations of the franchisor; other supervision, assistance, or services
12. Exclusive area or territory
13. Trademarks, service marks, trade names, logotypes, and commercial symbols
14. Patents and copyrights
15. Obligation of the franchisee to participate in the actual operation of the franchised business
16. Restriction on goods and services offered by franchisee*
17. Renewal, termination, repurchase, modification, and assignment of the franchise agreement and related information
18. Arrangements with public figures
19. Actual, average. projected, or forecasted franchisee sales, profits, or earnings*
20. Information regarding franchises of the franchisor
21. Financial statements
22. Contracts
23. Acknowledgment of receipt by prospective franchisee

Item 8 requires a franchisor to disclose whether the franchisee is obligated, by the franchise agreement or any other device or practice, to purchase or lease from the franchisor or its designees either goods, services, supplies, fixtures, equipment, inventory, or real estate relating to the establishment or operation of the franchised business. If the franchisee is so obligated, the product and supplier must be identified and the franchisor must disclose whether the franchisor, its parent, or persons affiliated with the franchisor, will or may derive income based on or as a result of any such required purchases or leases. The franchisor must also disclose the magnitude of these required purchases and leases in relation to all purchases and leases by the franchisee of goods and services which the franchisee will make or enter into in either the establishment or the operation of the franchised business.

Item 9 requires a franchisor to disclose whether the franchisee is obligated, either by the terms of the franchise agreement or any other device or practice of the franchisor, to purchase or lease in accordance with specifications issued by the franchisor, or from suppliers approved by the franchisor, goods, services, supplies, fixtures, equipment, inventory or real estate which relates to the establishment or operation of the franchised business. If the purchase or lease of these items is restricted, the products and services and the suppliers of each must be disclosed and the franchisor may include the reason for imposing such restrictions. The franchisor is also required to disclose how specifications are issued and modified and the manner in which approval of suppliers is granted or revoked. The franchisor must disclose whether, and for what categories of goods and services, the franchisor or persons affiliated with the franchisor are approved suppliers or the only approved suppliers, and if any, the precise basis by which the franchisor, its parent, or persons affiliated with the franchisor may derive income from purchases made from it or from other suppliers.

Item 16 requires disclosure of any restriction or condition imposed by the franchisor, whether by the franchise agreement or any other device or practice of the franchisor, to restrict the franchisee in the goods or services offered for sale or limit the customers to whom it may sell such goods or services. If the franchisee is restricted, the franchisor must describe whether the restrictions are conditioned on meeting certain defined sales efforts or results. The franchisor must also describe any obligation of the franchisee to sell or provide all the goods and services authorized by the franchisor.

Item 19 is similar to the earnings claims document described in the Federal Trade Commission rule.[436] Item 19 is generally considered to be more difficult to prepare than an earnings claims document, however, and this may be a factor in a franchisor's choice of format.[437]

§9.70 —What does the Federal Trade Commission rule format require?

The Federal Trade Commission Rule (FTC) rule format consists of the following 20 categories of information;[438] the two asterisked items are of particular interest and are discussed below in greater detail:

1. Identifying information as to the franchisor
2. Business experience of the franchisor's directors and executive officers
3. Business experience of the franchisor
4. Litigation history
5. Bankruptcy history
6. A description of the franchise
7. The initial funds required to be paid by a franchisee
8. Recurring funds to be paid by a franchisee
9. Affiliated persons the franchisee is required or advised to do business with by the franchisor

---

436 See **§9.72.**

437 See **§9.71.**

438 16 CFR §436, §436.1 n 3 (1982).

10. Obligations to purchase*
11. Revenues received by the franchisor in consideration of purchases by a franchisee
12. Financing arrangements
13. Restriction of sales*
14. Personal participation required of the franchisee in the operation of the franchise
15. Termination, cancellation, and renewal of the franchise
16. Statistical information concerning the number of franchised and company-owned outlets
17. Site selection
18. Training programs
19. Public figure involvement in the franchise
20. Financial information concerning the franchisor

Item 10 requires disclosure of any real estate, services, supplies, products, inventories, signs, fixtures, or equipment which relate to either the establishment or the operation of the franchised business which the franchisee is required, either directly or indirectly, to purchase or lease. This item of disclosure combines disclosure matters required by the Guidelines for items 8 and 9 of the Uniform Franchise Offering Circular (UFOC) format.[439] If a required purchase, lease, or rental must be made from a person or among a group of persons specified by the franchisor, not only the name and address of such a supplier but also the business justification for restricting the purchase list and the manner in which the franchisor issues and changes approved suppliers must be given. A list of required purchases and required suppliers may be given in a separate document provided it is referenced in the FTC rule basic disclosure document.

Item 13 of the FTC rule format is analogous to the disclosure required by the guidelines for Item 16 of the UFOC format.[440] The franchisor must describe and disclose whether the franchisee is (1) limited in the types of products or services it may sell; (2) limited in the customers to whom it may sell; (3) limited in the geographical area in which it may sell; or (4) granted territorial protection by the franchisor.

This disclosure is required whether these limitations are the result of the terms of the franchise agreement or any other device or practice of the franchisor, including a written or verbal understanding. Disclosure should describe the specific limitations and the franchisor's reasons for imposing these limitations. If a franchisee is limited in its right to sell competing goods or services, or required to sell either all goods or services offered by the franchisor or

---

[439] See **§9.69.**

[440] *Id.*

prohibited from selling some goods or services offered by the franchisor, these restrictions must be disclosed.

§9.71 —Which disclosure format is preferable?

While it is generally easier to prepare a disclosure document according to the Federal Trade Commission (FTC) rule format rather than the Uniform Franchise Offering Circular (UFOC) format, the UFOC is accepted, with only minor variation, in the 15 states which require franchise registration and/or disclosure,[441] whereas the FTC rule format is accepted only in the states of Hawaii, Illinois, Michigan, New York, North Dakota, and Wisconsin. Therefore, it is usually sensible for a franchisor who has plans to franchise nationally to use the UFOC format.

There are some specific areas, however, in which one format or the other may be more desirable. For example, the UFOC format requires disclosure of bankruptcy histories reflecting the previous 15 years; the FTC rule format requires disclosure for only the previous 7 years. The UFOC format requires disclosure of the numbers of cancellations, terminations, and nonrenewals during the most recent 3 fiscal years; the FTC rule format requires such disclosure only during the franchisor's most recent fiscal year. The FTC rule format requires disclosure of bankruptcy information for the franchisor's parent or holding company; the UFOC format requires disclosure of bankruptcy histories only for predecessors of the franchisor. The FTC rule format requires disclosure of the business justification for certain practices of the franchisor as, for example, placing limitations on sales, approving suppliers, limiting geographic areas, and limiting customers; the UFOC format does not. Generally, it is easier to prepare earnings claims according to FTC guidelines than for item 19 of the UFOC format, and an earnings claims document according to the FTC rule format is required for media claims.[442] However, earnings claims must meet UFOC format guidelines for use in registration states. A franchisor should compare the items of disclosure required by both formats and evaluate marketing practices with respect to the states in which the franchisor wishes to develop a marketing plan, in order to make an informed decision concerning which format should be utilized.

§9.72 What are earnings claims?

The definition of an earnings claim under the FTC rule[443] is very broad, and includes any "oral, written, or visual representation to a prospective franchisee or for general dissemination in the media which states or suggests a specific level or range of potential, or actual sales, income, growth, or net profits." The

---

441 See **§9.28.**

442 See **§9.72.**

443 16 CFR §436, §436.1(b)(3) (1982).

suggestion of the specific level may include any statement from which a particular level of income could be calculated as, for example, "100 per cent return on investment within the first year of operation" or "enough money to buy a new Porsche" as well as such claims as "earn a $10,000 profit." Earnings claims do not include what the FTC rule characterizes as *mere puffery* such as "make big money" or "opportunity of a lifetime." Earnings claims include statements concerning historical results of the franchisor, or of franchisees of the franchisor, as well as projections of future results.

If earnings claims are made, whether made directly to the prospective franchisee or in the media, the FTC rule requires a document called an earnings claim document which imposes the following standards:

1. A reasonable basis must exist to support the accuracy of the claim
2. Material sufficient to substantiate the accuracy of the claim must be in the franchisor's possession at the time the claim is made
3. The claim must be geographically relevant to the prospective franchisee's proposed location

An earnings claim document, prepared according to specifications detailed in the Guidelines, must be furnished to the prospective franchisee at the time for making disclosure as required by the FTC rule.[444]

State law does not deal specifically with earnings claims for dissemination in the media, but advertising must be submitted for approval in states having franchise sale registration laws, thereby giving state administrators the opportunity to restrict excessive claims or require that claims be included in the offering circular and meet the standards for inclusion.[445]

§9.73 Who must make disclosure?

Under the Federal Trade Commission (FTC) rule,[446] disclosure must be made by franchisors and franchise brokers. A *franchisor* is a *person* (any individual, group, association, partnership, corporation or other business entity) who offers a franchise as defined in the FTC rule. A *franchise broker* is any *person* other than a franchisor who sells, offers for sale, or arranges the sale of a franchise. Subfranchisors will be considered franchise brokers.

Under state law any person who makes an offer of a franchise or sells a franchise must provide an offering circular/disclosure document to the prospective franchisee which provides certain information[447] concerning the fran-

---

[444] See **§9.75.**

[445] *Final Guides to the Franchising and Business Opportunity Ventures Trade Regulation Rule,* 44 Fed Reg 49966, 49982 (1979).

[446] 16 CFR §436, §436.1(a) (1982); *Final Guides to the Franchising and Business Opportunity Ventures Trade Regulation Rule,* 44 Fed Reg 49966, 49969 (1979).

[447] See **§9.69.**

chisor and any subfranchisor.[448]

§9.74 Who must receive disclosure?

A prospective franchisee is defined by the Federal Trade Commission (FTC) rule[449] as any person, including any representative, agent, or employee of that person, who approaches or is approached by a franchisor or franchise broker, or any representative, agent or employee thereof, for the purpose of discussing the establishment, or possible establishment, of a franchise relationship involving such person. The characterization as a *prospective franchisee* is, to a certain extent, within the franchisor's control, since the franchisor can, in ordinary circumstances, control the length of the discussion to keep it brief, and the subject matter to keep it general, and can disclaim the ability to discuss the possible sale of a franchise at that time.[450]

State law requires disclosure to offerees of a franchise. Prospective franchisees under the FTC rule are not necessarily offerees.

§9.75 —When must disclosure be provided?

The Federal Trade Commission (FTC) rule requires that the disclosure document or the offering circular, whether it is a Uniform Franchise Offering Circular (UFOC) format or FTC rule format offering circular, must be provided to the prospective franchisee at the earlier of the first personal meeting, or the "time for making of disclosure." The latter term is defined as 10 business days prior to the earlier of:

1. the execution by a prospective franchisee of any franchise or other agreement imposing a binding legal obligation on the prospective franchisee in connection with the sale or proposed sale of a franchise
2. the payment by a prospective franchisee of any consideration in connection with the sale or proposed sale of a franchise. This does not include a payment which a prospective franchisee voluntarily makes as, for example, the fee paid to a lawyer or counselor reviewing the proposed investment[451]

---

448 *Uniform Franchise Offering Circular Guidelines,* Bus Fran Guide (CCH) ¶5700 *et seq,* ¶¶5796, 5801 (1980).

449 *Final Guides to the Franchising and Business Opportunity Ventures Trade Regulation Rule,* 44 Fed Reg 49966, 49969 (1979) [hereinafter cited as Guidelines].

450 Guidelines, *supra* note 449, at 49970.

451 *Final Guides to the Franchising and Business Opportunity Ventures Trade Regulation Rule,* 44 Fed Reg 49966, 49970 (1979) (hereinafter cited as Guidelines).

Since state statutes require the delivery of the offering circular at times which are the same as, or later than, those times specified by the FTC rule,[452] the FTC rule preempts[453] and controls the time of disclosures. In states requiring registration prior to the offer of a franchise, however, the offering circular proposed to be delivered to prospective franchisees must be effectively registered with the state authorities before meeting the timing requirements of the FTC rule. Since this process requires a franchisor to submit an application[454] which is reviewed by a state franchise examiner who may require additional detail in disclosure or the adaptation of provisions of the franchise agreement to state law before the state administrator is satisfied that the application complies with state statutes, regulations, and policies, the franchisor must anticipate some delay before it will be notified that the registration is effective. Registration does not imply an endorsement or recommendation by the state.

If a transaction is exempt or excluded from coverage under the FTC rule, then state requirements will govern time of disclosure. These will range from ten business days to two days prior to the execution of a binding agreement between the parties or the receipt of consideration by the franchisor.

§9.76 —Are there other areas in which the Federal Trade Commission rule is controlling over state law?

The Federal Trade Commission rule attempts to set a federal standard of minimum disclosure while permitting concurrent protection afforded by state law.[455] As a general rule, state laws are preempted only to the extent that they provide less protection than the FTC rule.[456]

The FTC rule acknowledges that the Uniform Franchise Offering Circular (UFOC) format provides protection[457] equal to or greater than that of the FTC rule format for disclosure. Nor does the FTC rule preempt state laws or regulations concerning registration of salespersons, bonding and escrow re-

---

[452] Cal Corp Code §31119 (Deering 1976 & Supp 1982); Hawaii Rev Stat §482E-5(d) (1976 & Supp 1980); Ill Ann Stat ch 121 1/2 §704(2) (Smith-Hurd Supp 1982-83); Ind Code Ann §23-2-2.5-9 (Burns Supp 1982); Md Ann Code art 56, §357 (1979 & Supp 1982); Mich Comp Laws Ann §445.1516 (Supp 1982-83); Minn Stat Ann §80C.06.5 (West Supp 1982); NY Gen Bus Law §683.8 (McKinney Supp 1981-82); ND Cent Code §51-19-08.6 (1981); RI Gen Laws §19-28-5.I (Supp 1980); SD Codified Laws Ann §37-5A-47 (1977 & Supp 1982); Va Code §13.1-565(c) (1978 & Supp 1982); Wash Rev Code Ann §19.100.080 (1978 & Supp 1982); Wis Stat Ann §553.27(4) (West Supp 1982).

[453] Guidelines, *supra* note 451, at 49971.

[454] See §9.67.

[455] *Final Guidelines to the Franchising and Business Opportunity Ventures Trade Regulation Rule,* 44 Fed Reg 49966, 49971 (1979) (hereinafter cited as Guidelines].

[456] *Id.*

[457] Guidelines, *supra* note 455, at 49970. See also §9.71.

quirements, or substantive regulation of the franchise relationship.[458]

Regulation by the FTC rule generally preempts the matter of the time at which disclosure must be made[459] and the form and content of earnings claims which are made in the media.[460]

§9.77 What do the state substantive laws require?

Besides the substantive laws dealing with termination and nonrenewal, as referred to in Chapter 7, certain states have specific prohibitions on fraud and misrepresentation as related to the sale of franchises.[461]

In addition, specific state laws relate to the obligation of the franchisor to repurchase proprietary items, the limitations placed on the enforceability of covenants not to compete, and other matters. These substantive state laws must be referred to in the offering circular in certain states. In addition, some states[462] require the prospective franchisee to execute a franchise agreement which has been conformed to include these applicable state law provisions. The franchise agreement may be conformed by the execution of an addendum modifying the franchise agreement as to the required matter.

§9.78 What are the consequences of failing to comply with the franchise laws?

→ les csq de la Violaº des lois s/ franchise

The Federal Trade Commission (FTC) may bring civil actions which seek penalties, injunctive relief, and/or consumer redress. The FTC may also issue cease and desist orders.[463]

Civil penalties allow for recovery of up to $10,000 a day for each violation. In order to prove such violation, the FTC must show *actual knowledge,* or *knowledge fairly implied* that the act complained of violates the FTC rule. Also, a $10,000 penalty is available if a franchisor engages in an act or practice which violates a previously issued cease and desist order, if the franchisor had "actual knowledge of the unlawfulness of the act or practice." In order to be able to provide actual knowledge or knowledge fairly implied, the FTC has sent *notice letters* accompanied by copies of the FTC rule, or, in the case of the cease and desist order, a synopsis of the FTC's decisions relating to unfair and deceptive

---

458 Guidelines, *supra* note 455, at 49971.

459 See **§9.75.**

460 See **§9.72.**

461 See **app G.**

462 Typically, this is required by all states listed in **app J,** depending upon the terms of the franchise agreement.

463 *See* FTC v HN Singer, Inc, Bus Fran Guide (CCH) ¶7698, *modified,* Bus Fran Guide (CCH) ¶7775 (1981), *affd,* Bus Fran Guide (CCH) ¶7791 *enforcing* Bus Fran Guide (CCH) ¶7901 (1982); FTC v Enamelcraft, Inc, Bus Fran Guide (CCH) ¶7704 (Sept 9, 1981); FTC v Marketing Assocs, Inc, Bus Fran Guide (CCH) ¶7679 (July 7, 1981).

acts or practices.[464]

Although courts have generally found no private cause of action in the FTC rule, some states have enacted *Little FTC Acts* which may elaborate upon or merely adopt the standard of §5 of the Federal Trade Commission Act, which prohibits "unfair or deceptive acts or practices" or "unfair methods of competition."[465] Many of these statutes provide that federal judicial interpretation of the FTC Act may offer guidance to the state courts. These statutes commonly state that businesses, including franchises, are objects of the statute's protection and do provide a private cause of action for damages, as has been affirmed in a recent case.[466]

State franchise statutes give authority to the state administrator directly, or through the state attorney general, to bring an action on behalf of the people of the state to enjoin unlawful acts or practices or to enforce compliance with the franchise laws.[467]

Violations of state franchise laws may result, in some states, in civil penalties for each violation, including violations of any injunction issued pursuant to the franchise law. These penalties may involve amounts of up to $25,000.[468]

Some states authorize the imposition of jail sentences as well as penal fines for violations of the franchise laws. Generally, these are limited to willful violations.[469]

Besides the ability to seek injunctive relief in court, state administrators may be vested with authority to issue cease and desist orders or stop orders denying

---

464 15 USC §45(m)(1)(A).

465 15 USC §45 (1981).

466 Bailey Employment Sys v Hahn, 545 F Supp 62 (1982).

467 Cal Corp Code §31400 (Deering 1979 & Supp 1982); Ill Ann Stat ch 121 1/2 §718(b) (Smith-Hurd Supp 1982-83); Ind Code Ann §23-2-2.5-32 (Burns Supp 1982); Md Ann Code art 56, §363 (1979 & Supp 1982); Mich Comp Laws Ann §445.1535 (Supp 1982-83); Minn Stat Ann §80C.16 (West Supp 1982); NY Gen Bus Law §689(2) (McKinney Supp 1981-82); ND Cent Code §51-19-13.1 (1981); Or Rev Stat §650.065 (1977); RI Gen Laws §19-28-10 (Supp 1980); SD Codified Laws Ann §37-5A-75 (1977 & Supp 1982); Va Code §13.1-568 (1978 & Supp 1982); Wash Rev Code Ann §19.100.210 (1978 & Supp 1982); Wis Stat Ann §553.54 (West Supp 1982).

468 For example, Cal Corp Code §§31300-31306 (Deering 1979 & Supp 1982); Ill Ann Stat ch 121 1/2 §719 (Smith-Hurd Supp 1982-83); Ind Code Ann §23-2-2.5-27 (Burns Supp 1982); Mich Comp Laws Ann §445.1538 (Supp 1982-83); Minn Stat Ann §§80C.16 (West Supp 1982); NY Gen Bus Law §690 (McKinney Supp 1981-82); SD Codified Laws Ann §§37-5A-72 and -78 (1977 & Supp 1982); Va Code §13.1-570 (1978 & Supp 1982); Wash Rev Code Ann §§19.100.210(2) and (3) (1978 & Supp 1982).

469 Ill Ann Stat ch 121 1/2 §720 (Smith-Hurd Supp 1982-83); Ind Code Ann §23-2-2.5-37 (Burns Supp 1982); Md Ann Code art 56, §365A (1979 & Supp 1982); Mich Comp Laws Ann §445.1538 (Supp 1982-83); Minn Stat Ann §80C.16.3 (West Supp 1982); NY Gen Bus Law §§690 and 692 (McKinney Supp 1981-82); ND Cent Code §51-19-14 (1981); Or Rev Stat §650.085 (1977); RI Gen Laws §19-28-11 (Supp 1980); SD Codified Laws Ann §§37-5A-76 and 79 (1977 & Supp 1982); Va Code §13.1-569 (1978 & Supp 1982); Wash Rev Code Ann §19.100.210(3) (1978 & Supp 1982); Wis Stat Ann §553.52 (West Supp 1982). *But see* People v Gonda, 138 Cal App 3d 774, 188 Cal Rptr 295 (1982).

the effectiveness of any franchise registration upon certain findings. These findings include: (1) the failure to comply with the provisions of the franchise law; (2) fraud, deceit, or misrepresentation to prospective franchisees; (3) conviction of an offense, or other involvement in litigation which is likely to create an unreasonable risk to prospective franchisees; (4) use of an offering circular which is materially incomplete, or misleading; (5) performance of illegal activities as part of the franchisor's method of business; (6) failure to demonstrate that adequate financial arrangements have been made; (7) failure to process diligently a registration application; (8) use of prohibited advertising; and (9) offer or sale of an unregistered franchise.[470]

Most state franchise laws authorize lawsuits by injured franchisees for damages, and, in some cases, injunctive relief, including attorneys' fees and costs of bringing the suit. For example, Illinois law specifically allows that a franchisee may bring an action against the franchisor to recover damages sustained by reason of a violation. If successful, the franchisee is entitled to damages and the costs of the action, including reasonable attorneys' fees.[471] Most states allow franchisees to sue for rescission or damages, but not both.[472]

§9.79 What are the implications of state and federal securities laws in the sale of a franchise?

A *franchise,* as defined by state law and the Federal Trade Commission (FTC) rule, without more, has not been held to be subject to federal securities law requirements.[473]

The state securities laws are more likely to be applicable to franchises, because, in the opinion of some state securities administrators, the franchise may be a security when the franchise fee required to be paid to the franchisor is for the purpose of raising capital for the franchisor to use in meeting its

---

[470] Some examples are found in the following state statutes: Mich Comp Laws Ann §§445.1513, 445.1530 (Supp 1982-83); Minn Stat Ann §80C.12 (West Supp 1982); ND Cent Code §51-19-09 (1981); RI Gen Laws §19-28-10.C (Supp 1980); Wash Rev Code Ann §19.100.248 (1978 & Supp 1982); Wis Stat Ann §553.54 (West Supp 1982).

[471] Ill Ann Stat ch 121 1/2 §721 (Smith-Hurd Supp 1982-83).

[472] Cal Corp Code §31300 (Deering 1979 & Supp 1982); Hawaii Rev Stat §482E-9 (1976 & Supp 1980); Ill Ann Stat ch 121 1/2 §721 (Smith-Hurd Supp 1982-83); Ind Code Ann §23-2-2.5-28 (Burns Supp 1982); Mich Comp Laws Ann §§445.1531, .1534 (Supp 1982-83); Minn Stat Ann §80C.17 (West Supp 1982); NY Gen Bus Law §691 (McKinney Supp 1981-82); Nd Cent Code §51-19-12 (1981); Or Rev Stat §650.085 (1977); RI Gen Laws §19-28-9 (Supp 1980); SD Codified Laws Ann §37-5A-83 (1977 & Supp 1982); Va Code §13.1-571 (1978 & Supp 1982); Wash Rev Code Ann §19.100.190(2) (1978 & Supp 1982); Wis Stat Ann §553.51 (West Supp 1982).

[473] Mr Steak, Inc v River City Steak, Inc, 324 F Supp 640 (D Colo 1970), *modified,* 460 F2d 666 (10th Cir 1972); Chapman v Rudd Paint Varnish Co, 409 F2d 635 (9th Cir 1969). *But see* SEC v Glenn W Turner Enters, Inc, 474 F2d 476 (9th Cir), *cert denied,* 414 US 821 (1973); SEC v Quality Care, Inc, CA 82-1438 (DDC May 25, 1982).

obligations to franchisees.[474] However, franchises sold under state franchise statutes are specifically exempt under the securities laws of some states.[475]

---

[474] Opinion of Okla Sec Commn, Dept of Sec re Fashion Flair, Inc, *reprinted in* Bus Fran Guide (CCH) ¶7577 (1980).

[475] Cal Corp Code §25019(4) (West 1968 & Supp 1970).

Glossary

A

Agency (and related terms) An arrangement whereby a manufacturer of goods sells its products through an intermediary while retaining ownership and legal possession of the goods.

Area franchise An agreement whereby the grantee is granted the exclusive right, for a consideration, to establish a number of individual franchised units within a designated territory. The term is also used in state franchise statutes to refer to an agreement whereby the grantee is granted the right, for a consideration, to sell or negotiate the sale of franchises in the name, or on behalf, of the grantor.

Area of primary responsibility The geographic area within which a distributor of a manufacturer's products is to be primarily responsible for the sale of such products, and to which the distributor is expected to devote its principal effort to cultivate sales.

B

Boycott An agreement to refuse to deal with a business or businesses.

Brokerage fee A payment made by either Seller or Buyer to an intermediary for arranging and facilitating a purchase or sale.

Business opportunity A sale or lease or offer for sale or lease of any products, equipment, supplies, or services which are sold or offered for sale to the purchaser/investor for the purpose of enabling the purchaser/investor to start a business and in which Seller makes certain representations with respect to the identification of customers, sites for the operation of its business, repurchase of inventory, guaranty of income, refund of the price paid to Seller, or a sales program or marketing program provided by Seller.

C

Class action A lawsuit in which one or a small number of representative plaintiffs asserts legal claims on behalf of a group of claimants who are similarly situated with respect to the subject matter of the action as the representative parties, and who will be bound by the outcome of the action.

Colgate doctrine A principle of law based on the decision of the Supreme Court in *United States v Colgate & Co,* 250 US 300 (1919), which recognizes the legal right of a supplier that is not a monopolist to select those customers with whom it will deal.

Combination Collaborative conduct among two or more persons for the purpose of achieving a common goal whether it be an express agreement or merely a unity of purpose, common design or meeting of the minds.

Competitor A business that functions on the same level of distribution and in the same product market and geographic market as another business.

Competitive allowance A discount or payment made by a supplier to a customer in connection with a sale of goods which is intended to enable the supplier to meet a lower price offered by a competitor, or which is intended to enable the customer to compete more effectively in the sale of the supplier's products.

Conscious parallelism of action Similar conduct engaged in by competitors, not the product of any communication or joint action, which would be against the economic interests of any individual competitor if engaged in solely by it and not by its competitors.

Consignment (and related terms) An arrangement whereby a manufacturer sells its goods through distributors or dealers, relinquishing possession while retaining ownership of the goods.

Conspiracy Any agreement, express or implied, to accomplish an unlawful purpose, or to accomplish some purpose not in itself unlawful by unlawful means, and which requires voluntary assent to a common scheme or plan; a joint undertaking extending over a period of time with a common purpose, intent or design resulting from a combination or agreement, express or implied, to accomplish an unlawful end or to accomplish a lawful end by an unlawful means.

Contract An agreement, express or implied, based upon certain consideration, to perform a particular act.

Contribution A claim by one of several joint tort-feasors to be reimbursed by other participants in the same tort, which exists at common law and under the statutes of many states, when one joint tort-feasor has been compelled to pay a disproportionate share of a judgment that arose from a common tort.

Cooperative A form of collective business organization which usually exists to process, manufacture or sell the output of its owners or members.

Cooperative advertising Advertising which invites the public to purchase a manufacturer's products at a dealer's place of business and where the cost of the advertising is borne by the manufacturer alone or shared by the manufacturer and dealer.

Customer One who buys or leases goods from a Seller or lessor.

Customer Restriction An agreement limiting the classes of persons or restricting particular persons to whom a Buyer may sell goods.

D

Dealer A term that usually is intended to be synonymous with retailer, to describe a purchaser of goods for resale to consumers or end users.

Delivered price A delivered price is one which includes delivery charges (cost to Buyer's destination). In UCC terms, it is a CIF price.

Discount A discount is a deduction from the price of goods.

Distributor A business that functions at the wholesale level, purchasing goods for resale to retailers or dealers; in some instances, the term may describe a business that does not purchase for its own account, but receives goods on consignment, and resells them on behalf of a supplier.

Dual distribution A method of selling goods in which a business competes on more than one level in the chain of distribution, as, for example, when an automobile manufacturer that sells cars to independent dealers also competes with those dealers through the operation of company-owned dealerships.

E

End user A person or business at the end of the chain of distribution that uses or consumes the particular product, rather than purchasing the product for resale.

Exclusive dealing An agreement whereby Seller agrees to sell its goods only to a single Buyer in a particular geographical area, or an agreement whereby a Buyer of goods agrees with a Seller that Buyer will purchase only the Seller's goods, and will refrain from purchasing the goods of the Seller's competitors.

Exclusive distributorship Any one of three arrangements: (1) an agreement by Seller to sell its goods only to the Buyer in a particular location or geographic area; (2) an agreement by a Buyer to purchase, resell, and deal in the goods of a particular supplier to the exclusion of the goods of a competitor; and (3) an agreement by a Buyer to sell the goods of a supplier only in a particular geographic area.

F

Franchise An agreement under which a grantee (franchisee) is granted the right to engage in the business of offering, selling, or distributing goods or services under a marketing plan or system prescribed in substantial part by the grantor (franchisor); the operation of the business pursuant to such plan or system is substantially associated with the grantor's trademark, service marks, trade name, or logotype designating the grantor or its affiliate; and the grantee is required to pay, directly or indirectly, a fee.

Full-Line forcing The sale of a particular type or size of goods on condition that the purchaser purchase a complete inventory of goods of a similar type, size or series from the same manufacturer.

Functional discounts Functional discounts are different prices charged to purchasers at different functional levels of distribution; a higher price is generally charged to the purchaser at the level farthest from the supplier in the chain of distribution. For example, a retailer may be charged more for goods than a wholesaler.

G

Goodwill An intangible property interest in a business that is derived from the business' reputation for quality and customer identification of the business name.

Goods A tangible product or item, othan than real property.

H

Horizontal market division An agreement between businesses that compete on the same level in the chain of distribution to divide either geographic areas (territorial allocation) or customers (customer allocation) among themselves for the purpose of eliminating competition.

Horizontal restraints Agreements between persons or businesses that function on the same level in a chain of distribution to restrict or eliminate competition.

House accounts House accounts are usually large end user customers to whom the supplier reserves the right to sell directly, usually to the exclusion of wholesalers, jobbers or dealers at lower levels in the chain of distribution.

I

Indirect purchaser doctrine An interpretation of §4 of the Clayton Act by the Supreme Court in *Illinois Brick Co v Illinois,* 431 US 720 (1977), under which (with certain exclusions) only a purchaser purchasing directly from a member of a horizontal price-fixing conspiracy is deemed to have suffered injury cognizable under the antitrust laws and is, therefore, entitled to sue for treble damages.

Injury to competition An adverse impact on the competitive conditions that exist in a particular market, as distinguished from an adverse impact on the business of the individual plaintiff.

Interstate commerce A practical concept that relates to business that is conducted in two or more states; a plaintiff attacking conduct under the Sherman Act or Clayton Act may establish the necessary connection with interstate commerce in either of two ways: by demonstrating that the alleged anticompetitive conduct occurred in interstate commerce, or by showing that the conduct had a substantial effect on the interstate commerce. A plaintiff seeking to establish a Robinson-Patman Act violation generally must demonstrate that products involved in a discriminatory sale actually moved across state lines.

Interbrand competition Competition between Sellers of different brands of similar goods, as, for example, the competition which exists between Coca-Cola and Pepsi-Cola.

Intrabrand Competition Competition between Sellers of the same brand of goods, as, for example, the competition which exists between competing Sellers of Ford automobiles.

J

Jobber One who purchases goods for resale to retailers. Jobbers do not usually maintain an inventory, or take physical possession of the goods, but arrange for them to be shipped directly from the supplier to the jobber's customer.

L

License An agreement under which an owner of a trademark or service mark (the *licensor*) grants to another person (the *licensee*) the limited right to use the trademark or service mark subject to adequate control by the licensor over the quality of goods or services provided by the licensee.

List price The price stated on a printed price list usually prepared by the manufacturer, which may or may not be the actual selling price.

Location restriction An agreement under which Seller obligates itself to sell goods to Buyer at a particular location, and a requirement that Buyer offer goods for resale only from a specified location.

M

Market A term referring to a particular class of products and/or a certain geographic area.

Market share The portion or percentage of a particular market possessed by a business.

Monopoly power The power to control prices or exclude competition.

P

Postsale services Services provided to an end user following the end user's purchase of a product. Postsale services include, for example, warranty service, product maintenance and repair services.

Presale services Services provided in connection with and to induce the sale of a product to the end user. Presale services include, for example, advertisements, product demonstrations, and training of salespersons.

Preticketing A form of suggested resale pricing by a supplier under which the goods are preprinted or tagged by the supplier with a suggested resale price. Potato chips, for example, are commonly sold with the suggested resale price preprinted on the bag.

Price The amount actually paid by a purchaser of goods.

Price discrimination Seller's charging unequal prices for goods of like grade and quality to competing purchasers in reasonably contemporaneous transactions.

Price-fixing Unlawful price-fixing consists of two types of agreements: (1) agreements between competitors coordinating pricing strategies (horizontal price-fixing agreements); (2) agreements between Buyers and Sellers whereby Buyer agrees that it will resell Seller's goods at an agreed-upon price or within a certain price range (vertical price-fixing agreements).

Price promotions Special discounts, generally of limited duration, given by a supplier to its customers, which are intended to increase sales of the supplier's products.

Price support A commitment, by a government or by a business, to take steps to insure a minimum price at which a product may be sold.

Profit pass-over clause A provision in a distribution or dealer agreement under which the distributor or dealer that makes a sale outside of its area of primary responsibility agrees to pay compensation (part of the profit) to the distributor or dealer in whose area the sale was made.

Promotional allowance A discount or payment made by a supplier to a customer in connection with a sale of goods whereby the supplier pays its customer for advertising the supplier's products for resale.

R

Rebate A refund of a portion of the purchase price of goods.

Reciprocal dealing Either the use of buying power to secure an advantage in the sale of one's products, or an agreement between two persons to purchase one another's products.

Refusal to deal Conduct whereby a person refuses initially or ceases to purchase the goods or services of a particular business or refuses to sell its own goods or services to a particular business. The legality of the refusal to deal depends upon whether it is a unilateral decision or the result of concerted action, and whether its purpose or effect is anticompetitive.

Relevant market The most narrowly defined market, both in product and geographic terms, so that products produced in areas not included within the geographic definition, or other products produced in the same area, but not included in the product definition, cannot compete on equal terms with those products included in the market.

Requirements contract An agreement under which Buyer agrees to purchase all the goods of a designated type that the Buyer may require for use in its business and Seller obligates itself to provide all such goods needed by the Buyer.

Resale The passing of title in goods from Seller to Buyer for a price, where the Seller did not manufacture the goods but purchased them for the purpose of sale rather than its own use or consumption.

Resale price maintenance A practice by which a seller of goods requires its purchasers to resell the goods at specified prices.

Retailer One who sells goods to consumers.

S

Sale The passing of title in goods from Seller to Buyer for a price.

Service Any result of useful labor which does not produce a tangible product or commodity.

Service mark A word, name, symbol, device, or any combination thereof adopted and used in the sale or advertising of services to identify the services of the person providing them and to distinguish them from the services of others.

T

Territorial restriction An agreement limiting the geographic area in which a Buyer may sell the goods of a supplier.

Trade name A word or phrase adopted by a business and used to symbolize the reputation of the business as a whole.

Trademark A sign, symbol or device adopted and used by a manufacturer and affixed to its goods for the purpose of distinguishing its goods from goods of the same general nature manufactured or sold by others.

Transshipping The practice of retailers' reselling products to other retailers.

Treble damages Triple damages; §4 of the Clayton Act allows a successful antitrust plaintiff to recover threefold its actual damages.

Tying An agreement under which a Buyer is required to purchase undesired products of a Seller as a condition to purchasing the Seller's desired products.

V

Vertical customer restrictions Agreements between Buyers and Sellers whereby Buyer agrees that it will resell Seller's goods only to a limited class of persons or to particular persons.

Vertical integration The performance by one business entity of functions on more than one level of distribution; for example, when a manufacturer *integrates forward* to perform distribution and/or retailing functions.

Vertical restraint A restriction imposed by Seller on Buyer which limits Buyer's discretion to resell Seller's products. Vertical restraints include resale price maintenance, customer restrictions, territorial restrictions, and location restrictions.

W

Wholesaler One who purchases goods for resale to retailers and usually maintains an inventory of such goods from which orders are filled, as distinguished from a *jobber* who usually arranges for direct shipment (or *drop shipment*) from the supplier directly to the retailer.

Appendix A
Sherman Antitrust Act
15 USC §§1, 2

§ 1.

Every contract, combination in the form of trust or otherwise, or conspiracy, in restraint of trade or commerce among the several States, or with foreign nations, is declared to be illegal. Every person who shall make any contract or engage in any combination or conspiracy hereby declared to be illegal shall be deemed guilty of a felony, and, on conviction thereof, shall be punished by fine not exceeding one million dollars if a corporation, or, if any other person, one hundred thousand dollars or by imprisonment not exceeding three years, or by both said punishments, in the discretion of the court.

§ 2.

Every person who shall monopolize, or attempt to monopolize, or combine or conspire with any other person or persons, to monopolize any part of the trade or commerce among the several States, or with foreign nations, shall be deemed guilty of a felony, and, on conviction thereof, shall be punished by fine not exceeding one million dollars if a corporation, or, if any other person, one hundred thousand dollars or by imprisonment not exceeding three years, or by both said punishments, in the discretion of the court.

Appendix B
Selected Provisions of the Clayton Act as codified at 15 USC §12 *et seq.*

§ 12.

(a) "Antitrust laws," as used herein, includes the Act entitled "An Act to protect trade and commerce against unlawful restraints and monopolies," approved July second, eighteen hundred and ninety; sections seventy-three to seventy-seven, inclusive, of an Act entitled "An Act to reduce taxation, to provide revenue for the Government, and for other purposes," of August twenty-seventh, eighteen hundred and ninety-four; an Act entitled "An Act to amend sections seventy-three and seventy-six of the Act of August twenty-seventh, eighteen hundred and ninety-four, entitled 'An Act to reduce taxation, to provide revenue for the Government, and for other purposes,' " approved February twelfth, nineteen hundred and thirteen; and also this Act.

"Commerce," as used herein, means trade or commerce among the several States and with foreign nations, or between the District of Columbia or any Territory of the United States and any State, Territory, or foreign nation, or between any insular possessions or other places under the jurisdiction of the United States, or between any such possession or place and any State or Territory of the United States or the District of Columbia or any foreign nation, or within the District of Columbia or any Territory or any insular possession or other place under the jurisdiction of the United States: *Provided,* That nothing in this Act contained shall apply to the Philippine Islands.

The word "person" or "persons" wherever used in this Act shall be deemed to include corporations and associations existing under or authorized by the laws of either the United States, the laws of any of the Territories, the laws of any State, or the laws of any foreign country.

(b) This Act may be cited as the "Clayton Act".

[for §§13-13b see Appendix C, Robinson-Patman Act]

§ 14.

It shall be unlawful for any person engaged in commerce, in the course of such commerce, to lease or make a sale or contract for sale of goods, wares, merchandise, machinery, supplies, or other commodities, whether patented or unpatented, for use, consumption, or resale within the United States or any Territory thereof or the District of Columbia or any insular possession or other place under the jurisdiction of the United States, or fix a price charged therefor, or discount from, or rebate upon, such price, on the condition, agreement, or understanding that the lessee or purchaser thereof shall not use or deal in the goods, wares, merchandise, machinery, supplies, or other commodities of a competitor or competitors of the lessor or seller, where the effect of such lease, sale, or contract for sale or such condition, agreement, or understanding may be to substantially lessen competition or tend to create a monopoly in any line of commerce.

§ 15.

Any person who shall be injured in his business or property by reason of anything forbidden in the antitrust laws may sue therefor in any district court of the United States in the district in which the defendant resides or is found or has an agent, without respect to the amount in controversy, and shall recover threefold the damages by him sustained, and the cost of suit, including a reasonable attorney's fee. The court may award under this section, pursuant to a motion by such person promptly made, simple interest on actual damages for the period beginning on the date of service of such person's pleading setting forth a claim under the antitrust laws and ending on the date of judgment, or for any shorter period therein, if the court finds that the award of such interest for such period is just in the circumstances. In determining whether an award of interest under this section for any period is just in the circumstances, the court shall consider only—

(1) whether such person or the opposing party, or either party's representative, made motions or asserted claims or defenses so lacking in merit as to show that such party or representative acted intentionally for delay, or otherwise acted in bad faith;

(2) whether, in the course of the action involved, such person or the opposing party, or either party's representative, violated any applicable rule, statute, or court order providing for sanctions for dilatory behavior or otherwise providing for expeditious proceedings; and

(3) whether such person or the opposing party, or either party's representative, engaged in conduct primarily for the purpose of delaying the litigation or increasing the cost thereof.

[§15a, suits by United States omitted]

§ 15b.

Any action to enforce any cause of action under sections 15, 15a, or 15c of this title shall be forever barred unless commenced within four years after the cause of action accrued. No cause of action barred under existing law on the effective date of this section and sections 15a and 16 of this title shall be revived by said sections.

[§15c, actions by state attorneys general as parens patriae, and §§15d-15h omitted]

§ 16.

(a) A final judgment or decree heretofore or hereafter rendered in any civil or criminal proceeding brought by or on behalf of the United States under the antitrust laws to the effect that a defendant has violated said laws shall be prima facie evidence against such defendant in any action or proceeding brought by any other party against such defendant under said laws as to all matters respecting which said judgment or decree would be an estoppel as between the parties thereto: *Provided,* That this section shall not apply to consent judgments or decrees entered before any testimony has been taken. Nothing contained in this section shall be construed to impose any limitation on the application of collateral estoppel, except that, in any action or proceeding brought under the antitrust laws, collateral estoppel effect shall not be given to any finding made by the Federal Trade Commission under the antitrust laws or under section 45 of this title which could give rise to a claim for relief under the antitrust laws.

[§§16b-16i, consent judgments, omitted]

[§17, labor and agricultural organization exemption omitted]

[§§18-18a, mergers and acquisitions omitted]

[§19, interlocking directorates and officers omitted]

[§20, acquisitions by common carriers omitted]

[§21, enforcement provisions omitted]

§ 22.

Any suit, action, or proceeding under the antitrust laws against a corporation may be brought not only in the judicial district whereof it is an inhabitant, but also in any district wherein it may be found or transacts business; and all process in such cases may be served in the district of which it is an inhabitant, or wherever it may be found.

[§23, subpoenas for witnesses in suits by United States omitted]

§ 24.

Whenever a corporation shall violate any of the penal provisions of the antitrust laws, such violation shall be deemed to be also that of the individual directors, officers, or agents of such corporation who shall have authorized, ordered, or done any of the acts constituting in whole or in part such violation, and such violation shall be deemed a misdemeanor, and upon conviction therefor of any such director, officer, or agent he shall be punished by a fine of not exceeding $5,000 or by imprisonment for not exceeding one year, or by both, in the discretion of the court.

§ 25.

The several district courts of the United States are invested with jurisdiction to prevent and restrain violations of this Act, and it shall be the duty of the several United States attorneys, in their respective districts, under the direction of the Attorney General, to institute proceedings in equity to prevent and restrain such violations. Such proceedings may be by way of petition setting forth the case and praying that such violation shall be enjoined or otherwise prohibited. When the parties complained of shall have been duly notified of such petition, the court shall proceed, as soon as may be, to the hearing and determination of the case; and pending such petition, and before final decree, the court may at any time make such temporary restraining order or prohibition as shall be deemed just in the premises. Whenever it shall appear to the court before which any such proceeding may be pending that the ends of justice require that other parties should be brought before the court, the court may cause them to be summoned whether they reside in the district in which the court is held or not, and subpoenas to that end may be served in any district by the marshal thereof.

§ 26.

Any person, firm, corporation, or association shall be entitled to sue for and have injunctive relief, in any court of the United States having jurisdiction over the parties, against threatened loss or damage by a violation of the antitrust laws, including sections 13, 14, 18, and 19 of this title, when and under the same conditions and principles as injunctive relief against threatened conduct that will cause loss or damage is granted by courts of equity, under the rules governing such proceedings, and upon the execution of proper bond against damages for an injunction improvidently granted and a showing that the danger of irreparable loss or damage is immediate, a preliminary injunction may issue: *Provided,* That nothing herein contained shall be construed to entitle any person, firm, corporation, or association, except the United States, to bring suit in equity for injunctive relief against any common carrier subject to the provisions of the Act to regulate commerce, approved February fourth, eighteen hundred and eighty-seven, in respect of any matter subject to the regulation, supervision, or other jurisdiction of the Interstate Commerce Commission. In any action under this section in which the plaintiff substantially prevails, the court shall award the cost of suit, including a reasonable attorney's fee, to such plaintiff.

[§26a, restrictions on purchase of gasohol omitted]
[§27, severability omitted]
[§28, expedited actions by United States omitted]
[§29, appeal procedures, omitted]
[§30, depositions for suits in equity omitted]
[§31, Panama Canal closed to violators omitted]

Appendix C
Robinson-Patman Act Amendment to §2 of the Clayton Act
15 USC §§13-13b

§ 13.

(a) It shall be unlawful for any person engaged in commerce, in the course of such commerce, either directly or indirectly, to discriminate in price between different purchasers of commodities of like grade and quality, where either or any of the purchases involved in such discrimination are in commerce, where such commodities are sold for use, consumption, or resale within the United States or any Territory thereof or the District of Columbia or any insular possession or other place under the jurisdiction of the United States, and where the effect of such discrimination may be substantially to lessen competition or tend to create a monopoly in any line of commerce, or to injure, destroy, or prevent competition with any person who either grants or knowingly receives the benefit of such discrimination, or with customers of either of them: *Provided,* That nothing herein contained shall prevent differentials which make only due allowance for differences in the cost of manufacture, sale, or delivery resulting from the differing methods or quantities in which such commodities are to such purchasers sold or delivered: *Provided, however,* That the Federal Trade Commission may, after due investigation and hearing to all interested parties, fix and establish quantity limits, and revise the same as it finds necessary, as to particular commodities or classes of commodities, where it finds that available purchasers in greater quantities are so few as to render differentials on account thereof unjustly discriminatory or promotive of monopoly in any line of commerce; and the foregoing shall then not be construed to permit differentials based on differences in quantities greater than those so fixed and established: *And provided further,* That nothing herein contained shall prevent persons engaged in selling goods, wares, or merchandise in commerce from selecting their own customers in bona fide transactions and not in restraint of trade: *And provided further,* That nothing herein contained shall prevent price changes from time to time where in response to changing conditions affecting the market for or the marketability of the goods concerned, such as but not limited to actual or imminent deterioration of perishable goods, obsolescence of seasonal goods, distress sales under court process, or sales in good faith in discontinuance of business in the goods concerned.

(b) Upon proof being made, at any hearing on a complaint under this section, that there has been discrimination in price or services or facilities furnished, the burden of rebutting the prima-facie case thus made by showing justification shall be upon the person charged with a violation of this section, and unless justification shall be affirmatively shown, the Commission is authorized to issue an order terminating the discrimination: *Provided, however,* That nothing herein contained shall prevent a seller rebutting the prima-facie case thus made by showing that his lower price or the furnishing of services or facilities to any purchaser or purchasers was made in good faith to meet an equally low price of a competitor, or the services or facilities furnished by a competitor.

(c) It shall be unlawful for any person engaged in commerce, in the course of such commerce, to pay or grant, or to receive or accept, anything of value as a commission, brokerage, or other compensation, or any allowance or discount in lieu thereof, except for services rendered in connection with the sale or purchase of goods, wares, or merchandise, either to the other party to such transaction or to an agent, representative, or other intermediary therein where such intermediary is acting in fact for or in behalf, or is subject to the direct or indirect control, of any party to such transaction other than the person by whom such compensation is so granted or paid.

(d) It shall be unlawful for any person engaged in commerce to pay or contract for the payment of anything of value to or for the benefit of a customer of such person in the course of such commerce as compensation or in consideration for any services or facilities furnished by or through such customer in connection with the processing, handling, sale, or offering for sale of any products or commodities manufactured, sold, or offered for sale by such person, unless such payment or consideration is available on proportionally equal terms to all other customers competing in the distribution of such products or commodities.

(e) It shall be unlawful for any person to discriminate in favor of one purchaser against another purchaser or purchasers of a commodity bought for resale, with or without processing, by contracting to furnish or furnishing, or by contributing to the furnishing of, any services or facilities connected with the processing, handling, sale, or offering for sale of such commodity so purchased upon terms not accorded to all purchasers on proportionally equal terms.

(f) It shall be unlawful for any person engaged in commerce, in the course of such commerce, knowingly to induce or receive a discrimination in price which is prohibited by this section.

§ 13a.

It shall be unlawful for any person engaged in commerce, in the course of such commerce, to be a party to, or assist in, any transaction of sale, or contract to sell, which discriminates to his knowledge against competitors of the purchaser, in that, any discount, rebate, allowance, or advertising service charge is granted to the purchaser over and above any discount, rebate, allowance, or advertising service charge available at the time of such transaction to said competitors in respect of a sale of goods of like grade, quality, and quantity; to sell, or contract to sell, goods in any part of the United States at prices lower than those exacted by said person elsewhere in the United States for the purpose of destroying competition, or eliminating a competitor in such part of the United States; or, to sell, or contract to sell, goods at unreasonably low prices for the purpose of destroying competition or eliminating a competitor.

Any person violating any of the provisions of this section shall, upon conviction thereof, be fined not more than $5,000 or imprisoned not more than one year, or both.

§ 13b.

Nothing in sections 13 to 13b and 21a of this title shall prevent a cooperative association from returning to its members, producers, or consumers the whole, or any part of, the net earnings or surplus resulting from its trading operations, in proportion to their purchases or sales from, to, or through the association.

Appendix D
Selected Provisions of the Federal Trade Commission Act
15 USC §41 *et seq*

§ 44.

The words defined in this section shall have the following meaning when found in sections 41 to 46 and 47 to 58 of this title, to wit:

"Commerce" means commerce among the several States or with foreign nations, or in any Territory of the United States or in the District of Columbia, or between any such Territory and another, or between any such Territory and any State or foreign nation, or between the District of Columbia and any State or Territory or foreign nation.

"Corporation" shall be deemed to include any company, trust, so-called Massachusetts trust, or association, incorporated or unincorporated, which is organized to carry on business for its own profit or that of its members, and has shares of capital or capital stock or certificates of interest, and any company, trust, so-called Massachusetts trust, or association, incorporated or unincorporated, without shares of capital or capital stock or certificates of interest, except partnerships, which is organized to carry on business for its own profit or that of its members.

"Documentary evidence" includes all documents, papers, correspondence, books of account, and financial and corporate records.

"Acts to regulate commerce" means the Act entitled "An Act to regulate commerce", approved February 14, 1887,[1] and all Acts amendatory thereof and supplementary thereto and the Communications Act of 1934 and all Acts amendatory thereof and supplementary thereto.

"Antitrust Acts" means the Act entitled "An Act to protect trade and commerce against unlawful restraints and monopolies", approved July 2, 1890; also sections 73 to 77, of an Act entitled "An Act to reduce taxation, to provide revenue for the Government, and for other purposes", approved August 27, 1894; also the Act entitled "An Act to amend sections 73 and 76 of the Act of August 27, 1894, entitled 'An Act to reduce taxation, to provide revenue for the Government, and for other purposes' ", approved February 12, 1913; and also the Act entitled "An Act to supplement existing laws against unlawful restraints and monopolies, and for other purposes", approved October 15, 1914.

§ 45.

(a)(1) Unfair methods of competition in or affecting commerce, and unfair or deceptive acts or practices in or affecting commerce, are declared unlawful.

(2) The Commission is empowered and directed to prevent persons, partnerships, or corporations, except banks, savings and loan institutions described in section 57a(f)(3) of this title, common carriers subject to the Acts to regulate commerce, air carriers and foreign air carriers subject to the Federal Aviation Act of 1958, and persons, partnerships, or corporations insofar as they are subject to the Packers and Stockyards Act of 1921, as amended, except as provided in section 406(b) of said Act, from using unfair methods of competition in or affecting commerce and unfair or deceptive acts or practices in or affecting commerce.

§ 52.

(a) It shall be unlawful for any person, partnership, or corporation to disseminate, or cause to be disseminated, any false advertisement—

> (1) By United States mails, or in or having an effect upon commerce by any means, for the purpose of inducing, or which is likely to induce, directly or indirectly the purchase of food, drugs, devices, or cosmetics; or
>
> (2) By any means, for the purpose of inducing, or which is likely to induce, directly or indirectly, the purchase in or having an effect upon commerce of food, drugs, devices, or cosmetics.

(b) The dissemination or the causing to be disseminated of any false advertisement within the provisions of subsection (a) of this section shall be an unfair or deceptive act or practice in or affecting commerce within the meaning of section 45 of this title.

§ 53.

(a) Whenever the Commission has reason to believe—

> (1) that any person, partnership, or corporation is engaged in, or is about to engage in, the dissemination or the causing of the dissemination of any advertisement in violation of section 52 of this title, and
>
> (2) that the enjoining thereof pending the issuance of a complaint by the Commission under section 45 of this title, and until such complaint is dismissed by the Commission or set aside by the court on review, or the order of the Commission to cease and desist made thereon has become final within the meaning of section 45 of this title, would be to the interest of the public.

the Commission by any of its attorneys designated by it for such purpose may bring suit in a district court of the United States or in the United States court of any Territory, to enjoin the dissemination or the causing of the dissemination of such advertisement. Upon proper showing a temporary injunction or restraining order shall be granted without bond. Any such suit shall be brought in the district in which such person, partnership, or corporation resides or transacts business.

(b) Whenever the Commission has reason to believe—

> (1) that any person, partnership, or corporation is violating, or is about to violate, any provision of law enforced by the Federal Trade Commission, and
>
> (2) that the enjoining thereof pending the issuance of a complaint by the Commission and until such complaint is dismissed by the Commission or set aside by the court on review, or until the order of the Commission made thereon has become final, would be in the interest of the public—

the Commission by any of its attorneys designated by it for such purpose may bring suit in a district court of the United States to enjoin any such act or practice. Upon a proper showing that, weighing the equities and considering the Commission's likelihood of ultimate success, such action would be in the public interest, and after notice to the defendant, a temporary restraining order or a preliminary injunction may be granted without bond: *Provided, however,* That if a complaint is not filed within such period (not exceeding 20 days) as may be specified by the court after issuance of the temporary restraining order or preliminary injunction, the order or injunction shall be dissolved by the court and be of no further force and effect: *Provided further,* That in proper cases the Commission may seek, and after proper proof, the court may issue, a permanent injunction. Any such suit shall be brought in the district in which such person, partnership, or corporation resides or transacts business.

(c) Whenever it appears to the satisfaction of the court in the case of a newspaper, magazine, periodical, or other publication, published at regular intervals—

> (1) that restraining the dissemination of a false advertisement in any particular issue of such publication would delay the delivery of such issue after the regular time therefor, and
>
> (2) that such delay would be due to the method by which the manufacture and distribution of such publication is customarily conducted by the publisher in accordance with sound business practice, and not to any method or device adopted for the evasion of this section or to prevent or delay the issuance of an injunction or restraining order with respect to such false advertisement or any other advertisement,

the court shall exclude such issue from the operation of the restraining order or injunction.

§ 55.

For the purposes of sections 52 to 54 of this title—

(a)(1) The term "false advertisement" means an advertisement, other than labeling, which is misleading in a material respect; and in determining whether any advertisement is misleading, there shall be taken into account (among other things) not only representations made or suggested by statement, word, design, device, sound, or any combination thereof, but also the extent to which the advertisement fails to reveal facts material in the light of such representations or material with respect to consequences which may result from the use of the commodity to which the advertisement relates under the conditions prescribed in said advertisement, or under such conditions as are customary or usual. No advertisement of a drug shall be deemed to be false if it is disseminated only to members of the medical profession, contains no false representation of a material fact, and includes, or is accompanied in each instance by truthful disclosure of, the formula showing quantitatively each ingredient of such drug.

Appendix E
Federal Trade Commission Franchising Rule
16 CFR Pt 436

PART 436—DISCLOSURE REQUIREMENTS AND PROHIBITIONS CONCERNING FRANCHISING AND BUSINESS OPPORTUNITY VENTURES

AUTHORITY: 38 Stat. 717, as amended, 15 U.S.C. 41-58.

SOURCE: 43 FR 59614, Dec 21, 1978, unless otherwise noted.

§ 436.1 The Rule.

In connection with the advertising, offering, licensing, contracting, sale, or other promotion in or affecting commerce, as "commerce" is defined in the Federal Trade Commission Act, of any franchise, or any relationship which is represented either orally or in writing to be a franchise, it is an unfair or deceptive act or practice within the meaning of section 5 of that Act for any franchisor or franchise broker:

(a) To fail to furnish any prospective franchisee with the following information accurately, clearly, and concisely stated, in a legible, written document at the earlier of the "time for making of disclosures" or the first "personal meeting":

(1)(i) The official name and address and principal place of business of the franchisor, and of the parent firm or holding company of the franchisor, if any;

(ii) The name under which the franchisor is doing or intends to do business; and

(iii) The trademarks, trade names, service marks, advertising or other commercial symbols (hereinafter collectively referred to as "marks") which identify the goods, commodities, or services to be offered, sold, or distributed by the prospective franchisee, or under which the prospective franchisee will be operating.

(2) The business experience during the past 5 years, stated individually, of each of the franchisor's current directors and executive officers (including, and hereinafter to include, the chief executive and chief operating officer, financial, franchise marketing, training and service officers). With regard to each person listed, those persons' principal occupations and employers must be included.

(3) The business experience of the franchisor and the franchisor's parent firm (if any), including the length of time each: (i) Has conducted a business of the type to be operated by the franchisee; (ii) has offered or sold a franchise for such business; (iii) has conducted a business or offered or sold a franchise for a business (A) operating under a name using any mark set forth under paragraph (a)(1)(iii) of this section, or (B) involving the sale, offering, or distribution of goods, commodities, or services which are identified by any mark set forth under paragraph (a)(1)(iii) of this section; and (iv) has offered for sale or sold franchises in other lines of business, together with a description of such other lines of business.

(4) A statement disclosing who, if any, of the persons listed in paragraphs (a)(2) and (a)(3) of this section:

(i) Has, at any time during the previous seven fiscal years, been convicted of a felony or pleaded nolo contendere to a felony charge if the felony involved fraud (including violation of any franchise law, or unfair or deceptive practices law), embezzlement, fraudulent conversion, misappropriation of property, or restraint of trade;

(ii) Has, at any time during the previous seven fiscal years, been held liable in a civil action resulting in a final judgment or has settled out of court any civil action or is a party to any civil action (A) involving allegations of fraud (including violation of any franchise law, or unfair or deceptive practices law), embezzlement, fraudulent conversion, misappropriation of property, or restraint of trade, or (B) which was brought by a present or former franchisee or franchisees and which involves or involved the franchise relationship; *Provided, however,* That only material individual civil actions need be so listed pursuant to this paragraph (4)(ii), including any group of civil actions which, irrespective of the materiality of any single such action, in the aggregate is material;

(iii) Is subject to any currently effective State or Federal agency or court injunctive or restrictive order, or is a party to a proceeding currently pending in which such order is sought, relating to or affecting franchise activities or the franchisor-franchisee relationship, or involving fraud (including violation of any franchise law, or unfair or deceptive practices law), embezzlement, fraudulent conversion, misappropriation of property, or restraint of trade.

Such statement shall set forth the identity and location of the court or agency; the date of conviction, judgment, or decision; the penalty imposed; the damages assessed; the terms of settlement or the terms of the order; and the date, nature, and issuer of each such order or ruling. A franchisor may include a summary opinion of counsel as to any pending litigation, but only if counsel's consent to the use of such opinion is included in the disclosure statement.

(5) A statement disclosing who, if any, of the persons listed in paragraphs

(a)(2) and (a)(3) of this section at any time during the previous 7 fiscal years has:

(i)Filed in bankruptcy;

(ii) Been adjudged bankrupt;

(iii) Been reorganized due to insolvency; or

(iv) Been a principal, director, executive officer, or partner of any other person that has so filed or was so adjudged or reorganized, during or within 1 year after the period that such person held such position in such other person. If so, the name and location of the person having so filed, or having been so adjudged or reorganized, the date thereof, and any other material facts relating thereto, shall be set forth.

(6) A factual description of the franchise offered to be sold by the franchisor.

(7) A statement of the total funds which must be paid by the franchisee to the franchisor or to a person affiliated with the franchisor, or which the franchisor or such affiliated person imposes or collects in whole or in part on behalf of a third party, in order to obtain or commence the franchise operation, such as initial franchise fees, deposits, downpayments, prepaid rent, and equipment and inventory purchases. If all or part of these fees or deposits are returnable under certain conditions, these conditions shall be set forth; and if not returnable, such fact shall be disclosed.

(8) A statement describing any recurring funds required to be paid, in connection with carrying on the franchise business, by the franchisee to the franchisor or to a person affiliated with the franchisor, or which the franchisor or such affiliated person imposes or collects in whole or in part on behalf of a third party, including, but not limited to, royalty, lease, advertising, training, and sign rental fees, and equipment or inventory purchases.

(9) A statement setting forth the name of each person (including the franchisor) the franchisee is directly or indirectly required or advised to do business with by the franchisor, where such persons are affiliated with the franchisor.

(10) A statement describing any real estate, services, supplies, products, inventories, signs, fixtures, or equipment relating to the establishment or the operation of the franchise business which the franchisee is directly or indirectly required by the franchisor to purchase, lease or rent; and if such purchases, leases or rentals must be made from specific persons (including the franchisor), a list of the names and addresses of each such person. Such list may be made in a separate document delivered to the prospective franchisee with the prospectus if the existence of such separate document is disclosed in the prospectus.

(11) A description of the basis for calculating, and, if such information is readily available, the actual amount of, any revenue or other consideration to be received by the franchisor or persons affiliated with the franchisor from suppliers to the prospective franchisee in consideration for goods or services which the franchisor requires or advises the franchisee to obtain from such suppliers.

(12)(i) A statement of all the material terms and conditions of any financing arrangement offered directly or indirectly by the franchisor, or any person affiliated with the franchisor, to the prospective franchisee; and

(ii) A description of the terms by which any payment is to be received by the franchisor from (A) any person offering financing to a prospective franchisee; and (B) any person arranging for financing for a prospective franchisee.

(13) A statement describing the material facts of whether, by the terms of the franchise agreement or other device or practice, the franchisee is:

(i) Limited in the goods or services he or she may offer for sale;

(ii) Limited in the customers to whom he or she may sell such goods or services;

(iii) Limited in the geographic area in which he or she may offer for sale or sell goods or services; or

(iv) Granted territorial protection by the franchisor, by which, with respect to a territory or area, (A) the franchisor will not establish another, or more than any fixed number of, franchises or company-owned outlets, either operating under, or selling, offering, or distributing goods, commodities or services, identified by any mark set forth under paragraph (a)(1)(iii) of this section; or (B) the franchisor or its parent will not establish other franchises or company-owned outlets selling or leasing the same or similar products or services under a different trade name, trademark, service mark, advertising or other commercial symbol.

(14) A statement of the extent to which the franchisor requires the franchisee (or, if the franchisee is a corporation, any person affiliated with the franchisee) to participate personally in the direct operation of the franchise.

(15) A statement disclosing, with respect to the franchise agreement and any related agreements:

(i) The term (i.e., duration of arrangement), if any, of such agreement, and whether such term is or may be affected by any agreement (including leases or subleases) other than the one from which such term arises;

(ii) The conditions under which the franchisee may renew or extend;

(iii) The conditions under which the franchisor may refuse to renew or extend;

(iv) The conditions under which the franchisee may terminate;

(v) The conditions under which the franchisor may terminate;

(vi) The obligations (including lease or sublease obligations) of the franchisee after termination of the franchise by the franchisor, and the obligations of the franchisee (including lease or sublease obligations) after termination of the franchise by the franchisee and after the expiration of the franchise;

(vii) The franchisee's interest upon termination of the franchise, or upon refusal to renew or extend the franchise, whether by the franchisor or by the franchisee;

(viii) The conditions under which the franchisor may repurchase, whether by right of first refusal or at the option of the franchisor (and if the franchisor has the option to repurchase the franchise, whether there will be an independent appraisal of the franchise, whether the repurchase price will be determined by a predetermined formula and whether there will be a recognition of goodwill or other intangibles associated therewith in the repurchase price to be given the franchisee);

(ix) The conditions under which the franchisee may sell or assign all or any interest in the ownership of the franchise, or of the assets of the franchise business;

(x) The conditions under which the franchisor may sell or assign, in whole or in part, its interest under such agreements;

(xi) The conditions under which the franchisee may modify;

(xii) The conditions under which the franchisor may modify;

(xiii) The rights of the franchisee's heirs or personal representative upon the death or incapacity of the franchisee; and

(xiv) The provisions of any covenant not to compete.

(16) A statement disclosing, with respect to the franchisor and as to the particular named business being offered:

(i) The total number of franchises operating at the end of the preceding fiscal year;

(ii) The total number of company-owned outlets operating at the end of the preceding fiscal year;

(iii) The names, addresses, and telephone numbers of (A) The 10 franchised outlets of the named franchise business nearest the prospective franchisee's intended location; or (B) all franchisees of the franchisor, or (C) all franchisees of the franchisor in the State in which the prospective franchisee lives or where the proposed franchise is to be located, *Provided, however,* That there are more than 10 such franchisees. If the number of franchisees to be disclosed pursuant to paragraph (a)(16)(iii)(B) or (C) of this section exceeds 50, such listing may be made in a separate document delivered to the prospective franchisee with the prospectus if the existence of such separate document is disclosed in the prospectus;

(iv) The number of franchises voluntarily terminated or not renewed by franchisees within, or at the conclusion of, the term of the franchise agreement, during the preceding fiscal year;

(v) The number of franchises reacquired by purchase by the franchisor during the term of the franchise agreement, and upon the conclusion of the term of the franchise agreement, during the preceding fiscal year;

(vi) The number of franchises otherwise reacquired by the franchisor during the term of the franchise agreement, and upon the conclusion of the term of the franchise agreement, during the preceding fiscal year;

(vii) The number of franchises for which the franchisor refused renewal of the franchise agreement or other agreements relating to the franchise during the preceding fiscal year; and

(viii) The number of franchises that were canceled or terminated by the franchisor during the term of the franchise agreement, and upon conclusion of the term of the franchise agreement, during the preceding fiscal year.

With respect to the disclosures required by paragraphs (a)(16) (v), (vi), (vii), and (viii) of this section, the disclosure statement shall also include a general categorization of the reasons for such reacquisitions, refusals to renew or terminations, and the number falling within each such category, including but not limited to the following: failure to comply with quality control standards, failure to make sufficient sales, and other breaches of contract.

(17) (i) If site selection or approval thereof by the franchisor is involved in the franchise relationship, a statement disclosing the range of time that has elapsed between signing of franchise agreements or other agreements relating to the franchise and site selection, for agreements entered into during the preceding fiscal year; and

(ii) If operating franchise outlets are to be provided by the franchisor, a statement disclosing the range of time that has elapsed between the signing of franchise agreements or other agreements relating to the franchise and the commencement of the franchisee's business, for agreements entered into during the preceding fiscal year.

With respect to the disclosures required by paragraphs (a)(17) (i) and (ii) of this section, a franchisor may at its option also provide a distribution chart using meaningful classifications with respect to such ranges of time.

(18) If the franchisor offers an initial training program or informs the prospective franchisee that it intends to provide such person with initial training, a statement disclosing:

(i) The type and nature of such training;

(ii) The minimum amount, if any, of training that will be provided to a franchisee; and

(iii) The cost, if any, to be borne by the franchisee for the training to be provided, or for obtaining such training.

(19) If the name of a public figure is used in connection with a recommendation to purchase a franchise, or as a part of the name of the franchise operation, or if the public figure is stated to be involved with the management of the franchisor, a statement disclosing:

(i) The nature and extent of the public figure's involvement and obligations to the franchisor, including but not limited to the promotional assistance the public figure will provide to the franchisor and to the franchisee;

(ii) The total investment of the public figure in the franchise operation; and

(iii) The amount of any fee or fees the franchisee will be obligated to pay for such involvement or assistance provided by the public figure.

(20) (i) A balance sheet (statement of financial position) for the franchisor for the most recent fiscal year, and an income statement (statement of results of operations) and statement of changes in financial position for the franchisor for the most recent 3 fiscal years. Such statements are required to have been examined in accordance with generally accepted auditing standards by an independent certified or licensed public accountant.

Provided, however, That where a franchisor is a subsidiary of another corporation which is permitted under generally accepted accounting principles to prepare financial statements on a consolidated or combined statement basis, the above information may be submitted for the parent if (A) the corresponding unaudited financial statements of the franchisor are also provided, and (B) the parent absolutely and irrevocably has agreed to guarantee all obligations of the subsidiary;

(ii) Unaudited statements shall be used only to the extent that audited statements have not been made, and provided that such statements are accompanied by a clear and conspicuous disclosure that they are unaudited. Statements shall be prepared on an audited basis as soon as practicable, but, at a minimum, financial statements for the first full fiscal year following the date on which the franchisor must first comply with this part shall contain a balance sheet opinion prepared by an independent certified or licensed public accountant, and financial statements for the following fiscal year shall be fully audited.

(21) All of the foregoing information in paragraph (a) (1) through (20) of this section shall be contained in a single disclosure statement or prospectus, which shall not contain any materials or information other than that required by this part or by State law not preempted by this part. This does not preclude franchisors or franchise brokers from giving other nondeceptive information orally, visually, or in separate literature so long as such information is not contradictory to the information in the disclosure statement required by paragraph (a) of this section. This disclosure statement shall carry a cover sheet distinctively and conspicuously showing the name of the franchisor, the date of issuance of the disclosure statement, and the following notice imprinted thereon in upper and lower case bold-face type of not less than 12 point size:

Information for Prospective Franchisees Required by Federal Trade Commission

* * * * *

To protect you, we've required your franchisor to give you this information. *We haven't checked it, and don't know if it's correct.* It should help you make up your mind. Study it carefully. While it includes some information about your contract, don't rely on it alone to understand your contract. Read all of your contract carefully. Buying a franchise is a complicated investment. Take your time to decide. If possible, show your contract and this information to an advisor, like a lawyer or an accountant. If you find anything you think may be wrong or anything important that's been left out, you should let us know about it. It may be against the law.

There may also be laws on franchising in your state. Ask your state agencies about them.

FEDERAL TRADE COMMISSION,
Washington, D.C.

Provided, That the obligation to furnish such disclosure statement shall be deemed to have been met for both the franchisor and the franchise broker if either such party furnishes the prospective franchisee with such disclosure statement.

(22) All information contained in the disclosure statement shall be current as of the close of the franchisor's most recent fiscal year. After the close of each fiscal year, the franchisor shall be given a period not exceeding 90 days to prepare a revised disclosure statement and, following such 90 days, may distribute only the revised prospectus and no other. The franchisor shall, within

a reasonable time after the close of each quarter of the fiscal year, prepare revisions to be attached to the disclosure statement to reflect any material change in the franchisor or relating to the franchise business of the franchisor, about which the franchisor or franchise broker, or any agent, representative, or employee thereof, knows or should know. Each prospective franchisee shall have in his or her possession, at the "time for making of disclosures," the disclosure statement and quarterly revision for the period most recent to the "time for making of disclosures" and available at that time. Information which is required to be audited pursuant to paragraph (a)(20) of this section is not required to be audited for quarterly revisions, *Provided, however,* That the unaudited information be accompanied by a statement in immediate conjunction therewith that clearly and conspicuously discloses that such information has not been audited.

(23) A table of contents shall be included within the disclosure statement.

(24) The disclosure statement shall include a comment which either positively or negatively responds to each disclosure item required to be in the disclosure statement, by use of a statement which fully incorporates the information required by the item. Each disclosure item therein must be preceded by the appropriate heading, as set forth in Note 3 of this part.

(b) To make any oral, written, or visual representation to a prospective franchisee which states a specific level of potential sales, income, gross or net profit for that prospective franchisee, or which states other facts which suggest such a specific level, unless:

(1) At the time such representation is made, such representation is relevant to the geographic market in which the franchise is to be located;

(2) At the time such representation is made, a reasonable basis exists for such representation and the franchisor has in its possession material which constitutes a reasonable basis for such representation, and such material is made available to any prospective franchisee and to the Commission or its staff upon reasonable demand.

Provided, further, That in immediate conjunction with such representation, the franchisor shall disclose in a clear and conspicuous manner that such material is available to the prospective franchisee; and *Provided, however,* That no provision within paragraph (b) of this section shall be construed as requiring the disclosure to any prospective franchisee of the identity of any specific franchisee or of information reasonably likely to lead to the disclosure of such person's identity; and *Provided, further,* That no additional representation as to a prospective franchisee's potential sales, income, or profits may be made later than the "time for making of disclosures";

(3) Such representation is set forth in detail along with the material bases and assumptions therefor in a single legible written document whose text accurately, clearly, and concisely discloses such information, and none other than that provided for by this part or by State law not preempted by this part. Each prospective franchisee to whom the representation is made shall be furnished with such document no later than the "time for making of disclosures"; *Provided, however,* That if the representation is made at or prior to a

"personal meeting" and such meeting occurs before the "time for making of disclosures", the document shall be furnished to the prospective franchisee to whom the representation is made at that "personal meeting";

(4) The following statement is clearly and conspicuously disclosed in the document described by paragraph (b)(3) of this section in immediate conjunction with such representation and in not less than twelve point upper and lower-case boldface type:

CAUTION

These figures are only estimates of what we think you may earn. There is no assurance you'll do as well. If you rely upon our figures, you must accept the risk of not doing as well.

(5) The following information is clearly and conspicuously disclosed in the document described by paragraph (b)(3) of this section in immediate conjunction with such representation:

(i) The number and percentage of outlets of the named franchise business which are located in the geographic markets that form the basis for any such representation and which are known to the franchisor or franchise broker to have earned or made at least the same sales, income, or profits during a period of corresponding length in the immediate past as those potential sales, income, or profits represented; and

(ii) The beginning and ending dates for the corresponding time period referred to by paragraph (b)(5)(i) of this section, *Provided, however,* That any franchisor without prior franchising experience as to the named franchise business so indicate such lack of experience in the document described in paragraph (b)(3) of this section.

Except, That representations of the sales, income or profits of existing franchise outlets need not comply with this paragraph (b).

(c) To make any oral, written or visual representation to a prospective franchisee which states a specific level of sales, income, gross or net profits of existing outlets (whether franchised or company-owned) of the named franchise business, or which states other facts which suggest such a specific level, unless:

(1) At the time such representation is made, such representation is relevant to the geographic market in which the franchise is to be located;

(2) At the time such representation is made, a reasonable basis exists for such representation and the franchisor has in its possession material which constitutes a reasonable basis for such representation, and such material is made available to any prospective franchisee and to the Commission or its staff upon reasonable demand,

Provided, however, That in immediate conjunction with such representation, the franchisor discloses in a clear and conspicuous manner that such material is available to the prospective franchisee; and *Provided, further,* That no provision within paragraph (c) of this section shall be construed as requiring the disclosure to any prospective franchisee of the identity of any specific franchisee or of information reasonably likely to lead to the disclosure of such person's identity; and *Provided, further,* That no additional representation as to the sales, income, or gross or net profits of existing outlets (whether franchised or company-owned) of the named franchise business may be made later than the "time for making of disclosures";

(3) Such representation is set forth in detail along with the material bases and assumptions therefor in a single legible written document which accurately, clearly and concisely discloses such information, and none other than that provided for by this part or by State law not preempted by this part. Each prospective franchisee to whom the representation is made shall be furnished with such document no later than the "time for making of disclosures",

Provided, however, That if the representation is made at or prior to a "personal meeting" and such meeting occurs before the "time for making of disclosures," the document shall be furnished to the prospective franchisee to whom the representation is made at that "personal meeting";

(4) The underlying data on which the representation is based have been prepared in accordance with generally accepted accounting principles;

(5) The following statement is clearly and conspicuously disclosed in the document described by paragraph (c)(3) of this section in immediate conjunction with such representation, and in not less than twelve point upper and lower case boldface type:

CAUTION

Some outlets have [sold] [earned] this amount. There is no assurance you'll do as well. If you rely upon our figures, you must accept the risk of not doing as well.

(6) The following information is clearly and conspicuously disclosed in the document described by paragraph (c)(3) of this section in immediate conjunction with such representation:

(i) The number and percentage of outlets of the named franchise business which are located in the geographic markets that form the basis for any such representation and which are known to the franchisor or franchise broker to have earned or made at least the same sales, income, or profits during a period of corresponding length in the immediate past as those sales, income, or profits represented; and

(ii) The beginning and ending dates for the corresponding time period referred to by paragraph (c)(6)(i) of this section,

Provided, however, That any franchisor without prior franchising experience as to the named franchise business so indicate such lack of experience in the document described in paragraph (c)(3) of this section.

(d) To fail to provide the following information within the document(s) required by paragraphs (b)(3) and (c)(3) of this section whenever any representation is made to a prospective franchisee regarding its potential sales, income, or profits, or the sales, income, gross or net profits of existing outlets (whether franchised or company-owned) of the named franchise business:

(1) A cover sheet distinctively and conspicuously showing the name of the franchisor, the date of issuance of the document and the following notice imprinted thereon in upper and lower case boldface type of not less than twelve point size:

INFORMATION FOR PROSPECTIVE FRANCHISEES ABOUT FRANCHISE [SALES] [INCOME] [PROFIT] REQUIRED BY THE FEDERAL TRADE COMMISSION.

To protect you, we've required the franchisor to give you this information. *We haven't checked it and don't know if it's correct.* Study these facts and figures carefully. If possible, show them to someone who can advise you, like a lawyer or an accountant. Then take your time and think it over.

If you find anything you think may be wrong or anything important that's been left out, let us know about it. It may be against the law.

There may also be laws on franchising in your State. Ask your State agencies about them.

FEDERAL TRADE COMMISSION,
Washington, D.C.

(2) A table of contents.

Provided, however, That each prospective franchisee to whom the representation is made shall be notified at the "time for making of disclosures" of any material change (about which the franchisor, franchise broker, or any of the agents, representatives, or employees thereof, knows or should know) in the information contained in the document(s) described by paragraphs (b)(3) and (c)(3) of this section.

(e) To make any oral, written, or visual representation for general dissemination (not otherwise covered by paragraph (b) or (c) of this section) which states a specific level of sales, income, gross or net profits, either actual or potential, of existing or prospective outlets (whether franchised or company-owned) of the named franchise business or which states other facts which suggest such a specific level, unless:

(1) At the time such representation is made, a reasonable basis exists for such representation and the franchisor has in its possession material which constitutes a reasonable basis for such representation and which is made available to the Commission or its staff upon reasonable demand;

(2) The underlying data on which each representation of sales, income or profit for existing outlets is based have been prepared in accordance with generally accepted accounting principles;

(3) In immediate conjunction with such representation, there shall be clearly and conspicuously disclosed the number and percentage of outlets of the named franchise business which the franchisor or the franchise broker knows to have earned or made at least the same sales, income, or profits during a period of corresponding length in the immediate past as those sales, income, or profits represented, and the beginning and ending dates for said time period;

(4) In immediate conjunction with each such representation of potential sales, income or profits, the following statement shall be clearly and conspicuously disclosed:

CAUTION

These figures are only estimates; there is no assurance you'll do as well. If you rely upon our figures, you must accept the risk of not doing as well.

Provided, however, That if such representation is not based on actual experience of existing outlets of the named franchise business, that fact also should be disclosed;

(5) No later than the earlier of the first "personal meeting" or the "time for making of disclosures," each prospective franchisee shall be given a single, legible written document which accurately, clearly and concisely sets forth the following information and materials (and none other than that provided for by this part or by State law not preempted by this part):

(i) The representation, set forth in detail along with the material bases and assumptions therefor;

(ii) The number and percentage of outlets of the named franchise business which the franchisor or the franchise broker knows to have earned or made at least the same sales, income or profits during a period of corresponding length in the immediate past as those sales, income, or profits represented, and the beginning and ending dates for said time period;

(iii) With respect to each such representation of sales, income, or profits of existing outlets, the following statement shall be clearly and conspicuously disclosed in immediate conjunction therewith, printed in not less than 12 point upper and lower case boldface type:

CAUTION

Some outlets have [sold] [earned] this amount. There is no assurance you'll do as well. If you rely upon our figures, you must accept the risk of not doing as well.

(iv) With respect to each such representation of potential sales, income, or profits, the following statement shall be clearly and conspicuously disclosed in immediate conjunction therewith, printed in not less than 12 point upper and lower case boldface type:

CAUTION

These figures are only estimates. There is no assurance that you'll do as well. If you rely upon our figures, you must accept the risk of not doing as well.

(v) If applicable, a statement clearly and conspicuously disclosing that the franchisor lacks prior franchising experience as to the named franchise business;

(vi) If applicable, a statement clearly and conspicuously disclosing that the franchisor has not been in business long enough to have actual business data;

(vii) A cover sheet, distinctively and conspicuously showing the name of the franchisor, the date of issuance of the document, and the following notice printed thereon in not less than 12 point upper and lower case boldface type:

INFORMATION FOR PROSPECTIVE FRANCHISEES ABOUT FRANCHISE [SALES] [INCOME] [PROFIT] REQUIRED BY THE FEDERAL TRADE COMMISSION

To protect you, we've required the franchisor to give you this information. *We haven't checked it and don't know if it's correct.* Study these facts and figures carefully. If possible, show them to someone who can advise you, like a lawyer or an accountant. If you find anything you think may be wrong or anything important that's been left out, let us know about it. It may be against the law. There may also be laws about franchising in your State. Ask your State agencies about them.

FEDERAL TRADE COMMISSION,
Washington, D.C.

(viii) A table of contents;

(6) Each prospective franchisee shall be notified at the "time for making of disclosures" of any material changes that have occurred in the information contained in this document.

(f) To make any claim or representation which is contradictory to the information required to be disclosed by this part.

(g) To fail to furnish the prospective franchisee with a copy of the franchisor's franchise agreement and related agreements with the document, and a copy of the completed franchise and related agreements intended to be executed by the parties at least 5 business days prior to the date the agreements are to be executed.

Provided, however, That the obligations defined in paragraphs (b) through (g) of this section shall be deemed to have been met for both the franchisor and the franchise broker if either such person furnishes the prospective franchisee with the written disclosures required thereby.

(h) To fail to return any funds or deposits in accordance with any conditions disclosed pursuant to paragraph (a)(7) of this section.

§ 436.2 Definitions.

As used in this part, the following definitions shall apply:

(a) The term "franchise" means any continuing commercial relationship created by any arrangement or arrangements whereby:

(1)(i)(A) a person (hereinafter "franchisee") offers, sells, or distributes to any person other than a "franchisor" (as hereinafter defined), goods, commodities, or services which are:

(*1*) Identified by a trademark, service mark, trade name, advertising or other commercial symbol designating another person (hereinafter "franchisor"); or

(*2*) Indirectly or directly required or advised to meet the quality standards prescribed by another person (hereinafter "franchisor") where the franchisee operates under a name using the trademark, service mark, trade name, advertising or other commercial symbol designating the franchisor; and

(B)(*1*) The franchisor exerts or has authority to exert a significant degree of control over the franchisee's method of operation, including but not limited to, the franchisee's business organization, promotional activities, management, marketing plan or business affairs; or

(*2*) The franchisor gives significant assistance to the franchisee in the latter's method of operation, including, but not limited to, the franchisee's business organization, management, marketing plan, promotional activities, or business affairs; *Provided, however,* That assistance in the franchisee's promotional activities shall not, in the absence of assistance in other areas of the franchisee's method of operation, constitute significant assistance; or

(ii)(A) A person (hereinafter "franchisee") offers, sells, or distributes to any person other than a "franchisor" (as hereinafter defined), goods, commodities, or services which are:

(*1*) Supplied by another person (hereinafter "franchisor"), or

(*2*) Supplied by a third person (e.g., a supplier) with whom the franchisee is directly or indirectly required to do business by another person (hereinafter "franchisor"); or

(*3*) Supplied by a third person (e.g., a supplier) with whom the franchisee is directly or indirectly advised to do business by another person (hereinafter "franchisor") where such third person is affiliated with the franchisor; and

(B) The franchisor:

(*1*) Secures for the franchisee retail outlets or accounts for said goods, commodities, or services; or

(*2*) Secures for the franchisee locations or sites for vending machines, rack displays, or any other product sales display used by the franchisee in the offering, sale, or distribution of said goods, commodities, or services; or

(*3*) Provides to the franchisee the services of a person able to secure the retail outlets, accounts, sites or locations referred to in paragraph (a)(1)(ii)(B) (*1*) and (*2*) above; and

(2) The franchisee is required as a condition of obtaining or commencing the franchise operation to make a payment or a commitment to pay to the franchisor, or to a person affiliated with the franchisor.

(3) Exemptions. The provisions of this part shall not apply to a franchise:

(i) Which is a "fractional franchise"; or

(ii) Where pursuant to a lease, license, or similar agreement, a person offers, sells, or distributes goods, commodities, or services on or about premises occupied by a retailer-grantor primarily for the retailer-grantor's own merchandising activities, which goods, commodities, or services are not purchased from the retailer-grantor or persons whom the lessee is directly or indirectly (A) required to do business with by the retailer-grantor or (B) advised to do business with by the retailer-grantor where such person is affiliated with the retailer-grantor; or

(iii) Where the total of the payments referred to in paragraph (a)(2) of this section made during a period from any time before to within 6 months after commencing operation of the franchisee's business, is less than $500; or

(iv) Where there is no writing which evidences any material term or aspect of the relationship or arrangement.

(4) Exclusions. The term "franchise" shall not be deemed to include any continuing commercial relationship created solely by:

(i) The relationship between an employer and an employee, or among general business partners; or

(ii) Membership in a bona fide "cooperative association"; or

(iii) An agreement for the use of a trademark, service mark, trade name, seal, advertising, or other commercial symbol designating a person who offers on a general basis, for a fee or otherwise, a bona fide service for the evaluation, testing, or certification of goods, commodities, or services;

(iv) An agreement between a licensor and a single licensee to license a trademark, trade name, service mark, advertising or other commercial symbol where such license is the only one of its general nature and type to be granted by the licensor with respect to that trademark, trade name, service mark, advertising, or other commercial symbol.

(5) Any relationship which is represented either orally or in writing to be a franchise (as defined in this [sic] paragraphs (a)(1) and (2) of this section) is subject to the requirements of this part.

(b) The term "person" means any individual, group, association, limited or general partnership, corporation, or any other business entity.

(c) The term "franchisor" means any person who participates in a franchise relationship as a franchisor, as denoted in paragraph (a) of this section.

(d) The term "franchisee" means any person (1) who participates in a franchise relationship as a franchisee, as denoted in paragraph (a) of this section, or (2) to whom an interest in a franchise is sold.

(e) The term "prospective franchisee" includes any person, including any representative, agent, or employee of that person, who approaches or is approached by a franchisor or franchise broker, or any representative, agent, or employee thereof, for the purpose of discussing the establishment, or possible establishment, of a franchise relationship involving such a person.

(f) The term "business day" means any day other than Saturday, Sunday, or the following national holidays: New Year's Day, Washington's Birthday, Memorial Day, Independence Day, Labor Day, Columbus Day, Veterans' Day, Thanksgiving, and Christmas.

(g) The term "time for making of disclosures" means ten (10) business days prior to the earlier of (1) the execution by a prospective franchisee of any franchise agreement or any other agreement imposing a binding legal obligation on such prospective franchisee, about which the franchisor, franchise broker, or any agent, representative, or employee thereof, knows or should know, in connection with the sale or proposed sale of a franchise, or (2) the payment by a prospective franchisee, about which the franchisor, franchise broker, or any agent, representative, or employee thereof, knows or should know, of any consideration in connection with the sale or proposed sale of a franchise.

(h) The term "fractional franchise" means any relationship, as denoted by paragraph (a) of this section, in which the person described therein as a franchisee, or any of the current directors or executive officers thereof, has been in the type of business represented by the franchise relationship for more than 2 years and the parties anticipated, or should have anticipated, at the time the agreement establishing the franchise relationship was reached, that the sales arising from the relationship would represent no more than 20 percent of the sales in dollar volume of the franchisee.

(i) The term "affiliated person" means a person (as defined in paragraph (b) of this section):

(1) Which directly or indirectly controls, is controlled by, or is under common control with, a franchisor; or

(2) Which directly or indirectly owns, controls, or holds with power to vote, 10 percent or more of the outstanding voting securities or a franchisor; or

(3) Which has, in common with a franchisor, one or more partners, officers, directors, trustees, branch managers, or other persons occupying similar status or performing similar functions.

(j) The term "franchise broker" means any person other than a franchisor or a franchisee who sells, offers for sale, or arranges for the sale of a franchise.

(k) The term "sale of a franchise" includes a contract or agreement whereby a person obtains a franchise or interest in a franchise for value by purchase, license, or otherwise. This term shall not be deemed to include the renewal or extension of an existing franchise where there is no interruption in the operation of the franchised business by the franchisee, unless the new contracts or agreements contain material changes from those in effect between the franchisor and franchisee prior thereto.

(1) A "cooperative association" is either (1) an association of producers of agricultural products authorized by section 1 of the Capper-Volstead Act, 7 U.S.C. 291; or (2) an organization operated on a cooperative basis by and for independent retailers which wholesales goods or furnishes services primarily to its member-retailers.

(m) The term "fiscal year" means the franchisor's fiscal year.

(n) The terms "material," "material fact," and "material change" shall include any fact, circumstance, or set of conditions which has a substantial likelihood of influencing a reasonable franchisee or a reasonable prospective franchisee in the making of a significant decision relating to a named franchise business or which has any significant financial impact on a franchisee or prospective franchisee.

(o) The term "personal meeting" means a face-to-face meeting between a franchisor or franchise broker (or any agent, representative, or employee thereof) and a prospective franchisee which is held for the purpose of discussing the sale or possible sale of a franchise.

§ 436.3 Severability.

If any provision of this part or its application to any person, act, or practice is held invalid, the remainder of the part or the application of its provisions to any person, act, or practice shall not be affected thereby.

NOTE 1: The Commission expresses no opinion as to the legality of any practice mentioned in this part. A provision for disclosure should not be construed as condonation or approval with respect to the matter required to be disclosed, nor as an indication of the Commission's intention not to enforce any applicable statute.

NOTE 2: By taking action in this area, the Federal Trade Commission does not intend to annul, alter, or affect, or exempt any person subject to the provisions of this part from complying with the laws or regulations of any State, municipality, or other local government with respect to franchising practices, except to the extent that those laws or regulations are inconsistent with any provision of this part, and then only to the extent of the inconsistency. For the purposes of this part, a law or regulation of any State, municipality, or other local government is not inconsistent with this part if the protection such law or regulation affords any prospective franchisee is equal to or greater than that provided by this part. Examples of provisions which provide protection equal to or greater than that provided by this part include laws or regulations which require more complete record keeping by the franchisor or the disclosure of more complete information to the franchisee.

NOTE 3: [As per § 436.1(a)(24) of this part]:

DISCLOSURE STATEMENT

Pursuant to 16 CFR 436.1 et seq., a Trade Regulation Rule of the Federal Trade Commission regarding Disclosure Requirements and Prohibitions Concerning Franchising and Business Opportunity Ventures, the following information is set forth on [name of franchisor] for your examination:

1. Identifying information as to franchisor.
2. Business experience of franchisor's directors and executive officers.
3. Business experience of the franchisor.
4. Litigation history.
5. Bankruptcy history.
6. Description of franchise.
7. Initial funds required to be paid by a franchisee.
8. Recurring funds required to be paid by a franchisee.
9. Affiliated persons the franchisee is required or advised to do business with by the franchisor.
10. Obligations to purchase.
11. Revenues received by the franchisor in consideration of purchases by a franchisee.
12. Financing arrangements.
13. Restriction of sales.
14. Personal participation required of the franchisee in the operation of the franchise.
15. Termination, cancellation, and renewal of the franchise.
16. Statistical information concerning the number of franchises (and company-owned outlets).
17. Site selection.
18. Training programs.
19. Public figure involvement in the franchise.
20. Financial information concerning the franchisor

Appendix F
State Alcoholic Beverage Dealer Laws

Ariz Rev Stat Ann §§44-1565 to 44-1567 (Supp 1981-1982)
Conn Gen Stat Ann §30-17 (West Supp 1982)
Idaho Code §§23-1033A (1977) & 23-1328A (Supp 1982)
Ind Code Ann §7.1-5-5-9 (Burns 1978)
Kan Stat Ann §§41-410, 41-2705 (1981)
Me Rev Stat Ann tit 28, §§665-679 (Supp 1982-1983)
Md Ann Code art 2B, §§203A-203G (1957)
Mass Gen Laws Ann ch 138, §25E (West Supp 1982-1983)
Minn Stat Ann §§325B.01 to 325B.17 (West 1981)
Mo Ann Stat §407.413 (Vernon 1979)
Mont Code Ann §§16-3-221 to 16-3-226 (1979)
Neb Rev Stat §§87-401 to 87-410 (Supp 1980)
Nev Rev Stat §§598.290 to 598.350 (1981)
NH Rev Stat Ann §§181:36 to 181:44 (Supp 1981)
NM Stat Ann §§60-8A-3 to 60-8A-19 (Supp 1981)
NC Gen Stat §18B-1117 (Supp 1981)
ND Cent Code §§5-04-01 to 5-04-17 (Supp 1981)
Ohio Rev Code Ann §§1333.82 to 1333.87 (Page 1979)
Pa Stat Ann tit 47, §§4-431, 4-492 (Purdon 1969 & Supp 1982-1983)
SC Code Ann §§61-9-1010 to 61-9-1050 (Law Co-op 1976)
Vt Stat Ann tit 7, §§701-708 (Supp 1981)
Va Code §§4-118.3 to 4-118.20 (Supp 1981)
W Va Code §§11-16-12a, 11-16-13b (1976)

Appendix G
Anti-Fraud Provisions

Ark Stat Ann §§70-801 to 70-826 (1979)

Del Code Ann tit 6, §§2551-2556 (1974 & Supp 1982)

Fla Stat Ann §817.416 (West 1976 & Supp 1983)

PR Laws Ann tit 10, §§278-278d (1976 & Supp 1981)

VI Code Ann tit 12A, §§130-139 (1982)

Appendix H
Business Opportunities Laws

Ala Code §8-19-5(20) (Supp 1981)
Cal Civ Code §§1812.200 to 1812.220 (West Supp 1982)
Conn Gen Stat Ann §§36-503 to 36-521 (West 1981 & Supp 1982)
Fla Stat Ann §§559.80 to 559.815 (West Supp 1982)
Ga Code Ann §§10-1-410 to 10-1-416 (1981)
Iowa Code Ann §§523B.1 to 523B.11 (West Supp 1982-1983)
Ky Rev Stat Ann §§367.801 to 367.990 (Bobbs-Merrill Supp 1980)
La Rev Stat Ann §§51:1821 to 51:1824 (West Supp 1982)
Me Rev Stat Ann tit 32, §§4691 to 4700-B (Supp 1982-1983)
Md Ann Code art 56, §§401-415 (Supp 1981)
Neb Rev Stat §§59-1701 to 59-1761 (Supp 1980)
NH Rev Stat Ann §§358-E:1 to 358-E:6 (Supp 1979)
NC Gen Stat §§66-94 to 66-100 (1981 & Supp 1981)
Ohio Rev Code Ann §§1334.01 to 1334.99 (Page Supp 1981)
SC Code Ann §§39-57-10 to 39-57-80 (Law Co-op Supp 1981)
Tex Rev Civ Stat Ann art 5069-16.01 to art 5069-16.15 (Vernon Supp 1982)
Utah Code Ann §§13-15-1 to 13-15-6 (Supp 1981)
Va Code §§59.1-262 to 59.1-269 (1982)
Wash Rev Code Ann §§19.110.010 to 19.110.930 (Supp 1982)

Appendix I
State Farm Equipment Dealer Laws

1981 Ala Acts 776

Ark Stat Ann §§70-819 to 70-826 (1979)

Ga Code Ann §§13-8-11 to 13-8-25 & 13-8-31 to 13-8-45 (Supp 1982)

Idaho Code §§28-23-101 to 28-23-111 (1980)

Kan Stat Ann §§16-1001 to 16-1006 (1981)

La Rev Stat Ann §§51-481 to 51-488 (West Supp 1982)

Minn Stat Ann §§325E.05-325E.06 (West 1981)

Miss Code Ann §§75-77-1 to 75-77-19 (Supp 1982)

Neb Rev Stat §§69-1501 to 69-1504 (1943)

ND Cent Code §§51-07-01, 51-20-01 (Supp 1981)

1981 ND Sess Laws House Bill 1375

1982 Okla Sess Laws House Bill 1872

SD Comp Laws Ann §§37-5-1 to 37-5-9 (1977)

Tenn Code Ann §§47-19-101 to 47-19-110 (Supp 1979)

Wash Rev Code Ann §§19.98.010 to 19.98.910 (1981)

Appendix J
State Franchise Laws Applicable To Sales Of Franchises

15

Cal Corp Code §§31000-31516 (Deering 1979 & Supp 1982)
Hawaii Rev Stat §§482E-1 to 482E-12 (1976 & Supp 1980)
Ill Ann Stat ch 121 1/2 §§701-740 (Smith-Hurd Supp 1982-1983)
Ind Code Ann §§23-2-2.5-1 to 23-2-2.5-50 (Burns Supp 1982)
Md Ann Code art 56, §§345-366 (1979 & Supp 1982)
Mich Comp Laws Ann §§445.1501 to 445.1545 (Supp 1982-1983)
Minn Stat Ann §§80C.01 to 80C.22 (West Supp 1982)
NY Gen Bus Law §§680-695 (McKinney Supp 1981-1982)
ND Cent Code §§51-19-01 to 51-19-17 (1981)
Or Rev Stat §§650.005 to 650.085 (1977)
RI Gen Laws §§19-28-1 to 19-28-15 (Supp 1980)
SD Codified Laws Ann §§37-5A-1 to 37-5A-87 (1977 & Supp 1982)
Va Code §§13.1-557 to 13.1-574 (1978 & Supp 1982)
Wash Rev Code Ann §§19.100.010 to 19.100.940 (1978 & Supp 1982)
Wis Stat Ann §§553.01 to 553.78 (West Supp 1982)

Appendix K
State Franchise Termination Laws 16

Ark Stat Ann §§70-807 to 70-818 (1979)
Cal Bus & Prof Code §§20000-20043 (West Supp 1983)
Conn Gen Stat Ann §§42-133e to 42-133i (West Supp 1982)
Del Code Ann tit 6, §§2551-2556 (Supp 1980)
Hawaii Rev Stat §§482E-1 to 482E-12 (Supp 1980)
Ill Ann Stat ch 121 1/2, §§704.3 to 704.4 (Smith-Hurd Supp 1982-1983)
Ind Code Ann §23-2-2.7 (Burns Supp 1982)
Mich Stat Ann §19.854(27) (Callaghan 1975)
Minn Stat Ann §80C.14 (West Supp 1982)
Miss Code Ann §75-24-53 (Supp 1982)
Mo Ann Stat §§407.400 to 407.420 (Vernon 1979)
Neb Rev Stat §§87-401 to 87-410 (Supp 1980)
NJ Stat Ann §§56:10-1 to 56:10-15 (West Supp 1982-1983)
Va Code §§13.1-557 to 13.1-574 (1978 & Supp 1982)
Wash Rev Code Ann §§19.100.180 (1978)
Wis Stat Ann §§135.01-135.07 (West 1974 & Supp 1982-1983)

Appendix L
State Motor Vehicle Dealer Laws

46

Ala Code §8-20-1 to 8-20-12 (Supp 1982)
Ariz Rev Stat Ann §28-1304.02 (Supp 1981-1982)
Ark Stat Ann §§75-2301 to 75-2312 (Supp 1977)
Cal Veh Code §§3060-3069 (West Supp 1982)
Colo Rev Stat §§12-6-101 to 12-6-123 (1978)
Conn Gen Stat Ann §§14-67a to 14-67d (West Supp 1982)
Fla Stat Ann §§320.60 to 320.70 (Supp 1982)
Ga Code Ann §§84-6601 to 84-6613 (1979)
Hawaii Rev Stat §§437-1 to 437-42 (1976 & Supp 1980)
Idaho Code §§49-2401 to 49-2420 (Supp 1982)
Ill Ann Stat ch 121 1/2, §§751-764 (Smith-Hurd Supp 1982-1983)
Ind Code Ann §§9-10-1-1 to 9-10-5-5 (Burns Supp 1982)
Iowa Code Ann §§322A.1 to 322A.17 (West Supp 1982-1983)
Kan Stat Ann §§8-2401 to 8-2424 (Supp 1981)
Ky Rev Stat Ann §§190.010 to 190.080 (Bobbs-Merrill 1980)
La Rev Stat Ann §§1251-1256.1 (West Supp 1982)
Me Rev Stat Ann tit 10, §§1171-1186 (West Supp 1982-1983)
Md Transp Code Ann §§15-201 to 15-213 (Supp 1982)
Mass Gen Laws Ann ch 93B (West Supp 1982-1983)
Mich Comp Laws Ann §§445.1561 to 445.1583 (Supp 1982-1983)
Minn Stat Ann §80C.14 (West Supp 1982)
Miss Code Ann §§63-17-51 to 63-17-139 (1972 & Supp 1982)
Mo Rev Stat §§407.810 to 407.835 (Supp 1983)
Mont Code Ann §§61-4-201 to 61-4-211 (1979)

Neb Rev Stat §§60-1420 to 60-1435 (1974)

Nev Rev Stat §§482.36311 to 482.36425 (1981)

NH Rev Stat Ann §§357-C:1 to 357-C:15 (Supp 1981)

NJ Stat Ann §§56:10-1 to 56:10-15 (West Supp 1982-1983)

NM Stat Ann §§57-16-1 to 57-16-16 (1978)

NY Gen Bus Law §§195-198 (McKinney Supp 1981-1982)

NC Gen Stat §§20-285 to 20-308 (1978 & Supp 1981)

ND Cent Code §§51-07-01 to 51-07-03 (1974 & Supp 1981)

Ohio Rev Code Ann §§1333.71 to 1333.81 (Page Supp 1981)

Okla Stat Ann tit 47, §§561-580.1 (West Supp 1981-1982)

Pa Stat Ann tit 63, §§801-816 (Purdon Supp 1979-1980)

RI Gen Laws §§31.6.1.1 to 31.6.1.17 (Supp 1978)

SC Code Ann §§56-15-10 to 56-15-130 (Law Co-op 1976 & Supp 1980)

SD Comp Laws Ann §§32-6A-1 to 32-6A-16 (1976 & Supp 1982)

Tenn Code Ann §§59-1702 to 59-1722 (Supp 1978)

Tex Rev Civ Stat Ann art 4413(36), §§4.01-7.01 (Vernon 1976 & Supp 1978-1979)

Utah Code Ann §§41-3-2 to 41-3-27 (1970 & Supp 1979)

Va Code §§46.1-516 to 46.1-550 (1974 & Supp 1979)

Vt Stat Ann tit 9, §§4083-4100 (Supp 1982-1983)

Wash Rev Code Ann §§46.70.00 to 46.70.920 (Supp 1970 & Supp 1982)

Wis Stat Ann §218.01(3)(17) (West Supp 1979-1980)

Wyo Stat Ann §§40-15-101 to 40-15-109 (Supp 1982)

Appendix M
State Petroleum Dealer Laws

Alaska Stat §§45.50.800 to 45.50.850 (1981)

Ariz Rev Stat Ann §§44-1551 to 44-1560 (Supp 1981-1982)

Ark Stat Ann §§53-1101 to 53-1103 (Supp 1981)

Cal Bus & Prof Code §§20999-20999.4 & 21140 to 21149 (West 1976 & Supp 1983)

Conn Gen Stat Ann §§42-133k to 42-133n (West Supp 1982)

Del Code Ann tit 6, §§2901-2911 (Supp 1980)

DC Code Ann §10-213 (1973)

Ga Code Ann §§10-1-230 to 10-1-241 (1982)

Hawaii Rev Stat §§486H (Supp 1980)

Iowa Code Ann §§323.1 to 323.14, 323A.1 to 323A.3 (West Supp 1982-1983)

La Rev Stat Ann §§1451-1454 (West 1974)

Me Rev Stat Ann tit 10, §§1451-1456 (1980)

Md Com Law Code Ann §§11-301 to 11-308 (Supp 1982)

Mass Gen Laws Ann ch 93E (West Supp 1982-1983)

Minn Stat Ann §§80C.14 to 80C.145 (West Supp 1982)

Nev Rev Stat §§598.650 to 598.680 (1979)

NH Rev Stat Ann §§339-C:1 to 339-C:9 (Supp 1981)

NJ Rev Stat §§56:6-19 to 56:6-32 (Supp 1982-1983)

NM Stat Ann §§70-8-1 to 70-8-6 (1978 & Supp 1982)

NY Gen Bus Law §§199-a to 199-j (McKinney 1981-1982)

1975 Pa Laws 126

RI Gen Laws §§5-55-1 to 5-55-9 (1976)

Tenn Code Ann §§69-701 to 69-707 & 69-721 to 69-724 (Supp 1979)

1975 Utah Laws 6
Vt Stat Ann tit 9, §§4101-4109 (Supp 1981)
Va Code §§59.1-21.8 to 59.1-21.18:1 (Supp 1980)
W Va Code §§47-11C-1 to 47-11C-8 (1976)

Cases

A

B

C

D

E

F

G

H

I

J

K

L

M

N

O

P

Q

R

S

T

U

V

W

Y

Z

Statutes

Arkansas

California

Colorado

Connecticut

Delaware

Idaho

Illinois

Ill Ann Stat ch 121 1/2, §720 (Smith-Hurd Supp 1982-83) **§9.78**

Ill Ann Stat ch 121 1/2, §721 (Smith-Hurd Supp 1982-83) **§9.78**

Ill Ann Stat ch 121 1/2, §751-764 (Smith-Hurd Supp 1982-83) **§§7.06, 7.15**

Indiana

Ind Code Ann §7.1-5-5-9 (Burns 1978) **§7.15**

Ind Code Ann §§9-10-1-1 to 9-10-5-5 (Burns Supp 1982) **§§7.06, 7.15**

Ind Code Ann §§23-2-2.5-1 to 23-2-2.5-50 (Burns Supp 1982) **§§9.02, 9.28**

Ind Code Ann §23-2-2.5-1(a) (Burns Supp 1982) **§9.28**

Ind Code Ann §23-2-2.5-1(a)(3) (Burns Supp 1982) **§9.32**

Ind Code Ann §23-2-2.5-1(g) (Burns Supp 1982) **§9.37**

Ind Code Ann §23-2-2.5-1(i) (Burns Supp 1982) **§9.32**

Ind Code Ann §23-2-2.5-1(i)(3) (Burns Supp 1982) **§9.35**

Ind Code Ann §§23-2-2.5-3(a) and (b) (Burns Supp 1982) **§9.37**

Ind Code Ann §23-2-2.5-4 (Burns Supp 1982) **§9.37**

Ind Code Ann §23-2-2.5-5 (Burns Supp 1982) **§9.38**

Ind Code Ann §23-2-2.5-9 (Burns Supp 1982) **§§9.67, 9.75**

Ind Code Ann §23-2-2.5-27 (Burns Supp 1982) **§9.78**

Ind Code Ann §23-2-2.5-28 (Burns Supp 1982) **§9.78**

Ind Code Ann §23-2-2.5-32 (Burns Supp 1982) **§9.78**

Ind Code Ann §23-2-2.5-37 (Burns Supp 1982) **§9.78**

Ind Code Ann §23-2-2.7 (Burns Supp 1982) **§§7.08, 7.15, 7.16, 7.31, 7.36, 7.38, 7.39. 7.46, 9.02, 9.28**

Ind Code Ann §23-2-2.7(4) (Burns Supp 1982) **§9.55**

Ind Code Ann §23-2-2.7(6) (Burns Supp 1982) **§9.55**

Ind Code Ann §23-2-2.7-1(1) (Burns Supp 1982) **§9.50**

Ind Code Ann §23-2-2.7-1(9) (Burns 1982) **§9.62**

Ind Code Ann §23-2-2.7-2(4) (Burns Supp 1982) **§§9.48, 9.49**

Ind Code Ann §23-2-2.7-2(5) (19) **§9.57**

Ind Code Ann §24-5-0.5-1 to 25-5-0.5-9 (Burns 1982 & Supp 1982) **§9.57**

Iowa

Iowa Code Ann §§322A.1 to 322A.17 (West Supp 1982-1983) **§§7.06, 7.15**

Iowa Code Ann §§323.1 to 323.14, 323A.1 to 323A.3 (West Supp 1982-1983) **§§7.07, 7.15**

Iowa Code Ann §§523B.1-523B.11 (West Supp 1982-1983) **§§9.02, 9.27**

Iowa Code Ann §523B.1.b(3) (West Supp 1982-1983) **§9.27**

Iowa Code Ann §714.16 to 714.22 (West 1979 & Supp 1982-1983) **§9.57**

Kansas

Kan Stat Ann §§8-2401 to 8-2424 (Supp 1981) **§§7.06, 7.15**

Kentucky

Louisiana

Maine

Maryland

Massachusetts

Michigan

Minnesota

Minn Stat Ann §80C.17 (West Supp 1982) **§9.78**

Minn Stat Ann §§325B.01 to 325B.17 (West 1981) **§7.15**

Minn Stat Ann §§325E.05 to 325E.06 (West 1981) **§7.15**

Minn Stat Ann §§325F.67 to 325F.70, 8.31 (West 1981) **§9.57**

Mississippi

Miss Code Ann §§63-17-51 to 63-17-139 (1972 & Supp 1982) **§§7.06, 7.15**

Miss Code Ann §§75-24-1 to 75-24-23 (Supp 1982) **§9.57**

Miss Code Ann §75-24-53 (Supp 1982) **§§7.08, 7.15, 7.16, 7.24, 7.31, 7.36, 7.45, 7.46, 9.02, 9.28, 9.34**

Miss Code Ann §§75-77-1 to 75-77-19 (Supp 1982) **§7.15**

Missouri

Mo Ann Stat §§407.010 to 407.200 (Vernon 1979 & Supp 1983) **§9.57**

Mo Ann Stat §407.413 (Vernon 1979) **§7.15**

Mo Ann Stat §416.141 (Vernon 1974) **§6.01**

Mo Rev Stat §§407.400 to 407.420 (1979) **§§7.08, 7.15, 7.16, 7.24, 7.31, 7.36, 7.46, 9.02, 9.28, 9.34**

Mo Rev Stat §§407.810 to 407.835 (Supp 1983)**§§7.06, 7.15**

Mo Rev Stat §416.031(3) (1969 & Supp 1975) **§4.02**

Montana

Mont Code Ann §§16-3-221 to 16-3-226 (1979) **§7.15**

Mont Code Ann §§30-14-101 to 30-14-142 (1981) **§9.57**

Mont Code Ann §§61-4-201 to 61-4-211 (1979) **§§7.06, 7.15**

Nebraska

Neb Rev Stat §§59-1601 to 59-1623 (1978) **§9.57**

Neb Rev Stat §§59-1701 to 59-1761 (Supp 1980) **§§9.02, 9.27**

Neb Rev Stat §§60-1420 to 60-1435 (1974) **§§7.06, 7.15**

Neb Rev Stat §§69-1501 to 69-1504 (1943) **§7.15**

Neb Rev Stat §§87-401 to 87-410 (Supp 1980) **§§7.08, 7.15, 7.16, 7.22, 7.24, 7.31, 7.36, 7.41, 7.46, 9.02, 9.28, 9.34**

Neb Rev Stat §87-404 (Supp 1980) **§9.59**

Neb Rev Stat §87-404(2)(a) (Supp 1980) **§9.59**

Neb Rev Stat §87-404(2)(b) (Supp 1980) **§9.59**

Neb Rev Stat §87-404(2)(d) (Supp 1980) **§9.59**

Neb Rev Stat §87-404(2)(f) (Supp 1980) **§9.59**

Neb Rev Stat §87-406 (Supp 1978) **§9.45**

Nevada

Nev Rev Stat §§482.36311 to 482.36425 (1981) **§§7.06, 7.15**

Nev Rev Stat §§598.290 to 598.350 (1981) **§7.15**

Nev Rev Stat §§598.360 to 598.640 (1979) **§9.57**

Nev Rev Stat §§598.650 to 598.680 (1979) **§§7.07, 7.15**

New Hampshire

NH Rev Stat Ann §§181:36 to 181:44 (Supp 1981) **§7.15**

NH Rev Stat Ann §§339-C:1 to 339-C:9 (Supp 1981) **§§7.07, 7.15**

NH Rev Stat Ann §§357-C:1 to 357-C:15 (Supp 1981) **§§7.06, 7.15**

NH Rev Stat Ann §§358-A:1 to 358-A:13 (Supp 1981-1983) **§9.57**

NH Rev Stat Ann §§358-E:1 to 358E:6 (Supp 1979) **§§9.02, 9.27**

New Jersey

NJ Rev Stat §§56:6-19 to 56:6-32 (Supp 1982-1983) **§§7.07, 7.15**

NJ Stat Ann §§56:8-1 to 56:8-25 (West Supp 1982-1983) **§9.57**

NJ Stat Ann §56:9-1 *et seq* (West 1981-1982) **§6.01**

NJ Stat Ann §§56:10-1 to 56:10-15 (West Supp 1982-1983) **§§7.06, 7.08, 7.15, 7.16, 7.22, 7.24, 7.31, 7.36, 7.41, 7.46, 9.02, 9.28, 9.34**

NJ Stat Ann §56:10-5 (West Supp 1982-1983) **§9.59**

NJ Stat Ann §56:10-5(2) (West Supp 1982-1983) **§9.59**

NJ Stat Ann §56:10-7 (West Supp 1982-1983) **§9.45**

New Mexico

NM Stat Ann §§57-12-1 to 57-12-20 (1978) **§9.57**

NM Stat Ann §§57-16-1 to 57-16-16 (1978) **§§7.06, 7.15**

NM Stat Ann §§60-8A-3 to 60-8A-19 (Supp 1981) **§7.15**

NM Stat Ann §§70-8-1 to 70-8-6 (1978 & Supp 1982) **§§7.07, 7.15**

New York

NY Exec Law §63 (McKinney 1982) **§9.57**

NY Gen Bus Law §§195-198 (McKinney Supp 1981-1982) **§§7.06, 7.15**

NY Gen Bus Law §§199-a to 199-j (McKinney 1981-1982) **§§7.07, 7.15**

NY Gen Bus Law §340 *et seq* (McKinney 1968 & Supp 1980-1981) **§6.01**

NY Gen Bus Law §340 (Consol 1968) **§4.02**

NY Gen Bus Law §§349-349a (McKinney Supp 1982-1983) **§9.57**

NY Gen Bus Law §§680-695 (McKinney Supp 1981-1982) **§§9.02, 9.28**

NY Gen Bus Law §681.3 (McKinney Supp 1981-1982) **§§9.28, 9.32, 9.33, 9.37**

NY Gen Bus Law §681.7 (McKinney Supp 1981-1982) **§9.32**

NY Gen Bus Law §681.7(a) (McKinney Supp 1981-1982) **§9.35**

NY Gen Bus Law §681.7(e) (McKinney Supp 1981-1982) **§9.36**

NY Gen Bus Law §681.7(f) (McKinney Supp 1981-1982) **§9.36**

NY Gen Bus Law §681.7(g) (McKinney Supp 1981-1982) **§9.36**

NY Gen Bus Law §683.8 (McKinney Supp 1981-1982) **§§9.67, 9.75**

North Carolina

North Dakota

Ohio

Ohio Rev Code Ann §§1333.82 to 1333.87 (Page 1979) **§7.15**

Ohio Rev Code Ann §§1334.01 to 1334.99 (Page Supp 1981) **§§9.02, 9.27**

Ohio Rev Code Ann §§1345.01 to 1345.13 (Page 1979 & Supp 1983) **§9.57**

Oklahoma

1982 Okla Sess Laws 1872 **§7.15**

Okla Stat Ann tit 15, §§751-763 (West Supp 1982-1983) **§9.57**

Okla Stat Ann tit 47, §§561 to 580.1 (West Supp 1981-1982) **§§7.06, 7.15**

Oregon

Or Rev Stat §§646.605 to 646.656 (1981) **§9.57**

Or Rev Stat §§650.005 to 650.085 (1977) **§§9.02, 9.28**

Or Rev Stat §650.005(4) (1977) **§9.28**

Or Rev Stat §650.005(4)(c) (1977) **§9.32**

Or Rev Stat §650.005(6) (1977) **§9.36**

Or Rev Stat §650.020(6)(a) (1977) **§9.67**

Or Rev Stat §650.065 (1977) **§9.78**

Or Rev Stat §650.085 (1977) **§9.78**

Pennsylvania

1975 Pa Laws 126 **§§7.07, 7.15**

Pa Cons Stat Ann §§201-1 to 201-9 (Purdon Supp 1982-1983) **§9.57**

Pa Stat Ann tit 47, §§4-431, 4-492 (Purdon 1969 & Supp 1982-1983) **§7.15**

Pa Stat Ann tit 63, §§801 to 816 (Purdon Supp 1979-1980) **§§7.06, 7.15**

Puerto Rico

PR Laws Ann tit 10, §§278 to 278d (1976 & Supp 1981) **§9.34**

Rhode Island

RI Gen Laws §§5-55-1 to 5-55-9 (1976) **§§7.07, 7.15**

RI Gen Laws §§6-13.1-1 to 6-13.1-11 (1969 & Supp 1980) **§9.57**

RI Gen Laws §§19-28-1 to 19-28-15 (Supp 1980) **§§9.02, 9.28**

RI Gen Laws §19-28-3(c) (Supp 1980) **§9.28**

RI Gen Laws §19-28.3(c)3 (Supp 1980) **§§9.32, 9.36**

RI Gen Laws §§19-28-3(i)(1) (Supp 1980) **§9.35**

RI Gen Laws §19-28-3(j) (Supp 1980) **§§9.32, 9.36**

RI Gen Laws §19-28-4(a) (1981) **§9.38**

RI Gen Laws §19-28-4(b) (Supp 1980) **§9.37**

RI Gen Laws §19-28-4(c) (Supp 1980) **§9.37**

RI Gen Laws §19-28-4(d) (Supp 1980) **§9.37**

RI Gen Laws §19-28-5.I (Supp 1980) **§§9.67, 9.75**

RI Gen Laws §19-28-9 (Supp 1980) **§9.78**

RI Gen Laws §19-28-10 (Supp 1980) **§9.78**

RI Gen Laws §19-28-10.c (Supp 1980) **§9.78**

RI Gen Laws §19-28-11 (Supp 1980) **§9.78**

South Carolina

South Dakota

Tennessee

West Virginia

Wisconsin

Wyoming

Index

A

M

N

P

Q

R

S

U

V

W